T0391957

The Postwar Antisemite

The Postwar Antisemite

Culture and Complicity after the Holocaust

LISA SILVERMAN

OXFORD
UNIVERSITY PRESS

Oxford University Press is a department of the University of Oxford.
It furthers the University's objective of excellence in research, scholarship,
and education by publishing worldwide. Oxford is a registered trade mark of
Oxford University Press in the UK and in certain other countries.

Published in the United States of America by Oxford University Press
198 Madison Avenue, New York, NY 10016, United States of America.

© Oxford University Press 2025

All rights reserved. No part of this publication may be reproduced, stored in a retrieval system, transmitted, used for text and data mining, or used for training artificial intelligence, in any form or by any means, without the prior permission in writing of Oxford University Press, or as expressly permitted by law, by license or under terms agreed with the appropriate reprographics rights organization. Inquiries concerning reproduction outside the scope of the above should be sent to the Rights Department, Oxford University Press, at the address above.

You must not circulate this work in any other form
and you must impose this same condition on any acquirer.

Library of Congress Cataloging-in-Publication Data
Names: Silverman, Lisa, 1969– author
Title: The postwar antisemite : culture and complicity after the Holocaust / Lisa Silverman.
Description: New York : Oxford University Press, 2025. |
Includes bibliographical references and index.
Identifiers: LCCN 2025016072 (print) | LCCN 2025016073 (ebook) |
ISBN 9780197697726 hardback | ISBN 9780197697757 | ISBN 9780197697733 epub
Subjects: LCSH: Holocaust, Jewish (1939–1945) | Rationalization (Psychology) |
Excuses | Reasoning | Evil, Non-resistance to | Ethical problems |
Immorality | Conscience | Prejudices
Classification: LCC D804.3 .S5853 2025 (print) | LCC D804.3 (ebook)
LC record available at https://lccn.loc.gov/2025016072
LC ebook record available at https://lccn.loc.gov/2025016073

DOI: 10.1093/9780197697757.001.0001

Printed by Marquis Book Printing, Canada

The manufacturer's authorized representative in the EU for product safety is
Oxford University Press España S.A., Parque Empresarial San Fernando de Henares,
Avenida de Castilla, 2 – 28830 Madrid (www.oup.es/en or product.safety@oup.com).
OUP España S.A. also acts as importer into Spain of products made by the manufacturer.

To my parents, Paula Silverman (1938–2022) and Harry Silverman (1933–2023) in loving memory

Contents

Acknowledgments ix

Introduction: Ida Ehre Breaks Down at the Bundestag 1

PART I. WEST GERMANY:
THE PATRIOT AND THE ANTISEMITE

1. Harlan's Jews: Dora Gerson, Julius Bab, and the Legacy of
   Jud Süss 23

2. Harlan's Antisemites: Karena Niehoff Testifies in Hamburg 56

PART II. EAST GERMANY:
THE ANTI-FASCIST AND THE ANTISEMITE

3. Alice Haas Disappears from *Affaire Blum* 101

4. Accused as Jews: Anna Seghers and Victor Klemperer 130

PART III. AUSTRIA:
THE VICTIM AND THE ANTISEMITE

5. Hilde Spiel Returns to Vienna: *Das andere Leben*,
   The Emperor Waltz, and *The Third Man* 167

6. False Accusations: *Der Prozess* and *1. April 2000* 201

PART IV. THE UNITED STATES:
THE ANTI-RACIST AND THE ANTISEMITE

7. Laura Z. Hobson Stands Up for Josephine Baker:
   Gentleman's Agreement 241

Notes 257
Bibliography 307
Index 329

Acknowledgments

This book represents the culmination of many years of learning, researching, and teaching about Jewish history and the power and persistence of antisemitism. I owe a debt of gratitude to the many people who have helped me along the way. Chaya Halberstam and Ravit Reichman began their academic journeys with me at Yale and have accompanied me ever since; their intellect, humor, friendship, and love mean the world to me. Friends and colleagues in Milwaukee have provided an ideal working environment and I am deeply grateful for their enthusiasm and encouragement. I am thankful in particular to Jasmine Alinder, Aneesh Aneesh, Rachel Baum, Joel Berkowitz, Erica Bornstein, Rachel Buff, Winson Chu, Carolyn Eichner, Christine Evans, Karolina May-Chu, Arijit Sen, and Vaishali Wagh. Grants from a fund established by our inimitable colleague Bruce Fetter at the Department of History of the University of Wisconsin-Milwaukee provided helpful support for my research, as did generous funds provided by the Sam and Helen Stahl Center for Jewish Studies.

I was honored to serve as Michael Hauck Guest Professor at the Fritz Bauer Institute for the History and Impact of the Holocaust at the Goethe University in Frankfurt am Main. There I benefited greatly from exchanges with Sybille Steinbacher, Tobias Freimüller, Hannah Hecker, Sarah Crane, Veronika Duma, and Werner Renz. The assistance of Manuela Ritzheim, Josefine Ruhe, Christopher Gomer, and Nathalie Schüler aided me enormously. I am especially grateful to Alix and Oliver Puhl for their generosity. A fellowship from the Vienna Wiesenthal Institute for Holocaust Studies provided the opportunity to complete research in Austria among a group of terrific scholars, including Rasa Baločkaitė, Roland Clark, Tim Corbett, Kinga Frojimovics, Nikolaus Hagen, Dagi Knellessen, Lovro Kralj, and György Majtényi. Many thanks are due to Éva Kovács, Béla Rasky, and Marianne Windsperger for facilitating such a productive stay. My term as a fellow at the Frankel Center for Advanced Judaic Studies at the University of Michigan, under the leadership of Deborah Dash Moore and Jonathan Freedman, likewise led to countless enriching and thought-provoking exchanges with Maya Barzilai, Lois Dubin, Jennifer Glaser, Harvey Goldberg, Kathryn Lavezzo,

X   ACKNOWLEDGMENTS

Tatjana Lichtenstein, Jessica Marglin, Isaac Oliver, Ranen Omer-Sherman, Laurence Roth, Andrea Siegel, and Orian Zakai.

Dan Magilow meticulously read every chapter and offered sage advice on a moment's notice. Darcy Buerkle, Abigail Gillman, and Kerry Wallach spent valuable time reading drafts and lending their keen insight and expertise to pivotal points. I am also grateful to the many other scholars who served as consistent sources of encouragement and wisdom, offering constructive comments and pointing me toward vital sources, including Elizabeth Anthony, Jörg Becker, Steven Beller, Michael Berkowitz, Tobias Brinkmann, Robert Dassanowsky, Maria Fritsche, Jay H. Geller, Alys X. George, Deborah Holmes, Malachi Hacohen, Alan Lareau, Paul Lerner, Sander L. Gilman, Rachel Gordan, Raphael Gross, Laura Morowitz, Bill Niven, Marcus Pyka, Till van Rahden, Warren Rosenblum, Marsha Rozenblit, Caroline Rupprecht, Georg Spitaler, and Frances Tanzer. Skillful editing by Rebecca Steinitz and Erin Trapp were crucial to the completion of this project. Liz Gillespie spent valuable time creating imaginative and original cover art. Deep appreciation is due to Jason Heilman for his savvy translation advice.

At Oxford University Press, I benefited greatly from Nancy Toff's experience, guidance, and humor over the course of publishing two monographs. Thanks are due as well to Meredith Taylor and two anonymous readers of this manuscript. The dedication and helpfulness of the staff of all of the archives in Austria, Germany, Israel, the Netherlands, and the United States were essential to the completion of this project. I owe a special debt of gratitude to Erika Brunngraber, Maren Kaiser, Andrew Kasiske, Susan Lowy Lubow, Ariane Niehoff-Hack, and Efram Wolff, who were so generous in sharing their families' stories and photographs.

I am deeply grateful to friends and family who provided boundless comfort and support over so many years. My dear friend Christoph Meinrenken braved challenging conditions to assist with my research. In Vienna, Elana Shapira's sharp insight always kept me on track. She and Sandra Brandeis-Crawford, Dieter Hecht, Louise Hecht, and Anton Legerer remain indispensable sources of friendship. Many thanks are also due to Willy Essl, Anneke Essl, Thomas Vitzthum, Antonia Vitzthum, and Elsa Vitzthum for always making me feel right at home.

My partner Georg Essl was always willing to hear about my adventures in the archives and help me refine ideas. My sister Jill Silverman sacrificed a great deal of her time so I could pursue research wherever it took me. Their incredible generosity and love are what made it possible for me to complete

ACKNOWLEDGMENTS xi

this project while we cared for our beloved parents, whom we miss every day. It is to Paula and Harry Silverman that I dedicate this book in loving memory.

All translations are my own unless otherwise indicated.

Portions of Chapter 1 and Chapter 2 appeared in Lisa Silverman, "Der Nachkriegsantisemit. Veit Harlan, Jud Süss und Antisemitismus nach dem Holocaust," *Einsicht. Bulletin des Fritz Bauer Instituts* 14, no. 23 (2022): 70–79.

Portions of Chapter 5 appeared in Lisa Silverman, "Review of Herzog, Hillary Hope, *Vienna Is Different: Jewish Writers in Austria from the Fin de Siècle to the Present*; Spiel, Hilde, *Return to Vienna: A Journal.*" HABSBURG, H-Net Reviews. June, 2012.

Portions of Chapter 5 and Chapter 6 appeared in Lisa Silverman, "Absent Jews and Invisible Antisemitism in Postwar Vienna: *Der Prozess* (1948) and *The Third Man* (1949)," *Journal of Contemporary History* 52, no. 2 (2017): 211–28.

Introduction

Ida Ehre Breaks Down at the Bundestag

In November 1988, the esteemed actor and theater director Ida Ehre traveled from Hamburg to Bonn to recite Paul Celan's poem "Todesfuge" (Death fugue) at a ceremony at the Bundestag (lower house of the West German parliament) to commemorate the fiftieth anniversary of the November pogroms, the so-called Kristallnacht.[1] The murders, arrests, and vandalism of that infamous night marked a turning point for many Jews, who realized they could no longer rationalize Hitler's anti-Jewish policies as fleeting or harmless. Many decided to flee, including Ehre, who suffered a stone flung through her bedroom window.[2] With her non-Jewish husband, Bernhard Heyde, and their daughter, Ruth, she boarded a ship bound for Chile in August 1939, only to find her journey interrupted by the start of the Second World War on September 1. The ship returned to Hamburg, where she spent the war, protected by her mixed marriage, although she was denounced, arrested, and imprisoned for six weeks in 1943. Her mother and sister were murdered by the Nazis.[3]

When the war ended, she re-established the Hamburg Kammerspiele (theater), where in 1947 she produced Wolfgang Borchert's popular postwar drama, *Draußen vor der Tür* (The man outside), about a German soldier who commits suicide when he is rejected by society after his return home.[4] In those early postwar years, she also performed on stage and in films such as Helmut Käutner's *In jenen Tagen* (Seven journeys, 1947), in which she drew upon her own experiences of Nazi persecution to play her Jewish character. At a time when very few German Jews returned to their homeland, Ehre relished living and working in Germany and staging performances for German audiences.[5] Although most members of the theater-going public were welcome, she reportedly did not allow Veit Harlan, the director of the antisemitic Nazi propaganda film *Jud Süss*, and his wife and the film's star, actor Kristina Söderbaum, to attend her theater in Hamburg.[6] But they were

The Postwar Antisemite. Lisa Silverman, Oxford University Press. © Oxford University Press 2025.
DOI: 10.1093/9780197697757.003.0001

2 INTRODUCTION

exceptions. By 1988, she had spent decades tiptoeing around German discomfort about antisemitism and Jews.

This history made Ehre the perfect choice for an event that was intended to be a significant step forward in West Germany's public memory of the Holocaust. It was the first commemoration of the November pogroms at the Bundestag, and Ehre was the only non-politician invited to speak. However, all did not go as planned. After she delivered a moving reading of Celan's poem, President of the Bundestag Philipp Jenninger, a member of the conservative Christian Democratic Union (CDU), spoke. After noting that he and several colleagues had attended a memorial ceremony hosted by the Central Council of Jews in Germany at the main synagogue in Frankfurt the night before, he claimed that this subsequent memorial event at the Bundestag was important because "it is not the victims, but rather we, in whose midst the crimes occurred, who must remember and be accountable, because we Germans want to achieve a clear understanding of our history and of the political lessons for our present and future."[7]

Jutta Oesterle-Schwerin, a representative from the left-wing Grüne (Green) party, immediately shouted out in protest after his distinction between Jewish "victims" and "we Germans."[8] As the speech went on, Jenninger described how Germans saw Hitler's early years as a "triumphal procession" and "glorious times," utterly sidestepping the widespread anti-Jewish measures and violence of those same years. Without establishing sufficient critical distance from what he was asking, Jenninger posed rhetorical questions from the Nazi era, such as "Hadn't Jews deserved being put back in their place?"[9] After a few more outbursts from the audience, several incensed parliamentarians walked out mid-speech.

Caught off guard by the widespread negative reaction and deeply offended that his speech had been interpreted as perpetuating antisemitism instead of opposing it, Jenninger deflected responsibility in a television interview later that night, where he petulantly remarked, "You have to learn that you can't call everything by its name in Germany."[10] The next day, images of an anguished Ehre seated next to Jenninger accompanied newspaper articles about the speech around the globe.[11] Some photographs showed Ehre with her head bowed, arms propped on the arms of her chair, and interlaced fingers covering her face (Figure I.1). Others showed her cradling her forehead in her hand, her head sunk in dismay.

The ensuing public furor led to Jenninger's resignation, effectively ending his career as an elected government official. But he was soon appointed to a

Figure I.1. Photographs featuring an emotionally distraught Ida Ehre seated next to Bundespräsident Philipp Jenninger were published in newspapers around the world in the days following the Bundestag commemoration event on November 10, 1988. © *Bundesregierung/Lothar Schaack.*

plum ambassadorship in Vienna and remained employed as a civil servant until his retirement. Jenninger ultimately issued a highly qualified apology, but his bitterness about the incident lasted for decades. In a 2006 interview, he insisted that he had intended the speech as a frank answer to the questions young Germans often asked about why their parents had become Nazis. Noting that he had received anonymous, threatening phone calls even before the event, he positioned himself as its greatest victim. Significantly, he blamed the uproar that evening not only on an audience member who yelled *Alt-Nazi* (old Nazi), but also on Ehre's reading of Celan's poem.

He said he and the audience were shocked when Ehre "roared the horrifying line from the poem into the audience, 'Der Tod ist ein Meister aus Deutschland' [Death is a master from Germany]," claiming that psychologists had analyzed the events and determined that the poem and his speech "simply weren't a good fit" and asserting that he should have delivered a "guilt and shame" speech instead. In fact, the juxtaposition of the texts was perhaps the most telling element of that day. As a poem that speaks with the

4   INTRODUCTION

full awareness of Jewish suffering, implicating Germany as a national executioner, Celan's words underscored how Jenninger's effort to rationalize German willingness to follow Hitler entirely missed the point.[12]

As well as criticizing the poem, Jenninger implicated Ehre's reading in his distress: "I had my first heart attack during the speech. I didn't notice it directly, I just felt my body trembling. I thought it was due to Ida Ehre's presentation and the turmoil I described.... So I was physically and psychologically very much weakened during this speech."[13] Like many Germans after the war, Jenninger was deeply invested in his self-identification as a good, moral person. Hearing himself called a Nazi and watching legislators walk out of his speech about the Holocaust would have challenged his very sense of self. Yet, in the following weeks he received thousands of letters and expressions of support from individuals who believed he had been unfairly punished for speaking the truth.[14] Nevertheless, Jenninger focused his energy on refuting the accusation of antisemitism and positioning himself as the event's true victim.

The emotionally charged images of Ehre with her head in her hands turned her into a symbol of the embarrassment, shame, and anger of many Germans over Jenninger's speech. However, Ehre maintained that her own presentation of the poem, not the speech, was the cause of her emotional distress—an explanation that seemed to satisfy Jenninger alone.[15] Few others seemed prepared to take Ehre at her word. Former German Chancellor Helmut Schmidt said, "I was there. I remember that she quoted Celan's 'Todesfuge' on this occasion, recited in the Bundestag. And the President of the Bundestag, Jenninger, made a well-intended speech, which, however, seemed absurdly twisted to such an extent that it spread consternation and horror in Parliament, and I remember Ida Ehre's face, which was also horrified."[16]

The Bundestag event and its aftermath represent the culmination of decades of post-Holocaust culture that was designed to comfortably distance non-Jews from associations with antisemitism. This book delves deep into the immediate postwar period to examine how trials, films, and literature helped create this comfortable distance by constructing a mythical, imagined Antisemite in the form of an outsider who threatened non-Jews as well as Jews. This figure served to restrict antisemitism to the intentional words and deeds of a circumscribed group of bad people, thus shielding Germans and Austrians from coming to terms with their complicity in Nazi atrocities and insulating them from broader accusations of antisemitism.

INTRODUCTION 5

By now, scholarship has grown to encompass myriad methods of identifying and thinking about antisemitism. In general, the notion of antisemitism as the mindset of a few bad apples is considered a fallacy. Recent sociological studies about prejudices suggest that it is better described not exclusively as a personal trait, but as a system of thought that remains embedded in culture, often in unstated or invisible ways, like other forms of discrimination into which we are all socialized.[17] That means that, like it or not, we all run the risk of expressing and engaging prejudices, regardless of how we feel about them. I build upon these notions and frame antisemitism as one iteration of what I have defined elsewhere as "Jewish difference": the hierarchical social framework that encompasses the relationship between the constructed categories of Jew and non-Jew.[18] This term allows us to separate antisemitism from the broader framework that generates iterations of the Jew and non-Jew, just as we separate sexism and misogyny from the framework of gender.[19]

Jewish difference is best understood as one of a number of analytic categories, like gender, sexuality, race, and class, that not only intersect and overlap via broadly understood social codes, but also use each other's terms to express their power.[20] It is a deeply embedded ordering system of imagined ideals that remains distinct from the people it affects: Jews, non-Jews, and individuals of every possible degree of self-identification in between. This ordering system forms not only the basis for violence against Jews, but also the foundation for opportunistic support for and celebration of Jews, as well as moments in which responses to and attitudes about Jews may be more ambiguous, displaced, contradictory, or suppressed.[21] *All* of these responses stem from a deeply embedded, hierarchical binary system of thought in which the constructed Jew functions as the quintessential Other, who, in the absence of being recognized and destabilized, continues to be perpetuated.[22]

Crucially, this analytic framework also illuminates how the absence of explicit antisemitism in a narrative does not necessarily mean that its deeply embedded cultural stereotypes have been erased.[23] They often still appear in coded or subtle terms and are applied to Jews or to people only imagined to be Jewish. Jewish difference enables us to consider how antisemitism targets people with varying relationships to Judaism, including self-professed Jews, former Jews, people whose parents converted before they were born, or people only imagined to be Jewish. While self-identifications of the Jews considered in this book varied widely, I include their experiences with the conviction that Jewish self-identification should not form the ontological

6 INTRODUCTION

foundation of a study of antisemitism after the Holocaust. This flexibility is more in keeping with most people's lives and works, which distinguished between Jews and non-Jews (as people), on the one hand, and the Jewish and non-Jewish (as cultural categories), on the other.[24] Moreover, it allows us to better understand how the discursive logic of narratives intended to oppose antisemitism can still reflect and reinforce the constructed categories of Jewish difference that make antisemitism possible, rather than destabilize them.

Given that the power of the figural Antisemite hinges on its liminal position between Jew and non-Jew, it is not surprising that many of those who either engaged or sought to avoid its terms grappled with such liminality in their daily lives. Numerous individuals discussed in this book were targeted by the Nazis because of their mixed Jewish/non-Jewish parentage, grew up with Jewish parents and converted or left the Jewish community, grew up with parents who converted from Judaism before they were born, or were married to non-Jews. Non-Jews married to Jews were also often especially attuned to the power and pliability of the constructed categories of Jewish difference.[25]

Contextualizing antisemitism—whether subtle innuendo, negative stereotype, or violent act—as one iteration of this broader ordering system of Jewish difference illuminates how, after the genocide of Europe's Jews, a figural Antisemite allowed people to imagine themselves not simply as individuals who did not hate Jews, but as individuals operating outside the entire framework of social constructions that made antisemitism possible. Ironically, however, this idealized Antisemite, who shouldered the blame for antisemitism so that others could disavow it, ultimately contributed to its perpetuation and power by holding the framework of Jewish difference in place, rather than calling it into question. The Antisemite was mutable: while it often was presented as an adult, non-Jewish male, it could appear as a woman, a child, or even—a Jew. Indeed, this Antisemite was most effective when occupying both sides of the threshold of Jewish difference via a mix of Jewish- and non-Jewish-coded characteristics.[26] As such, the Antisemite reflected the convergence of abstract, negative stereotypes about Jews and the growing need to demonstrate pro-Jewish attitudes in the postwar period.[27]

One way this postwar Antisemite operated was by enabling people to imagine non-Jews as its primary target. The thematization of non-Jews as victims had already begun during the Second World War, when Nazis portrayed Bolsheviks and Jews as threats from the East to encourage support for the war.[28] These characterizations drew upon age-old antisemitic portrayals of Jews as criminals, murderers, and vermin—which the Nazis used to argue that Jews were dangerous to the health of the German nation.[29] After the war, claiming victim status allowed non-Jews to imagine themselves as targets of revenge on the part of the Allied Forces and returning Jews, who were often merged into one imagined force of vengeance.[30] The stereotype of the supposedly vengeful Jew became a critical buttress for this narrative of victimization.[31]

The expansion of its victim pool allowed antisemitism to signify not only hatred of Jews, but also the corruption of culture in general, and opposing it was thus transformed into a far-reaching humanitarian value. On the surface, this might not sound problematic—after all, antisemitism is not a problem for Jews alone to solve. But framing antisemitism in this manner dilutes the impact of the specific ways it targets and hurts Jews.[32] Foregrounding the Antisemite's non-Jewish victims emerged as the concept of guilt and, more specifically, collective guilt became associated with debating German *Vergangenheitsbewältigung*, or working through the past.[33] But the idea of charging Germans with collective guilt was also propagated by Germans themselves; in fact, it aided in their self-fashioning as powerless victims of an unjust accusation.[34] In July 1946, Moses Moskowitz wrote, "Perhaps the most common mechanism by which the German masses avoid a sense of guilt for the fate of the first and most tragic victims of Nazism, the six million Jewish dead, is to convince themselves that they, too, have been victims of Nazism, and possibly in greater measure than any other people."[35]

Postwar narratives of non-Jewish victimhood often reinforce antisemitism even when those who invoke this victimhood intend the exact opposite. Appropriating the language of a taboo on antisemitism while continuing to place Jews at a disadvantage by making them secondary to non-Jews was a crucial strategy that post-1945 cultural narratives use to perpetuate antisemitism under the guise of opposing it. This was evident in Jenninger's interview about the aftermath of his speech, when he usurped the role of the victim from an elderly Jewish woman who had been persecuted by the Nazis and redirected public sympathy back upon himself. He did not deny the existence of the Antisemite: rather, he identified himself as its victim.[36] In doing so, he drew upon an oft-repeated, postwar narrative cycle in which West Germans, East Germans, and Austrians constructed a figural Antisemite who was a powerful entity separate from them and then imagined themselves to be its primary victims. Examining how the Antisemite emerged in

8   INTRODUCTION

these three countries as they configured new national and geopolitical self-understandings shows how its pliability allowed each country to shape a sense of victimhood and distance from antisemitism.[37]

After the Allied Forces emerged victorious, the sense of persistent national victimization, first by the Nazis and then by the Allied Occupation Forces, became a powerful narrative. Compulsory German and Austrian denazification proceedings also contributed to this narrative of victimhood, as the label "Nazi" soon became shorthand for authoritarianism and antisemitism.[38] The figural Antisemite thus came to be particularly useful after 1945, as formal renunciations of antisemitism and pro-Jewish assertions proliferated in a matrix of relationships among the Allied Forces, the general population, and Jewish re-émigres. Usurped Jewish victimhood, Jewish absence, and philosemitism all played a role in these national variations on the Antisemite.[39]

Each category was weighted according to the country's political and cultural needs. West Germany bore the most historical and moral responsibility for the Holocaust, and West Germans grappled most openly with antisemitism and issues surrounding collective guilt for Nazi crimes. West Germany found its victimhood by focusing on high-level Nazis, like Hitler and the war criminals tried at Nuremberg, who were guilty not only of perpetrating antisemitism but also of forcing others to follow their orders. This focus on high-level defendants helped exonerate everyone else from complicity in Nazi crimes and, again, to subordinate Jewish victimhood.[40] The Antisemite who emerged in the widely publicized trials of Nazi filmmaker Veit Harlan for crimes against humanity between 1948 and 1950 provided a prominent model that individuals could use to embody a German patriotism and morality that disavowed Nazi complicity.

In the Soviet-occupied zone out of which East Germany emerged in 1949, government officials grew to focus on casting former Nazi functionaries in the leadership of West Germany as fascists responsible for the persistence of antisemitism there.[41] The state set the cultural agenda via the creation of a capitalist Antisemite who supported the political goal of assigning responsibility for Nazism to West Germany and targeted communists as its primary victims. Envisioning the Antisemite as a capitalist and fascist helped frame the nascent nation as a bastion of anti-fascist resistance as it subsumed the persecution of Jews as part of a broader class war.[42] Shaping the Antisemite as a symbol of capitalist oppression enabled East Germany to evoke—and by extension claim to embody—an ideal Germany that had no antisemitism, in contrast to the capitalist society of the West (Germany) that fostered it.[43]

During this period, Austrians walked a fine, precarious line between maintaining a sense of self-identification separate from the culture and deeds of their East and West German neighbors and laying claim to the German language and culture they shared.[44] By continuously keeping with its treasured status as "Hitler's first victim," bestowed upon their country by the Allied Forces, whose Moscow Declaration of 1943 set forth this disingenuous myth (ignoring the many Austrians who embraced the *Anschluss*, Hitler's annexation of Austria to Nazi Germany in 1938), Austria modeled how an entire country could usurp Jewish victimhood, a fantasy that depended in part upon erasing both Jews and Antisemites from Austria's past and future.[45] Meanwhile, in the United States, the Antisemite helped audiences imagine that its most dangerous iteration existed only in Hitler's Europe. It also exposed the degree to which the constructed Antisemite was not a phenomenon limited to Europe and often relied upon race and gender for its narrative power.[46]

Antisemitism is sometimes referred to as the "longest hatred," and its effects around the globe persist to this day—indeed, they are once again increasing. The recent surge in acts of antisemitic violence cannot be separated from the growing acceptance of verbal and visual public expressions of antisemitism. The seeds for this acceptance were sown immediately after 1945, when the Antisemite was reconfigured without challenging, or even addressing, the terms of Jewish difference. This book focuses largely on East and West Germany and Austria in the decade after 1945 because the Nazi persecution of Jews began on those territories, and their postwar absence of Jews was most relevant to the construction of the postwar Antisemite—and to understanding that figure today. Although the Nazis and their helpers decimated the Jewish communities in all three countries, West Germany, once home to the largest number of Jews among the three, took on the brunt of responsibility for addressing Nazi crimes and remained closely watched for its postwar engagement with Jews and antisemitism.[47] This commitment helps explain the uproar over Jenninger's speech and the ways it illustrated the enduring tension between personal and political understandings of the Antisemite.[48]

The persistence of animosity toward Jews in early postwar Europe was widely recognized at the time. Sporadic outbursts of antisemitic violence included Poland's Kielce Pogrom of July 4, 1946, which killed 42 Jews and

10   INTRODUCTION

wounded more than 50. Between November 1944 and 1947, around one thousand Jews were killed in Poland.[49] In 1946, there were pogroms in thirteen communities in Hungary.[50] Antisemitic accusations persisted as well. In 1948, a woman in Memmingen, Germany, accused a Jewish concentration camp survivor of kidnapping her four-year-old son to use his blood for a Jewish ritual, and three Jews in Bayreuth were rumored to have carried out a ritual murder on a local citizen who had disappeared.[51] In 1946, an Austrian from Bad Ischl spread the rumor that former Jewish concentration camp inmates had infested candy with tuberculosis bacteria and given it to children, making them sick.[52] Jewish cemeteries were desecrated, Jewish institutions were defaced with swastikas and anti-Jewish slogans, and Jews were verbally assaulted. While few non-Jews openly supported these acts, the most frequent response was indifference.[53]

Journalists also reported on the persistence of widespread antisemitic attitudes. In articles in *Commentary* in 1946, Hal Lehrman painted a lurid portrait of economic depression, overcrowded conditions, and antisemitic attitudes in Austria, and Moses Moskowitz claimed that few of the Germans he interviewed over the course of a year "were free from anti-Jewish bias of one kind or another."[54] However, news reports and films about the murder of Jews, which the Allied Forces forced people to view, made many want to distance themselves from any association with antisemitism.[55] As Moskowitz wrote: "Indeed, there is hardly a German who doesn't express horror at the mention of concentration camps and crematoria."[56] Writing for the *Menorah Journal* in the fall of 1947, Heinz Liepman offered a similarly bleak outlook, noting the disconnect between the "beautifully phrased" articles about "collective guilt" in magazines and newspapers and the unwillingness of Germans to address antisemitic acts: "But we have not heard a single German statesman, politician, editor, or intellectual protest against any of these happenings or suggest a way to help the surviving German Jews."[57] And West Germans remained sensitive to how the outside world viewed them. By September 1951, when West German Chancellor Konrad Adenauer finally made an official statement against antisemitism, the constructed Antisemite had already emerged as a pervasive narrative device in trials, literature, films, and dramas.[58]

In fact, postwar antisemitism often functioned silently and invisibly, in coded terms, at times reinforced through people convinced they were avoiding it. The continuation of hidden prejudices against Jews in the face of their decimation formed part of an ironic phenomenon so widespread in postwar Europe that the journalist Paul Lendvai aptly dubbed it "antisemitism without Jews."[59] As Austrian journalist Artur Rosenberg noted in a 1946 article for *Neues Österreich*, conspicuous antisemitism became publicly unacceptable, particularly in the media, entertainment, and politics.[60] At the same time, in a pattern familiar from other taboos, it became more likely to rear its head via code words, dog whistles, and backhanded efforts to deny its existence. Examples of this include Mayor Theodor Körner's 1947 attempt to blame the "foreign press" for circulating the accusation that Vienna was antisemitic, and the common postwar joke from the Jewish perspective, critiquing that misplaced blame: "'Die Nazis haben ja alles ramponiert,' raunzte ein Alt-Wiener, 'selbst den Antisemitismus'" (The Nazis ruined everything, complained the old man from Vienna, even antisemitism).[61] Given how few people were willing to own up to antisemitic attitudes, despite their ubiquity, psychologist Bernd Marin aptly termed this new taboo "antisemitism without antisemites."[62]

Viennese-born Germanist and Auschwitz survivor Ruth Klüger noted early on that postwar German-language literature tended to exclude Jews and to portray all Central Europeans as victims. Instead of facing the past critically, their authors resurrected Jewish stereotypes in characters that indirectly evoked Jews as both victims and victimizers.[63] The much-recited dark joke, "The Germans will never forgive the Jews for Auschwitz," makes this point succinctly. Indeed, several postwar polls indicated that significant proportions of the population blamed Jews for their own persecution during the war, which was one step on the path to conflating Jews with the idealized Antisemite.[64]

New postwar prescriptions for positive representations of Jews and negative representations of Antisemites resulted in the development of the constructed Antisemite as a non-Jewish/evil/Nazi/Nazi-aligned character who was nevertheless described in stereotypical terms associated at least in part with Jewishness.[65] These codes enabled the postwar Antisemite to be ugly or beautiful, seductive or anodyne, urban or rural, socialist or capitalist, or corrupt, urban, depraved, materialist, decadent, and immoral, depending on the demands of the narrative it intended to serve. This elasticity met the political and cultural demands for a negative postwar Antisemite while implicitly allowing antisemitism to persist and opening up space for non-Jews to take the place of the Antisemite's Jewish victims. Indeed, the Antisemite's victims were often depicted as so-called good Germans: non-Jewish

12 INTRODUCTION

characters defined by moral purity, opposition to antisemitism, and martyrdom.[66]

Before 1933, Jewish characters in texts and films often represented negative qualities such as conspicuous consumption, insatiable greed, deviant sexuality, and rootlessness. After 1933, to align with the Nazi agenda, authors and filmmakers often replaced Jewish characters with Aryans coded with Jewish characteristics who became the locus for such negative qualities, sometimes called "white Jews."[67] After 1945, even narratives seeking to oppose antisemitism nevertheless included characters with the negative characteristics previously reserved for Jews and "white Jews," at times mixing Jewish- and non-Jewish-coded features.[68]

Important studies of antisemitism after 1945 have drawn attention to how Central Europeans sought to deflect guilt for the crimes of the Nazis by trying to halt discussion of the Holocaust—commonly referred to as *einen Schlußstrich ziehen* (to draw a line under)—and blaming Jews for continually bringing it up, which is sometimes referred to as "secondary antisemitism."[69] There is a rich history of delineations of various types of Jew-hatred, such as the violent acts sometimes referred to in German as *Radauantisemitismus* (hooligan antisemitism; literally "antisemitism that makes a racket"); the persistence of dormant prejudices, known as latent antisemitism; identifying good Jews in order to denigrate bad Jews, sometimes called selective antisemitism; and the phenomenon of celebrating Jews by deploying positive stereotypes or opposing negative stereotypes, often referred to as philosemitism and anti-antisemitism, respectively.[70] Although these terms are useful in various contexts, a preoccupation with these distinctions runs headlong into the argument that the struggle for the authority to define the Antisemite, and thus to make such distinctions, is one of antisemitism's most powerful and persistent postwar legacies.

After 1945, a widespread desire for comfort and distance from antisemitism writ large became an end in itself. To service that desire, many narratives that oppose antisemitism, as well as individual attempts to avoid being called antisemitic, can be understood as attempts to assert the authority to define the imagined, so-called Antisemite. This approach helps explain how so many early postwar narratives that aimed to avoid or counteract antisemitism in fact subtly reinforced the familiar ordering framework of Jewish difference, which inevitably located the Jewish as subordinate to the non-Jewish. In so doing, they often reproduced antisemitic effects and perpetuated antisemitism as a powerful narrative force.

INTRODUCTION 13

Inventing the Antisemite

In his now-famous *Réflexions sur la question juive* (1946; *Anti-Semite and Jew*), the philosopher Jean-Paul Sartre observed, "If the Jew did not exist, the anti-Semite would invent him," articulating a figural Jew whose presence in popular consciousness has persisted for decades.[71] To be sure, Sartre's book bravely highlighted a number of truths about antisemitism in postwar Europe that few others were willing to confront. After the Holocaust, many people were relieved to find a well-respected non-Jewish intellectual denouncing the hatred of Jews so openly, while also clearly pointing out that this hatred was based in fantasy rather than fact.

Even contemporaneous Jewish émigré scholars of antisemitism who engaged deeply and scientifically with the topic in the years immediately following the Holocaust praised the essay. In their study *Anti-Semitism and Emotional Disorder: A Psychoanalytic Interpretation* (1950), social psychologist Marie Jahoda and psychoanalyst Nathan Ackerman acknowledged their debt to it: "Recently, Jean Sartre, in his *Portrait of an Anti-Semite*, has given an intuitive description which contains many similarities to ours."[72] Max Horkheimer and Theodor Adorno referenced Sartre's "brilliant paper" in their influential study *The Authoritarian Personality* (1950), noting that they found it remarkable how closely his portrait of the Antisemite resembled their empirical observations and quantitative analysis.[73] In the decades since, countless scholars and others have praised what they perceive as Sartre's astute articulation of the constructed Jew as an expression of self-serving nonsense by naïve or irrational individuals.[74]

However, Sartre's much-quoted line in fact ascribes a great deal of power to a figural Antisemite who bears full responsibility for demonizing Jews and, crucially, is distanced from Sartre and his readers. Few people realize the connections between this sentence and a statement in *Hitler m'a dit* (*Hitler Speaks: A Series of Political Conversations with Adolf Hitler on His Real Aims*), a book first published in 1939 by former Nazi party member Hermann Rauschning, which Sartre read at the time.[75] The book was later acknowledged to be a fraudulent account of the author's discussions with Hitler that never happened.[76] Sartre likely adapted his famous formulation from a passage in which Rauschning imagines Hitler's response when asked whether he wanted to completely destroy Jews: "No, replied Hitler, on the contrary, if the Jew did not exist, we would have to invent him."[77] Sartre's recycling of Hitler's words as imagined by Rauschning positions the Antisemite and its

14   INTRODUCTION

constructed, demonized Jew within a system of categorization that is theirs alone—everyone else can live their lives outside it.[78] As such, his text asserts his own authority to define the Antisemite as an entity separate from himself and his readers.[79]

Sartre's oft-quoted formulation became popular among Jews and non-Jews alike, in part because it allowed readers to envision a society largely free of Antisemites. For non-Jews, it meant they didn't have to be blamed for antisemitism. For Jews, the belief that most non-Jews were not Antisemites helped uphold a fantasy of inclusion among non-Jews. The naïve belief that one could stand comfortably outside the self-contained, constructed categories of the "Antisemite" and its "Jew" gained traction at a time when people wanted to distance themselves from antisemitism but were unable to part with the powerful terms of Jewish difference that continued to inform trials, films, and literature. The idea of a constructed Jew that was the product of the Antisemite's imagination allowed often well-intentioned people to believe they did not participate in perpetuating deeply engrained stereotypes and practices that placed Jews at a disadvantage.

Scholars have long acknowledged the historical importance of the figure of the Jew who functions as an imagined Other in a broader social framework.[80] Determining who can serve as this Other is often framed by scholars as the arbitrary, political power of antisemitism, as in the case of fin-de-siècle Viennese mayor Karl Lueger, who supposedly offered the phrase "Wer Jude ist bestimme ich!" (I determine who is a Jew!).[81] In other words: the decision where and when to deploy antisemitism is his alone. This statement suggests that what is most powerful about antisemitism is that the speaker can decide how to define its target.[82]

After the Second World War, the figural Antisemite came to stand in for the figural Jew as the primary Other whom a wide range of narratives claimed authority to define—and imbue with negative qualities.[83] The locus of antisemitism's narrative power thus shifted to the imagined phrase "I determine who is an Antisemite," as the ability to determine who was an Antisemite now conferred moral authority, especially in countries where large numbers of Jews had been killed or displaced. The Antisemite thus became an important and powerful rhetorical device that helped distance everyone else from the horrors of the Holocaust, the stigma of Nazism, and the immorality that came to be associated with both, while offering Jews and non-Jews alike the illusion that antisemitism was not integral to the culture they loved, but rather limited to a finite number of individuals, times, and places.

It is for this reason that postwar narratives often hinge on the various ways in which filmmakers, writers, and other public figures manipulated, shaped, and recast stereotypes about Jews according to their and their audience's needs for addressing antisemitism. How they do so is best understood by foregrounding the constructed, symbolic substance of what people understand as Jewish and not Jewish and by investigating how these codings are used to make cultural artifacts meaningful to people's everyday lives.

It is difficult to untangle a study of postwar antisemitism from issues surrounding the Holocaust and guilt for Nazi crimes. Holding individuals accountable for their treatment of Jews between 1933 and 1945 is different from evaluating their degree of complicity in the perpetuation of antisemitism in their words and deeds after the war. The expression of antisemitic prejudices, like their absence, can be useful historical evidence, but a study of antisemitism needs to be able to examine how people used those expressions to define the Antisemite—without reinscribing that very process. If we continue to place a premium on defining the Antisemite, rather than analyzing how the discursive logic of antisemitism continues to function in narratives that purport to disavow it, then we risk complicity in that very system. We also risk falling prey to the simplistic postwar logic used by those who insisted that their acts of kindness to individual Jews were more important than any antisemitic prejudices they might have casually (or purposefully) expressed or acted upon.[84]

To understand postwar antisemitism, it is helpful to shift our attention away from the guilt of those directly involved in the genocide of the Jews toward the more widespread activity of continuing to engage in—rather than actively destabilizing and destroying—an antisemitized culture that perpetuates harmful stereotypes and beliefs about Jews.[85] This means recognizing the deep-seated, continued presence of Jewish difference in postwar culture as an ordering system that has the potential to inform *everybody's* actions and ideas. Because nobody can avoid being socialized into this system of beliefs, everyone is at risk of deploying it in some form, at some time. However, people can become more self-reflexive: they can recognize and take responsibility for their roles in perpetuating it, instead of deflecting, denying, or being complacent about it. To be sure, participation in this system is often neither conscious nor intentional.[86] But the term

16   INTRODUCTION

"unconscious antisemitism" obscures how this system remains powerful precisely because its advantages remain invisible to the person who benefits from them. In other words, antisemitism often functions because of, not in spite of, a lack of intent. The term "complicity" need not signal a moral evaluation of individual behavior. Instead, it can emphasize how systems of difference maintain their power precisely because we are not aware of how they operate.

We can look to the cultures of early postwar East and West Germany and Austria in order to understand how the experience of complicity in perpetuating antisemitism after the Holocaust was distinctly different from bearing responsibility for the crimes of others in the past.[87] Popular cultural narratives resonated precisely because, rather than simply exploring individual prejudices, they provided comfortable ways for Germans and Austrians to avoid confronting their own complicity in perpetuating a system that gave them advantages as non-Jews. Rather than trying to determine whether to label people as Antisemites or victims, a more fruitful approach is to allow the complexities of each individual's life and work to reveal the discursive logic of antisemitism embedded in their assertions of the authority to assign those labels.[88]

Jewish Victims

Jewish victims of Nazi persecution who lived in or returned to Europe faced particular challenges engaging with and responding to the Antisemite after the war. They had to re-establish their lives in the shadow of a de facto, worldwide Jewish ban/boycott of German language and culture and a lack of support for re-establishing their lives in the "land of the murderers."[89] And yet, by 1948, over a hundred Jewish communities had been re-established in Germany, with Jewish populations of 8,000 in Berlin and 3,300 in Munich, though most others had fewer than fifty members.[90] In Vienna, from 1948 up until 1959, the Jewish community had around 8,000 members.[91] These communities included former displaced persons (DPs) from Eastern Europe, as well as German and Austrian Jews. And yet, the years of shared suffering of Jews under the Nazis did not eliminate the strong cultural and political differences among them, which often re-emerged after the war.[92]

Hal Lerhman, writing in *Commentary*, described the dreary state of affairs for the few Jews in Vienna in the early postwar years. He also lamented the demise of Vienna's prewar cultural life, in which Jews had played major roles: "At the moment, this capital of deathless song and café wit is less concerned with yesterday's *Wienerlieder* and today's feuilleton than with scrounging enough food somehow to keep alive until tomorrow."[93] Nevertheless, cultural life quickly re-established itself in Austria and Germany, and a handful of re-émigrés reclaimed their cultural prominence in Vienna.[94] The suppression of antisemitism made it possible for re-émigrés to rebuild their lives and participate successfully in the public sphere. Yet they paid a price for this role. They had to carefully circumscribe the way they spoke about their own suffering if they wanted to continue to write, publish, and perform for broad audiences.[95] But the cost of achieving popularity was typically a tacit agreement to remain silent about their audience's complicity, or at least to allow those audiences to be comfortable while considering it.[96]

Jews were a minority group with the most to lose from the ordering system of which antisemitism was a critical component. Thus, the choices and actions of Jews, even if they appeared aligned with antisemitism or had antisemitic effects, must always be contextualized within a system that disadvantaged them. After the war, as before, even those who did not self-identify as Jews were subject to its consequences. Jews who returned to Europe were often shut out of the emotional communities formed by non-Jews.[97] Austrian-Jewish actor Fritz Kortner highlighted these communities when he chronicled his return to Germany in 1945: "I fought to recognize my equal rights in the misfortune and misery I suffered."[98] Writer Hilde Spiel expressed similar sentiments when she described returning to Vienna from exile and being told by an acquaintance how lucky she was not to have had to live through the destruction of the city.[99] Austrian director Willi Forst undermined his open request for Austrian exiles to return by stressing their responsibility to help rebuild the country while implying that they been comfortably lounging around swimming pools in Hollywood while Austrians suffered at home.[100]

In 1950, at Max Horkheimer's installation as rector of the University of Frankfurt after his years of exile in the United States, Walter Leiske, the mayor of Frankfurt am Main, suggested that the return of Jews to West Germany was valued for how it might serve the efforts of non-Jewish Germans to come to terms with the past.[101] Horkheimer's private letters from the immediate postwar period indicate that he felt the need to tread carefully as a Jewish re-émigré, despite his prestigious position.[102] Just as Jews who returned to Austria and Germany did not share the wartime experiences of non-Jews, they didn't share their postwar resentment at having to face guilt and

18   INTRODUCTION

responsibility for antisemitism—a resentment that was sometimes projected onto Jewish re-émigrés themselves.

Fritz Kortner addressed this issue in his screenplay for director Josef von Báky's *Der Ruf* (The last illusion, 1949), in which he also starred. It was the first film to deal directly with the return of Jews to Germany and one of a number of films that engaged the issue of postwar antisemitism.[103] Kortner, who spent the war years in exile in Hollywood, cast himself as an exiled Jewish philosophy professor who returns to Germany after the war to take up his old position, only to face antisemitism from a group of his students, the leader of whom turns out to be his own son from his pre-war marriage to his non-Jewish wife.[104] Unsurprisingly, given its depiction of the persistence of antisemitism among Germans, the film was a box-office failure despite a number of positive press reviews.[105]

Journalists like Karena Niehoff, who testified publicly against Veit Harlan, and Heinz Liepman, who dared to publish newspaper articles that called out former Nazis in positions of power, faced threats of violence and insults.[106] It is no wonder that actors like Karl Farkas and Ida Ehre appeased audiences in order to maintain their careers. Cabaret director and performer Stella Kadmon was involved in highly critical political cabaret before she fled Austria in 1938; in postwar Vienna, she toned down the politics of her cabarets, and even her anti-fascist plays portrayed antisemitism in a way that let Austrians and Germans off the hook.[107] Although Jews did not operate outside the system of Jewish difference that generated antisemitism, the fact that they could be disadvantaged by it, seemingly at will, means that we must consider their engagement with antisemitic stereotypes differently.

Jews who immersed themselves in postwar culture had to walk a fine line in their public relationships with non-Jewish Germans and Austrians. For some, postwar antisemitism also complicated the choices they made in their private lives. Ida Ehre had no difficulty excluding Veit Harlan and his wife from her theater. Yet she maintained a close friendship with another Nazi star director, Wolfgang Liebeneiner, and his wife, actor Hilde Krahl, who had been a member of the Nazi party.[108] Though Ehre is rarely credited for her role in adapting Wolfgang Borchert's radio play *Draußen vor der Tür* (The man outside) for the stage, she ensured that it debuted at her Hamburger Kammerspiele under the direction of Liebeneiner, who went on to direct an adapted version as his first post-Nazi era film, retitled *Liebe 47*.[109] Ehre described her friends:

For me, Hilde Krahl and Wolfgang Liebeneiner became a ray of hope after this evil, darkest, worst time of my life, which had been behind me in the previous twelve years. I never had the feeling that the two of them could have done anything they were accused of during the Nazi era. That is why it struck me deeply when many people said to me at the time: "How can you, how can you prefer these two when they achieved this and that during the Nazi era." I listened to that and didn't want to believe it.[110]

Ehre's denial was powerful, but so was her need for her friends.

Ehre survived the war in no small part due to her privileged position as the wife of Bernhard Heyde, a self-proclaimed German nationalist who, she implies, refused to sleep with her after 1934 because she was a Jew. Ehre only admitted this decades later:

My husband was a strange person, a very torn, ambiguous person. He never stopped loving me, even then, in 1934, when he told me that he could no longer live with me "maritally." He had his view of the world, and sometimes I couldn't understand that. But he had tremendous humor and wit, and yet I was infinitely grateful to him for everything he had done for us. That's probably why I stayed with him, although this loyalty came at a high price.[111]

Ehre's marriage and postwar connections to Germans associated with Nazi ideology complicate our understanding of her postwar position as a Jewish victim of Nazi persecution in West Germany, whose status limited her options.[112]

Journalist Ralph Giordano described how the immediate years after the Second World War were especially difficult for victims of Nazi persecution, given the broader population's denial of complicity in both Nazism and antisemitism: "For me, the most morally devastating experiences with my German environment do not happen in the period before liberation, but in the months immediately afterwards, in which there is such untruthfulness, cowardice and hypocrisy."[113] Writing in 1947 about Jews who returned to Hamburg, Heinz Liepman observed, "Over two years have passed since the powers of freedom and decency won the war; but the wrong hasn't been righted yet, and the survivors of the greatest massacre in the history of our world are still standing outside the gates of their houses, and the Nazis are

20 INTRODUCTION

still inside."[114] Having reported on the Nuremberg trials and the trials of Veit Harlan, Liepman was well aware that it was important to bring powerful figures to trial—but also that blaming major figures allowed those who played smaller roles in the war, including politicians, to ignore both their own culpability (or at least complicity) and the presence of former Nazis in positions of power. As Rabbi Joachim Prinz, who left Berlin for the United States in 1937, cautioned in July 1949, "We must make it our business to watch the political developments in Germany carefully. There is no question in my mind that Germany might become the headquarters of world anti-Semitism."[115]

Only by remaining mindful of how other systems of difference, such as gender, sexuality, class, and race, remain crucial to the persistence of the figural Antisemite can we begin to understand and undermine its narrative power.[116] To highlight the particular salience of gender to its analysis, the experiences of women who were vulnerable to the Nazis provide crucial context for understanding how the Antisemite figures in popular events and works created by men who were often, unsurprisingly, more prominent. Although many have examined the significance of Jenninger's speech to the history of Holocaust memorialization in West Germany, they overlook Ida Ehre's role in the event. Jenninger's defensive outrage at her reading of Celan's poem and his portrayal of himself as her victim typified a common response to postwar associations with antisemitism that further entrenched the idea that the true victims of the Nazis were non-Jews. Ehre's denial that the delivery of Jenninger's speech had troubled her underscores her experience as a Jewish woman facing German discomfort with being associated with antisemitism.[117] Jenninger's emotional response to the criticism of his speech, conditioned by a sense of male entitlement, reflects the powerful role of the imagined Antisemite in the precarious postwar emotional landscape that Jewish and non-Jewish writers, actors, filmmakers, and directors had to navigate to create popular culture.[118]

For years, many people debated whether Jenninger's speech was truly harmful and questioned whether his critics were self-serving opportunists or if they were actually concerned with working through the German past. Regardless of their merit, these analyses tend to reduce the historical significance of this moment. The events at the Bundestag, which resonated around the world, underscore what early postwar trials, films, and literature revealed decades earlier: not only that words matter, but also that, after the Holocaust, the question of who speaks about antisemitism and how they speak gained new and highly influential power.

PART I
WEST GERMANY
The Patriot and the Antisemite

1

Harlan's Jews

Dora Gerson, Julius Bab, and the Legacy of *Jud Süss*

On April 25, 1935, Dora Gerson recorded several songs in the cellar of a Berlin synagogue, including "Vorbei" (Gone, beyond recall), a haunting German ballad about lost love, and "Niggun" (Melody), based on the Yiddish folk song "Der Rebbe hot gehaissen frailech sain" (The Rabbi says be merry).[1] That spring, along with the recording session, Gerson performed in late-night variety shows for Jewish youths and a few other events that still welcomed Jews.[2] But these meager opportunities were a far cry from the broad range of dramatic, cabaret, and film performances that, in the dozen years before Hitler came to power in 1933, had critics calling her "one of the best chansonnières," able to "produce every shade of joy and sorrow, intelligence and humor, all streaming from a fount of wonderful vitality and naturalness."[3]

Dorothea (Dora) Gerson (Figure 1.1) was born in Berlin in 1899 to Max and Johanna Hermine Gerson.[4] She studied at Max Reinhardt's drama school, then began acting professionally, including at Berlin's esteemed Volksbühne and with Erwin Piscator's avant-garde Bühne. In 1920, she appeared in two silent film adaptations of Karl May novels.[5] In 1922, she married Veit Harlan, who had also recently begun his acting career. They performed in the traveling Holtorf Troupe before splitting up in 1924. Though the marriage had been brief, its consequences on their later lives would be profound. For it was Gerson and other Jews affiliated with Harlan who became central touchstones to his postwar self-fashioning as the victim of the Antisemite.

Gerson's colleagues provided many testaments to her unique qualities as a beloved performer. Austrian-Jewish actor and director Leo Lindtberg described her as a "magnificent actor" who was "beautiful, warm-hearted and gifted."[6] Pianist Herman Kruyt admired the polish and emotional nuance of her singing.[7] Colleague Lale Anderson highlighted her sex appeal, and composer Curt Bry commented on her inner strength, soulfulness, and

The Postwar Antisemite. Lisa Silverman, Oxford University Press. © Oxford University Press 2025.
DOI: 10.1093/9780197697757.003.0002

Figure 1.1. Performer Dora Gerson faced increasingly narrow career opportunities in Germany in the 1930s as her ex-husband Veit Harlan's participation in the film world increased. *Courtesy of Cabaret Ping Pong Archive administered by Efram Wolff Studios.*

ability to move audiences.[8] But not everyone loved her: an especially harsh Berlin critic described her as a "splendidly sloppy woman" who "blared and howled across the stage," adding, "We haven't heard such wonderfully wrong singing in a long time. Apparently, you can even be a slut with grace."[9] Nevertheless, her career thrived in Weimar-era Berlin.

Then everything changed. Even before the Nazi government implemented systematic legal restrictions on them, they prevented Jews—the most visible representatives of the "Jewish spirit" they vilified—from performing on stage and screen.[10] In 1933, Gerson and three other Jewish actors were dismissed from Werner Finck's cabaret Katakombe (Catacombs), which continued to perform without them until Nazis censors shut it down in 1935.[11] At that point, Gerson, along with many other German-Jewish émigrés, went to Holland, where she became the star of Kurt Egon Wolff's newly formed cabaret Ping-Pong.[12] Jewish entertainers had more opportunities in Holland, but there too the environment was volatile. While unemployment rose and political criticism became increasingly dangerous, Ping-Pong adapted by performing literary parodies, where it was easier to insert subversive political positions.[13] For instance, a rendition of Shakespeare's *Hamlet* contained the line: "To be or not to be—tell me, Prince Hamlet, who is a Jew or a non-Jew these days, that is the so-called race question."[14]

In 1934, after Ping-Pong was unable to extend work permits in the Netherlands, the troupe traveled to Zurich. Gerson was such a hit with Swiss audiences that she was invited to stay and perform with the newly founded Zurich cabaret, Das Cornichon (The pickle). When Wolff asked her to return to Holland in August to perform with Ping-Pong again, her response revealed some of the challenges she faced: "I must have enough money to get out of Holland, and so far I haven't even got the money to get in. So I can't leave here tomorrow, neither to Stuttgart nor to Holland. Yesterday morning I again telephoned my mother, who was unfriendly and very disagreeable."[15] Her concerns notwithstanding, she did return to Amsterdam in 1934, when she was unable to renew her residence permit for Switzerland. By then Ping-Pong had disbanded, so she performed in other cabarets run by émigrés, including one led by composer Rudolf Nelson.[16]

Gerson occasionally returned to her apartment in the Künsterkolonie Schmargendorf, a Berlin residence for artists, although opportunities for performing as a Jew in Germany were scarce. She made her April 1935 recordings for Lukraphon, a label of the Jüdischer Kulturbund (Jewish Cultural Association). Literary and cultural critic Julius Bab, who had been

26 THE POSTWAR ANTISEMITE

a witness at Gerson and Harlan's wedding, co-founded the Kulturbund deutscher Juden (Cultural Association of German Jews) to provide opportunities for Jewish performers to work after the Nazis banned Jews from working in entertainment and culture in June 1933. In 1935, the Nazis forced the group to change its name to Jüdischer Kulturbund because they saw the term "German Jew" as a contradiction in terms. Its performances were restricted to Jewish performers and audiences and faced strict censorship and oversight; they were expressly forbidden from performing anything that the censor deemed "especially German."[17]

As Gerson exhausted herself chasing ever-narrowing opportunities to perform in Europe, her ex-husband Veit Harlan's career in Berlin was ascending. In 1934, he landed his first leading film role in Arzén von Cserépy's *Nur nicht weich werden, Susanne!* (Don't lose heart, Susanne!), an antisemitic comedy in which he heroically saved German cinema from the Jews.[18] Hans Hömberg's screenplay was based on a 1933 novel by Willi Krause (pseud. Peter Hagen), a committed Nazi who served as editor and film critic for Goebbels's newspaper *Der Angriff*, where the novel was first serialized, and as Reichsdramaturg, a powerful position where he could censor, approve, or reject scripts.[19] The film is billed as a comedy, but its message is dead serious. By satirizing Jews and Jewish film and promoting an Aryan German alternative, von Cserépy used explicitly antisemitic stereotypes and plot devices to teach viewers how to eradicate Jewish influence from German cinema.[20]

Harlan plays Georg Brinkmann, a working-class chauffeur with a strong Berlin accent, whose bravery and heroism save his girlfriend Susanne (Jessica Vihrog), an aspiring actor, from the clutches of the criminal, deviant, greedy Jews who have corrupted the German film industry.[21] The Jewish characters in the film, all male, are ripped straight from the pages of Julius Streicher's antisemitic tabloid *Der Stürmer*; they are portrayed through unmistakably negative Jewish stereotypes, including names associated with money, Yiddish-inflected language, exaggerated gesticulating, remorseless criminal activity in pursuit of profit, and sexual aggression toward a young, pure, blond German woman.[22]

In one scene, Brinkmann emerges victorious from an aggressive barroom brawl, having broken the bones of a man named Wiesenthal; a brief cut from the fight to Susanne cheering on the sidelines implies that violence against Jews is desirable. This scene foreshadows Brinkmann's ultimate success in ousting the Jewish producer of Susanne's movie, paving the way for a German director to take over. The film's final scenes feature Georg and Susanne in their vegetable garden in the countryside, highlighting their abandonment of the corrupt, urban, Jewish-linked entertainment industry for a comfortable, pastoral life where they can harvest the fruits of the earth and live according to traditional gender roles.[23]

Suffused with tropes of antisemitic propaganda from start to finish, *Susanne* aimed to build support for the Nazi project of expunging Jews from the German culture industry, even at the cost of violence. Like almost all comedies produced in Nazi Germany, the film was a critical and commercial failure. This has led most scholars to assume it was of little importance as a form of Nazi propaganda. Indeed, one contemporary critic felt that *Susanne* was not antisemitic enough, and even Goebbels said it was a lousy film.[24] But its lack of success at the time of its release did not mean it had no effect. Several Viennese critics touted the film when it was shown there in September 1938, six months after the *Anschluss*; one review in the Nazi *Völkischer Beobachter* lauded its "realistic" portrayal of Jewish depravity and took note of Harlan's apt portrayal of Brinkmann.[25]

In 1934, Harlan could hardly claim to have been forced into participating in an antisemitic role in a film with such explicitly Nazi origins and content, and, indeed, he later asserted that "the pressure exerted by the National Socialism on persons connected with the production of films did not start until shortly before the war."[26] It is no wonder, then, that after the war he omitted the film from the otherwise exhaustive lists of his work experiences in his denazification questionnaires, essays, texts, interviews, and autobiography. Instead, he carefully drew attention to his other achievements around that time, such as directing his first film, *Krach im Hinterhaus* (Trouble backstairs), released in December 1935, which won the favor of Goebbels, who put Harlan on his radar for future projects. By 1939, Harlan had become Goebbels's star director, responsible for the wildly successful antisemitic propaganda film *Jud Süss*, which became an important tool for fostering support among German audiences for the genocidal attack on the Jews.[27]

But to overlook *Susanne* is to ignore the lessons it taught Harlan about the pitfalls of crass portrayals of Jewish difference on film, which he in turn used to shape *Jud Süss*.[28] The plot of *Jud Süss* focuses on the historical figure of Joseph Süss Oppenheimer (1698–1738), who in 1733 became the Court Jew of Karl Alexander, the Duke of Württemberg. Historically, Court Jews provided banking and financial services for European royalty, especially in Germany and Austria, in return for social and financial privileges from which Jews were generally excluded. Some amassed a great deal of wealth

28 THE POSTWAR ANTISEMITE

as a result. Oppenheimer was one of them, but after Karl Alexander's death, he was put on trial for crimes, including fraud and embezzlement, and in 1738, he was hanged. Beginning in the nineteenth century, Oppenheimer's story was repeatedly depicted in literature and film, including an 1827 novella by the German author Wilhelm Hauff, a 1916–1917 drama and 1925 novel by German-Jewish author Lion Feuchtwanger, and a 1934 British film adaptation based on Feuchtwanger's novel and directed by German-Jewish director Lothar Mendes. While all of these works portrayed Süss as a flawed individual, it was Feuchtwanger who presented him as most complex—a tragic figure whose own failings caused his fate.

From the start, Goebbels intended the film to foster antisemitism. Produced on a lavish budget and featuring several stars, including the director's third wife Kristina Söderbaum, Harlan's version portrays Süss as a conniving, dishonest swindler who attempts to demean Germans and bilk them out of their wealth. Posters featuring Süss as a diabolical figure trumpeted the film's intent, as did the insistence that it was historically based. Yet in a dramatic and egregious departure from historical events, Goebbels and Harlan's Süss is put to death for having had what the film euphemistically terms "sexual relations" (although the film depicts it as rape) with a Christian woman, Dorothea Sturm, the daughter of a prominent district councilor, who is played by Söderbaum.

Still, when Harlan was put on trial for crimes against humanity in 1948 because of *Jud Süss*, he and a number of colleagues testified in his defense that he had downplayed the explicit, crude antisemitism called for in earlier versions of the screenplay and added scenes to foreground Süss's cleverness, charm, and sex appeal. But in a postwar autobiographical essay submitted as part of his denazification hearing, Harlan revealed the real reasons he presented an erotically charged—rather than repulsive—villain. He claimed to have told Goebbels: "The audience could only get the impression that the whole [earlier] picture was repulsive and sordid—but not the Jew. In staging a film, I was driven only by aesthetics and would not be able to create a dramatized '*Stürmer*.'"[29] In this revealing statement, Harlan asserts a truth: in order to transmit *any* effective message about Jews, the film needed to be appealing and its protagonists attractive. In the end, his film's Jud Süss encompasses the negative qualities that Goebbels was looking for—the merciless, vengeful Jew who corrupted Christian women—along with the eroticism of a woman's attraction to a non-Aryan "Other."

By the time Harlan began rewriting the script for *Jud Süss* in 1939, Gerson, his Jewish ex-wife, had relocated to the Netherlands for good. There, in 1937, she married textile manufacturer Max Sluizer, with whom she had two children, Miriam, born on November 19, 1937, and Abel Juda, born on May 21, 1940 (Figure 1.2), shortly after the Germans invaded the Netherlands.[30] The dangers the German occupation of the Netherlands posed to Jews made it clear that the family needed to leave. Desperately seeking a way to emigrate, Gerson wrote to Harlan in 1942, asking for assistance. She also asked a friend to intervene with him on her behalf. Though Harlan later often insisted that he had never refused a request to help Jews, he did not respond to her plea.[31] That same year, the family paid a smuggler to bring them to Switzerland via France. When they reached the French border, Gerson was asked to sedate the children so they would not betray the group to the Nazis. Gerson refused, the children cried, and the family was discovered, arrested, and deported to Auschwitz-Birkenau, where they were murdered on February 14, 1943.[32]

Figure 1.2. Dora Gerson relaxes with her children Miriam and Abel Juda at their home in Amsterdam, shortly before the family went into hiding in France. After the cries of one of the children revealed their location, Gerson, her husband Max Sluizer, and the children were deported and murdered in Auschwitz in 1943. *Courtesy of Cabaret Ping Pong Archive administered by Efram Wolff Studios.*

30   THE POSTWAR ANTISEMITE

On the first day of his trial in 1949, Harlan admitted that he was aware of the circumstances of Gerson's death, as well as her request for his help.[33] This makes it all the more remarkable that he consistently portrayed himself as her victim. After a radio interview that aired in Zurich in April 1962, journalist Katja Wyler-Salten commented, "It would have been better if he had kept quiet about his first Jewish wife, the actor Dora Gerson, who, according to a report by her divorce lawyer, was deported and who was also a victim of the Nazi incitement against Jews, which was greatly aided by the film 'Jud Süss'."[34] Although Harlan never mentions the fate of Gerson and her husband and children in the 500-page manuscript of his autobiography, he does express anger at Wyler-Salten's implication that he played a role in the Nazis' murder of the Jews. Perversely, he also complains that Gerson's leaving *him* was the real "tragic story," asserting that "[f]or me this divorce was a terrible blow."[35] In the juxtaposition between Wyler-Salten implying that Harlan was an Antisemite responsible for Gerson's death and Harlan insisting he was Gerson's victim, we can see how Harlan at once explicitly disavowed antisemitism and implicitly replaced the Jew with himself as the victim, thus repositioning the Jew as villain and deploying the narrative trope that transformed the figural Jew into the postwar Antisemite—thus arrogating the power to determine the Antisemite.

After the war, Harlan boasted about his victimization at the hands of his Jewish ex-wife as if it were a badge of bravery. At times, he claimed that his intimate relationship with a Jewish woman got him into trouble with Goebbels. But he also cast himself as the victim of Gerson and her family's religious prejudices, insisting that she left him "only because she claimed she could not live with a non-Jew" and "the Orthodox Jews in the large Gerson family brought my wife so far as to convert to their Orthodox opinion. We broke up and she married a Jew."[36] This formulation once again positions him as her victim and further aligns her with religious prejudice, which lies at the heart of antisemitism.[37] Harlan would present himself as a victim during his denazification trials, his 1949 and 1950 trials for crimes against humanity, and long thereafter, first as a victim of the Nazis, of the state prosecutor, the Allied Occupation Forces, the press, and, ultimately, the Jews.[38]

Harlan took his first stab at using his own victimization as a defense against accusations of antisemitism when he initiated his own denazification trial in Hamburg after the war. His role in *Jud Süss* was preventing him from obtaining a filmmaking license, for which exoneration by the denazification commission was a prerequisite, so in July 1946, his lawyers sent the

Hamburg denazification committee a letter outlining his request to appear before them and the reasons why he should be exonerated. They enclosed Harlan's completed questionnaire about his Nazi-related activities and a forty-page autobiographical essay written in May 1945, titled "My Attitude Toward National Socialism."

Harlan wrote the essay to defend himself and Söderbaum against accusations that their participation in *Jud Süss* aligned them with Nazis. In it, he first used the tactics he would turn to repeatedly in his trials and postwar writings, which demonstrate his skill at separating the "Jewish" from actual Jews to create a narrative of self-exculpation acceptable to postwar audiences. By blaming (bad) Jews who obstructed his career and praising—and identifying with—(good) Jews who supported him, he positioned himself to stand in for the (good) Jew as the Antisemite's true victim—while also aligning antisemitism with the (bad) Jew. In the essay, he started off by condemning the (bad) Jews who harmed him: "As, to my knowledge, my Jewish colleagues after emigrating to foreign countries have put me on a so-called 'black-list' . . . and as many foreign newspapers . . . have called me the 'Nazi Film Producer No. 1,' I must of necessity defend myself against these publications, the more so as the subsistence of my wife as well as my own are endangered."[39] The first subheading, "The Main Point of Attack Against Us," underscores his self-victimization. In what follows, he claims that resisting Goebbels and Hitler in minor matters might have been possible for him, but that "in the really important question as to whether one favoured anti-Semitism or not, resistance simply meant being locked-up [*sic*] in a concentration camp."[40] According to this statement, favoring antisemitism is not a good measure of whether someone was an Antisemite. And in the rest of the essay, he outlines all of his actions that he insists mean he is not an Antisemite: he was not a Nazi party member, did not willingly and gladly work for the Nazis, and he assisted some Jews after 1933.

To buttress his disavowal of antisemitism, Harlan walked a thin line between dissociating from and identifying with the Prague Jews whom he hired to work on *Jud Süss*. First, he asserts that the Jews participated eagerly and were paid "extraordinarily well," but also claims he had been pressured into working on the film and only did so reluctantly. Then he goes on to state that neither the Jews nor he and his wife could be blamed for submitting to Goebbel's "incredible power" (Figure 1.3), aligning himself and Söderbaum with the Jews as victims of the Nazi. The essay also included a four-page section labeled "The Assistance I Rendered to Artists Married to Jewish

Figure 1.3. Joseph Goebbels (far left) congratulates Veit Harlan after the premiere of his 1942 film *Der grosse König*. Behind them are Fritz Hippler, chief of the Film Bureau in the Ministry of Propaganda (center) and actor Otto Gebuehr (left). *Ullstein Bild Dtl. via Getty Images.*

Partners," which further associates him with Jews against the Antisemite, who is clearly someone other than himself.[41]

This alignment, which persisted for years, turned out to be social as well as rhetorical. Harlan tried to get prominent Jews to support him so he could further distance himself from the Antisemite. When that support was not forthcoming, he framed them as bad Jews and himself as their victim. By using Jewish characteristics to describe himself and his victimhood, he effectively cast Jews as Antisemites. If Harlan had gained his authority to define the Antisemite in *Jud Süss*, he used this authority after the war to claim that he was the Antisemite's true victim. Harlan's efforts to reshape the terms of his relationship with German Jews as self-victimization created a rhetoric of deflection, obfuscation, and denial that others could draw upon to justify their activities between 1933 and 1945—and that enabled the powerful postwar redefinition of the Antisemite as a liminal figure that combined stereotypes about Jews with an overarching power to victimize everyone, including non-Jews.

Though Harlan was acquitted for crimes against humanity in 1950 and subsequently returned to filmmaking, critical newspaper articles and protests against his films kept him constantly on the defensive, and he remained deeply concerned about his career, his reputation, and his legacy. He never stopped curating his image and trying to rid himself of the taint of *Jud Süss*.[42] Until the end of his life, he continued to highlight associations with Jews that framed him in a positive light, while accusing unsupportive Jews of victimizing him, just as he had done with Dora Gerson.

Harlan's relationships with a number of prominent German Jews reflect his preoccupation with positioning himself as a victim of the Antisemite. Harlan made great efforts to persuade the writer Julius Bab to issue a public statement of support for him; when Bab refused, Harlan cast himself as Bab's victim and aligned Bab with the Antisemite. Harlan already viewed himself as the victim of German Jewish émigré writer Lion Feuchtwanger, who published an open letter in 1941 castigating him and a number of other actors for their roles in creating *Jud Süss*; as the author of a novel with the same title, Feuchtwanger figured as an authority on defining the Antisemite, so Harlan could not resist challenging him when he republished the letter after the war. Finally, in a publicity stunt that epitomized his desire to be seen as the Antisemite's ultimate victim, Harlan asked Berlin-born Auschwitz survivor Norbert Wollheim, head of the Central Committee of Liberated Jews in the British Zone, to allow him to appear before a Jewish honor court, a system designed by Jews for Jews accused of collaborating during the war. Wollheim not only rejected this request but provided damaging testimony at Harlan's trials for crimes against humanity, thus becoming another victimizer.

Harlan's final act of self-justification was his autobiography, titled "Wie es war... Erlebnisse eines Filmregisseurs unter seinem allerhöchsten Chef, dem 'Schirmherrn des deutschen Films,' Dr. Josef Goebbels" (How it was: A film director's experiences under his very highest boss, the 'guardian of German films,' Dr. Josef Goebbels). Although the original title indicates how highly Harlan esteemed his former boss, the title of the much-abbreviated autobiography published two years after his death in 1966, *Im Schatten meiner Filme* (In the shadow of my films), reflected Harlan's editor's efforts to cast him as a victim of his films' legacy. To create this representation, he edited out numerous passages where Harlan in fact reinforced his self-serving descriptions of Jews and the liminal, Jewish-coded, all-powerful Antisemite who turned Harlan into a victim.

34   THE POSTWAR ANTISEMITE

A German Patriot: Julius Bab

In 1948, a week after Harlan was charged with crimes against humanity, he found out that Rabbi Joachim Prinz, a prominent German-Jewish émigré, would be stopping in Hamburg on his return from Montreux, Switzerland, where Prinz was leading the U.S. delegation to the World Jewish Congress. In a meeting that was never publicly reported, Harlan pressed Prinz for his personal support as well as for support from the Hamburg Jewish community.[43] According to Heinz Liepman, who described the meeting in a letter to state prosecutor Gerhard Kramer,

> Harlan added that antisemitism was growing in Germany and that only men like him could oppose it. He further noted that he was ready to support the Jews—not as repentance for his acts or for ideological reasons, but as a form of exchange that he was ready to do when the Jews would in return give up their resistance to Harlan.[44]

Harlan frequently asserted that he was invulnerable to accusations of antisemitism. Nevertheless, he persistently sought support from (good) Jews whose judgment, he believed, would carry extra weight with the public and thus serve as a counterweight to the (bad) Jews who supported the accusations against him.

During the early years of denazification, Harlan had reason to hope that writer Julius Bab, a close friend of his father, the dramatist Walter Harlan, would be one of those supporters. After all, Harlan's father had been accused of antisemitism, too. Shortly after delivering the eulogy at Walter Harlan's funeral in 1931, Bab had published an article defending his friend against such accusations, which were alleged to have been made by Jewish authors, including Hans Rehfisch, at a meeting of the Verband Deutscher Bühnenschriftsteller (Association of German Dramatists) in Berlin earlier that year (Walter Harlan was the long-time chairman of the Association).[45] Bab had also served as something of a mentor to Veit and helped him begin his acting career at Berlin's Volksbühne. Yet, there is no evidence that the two continued to have a relationship after Walter's death.[46] From 1933 on, Bab was focused on the encroachments of the Nazi regime and the Kulturbund. In 1939, he finally fled Germany, first to France, then in 1940 to New York, where he and his wife Elisabeth settled for good.[47]

HARLAN'S JEWS 35

Bab's role in the Kulturbund is key to understanding the depth of his German patriotism and his devastation at having to leave Germany behind. From the start, Bab and the other Kulturbund founders were highly attuned to the risks of their new endeavor. Member subscriptions, their only source of funding, were a constant challenge, as some Jews believed the organization represented a capitulation to the exclusion of Jews from German culture and supported the Nazi case that they did not treat Jews badly.[48] But Bab felt the Nazis had left them with no other options. In a letter to Jewish actor and director Fritz Wisten in May 1933, he wrote, "Basically, the men in charge want nothing less than to create a ghetto, and that's what this company unfortunately and inevitably comes down to"; in a June letter, he added, "it's a bitter pill to swallow, a ghetto company, of course we want to do so well the Germans will have to be ashamed of themselves."[49] He wrote to Jewish writer Georg Hermann that the group was an attempt to "make this ghetto corner, into which we have been undeniably and pretty much permanently forced into, more bearable."[50] When his writer friend Hans Franck, who had joined the Nazi party, entered Bab's house wearing a swastika in 1933, Bab broke with him in a devastating farewell letter, making clear the connection between Franck's actions and the reluctant establishment of the Kulturbund: "in it, theater will be performed, music will be made, and lectures given, etc. by Jews for Jews. It is all that I have rejected and fought against for 30 years; it is the ghetto—it is what your party comrades want and are forcing."[51]

Publicly, Bab did his best to promote the Kulturbund as a way for Jews to keep a foothold in German culture and patriotism. In a 1933 article, he wrote, "We drew our strength from twofold roots, we were Jews and Germans, and we still are. But we sense the axe taken to these roots; our Germanness is threatened, especially in the most severe, spiritual sense."[52] The Kulturbund's leadership framed membership as a way to continue to engage with the humanistic values that made them proud to be German, rather than a return to an isolated ghetto. Indeed, for many Jews, it was a matter of spiritual survival to see the Nazis as an aberration in German culture, a bug rather than a feature, as we would put it today. But participating in the Kulturbund was also a way to avoid despair: the Kulturbund's performances and other events offered a sense of dignity, comfort, and community to Jews who were becoming increasingly isolated and frightened as their worlds collapsed. Bab's commitment to this effort withstood a stone thrown through his window, the loss of his apartment to an Aryan tenant, and arrest; when he finally left

36   THE POSTWAR ANTISEMITE

Germany, he endured internment in a French concentration camp and impoverishment when he and his wife arrived in the United States.[53]

On April 15, 1947, Bab published an article about actor Hilde Körber, Veit Harlan's second wife, in which he mentioned Veit's "unscrupulous ambition" in corrupting his father's works with antisemitism under the Nazis.[54] Its publication prompted Harlan to begin corresponding with Bab in New York on August 23. His aim was to convince Bab that he was not an Antisemite, and also to seek his help in convincing the Hamburg denazification commission that he should be allowed to return to filmmaking. Six days earlier, Harlan had written to the commission and insisted that his work on *Jud Süss* was mitigated by the fact that he had helped every Jew or person married to a Jew who asked him for assistance.[55] His lawyers concurred, adding explicitly that Harlan was not antisemitic: "Mr. Harlan's aversion to National Socialism was rooted precisely in the complete rejection of antisemitism. Mr. Harlan never made a secret of this rejection, and he stood up for and helped Jews at every opportunity."[56]

A close analysis of his first letter to Bab reveals the rhetorical techniques that Harlan used to define the Antisemite as someone he was not, who victimized him as much as, if not more than, Jews. He begins by stressing that others had enabled this initial contact, as if to disavow his own self-serving motivation: his son Thomas gave him Bab's address, his sister Esther told him that Bab planned to publish an extended version of one of their father's plays, and Körber informed him that Bab had "with great regret taken note of [Harlan's] activity against Judaism." Harlan initiates his defense by refuting this statement and simultaneously asserting their relationship: "and so I hereby inform you that neither outside nor inside have I ever become different from the way you knew me."[57]

Harlan continues to disclaim responsibility for his own actions, displacing them onto "those Germans" and flinging about passive and subjunctive constructions:

> The unfortunate entanglement in which those Germans who found themselves directly under the command of Goebbels due to their occupation cannot be described exactly. Everyone is looking for an excuse. I would be ashamed if I tried to repair a relationship between the two of us with cheap words, if had been the one who rudely tore that relationship apart. Nor would I ask for mercy from any Jew if I were one of those whose essence it was to deal mercilessly with the Jews. I read terrible things about myself in

foreign newspapers, including a lot of lies, because of course I was never in this [word unreadable] party or one of its branches.[58]

Deflecting responsibility for the break in their relationship, he suggests that he is not among those who need to beg Jews for forgiveness, subtly defining the Antisemite as someone "whose essence it was to deal mercilessly with the Jews." In contrast, Harlan outlines his own victimization at the hands of the Nazis, and finally makes two direct declarations: what has been printed about him is untrue, and he was not a party member. He evokes conversations they had in 1933 about an article published in the *Völkischer Beobachter* that contained disparaging statements about Bab which Harlan claimed had been falsely attributed to him. Although he does not mention it in the letter, Harlan knew that the denazification commission saw this interview as early evidence that he was aligned with Nazi ideology.

Harlan then attempts to bolster his relationship with Bab by referencing a mutual Jewish acquaintance—further emphasizing his good relationships with (good) Jews—and his father Walther, the source of their connection. Lucie Mannheim, an actor living in exile in Great Britain, had recently visited him, and, he writes, "I gained much more confidence from her visit, because she had such a touchingly unswerving attitude towards me—this eternal *Berliner Range* [an awkward/gawky youth from Berlin] that almost shook me. We also spoke of you."[59] Through his condescending description of Mannheim, Harlan wields misogyny as another connection between the men. Identifying himself with his father, he applies further pressure for Bab's support: "I now have white hair and a white goatee and apparently resemble my father. I doubt myself whether I resemble him very much on the inside, although many say so. But in any case, I am close to him and from this closeness I write to you and his eyes read this letter as well, just as they will read the one that you might answer me."[60]

Harlan's letters to Bab register a significant decline in amiability over the next several months. In the next, dated October 6, 1947, Harlan complains about Bab's references to Harlan's 1939 film *Das unsterbliche Herz* (The immortal heart), which had recently played in New York. Where Bab claimed that the film added "antisemitic roles" to Walter Harlan's play *Das Nürnbergische Ei* (The Nuremberg egg), on which it was based, Harlan insists that he actually *decreased* the antisemitism of his father's play: "In any case, I left out the punch line that is in my father's play, where the curmudgeon Güldenbeck talks about the Jew Mesech."[61] In addition to asserting

38 THE POSTWAR ANTISEMITE

himself as the authority on antisemitism, Harlan continues to characterize himself as a victim of the Nazis by complaining about the difficulties he faced while working under the demanding and watchful eye of Goebbels, who, he asserts, was wary of him because of his marriage to Dora Gerson. By reminding Bab that he was a witness at Harlan and Gerson's 1922 wedding, Harlan begins to subtly implicate Bab in Goebbels's victimization.

Once again citing his associations with Jews to place himself in the victim role, Harlan further reminds Bab that Jews—actor Fritz Kortner and writer Francesco von Mendelssohn—had also served as witnesses at his wedding to Hilde Körber in 1929.[62] Similar to the first letter, Harlan closes with a reference to his father and pressures Bab for support even more strongly, again bringing up the false claims in the 1933 *Völkischer Beobachter* that he insists they discussed.[63] In a reply to Harlan on November 15, 1947, Bab claims to have heard from several sources that certain roles have severely antisemitic overtones, complaining: "You're telling me the opposite! What am I supposed to think?" Nevertheless, the rest of his letter maintains a cordial tone.[64]

In his reply, dated December 6, 1947, Harlan responds to their debate about the film's antisemitism with details about his Nazi-era generosity toward individual Jews, a tactic he would continue to pursue in later years. He also returns to the topic of *Das unsterbliche Herz*, first asking how Bab could accuse him of embedding an antisemitic character in the film when he had cast the "half-Jew" Paul Henckels as Güldenbeck, then describing how well he had treated Henckels and his Jewish wife, Thea Grodzinsky. In an ironic statement, Harlan adds that, if he *had* planned to embed an antisemitic character in the film, he probably would have decided against Henckels, who would be more likely to play a Jew.[65] Again, Harlan wants to show he knows better than Bab how to define antisemitism and thus shape the Antisemite. It is an early example of postwar antisemitism, echoed by others over decades, and brings into sharp relief the mechanisms and rhetoric used to construct the postwar Antisemite.

Six days later, on December 12, 1947, the Hamburg denazification commission issued its preliminary decision: a majority of its members voted to exonerate Harlan. It was customary for the committee to wait a week or two before announcing its final decision, but the next day an unknown source leaked the vote to the radio and newspapers, catalyzing a public outcry from those who wanted to see Harlan held to account.[66] The strong negative reaction from the press, the Jewish community, the Hamburg branch of the Social Democratic Party (SPD), and the Association of Film Producers in

HARLAN'S JEWS   39

the British Zone, among others, threw the committee into disarray.[67] In the end, it decided to reconsider the case.[68]

In the meantime, Harlan learned that state prosecutor Gerhard Kramer was considering whether to charge him with crimes against humanity. On May 29, 1948, Harlan wrote to Bab that he had visited Kramer's office, where they discussed the sworn statement of author Hans Rehfisch about the 1933 *Völkischer Beobachter* interview. Rehfisch, who had fled to New York years earlier, testified that Harlan had falsely accused him of leading the group of writers who accused Walter Harlan of antisemitism in 1931 and causing his heart attack. Rehfisch stated that he had never accused Walter Harlan of anything dishonorable, including antisemitism.[69] In the cover letter that he included with his statement, Rehfisch claims that he was not surprised about Harlan's association with the National Socialists given his extreme opportunism.[70]

In his letter to Bab, Harlan replaces his father with himself as Rehfisch's victim and places the Jewish writer in the role of the Antisemite: "With several perjuries, Mr. Rehfisch tried to deliver me up to the vengeance that prevails in Germany today, and in doing so he committed exactly the crime against me of which he accuses me."[71] He tells Bab how upset he was about the renewed denazification proceedings but professes certainty that he will once again be exonerated and able to return to work. And he continues to assert his victim status: "But it will be a long time before the audience, which for three years was presented with Veit Harlan as the 'murderer of Auschwitz,' learns that they have only been fed with lies and filth. Maybe I'll never get rid of it entirely."[72] Harlan could not have known that Kramer had already informed Bab about Rehfisch's testimony and had inquired whether Bab had been a witness at the meeting in 1931 at which Walter Harlan died (he had not).[73]

The following month, Harlan again asserted his authority to define the Antisemite, chastising Bab for, as Harlan saw it, erroneously identifying the actor Werner Krauss as an Antisemite. To show he knows better, Harlan first expounds on his firsthand knowledge of the tense relationship between Krauss and Goebbels. Then, a few lines later, he effectively concedes the point, arguing that Krauss was not a "Nazi-quality antisemite." To support his claims for Krauss's virtue and his own, he points out that he was forced to hire Krauss to play the role of several Jews in *Jud Süss* and that Krauss portrayed the rabbi as "the most sympathetic character in the film" (the critics did not agree).[74] In response, Bab rejected Harlan's rosy characterization of Krauss

40   THE POSTWAR ANTISEMITE

with a well-sourced anecdote about the actor's admiration for Hitler and lack of sympathy for exiled Jewish actor Elisabeth Bergner.[75]

Taking another tack, Harlan contends that geographical distance stands in the way of Bab making a fair judgment: "You are wrongly oriented. The tidal wave of hatred probably makes any true orientation impossible from so far away. You will probably also consider this letter to be subjective and a form of self-defense. Probably the most primitive as well as the most complicated differences are fought out today in Germany with the weapon: 'You're a Nazi'!" He closes by again bringing up the *Völkischer Beobachter* interview and insisting that Bab validate his claim that he was falsely accused.[76] By this time, Bab was also feeling pressure from Kramer, the prosecutor, who had inquired about his relationship to Harlan as he considered putting Harlan on trial. On June 28, 1948, Bab briefly informed Harlan that he had told Kramer he did not remember the interview in the *Völkischer Beobachter*.[77] Less than a month later, on July 15, 1948, Kramer formally charged Harlan with crimes against humanity.

Six months later, Bab faced renewed pressure to denounce Harlan—this time from Norbert Wollheim, head of the Central Committee of Liberated Jews in the British Zone of Germany, who mistakenly believed that Bab had written articles supporting Harlan, given Harlan's constant and unjustified use of Bab's name as he attempted to repair his reputation. On March 10, 1949, Wollheim wrote to Manfred George, editor of *Aufbau*, the leading German-language Jewish newspaper in New York, requesting him to ask Bab to stop supporting Harlan, which was damaging to the prosecution and the public.[78] Bab replied that Harlan was not his close friend and explained that he had written only about *Das unsterbliche Herz*, Harlan's 1939 film based on his father's play, and had neither seen nor written about *Jud Süss*. He added a sentence that lightly disavowed both Harlan and his prosecution, which Harlan found sufficiently useful to eventually publish: "My personal relationships with my old friend's son are of no public concern. I know his weaknesses—and those of other people. But I don't like active or passive burning pyres."[79]

Bab's private correspondence during the two years of Harlan's trial confirms that any esteem he held for his old friend's son had waned. By 1951, Bab had apparently had enough. On February 4, 1951, he published an article entitled "Immer noch Fall 'Veit Harlan!'" (The case of Veit Harlan yet again) in another New York German-language newspaper. Though the title was reminiscent of his 1931 article, "Der Fall Harlan," where he defended

Walter Harlan against charges of antisemitism, here he distanced himself from his friend's son, complaining that "Veit Harlan always mentions my name first as evidence that he is not an Antisemite!" Still, he also remains cautiously judicious, claiming that he cannot judge whether Harlan was a Nazi or Antisemite because he had not seen *Jud Süss*. Echoing his earlier observation that he disliked "burning pyres," Bab points out that Harlan should not be the only one held to account, but he also maintains that the director should not escape responsibility for his actions: "He has completely lost sight of the particularly bad consequences of his Nazi service. In this mood, he sees himself as the one who has been hurt, the one wrongly prevented from doing his work." Ultimately, he urges people to wait and see about Harlan's forthcoming films and indicates that boycotting them should be a personal choice.[80]

Bab's article provoked a furious explosion from Harlan in the form of a letter whose six pages overflow with insults and self-justifications. "I have become skeptical whether a Jew in America can still understand a normal German who has stayed here," he rants, before lecturing Bab about his own bravery: "If you read my decision you will see that I acted against Goebbels with extraordinary courage." Most significantly, he articulates what he believed to be the unique pattern of his victimization, first by the Nazis, then, after the war, by those whom the Nazis had persecuted, including Jews: "But for me, it has been said for 10 years, first through Goebbels, then through the SD [Sicherheitsdienst des Reichsführers-SS, the Nazi intelligence agency] and today through the VVN [Vereinigung der Verfolgten des Naziregimes, Union of Persecutees of the Nazi Regime] through the Jewish community or through the SPD [Social Democratic Party] so that I should actually be squashed." He apparently could not resist comparing the German government's costs for compensating Jewish concentration camp victims to the costs of his trial. He concludes by once again excluding Bab from the German community: "I don't think you can know what is essential in Germany at the moment."[81]

Four months later, in his final letter to Bab, Harlan intensified his attack on his father's old friend, directly accusing him of evading responsibility for his own support of Nazi antisemitism by leaving the country where Harlan was being persecuted for what he claims were comparable actions:

> If you had lived in my house the whole time, like my wife did, and if you had experienced the time when I got the terrible assignment, what I did about

42 THE POSTWAR ANTISEMITE

it and how I then staged it, then you would know that I had no connection with these people. I was no more in contact with these people than you were, when you were in charge of the Kulturbund der Deutschen Juden at the time—which was headed by Mr. Hinkel. Your fate has separated you from this gruesome connection. Mine didn't do that. In your own way—I hope it goes without saying that I say it uncritically and without reproach—you served antisemitism by joining an organization that had a purely National Socialist character and was led by one of the grimmest National Socialists—an organization that had sprung from the head of Goebbels, which he let exist as long as it suited him, in order to then go on in his plan of annihilation.[82]

To accuse Bab of having "served antisemitism" by founding the Kulturbund was to willfully ignore the antisemitic persecution Bab had faced in Germany, even as Harlan's career ascended, as well as the suffering his friends and family had endured under the Nazi regime. In this context, Harlan's petulant and overblown claim that Bab, the man who stood up for his father, "suddenly takes the side of those who want nothing more and nothing less of me than despair and death" is especially grotesque. Harlan continues to insist that he was the greatest victim, unjustly associated with "gigantic crimes" whose victims had nothing to do with him and should not be allowed to minimize his victimhood: "It is not acceptable that a logic prevails according to which my misfortune or my despair must not count in relation to the despair of millions with which I 'was somehow connected.'"[83]

Before Bab left Germany in 1939, he wrote an essay titled "Leben und Tod des deutschen Judentums" (Life and death of German Jewry).[84] Although by 1943, he claimed to no longer believe in the possibility of symbiosis between German and Jewish culture, his deep connections to German culture made it difficult for him to find secure footing as a writer in the United States, which left him and Elisabeth in dire economic straits. Bab lost his homeland, his readership, his deepest sense of German self-identification, and his livelihood.[85] In contrast, Harlan was acquitted and returned to filmmaking, though some continued to protest against him and boycott his films. It is no wonder that their correspondence ended with Harlan's insulting accusation that Bab had helped support Nazi antisemitism. There is no question that of the two, Bab was, materially, the greater victim of the Nazis. Still, Harlan continued his pattern of trying to convince German Jews that he was the ultimate victim of the Antisemite.

Harlan as Jud Süss

Harlan's letters to Lion Feuchtwanger and Norbert Wollheim during this time shed additional light on how Jews figured in his efforts to redefine the Antisemite. By reversing the positions of the Antisemite and Jew as he had portrayed them in *Jud Süss*, he put himself in the role of his infamous Jewish protagonist. These letters further show how he cast Jews who did not support his authority to determine the Antisemite as Antisemites themselves, a deft maneuver intended to further boost his own image and authority.

On December 12, 1947, the day the denazification commission reached its unofficial decision to exonerate him, Harlan penned a vitriolic open letter to Lion Feuchtwanger in response to the recent republication of a scathing open letter Feuchtwanger had written in 1941, castigating Harlan and several other Berlin actors for participating in the antisemitic Nazi film version of *Jud Süss*, whose origin point was his 1925 novel.[86] Six years later, Harlan angrily remonstrated Feuchtwanger in terms similar to those he had used with Bab, insisting that Jews could not understand what he and other Germans experienced under the Nazis, because they were not there.[87] Moreover, as with Bab, Harlan proposed that Feuchtwanger, not Harlan, was the actual Antisemite.

The heart of this claim is Harlan's assertion that Feuchtwanger's novel was itself antisemitic propaganda, since its narrative aims to "cleanse" a "criminal" simply because he was a Jew. Harlan also blames Feuchtwanger for Goebbels's decision to make a film about Jud Süss, saying the author should have written a novel about a more noble Jew, such as Moses, Heinrich Heine, or Einstein. In contrast, he boasts that he made both Feuchtwanger's story and the historical figure of Süss *less* antisemitic by having his Süss act selflessly in the interests of the Jewish people, which leads to his death at the hands of brutal Antisemites. Harlan insists that the "baskets of love letters" received by actor Ferdinand Marian, who played Süss, meant that audiences sympathized with him, rather than hating him.[88] Then Harlan makes his characteristic turn, linking the death of his film Süss—victimized, martyred, sympathetic, and seductive—to his own fate, tossing in another poke at Gerson, his Jewish ex-wife, along the way:

> The Jew has to die because—as it is said in the style of the time—he "had become physically entangled with a Christian." Even in the Nazi era it was clear to every normal person that this is not a crime at all. I myself was

44 THE POSTWAR ANTISEMITE

married to a Jew who left me to marry a Jew. So if we looked to this motive for his conviction, which historically did not even exist, it becomes clear that real crimes for which people are rightly convicted are not given as reasons for conviction in the film.[89]

Harlan's awareness of the Nazi anti-miscegenation laws outlawing sexual relationships between Jews and Christians make his denial of their concept of *Rassenschande* (racial defilement) especially egregious.

Harlan maintains that his Süss's only crime is "seducing" the film's heroine, Dorothea (played by his wife Kristina Söderbaum), and that Süss's insistence on remaining loyal to the Jews even in the face of death renders him a hero—a depiction that clearly resonates with his own self-representation as a loyal German patriot, guilty only of having once loved a Jewish woman, for which he paid a heavy price. But the film Süss does not seduce Dorothea; he kidnaps and rapes her. He also arrests and tortures her fiancé, whose screams Dorothea can hear during the rape. It is not much of a leap to see this scene—which Harlan himself apparently inserted into the screenplay—as a revenge fantasy about Gerson. Harlan closes the letter by repeating the comparison to the Jews of Prague in his 1945 denazification essay. He says that if he were guilty of cowardice, so were the Jews in Prague, including the rabbi, who agreed to perform a religious ritual for his film. Both parties, he insists, participated in the film because they feared being imprisoned by the Nazis. As he put it, "I'm the last one who doesn't understand their fear."[90] In a final act of triangulation, Harlan submits that their shared lack of resistance was actually a virtue derived from their shared difference from the Nazis: "The antisemites came and we didn't have the violence to stop them in their intentions."[91]

Six days later, on December 18, 1947, Harlan wrote to Norbert Wollheim, chair of the Central Committee of Liberated Jews in Germany's British Zone. Born in Berlin in 1913, Wollheim was expelled from the University in Berlin, where he was studying law, in 1933, and he was dismissed from his job at the mining company Rawack and Grünfeld AG in 1938. Between November 1938 and August 1939, he helped arrange for over twenty *Kindertransporte* (children's transports).[92] In 1943, along with his pregnant wife and three-year-old son, he was deported to Auschwitz, where he survived as a slave laborer for the chemical firm I. G. Farben, whom he later successfully sued for compensation for surviving laborers. His other family members were gassed.[93] In 1949, Wollheim testified at Harlan's first trial for crimes against humanity about the detrimental effects of *Jud Süss*, which he had heard about firsthand from I. G. Farben's non-Jewish laborers.[94]

Harlan was reacting to an open letter Wollheim had written on behalf of the Central Committee in response to the denazification committee's preliminary decision. In that letter, excerpted in *Die Welt* on December 18, 1947, alongside excerpts from Harlan's open letter to Feuchtwanger, Wollheim sarcastically lauded Harlan as the successful star of a pathetic comedy for convincing the court to accept his flimsy excuse that his film demonstrated great sympathy for Jews.[95] In his letter to Wollheim, Harlan asked to appear in person before the Central Committee. Per usual, he insisted that he had never been an Antisemite and used Gerson and Bab to support his claim: "My first wife was fully Jewish; that she left me in 1923 to marry a Jew was certainly not due to my racial attitudes. My witness at the time was Julius Bab, to whom I feel just as connected today as back then and during the Hitler era."[96] Curiously, the letter goes on to reframe Harlan's initial request to appear before the Committee as a request to appear before what he called a "Jewish court"—but only so long as it is "objective" and "not vengeful," a reference to the common stereotype of vengeful Jews.[97]

Jewish honor courts emerged after the war as way for Jews to try Jews accused of collaborating with the Nazis. These courts had no legal standing, but they imposed moral judgments about whether the accused were guilty of betraying the Jewish people. The verdict would be publicized within the Jewish community, and a defendant might be banned from holding public office in the community or might even be excluded from membership.[98] Harlan's request was perhaps his most audacious attempt to associate himself with Jews and the Süss that *he* created for his film. In the implicit assumption that a Jewish honor court would find him innocent, he aligned himself with his (good) Jewish friends at the same time as he cautioned them to resist the (bad) Jewish impulse to seek revenge rather than justice, suggesting once again that he knew Jews better than they knew themselves.

It is not clear whether Harlan published this letter. But before Wollheim even had a chance to reply, newspapers reported that Harlan had asked to appear before a Jewish honor court to prove that *Jud Süss* was not antisemitic.[99] On January 3, 1948, Wollheim tersely informed him that his request would be impossible as the honor court only served Jews, adding that such an appearance would be inappropriate under any circumstances given the ongoing investigation of the denazification commission.[100] Harlan surely knew that these courts only served Jews and could not have been surprised

46 THE POSTWAR ANTISEMITE

by Wollheim's refusal. The newspaper articles about his request were effective enough: They invited the public to imagine Harlan as a German patriot facing Jewish accusers, that is, as the ultimate victim, just like Harlan's Süss.[101]

The Last Word: Veit Harlan's Autobiography

Harlan completed his 500-manuscript-page autobiography in 1960, but plans for its publication did not begin until after his death in 1964, and his editor made significant cuts to produce the 245-page version that appeared in 1966. The passages that were edited out further illuminate the contours of Harlan's postwar Antisemite, for it appears his editor felt the need to excise many references to Jews and antisemitism to protect Harlan's legacy from the accusations that had dogged the last two decades of his life—accusations those references went a long way to prove.

It is unclear exactly how Hans Carl Opfermann, a scientist who specialized in in photo-optic-related engineering for processing color photography, became the editor of Harlan's autobiography.[102] By Opfermann's own account, he and Harlan never spoke of it directly. Opfermann claimed that he and Harlan first met on the set of Harlan's 1937 film, *Kreutzersonata* (The Kreutzer sonata), where they got along well because, as Opfermann put it, he was used to being around "dictatorial" people like Harlan. When an interviewer asked about editing the autobiography, Opfermann referred vaguely to having handled various issues for Harlan in Hamburg "that had to do with the collapse of the Third Reich." He said he was not surprised that Harlan had gotten along so well with Goebbels and Hitler, and he assured the interviewer that he, Opfermann, had one of these "famous white vests," a phrase associated with the term *Persilschein* (clean bill of health) that was used to signal being cleared by the denazification process.[103]

Opfermann also got along well with Harlan's wife, Kristina Söderbaum. Apparently the idea of publishing the autobiography came up after Harlan's death, as they were discussing the family's debts. Opfermann advised that publishing the autobiography could be lucrative, though he knew the issues surrounding *Jud Süss* might elicit "difficulties." He reported that an editor with the publisher Sigbert Mohn was keen to acquire the book and agreed that Opfermann should edit the manuscript, cut Harlan's "tremendous, widespread opinions," and include a critical commentary "to put Veit's memory in the right light."[104] Those deleted opinions provide a rich repository of unguarded statements about Harlan's admiration for Goebbels, Hitler, and other Nazis; his relationships with Jews before and after the Second World War; and, perhaps most importantly, the origins of his self-determined authority to define the Antisemite.

Some of Opfermann's edits were simply stylistic and mechanical. They were designed to make the lengthy manuscript more readable, for instance by omitting lengthy descriptions of film plots, detailed film exposés, and Harlan's postwar travels. But Opfermann was a self-proclaimed German nationalist, and his most drastic cuts to the manuscript toned down Harlan's enthusiasm for the Nazis and the harmful behavior of Nazi officials.[105] He cut back on Harlan's self-serving language, eliminating passages where he seemed to go too far in serving himself up as the ultimate victim, including a description of his treatment as "an infuriating act of outrageous injustice."[106] He also deleted Harlan's sardonic reference to being part of a "proud community" of prominent artists who had been judged as Antisemites immediately after the war, including conductor Wilhelm Furtwängler, writer Knut Hamsun, and actor Werner Krauss. Perhaps Opfermann felt Harlan came too close to admitting he was an Antisemite when he lamented that Furtwängler had been forgiven, Hamsun had died, and the "great German actor" Krauss had endured merely a few years of being publicly "pissed on" by lesser actors, before going to Austria, where he was awarded a medal for his service to the nation. "The only one left was Veit Harlan," he noted, inadvertently implying there was a reason for that![107] Opfermann removed other instances in which Harlan foregrounded his victim status, such as complaints about newspapers referring to him as a "criminal Nazi."[108] He cut most of Harlan's specific—and frequent—mentions of journalists he felt had wronged him and his allegation that an "abundance of genuine, enthusiastic Nazis" working for newspapers in Munich and Berlin were happy to conduct a "witch hunt" against him without admitting their own antisemitism.[109] Taken together, these fulsome edits obscure Harlan's own culpabilities while consolidating his authority to define the Antisemite.

The original manuscript contains many passages that undermine Harlan's postwar efforts to distance himself from the Nazis. He boasts, for instance, about his singular ability to negotiate with Nazi leaders like Goebbels and still remain safe, how much money his films made for the Nazis (although he did not see much of it), and how many millions he lost out on by not joining the Nazi party.[110] In general, excising these and other such passages

48 THE POSTWAR ANTISEMITE

minimized Harlan's pride in the recognition he received from Nazi leaders and downplayed his intimate knowledge of Goebbels.

By omitting Harlan's boasts about not fearing his boss, unlike others who worked for Goebbels, Opfermann ensured that the published book would not contradict Harlan's public representations of their relationship. In the unedited manuscript, Harlan seems relieved to finally be free to describe how he manipulated Goebbels. But Opfermann censored such bravado, cutting lines such as: "In this way I could sometimes achieve effects that a shy, humble, or even fearful person could never achieve. I turned my insolence into a weapon, and even if he got angry every now and then because I had gone too far, it didn't hurt in the end."[111] Harlan's assertion that "telling Goebbels when a mess was a mess wasn't so dangerous, and I did it many times" also went on the chopping block.[112] This sense that he persistently stood up to Goebbels without consequences is a far cry from his public insistence that he was Goebbels's victim. Opfermann also removed a passage in which Harlan admits to Nazi leader Oswald Pohl that he never missed a chance to make good use of his ability to manipulate Goebbels.[113] In short, Opfermann's cuts maintained Harlan's earlier contentions at his trials that Goebbels had been fully in charge and responsible for the film's antisemitism.

Harlan's sympathy for the losses experienced by Nazi party officials in the postwar period further undermine his efforts to distance himself from them—and were also cut. Opfermann deleted pages where Harlan mourns Goebbels's death and the loss of his beloved office, including the "treasured paintings" destroyed when the Ministry of Propaganda was bombed.[114] In another deleted passage, Harlan reverently describes his visit to the Landsberg penitentiary, where he expresses deep sympathy for a dead Nazi and the crying widows of Nazis and awe at visiting the place where Hitler wrote *Mein Kampf* and the graves of hanged Nazis (though he never references the genocide they helped perpetrate).[115] These passages reveal that at the end of his life Harlan felt he could finally be open about his reverence for these Nazis.

Opfermann particularly targeted statements about Goebbels, the Nazi Harlan most admired, for deletion. In addition to altering the book's title to make it less deferential to Harlan's boss, Opfermann excluded many instances of Harlan's praise for Goebbels, like this one, where a brief disclaimer does little to hide his admiration: "To be sure, scores of people suffered greatly under him. But nobody has ever disrespected the speed and precision of his thinking, his ability to verbally formulate the most difficult thoughts in a way that even simple people could understand, and the power of suggestion that he undoubtedly possessed."[116] The specificity of the praise reveals how close Harlan felt to Goebbels and how carefully he observed him. Another seemingly objective statement reveals Harlan's sympathy by brooking no objections: "Goebbels had a resolve in his thinking and acting that undoubtedly made him the most important among the National Socialists and at the same time the most dangerous" ("dangerous" here seems as potentially positive as it could be negative).[117]

Opfermann also edited out comments about Goebbels's positive role in German film. Harlan points out that Goebbels managed to get good films out of his artists, and his leadership style allowed artists the freedom to earn money. He makes the same point obliquely when he insists that the best Nazi films represented the best of German national culture and should not be rejected out of hand: "I ask that some people may consider whether you are not afraid of a tradition now and then, just because it once went through Goebbels's hands"[118]—this too was cut. Opfermann edited an anecdote about offering the "Heil Hitler" salute and singing the Nazi song "Deutsch ist die Saar" (The Saar is German) to a Nazi official from the Ministry of Propaganda who visited one of their film sets to ensure they were using swastikas properly. The published version of the story includes Harlan's sober observation that the song was "manageable," but leaves out the part where he says, "It is a beautiful song and it also sounded very nice when the miners played it, even though it was more Nazi than artistic at the time."[119]

Opfermann removed Harlan's compliments about Goebbels's knowledge of Nietzsche, ability to handle money, sensitivity, work ethic, and enthusiasm.[120] The published book includes Harlan's contention that Goebbels did not have a real conscience, but it omits the next sentence in which he muses that Goebbels probably shared that trait with numerous successful politicians or leaders, "who wielded or wield unusual violence," claiming that Goebbels was still "incredibly confident" up until his death.[121] Ultimately the book includes many of Harlan's straightforward assessments of Goebbels's character, but his more laudatory comments about Goebbels's actions and their effects have largely been removed.

Harlan's penchant for creating false equivalencies among Jews, members of the Nazi party, and Germans in order to suggest that they were all victims of Hitler's rule surfaces at several points in the original manuscript, only to be removed by his protective editor. Harlan's explicit comparison between Dora Gerson and Hitler is one of the most striking of these passages: "I did not understand the wall that my wife at that time erected between us . . . just

50 THE POSTWAR ANTISEMITE

as I will never understand the wall that Hitler built using police brutality between the hearts of those people who loved each other and were no longer allowed to connect because something was wrong with their 'Aryanism.'"[122] This slippery analogy implies that if the Gerson family's prejudice is the same as Hitler's, Harlan is essentially the victim of Jews, antisemitism, and Nazi ideology.

In another remarkable passage, Harlan sets up a parallel between a slur used against a Jew "in the past" (presumably before 1945) and a postwar slur against someone accused of being a Nazi:

> One says "Cheeky Nazi lout." In the past, "cheeky Jewish lout" overruled the right and truth of a Jew. One is no less moral than the other . . . I heard statements from Jews whose fate was the most unspeakable cruelty. My own fate, having to face the false allegations, then seemed shamefully easy to me. But who can ask me to measure the minor tragedy of my fate, which is also one of the foundations of me and my family, by the outrageous things that had happened via the Nazis. I don't think I behaved in such a way that I lost my right to life, work and justice.[123]

This passage, unsurprisingly deleted by Opfermann, is both offensive and telling, not least because it underscores Harlan's struggle to convince others that he has the authority to determine who is an Antisemite. Pointing to the shift in power discussed in this book's Introduction—from Karl Lueger's fin-de-siècle "I determine who is a Jew" to the post-1945 "I determine who is an Antisemite"—it demonstrates Harlan's understanding that positioning himself in the place of the Jewish victim was the best way to take advantage of this shift.

Harlan consistently asserted that his German patriotism was incompatible with antisemitism, and Opfermann cut many statements in which Harlan remained unrepentant about his German patriotism and his affinities for German nationalists and avowed Antisemites. These statements make Harlan's logic clear: if German patriotism is incompatible with antisemitism, Harlan, a true German patriot, cannot be an Antisemite. Too often, however, or at least too often for Opfermann, Harlan's German patriotism comes awfully close to the Nazis. Take, for instance, his mention of the *Deutschlandlied*, which was closely identified with the Nazis: "'Deutschland, Deutschland über alles' still applies to me. It differentiates me from some of my colleagues, even from one of my sons. I bet a lot of people think that it's a sign of old age or a nationalism. But it is nothing more than feeling my roots."[124] Opfermann omitted this passage, along with another in which Harlan insists that his German patriotism was always perfectly calibrated: "The word *Vaterlandsliebe* [love of the fatherland], which has become old-fashioned today, means a lot to me. Times can do little to change that just as Hitler could do little to change that. In this sense, I still consider myself more modern today than those who have lost this love."[125] By reframing the German patriotic spirit as pre-Hitler, Harlan separates it from the Nazis and, by extension, the Antisemite. And yet, his correspondence with Bab shows he had little understanding for German Jews who shared his old-fashioned German patriotic spirit—until their motherland turned on them.[126]

Alfred Braun, who served as a directorial assistant on *Jud Süss*, testified in 1948 that Harlan "felt very German and patriotic, almost until the end believed that Germany would survive the war well."[127] But Opfermann nevertheless downplayed Harlan's patriotism, for instance by omitting passages in which Harlan reflects on his choice not to leave Germany: "My heart is German, I am at home here. I will stay here as long as I am not driven out by force."[128] Harlan often juxtaposes such passages with backhanded compliments about Jews who never got over leaving Germany, for example: "I sense the tragedy of the original Berliner Paul Graetz [an actor and Weimar cabaret luminary], to whom I was very attached. He died of homesickness in America because he loved his hometown more than he loved being safe from Hitler in Hollywood."[129] The inappropriate use of love in this fairly irrational comparison between the longing of a Jew for his homeland and the implied loss of faith in that homeland on the part of other German Jewish émigrés in Hollywood perhaps says too much about Harlan's belief in the power of his love for Germany and his lack of sympathy for those who lost that love as a result of persecution. The problem with Harlan's insistence that German patriotism was incompatible with antisemitism (a view many German Jews shared) was that his comments and actions indicated that he excluded Jews as well as Antisemites from his version of German patriotism.

For Harlan, as for many both before and after the war, there was antisemitism, and then there was antisemitism. Harlan was scornful of the crude, violent antisemitism of Goebbels and other high-ranking Nazis. But Opfermann omitted other passages where Harlan claims that there are degrees of antisemitism. He writes of the feared Nazi propagandist Julius Streicher, "You didn't have to be an anti-Nazi, you could even have

52   THE POSTWAR ANTISEMITE

been anti-Semitic—and yet you would have known from the first second what kind of person you were dealing with."[130] In other words, he implies that Streicher's particular brand of violent, crass antisemitism made milder antisemites cringe. This is similar to a comment about Werner Krauss in a letter to Bab: "If Krauss had been an antisemite of Nazi quality—then I couldn't possibly have missed it."[131]

This dynamic worked in the opposite direction as well: Harlan expressed sympathy for Norwegian writer Knut Hamsun, who had also been accused of being an Antisemite, commenting that his portrayal of Jewish characters in his 1917 novel *Segen der Erde* (Growth of the soil) as "materialistic exploiters," had not been done in a "mean, antisemitic way."[132] A similar logic is at work when he implies that he could have made *Jud Süss* more antisemitic if he wanted to, including by drawing upon "gruesome and untrue" stories from the New Testament about how the Jews tortured and killed Jesus—and, conversely, to point out that he would not have portrayed Jews and their rituals with such respect if he had wanted the film to be more antisemitic.[133] This hierarchy of antisemitic attitudes typifies Harlan's engagement with Jewish difference: distinguishing between greater and lesser degrees of antisemitism helped him establish his authority to determine the Antisemite, whether he was creating antisemitic films for Goebbels during the war or trying to repair his reputation afterward.

Then there is the matter of Harlan's descriptions of Jews, again cut by Opfermann, which further his relativism and the extreme standard it sets for so-called true antisemitism. Harlan repeats ugly stories about Jews with authority. His language about Jews also betrays his negative inclinations, as in his observation about the religious service he asked Jews to perform on the set of *Jud Süss*: "The Hasidic service had a demonic effect. The strangeness, which was performed with great temperament, emanated a strong suggestion—it was like an evocation."[134] This deleted remark corroborated the vision for the Purim scene that he described in a 1940 interview for *Der Film*, which appeared two months before filming began, where he also revealed his intention to depict Süss via the classic antisemitic trope of the disguised Jew: "a victory festival that is interpreted by the Jews as the festival of revenge on the Gojims [*sic*], the Christians. Here I show ancient Jewry, how it was then and how it is still preserved today in the former Poland. Only Jud Süss stands in contrast to this ancient Jewry, the elegant court financial advisor, the clever politician; in short: the disguised Jew."[135] In the published book, Opfermann included Harlan's glowing description of the

Prague Jewish community, whose members were so eager to participate in the film that their rabbi gifted him a Torah.[136] But he cut Harlan's lengthy descriptions of other antisemitic films he *could* have made for Goebbels.[137]

For Harlan, Hitler and the Nazis represent the absolute image of the Antisemite, while Harlan and the millions of other Germans who voted for him without knowing what his antisemitism was capable of represent not his true believing supporters, but rather the antitheses of the Antisemite. Harlan thus transforms one end of the antisemitism spectrum into an absolute signifier, the Antisemite, and then relativizes the rest of the spectrum. This structure of disavowal has two purposes: on one hand, it denies antisemitism; on the other, it maintains the Antisemite to the benefit of non-Jews.

Harlan and the Aftermath of *Jud Süss*

Harlan and his wife remained bitter about *Jud Süss* to the ends of their lives.[138] According to Kristina Söderbaum in a television interview, "What the film did for us? I can tell you precisely: it ruined our lives. That's what it did. At that time, one could never have imagined it. That it would be used in such a way. That it could simply wreck a person's whole life."[139] Like her husband, she was unable, or perhaps unwilling, to recognize the film's impact on Jewish suffering and instead remained laser-focused on their personal losses and sense of victimization. Long after the war, Harlan's son Thomas lamented his father's lack of self-reflection: "The reality is that the non-antisemite was the best whetstone, and that's the worst and most infamous thing about it: That the one who did it didn't understand what he had been asked to do. And when he understood, or was able to understand, that he still didn't realize that maybe one should not be allowed to continue in the field."[140]

By describing his father as a non-antisemite, Thomas seems to be using his father's definition of the Antisemite as a hardcore Nazi in contradistinction to someone who openly stated how much he hated antisemitism. Nevertheless, Thomas crystallizes what was at stake in debating this issue after the war. Like so many others, his father was mainly concerned with proving to the world that Antisemites existed, but he was not one. To do this, he had to establish his authority to define the Antisemite, over and above any Jews, in order to show that he was the Antisemite's true victim.[141] Harlan's writings

54 THE POSTWAR ANTISEMITE

over the years display his unchanging love for German patriotism, desire for career success, and belief in himself as an artist. His relationships with Jews were always subservient to his own needs and desires: while he was willing to help certain Jews and even married one, he was also willing to denigrate Jews when it suited his purposes. His words in the first letter he wrote Julius Bab after the war ring true: "Neither outside nor inside have I ever become different from the way you knew me."[142] Indeed, his postwar letters and texts indicate that he never reflected upon or changed his views, which remained consistent before, during, and after the Nazi regime.

Harlan's efforts to reclaim his reputation underscore a key point: after the war, it was of paramount importance for non-Jews to be able to claim they had the authority to determine the Antisemite, so they could position themselves as victims when needed. Harlan's trials and texts reveal the useful strategies he provided for portraying victimhood at the hands of the Antisemite or Jew, or framing oneself as the Jews' savior. By thus presenting Jews as either morally compromised or impossibly good, but never as multi-faceted, complex individuals, he engaged Jewish difference for narrative effect while still adhering to the new taboo against antisemitism.

Julius Bab and his wife Elisabeth returned to Germany twice, in 1951 and 1953. Elisabeth described the trips as a *Triumphzug* (parade of triumph) for her husband. While they saw old friends and enjoyed German theater performances, they were sad to see the destroyed streets and overgrown graves of loved ones and to feel the absence of many other friends. And despite their impoverished, uprooted existence in New York, despite offers to stay, despite his previous deep patriotism and love of German culture, Bab did not want to remain in Germany. In a letter to German-Jewish director and screenwriter Ludwig Berger, he wrote: "I don't want to go back to Germany (where I could live much more comfortably). Too many unhanged murderers are walking around there, and I don't want to be in a position to unwittingly shake hands with the man who pushed my niece's little children into the gas chamber."[143] The world of Jewish life as he knew it was gone forever, as evoked in the poignant words of "Vorbei," the last recording Dora Gerson made in Berlin: "Gone, beyond recall—a final word, a last greeting—gone."[144]

Not all German and Austrian Jews shared this sentiment after the war. But Bab could not maintain the fantasy that one could remain a German patriot simply by convincing oneself that the true definition of being German meant that one was protected from accusations of antisemitism. His experiences between 1933 and 1945 had already proven to him that too many people believed that the true definition of being German did not include being Jewish. As Gerson's lyrics about loss "beyond recall" show, the postwar debate about Harlan's antisemitic legacy omitted the most significant fact of this period: everything that Jews had lost, through death, destruction, and displacement, which they could never recover or return to after the Holocaust. Yet the ultimate significance of Gerson to this story is not her absence from it, that is, her death at the hands of the Nazis, but the way Harlan turned her into his Jewish persecutor as part of the postwar struggle over the authority to define the Antisemite. Harlan's fame made this dynamic visible, allowing us to consider the moral logic that informs complicity in antisemitism as a system of thought and to understand how those who believe they have no part in that system can nevertheless transform and perpetuate it.

2

Harlan's Antisemites

Karena Niehoff Testifies in Hamburg

On April 14, 1950, twenty-nine-year old journalist Karena Niehoff prepared to exit the courthouse on Hamburg's Sievekingplatz, where the film director Veit Harlan was on trial for committing a crime against humanity for directing the 1940 Nazi propaganda film, *Jud Süss*. Niehoff appeared at Harlan's trial as a witness because she worked from 1940 to 1941 as an assistant to the film's recently deceased screenwriter Ludwig Metzger, rendering her testimony particularly important.[1] The trial was done for the day and the famous director had left long ago. But Niehoff looked out the window to see a lingering crowd of hostile onlookers with a few policemen keeping them at bay. Other journalists told her they were waiting especially for her and already were issuing threats due to her provocative testimony against Harlan. She took a step back from the window when she realized they recognized her red beret.

Once Niehoff was outside, the police ushered her into a waiting car as the crowd hooted, spit, yelled "Go home, foreigner!," and hurled other antisemitic insults, including the especially spiteful invective *"Judensau!"* (Jew pig!) (Figure 2.1).[2] Given the desire of many to carefully craft an image of West Germany as free from antisemitism five years after the Holocaust, this display of explicit antisemitism became the subject of international news, further underscoring the trial's significance in postwar culture.

Niehoff, who was born in Berlin in 1920 to a Jewish mother and non-Jewish father, had spent much of the war jailed or in hiding. After 1933, she was expelled from high school for refusing to participate in nationalist classes and for being a so-called *Halbjüdin* (literally "half-Jew" in Nazi terminology), according to the Nazis.[3] In 1943, a grocer denounced her when she tried to reuse a ration card to obtain bread for her Jewish mother, aunt, and grandmother. She served nearly the entire six months of a sentence handed to her by a judge who characterized her offense as an act of sabotage. The Gestapo arrested her again on January 11, 1944, when she refused to reveal

The Postwar Antisemite. Lisa Silverman, Oxford University Press. © Oxford University Press 2025.
DOI: 10.1093/9780197697757.003.0003

HARLAN'S ANTISEMITES 57

Figure 2.1. This illustration from the April 21, 1950, edition of the *Allgemeine Wochenzeitung der Juden in Deutschland* depicts Karena Niehoff exiting the courthouse in Hamburg into a crowd yelling out antisemitic jeers and catcalls, including *"Judensau"* (Jewish pig). *Jüdische Allgemeine/Staatsbibliothek zu Berlin.*

the address of her mother, Rose, who had gone into hiding. She remained imprisoned until February 25. Three months later, she was arrested a third time because of her work for Shigeki Sakimura, a Japanese economist accused of treason. This time, she was incarcerated in the Fehrbellin labor education camp until August 18. When the Gestapo called her in for questioning shortly after her release, she decided she could not risk future imprisonment and went into hiding, where she remained until the end of the war in May 1945.

After the war, Niehoff was reunited with Rose, who had been deported to Theresienstadt in June 1944 after a neighbor denounced her.[4] To earn money, Niehoff started working as a journalist for various newspapers.[5] She often traveled for her articles, including to the Soviet occupation zone. In 1946, she reported on the Nuremberg trials, reserving her most biting criticism for the audience in attendance, rather than the Nazis defendants. Her description of the disinterest, distance, and irony with which the citizens of Nuremberg watched the endless procession of cars and journalists in town for the historic trials was especially memorable.[6] She depicted the journalists at the trial as self-righteous and smug, imagining them thinking, "I am so

58 THE POSTWAR ANTISEMITE

wonderfully innocent and can sit in the audience in a white vest and marvel at the world theater of the damned." By comparison, she described the accused Nazis as a "ghost gallery of exhausted desert hikers," a far cry from their depiction as gruesome, evil monsters in most media.[7]

Critical observations about her fellow Germans and their antisemitism and unacknowledged relationship to Nazi crimes peppered Niehoff's postwar reporting on topics ranging from penicillin to pedagogy to displaced persons (DPs). In one article from 1947, she linked persistent casual antisemitism after the war to the attitudes that Germans "picked up" under the Nazi regime:

> Even for those who were just "bystanders," nothing collapsed and there was no need to laboriously patch anything up. Like their houses, they remained intact inside. . . . It is very convenient and very practical, and that is why—albeit without passion—one picked up some useful things on the roadside of Nazi ideology, which one cannot separate from today. Things don't move that fast in this country. So one sits down in the courtyards and small businesses of the few, long-established Jews, who were farmers and artisans like themselves, with comfort and without a pounding heart. That is why the youngsters today insult the only Jewish child in a village.[8]

Her description of German bystanders as "intact inside," like their houses, suggests that what had happened in Germany was less a process of national damage and reconciliation than one of superficial external changes masking a persistent consistency. In other words, Nazi ideology could not be separated from the postwar conditions in which Germans continued to live their lives without reckoning with the absence of Jews from their communities—and how that absence came to be. Niehoff's testimony against Harlan that day revealed similar uncomfortable truths about postwar antisemitism—surely one reason why it elicited such violent response.

By 1950, nearly two years had passed since the occupying forces in the British military zone had charged Harlan with committing a crime against humanity for directing the 1940 Nazi propaganda film, *Jud Süss*. To have committed a crime against humanity was the harshest possible accusation under the postwar laws set up to administer justice for Nazi crimes. Harlan was first acquitted on April 23, 1949, with the rationale that a clear connection between the film and inhumane acts could not be proved. But the British military government overturned that decision on December 12, 1949, noting that "[a]nyone who made a hate film against the Jews in 1940 cannot claim that they were not responsible for the film's effects because the Jews would have been persecuted anyway."[9] The second trial, where Niehoff testified, began on March 29, 1950. Harlan was acquitted again only a month later.

By the time the war ended, Harlan had starred in and directed dozens of successful films for the Nazis, becoming a household name along the way. But the decision to charge him with crimes against humanity for directing a film nevertheless sparked controversy. His fame made his fate a linchpin for the question of whether someone who had never joined the Nazi party, served in the military, or physically harmed anyone could be culpable for Nazi crimes. Leading Nazis had already been arrested, put on trial, convicted, and executed for their murderous deeds. But the complicity of others who had benefited from the Nazi regime was still unclear. The question remained: What should happen to people who did not personally harm Jews but still benefited from their expropriation and murder?

Commentary on Harlan's trials at the time focused on whether he deserved to shoulder the blame for creating culture for the Nazis when so many other artists had also maintained successful careers under the regime. As writer Norbert Muhlen observed,

> It seems that he was a rather representative member of that largest class of Germans which cannot be fitted snugly into the customary triptych of "real" Nazis, non-Nazis, and anti-Nazis. In Harlan's case, as in so many others, a mixture of various motives, none of them being a fanatical enthusiasm for the totalitarian system, produced that irresponsible submission to and support of the Nazi dictatorship which was its real source of popular strength.[10]

Muhlen frames Harlan as representative of what is typically described as the problem of German guilt. Others used the trials to vilify or defend his artistic merit by gauging the degree of antisemitism in his life and works. Harlan's well-publicized trials and the events surrounding them highlight the postwar power struggle for the authority to define the Antisemite, a struggle Harlan believed he needed to win in order to be acquitted. His trials for crimes against humanity served as the ultimate public testing ground for that authority by putting his account before the court and the broader community of West Germans, who would similarly choose to accept or reject it. The trials thus became a way of establishing a public narrative not only about

60 THE POSTWAR ANTISEMITE

who bore responsibility for Nazi crimes but also about the perpetuation of postwar antisemitism.

The fact that Niehoff, an outspoken, Jewish, female critic, triggered years of particularly vindictive retaliation from Harlan and his supporters suggests that she posed the trial's greatest challenge to this authority. The outcry she provoked shows how antisemitism and gender constructions shaped the various narratives put forth at the trial. Despite the postwar societal taboos against explicit antisemitism, deeply ingrained cultural practices built on age-old prejudices against Jews persisted, often via coded references. When these ingrained practices erupted explicitly, as they did on April 14, 1950, they exposed how central the struggle to define and manage expressions of antisemitism was to the construction of postwar West German self-understandings.

After 1945, Germans and Austrians under Allied occupation faced new legal and social consequences for explicit expressions of Jew-hatred. However, targeting a small number of bad people as Antisemites hardly eradicated antisemitism or the coding system of Jewish difference from which it stemmed. Instead of prompting critical reflections on the role of stereotypes about Jews, both positive and negative, in European culture, this new state of affairs created the belief that being associated with antisemitism in any form was the worst possible moral offense. In turn, calling someone an Antisemite became an effective means to gain and maintain power in a variety of social situations. Those who were able to wield it could maintain the societal advantages supplied by antisemitism while appearing to oppose it. Harlan's trials demonstrate how the postwar courtroom also marked a shift in this narrative power, from being able to determine who was a Jew to being able to determine who was an Antisemite.

Although the trials ostensibly concerned Harlan's complicity in Nazi crimes against Jews, the words of the prosecution, defense, witnesses, newspapers, and Harlan's supporters, during and after the trial, constitute the context of ongoing complicity that Niehoff described with such clarity in her accounts of the Nuremberg trials and postwar German life. Niehoff reminds us that the question of what it meant to be a good German cannot be understood apart from the effort to claim the authority to define the Antisemite. Harlan's defense presented him as a true German patriot and claimed that a true German patriot could not be an Antisemite. This argument resonated strongly for West Germans who were upset about the loss of the war, wanted

HARLAN'S ANTISEMITES   61

to rebuild their careers, and also wanted to think of themselves as good and loyal Germans. But Niehoff stood in its way.

Harlan's Antisemite

Though Harlan was certainly aware that many Germans were undergoing similar uncomfortable evaluations of their activities under the Nazi regime, he firmly believed that his prominent role as the Nazis' most successful filmmaker meant that he alone was being blamed for things others had also done.[11] He was not wrong in recognizing his role as scapegoat. But where he could have acknowledged complicity and then insisted that others also be held accountable, he instead refused to be associated with any harm caused to Jews and highlighted his role as the Antisemite's main victim. This meant that his defense had to convince others that he had the authority to define the Antisemite.

Harlan and his supporters had various shifting ways to rationalize his behavior—and by extension the behavior of all Germans who survived or even flourished during the war. To begin, they held that career advancement and financial gains achieved while the Nazis were in power could be balanced out by kindness and personal relationships with individual Jews. Harlan sometimes conceded that under the Nazis, his career had thrived, he had great authority over his films, and he enjoyed significant advantages, only to contradict himself by claiming that these advantages counted for little when, as he liked to point out, he could have been killed at any moment for resisting orders. At certain times, he positioned himself as a German patriot who acceded to or resisted the Nazis as needed. Sometimes he claimed to stand completely outside the system of Antisemites and their targets; at other times he asserted that he was the Antisemite's main victim.

The trials revealed the development of a postwar coding system of Jewish difference that continued to confer its benefits on non-Jews. Unsurprisingly, Harlan often expressed anger, hurt, and disbelief at the accusation that he had willingly participated in antisemitic Nazi propaganda. One way he responded to this accusation was by continuing to emphasize his close relationships to Jews, including his first wife, Dora Gerson. Witnesses for the defense highlighted his generosity and how he used his clout with Goebbels to help friends and associates affected by the Nuremberg Laws.

62   THE POSTWAR ANTISEMITE

Irene Meyer-Hanno, communist actor Hans Meyer-Hanno's Jewish wife, testified that Harlan had assisted the couple after her husband's arrest, and Paul Henckels, whose father was a Jew, testified that Harlan had invited him and his wife to a party where prominent Nazis would also be in attendance.[12] These testimonials reinforced Harlan's definition of an Antisemite as a person who wants nothing to do with Jews, speaks disparagingly about them, and categorically refuses to help them—because they intentionally, maliciously hate Jews. He explained that he depicted Antisemites in *Jud Süss* as people who hurt Jews simply because they are Jews, not because of anything they have done: "And everyone who sees the film today can say: that's how the Nazis were and that's how they are presented in my film, true to life."[13]

Harlan defined the Antisemite as someone who shunned all Jews so that he could both draw on his personal relationships with Jews to prove that he was not an Antisemite and disparage Jews by casting them as Antisemites when it suited his purposes. Indeed, another critical element of his self-defense was the contention that since Antisemites *and* Jews had treated him badly, he could not be accused of antisemitism, regardless of anything else he had done. This contention, like others, required him to define the Antisemite as a figure who not only was separate from himself but also had the power to make him its victim. In this respect, his film *Jud Süss* served an even more important purpose: it related the history of a Jew put on trial, convicted, and sentenced to death by Antisemites, so by associating himself with his own protagonist, Harlan could cast himself as the victim of those who put him on trial and testified against him, not least of all Niehoff.

Whose Antisemitism? The *Jud Süss* Screenplay

By her own account, Karena Niehoff worked for Metzger until their political differences became too much for her, but they remained on friendly terms after the war. In fact, evidence suggests that Niehoff crafted her testimony to rebut the defense's portrayal of Metzger as the antisemitic mastermind behind *Jud Süss*. Though Niehoff conceded that Metzger was a German nationalist and a committed National Socialist, she insisted that he was not an Antisemite and that he had not written the screenplay to specifically target Jews. In other words, Niehoff's account of Metzger challenged Harlan's authority to define the Antisemite by asserting her own authority and definition, which helps explain why her testimony provoked such a heated reaction.

The defense argued that Harlan had no choice but to carry out Goebbels's request to direct the antisemitic propaganda film, and that once he did, he focused on improving its artistic quality and lessening its antisemitism, which included forgoing what was characterized as the "*Stürmerisch*" style of antisemitism contained in Metzger's draft, a reference to Julius Streicher's infamous antisemitic newspaper *Der Stürmer*. Harlan had learned his lesson about the pitfalls of such explicit representations of Antisemites from his role in the unsuccessful *Susanne* of 1934: less explicit antisemitism would make his film more rhetorically powerful. So it is not surprising that in order to make his film more effective, Harlan toned down some of the original screenplay's more egregious and distasteful examples of antisemitism and played up its portrayal of protagonist Jud Süss as elegant and seductive.[14] At times, argued Harlan, Goebbels himself insisted that Harlan reverse some of his efforts in this direction. He pointed out instances where he tried to lessen the film's antisemitic effect, such as when Goebbels insisted that a character call out "Jude, Jude!" when he had suggested the less offensive phrase "Jud Süss."[15] Harlan's preferred ending for the film had been for Süss to die a martyr after a heroic speech about his love for the Jews, which Goebbels insisted on changing to one in which Süss dies a humiliating death for all to see, as a coward. At the time, Harlan and his supporters played up these narrative choices to claim that any antisemitic effect of the film occurred in spite of, rather than because of, Harlan.[16]

This cynical view overlooks the important context of such "improvements:" Harlan toned down some of the film's most negative representations to make it more effective as a work of antisemitic propaganda. For this reason, it is astounding that the (second) acquittal decided that, while Harlan's film incited antisemitism, Harlan himself could not be held accountable for it.[17] It is simply not convincing that making the film more tasteful means that it was not perpetuating antisemitism, and points to the postwar shift in how the Antisemite was defined, and who was allowed to define it.

Niehoff's testimony that day hinged on her stated familiarity with Metzger and his original draft for *Jud Süss*, which she claimed to have read while working for him. It is a claim she had already made in a witness statement in Berlin the year before the trial, when she described her judicious comparison of the screenplay and film: "I read the book [screenplay] very carefully and later observed the film carefully, and noted the differences."[18] She seems to

64 THE POSTWAR ANTISEMITE

have entered the Hamburg courtroom determined to counter the defense's attempt to portray Metzger as the Antisemite responsible for *Jud Süss*. She later alluded to the fact that she had been aware of the smear campaign against Metzger and wanted to counteract it.[19] More than a decade later, she wrote to Metzger's daughter Gunhild that she had admired Metzger despite their differences, visited him at his deathbed, and soon after his death "had the opportunity to prove her friendship" and "perhaps Gunhild's mother had told her about it."[20] Metzger's widow, Astrid, later said that Niehoff had shown "great courage" by testifying against Harlan on her husband's behalf.[21]

Niehoff's testimony reinforced what Metzger himself had argued about the film before his death, when he firmly attributed *Jud Süss*'s screenplay's antisemitism to Harlan. Metzger wrote an initial précis for the film, and writer Eberhard Wolfgang Möller, a Nazi party member, wrote dialogue and scenes to produce their first jointly authored draft of the screenplay. Immediately after the war, in a sworn statement for his denazification proceedings, Metzger asserted that not a single word or sentence in the final screenplay was actually his, because when Harlan took over the project, he admitted revising it entirely to conform with the Ministry of Propaganda's political directives in a letter to Metzger dated January 30, 1940:

> In its current version, the script is a fundamentally different artistic script with completely different dialogues and numerous scenes that I invented. It will be yes, finally, the version that I have just written, and even though, as you rightly judge, I have largely left the original plot structure, the character of the film has changed completely. Large parts are completely new. I even wrote a completely different conclusion and added other scenes that you don't even know about.[22]

In a 1947 statement, Harlan confirmed that he "rewrote" the script when he came on board as the film's director in 1939.[23] Metzger insisted that Harlan, not Möller, was responsible for the film's most antisemitic scenes: "It is also clear that the actual tendentious Jewish scenes were not available in Möller's screenplay, but were freely invented by Harlan. This is the entire Frankfurt complex with its Jewish scenes, the expansion of the diverse Werner Krauss roles, and also the entire plot of the demolished house."[24] Niehoff confirmed his account at the trial, when she argued—in contrast to all of the other witnesses—that Harlan's version was much more negative than Metzger's. But she also added her own observations. For example, when the judge claimed that there would have been no *Jud Süss* film without Metzger, she replied, "Then Harlan would have made a different antisemitic film!"[25]

Harlan did indeed remove some particularly antisemitic instances from the Metzger-Möller screenplay, but he also added antisemitic scenes and embellishments, including Süss's partial demolition of a blacksmith's house and the rape scene.[26] Perhaps not surprisingly, Metzger's defenses for his wartime activities sound a lot like Harlan's, from his insistence that he hadn't been "political," voted for Hitler, or joined the Nazi party, though it would have been better for his career if he had, to his belief that he had thought Hitler would be a capable statesman who would do good for Germany and the world. After reviewing his activities during the Nazi era, the Allied Forces found him sufficiently culpable to blacklist him.[27] Like Harlan and others, Metzger also insisted that his German patriotism had nothing to do with antisemitism, making him part of the ongoing collective effort to detach the Antisemite, and thus the Nazi, from German patriotism, which in turn allowed individuals to insist that because they were not Antisemites, they could remain committed German nationalists without being Nazis.

Again sounding like Harlan, Metzger wrote, "I am not an antisemite—I was friends with Jews long before 1933, and acted for them as a manager, and I myself once wanted to marry a Jewish woman; in 1936 I lived in a half-Jewish household, for over a half a year I feared the Nürnberg laws and was ready to personally carry all their consequences." He insisted he had never spread Nazi ideology and said that at the time he was involved with *Jud Süss*, he never could have imagined the catastrophe that would come to his country.[28]

Clearly, both Metzger and Harlan wrote screenplays for an antisemitic film, and both insisted after the war that they were not antisemitic. Without Metzger to testify on his own behalf, Harlan had a good chance of making sure his version of events painted Metzger as the Antisemite. But by testifying in support of Metzger and challenging Harlan's attempt to cast him as the arch Antisemite of *Jud Süss*, Niehoff undermined Harlan's authority to make that very determination. As a witness, Niehoff herself became caught up in this discourse of authority, though she must have been aware that the cost of lending credibility to Metzger's defense was to risk becoming a target of antisemitism herself, as occurred inside and outside the courthouse. Yet, her role in the trial and the challenge she presented to Harlan's authority also meant that he and others, including the judge and the mayor of Hamburg, were able to denigrate her without explicitly positioning themselves as

66 THE POSTWAR ANTISEMITE

antisemites. They could take advantage of her liminal position as "not quite" a Jew, and as a woman, to place themselves in positions of power over her, even as they portrayed Harlan and others as her victims. In other words, antisemitism, the implicit disavowal of antisemitism, and misogny all allowed Harlan and his allies to more easily cast Niehoff as the persecutor.

Niehoff's Testimony: Conflicting Accounts

The contentious and often hostile atmosphere in the courtroom on the day of Niehoff's testimony produced conflicting accounts of what happened—and who was to blame. One way of reading the conflict is to understand that the questions of responsibility at stake were so fraught that they leapt the bounds of the trial's content, in the past, and infiltrated its context, in the present and then the future, for while Harlan's anger at the young female journalist began in the courtroom, it resonated for years thereafter.

In Harlan's autobiography, he describes how Niehoff insulted him with a comment about his wife, after which an "anonymous person" yelled out "Frechheit":

> In the air of the courtroom, there were no doubt special explosives and there was a dull feeling that there would be an explosion. She had clearly prepared herself. This explosion came when a few well-formulated defensive remarks by Miss Niehoff made the audience laugh, whereupon the Attorney General Dr. Kramer exclaimed: "It is unbearable to have to negotiate under this pressure. There is only a Nazi audience in the room!!" Of course, this elicited an outraged response at the senior public prosecutor—including a loud "How dare you!!"[29]

Though Harlan's phrasing distances himself from this outburst, other accounts make it clear that it was his. In a passage deleted from the published version of his autobiography, Harlan similarly argued that Niehoff and the prosecutor had orchestrated the entire sequence of events, attributing to them the skills of a film director (and thus usurping *his* role):

> It was clear to everyone who was clear-sighted and certainly also to the senior public prosecutor, who had called the entire audience "Nazis," that this scandal had been violently provoked. It was precisely the interrogation

of the witness Niehoff, who had openly harmed the dignity of the court with her remarks—and caused the unrest in the audience—and who must have been chosen from the outset for this "bomb"—which was to burst—because the various explosions the ones that preceded the main bomber burst increased according to a pattern that directors know how to use.[30]

This exchange was presided over by Walter Fritz Tyrolf, a former Nazi party member who had served as a judge under Hitler. In a letter to one of his former colleagues, Harlan described him as a "typical NSDAP [Nazi]-judge, who was even in the SA [Storm Troopers]" as well as a "thoroughly honorable man."[31] Long after Harlan's death in 1964, his son Thomas brought to light the harsh verdicts Tyrolf issued during the Nazi regime, including death penalties for crimes such as robbery. He also noted Tyrolf's sympathy for Harlan and the role it likely played in his father's acquittals.[32] In other words, the trial and its accompanying outbursts took place in the shadow of the failure of the denazification process to remove former Nazis from power.[33]

Harlan reconstructed Niehoff's testimony to his advantage, rendering his own interjection anonymous, ignoring its role in setting other disturbances in motion, and blaming Niehoff for egging on the crowd by calling them Nazi pigs and insulting his wife.[34] But evidence from the proceedings contradict some of these points. According to a handwritten trial transcript, which the prosecutor's account corroborated, Harlan was the first to cause a stir: "A remark made by the defendant to the witness Niehoff was reprimanded. The defendant apologized. The witness Niehoff was also made aware of her previous statements to the court, the public prosecutor's office, the senior public prosecutor in Berlin, and the defense, during the preliminary trial. Interjections from the audience disturbed the progress of the proceedings."[35] At that point, Judge Tyrolf barred the public from the room while he investigated the disturbance. The transcript indicates that two men, both residents of Hamburg, were reprimanded and barred from returning. Niehoff continued her testimony with only the press in the audience.

A number of other sources, some of them conflicting, provide more details of the testimony and ensuing events. According to a statement Niehoff gave police six days later, her exchanges with Tyrolf triggered additional responses from the courtroom audience. The first occurred after Tyrolf suggested that her status as a *Halbjüdin* was the reason she opposed the Nazi regime, a point she immediately clarified:

68   THE POSTWAR ANTISEMITE

When the judge explained that it was understandable that, as a *Halbjüdin*, I was opposed to the Nazi regime, I interrupted him vigorously—with the words "wait a minute," as other people told me afterwards—and explained that I would also have been a Nazi opponent even if I hadn't known that I was a *Halbjüdin*. After this explanation from me, there was laughter and movement in the audience, but it wasn't clear to me from this outburst if the public was against me.

The second outburst she described occurred when the judge asked her what Metzger had said about Harlan's wife, Kristina Söderbaum. She stated that "the audience continued to laugh when I spoke of Harlan sending his wife 'into the water' in almost all of his films." Niehoff was referring to the fact that in Harlan's films such as *Jugend* (1938) and *Die goldene Stadt* (1942), Söderbaum often played characters who commit suicide by drowning themselves; the joke, to German audiences, was that she was a *Reichswasserleiche* (official corpse of the Third Reich's waters). Kramer's account confirmed Niehoff's statement. He wrote that Niehoff testified that Metzger told her Harlan changed the screenplay "so that Dorothea Sturm, portrayed by his wife, would 'go into the water.' Metzger said Harlan always lets his wife 'go into the water.' The accused then said in a low voice to the witness: 'How dare you!' At my request, the defendant's exclamation was reprimanded by the judge."[36] It becomes clear here that Harlan's retort reflected his repeated efforts to position himself as the victim of Niehoff's challenge to his masculinity and to defend his own character.

Shared hostility toward Niehoff united Harlan, the audience, and even the judge.[37] According to Niehoff, the hostility first surfaced when she asserted that "decent" Nazis were stupid and recounted how she had told Metzger that Germany had to lose the war:

Finally, there was unrest in the audience when I said that Metzger was the only decent Nazi I knew, based on the fact that he was stupid. I added that I had never met any decent Nazis whom I could describe as smart. During further descriptions of my conversations with Metzger, the judge asked whether I would have criticized Metzger for his involvement in the *Jud Süss* film, and I explained that this was the case, and I told him that someday he would be called to account for it. When Metzger dismissed this by saying that Germany would win the war, I declared not only that the Nazis would lose the war, but also that they must lose it. This statement also caused unrest in the audience, which I now determined to be politically tinged and directed against me.[38]

The audience's dissatisfaction with her criticism of Metzger and rejection of Nazi Germany transformed her from a German witness to a Jewish one, a move made easier by her status as a so-called *Halbjüdin*, as Tyrolf pointed out when questioning her. This process worked to secure Harlan's place—rather than Niehoff's—as the real arbiter of the Antisemite. In turn, the dismissal of Niehoff's authority paved the way for new expressions of antisemitism and misogyny toward her, even from the judge himself. Returning to her status as a *Halbjüdin*, the judge asked when Metzger first learned of her identity. Niehoff replied that he only found out after *Jud Süss* was completed:

> Then the judge asked with a smile: "Didn't he already notice it?" There was a loud laugh from the audience, which could only have been perceived as antisemitic. I turned to the audience and asked, "What is there to laugh about?" As the laughter intensified, the prosecutor jumped up and explained that it was intolerable to continue in such an atmosphere. He asked the judge to stop these Nazi demonstrations. The audience laughed again at the prosecutor's statement.[39]

Although Niehoff does not mention it, a newspaper later reported that after the judge asked her whether Metzger had noticed that she was a Jew, a woman in the courtroom audience exclaimed, "Das sieht man doch!" (That's quite obvious!), which elicited further laughter.[40] Clearly, her criticism of German nationalism had further undermined her efforts to describe the Antisemite, underscoring the fact that in the liminal position of *Halbjüdin*, she could never be a true German patriot and thus could never have the authority to define the Antisemite.

This positioning of Niehoff both as the target of antisemitism and as someone who lacks the authority to define the Antisemite and criticize men relies on her liminal position. As these courtroom accounts show, one way others dismissed her was by pointing to apparent contradictions between how she identified herself and how others identified her, refusing to let the categories of Jew and German overlap. Niehoff's description of her conversation with a man who distanced himself from the antisemitic crowd underscored this point:

70 THE POSTWAR ANTISEMITE

He said that he did not like the insults spoken against me, but he did not understand why I said at the trial that Germany must lose this war, because as a *Halbjüdin* I am "also" a German. I acknowledged his resentment with the remark that not only people who are "also" Germans, but who, in his view, are "real" Germans—that is, not at all Jewish—could have wanted or even prayed for this war to be lost by Germany as well, since these were the best, the smartest and the finest Germans.[41]

Although the man decried the antisemitic outbursts, he believed that Niehoff's status as a *Halbjüdin* did not justify her lack of German patriotism and failure to support the Nazis, which *would* have been justified if she had been, in Nazi terminology, a *Volljüdin* (full Jew). His view reflected the common prewar notion that Jews were not fully German, which still persisted after the war. In many ways, the trials themselves validated his assumptions about Jews and Germans, as well as how even those who believed they were not Antisemites could perpetuate those assumptions.

Niehoff's account goes on to note that when a number of people, including journalist Egon Giordano, himself a "half Jew," stood up to protest the antisemitic tenor of the outbursts, Judge Tyrolf cleared the room and suspended the trial—all so quickly that it left her a little dazed. After the trial resumed, Niehoff's testimony continued uninterrupted. But when the day's proceedings ended, she and other journalists were met with insults in the courtroom hallway: "Make sure you get out of Germany"; "We don't need such people here"; and "Here comes her protector; he's probably a Jew, too!," which may have been a reference to Manfred Jackson, a journalist for the *Jewish Chronicle* and the *Allgemeine Wochenzeitung der Juden in Deutschland*.[42] Niehoff described her efforts to defend herself:

At that moment I was insulted by a woman who called out "Judensau." I couldn't see this woman clearly. I only noticed that she was a small person. The journalist Dieberitz looked around for the caller and tried unsuccessfully to catch her. In my excitement, which was increased by the fact that people crowded around me and took hold of my sleeves, I turned around and said: "Leave me alone. It's starting again like in 1932 that the Jews are to be thrown out of Germany and insulted; there seem to be substantial Nazis here." It is also possible that I spoke of "Nazi gangs," but I know I didn't say "Nazi pigs" and I didn't say "all Germans." Also, my words were simply a reaction to the attacks against me.

In response to these attacks, as well as to the crowd that gathered outside before she left, Kramer insisted that she leave with police protection. As Niehoff exited the building, the crowd turned its attention to her:

> When I stepped out of the courthouse, I was greeted by the crowd on the opposite side of the street with hoots, whistles, and incomprehensible shouts. After a moment's hesitation, I got into the car some people were standing in front of. However, they were pushed back by the police and the car drove at a high speed around the building across the opposite side of Sievekingplatz towards the city. A number of demonstrators had run across the square, some of whom threatened with their clenched fists when I drove past. Some also spat in front of the car. Among these people I remember a woman because of her particularly wild facial expression. I had noticed this woman after the scenes in front of the courtroom. There, journalists had drawn my attention to her and expressed their suspicion that she was the woman who had called out "Judensau." They told me she had denied it. It was a small person with dark blond hair, around 40 years old. I think I saw her again in the courtroom the following Monday. I intended to identify her after the trial. But apparently she noticed that I looked over at her a few times, and so when I looked back at her place after a while, she was gone.[43]

Newspapers in both East and West Germany and abroad reported on the events at the courthouse that day, providing further varying accounts. In West Germany, the *Allgemeine Wochenzeitung der Juden in Deutschland* noted with dismay that the "loutish behavior from these *Stürmer* anti-Semites should make Germans reconsider their claim that 'we' see the German situation via dark glasses; rather, it proves that for many Germans the nourishment for antisemitism is present again." The paper also disapprovingly noted that, although Bundeskanzler Adenauer and Dr. Heinemann, head of the Protestant church in Germany, had condemned the worst of the crowd in a radio address, they had not criticized Judge Tyrolf and the police for allowing the antisemitic statements: "We summarize: A witness is insulted as a '*Judensau*' without effective action against the hooligans, and anti-Semitic statements and threats are tolerated in the courtroom itself."[44] The East German *Berliner Zeitung* used the opportunity to cast West Germany's government as the antisemitic successor to the Nazi regime with the hyperbolic headline "*Kristallnacht*-Atmosphere in Hamburg: Harlan Trial in Adenauer's "Freedom Air"/Ruckus Democracy for Antisemites."[45] On the

72 THE POSTWAR ANTISEMITE

other hand, American representatives of the Allied Forces, already worried about how the trial might affect the rebuilding of West Germany's reputation, downplayed the events. U.S. High Commissioner McCloy's op-ed in the *Süddeustche Zeitung* was headlined "The German People Are Not Antisemitic."[46]

When the trial resumed the following Monday, April 17, Judge Tyrolf mentioned the "deeply regrettable" events of April 14, but said nothing more about what had transpired. In Tyrolf's own account, he unsurprisingly downplayed the courtroom commotion as little more than good-natured ribbing, stating that he had merely cracked a smile at the "still young, very clever and spirited witness," at which point the audience also grinned. Disputing the newspaper accounts, he continued:

> It is incorrect that the audience made anti-Semitic statements during my questioning of the witness Niehoff, in particular when I asked the witness whether the author of the screenplay "Jud Süss,"—Metzger—who had since passed away, and who also inspired the idea for this film, apologized for the anti-Semitic content of this screenplay, because he knew or noticed that the witness was half-Jewish. The audience smiled for a moment at my question, but was immediately calm again.[47]

Tyrolf suggested that what he carefully refers to as "these tensions" in the courtroom actually stemmed not from Niehoff, for whom he retained a paternalistic condescension, but from two other incidents, one of which was the testimony of another Jew.

Early in the trial, he noted, the prosecutor read aloud a letter from Norbert Wollheim, a survivor of Auschwitz and chairman of the Central Committee of Liberated Jews in the British Zone, who appeared as a witness during the first trial but refused to appear for the second. In the letter, Wollheim expressed his disappointment with the first acquittal and said he would not return to the court as he had nothing further to add to his original testimony.[48] Tyrolf denounced the content of the letter as "violent attacks against the objectivity of the court," which he believed led to the "tensions," using the familiar strategy of inflaming critical language in a description of prejudice or protest to turn it into the cause.[49] Framing the Jewish Wollheim as the attacker, Tyrolf positioned not only Harlan, but also the justice system itself, as the victims of vengeful Jewish forces.

The second inciting incident Tyrolf referenced was a courtroom discussion about prohibiting a public screening of Harlan's film on the basis that it would disturb public order. When the prosecutor claimed that the screening would also be a danger to "morality," the audience laughed. According to Tyrolf, "This laugh was undoubtedly improper, but could not in any way be perceived as a Nazi or antisemitic statement. They were obviously laughing because the reference to the threat to morality from a public screening of the film was considered funny."[50] This appeal to commonsense humor trivialized the trial's central question about the antisemitic effects of Nazi-era propaganda films. With his ability to delegitimize criticism of the legal system and to trivialize the content and potential harm of the film under discussion, Tyrolf wielded the postwar power to determine who was an Antisemite, or at least, a Nazi.

Tyrolf wielded that power again when he explained his decision to acquit Harlan in his second verdict: "Antisemitism itself is not punishable if the laws of humanity are not disregarded."[51] The defense's effort to prove Harlan was not an Antisemite by smearing Metzger had worked. Tyrolf determined that Metzger's screenplay was "more antisemitic" because, among other reasons, the Jews speak in jargon, the main character Jud Süss is portrayed as a "*schmutziger Jude*" (dirty Jew) driven into the town in a garbage truck, and "*mehrere sexuelle Szenen*" (numerous sexual scenes) show Süss procuring girls for the Duke and disreputable girls for himself (unlike Harlan's screenplay, which contained a love scene).[52]

The defense also had a positive strategy, and it too succeeded. Many witnesses argued that Harlan's goal was to create a high-quality artistic film, not to stir up hatred against Jews. This meant avoiding the *Stürmerisch* antisemitism Harlan had learned from his past experience. Assistant director Wolfgang Schleif testified that during a break from filming one day, actors Werner Krauss and Ferdinand Marian took photographs of themselves caricaturing Jews. Schleif claimed Harlan became so upset when he saw the photos that he demanded they not be used; he was later dismayed when the Terra film company included them in their advertising materials.[53] By affirming that making the film more tasteful made it less antisemitic, the court reinforced its definition of the Antisemite as crass, explicit, and Nazi-affiliated—and in so doing, reinforced the fact that former Nazi party members, like Tyrolf, now had the power to define who was an Antisemite.

A photograph from the day of the acquittal highlights the delight and relief of Harlan and his ebullient fans, who carried him out on their shoulders (Figure 2.2). But in a passage cut from the published version of his autobiography, he could not resist turning that moment of triumph into another episode of victimization:

> I knew immediately that this ending would have a dangerous aftermath for me, but I didn't have the strength to fight off the raging crowd and my requests to those who carried me had absolutely no effect. Of course, it was not anti-Semites who carried me out, but people who loved the film *Die goldene Stadt* or *Immensee* and *Opfergang* and who kept calling out the titles of these films again and again. Apparently the press did not want to hear it—although it was unmistakable—the next day many newspapers and radio stations said that "neo-Nazis" had carried me out.[54]

In a telling juxtaposition, he claimed that the people who celebrated his acquittal were not Antisemites but rather fans of his *other* films, indirectly

Figure 2.2. On April 23, 1949, a jubilant crowd outside the courthouse in Hamburg carried Veit Harlan on their shoulders after he was found not guilty of having committed crimes against humanity. *Bundesarchiv, Bild 183-R76220.*

HARLAN'S ANTISEMITES   75

suggesting that people who loved *Jud Süss* could be Antisemites. However, he went on to insist yet again that *Jud Süss* was not antisemitic propaganda, and the people who said it were politically motivated by the fact that Germans had lost the war.[55] This passage, too, was omitted from the published autobiography.

Hamburg's Antisemites

A number of national and international newspapers reported on the incident involving Niehoff and the antisemitic atmosphere in Hamburg. Even the West German chancellor decried the reports, putting Hamburg Mayor Max Brauer on the defensive. On April 19, Brauer held a press conference at the town hall, where he, like Harlan, blamed the disturbances on the twenty-nine-year-old female journalist from Berlin. As the *Hamburger Freie Presse* reported, Brauer denied that there had been any "large antisemitic demonstration," characterizing the disturbances as the *"geschickteste Trickfilm"* (cleverest cartoon) that the communists had ever constructed. He claimed Niehoff had started it by calling Germans "Nazi pigs" and said it was true that a woman had called out *"Judensau,"* but she was a puppet planted by the communists: "Insulted and offended they came from the same camp; they just put on different caps and just changed their treasure chest of quotes. One shouted 'Judensau,' the other 'Nazi pig' and both winked cheerfully, both playing the role of 'agent provocateurs.'"[56] He made much of the fact that just two weeks before she testified in Hamburg, Niehoff had been released from six weeks of imprisonment in East Germany on suspicion of spying for West German newspapers, though the authorities found no evidence of such a plan.[57] He topped things off by saying there was no antisemitism in Germany.

Brauer's denials and deflections relied upon an image of the Antisemite as a communist in disguise, which placed the Antisemite and the Antisemite's victim together, allowing him to conveniently position the city of Hamburg and himself as neither Antisemite nor putative victim, but rather the *real* victim of the Antisemite. Some journalists and communist leaders recognized the communist plot accusations as a blatant attempt to deny antisemitism in Hamburg.[58] One German Jew from Stuttgart wrote to Brauer, calling him out on deflecting the charge of antisemitism by scapegoating communists and pleading with him to do the right thing: "You, as a German civil servant,

76 THE POSTWAR ANTISEMITE

should have the greatest interest in making up for what your predecessors did badly by having an open, objective democratic attitude."[59] Brauer's office replied that the mayor found the form and content of his letter "unsuitable for a factual answer."[60]

The newspaper reports of the mayor's accusation seriously damaged Niehoff's own journalism career. Georg Zivier of *Die Neue Zeitung* in Berlin informed her that the Society for Christian-Jewish Cooperation did not support her because "one should not accuse anyone of antisemitism if the person insulted is himself a provocateur."[61] Niehoff wrote to Brauer's office several times, pleading with him to retract his statement, which he repeatedly refused to do. In the burgeoning years of the Cold War, spinning the incident as a communist plot was too powerful a draw for this socialist mayor, who asserted his staunch opposition to antisemitism at every turn, even traveling to the United States to meet with Jewish organizations to show his support for Jews.[62] Other Social Democrats tried to get Brauer to back off his unjustified attack on Niehoff, but their efforts were in vain.[63] Brauer claimed that newspaper reports had misquoted him and that he had never specifically named Niehoff, despite later witness statements to the contrary (journalist Manfred Jackson, who attended and spoke out at the press conference, confirmed that the newspapers had accurately reported Brauer's speech).[64]

With her health and career suffering, Niehoff initiated a libel lawsuit against the mayor in July 1950, beginning a lengthy battle with the city of Hamburg that she ultimately lost.[65] As late as 1957, Hamburg authorities were still seeking to recover the costs of the lawsuit, but Niehoff was not having it, using the occasion of her refusal to remind them that she had been their victim, not vice versa, and that it was an "'unreasonable harshness' that cost me—the innocent victim of political interests—hardly any less strength and health than had the injustice done to me previously by the two dictatorships."[66]

As these events unfolded in Hamburg over the course of 1950, Erich Lüth was initiating a campaign for widespread boycotts of Harlan and his films. Lüth, who served as Brauer's press director from 1946 to 1953 and again from 1957 to 1961, was intimately acquainted with the proceedings of Harlan's trial and Niehoff's lawsuit. He had announced his opposition to Harlan in a press conference and claimed that *Jud Süss* had made Harlan "antisemitic activist Nr. 1 of the Third Reich" in an article for *Film-Echo*.[67] On September 20, 1950, as Niehoff was enmeshed in her lawsuit against Brauer, Lüth took the opportunity of his opening speech at Hamburg's Week of German Film

HARLAN'S ANTISEMITES 77

to speak out against Harlan's acquittal and to call for protests and boycotts in anticipation of Harlan's return to filmmaking.[68]

Lüth maintained that protesting and boycotting Harlan's films was not only the right of upstanding German citizens but also their duty. Although Harlan and his film production company initiated an injunction against Lüth that curbed his immediate activities, others—including but not limited to students, members of the Jewish community, and DPs—took up the cause, leading protests at cinemas showing Harlan's films from 1951 through 1959. The greatest wave of protests occurred between 1951 and 1954, with nearly seventy events throughout West Germany, Austria, and Switzerland. These events, often reported in the press, drew their own opposition, with passersby yelling insults such as "Jewish mercenaries" at protesters, reflecting the continued support for Harlan and antisemitism in Germany.[69] At a showing of Harlan's film *Hanna Amon* in Freiburg on January 11, 1952, small groups of students handed out flyers and tried to disrupt the showing with calls of protest, loud whistles, and stink bombs; in response, cinemagoers yelled "*Judenlümmel*" (Jewish beasts) and "*Juden raus*" (Jews get out), while the protesters countered with "*Nazis, die nichts hinzugelernt haben*" (Nazis who haven't learned anything). Several demonstrators were injured by the police.[70] Incredibly, Harlan positioned himself as the ultimate target of the antisemitic slurs, which he maintained had been staged by his enemies: "In any case, this weapon has become the best weapon against me in my opponents' hands. Because in this day and age, "Jew lout, Jew servant, Jew mercenary, Jew swine" sounds so terrible in people's ears that these screamers are certainly able to turn a lot of people against me who were previously on my side."[71]

These were not the only West German protests against antisemitic films, but most of the others focused on explicitly antisemitic content, such as the depiction of the Jewish character Fagin in the English film *Oliver Twist*, which premiered in Berlin at the end of February 1949.[72] In contrast, Lüth's call to boycott Harlan's postwar films arose from the conflicts around the trial and focused on the controversial character of Harlan himself—though the notoriety that his accusations brought Lüth when he set himself up as Harlan's nemesis also played a role. The boycotts did not halt the screening of Harlan's postwar films, despite spurring protests and counter-protests.[73]

The larger context of Lüth's pro-Jewish acts in postwar West Germany is relevant here. One problem with the development of philosemitism in Germany after 1945 was that Germans could use it in an abstract and non-binding

78 THE POSTWAR ANTISEMITE

way to avoid any potential social cost of actively rejecting antisemitism.[74] In contrast, Lüth backed up his words with action. Norbert Wollheim and other Jewish leaders also considered Lüth an important ally in their efforts to combat the continued presence of antisemitism.[75] However, his rejection of antisemitism also included a drive for the authority to define an Antisemite that excluded himself and many others. For example, his protests against Harlan did not preclude him from inviting Wolfgang Liebeneiner to become a member of his organization promoting German-Jewish reconciliation.[76]

On January 24, 1954, Benjamin Sagalowitz, head of the press agency of the Union of Jewish Communities in Switzerland, wrote to Lüth about Harlan's attempts to pressure the Jewish community into supporting his public burning of a negative of the film *Jud Süss* that had recently been discovered in Zurich as a form of reconciliation. Harlan envisioned a press conference, at which he would speak. In a quid pro quo reminiscent of his offer to Rabbi Joachim Prinz in 1948, he asked that the Swiss Jewish community in return agree not to boycott his films. Sagalowitz was deeply disturbed by this offer: "I hate this deal with all my heart. It revitalizes Harlan and his pathetic business cycle in its entirety. *Jud Süss* served its purpose and today Harlan seems ready to destroy the negative in order to enable the showing of his new films in Switzerland."[77] Unsurprisingly, the community did not accept Harlan's offer. Sagalowitz's response made it clear that they knew other copies of the film had already been shown in Arab countries, so the destruction of this negative would have no practical use as a deterrent to future screenings. If Harlan wanted to publicly express his regret over *Jud Süss*, Sagalowitz noted, he could do so without the Swiss Jewish community.[78]

Harlan's second-to-last film, *Das dritte Geschlecht* (1957; released in West Germany as *Anders als du und ich* (§175)) also led to protests, but for different reasons. The film was one of the first in postwar German cinema to tackle homosexuality. Sex between adult men was illegal in West Germany until 1969 because of a holdover law from the Nazi era, and, like antisemitism, homosexuality was generally a taboo topic.[79] The film describes the efforts of middle-class parents Werner and Christa Teichmann to correct what they suspect is their son's preference for men after he starts spending most of his time with his friend Manfred, a poet and writer. Its stellar cast included Paula Wessely and Hilde Körber, and the opening credits boast that it was completed under the direction of sexologist Dr. Hans Giese, who had been a Nazi party member.[80]

Perhaps most relevant here, however, is that the film opens with a trial: Christa Teichmann (Wessely) has been accused of procuring sex for her seventeen-year-old son Klaus by asking the family's live-in helper, Gerda (Körber), to seduce him. We soon learn, however, that she has broken the law at the recommendation of a doctor who has advised her that Klaus's problem could be fixed by love. The sympathetic portrayals of Klaus, Christa, and Gerda, in particular, contrast sharply with the harsh courtroom judge, whose icy, harsh demeanor and determination to uphold the law clearly liken him to a Nazi. Meanwhile, almost every homosexual character is depicted negatively, and the archvillain is a homosexual predator, antique dealer Dr. Boris Winkler, played by Friedrich Joloff, whose unsubtle depiction as a sexual deviant is enhanced by shadows, crooked camera angles, abstract art, and atonal music. In this case, the tropes used to depict homosexuality are closely linked to those used to signify Jews. These negative depictions, along with the film's constant association of homosexuality with modern art and music, led to criticism and protests.[81]

The protests allowed Harlan to portray himself once again as the ultimate victim. His excuses for the film's homophobia mirrored his excuses for the antisemitism of *Jud Süss*: the West German censorship board had found his original version too sympathetic to homosexuality. The censors, like Goebbels, made him cut all the scenes that featured positive depictions of gay men and altered the final scene so that the police arrested Winkler rather than allowing him to flee, which, Harlan insisted, would have shown sympathy toward homosexuals: "The same thing that happened when Goebbels changed '*Jud Süss*' is repeated—if not to the horrible extent, then in character. The film was made into a hate film against homosexuals, which it certainly wasn't before. The law required it."[82] Christa, like Harlan, is treated unfairly by the law, and her victimizer is a homosexual coded as Nazi and Jew, a liminal Antisemite who targets decent Germans.

Just as Harlan's postwar letters and articles distinguished between good and bad Jews, here he uses good homosexuals as a counterweight to bad homosexuals, a strategy that allows the film to continue to rely upon homophobic tropes, including ones he considered sympathetic. In another passage cut from his published autobiography, Harlan suggested that Jews were to blame for criticism of the film, claiming it must have come from a "conspiracy of certain press circles" intent upon his ruin.[83] Perhaps he had in mind Karena Niehoff's review of the film—which she described as

80 THE POSTWAR ANTISEMITE

"reminiscent of Nazi methods"—as he once again walked the familiar path of the victim to deny that he was the perpetrator.[84]

The aftermath of Harlan's trial impacted Niehoff and Lüth very differently: while Lüth's opposition to Harlan propelled him into the stratosphere, Niehoff struggled to put her life back together in the wake of the unwelcome negative attention she had received. Interestingly, Lüth did not support her, despite his general commitment to the Jewish people. Niehoff noted that he was uncooperative as she tried to get Brauer to retract his statement, putting her off or having his secretary respond to her requests. Immediately after Brauer's press conference, she got in touch with him to try to arrange a meeting with the mayor about a retraction, but, she reported, "Lüth reacted extremely coldly and did not see anything offensive about Brauer's remarks. 'By the way, they are true.'"[85] After Harlan's acquittal, and as her lawsuit against Brauer continued, Niehoff returned to Berlin, where she slowly rebuilt her reputation and career, becoming known for the biting social commentary of her essays and film reviews, which she apparently had no qualms about deploying against Harlan. But throughout the 1950s and 1960s, she continued to receive anonymous hate mail and suffered from panic attacks and other consequences of the trauma of wartime incarceration and hiding.[86]

In 1951, Harlan sued Lüth over his call for boycotts. Lüth had a great deal of financial and political support, and several parties passed passionate resolutions condemning Harlan's return to filmmaking. While the initial lawsuit resulted in an injunction against Lüth, the German Federal Constitutional Court overturned the injunction in 1958, upholding the right to boycott. The *Lüth-Urteil* (Lüth verdict) became West Germany's benchmark free speech decision, in another instance of a postwar German court asserting its authority to define the Antisemite—underscoring its power by catapulting it to the national level. For Harlan's detractors, Lüth became the symbol for the "Other Germany," as it was often called, which kept Harlan in the position of the Antisemite. In this context, it is notable how little sympathy there was for Karena Niehoff in Hamburg, even among Harlan's opponents, like Lüth. Her role and her legacy remain largely forgotten.

Damage Control: "Der Fall Veit Harlan"

Lüth's boycott campaign ensured that Harlan's 1950 acquittal did little to quell his critics. Harlan continued to vacillate between insisting that *Jud Süss* was not antisemitic because of his interventions and altogether denying responsibility for its antisemitism. His response to a January 1951 open letter from the chairman of the Association of Nazi Persecutees illuminates his ambivalence. Harlan calls himself a "Philosemite," says he was forced to make *Jud Süss*, and bemoans the frequent accusations of antisemitism he still receives. He also once again asserts his authority to define the Antisemite: "I have the right to declare that I feel that antisemitism, in whatever form it may appear, is a cultural disgrace and a presumption against God, who created the Jews and all other people."[87] In other words, the Antisemite threatens everyone, not just Jews—a formulation that allowed the general population to avoid examining how antisemitism continued to harm Jews in the postwar years.

Harlan's friends and sympathizers shared his sense that he was a target, and they actively supported his cause. One locus for this support was a lengthy article series, "Der Fall Veit Harlan: ein Tatsachenbericht" (The case of Veit Harlan: a factual report), which appeared over the course of 1952 in *Film und Mode Revue*. Harlan and his assistant Lu Schlage, the former secretary of SS officer and general major of the police Walter Abraham, put the series together and published it under a pseudonym that maintained Lu Schlage's initials: Leonard F. Schmidt.[88] While the medium was new, the message was familiar: how Schlage worked closely with editor-in-chief Harald Gloth to cast Harlan and his wife, Kristina Söderbaum, as victims of the Nazis, the press, and the Jews, while foregrounding their patriotism, generosity, talent, and Jewish supporters. Meanwhile, they demonized Nazi leaders like Goebbels, described as "fanatically" devoted to Hitler and greatly suspicious of Harlan and Söderbaum, once again setting up the contrast between the real Antisemite and the true Germans who remained steadfastly and bravely committed to Germany as they did their jobs and tried to help Jews.

Gloth, who became the editor of the magazine in 1950, was well suited to continue Harlan's rehabilitation.[89] Having joined the Hitler Youth in 1930 and the Nazi SA in 1932, he became editor of the "Junge Welt" (youth) section of the Nazi party Zentralverlag (main publisher) Franz Eher in 1939.[90] In 1940, the Verlag Die Heimbücherei, which published Nazi authors such as Möller (the third author of the *Jud Süss* screenplay), published his book, *Gesicht unterm Helm. Skizzen eines Infanteristen vom Westfeldzug* (The face under the helmet. Sketches of an infantryman from the Western Expedition), which makes clear his wartime allegiance to Hitler and the Nazis.[91] Gloth was also unhappy with the negative portrayal of Germany in postwar films, which clearly shaped his editorship.[92]

82 THE POSTWAR ANTISEMITE

Under Gloth, *Film und Mode Revue* began to print letters to the editor. One of the first letters complained about media depictions of Harlan's trials. The writer, a man in Würzburg, portrayed Germans as the Antisemite's real victims, noting that while *Jud Süss* may have served as propaganda for the "bestial antisemitic agitation of the Third Reich" and aimed to "stir up hatred against the Jews, which was basically non-existent" [*sic*], its director was under pressure from the Nazis, which meant the accusation that he had committed a crime against humanity was unjustified.[93] At the close of the letter, the writer suggested, "Perhaps you could raise the topic of the Veit Harlan Trial as a topic of discussion." Gloth was happy to take up the invitation.[94]

Over the next year, the majority of letters on the topic were sympathetic to Harlan. One writer found it incomprehensible that the director was still on trial since he had made such good films, had only been fighting for his existence, and *Jud Süss* would have been made regardless of his involvement.[95] Another noted that he had seen the film and thought it was a "great work" that "in no way aroused or strengthened antisemitic sentiment."[96] In 1952, at the height of the boycotts and protests, the magazine issued its own statement of support for Harlan. It splashed "Justice for Veit Harlan!" across its cover and a column inside asked, "Will Veit Harlan be burned?" The column began by condemning the demonstrations and lamenting the injustice of preventing Harlan from continuing his career. It quoted a cinema owner who claimed the court had ruled that Harlan was not an Antisemite and pointed out that "[e]very denazified coal merchant is allowed to freely sell coal again. Why should it be any different for Harlan?" It also cited Julius Bab's statement that "I don't like active or passive burning pyres."[97]

The correspondence between Gloth and Schlage reveals their surreptitious efforts to conceal any connection between Harlan and antisemitism. For instance, Schlage wrote to Gloth that she had composed a letter to the editor about the "horrible" Lüth that included the lines: "We all want peace. All peoples of the earth, including the Jews. With the Germans they will have it. They don't get it from the 'Lüths.' It is not opportunism that makes peace, but the Christian heart."[98] Unfortunately, she went on, she could not publish it, "But . . . something similar should appear under 'Letters to the editors' from other countries—in any case, it would be important to mention somewhere that Lüth, the 'propagandist of mass murder,' is banned by injunction. I leave it in your hands, but as I said, unfortunately I can't act as a writer, and I don't want to pretend either."

HARLAN'S ANTISEMITES 83

In response, Gloth mused over how they might use her letter, since it would need to sound as if it were written by someone "plausible." He also conferred with her about a photograph of Conrad Veit, who played the lead role in the 1934 British film *Jud Süss*, which he wanted to publish. However, they had received letters from readers who said the British *Jud Süss* was not as antisemitic as Harlan's. Aware that this issue had come up at the trial, he asked, "Do you know any details about this material? Who were the witnesses who testified to the strong antisemitic effect of the British *Jud Süss*? Can we name them? That would be very valuable for the caption."[99] Four days later, Schlage replied that Goebbels had insisted on making the German *Jud Süss* in "response" to the earlier English version, to support a new wave of antisemitism in England, but this information should not be printed as it would not be helpful to their cause. She also complained that Harlan was unfairly scapegoated because the press had been full of advertisements for the film, even before he was involved:

> The Jews were already anxious by then, and this fear, dear Herr Gloth, which the Jews already had in the fall of 1939, before Harlan had anything to do with it at all, is what Harlan is accused of today. The film couldn't have made them more anxious, as they hadn't seen it at all. But the big announcement in 1939 with the beginning of the war was what tormented them. And that had to be emphasized somehow and that was probably the only way.[100]

Clearly, the trials had not succeeded in closing the book on Harlan or *Jud Süss*.

Schlage strategized with Gloth about how she could support Harlan without revealing her identity, which would be damaging for them both. On April 1, 1952, she wrote to him with warm greetings from the Harlans, who were "deeply moved" by his efforts on their behalf. On April 4, however, she begged Gloth to state publicly that Harlan was not involved with the article series, as he was receiving letters that "completely unfairly named [him] as the author of the article." Harlan's response to one of those letters was typical: "I have as little to do with this report as I do with the countless other reports that are less favorable to me."[101] Without irony, Gloth asked Harlan to ensure that the reports on the trial that Lu Schlage sent him for the article series remained neutral, for the sake of Gloth's and the magazine's reputation.[102]

84   THE POSTWAR ANTISEMITE

The cover of the issue that contained the first article in the series featured Söderbaum resting her head on Harlan's shoulder and the words "Ehe im Sturm" (marriage in turmoil), setting the tone for what followed by emphasizing the couple's vulnerability—to the Nazis, public criticism, and Jews (represented by the "New York cinemas" who profited from Harlan's films after the war while he and his family lived in a one-room apartment).[103] The text and image evoke the film poster for *Ehe im Schatten* (Marriage in the shadows), director Kurt Maetzig's 1947 film based on the life of popular actor Joachim Gottschalk, a parallel that once again allowed Harlan to co-opt the suffering of others.[104] When Goebbels commanded Gottschalk to divorce his Jewish wife, Meta Wolff, in 1941, Gottschalk and Wolff instead killed themselves and their eight-year-old son Michael with poison gas. The article describes how Harlan tried to help Gottschalk and other actors with Jewish wives by offering them roles in his films. It suggests that Goebbels refused to help Harlan aid Gottschalk because Harlan had also been married to a Jewish woman. However, the article does not name Dora Gerson, nor does it mention the request for help she sent to Harlan or her and her family's murder in Auschwitz, erasing the actual Jewish woman even as it strategically uses the idea of her.

Ehe im Schatten figured in the article series not only as a parallel, but as the basis for an event it described as "shattering" for the Harlans. As the second installment of the series recounts, friends who knew about Harlan's efforts to help Gottschalk convinced the couple to attend the film's premiere in Hamburg's Waterloo Kino in April 1948, since it was also a memorial event for Gottschalk and Harlan had been one of his "noblest friends." However, his presence at the theater caused "significant unrest" among some in the audience, and the director of the theater forced them to leave. In recounting the event, the article drew the grotesque parallel between the martyred actor couple of Gottschalk and his wife and Harlan and Söderbaum.[105]

The series also deployed one of Harlan's favorite themes: his support for Jews during the years he worked for the Nazis, which supposedly canceled out the negative impact of his films. For example, it recounted how when the Jewish wife of Fritz Kühne, who was in charge of lighting for both *Jud Süss* and Harlan's 1945 film *Kolberg*, received a deportation order, Harlan successfully got the order rescinded. Tragically, Kühne and his wife committed suicide before Harlan and Söderbaum arrived at their home with the good news, but the deceased couple nevertheless left a note of gratitude in their intertwined hands: "Dear Professor and consort! Unfortunately all your great kindness and love was in vain. We have no strength to bear our fate. Too often our hearts were torn apart for an undeserved lot. Take our deepest thanks, dear both. God reward you both for what you have done for us. Your Loni and Fritz Kuehne with sincere gratitude." The article takes care to emphasize the broader implications of this sad anecdote: "This is what Veit Harlan looked like in the judgment of people who knew him at that time and experienced his love and helpfulness."[106] The anecdote extends the parallel between Harlan and Söderbaum and the Gottschalks to this third couple, who were similarly persecuted and explicitly expressed their gratitude from beyond the grave.

Harlan and Söderbaum's patriotism is another ongoing theme of the series, which gingerly decouples German patriotism from Antisemitism by both casting the Antisemite as unpatriotic and coding him as Jewish. The first article describes the moment in 1944 when Harlan and Söderbaum, having just received a warm welcome from the audience at a Hamburg theater, were suddenly attacked by Goebbels, who accused them of wanting to desert Germany, in what became an ongoing smear campaign. As elsewhere, the series carefully protects Harlan and Söderbaum's patriotism from associations with Nazis and Antisemites by insisting that neither Harlan nor his wife would have "turned their backs on Germany."[107] The series frequently points out that though the Harlans were targeted, they never abandoned their country, unlike those who left—though it never explicitly mentions that those who left were largely Jews, people married to Jews, or others targeted by the Nazis.

These implications are visually reinforced with photographs that portray Harlan and Söderbaum with their children as the perfect Aryan family, as well as a picture of Harlan's bombed-out house.[108] The article series marked the continuation of Harlan's victim narrative about the suffering that non-Jews who were neither committed Nazis nor Antisemites endured between 1933 and 1945, even when they outwardly appeared to have prospered. The Harlans thus became the new blond, patriotic, postwar German family, just like Hitler's perfect family, except that they too had suffered under the Nazis and survived, so they were now not only explicitly anti-Nazi but also themselves victimized.

Much of Harlan's moral repositioning relied on his ability to present himself as a victim. Rather than articulating the political stakes of those opposed to him, he instead focused on what he portrayed as their vicious and unfair attacks. He also complained about being victimized by the media, insisting

86 THE POSTWAR ANTISEMITE

that all the radio programs were against him and gave him no opportunity to publicly defend himself. But the retelling of the events at his trials in Hamburg formed a significant portion of the article series, which concluded, "Both jury trials against him have shown that Harlan was a good German and patriot but never a Nazi."[109] The articles further emphasized this point by citing various pronouncements Harlan made to newspapers at the time, for instance:

> It is not anti-Semitism that is on trial here, which would really belong to a historic world court, but only myself, for whom to be identified with anti-Semitism is a tragic mistake. The essential content of my life not only proves that I am not an anti-Semite, it also proves that I believe that anti-Semitism, especially where it appears in an aggressive and cruel form, is without culture, inhuman and un-Christian.[110]

When Harlan claims that only an abstract "historic world court" would have the authority to define the Antisemite, he suggests that the Antisemite's primary danger was to everyone, Jews and non-Jews alike, which meant that the Antisemite was a danger to him, and he, a true German patriot, was not an Antisemite.

One more way in which the article series illuminated how Harlan positioned himself, and all Germans, as victims of antisemitism was by rehearsing the good Jew/bad Jew narratives he liked to deploy, beginning in his letters to Bab. This narrative first appears in the series in an implicit comparison between Karena Niehoff and Ferdinand Marian, the actor who played Jud Süss, that identified them both in terms of the Nazi classification *Halbjuden*. Both historically and on screen, Jud Süss was the son of a Christian aristocrat and a Jewish mother and thus a *Halbjude*. Although Marian was not Jewish, his wife, actor Maria Byk, had a "half-Jewish" child from her first marriage to a Jew. The article suggests that Süss Oppenheimer, the *Halbjude* of Harlan's film, was a good, sympathetic Jew, while Niehoff, the *Halbjude* of his trial, was a bad Jew. The terms of this comparison were familiar tropes in the postwar era, presenting the good Jew as a figure with whom non-Jews could identify as they disassociated themselves from the Antisemite, and the morally compromised bad Jew as the Jew from whom they can continue to separate themselves. This schematization replaces questions of complicity with assertions of morality, a crucial move in Harlan's efforts to redeem himself.

Here, too, the article series used visual cues to buttress its narrative. A description of Niehoff's testimony, which was framed as impudent, unclear, contradictory, and purposefully damaging, was illustrated with two photographs of Ferdinand Marian in character, one as Jud Süss, the other as Don Pedro de Avila, a rich Puerto Rican landowner in the film *La Habanera* (1937), directed by Douglas Sirk (Figure 2.3). Don Pedro is pictured with Zarah Leander, a German actor and darling of Nazi cinema, who played Astrée, a young woman from Sweden unhappily married to Don Pedro. The film buffs who read *Film und Mode Revue* would have been expected to draw the parallel between German actor Leander, who played a Swedish woman in *La Habanera*, and Swedish actor Söderbaum, who played a German woman in *Jud Süss*. The visual juxtaposition between the protagonists of *Jud Süss* and *La Habanera* shows how Sirk's film, also made under Goebbels, played up Marian's dark looks to emphasize his foreignness. The caption explores the implications of this choice, specifically referencing how Marion's appearance in Sirk's film reflected a dark, unsympathetic "Jewish type" that Harlan's film avoided.[111]

This framing highlights Harlan's intimate knowledge of the subtle codes and messages with which German film engaged the terms of Jewish difference. He used these codes to make Jud Süss appear as non-Jewish as he could, giving him a light wig and desexualizing him by depicting him alone. The caption confirms these choices: "Harlan saw Jud Süss as an elegant, cultured cosmopolitan who also stood up for his Jewish brethren. This is clearly supported by Jud Süss's mask and demeanor, which Marian (our picture) gave the title hero according to Harlan's instructions.[112] Once again, Harlan flexes the muscle of his authority to determine the Antisemite. Under the Nazis, characters coded as wealthy cosmopolitans represented typical antisemitic stereotypes about Jews; to suggest that portraying Süss as an "elegant, cultured, cosmopolitan" is not a standard antisemitic portrait borders on ludicrous. The same can be said about the claim that he "is not drawn as a criminal," for in the film Süss rapes a non-Jewish woman.[113] As we have seen, Harlan relied on discussions of casting decisions to deflect attention from the content, ideology, and uses of his films and to elevate his work as more artistic. In this case, his distinction between his good Jew and Sirk's bad Jew deflects attention from the real issue of antisemitism by claiming authority to define the Antisemite, although in this case his own film's content conveniently undermined his case.

Figure 2.3. The *Film und Mode Revue* article series "Der Fall Veit Harlan" maintains that the depiction of Ferdinand Marian in Harlan's film *Jud Süss* (1942) (top) is less antisemitic than his appearance as the protagonist of Douglas Sirk's film *La Habanera* (1937) (bottom). *Courtesy of Deutsche Kinemathek.*

One key claim of the article series is that Harlan intended the relationship between Süss and Dorothea to be a love story; this notion helps us think about how Harlan derived and bolstered his sense of authority to define the Antisemite through his use of Jewish and non-Jewish women, both female characters and real-life female partners. The series claims that Harlan directed scenes of "genuine affection" between Süss and Dorothea which Goebbels later cut: "With Harlan, Joseph Süss Oppenheimer honorably asked Dorothea's father for her hand. He is dismissed by the old Sturm only because he is a Jew. The insult to Süss Oppenheimer by the family of the beloved woman then leads to the rape scene, which becomes a prerequisite for the later conviction of the perpetrator."[114] This framing justified the rape as reasonable in the face of her family's rejection of Süss (which of course echoes Harlan's rejection by Dora Gerson's family).

There was much discussion of these excised love scenes and their intended impact at the trial. But these arguments obfuscate the film's use of another pervasive antisemitic trope: corrupt, diabolical Jewish sexuality, in particular the Jewish man who defiles innocent German women.[115] Even if, as the article claims, the "attentive viewer" can "still perceive" the love story, they can also see the rapist, as they are set up to distinguish between the good Jew, the bad Jew, and the Antisemite. The position of the German spectator thus becomes akin to Harlan's position, as the one who makes these determinations, as the article bolsters the authority of both.

One final example from the series helps define the moral position Harlan created by asserting his authority to define the Antisemite. Under the heading "A Jew Congratulates Harlan," it lauds an unnamed Jewish man who had accused Harlan of crimes against humanity, but later recanted his accusation and visited him to congratulate him on his first acquittal. The article praised the man for having "much more respect" for Harlan's acquittal than others. It went on to make this good Jew the voice of reconciliation:

> I didn't know, he said, what the German people had to go through when we were in the concentration camps. It was only through this process that I became aware of the whole tragic fate that the German people went through under Hitler. I did not know, Mr. Harlan, all that you did for my Jewish comrades during the Nazi regime and how many of them owe you their life today. If every German had acted that way, such a misfortune would not have come over us Jews. Knowing this, I would never have joined the lawsuit.[116]

Dismissing the process of national reckoning and accountability that the trial was intended to establish, this passage reconfigures the courtroom as a space to raise Jewish consciousness about the harm experienced by the

90   THE POSTWAR ANTISEMITE

German people under Hitler. Not only was Harlan able to publicly exonerate himself, but he used a Jewish accuser to transform his own consciousness from bad Jew to good Jew. Ultimately, the trials granted Harlan the power to define the Antisemite, while his effort to re-narrativize that experience gave him the authority to oversee this moral transformation—even, or perhaps especially, for a Jew.

From *"Judensau"* to *"Saujud"*

Eleven years after delivering her contentious testimony in Hamburg, Karena Niehoff had another opportunity to reflect on antisemitic catcalls and imagery—this time, in her review of the film *Schwarzer Kies* (1961), directed by Helmut Käutner. The films of Käutner take up the terms set by Harlan's trials to claim a similar authority around defining the Antisemite. Käutner, whom one critic called the "second Ernst Lubitsch," was one of many German directors who were active during the Nazi era but whose careers were able to continue without interruption after 1945 because they had not been involved in creating propaganda films.[117] Though Käutner began his career in comedic and satirical cabaret in Berlin, he largely avoided political topics in the films he made under the Nazis (though critics have pointed out that he managed to insert some quasi-resistant tropes in films otherwise designed to entertain). This background may have helped him pass under the radar and avoid enraging the Nazis.[118]

West German theater and film critic Friedrich Luft described Käutner's activities between 1933 and 1945 with admiration: "He stayed in the film business, made the cinema to the end, but he never delivered a film that was even close to being 'brownish.' He had character. When the war was over, he was one of the very few filmmakers who could start again immediately. His vest was clean."[119] Though Luft does not mention it, Käutner was questioned about the one propaganda film he did make: *Auf Wiedersehen, Franziska* (1941; Goodbye, Franziska), a story about a woman who finds meaning when her husband, a foreign correspondent, is called to cover the war. Unlike Harlan, Käutner was able to convince the occupation authorities that the Nazis had forced him to change his film's ending.[120] In a 1973 television interview, actor Hans Söhnker asked Käutner whether he felt Harlan had been pressured into making *Jud Süss*. Käutner replied:

No. I know about Harlan, from long debates after the war. I hardly knew him before, I saw him briefly once or twice, and after the war, I thought it was my duty and also my right to talk to Harlan about why he did that and why a man who was such a great artist could sink to such depths and how that could be reconciled. And ... then it became completely clear to me that Harlan, for the sake of his career, wanted to be the most important man, the greatest man in Europe in the film sector, and so he acted ruthlessly, using any means necessary.[121]

Käutner thus seemed an unlikely candidate to be enveloped in a scandal over antisemitism. Seeming to add to the unlikelihood is the fact that Käutner was one of the filmmakers who chose to critically address the Nazi era in his early postwar films. In fact, he co-wrote and directed *In jenen Tagen* (In those days, 1947), the first of the West German *Trümmerfilme* (rubble films) that dealt with everyday German life under fascist rule.

The film comprises seven scenes that tell the stories of the successive owners of a car between 1933 and 1945, all narrated from the point of view of the car, a most objective witness, voiced by Käutner himself. Given the difficulty of filming in a studio in 1947 (unlike DEFA [Deutsche Film-Aktiengesellschaft] in the Soviet-occupied zone), the car motif cleverly allowed scenes to be filmed outside on the streets. Ida Ehre starred, and her role seemed as if it had been written with her in mind. Unlike the parts Ehre had played on stage, Sally Bienert, the only Jewish character in the film, was to some extent autobiographical: a Jewish victim of Nazi persecution married to a non-Jew, Wilhelm. She appears in the third scene, which takes place on and around the so-called *Reichskristallnacht*. The scene opens with the car parked in front of the Bienerts' frame store as Wilhelm and Sally pack it to the gills for a ride to their house in the countryside. In a scene typical of married couples in films, Sally bickers with her husband, but with specific reference to the times: while she complains that he is not dressed warmly enough, she also points out that he has not drawn white letters on their shop sign to show it is owned by Jews, as they have been ordered. The scene sets up Wilhelm, the non-Jewish husband whose Jewish wife is pushing him to carry out a Nazi directive, as the sympathetic victimized martyr in the relationship.

Wilhelm claims to be reluctant to carry out the order because everyone already knows that Sally is the actual owner of the store. This characteristically modest self-effacement serves to highlight more stereotypes about his Jewish wife: clad in fur, she henpecks her husband and owns both the store and, we

92   THE POSTWAR ANTISEMITE

soon learn, the car. In the next bit of dialogue, Sally complains that soon "we" won't be able to drive, meaning *she* won't be able, and exclaims, "And the car actually belongs to me!" These interactions highlight Sally's concerns with property, propriety, and money, engaging stereotypes of superficial, materialistic Jewish women that proliferated before the Nazi era, though audiences of the time would already have recognized Ehre as a Jew from her prominent nose and "typical" Jewish look. As a solution to their problems, Sally suggests to Wilhelm that they divorce, an act of benevolence one-upped by Wilhelm's self-sacrificing refusal to indulge it. Although Sally is the Jew targeted by the Nazis, Wilhelm is again received more sympathetically, a stance reinforced by a violent act of solidarity. Upon his return to the store that evening, he sees Nazi thugs looting other stores but sparing theirs because he failed to heed Sally when she told him to comply with the Nazi directive to mark it as Jewish. Guilty that the store has been spared, unlike the nearby Jewish store whose windows have been smashed, he grabs a cobblestone and throws it through their own storefront window.

Shattering his own store window after seeing the destruction of his neighbor's store suggests that he recognizes and feels guilty about his complicity in the persecution of Jews, which the intact window represented. At the same time, the shattered window transforms him into a Jewish victim, along with his wife. This is the last we see of Wilhelm and Sally; the following morning, we learn via a crowd gathered outside their home that the couple has committed suicide. Given his earlier willingness to throw the cobblestone, it is not a leap to imagine that Wilhelm instigates this act of martyrdom. As in *Ehe im Schatten*, the martyred German spouse was a popular motif of postwar films. Ehre's portrayal of Sally as the less sympathetic half of this couple was effective: as one contemporaneous reviewer noted, "The husband of that Jewish woman is memorable."[122] It is Wilhelm, not Sally, who captures our imagination and sympathy.[123]

Unlike Wolfgang Staudte's *Die Mörder sind unter uns* (Murderers among us, 1946), the very first rubble film produced by DEFA, Käutner's film has no central villain. Though it refers to Nazis, it keeps them anonymous and off screen, focusing instead on everyday, sympathetic Germans who make difficult, humane choices.[124] Like most rubble films, *In jenen Tagen* aimed to create a model of victimhood that allowed Germans to conflate their own suffering during and after the war with that of the Nazis' primary victims. It also created another foundational form of deflecting German complicity in the war by highlighting innocent German characters and avoiding the depiction of Nazis, even though it is set during the years of the Nazi regime.[125] In so doing, it evokes an Antisemite who remains unnamed and off screen and whose victims include both the Jew and her non-Jewish husband.[126]

In jenen Tagen provides valuable context for the evolution of Käutner's postwar relationship with Harlan and the controversy that would erupt years later over his film *Schwarzer Kies* and its portrayal of the Antisemite. Soon after the war ended, Käutner established the Interessengemeinschaft der Filmhersteller (Interest Group for Film Producers), for which he created a directory of film industry professionals in Hamburg who might help to rebuild the shattered film industry.[127] The list of seven directors included Veit Harlan and Wolfgang Liebeneiner, the two most powerful directors under the Nazis.[128] At that early postwar date, Käutner and Harlan were on friendly terms.[129] But for reasons that remain unclear, Käutner soon distanced himself from Harlan. When the Hamburg denazification committee asked him for a reference, Käutner claimed that Harlan had not been an "ideological Nazi" but rather a "ruthless opportunist" who grabbed every advantage in service of his career, though he also admitted that Harlan had passionately fought to save some of his endangered colleagues.[130]

In 1961, Käutner returned to the war's impact on Germany in *Schwarzer Kies*.[131] Though some films still focused on the experience of postwar Germany, their emphasis had shifted from the Nazis to how Germans coped with the Occupation Forces who were still a constant presence amidst the Cold War. Käutner's late rubble film fits this agenda. It takes place on an American military base in the early 1960s, where the German protagonist, Robert, sells gravel on the black market and frequents a thriving seedy bar that moonlights as a brothel. The title sequence features the death of a dog inadvertently buried in an enormous pile of black gravel, signaling the film's dark nature. Käutner clearly sought to portray the gritty world of postwar Germany, where underhanded dealings—and antisemitism—persisted, despite Hitler's demise and the presence of Allied military forces.

But the controversy around the film arose not from its darkness, but from its depiction of Jews and Antisemites, in particular one brief scene in which a former Nazi calls the bar owner a *Saujud* (Jewish pig) in a fit of rage. The head of the Central Council of Jews in Germany was so upset by the scene that he threatened to sue Käutner and the film company UFA (Universum-Film Aktiengesellschaft) if it was not removed. Though Käutner claimed there had been a misunderstanding and most people agreed that any offense

94 THE POSTWAR ANTISEMITE

was unintentional, he cut the offending scene out of deference to the Central Council.

Few believed Käutner wanted the film to promote antisemitism. But in defensively deflecting the charge, Käutner seemed to miss the point that, despite his best efforts, he had done exactly that. In an attempt at mitigation, he pointed to the fact that the actual bar in the film was owned by a Jew named Friedmann, with whom he had had several conversations about using the premises and had even offered Friedmann the chance to play the role of the barkeeper in the film.[132] Moreover, the actor who played the barkeeper, Max Buchsbaum, was also a Jew. As Käutner explained: "Incidentally, a Jewish innkeeper made his restaurant available for the outdoor shots and a Jewish actor played the role."[133] Although well-meaning, Käutner's logic seems to be that antisemitic stereotypes linking Jews to prostitution and vice were rendered harmless if one could find an actual Jew to fit its description.

Käutner's earlier casting decisions about Ida Ehre show that *Schwarzer Kies* was not the first time his well-meaning attempts to avoid antisemitic effects ended up negatively affecting Jews. When Ehre asked to play the role of Duchess Leuenstein in *Königskinder* (Royal children, 1950), his film about the royal family, Käutner replied that he could not allow her to play in the role of an aristocratic emigrant who returns as the heroine's enemy and has no understanding for postwar Germany: "It's just a comedy, but your occupying the role could be interpreted for both of us (including you) as antisemitism. You know from your own experience that we have to be very careful. I'll be casting a massive blonde Goy to avert any danger in this regard."[134] His own struggle with defining the Antisemite suggests that in the postwar era, avoiding negative stereotypes about Jews in films did little to dismantle them and in fact could continue to place Jewish actors like Ehre at a disadvantage.

To be sure, context matters, and in the case of *Schwarzer Kies*, Käutner did not intend the scenes in question to indicate support for the former Nazi character's views. On the other hand, an earlier version of the screenplay and the correspondence surrounding it underscore that, regardless of how Käutner described it in his interview, it was not merely by chance that the film featured a bar owned by a Jew. The original screenplay describes the owner of the bar, Loeb, as "an unmistakable Eastern Jew of proletarian type and indefinable age" who is first introduced to the audience leaning against the bar and cleaning his fingernails; another version refers to him to as a "Polish Jew."[135] Did Käutner and his team hunt around until they found a Jewish bar owner to lend this description credibility?

Officials at UFA expressed awareness of concerns about the dialogue in these and other scenes even before the film was shown. In a letter dated November 1, 1960, producer Paul Verhoeven wrote to Käutner about a number of scenes that were raising questions. Although he gives no details about the source of the concerns, he includes his defense of each point. About the scene in which the character Krahne states, "I'm not even a Jew," Verhoeven noted:

> Krahne speaks like one of those who have not yet died out in Germany. There are actually a number of people who express their antisemitism by saying that you have to be a Jew to do business in Germany. With this sentence by Krahne, a flash of light falls on the truth. I have no reason, after the author suggests this sentence, to make him refrain from this sentence.

Like Käutner, Verhoeven had made films for entertainment under the Nazis, but not outright propaganda films. Still, both of them knew they needed to proceed with caution when criticizing antisemitism. Here, Verhoeven limits Krahne's sentence to the Antisemite, whose portrayal he finds unproblematic. Then he turns to the next issue:

> When Roessler shouts 'Saujud' into the sudden silence, the reaction in the audience will undoubtedly be very strong. . . . I don't think the dramaturgical intent can be misunderstood. . . . I see no reason to induce the author to withdraw from the non-binding nature of this time-critical material. I am also sure that director Käutner is very clear about directing the actors in the mentioned settings.[136]

Verhoeven clearly believed that Käutner had represented the Antisemite accurately and critically, without tainting other characters, the film as a whole, or himself. During the Nazi era, Käutner possessed neither the power nor the status that Harlan had enjoyed. After the war, he attempted to depict and critique the persistence of antisemitism in his films. But even these well-intentioned attempts reinforced rather than destabilized the constructed categories of Jewish difference and revealed similarities between his and Harlan's struggles to define the Antisemite.

By 1961, when *Schwarzer Kies* appeared in theaters, Niehoff had established her reputation as an insightful cultural critic known for her biting critiques and sharp, savvy essays. In her review of *Schwarzer Kies*, she devoted only a short paragraph at the end to the antisemitism controversy,

96 THE POSTWAR ANTISEMITE

which speaks to how the experience of the trial, in which she herself was targeted as a *Judensau* only five years after the Holocaust, limited the realm of what it was possible for her to say. She conceded that the Jewish community had overreacted by misreading the character's words as the director's beliefs. But she also suggested that Käutner should have been more sensitive to the position of Jews in postwar Germany:

> A word about this controversy: Käutner, in particular, should have been immune to accusations of anti-Semitism. To associate the anti-Semitic remarks from the mouth of a—thin, but negatively conceived—character with Käutner himself seems to be ill-conceived hypersensitivity. But even so: such a misunderstanding has arisen among a leading group of German Jews, and perhaps not by accident. It is indeed difficult to bear, and not only for Jews, to find the word "Saujude" pounded out in a current German film—even the tone of indignation behind it does not remove the horror of proximity and the proximity to terror. And another thing that looks like a contradiction but is not: there is a philosemitism or a certain obtrusiveness in the way of expressing it that can easily and dangerously change dialecti-cally to its opposite: to emphasize that one "Is really not an anti-Semite at all" is, to be more precise, a sublime, unconscious reaction to something that is, at least, "different." Whoever says "the Jews," even if they do so with great affection, already distinguishes Jews from themselves. The Jews here with us are more in need of and more worthy of protection than they are in other countries, although not because of them, but because of us, because of the German past. But they are not a nature reserve in which their admirers and their enemies are allowed to sneak around with sharp field glasses for study purposes (or not allowed, depending on the city). Sensitivity is required not only to anti-Semitism but also to being foreign or alien. Individuals' written words and conversations can differentiate such questions—but films (probably this one too) usually brush them away so clumsily and good-naturedly. Could one imagine a German film, however self-critical, in which a German classified a German, be it the worst crim-inal or someone he personally hated, as a "German pig?" No, he would not do that, he would always be content with anger without a national sign. So there you go.[137]

Niehoff's take on postwar antisemitism did not deny that Jews should be distinguished in some ways from other Germans, but she implied that this distinction should be hers—and other Jews'—to make, as indeed she did, using the phrase "the Jews" right after she says that "Whoever says 'the Jews' ... already distinguishes Jews from themselves." Niehoff also recognized that what mattered most was the continued exclusion of Jews. Jews, she argues, may be in some ways a separate group, but that group should not be excluded from the idea of a collective Germany. By noting that a German would never denigrate another German with the epithet "German pig," she pinpoints exactly how the film's definition of the Antisemite, despite its critical intentions, is too narrow. The audience learns from the film that a good German would not call a Jew "*Saujude*," but the existence of this term for Jews, like the framework of Jewish difference, goes unquestioned.

Creating the figure of the Antisemite as mutually exclusive to the ideal German manifests precisely the kind of German nationalism that Harlan fought to maintain throughout his trials, with his definition of the Antisemite. Other German Jews also believed that maintaining this fantasy—that the "true German" was not an Antisemite—would enable their inclusion on its terms. While the Nazis aimed to definitively exclude Jews from the fabric of the German nation through extermination, postwar efforts to render antisemitism taboo did not revise the terms of Jewish inclusion, but rather added the Antisemite as another figure for exclusion. Karena Niehoff recognized the problematic nature of this barely revised differentiation, but there was little she alone could do about it.[138] Instead of rethinking German nationalism to include Jews, German culture, like Harlan, focused on externalizing Antisemitism, which did nothing to destabilize the terms of Jewish difference.

PART II
EAST GERMANY
The Anti-Fascist and the Antisemite

3

Alice Haas Disappears from *Affaire Blum*

Alice Haas (Figure 3.1) had been married and living in Germany for just over two years when the Magdeburg police arrested her husband for murder on June 18, 1926. Born Alice Kussi in 1900, she was raised in a prominent Jewish family in Prague, where on March 12, 1924, she wed Rudolf Haas, a businessman nine years her senior from a well-known Jewish family in Magdeburg.[1] Alice and Rudolf's fathers were successful businessmen: Julius Kussi, born in Kralovice in 1863, built a wholesale business specializing in drugs, spices, chemicals, and cosmetics, and Louis Haas, born in Bavaria in 1862, established Louis Haas AG, which became one of the largest machine building and repair companies in Sachsen-Anhalt. As expected, their sons followed them into the family businesses. While Alice's younger brother Bedrich remained in Prague to join their father's company, Alice accompanied Rudolf back to Magdeburg, where he ran Louis Haas AG.[2]

In Magdeburg, the newlyweds moved into an apartment on the tony Staatsbürgerplatz, not far from Rudolf's parents, Louis and Ottilie Haas, who lived in a villa on a row of elegant homes on the Markgrafenstraße overlooking the Elbe. As prominent members of the Jewish community, the Haases were a well-regarded, sociable couple who belonged to the liberal synagogue and donated generously to the local Jewish retirement home. On fine days, Alice and Rudolf strolled around the shops on Hasselbachplatz or in the cloister gardens. On warm days, Rudolf drove them around in his Lancia convertible. When Rudolf was at work, Alice stayed busy raising their twin sons, Hans and Alfred, who were born on May 25, 1925.[3]

It is hard to imagine how distraught Alice must have been that afternoon in June when the police arrested Rudolf for the murder of Hellmuth Helling, a bookkeeper who had been dismissed from Louis Haas AG more than a year earlier. Helling had disappeared without a trace on June 10, 1925, after he missed an appointment at the local tax inspector's office, where he had supposedly planned to reveal details about tax evasion at the firm. This missed appointment became the tenuous basis for the case against Haas constructed by police detective Wilhelm Tenholt, a right-wing nationalist and early

The Postwar Antisemite. Lisa Silverman, Oxford University Press. © Oxford University Press 2025.
DOI: 10.1093/9780197697757.003.0004

Figure 3.1. Alice Haas, née Kussi (later Hanselová), the Czech Jewish wife of Rudolf Haas, is replaced with a non-Jewish German woman in every German adaptation of the story of her husband's ordeal. *National Archives of the Czech Republic, Police Headquarters Prague II—General Register, 1941–1950, sig. H 755/6 box 2874, Alice Hanselová born 25.1.1900.*

member of the Nazi party, and the equally right-wing investigating judge, Johannes Kölling, who were more than ready to link Helling's disappearance to the Jewish industrialist. Their case hinged on Richard Schröder, a failed blacksmith's apprentice and ex-felon who had been caught cashing Helling's checks and pawning his watches. Instead of treating Schröder with suspicion as he concocted increasingly improbable stories about his involvement in the crime, they suggested to him that Haas might have been involved. The right-wing jurists then egged him on as he wove an implausible narrative implicating the wealthy Jew he had never met.[4] Schröder first claimed to have obtained the watches and checks from a mysterious man named Adolf. Later, he insisted that Haas and his chauffeur had kidnapped Helling and planned to get rid of him in Czechoslovakia.[5] Eventually they got Schröder to admit that he had shot Helling, stolen his possessions, and buried the body in the cellar below his apartment at Haas's direction. Haas remained in jail for seven weeks solely on the basis of Schröder's testimony.

This high-profile murder case became a lightning rod that exacerbated tensions over antisemitism in provincial and national politics and increased pressure on the German justice system. The Haas family first attempted to keep the story out of the newspapers, fearing the negative press would hurt the firm. When it became apparent that Tenholt and Kölling were clinging to their antisemitic conspiracy theory, Rudolf's brother-in-law Paul Crohn used his contacts in the government and press to spin the local crime into a national affair. Reports in local and national newspapers highlighted the political conflict between the right-wing nationalists sympathetic to Schröder and the Social Democratic left, which supported Haas. Thanks to the intervention of Crohn's friend Otto Hörsing, a Social Democratic politician and representative of the Prussian province of Sachsen, the authorities finally released Haas on August 10, 1926, and put Schröder on trial a month later. Schröder was found guilty and was sentenced to death on September 17, though his sentence was later commuted to life imprisonment.

In the wake of Crohn's public relations interventions, the case became known as the *Magdeburger Justizskandal* (Magdeburg justice scandal) and served as a galvanizing symbol for national efforts to reduce the influence of reactionary judges, who many believed were abusing their power. The antisemitism that was both the foundation of Tenholt and Kölling's case and a leitmotif for Schröder's supporters provided a useful rallying cry for this movement. Journalist Carl von Ossietzky, for example, sarcastically labeled the case a "small Germanic ritual murder." From France, left-wing

104 THE POSTWAR ANTISEMITE

Jewish playwright Ernst Toller wrote to a friend in Germany, "Are people participating in the Magdeburg justice carousel? Is it finally opening their eyes to the plague of justice that contaminates Germany?"[6] But for Jews in Germany, the case was also personal: it shook their collective trust in the integrity of German justice and its ability to protect them from antisemitism.[7] The typically reserved *Israelitisches Familienblatt*, for example, referred to it as the "Magdeburg Dreyfus Affair."[8] These two labels, the *Magdeburger Justizskandal* and the Magdeburg Dreyfus Affair, point to how the case's antisemitism was used in two distinct ways: to highlight the effects of individual and systemic prejudice against Jews and to criticize the Weimar justice system. As such, it revealed the power of antisemitic narratives to boost broader political concerns.

On the day of Haas's release, several newspapers featured smiling photographs of Rudolf and Alice, who were clearly relieved at his vindication. But these cheerful images masked the heavy toll the distressing incident took on the Haas family. According to Alice, both the death of her father, Julius Kussi, on December 6, 1926, at age sixty-three, and Rudolf's suicide in 1933, at age forty-two, were direct consequences of the stress they had suffered.[9] The case also left its mark on a young teacher, Robert A. Stemmle, who was born and raised in Magdeburg, attended Schröder's trial, and reported on the divisive scandal for the *Magdeburger Volksstimme*.[10] It made such an impression on him that he wrote a radio play about it with Willi Fehse, a fellow writer and teacher. Titled *Justizwillkür ges. gesch* (Arbitrary justice protected by law), it first aired on Hamburg's Nordische Rundfunk in 1930. However, it made no explicit mention of Jews or antisemitism, hinging instead on the injustice of a judge falsely accusing an innocent industrialist of murder.[11]

But seventeen years later, in a postwar milieu where filmmakers felt compelled to cement their anti-Nazi stances, Stemmle transformed his brief play about the abuse of power in German courts into the screenplay for a feature film about antisemitism. By then a well-known screenwriter and director, he suggested that the newly configured DEFA (Deutsche-Film Aktiengesellschaft), the first film production company established in the Soviet zone, make a film about the case. A story about an unfairly accused Jew was the perfect signal for DEFA's definitive break with Nazi filmmaking, and director Erich Engel's *Affaire Blum*, which premiered in 1948 to international acclaim, became a bright spot in Germany's postwar cinematic landscape.[12] The film plays an especially important role in this book's argument about the postwar Antisemite, for by downplaying some details of this historic antisemitic scandal and embellishing others, the filmmakers created an Antisemite that addressed the social and political needs of the newly developing East German state. But it suggests that creating a popular film opposing antisemitism in these early postwar years was anything but straightforward. The clashing sensibilities of non-Jewish German DEFA filmmakers and their (mainly) Jewish Soviet censors about the portrayal of the film's Antisemite complicated a fundamental obstacle: How can the film champion a wealthy Jewish industrialist and the evils of capitalism at the same time? What emerges is a film opposing antisemitism that, paradoxically, at times deploys antisemitic codes or downplays Jewishness to promote its message.

Indeed, the complex story around *Affaire Blum* evinces a key point: the authority to determine who was or was not the Antisemite became a concern not just in capitalist West Germany, but in East Germany as well, where it manifested itself in ways specific to the ideological and historical needs of the nascent state. The emergence of the German Democratic Republic (GDR) under the domination of a communist power to whom Germany had just lost the war created a relationship to their shared Nazi past that differed substantially from that of the Federal Republic of Germany (FRG).[13] East Germany was determined to replace Hitler's racist ideology with communist anti-fascism, so their approach to externalizing antisemitism must be understood in connection with their interest in conflating fascism with West Germany's capitalist system.[14] The fact that many Nazis were able to seamlessly transition into prominent careers in West Germany provided ample fodder for GDR initiatives aiming to embarrass the FRG government. East Germany undoubtedly helped foster the general perception that West Germany was more welcoming to former Nazis, and highlighting the continuation of antisemitic incidents there certainly played an important role in this project.[15]

To be sure, the GDR included more Jews in active leadership in politics and culture than did the FRG. However, as Jews they were also subject to expulsion, depending on party needs.[16] Most significant is that East German opposition to antisemitism emerged as a way to support an anti-fascist agenda, not as a means of supporting Jews. The official annual commemorations of the so-called *Kristallnacht* of November 9, 1938, known in East Germany as the Day of the Victims of Fascism, provide a good example. Although Jews were included in these events, their status as Jewish victims of Nazism was

106 THE POSTWAR ANTISEMITE

in general overlooked or subordinated, and depictions of their persecution as Jews decreased significantly between 1949 and 1953.[17] Rather than focus on what had happened to Jews under the Nazis, commemorative events were more useful as a means to attack contemporary West Germany as a successor to the Nazi state than they were as a way to sympathize with targets of an antisemitic regime.[18]

Jews in East Germany were caught between their hope for creating a new state free of Antisemites and the antisemitism they continued to encounter. In 1948, Jewish communists Stefan Heymann, who had survived Auschwitz, Buchenwald, and other camps, and Siegbert Kahn, who returned from exile in Great Britain, did their part by publishing pamphlets linking Nazi leaders and antisemitism with German industry and capital.[19] But explicit antisemitic acts, such as numerous desecrations of Jewish cemeteries, could not be ignored.[20] Implicit antisemitism continued, too. Thomas Eckert, whose mother and grandparents returned from the United States to East Berlin in 1949, recalls the strained relationship Jewish re-émigrés had with East Germany. Few among them wanted to highlight their Jewishness.[21] Their reluctance was justified, given the Stalinist purges in Eastern Europe starting in 1948, many of which especially targeted Jews, and restrictions placed by the East German government.[22]

Affaire Blum illustrates the nexus between liberal democracy, capitalism, and antisemitism that served the needs of the nascent East German state by shaping the postwar Antisemite as a symbol of capitalist, imperialist oppression. The film did so in part by using prewar Jewish codes to delineate an Antisemite who allowed all East Germans to be seen as the victims of both Nazism and capitalism.[23] As in West Germany, the construction of the East German Antisemite amid the new postwar taboo on antisemitism reflected the persistence of Jewish difference as a fundamental framework that often intersected with and overlapped with gender, class, and other ordering systems in order to create meaningful narratives, albeit in ways specific to the developing workers' state. The years between 1945 and 1949 functioned as a particularly important period of transition between the end of the Second World War and the beginning of the Cold War, when state attitudes about Jews and antisemitism, on the one hand, and Holocaust restitution, compensation, and memory, on the other, were not yet fixed.[24]

In the context of the emerging East German state, *Affaire Blum* shows how artists and filmmakers were compelled to balance their desires to distance themselves from Nazi crimes with the demands of Soviet military authorities and SED (Socialist Unity Party) functionaries to construct an Antisemite who would complement communist ideology. The most useful Antisemite was either a high-ranking Nazi ideologue or a bourgeois capitalist with right-wing leanings who pressured regular, working-class Germans into carrying out evil acts against Jews. While this postwar fantasy suggested that Antisemites could thrive only in capitalist West Germany and that East Germans lived in the noble, anti-fascist half of Germany, it also helped former Nazis reintegrate into East German society after the denazification processes ended in 1948.

The figural Antisemite in East Germany had to be pliable enough to serve all of these needs. In the standard narrative, the former fascist transforms with ease into a postwar West German capitalist, allowing the East German government to portray West Germany as the sole heir to German fascism and the home of the Antisemite. In *Affaire Blum*'s iteration of this narrative, the use of the *Magdeburger Justizskandal*, a historical instance of antisemitism in Weimar Germany, suggests that the antisemitic origins of the Holocaust persist in postwar West Germany, even as the Antisemite's main target shifts from Jews to Germans.[25] The film replaces Alice Haas, the Czech-Jewish wife of the Jewish industrialist, with Sabine, a non-Jewish German woman who bears the brunt of antisemitic attacks after her husband's imprisonment and becomes the heroic champion of his redemption. Transforming Alice and Rudolf into an interfaith couple frames marriage to a Jewish capitalist as the source of Sabine's suffering and marks Sabine herself as both a target of antisemitic oppression and a savior of the Jews.[26]

Swapping in a non-Jewish wife also perpetuates the prewar cinematic trope of dismissing or downplaying Jewishness, especially for women characters.[27] Advertising in interwar Germany often used Jewish-coded women, who were linked to the conspicuous consumption of luxury items, as marketing tools to generate consumer desire, but their images were gradually effaced as the "Aryan" woman became the ideal.[28] The disappearance of Alice's story from the film thus echoes the disappearance of Jewish women that began in the 1930s and furthers the post-1945 elevation of non-Jewish women as victims. In so doing, it advances a usable narrative for Germans seeking to distance themselves from Nazi perpetrators and to imagine themselves on the right side of history. In short, replacing Alice with Sabine allowed the film to refigure the *Magdeburger Justizskandal* (aka the Magdeburg Dreyfus Affair) through the narrative of capitalist oppression and without destabilizing traditional antisemitic tropes.[29]

Making Headlines

In December 1948, a line outside the Babylon Theater in Berlin (Figure 3.2) signaled excitement about the premiere of *Affaire Blum*. As a postwar German film focused on antisemitism, it created quite a stir. It begins with two lines of text: "You are viewing a film that is based upon facts. The affair took place over 20 years ago." The next shot is a montage of newspaper headlines, the first of the film's six. This technique not only reinforces the film's realism, evoking documentary rather than drama, but references the "great press storm" of July and August 1926, when German newspapers politicized the murder of Hellmuth Helling, one of the first times they did so—but far from the last.[30]

Although each newspaper montage appears for only a few seconds, they collectively reflect the centrality of media representation to the story. The first montage begins with an image of the September 4, 1926, edition of the *Mitteldeutscher Generalanzeiger* (a fictional newspaper clearly based on the

Figure 3.2. A crowd of eager moviegoers line up outside the Babylon Theater in Berlin for the premiere of director Erich Engel's *Affaire Blum* (1948), based on a screenplay by R. A. Stemmle. Karin Evans in the role of Sabine Blum (right) features prominently in the poster for the film. *Bundesarchiv, Bild 183-1984-0517-511/Walter Heilig.*

Magdeburger Generalanzeiger), whose headlines read "The Fascist Militia is mobilized" and "Mussolini announces death penalty." A voiceover narration begins, "These were restless times." Zooming in from this depiction of the general political atmosphere, the next headline references actual events from the mid-1920s: "Sensation in *Feme-Committee*. A former OCer unveiled / MP Jahnke as liaison / The meeting with a book printer / Today he will continue to testify." The *Feme-Committee* was a parliamentary committee that investigated the *Feme* murders, political assassinations of supposed traitors by right-wing paramilitary organizations (such as the Organization Consul, or OC) in the early 1920s.[31] This initial focus on right-wing violence is followed by headlines on an array of topics: One headline references the late 1925 "Potsdam Society Scandal," which involved a scam artist named Baron von Oppen who, among other things, proposed marriage to four different women; another reports on rising unemployment in Berlin, and another mentions that President Hindenburg was named an honorary citizen of the village of Bad Tölz, where Hitler delivered his first election speech.[32] Yet another headline from this fictional newspaper announces the publication of the second volume of *Mein Kampf*, and a final shot shows two photographs of the *Stahlhelm* (League of Frontline Soldiers), the largest right-wing paramilitary organization in Germany, which was headquartered in Magdeburg, with the headline "1011 cases of typhus in Hannover."

Only after this juxtaposition of Nazi tropes associated with Jews—sexual deviance, swindling, economic strife—and the doings of aristocrats, high-ranking Nazis, and right-wing paramilitary organizations does the montage turn to antisemitism. First, a partially obscured headline shows the words "rally, "antisemitic," and "18 injured." Then the full headline becomes visible: "Antisemitic Rally. An antisemitic rally in Stenger's Beerhall ended with four dead and 18 injured / The Leiferde assassin is brought to Hannover." The Leiferde assassin refers to Otto Schlesinger and Willi Weber, who derailed the Berlin-Cologne train near the town of Leiferde in Niedersachsen during an intended robbery on August 19, 1926, resulting in twenty-one deaths. They were convicted and sentenced to death that fall, but in 1927, they were pardoned after many prominent people, including Albert Einstein, wrote letters on their behalf. Because Schlesinger was assumed to be Jewish, the pardons led to antisemitic protests.[33] As the rally headline dissolves to reveal the newspaper's classified ads, the narrator points out that hundreds of people were seeking the few jobs advertised. The voiceover continues, "With the last ad begins the Affaire Blum," as the full text of the ad in question fills the

110   THE POSTWAR ANTISEMITE

screen: "We are looking for cashiers for savings and loan funds in the country with immediate effect. Independent post. Credentials. 1000.- RM deposit. Offers under 'trust' to the Mittel-DG [*Mitteldeutscher Generalanzeiger*] office." This is the ad that will lure the killer to his prey.

This first headline montage provides the film's political background: fascism in Italy, right-wing political murders in Germany, scam artists, economic woes, Hindenburg's politics, the rise of Hitler and the *Stahlhelm*, deadly diseases, violent right-wing antisemitism, and, finally, unemployment, which leads to the ad that initiates the narrative. The film thus situates the Antisemite firmly in the context of rejected right-wing German politics, legitimate economic despair, and overall social malaise, while fixing German antisemitism as the responsibility of prewar, right-wing German nationalist politicians and their woeful economic and social policies. By connecting antisemitism to economic policies, which threaten all Germans, the film refigures antisemitism as a consequence of economic exigencies, rather than the racializing logic of Jewish difference.

Explicitly and via its documentary style, the film lays down a claim to historical accuracy, yet it also carefully chooses when to downplay antisemitism and when to enhance it for the purpose of sustaining a critique of capitalism—and to avoid alienating general audiences. Its main tools for this task are the familiar codes of Jewishness that allow audiences to identify with both Jews and non-Jews as targets of the Antisemite, as well as to distance themselves from antisemitism. For example, by playing up the antisemitism of the Magdeburg police chief Konrat (based on the real-life investigating judge Kölling), the detective Schwerdtfeger (Tenholt), and Schwerdtfeger's lawyer son, Egon, and downplaying the antisemitism of the lower-class murderer, Karlheinz Gabler (Schröder), the film supports the fantasy that German nationalism could be decoupled from antisemitism—which, in East Germany, let former Nazis reintegrate into the body politic and become loyal communists. Taking it a step further, the film uses prewar *Jewish* codes to signal the evil intentions of Schwerdtfeger, Konrat, and Egon: they are cigar-smoking, upper-class fat cats whose loyalty is to their professions rather than the German state, which they are corrupting through their actions and support of antisemitism.

Journalism and publishing were other Jewish-coded industries in prewar German culture, while referring to them as the Jewish "Lügenpresse" (lying newspaper industry) was a popular Nazi slur.[34] Forty minutes into the film, the second montage of newspaper headlines deploys this trope—ostensibly to evoke Nazi Antisemites, but actually associating these Antisemites with Jews. The montage follows a newsroom scene in which a leering journalist gleefully announces that he has come up with a juicy headline: "Jewish Industry Tycoon Suspected of Murder." His colleague responds affirmatively, adding that they should add the name "Jakob Blum" to the headline, along with a picture. This scene exemplifies how the film applies Jewish codes to Antisemites. While the stereotypical journalist chomping at the bit for the story is coded Jewish, his dark mustache has been shaved at the ends to resemble Hitler, his newspaper is called *Völkisches Tageblatt* (National Daily Newspaper), and his exclamation, "Finally, some good propaganda," speaks for itself. The fruits of their antisemitic labor appear in the revised headline, "Jewish Head of Industry Under Suspicion of Murder," featured next to Blum's picture.

The headline segues into a close-up of the article that says, "A sensational arrest has left all German-minded circles extremely excited. The Jewish director of Blum Werke, Dr. Jakob Blum, has been arrested"; the headlines "Missing Bookkeeper" and "Arrests at Blum & Co."; an article about the arrest of Blum's chauffeur Karl Bremer, who is suspected of involvement in the disappearance of the missing bookkeeper, Platzer (Helling); the headline "Review of the Books in the Blum Company"; and finally, the explicitly antisemitic headline "A Victim of Jewish Financial Manipulation," which refers to Platzer. The next scene features Schwerdtfeger and his son, Egon, seated at a table in their bourgeois dining room reading newspapers as the judge's wife embroiders. This journalistic ramping up to full-on antisemitism helps facilitate the film's subtle reversal of terms, as Jakob Blum becomes less Jewish and more capitalist at the same time as he and his non-Jewish chauffeur become the victims of the Antisemite, figured as the Jewish-coded press.

Subsequent newspaper montages at once stress the scandal mongering of the press and the machinations of Magdeburg's right-wing lawyers and judges with headlines like "Judicial Scandal," "Secret Session of the Judges," and "Behind the Scenes of the Blum Affair." But the most poignant headline appears in the final minutes of the film, in the *Mitteldeutscher Generalanzeiger* on November 5, 1926: "Gabler sentenced to death." The film cuts from the headline to the modest kitchen of Bremer, Blum's chauffeur, whose wife tells him to stop pacing. Bremer holds up the newspaper and tells her to look at the headline, which points to a fate he narrowly escaped. Here, the audience is invited to sympathize with Bremer as a working-class, non-Jewish victim of the Antisemite. Furthering the class contrast, the film

112   THE POSTWAR ANTISEMITE

segues to Blum and his wife enjoying dinner at an elegant table. Sabine raises a glass and says, "To better days to come." Blum drinks, but when Sabine tells him that it is all over, Blum replies, "It isn't all over. It's just starting. Facing the court today as a witness, I had a feeling that everyone behind me would have preferred to see me in the dock instead of Gabler." In the couple's sole moment of disagreement, Sabine asserts her patriotic loyalty as she insists that Germany is a *Rechtsstaat* (state based on the rule of law). Blum kisses her hand and looks worriedly off in the other direction, hinting at the persistence of antisemitism and a foreshadowing of the Holocaust.

A Blum by Any Other Name

Robert A. Stemmle and Erich Engel, the director of *Affaire Blum*, enjoyed successful careers under the Nazis, though their films did not serve as anti-Jewish propaganda. While Engel's partial Jewish background put him in a precarious position after 1933 (though he claimed this did not keep him from sneaking a message of resistance into at least one of his films), after 1945, it helped him prove he was not a Nazi.[35] If making a postwar film critical of antisemitism was a way to bolster one's commitment to anti-fascism, it was an especially beneficial task for Stemmle, who had no genetic grounds for his defense. This did not mean that his desire to oppose antisemitism was insincere. Wolfgang Staudte, director of the rubble film *Die Mörder sind unter uns* (1946), the first feature film to address how Germans might grapple with Nazi crimes after the war, explicitly admitted that making the film was an essential first step toward postwar rehabilitation for Germans.[36] In so doing, he implicitly suggested that thematically appropriate films could also be critical steps toward individual rehabilitation for filmmakers.

Like Veit Harlan's *Jud Süss* (1940) and G. W. Pabst's *Der Prozess* (1948), *Affaire Blum* is based on a historical case of Jews falsely accused of crimes. However, *Affaire Blum* is set in the more recent past, and its documentary style underscores its factuality. Stemmle would later claim that he changed only the names in his narrative reconstruction, which he based on news reports, his personal experiences, and the recollections of police detective Otto Busdorf (called Bonte in the film), who had helped solve the original case and who served as an advisor on the film set.[37] Yet, close examination of *Affaire Blum* shows that while many facts remained the same, the film fundamentally changed critical plot and character elements to create an Antisemite that fit the social and political needs of the emergent East Germany.[38]

The multiple versions of the screenplay that Stemmle submitted to the Soviet Military Authority in Germany track some of the initial changes.[39] While an early draft of the screenplay dated September 13, 1947, was titled *Mordprozess Haas* (Haas murder trial), two months later, director Erich Engel referred to the project as "Affaire Blum" in a memo to DEFA managing director Alfred Lindemann.[40] It would appear that the protagonist's name was changed from Haas to Blum to more overtly signal his Jewishness, while the inclusion of the French word "Affaire" links the case to the Dreyfus Affair and its innocent Jewish victim (a connection that some people made at the time). Left-liberals had been yearning for a courtroom scandal like the Dreyfus Affair which they could use to highlight their dissatisfaction with the increasingly undemocratic courts by underscoring their antisemitism. In 1922, left-leaning liberals had supported the cause of Felix Fechenbach, a Social Democrat convicted of treason in a dubious trial. After his conviction, the Social Democrat newspaper *Vorwärts* announced that "Germany has its Dreyfus Affair," but at the time neither the Fechenbach case nor the Haas case received anywhere near the international attention of the Dreyfus Affair.[41]

Changing the name of the film's protagonist from Rudolf Haas to Jakob Blum also linked him to Léon Blum, a well-known Jewish journalist and France's first Socialist prime minister, who was not only politically aligned with the Soviet Military Authority in Germany but also had been one of the earliest journalists to champion Dreyfus, events recalled in his memoir, *Souvenirs sur l'Affaire* (1935). In several scenes, the film suggests that only Antisemites recognize the name Blum as Jewish and associate it with Léon Blum. In fact, the constellation of film characters that the screenplay invents, changes, or eliminates shows how the screenwriter, director, and censors together shaped the tale to suit the Soviet zone's efforts to make opposing antisemitism synonymous with communism. The fact that certain explicit references to antisemitism in early screenplays of *Affaire Blum* are later censored due to fears they might disrupt the film's pro-communist narrative complicates our understanding of these characters and how they related to the film's engagement with Jewish difference and creation of the Antisemite.

· 114 THE POSTWAR ANTISEMITE

The draft screenplay dated November 18, 1947, matches the film, with one notable exception: its ending. In the screenplay, a crowd of people in front of Blum's villa shout antisemitic slurs such as *"Juda—verrecke!"* (Perish, Jews!) in unison and throw stones through all of its windows, breaking the glass and knocking over the candles on the dinner table.[42] At a meeting on January 2, 1948, DEFA head Hans Klering, director Kurt Maetzig, DEFA chief dramaturg Wolfgang von Gordon, and the censor for the Soviet Military Authority, Major Samuil Simowski, engaged in a robust discussion of this scene.[43] Simowski said he would only allow what he called the "pogrom" scene to appear in the film if the crowd included recognizable members of the anti-Nazi *Reichsbanner Schwarz-Rot-Gold* (Black, Red, Gold Banner of the Reich), a German paramilitary group also known for its anti-communist stance. However, the Germans in the meeting knew that portraying the *Reichsbanner* as antisemitic would make no sense to audiences and instead convinced Simowski to eliminate the scene.[44] Simowski also insisted that the film not "overly emphasize" that Blum was an entrepreneur, as that would "strip the film of its clear character of class struggle."[45] This conversation reveals how compromises shaped the film. Simowski's desire to link antisemitism to anti-communism appears clearly in relation to his commitment to foregrounding class struggle, as communist imperatives overshadow the imperative to redress the harms done to Jews, even, or perhaps especially, when the nature of the Antisemite is the topic at hand.

The boundaries of the film's Antisemite were also influenced by decisions about the depictions of Jewish characters, including which characters to include. Eliminating the character of Haas's brother-in-law, Paul Crohn, streamlined the cast and enabled his actions and impacts to be distributed among non-Jewish characters. Crohn was something of a mysterious figure, not least because he was a Zionist who had running conflicts with the *Centralverein*, the mainstream German Jewish organization with which Haas was affiliated.[46] The newspaper campaign in support of Blum seems to emerge organically, unlike Haas's publicity campaign, which was spearheaded by Crohn; Blum's wife, Sabine, secures the cooperation of the president, which Crohn secured for Haas. The film thus shifts responsibility for saving its protagonist from the Jewish brother-in-law to the non-Jewish wife, further diminishing the significance of actual Jews to a story about antisemitism.

The first postwar films to deal explicitly with Jews, antisemitism, and the Holocaust were made by DEFA in the Soviet zone; these included not only

Affaire Blum but also Staudte's *Die Mörder sind unter uns* (1946) and Kurt Maetzig's *Ehe im Schatten* (1947).[47] This was not because the Soviet occupiers sought to address these topics, but rather because they collaborated on films with Germans returning from Soviet exile, prisons, and concentration camps, whereas American Occupation Forces sought more direct control over their re-education efforts. Some Soviet cultural officers who supervised and censored German filmmakers, like Sergei Tulpanow and Aleksandr Dymschitz, were scholars of German literature themselves, who maintained close, cooperative relationships with German émigré writers and others with whom they had been in contact during the war.[48]

Nevertheless, many Soviet military cultural officers responsible for overseeing these early German postwar films were themselves highly educated, middle-class Jews. German-Jewish historian Helmut Eschwege, who survived the war in Estonia and Palestine, noted that when he returned to Dresden in 1946, there were groups of Jews in the Soviet Army and "all the cultural and political officers were Jews." He claimed this was because Jews felt more secure in Germany than they did in the Soviet Union, where antisemitism was on the rise.[49] Interestingly, the records of the Soviet censorship of *Affaire Blum* indicate that Stemmle and other non-Jewish Germans sought to explicitly engage with antisemitism but were held back by Russian Jewish officers, including Simowksi, Mark Mogilewer, and Alexander Dymschitz, who, like many Jews after the Holocaust, wanted to avoid focusing on the persecution of Jews by Antisemites.[50]

Both Soviet Jewish occupiers and non-Jewish German filmmakers wanted to construct an Antisemite who was someone else, somewhere else. But what accounted for the differences in their approaches to antisemitism? Many German and Russian Jews remained deeply invested in the idea that German culture itself was free of antisemitism. Dymschitz, for example, echoed the fantasy of many Jews (and non-Jews) when he noted, "We knew that while Nazism could abuse German art, it could never kill it. We knew what a great contribution the German anti-fascist artists had made in the world struggle against Hitler fascism, because we knew that German art was still breathing within Germany, so we weren't fooled by the ruins, but set about digging up this art again."[51] In other words, he was determined to separate Germans from Nazis.

Ultimately, however, engagement with Jewish difference, including antisemitism, depended more on politics than religion, nationality, or aesthetics. The standard account of the period is that German communists who

116   THE POSTWAR ANTISEMITE

returned from exile marginalized the Holocaust in the service of undoing the Soviet Union's wartime alliance with the West, resulting in a state that officially ignored Jewish difference, which can be construed positively, negatively, or both. Recent scholarship has come to more nuanced understandings that take into consideration the presence of Jewish functionaries in the SED and limited attempts at recognition, such as providing restitution and commemorating Jewish holidays.[52] Nonetheless, the scholarly consensus that East Germany marginalized Jews and Jewish memory of the Holocaust remains intact and helps support the postwar pattern of marginalizing Jewish victimhood to promote the narrative of German victimhood.[53] While this pattern was also part of the construction of the Antisemite in West Germany, the form it took in East Germany served explicitly political purposes. Defining the Antisemite as a figure incompatible with communism helped bolster the idea that the state itself operated outside the system of Jewish difference according to which the Antisemite targets the Jew. But even as this idea reinforced the political and moral primacy of communism, it also opened the door to a new iteration of the Jewish-coded capitalist, which in turn enabled the construction of an anti-capitalist Antisemite.

Sabine: The Antisemite's Non-Jewish Victim/Hero

The filming of *Affaire Blum* took place between January 20 and July 9, 1948.[54] But in early February, director Erich Engel was called to testify at Veit Harlan's trial for crimes against humanity. It seems likely that as Engels went on to make his film about an innocent Jewish victim of Weimar antisemitism, he was still thinking about German filmmakers' complicity in Nazi crimes and how Harlan deployed his own victimization to defend himself against accusations of antisemitism. There is no question that his film similarly defines the Antisemite to position Germans as its victim—albeit for political rather than personal purposes—even as it aims to show the dangers of antisemitism before the war.

The filmmakers' decisions about which characters would be Jews reveal the contours of a postwar Antisemite designed to fit newly developing East German specifications. Essentially, this entailed splitting the antagonist in two: the Antisemite, whom the communist state opposes, and the industrialist, whom the communist state also opposes, even as he is the target of the Antisemite (in other words, the enemy of my enemy is not wholly my friend).

To do this, the screenplay maintains the historical identity of the German nationalists who try to frame the Jewish industrialist, which firmly associates them with antisemitism and Nazis; they are the overt bad guys. Traditionally, antisemitism targeted Jews as industrialists and capitalists, so to maintain its ability to protect the Jew and attack the capitalist, the film works hard to code Blum as non-Jewish in looks and affect. He is an anodyne character who displays little in the way of stereotypical Jewish characteristics or even personality, recognizable as a Jew only by his name and profession[55] and aligned primarily with his non-Jewish wife, Sabine.[56]

Transforming the Czech Jew Alice Kussi Haas into the non-Jewish Sabine Blum introduces gender as another strategy for splitting antisemitism and Jews. The actors who play Jakob (Kurt Ehrhardt) and Sabine (Karin Evans) Blum look neither conventionally Jewish nor Aryan, which in effect renders them blank cultural slates. The Blums do not appear until Jakob's arrest at home (a detour from the historical record, as Haas was arrested at his factory), a full half hour into the film. The scene begins with a distressing visit from the police waking Jakob and Sabine in their darkened bedroom.[57] Although the Blums are not visually coded as Jews, their surroundings nevertheless evoke stereotypes about Jewish wealth through fancy bedclothes, elegant furniture and woodwork, Sabine's fashionable nightgown, and the white scarf Jakob wears over his dark dressing gown. Placing Sabine at the scene of the arrest begins the process of beefing up her role in her husband's defense and transforming her from supportive spouse to co-protagonist. At every subsequent turn, Sabine is deeply involved in her husband's case, from asking the police what will happen to him, to mobilizing his lawyer and President Wilschinski (based on German President Hindenburg) on his behalf, to accompanying Bonte (based on Busdorf) to Düsseldorf to help secure the confession that will free her husband. As the police wait for Jakob to get dressed, we learn that they are also arresting his driver, Bremer, who lives directly downstairs in a literal representation of his lower social standing. If the nighttime arrest of an innocent man and his driver evokes the Gestapo invading homes to arrest Jews, adding Sabine and the working-class, non-Jewish Bremer to the scene (Haas's driver was brought to the police after Haas's arrest) gives the Antisemite non-Jewish victims from the beginning of the case.

An early, uncensored version of Stemmle's screenplay presents Jakob as a victim of antisemitism even before he is arrested, when two swastikas and the word *Saujude* (Jewish pig) are drawn in the dust on his car.[58] Omitting

118   THE POSTWAR ANTISEMITE

this scene dials down the antisemitism against him, but adding instances of antisemitic aggression against Sabine plays up her status as victim. When detective Schwerdtfeger refuses to allow Sabine to visit her husband just after he allows a visit between Gabler and his fiancée, we see the detective's antisemitism through its impact on Jakob's wife, rather than Jakob. The next scene shows Sabine in her living room, where a seven-armed menorah sits on the mantel and she tells Wormser, their lawyer and the only other Jewish character in the film, that she has found a swastika painted on their garage and received anonymous hate mail asking why she is married to a Jew. In the letter she reads aloud, adjacency to a Jew becomes the equivalent of being a Jew: "You're a German woman. Why did you marry a Jew? Did you know your lawyer is also a Jew? Whoever profits from the Jews also dies." In light of the strategic character shifts we've already seen, it should come as no surprise that Haas's lawyer Heinrich Braun was not Jewish. Making Wormser a Jew and assigning him stereotypically Jewish traits—like suggesting a large financial reward for information about the murderer—helps make Jakob Blum seem less Jewish in comparison.

Beyond minimizing Jakob's Jewishness, the film minimizes his very presence in the narrative. Instead, besides Sabine, it focuses on Gabler, the actual murderer, and Bonte, the detective from Berlin. Sabine plays a heroic role in freeing her husband from the clutches of antisemitic injustice when she persuades Gabler's fiancée Christina, a dental assistant, to testify against him, which allows Jakob to go free. By mobilizing a working-class woman to prove her Jewish husband's innocence, the film connects the machinations of its Antisemites and the violence of the capitalist system, which together constitute the perpetuation of antisemitism in the institutions of the German state.

When Jakob Blum and his driver are implicated in the murder at the police station lineup—another instance of a non-Jew accompanying the nominal Jewish victim of the Antisemite—Jakob accuses the judge of setting them up. The judge indignantly replies, "How dare you make this accusation in a German court! You're slandering German justice!" Jakob's response is to out-German his interlocutor: "Why are you stressing the word German? I'm German myself. Truth is not German, truth is universal." He not only makes the case that a Jew can be a German but also sets up Germans as the targets of those who would seek to undermine the truth, in this case, the Antisemite. In this scene, where Jakob Blum, the German Jew, insists upon his German-ness in the face of the Antisemite, he is surrounded by his wife and his driver, the parallel non-Jews who suffer along with him.

ALICE HAAS DISAPPEARS FROM *AFFAIRE BLUM*   119

According to this schema, antisemitism is a byproduct of political tensions and oppositions, the tool of greedy, biased individuals who also catch non-Jews in their web of persecution but who will be safely confined to West Germany after the war. The larger irony here is how a film that aimed to document the miscarriage of justice for German Jews in the Weimar period ends up sidelining German Jews as it helps shape the postwar East German Antisemite.

Jewish Indifference

Although Gabler, the murderer, and Bonte, the investigator from Berlin who pins the murder on him, are central to the plot of *Affaire Blum*, neither is associated with antisemitism. Given that Stemmle attempted to play up antisemitism in invented scenes that the Soviets censored, his choice not to depict Gabler and Bonte as antisemitic is notable, especially as their characters are modeled on individuals who were deeply implicated in Nazi party activities and right-wing German nationalism. Instead, the film portrays Gabler as an ordinary man deceived by the promises of right-wing German nationalism, and Bonte as an apolitical, objective detective interested only in finding out the facts of the case. Removing antisemitism from the depiction of Gabler sets up poverty as the rationale for his crimes and his right-wing nationalist activity. In so doing, the film establishes a moral rationale for reintegrating low-level Nazi functionaries and party members into the body politic (also a goal of West German and Austrian rehabilitation programs). Even more salient to how this film shapes the Antisemite is its placement of both the murderer and the man who uncovers his crime completely outside of the system of Jewish difference, which is what makes this narrative emphasis on reintegration succeed.

To be sure, Gabler appears suspicious from the very first scene, which shows the frosted glass of a front door from inside a home, as the shadow of a person in a cap comes into view and rings the doorbell. This visitor turns out to be Gabler, the man who placed the newspaper ad for a cashier that closes the opening montage. He is arriving at the home of Platzer, a book-keeper who has responded to the ad, to collect the deposit for the job. Gabler removes his cap to reveal blond hair and two *Schmisse* (dueling scars) on his face, unmistakable signs that he belongs to a right-wing *Burschenschaft* (fraternity), and immediately demands the deposit. Yet even as his appearance

120 THE POSTWAR ANTISEMITE

and behavior suggest nefarious purposes, his desperate need for cash also elicits sympathy.

Gabler convinces Platzer to accompany him on his bicycle to his home in Gross Helgendorf, assuring him that they will return in time for an appointment Platzer has scheduled that evening, and reminds him to bring the deposit. When they arrive, Gabler introduces Platzer to his fiancée, Christina Burman, who lives with him. The two men go into the next room. Moments later, Burman is horrified to hear shots fired, after which she runs into the room and sees that Gabler has murdered Platzer. Gabler's friend Fischer arrives and sees Platzer's bicycle in the garden. Thinking fast, Gabler claims to have bought the bicycle for Fischer, who obliges by buying it from Gabler and then sells it the next day to a man named Tischbein, whom he refers to as a communist. The next scene takes place in Gabler and Burman's shabby living room, where they, Fischer, and Fischer's girlfriend are drinking beer, singing nationalist songs, and showing off their swords and other right-wing paraphernalia, in a de facto mashup of German nationalism and poverty.

The first half of the film continues in this vein, portraying Gabler as a nasty lout. He cheats Fischer on the price of the bicycle, kicks him out of his house, and abuses his fiancée, all the while proclaiming his love for the fatherland. When Burman, upset about the murder, tells Gabler she keeps seeing Platzer's ghost, he drags her down to the cellar and for the first time recites his favorite saying, "Life is dangerous but good practice." In classic abuser fashion, he then tells her, "I'm just doing this for us," picks her up, carries her back to bed, asks her to be reasonable, and seeks her assurance that she loves him. And yet, though Gabler is an unmistakable German nationalist, he is also pathetic and inauthentic: his *Schmisse* are not the result of a duel, but rather self-inflicted to make it appear that he was a brave member of a prestigious *Burschenschaft*, when in fact he has never attended university.[59] Nor has he profited from the war years, unlike the film's upper-middle-class officials who easily manipulate him. That favorite saying, "Life is dangerous but good practice," has nothing to do with antisemitism or politics, but rather reflects the lived reality of the working class.

Gabler's activities immediately after the murder/robbery highlight the commercial activity the crime sets in motion: newly flush, he goes to a store where he purchases a gun, visits a café, orders a coffee, and tries to chat up a woman by offering her a coin for the telephone—all with Platzer's money. These interactions all involve financial transactions, and none of them have anything to do with Jews or Antisemites. They thus underscore commodification, trade, and other elements of capitalism as the driving forces for the murder, rather than antisemitism. While the murder and its immediate aftermath are infused with German nationalism, Jews are not its explicit target. Rather, the scenes set into motion by the murder foreground everyday exchange and capitalism. While the film introduces antisemitism—and by extension Jews—in its opening newspaper montage, they do not reappear until twenty-two minutes into the action, when Schwerdtfeger asks a colleague whether he has heard of the company Blum & Co. "A Jewish company," his colleague replies, leaving the phrase hanging. At this point, neither the colleague nor the audience know why he is asking about the company, so if Schwerdtfeger's question serves to open the door for the introduction of Jakob Blum, the colleague's response serves to introduce Jewish difference; it is notable that both introductions refer to a company, not a person. The repetition of this introductory conversation serves as emphasis when Schwerdtfeger tells Konrat, "I have an interesting case—do you know Blum & Co.?" to which Konrat replies, "Of course, a Jewish firm." Schwerdtfeger explains that Platzer had incriminating evidence of tax evasion at the company but was fired and then went missing on the very day he was going to report it. Here, as Schwerdtfeger links Blum & Co., which has twice been identified as Jewish, to accusations of financial malfeasance and implications of additional criminal activity, Jewish difference enters the realm of antisemitic possibility. Unlike the police, the audience knows why Platzer went missing and presumably realizes he was going to share his evidence against Blum & Co. at the appointment Gabler told him he would not miss (whose purpose Gabler did not know), so they are primed to see the police conspiracy for what it is.

The film also makes it clear that Schwerdtfeger and Konrat coax Gabler into parroting their antisemitic narrative that sets up Blum as the murderer. As they sit in Schwerdtfeger's living room with his son Egon, Konrat makes an explicitly antisemitic observation about Jews, and Egon notes that the case might be "a fine answer to the Rathenau affair" (the 1922 assassination of Jewish statesman Walther Rathenau) because "now people will see that sometimes a Jew can also kill, and not for politics but for money." The three of them laugh heartily at this last antisemitic barb. Later, as Schwerdtfeger and Konrat search through Blum's tax documents for incriminating evidence, they comment on the business's many branches, affiliates, and international subsidiaries. Schwerdtfeger notes that they are all "polished tricksters, including Blum." Konrat remarks, "I had a close look at his face,

122   THE POSTWAR ANTISEMITE

his whole physiognomy—swarthy complexion, the eyes, the nose, intelligent, but scheming." The proliferation of antisemitic tropes becomes almost comical, even as its implications are all too serious—at least for Jakob Blum. The film thus delimits Antisemites to, on the one hand, the cowardly anonymous troublemakers who threaten Jews and non-Jews alike by drawing swastikas and writing slurs on their property (cars and garage, in the case of Jakob and Sabine Blum) and, on the other, elite right-wing representatives of the state and its institutions, like Schwerdtfeger, Konrat, and Egon. These depictions further separate the actual murderer, Gabler, from antisemitism, for he neither expresses antisemitism nor kills for political reasons; instead, the determining factor of his life and crime is his desperate need for money due to the damaging effects of the capitalist system. Ultimately, then, the film uses Gabler to downplay the culpability of everyday Nazis, shift blame for antisemitism to the elite, and in so doing vindicate East Germany's antifascist communism. Its portrait of the liminal Antisemite as the elite, capitalist, right-wing, proto-Nazi leader who exploits working-class people gives ordinary Germans a pass, even if they happened to be antisemitic and to have joined the Nazi movement, for the film ultimately blames the capitalist system for the social ills that brought about Nazism.

The fact that Engel, Stemmle, and Gordon had worked in the film industry under the Nazis likely colored their portrayal of the Antisemite as an elite right-wing nationalist. Disconnecting antisemitism from Social Democrats and Communists suggests that antisemitism is not part of a broader, all-encompassing German system and that the poor, disadvantaged people whom these parties purport to represent cannot be held responsible for it. The way Schwerdtfeger, Konrat, and Egon use Gabler as their puppet is the film's key representation of this dynamic. Yet while Schwerdtfeger and Egon are kindly disposed toward Gabler, they also mock his attempts to pretend he has a degree from the prestigious university in Marburg and laugh at his self-inflicted *Schmisse*, further emphasizing their unsympathetic distance from the lower classes.[60] Even, or perhaps especially, when elite bourgeois capitalists force poor and working-class people to use antisemitism against other capitalists, they ultimately reveal themselves as the *real* Antisemites.

One final way in which *Affaire Blum* shapes its liminal Antisemite is by using the Nazi cinematic trope of replacing a traditionally Jewish character with a non-Jew who has traits that are just Jewish enough to perpetuate Jewishness in the narrative. In her study of Nazi film, Valerie Weinstein refers to the use of "white Jews," that is, Jewish-influenced Aryans, to drive home the point that the goal of the Nazis was to eliminate not only *Rassejuden* (Jews by race) but also *Gesinnungsjuden* (Jews in spirit).[61] Films that hinged upon the country/city divide, for instance, engaged the stereotypical association of Jews with the city and non-Jews with the country. *Affaire Blum* uses this distinction to affiliate its hero, Berlin police detective Bonte, with Jews by virtue of his association with the city, while otherwise representing him as non-Jewish to underscore how the Antisemite threatens non-Jews. Still, the film cannot help but reinscribe antisemitic stereotypes about Jews and non-Jews as it precariously tries to distance Bonte from both Jews and Nazis.

From the moment he arrives in Magdeburg, Bonte is cast as an outsider, valued primarily for his objectivity rather than his cleverness. He may be from Berlin, but he persistently resists the codes of Jewish urbanity, instead signaling a working-class embodiment of city life. Brainstorming ideas about how to help Jakob at dinner with Sabine, President Wilschinski, and Wormser, Bonte rejects Wormser's suggestion that they offer a financial reward for information about Platzer's killer, distancing himself from the Jew's focus on money. But he understands that Blum is likely being framed, refusing to buy in to the fabricated antisemitic narrative. He also resists the elegant meal's signifiers of wealth and elitism, instead uncouthly downing his brandy in one gulp and asking Sabine to confirm that the flavor is cherry. That he is apparently more interested in the drink than the conversation attests to his gruff, no-nonsense, yet likable anti-bourgeois neutrality. The dinner alone suggests that he is a savvy investigator impervious to antisemitism, bourgeois sensibilities, and capitalism, even as it does so by reinforcing stereotypical assumptions about all these things. By the end of the film, he emerges as its hero for cracking the case when he finds Christina and gets Sabine to persuade her to testify against Gabler.

The character of Bonte is based on Otto Busdorf, who, as previously noted, served as an advisor to Stemmle and Engel on the set of *Affaire Blum*. That his character emerged as the film's hero is thus hardly surprising. Floating over and above the fray of Jewish difference, Bonte is the perfect foil to Schwerdtfeger and Konrat, the film's villainous Antisemites. But the historical record is more complicated. While Busdorf opposed Tenholt and Kölling during the Haas case in the 1920s, all three men later became committed members of the Nazi party. Busdorf went so far as to join the Nazi SS and later secretly destroyed police documents related to its activities.[62] In this context, the creation of the enviable, ideal, and ultimately impossible character of Bonte becomes the only way to establish a narrative that locates

124 THE POSTWAR ANTISEMITE

Busdorf, and with him East Germany, outside of the engagement with Jewish difference and antisemitism from which they emerged.[63]

Reinscribing Antisemitism and the Liminal Antisemite in *Affaire Blum,* the Novel

Affaire Blum was an international hit, especially in the United States. One reviewer called it "suspenseful, powerful," and the "most impressive film to come from Germany since the war."[64] The *New York Times* described it as "a trenchant dramatic exposition of the way in which an innocent German Jew is almost destroyed by nascent Nazis—back in 1926," although it notes that the film was made in the Russian zone of Berlin, so it is no accident that the "good" people come from the "leftist" party.[65] In 1948, Stemmle published a novel based on the screenplay that gave him the opportunity to expand upon the narrative.[66] He does this in part by including more details about the characters' lives and interiority. However, he also reinscribes Jewish difference by reinstating both the scenes of antisemitism that Soviet military authorities censored from the screenplay and elements of Haas's life that corresponded with Jewish stereotypes.[67]

The novel rounds out Jakob's character by including his inner thoughts and expanding on his concern for his daughter, Ellen (a new and wholly fictional character). But it also flattens him by emphasizing his Jewishness— through scenes in which he is a victim of antisemitism and by attaching him to stereotypes about Jews, which in turn feed the novel's implicit antisemitism. For example, depicting him as a cosmopolitan admirer of modern art echoes antisemitic propaganda. While Jakob's neutral political stances and indifference to the impression he makes may work to obscure his true character, that in itself plays into negative stereotypes about inauthentic Jews, as does the insertion of these observations into a set of Jewish stereotypes, including penny pinching and modern art:

> Now, however, Blum placed little emphasis on making himself popular. He didn't look up or down, right or left. But apart from that, he was full of contradictions that did not make it easy to get to his real core. He could be stingy and haggle for pennies, on the other hand he often enough proved to be generous and giving as a patron and secret benefactor, especially towards his co-religionists. He valued modern art, especially graphics, and collected

ALICE HAAS DISAPPEARS FROM *AFFAIRE BLUM* 125

crazy stuff, as his wife called it. At the same time, he had a sentimental tendency towards popular simplicity, even kitsch. A philistine and cultured man of the world at the same time, he found pleasure in old-fashioned, home-made hams as well as Paul Klee, Picasso and Kandinsky. His avowed favorite was Walter Trier, of whom he owned a number of originals.[68]

Similarly, the novel's praise for Jakob's business prowess comes across as back-handed. The fact that he was born in Warsaw ties him to stereotypical depictions of Jews from Eastern Europe, known for their canny business sense. He knows how to flatter international customers' aesthetic preference for "idyllic landscapes of Upper Bavaria" and realistically painted mountains, and he "flood[s]" the Balkans, Turkey, Syria, Iraq, and lower Egypt with lush colored images of village life.[69]

Sabine Blum first appears in the novel hosting a dinner party, a bourgeois high-society gathering where the guests discuss politics, art, and theater.[70] That same night, the Blums receive word that Ellen, who is married to a Dutchman and lives in Amsterdam, has given birth to their first grandchild, and the police arrest Jakob.[71] As it does with Jakob, the novel again goes farther than the film in using Sabine to delineate its Antisemite. On the one hand, it includes more details about her efforts to support Jakob, including going to his office every morning to represent him while he is in jail. She is also more vigilant about antisemitism, noting that an antisemitic publisher in Leipzig has published a brochure in which someone named Theodor Fritsch (the name of a real-life antisemitic publisher) has written awful things about Jakob's past. On the other hand, the novel portrays Sabine as even more of a victim, to the point of being a martyr to her husband's cause, though she generously spares him her extended suffering:

> She hides more from him than she tells. She doesn't say anything about being so alone; that their son-in-law is behaving poorly in Amsterdam and Ellen's marriage is on the verge of collapse. Apart from Wormser and the little Rademacher, all their old friends and acquaintances have withdrawn. She says nothing about the difficulties that are stifling business, nothing about the business correspondence returned with: "We do not do business with murderers." She is powerless in the face of the bustle of competition, which has suddenly become so active that it threatens to kill the company. Sometimes she thinks she's ready for the madhouse. But she says nothing about that. Nothing of the worries, big and small: that Hedwig, the maid,

126 THE POSTWAR ANTISEMITE

has quit; that Mrs. Bremer got permission to visit her husband two weeks ago, but said nothing about it, and blames Blum for everything. She doesn't say anything about it. She smiles.[72]

Implicitly caused as much by her husband's Jewishness as by the accusation against him (not that the two can truly be separated), Sabine's tribulations mark her as the Antisemite's victim. For all that she identifies with her Jewish husband, she is not Jewish, and thus, as in the film, her victimization effectively deracinates the Antisemite.

Back home after the trial, Jakob tells Sabine that when he testified, he felt the people in the courtroom still wanted him to be on trial instead of Gabler. Sabine says, "You must start to believe in people again." He replies, "That is difficult." She responds, "I'll help you." With this exchange, the novel moves the process of postwar rehabilitation into the home and into the purview of a Christian woman, suggesting that the wounds of the past will be repaired by individual efforts to coexist peacefully—not targeted efforts (of Jews or anyone else) to address widespread antisemitism. Jakob has also learned that Antisemites endanger everyone. He tells Sabine, "I woke up. Now I know more than before. I know that it's just starting now. What happened to me, could happen to anyone. Anyone, at any time!"[73] Just then, he hears "*Juda— verrecke*!" (Perish, Jews!). Outside the window, a horde of young nationalists are shouting, with an adult directing them like a choir. One even throws a paving stone into the garden. But if it seems like the novel is offering a corrective to Jakob's universalist and Sabine's domestic erasure of antisemitism, it immediately backs off, for Bremer also hears the shouts and the police arrive. The mob runs away, leaving Jakob, Sabine, and Bremer, the Jew and his non-Jews, once again tied together as the Antisemite's victims.

At the end of the novel, the Blums have emigrated to Australia, where Jakob starts a successful new printing business with his son-in-law, Ellen's husband. While Sabine dies three years later, Ellen's son grows up to be a healthy twenty something who speaks several languages and has a thriving business. The novel's final scene describes a photograph Jakob has sent to Bonte from Australia: "White-haired, he sits at his desk with a strange-looking telephone wearing a broad suit jacket made of raw silk. In the foreground is a paving stone that serves as a paperweight. He writes: 'I have always taken it with me as a reminder of how it began.'"[74] This fictional presentation of Rudolf Haas's fate not only comforts readers with a happy ending for a Jewish Nazi victim but also suggests he is actually better off, having landed on his feet in his newly adopted country, where he dresses in silk and uses the newest technology. It even suggests that Blum is satisfied with turning the horrific violence of the Nazi youths who stormed his garden after the trial into a nostalgic memory of his former homeland—and that he is deeply bonded with the apolitical German detective who saved him. The novel thus once again aims for the comfort zone of German readers who might want to believe that Jewish exiles were actually better off outside Germany and displace the painful realities of Jewish suffering during and after the Holocaust.

The Fate of Alice Kussi

In fact, rather than film or fiction, antisemitism, German nationalism, and Nazis destroyed the Haas family. Rudolf's arrest and incarceration, followed by constant accusations and threats of government interference, took a heavy toll, as did the death in 1931 of one of the couple's six-year-old sons, Hans. At the end of February 1932, Rudolf and Alice moved to Prague.[75] After the Nazis came to power, the firm Louis Haas AG was forced into bankruptcy, broken up, and sold off. Late in the morning of Saturday, April 29, 1933, Rudolf hung himself in a storeroom near his family's apartment. He had apparently informed his brother-in-law and his lawyer of his intentions, and the suicide note found with his body read only, "Whoever finds me, I leave fifty crowns for the effort."[76]

After Rudolf's death, Alice remained in Prague to look after her mother and her remaining son, Alfred, whom she had enrolled in a German school. In 1938, Alice was increasingly worried about the Nazis. When she came across a 1926 letter from Herman Kussi, her father's cousin, she wrote to ask if he could help her family get visas to emigrate to the United States. In the letter she reminds Herman of her oil portrait, which he had admired on a visit to Prague; tells him about the deaths of her father, husband, and son and how she is now caring for her thirteen-year-old son and elderly mother; notes her inability to transfer her money out of the country; and bewails antisemitism: "The growing anti-Semitism makes me fear that it would happen to me as it happened to the Jews in Germany."[77] Though Herman made inquiries, he was unable to procure the visas. In 1941, Alice married a Czech Jew, Artur Hansel. Her mother was deported to Theresienstadt on July 16, 1942, then sent to Treblinka, where she was murdered on October 19. It is unclear whether Alice knew of her mother's fate when she, Artur,

128 THE POSTWAR ANTISEMITE

and Alfred were deported from Prague to Theresienstadt on March 6, 1943. Six months later, on September 6, 1943, Alfred was deported to Auschwitz, where he died. Alice was killed on April 7, 1944, in Theresienstadt; Artur was deported from Theresienstadt to Auschwitz on October 23, 1944, where he was murdered.[78]

Like the film and the novel, Stemmle and Engel's stage version of *Affaire Blum*, first performed in 1960 at the Berlin Volksbühne in the GDR, obscures Alice's murder by the Nazis. In Stemmle's essay for the program, which he lightly revised for publication in 1965, he touts the production as closely based on the life of Rudolf Haas and claims to now know even more about what really happened to the individuals involved.[79] Yet even in 1965, he writes, "Rudolf Haas committed suicide. His wife followed him voluntarily to her death."[80] Meanwhile, he claims that Otto Busdorf was a hero even after 1933, when he was "one of the first to be arrested and brought to the Oranienburg concentration camp," and denounces Tenholt as "one of the most-feared Gestapo agents," continuing to use his newly gathered facts to prop up the ideological rearrangements of his fictions. Sketches for the play's sets show the imprisonment of Gabler, Tischbein, Blum, and Bremer all in a row, suggesting a concentration camp and reinforcing the notion that they are all victims of the same forces. The program also includes a brief essay by Arnold Zweig, "Beginn und 'Endlösung,'" that emphasizes the basis of antisemitism in capitalism since Roman antiquity, and a two-page spread of eleven brief reports "Aus westdeutschen Blättern" (from West German newspapers) about antisemitic incidents in West German cities between 1959 and 1961. In short, the blame remains the same: West German capitalism.

The double erasure of Alice Haas's story from the film *Affaire Blum* and Stemmle's subsequent retellings of her fate as suicide is remarkable and disturbing. By removing first her Jewishness and then her death at the hands of the Nazis, the multiple and extremely popular iterations of *Affaire Blum* reinscribe a deeply antisemitic, historically particular set of events as a political fable. Besides demonstrating how stories of Jewish female suffering and struggle are exploited or overlooked for political drama, this eviction also demonstrates the extent to which the true horror of what the Nazis did could not be engaged in film in the postwar period—even in a supposedly fact-based film designed to oppose antisemitism. Ultimately, *Affaire Blum* instead minimizes antisemitism.

It is not surprising that Stemmle would end the novel by linking the events of the Kölling-Haas affair, as it came to be known, with the Holocaust. But given that Rudolf Haas actually committed suicide, that his wife Alice was murdered in the Holocaust, and that Busdorf became a Nazi, ending the novel with this suggestion of their lasting brotherhood feels like the rewriting of more than just their individual relationship. Blum found success in Australia but left his fellow non-Jewish Germans to fend for themselves at the hands of Nazis, suggesting that antisemitism was neither widespread nor deep-seated in German culture, but rather largely confined to capitalists. When the Antisemite is narrowly defined as a symbol of the bourgeois capitalist and right-wing nationalist, East Germany can at once refuse to reckon with it and define itself against it. As a figure that boosts the state's communist and anti-fascist cause, this Antisemite helps drive cultural narratives that promote models of justice or reconciliation that neither involve an engagement with Jewish difference nor destabilize its terms.

4

Accused as Jews

Anna Seghers and Victor Klemperer

In the fall of 1948, following months of travel abroad, the writer Anna Seghers (Figure 4.1) returned to her home in Berlin's eastern sector to an unlikely and ironic accusation: fostering antisemitism. Under the headline "*Stürmers* Echo" (a reference to Julius Streicher's infamous propaganda newspaper), the Berlin magazine *sie* accused Seghers of using antisemitic stereotypes to describe Jewish displaced persons (DPs) in an article titled "Passagiere der Luftbrücke" (Passengers of the air lift) that had recently appeared in *Aufbau: Kulturpolitische Monatsschrift*, an SED (Socialist Unity Party) newspaper. *sie* further asserted that Seghers had deliberately designed the article, at the behest of Soviet military authorities who had no love for DPs, to appeal to former Nazis whom the SED was trying to win over to its ranks.[1]

Needless to say, the accusations horrified Seghers, who had left the Jewish community in 1932 but had nevertheless been persecuted by the Nazis.[2] Indeed, as the editors of *sie* surely knew, her article's intent had been the exact opposite: to inspire sympathy for the plight of Jewish DPs by criticizing the German newspapers that described them in antisemitic terms reminiscent of Nazi propaganda, which included associating them with the black market and *Spekulantentum* (currency speculating).[3] For instance, the title alone of "Unerwünschte ausländische Gäste Berlins: UNRRA—Schützlinge als Gangster" (Unwanted foreign guests of Berlin: Gangsters in the care of UNRRA [United Nations Relief and Rehabilitation Administration]), an article that appeared in the Eastern zone's *Berliner Zeitung* on July 4, 1948, was enough to reveal its derogatory, antisemitic approach to its content.

Despite Seghers's intent and indignation, a case could be made that her artistic, allusive flair and oblique argumentation (both likely shaped by her background in fiction) rendered her text confusing and open to misreading. Additions and changes by *Aufbau* editors only made things worse. It is easy

The Postwar Antisemite. Lisa Silverman, Oxford University Press. © Oxford University Press 2025.
DOI: 10.1093/9780197697757.003.0005

Figure 4.1. Shortly after her return to Berlin in 1947, Anna Seghers posed for a series of portraits taken by photographer Fritz Eschen, whom the Nazis had also targeted for persecution as a Jew. *SLUB Dresden/Deutsche Fotothek/Fritz Eschen.*

to see how her use of derogatory language echoes the articles she was refuting and overpowers her critique:

> The UNRRA people were by no means dismissed with warm words of farewell, but rather with relief that one had gotten rid of the bad guests. The name was synonymous with "black market" and speculation. . . . The few newspapers that dealt with these transports said goodbye to the "scraps," to the "declassed elements." These were considered the darkest parts of the blackest market. To a certain extent its lifeblood. Disgusting, sick, black

132 THE POSTWAR ANTISEMITE

> blood.... They were the UNRRA gang, wholly repugnant to all and used by everyone.[4]

Without quotation marks, for instance, it is unclear whether the phrase "disgusting, sick, black blood" represents the author's thoughts or describes language used by others. In an earlier draft, the words "zu Recht" (rightly) are written and crossed out next to this phrase, suggesting that Seghers was conflicted about using it. She struggled to strike a balance between evoking sympathy for unjustly characterized DPs and distancing herself from their black market activity, which she found distasteful. Some of her attempts to arouse sympathy proved inartful at best and downright negative at worst: descriptions of pregnant women with their bosoms stuffed with chocolate, sugar, and coffee; mothers hiding cigarettes in their babies' diapers; "grossen Schieber" (big black market profiteers) who were registered in the camps but had beautiful big apartments at their disposal (referencing the stereotype of scheming Jews who returned to postwar Germany and took over property). It is easy to see how it was possible to misconstrue Seghers as upholding the hateful stereotypes about Jews that she was supposedly trying to discredit.[5]

Although she was upset at *sie* for claiming she had written the piece to co-opt former Nazis at the behest of the Soviets, Seghers placed blame for the incident largely on her editors at *Aufbau*. Their response to the accusations was in itself problematic: they reprinted the *sie* column with an afterword in which *Aufbau* accused *sie* of calling its author a "well poisoner," itself an antisemitic slur. They further claimed that the accusations against Seghers and *Aufbau* were designed as an "anti-Bolshevist" measure, rather than a sincere critique. And they even added another antisemitic dog whistle in the form of a description of DPs who had returned to Berlin to complete street corner black market deals in dollars, pounds, and other currencies.[6] Regardless of their intent, it demonstrates the powerful pull of antisemitic stereotypes, even in narratives that sought to undo them.

If the *Aufbau* editors did not care about their words' antisemitic potential, Seghers certainly cared about hers. In an angry, undated letter, she contended that, due to their edits and misprints, the published article had "a completely different character" from her original text:

> I wrote in my article that although they were mainly identified with the "black market" in Berlin, among the people in the UNRRA camp there

were great, even admirable people, such as the artists and the teachers and others. I said that the camp is a product of a crumbling society (not of the Jewish society, of course, but of the society we live in, the crumbling, capitalist post-war society), so that the black marketeers who have been locked up for years and shoved from one camp to another, could not have behaved differently.... I wanted to make a disgusting phenomenon understandable.[7]

Where she wanted to defend Jews against the antisemitic caricatures of the time, their editing had provided fodder to her opponents. While Seghers was upset that the edited article had riled up the "bad fools" at *sie*, she was particularly angry about the accusations that she had fostered antisemitism by focusing only on Jewish DPs who traded on the black market—accusations the *Aufbau* editors had not even cared to correct in their response. Yet, in the end, she obliquely acknowledged her struggle to create journalistic texts that could acknowledge complex realities and dismantle the antisemitism she aimed to critique:

It is of course wrong to deny in a people or in a group [**typed in typescript and then deleted by hand:** *that one loves*] precisely the mistakes that one wants to eliminate. You have to know them clearly and ruthlessly with their causes and effects, especially if you want to eliminate them. It is of course nonsense (about which you from "Aufbau" have not the slightest knowledge) to accuse me of all people of only drawing attention to these mistakes. Such accusations are so foolish and so thoughtless that I will not address them either here in this letter or later. I have written short stories and essays in which you can read about them and I too can write short stories and novels better than letters, probably better than articles.[8]

The antisemitism was certainly there for the critiquing. After the war, newspapers printed a stream of articles about the unsavory activities of DPs on the black market, often identifying them as Jews, implicitly or directly. Some insisted that Jewish organizations be held responsible for deporting "impudent and unscrupulous" DPs who were fixated on illegal black market schemes.[9] While it was common knowledge that virtually the entire population, including foreigners and members of the occupying forces, participated actively in the black market, newspaper articles and eyewitness reports still foregrounded the role of DPs and the real and imagined tensions they caused.[10] One article blamed the influence of "foreign" elements,

134 THE POSTWAR ANTISEMITE

clearly a code for Jews, for the black market activities of the general population.[11] Another described Jews as wealthy, privileged, "morally lax, natural criminals, and black marketers."[12] Such stereotypes were common in all zones of Germany and Austria. In a moment of rare candor, Baron Karl Karwinski, former police chief and minister of home security, as well as chief political advisor to the American Occupation Forces, summed up the general attitude: "Isn't it a pity that the Jews are now spoiling everything by making money out of Austria's misery! The DP camps are all black-market centers, while our own people are starving. This will be difficult for the Austrians to forget."[13]

These representations of continued antisemitism among the general population were exactly what Seghers was attempting to address; her failure points us once again to the struggle to define the Antisemite in those early transitional years—in this case, in an East German context. She did not deny the existence of antisemitic views among Germans, many of whom would always look for—and find—the worst, but she also believed that writers could awaken their ability to sympathize with Jews and saw herself as someone who could counteract antisemitism among her readership. Still, the exchange between *sie* and *Aufbau* emblematized the growing political tensions between West and East, showing how they could exploit her text's weaknesses to weaponize accusations of antisemitism to their own advantages.[14]

As the Soviet military occupation transitioned to the GDR, art and literature continued to play important roles in transmitting the government's anti-fascist messages. Communist writer Johannes Becher, who had spent the Nazi regime in exile, largely in the Soviet Union, was appointed to lead a new party commission "to draft measures for the ideological reeducation of the German people in an anti-fascist, democratic spirit and to formulate specific tasks that will be assigned to literature, radio, film, and theater."[15] This commission signaled the government's intent for culture to play a large role in its anti-fascist re-education project, leading the way for the development of a centralized program with carefully circumscribed parameters.

Like *Affaire Blum*, East German cultural policy cast Nazi fascism—and with it, the Antisemite—primarily in economic terms, setting up the GDR's rejection of capitalism as a radical break with Germany's fascist past. Opposing antisemitism was an important element of this cultural project, but it was rarely foregrounded as a specific theme, and the power to determine when and how to use it was guarded carefully.[16] On the one

ACCUSED AS JEWS   135

hand, in East Germany, as in West Germany and Austria, the Holocaust had rendered explicit antisemitism taboo—though unlike their West German counterparts, government officials in East Germany felt no pressure to use their opposition to it to prove their moral regeneration to the Western powers. In the early years of transition, focusing too explicitly on Nazi persecution of Jews worked against the East German goal of creating widespread outrage against fascism, since that goal required convincing people that the Nazis had harmed *all* Germans.[17]

Accordingly, though early GDR film and literature were very interested in the suffering of German civilians in the Nazi era, it rarely foregrounded Jewish topics or the Holocaust.[18] In many ways, this omission mirrored the West's approach to the recent past, which was to maintain that all Germans and "true" German culture had suffered at the hands of the Nazis. The twist in the East was to subsume Nazi persecution of Jews under a broader class war. Shaping the Antisemite as a symbol of capitalist oppression enabled East Germany to evoke—and by extension claim to embody—an ideal Germany that had no antisemitism, in contrast to the capitalist society of the West (Germany) that fostered it. But it also allowed them to continue to evoke negative stereotypes about Jews as powerful narrative devices to satisfy changing political aims.[19]

Party leaders may have wanted the SED to appear unified and monolithic in these goals, but reality suggests that life for artists in the Eastern zone was more complicated, particularly in the new state's early years.[20] Writers once persecuted as Jews who now sought to rebuild their careers in the GDR faced particular struggles as they navigated the tension between coming to terms with Nazi violence against Jews and supporting the new image of the East German state. The SED held that, having suffered under the Nazis, its members bore no legal or moral responsibility for Nazi crimes, which became an important foundation for East German state mythology that in turn was threatened by the very suggestion that Jews had suffered more.[21] In this context, opposition to antisemitism worked only when it was aimed at creating an image of West Germany as the cesspool of former Nazis, Nazi ideology, and capitalism.

The challenges for those who critically engaged antisemitism in the increasingly authoritarian environment of East Germany are evident in the early postwar texts of Anna Seghers and Victor Klemperer, who both joined Becher's commission. While both are recognized today as important writers,

136 THE POSTWAR ANTISEMITE

their reputations during their own lifetimes differed profoundly. Seghers was perhaps the most important German woman writer of the twentieth century, celebrated during her life with myriad prizes and awards.[22] Although Klemperer had a successful postwar career as a scholar, his prominence came later, through his meticulous, engaging diaries, which were first published in 1995. Seghers's and Klemperer's early postwar letters, diary entries, and published texts not only register their concerns about the widespread use of antisemitic stereotypes and the harm it caused, but also reflect their own occasional use of these stereotypes in their writing. They both shared a desire to engage critically with postwar antisemitism as manifested in the supposedly antisemitism-free East Germany, and both writers' attempts to do so were hampered by state officials. At the same time, this context revealed the pervasive structure of Jewish difference and its effects on their own lives and works, as the nascent East German state asserted its authority to shape the Antisemite and instrumentalize the terms of Jewish difference.

It might seem absurd to ascribe antisemitism to a government that not only claimed opposition to antisemitism as its creed but appointed Jews, former Jews, and their allies to positions of power. In fact, a number of Jews occupied leadership roles in East Germany as well as other communist states in Eastern Europe. However, the mere presence of these individuals in these governments did little to diminish the power and persistence of the deep-seated ordering system of Jewish difference that continued to operate in European culture after the Holocaust. Because of its deeply rooted presence, Jews in leadership roles were aware that their empowerment was conditional: they, too, remained vulnerable as potential targets of antisemitism. To navigate these circumstances, some Jews even preemptively targeted other Jews or ascribed antisemitism to others, including other Jews, as a political maneuver that sometimes led to dire consequences. This phenomenon reflects how the authority to determine the Antisemite played out under communist regimes.[23]

As a condition of their career successes, including their leadership positions on the cultural council, Seghers and Klemperer had to uphold a fantasy of a communist East German society that was free of Antisemites and was wholly welcoming to Jews and former Jews. Ironically, those instances in which they were accused of perpetuating antisemitism brought the power to define the Antisemite into bold relief, showing not only how the state asserted this power, but also the extent to which this authority could be used to mask its own complicity in its terms.

What's in a Name?

Born Netty Reitling into an Orthodox Jewish family in Mainz in 1900, Anna Seghers became interested in existential Christianity and Catholic culture years before she and her husband, László Radványi, left the Jewish community in 1932. Although she eventually became a committed communist, her writings reveal her continued respect for and interest in religion, both Judaism and Christianity. She met Radványi in the early 1920s, while studying art history and sinology at the Heidelberg University, where she completed a dissertation on "Jews and Jewry in the Works of Rembrandt." The topic reflected her early exposure to the art world through her father, a dealer in art and antiquities with his own store in Mainz, as well as her interest in representations of Jews, a theme she continued to explore in some of her fiction. Still, her early efforts to distance herself from her family's Jewish roots were undeniable, and her reluctance, even defensiveness, in response to biographical inquiries is well-documented. Although she, her husband, and their children survived the Nazi era in exile, her mother and aunt were murdered in the Holocaust, which added another layer of complexity to her engagement with postwar representations of Jews and Antisemites.

Although Seghers never wrote an autobiography, she invited readers to speculate on autobiographical elements in her work, noting that "the most important parts [of my life] are contained in my books."[24] She published her first work of fiction the same year she completed her dissertation on Jews and Rembrandt, using a pseudonym that allowed her to stylize herself as the descendant of a Protestant minister. The story, titled "Die Toten auf der Insel Djal. Eine Sage aus dem Holländischen: Nacherzählt von Antje Seghers" (The dead on the island of Djal. A legend from the Dutch retold by Antje Seghers), appeared in a special Christmas issue of the *Frankfurter Zeitung und Handelsblatt* in 1924.

Later, she claimed that she wanted to use the Dutch-sounding name Antje as a subtle way to attract attention: "I found this way of making myself known to my friends—but not directly. This name is so unusual that it was bound to attract attention when it suddenly appeared over a story in the newspaper. On the other hand, I could hide behind it."[25] This theme of masking while indirectly addressing her own self-identification, at once hiding her origins but making herself legible to those who knew her, reappeared in her fiction throughout her career. It undergirds the complicated and at times contradictory ways that her writing, both in exile and after the war, engages Jewish

138 THE POSTWAR ANTISEMITE

difference, ranging from the erasure of Jewishness to the reinforcement of negative stereotypes.

Beginning in 1928, Seghers published under the name Anna Seghers, which seems at least in part to have been an effort to mask her Jewishness, as she explained in an interview in 1973:

> I printed my first pieces under a pseudonym; my current name is a pseudonym, at first nobody knew who was behind it. Sometimes I would also casually walk around manuscripts to see the reactions. I was by no means sure of myself. At that time, I was good friends with a sinologist, whose judgment was important to me. He also brought me into contact with young people from other countries, with students who were unable to complete their studies in their home countries because of their political views, or who had immigrated with their parents.[26]

While she actively avoided stating the fact that she would have been recognized as a Jew if she published under her own name, her concern about "judgment" and her apparent identification with other students affected by prejudice surface the specter of antisemitism. In the same interview, she spoke highly of her parents, noting that she got along better with her father than her mother, though she also underscored how desperate she was to get away from her confining middle-class home.[27]

Seghers and Radványi, a Hungarian Jew and communist who had fled the Horthy regime, had two children together. In 1928, Seghers received the prestigious Kleist Prize for German literature and joined the Communist Party. After she was arrested in February 1933, following the burning of the Reichstag, she and the children fled Germany for France via Switzerland, where they waited for Radványi to join them. The family remained in Paris, where Seghers became deeply involved in engaging international writers and intellectuals in anti-fascist organizing efforts. After her husband's arrest and imprisonment in a concentration camp in France, she fled with their children to the south of France. In 1941, they sailed to New York, where they were denied entry, and ended up in Mexico, where they remained for the rest of the war. There, Seghers continued to write, participated in anti-fascist activities, and joined what became known as the Merker group after its leader, Communist Paul Merker.

Born in 1894 in Saxony, Merker served as a soldier during the First World War. He became a member of the Communist Party in 1920 and a leader

ACCUSED AS JEWS   139

of its Politburo's Central Committee in 1927, then spent the 1930s and early 1940s supporting the Communist Party and resisting the Nazis in exile (aside from a brief stint with the Communist underground in Berlin in 1934), in the United States, Leningrad, Paris, Vichy internment camps near Vernet and Marseilles, and Mexico, where he finally ended up in 1942. There, Merker worked closely with Jews (or those like Seghers who were targeted as Jews), including Egon Erwin Kisch, Alexander Abusch, Bruno Frei, Leo Zuckermann, Leo Katz, and Otto Katz.[28] The Merker group was intensely engaged with news about the murder of Jews in Europe, which was a topic of nearly every edition of the monthly party newspapers, *Freies Deutschland* and *Demokratische Post*, and the subject of two 1944 books by members. Between her involvement with the group and the stream of newspaper reports about mass executions of Jews in Minsk, Babi Yar, and Odessa, and deportations to the east from Paris, Vienna, and other cities, it is clear that Anna Seghers was well aware of the events in Europe while she was writing in Mexico.[29]

Seghers wrote and published the work for which she became famous, *Das siebte Kreuz* (*The Seventh Cross*), in exile in 1938–1939. This story about German political prisoners escaping a concentration camp was published in English translation in 1942.[30] In 1944, it became a successful film directed by a fellow Jewish exile, Fred Zinnemann, whose parents were killed by the Nazis.[31] While *Das siebte Kreuz* was explicitly anti-Nazi and anti-fascist, it barely engaged the plight of Jewish victims and altogether avoided the complicity of individual Germans with the Nazi regime. This novel and other texts by Seghers mirror later postwar works by Jews and non-Jews alike that deliberately chose, for political reasons, not to single out Jewish victims. Seghers's commitment to communism and idealization of Germans help explain this omission, as well as her focus on more universal themes, such as how ordinary people might resist powerful and fearful pressures. But learning about the murder of Jews like her mother and other friends and relatives at the hands of the Nazis in the mid-1940s, as well as her own experiences in exile, led to a shift in subsequent novels, such as *The Dead Stay Young* (1949), in which she does directly address how Germans chose to accept or resist the Nazis, and in which she also engages Jewish difference—both implicitly and explicitly.[32]

Meanwhile, Merker was beginning to make the argument that antisemitism might be more widespread in German society than most people wanted to believe. In opposition to generations of German-speaking socialist theorists

140 THE POSTWAR ANTISEMITE

who believed that antisemitism was not important and would disappear on its own, Merker suggested that it was not limited to a particular political class, but rather included all those who did not actively oppose it.[33] When Merker returned to East Germany after the war, he became a lone non-Jewish voice speaking out explicitly against antisemitism and for the reintegration of Jews into German society, including restitution of their property and compensation.[34] He urged Seghers to return to the Soviet zone and, at least at first, advocated for her when other SED functionaries considered her too international, since her early postwar works had as much to do with France as with Germany.

Though her husband remained in Mexico City, where he was a professor at the National University, Seghers returned to Berlin in 1947. She thrived there as a writer and served as president of the Kulturbund, and in 1947 she received the Büchner Prize, Germany's top literary award. Even so, she never felt entirely comfortable back in Germany. Appalled at the miserable state of intellectual, political, and spiritual life she found upon her return, Seghers became disillusioned with her own party—and her party with her. The explicit antisemitism surrounding the Slánsky trial in Czechoslovakia in 1952 provided added context for SED functionaries—including Jews such as Alexander Abusch—to question her loyalty to the party when she was in exile in Paris. They pushed her off the board of the Kulturbund, and Abusch accused her of being an enemy of Germany for acting too French and only speaking French, thereby evoking a long-standing antisemitic trope in German-speaking Europe of casting Jewish women as "too French" to signal their disloyalty.[35]

Seghers's disappointment over political and cultural developments in Germany led her to idealize the Soviet Union and the struggle for world peace. She envisioned herself an "international communist," and her novels promoted solidarity with the class struggle in all countries. Contrary to the general impression that it would be especially difficult to rehabilitate former members of the Hitler Youth, Seghers believed that young Germans could be transformed. And yet, there remained a persistent obliqueness around antisemitism in her work. To be sure, to some extent Seghers was following the party line by downplaying its persistence among East Germans. On the other hand, the fact that the Antisemite of her work in exile is drawn much more sharply suggests that her later depictions were influenced as much by personal experience as they were by pressure from above. The result, in her

ACCUSED AS JEWS 141

early postwar texts, is at once a complicated, though not complete, disavowal of the Antisemite and its (actively repressed) return, as if her convictions largely and finally, but not always, triumphed over her emotions.

Antisemites in Exile

Seghers engaged differently with the figure of the Antisemite over time. While in exile in 1943, she wrote a work that explicitly addresses German antisemitism: her autobiographical short story "Der Ausflug der toten Mädchen" (The excursion of the dead girls).[36] In it, her depiction of antisemitism is raw: she blames the hatred of Jews on the fascists who have corrupted the protagonist's school friend Marianne, who has no problem sitting on a bench with her Jewish teacher until the Nazis come to power. Marianne later marries a high-ranking Nazi official. Another teacher hangs a swastika flag in his living room window because he fears for his job. But the story also gives equal weight to the Nazis' non-Jewish victims, such as the protagonist's best friend Leni, whom the Gestapo beats when she refuses to provide them with information about her husband, and who later starves to death in a concentration camp. Seghers's anger toward the Nazis and the girls who collaborate with them is expressed as revenge and a desire for punishment, palpable from the graphic descriptions of their violent deaths.[37] The story associates antisemitism with the bad German, who is corrupted by the Nazis. Meanwhile, it keeps the good German free of its taint by making her the victim.

It is characteristic of Seghers's indirectness that even in an autobiographical story, she describes Leni, rather than the narrator, as "much too naïve to sense that the destinies of the boys and girls make up the destiny of a nation, the destiny of a people, so that sooner or later the sorrow or the joy of her school friend could cast a shadow or shine upon her."[38] The hope—or fantasy—that there are Germans who can exist outside the framework of Jewish difference is expressed through Leni, the non-Jew, whom Marianne despises and denounces.[39] While the narrator's mother (like Seghers's mother) suffers a "cruel, agonizing end in a remote village whither she had been banished by Hitler," it is clearly important to Seghers to place non-Jewish Germans alongside Jews as Nazi victims.[40] This equation allows the story to provide a nuanced description of the diverse forces that led people to

142 THE POSTWAR ANTISEMITE

Nazism while bracketing the role of antisemitism, which in turn creates the space for the idea that the Antisemite victimizes all Germans, regardless of whether they are Jewish.

Externalizing antisemitism to a narrow subset of Germans became more difficult when Seghers came face to face with them upon her return to Berlin in 1947. In a letter she wrote three weeks after her return, she described her need to address both the murder of Germany's Jews and how Germans participated in these crimes—and the difficulties she faced in doing so.[41] Amid the general alienation she felt back in Berlin, Seghers felt uneasy that she could no longer gauge the politics, honesty, or honor of the Germans she encountered. She used her landlord, a former army officer who was disgruntled about the Allied occupation, as her exemplar:

> For example, I had always believed that I knew exactly what a Nazi is, what a thief is, what an honest man is. But that was just my imagination. For example, my landlord. Is he a Nazi? Is he a democrat? Is he a thief? Is he honest? I still don't know. I only know that the four allies meet at least one of his needs: to bend often in all four directions. Otherwise, understandably, he does not like the disorder of the occupation. . . . "In my unit," he says, "there was always better order."[42]

She goes on to recount an exchange with the landlord, in which she pressed him on his annoyance with the occupation. However, in one of the frequent characteristics of her style, her prose segues so fluidly from one speaker and comment to the next that she ultimately ends up aligning with the landlord she seems to be challenging:

> Was there not a certain difference between the occupation of Amsterdam and Berlin? The famous Dutch livestock was destroyed for generations. I shyly ask whether it is true that the Dutch livestock has been destroyed for generations. —That is probably true. You'd need cattle at home. You would need cattle to feed troops. This prevents private raids and looting. —After all, for one reason or another there is a difference between the occupation of Amsterdam and that of Berlin. —I am prepared for a shrug of the shoulders, for mocking answers, for Nazi arguments, for "war is war" or the like. —But the answer is much stranger: So you mean, these are two different occupations? The thought has never crossed my mind. I have to think about that first.[43]

ACCUSED AS JEWS   143

The way Seghers leans in on slaughtered cattle as the difference between the occupations of Amsterdam and Berlin suggests that she may be circling around the topic of slaughtered Jews, including perhaps the ones wiped out by the landlord's occupying unit. But where she is oblique, he is oblivious: rather than try to escape responsibility, as she expects, the very idea that there might be a difference between the German occupation of Holland and the Allied occupation of Germany startles him. Jews are simply elided from his equation, not a part of the conversation he is having. And yet they are also barely present in the conversation she is having.

Seghers intended "Das wirkliche Blau" (The real blue), another story she wrote in Mexico (though it was not published until 1967), to focus on the victims of Nazi gas chambers. However, by referencing murder in the gas chambers only vaguely, she allows German participation in the Nazi genocide to slip away from the narrative. The story centers on a Mexican ceramicist who decorates his pots with a blue dye imported from Germany. When the Nazis come to power, halting the import of the dye, he sets off on an arduous journey to find the correct color in Mexico. Various well-meaning people help him along the way with food and advice, until he finally reaches his destination, where he obtains the desired dye and then returns home to his family. Seghers later claimed that she meant readers to associate the blue dye from Germany with the paint company that manufactured poison gas:

the narrative was interpreted completely one-sidedly and therefore incorrectly by some. The story is based on an impulse from earlier times. I don't know whether there are any real connections between the blue poison from the Hoechst paintworks, which the Nazis used to destroy people, and their blue dye, which had to be fetched from Germany for the Mexican potters. In my imagination, however, there were connections, and in reality it is also the case that these giant corporations always have a very "round" program that they earn money from: they produce funds to save lives, medicines, and they also provide funds here to destroy life, poison. It was not at all about presenting a technical or scientific fact, it was also not important to me to show a real incident, I rather wanted to get the readers' imagination moving; I don't just want to depict something out of reality, I want people to form an image of reality.[44]

By referring so obliquely to the murder of Jews in the Holocaust and the connection she imagines between the blue dye and the blue poison used by

144 THE POSTWAR ANTISEMITE

the Nazis, Seghers loses control of how her narrative is read, making it impossible for her readers to "form an image of reality" in the way she wants them to.

In the postwar era, Seghers aimed to combat antisemitism through her writing, because she believed in the transformative potential of stories. This commitment to the political potential of narrative was already evident in *Transit* (1944), a novel set in Marseilles in 1940.[45] Like her earlier texts, the novel addresses the choices of Germans under the Nazis while avoiding a direct reference to Jews even as it evokes their presence. An unnamed young German who has been freed from a Nazi concentration camp waits in Marseilles for passage to a safer destination. As he waits, he reads the manuscript of a German writer named Weidel who has just committed suicide. He is so transformed by the story that he ends up taking on the name of the writer. The reader learns almost nothing about the manuscript, except that its words overcome, nourish, and even merge with the protagonist—and are antithetical to the Nazis:

> And out of sheer boredom I began to read. I read on and on. I was spellbound, maybe because I'd never before read a book to the end. But no, that couldn't be the reason . . . I didn't know anything about writing. It wasn't my world. Yet I think the man who'd written this was an expert in his art. . . . I forgot my deadly boredom. And if I'd had fatal wounds I would have forgotten them, too while I was absorbed in reading. And as I read line after line, I also felt that this was my own language, my other tongue, and it flowed into me like milk into a baby. It didn't rasp and grate like the language that came from the throats of the Nazis, their murderous commands and objectionable insistence on obedience, their disgusting boasts. —*This* was serious, calm, and still.[46]

Refusing to share details of the story, because "I'd better not bore you with that," the protagonist instead describes how the story has "crazy characters, really mixed-up people; almost all of them got involved in bad, devious things, even those who tried to resist." But the author's language cleanses them: "They all became clear and pure, as if they had done their penance, as if they had already passed through a little purgatory, the small fire that was the dead man's brain." That this language is "my own language, my other tongue," and that it is most emphatically not "like the language that came

ACCUSED AS JEWS 145

from the throats of the Nazis ... murderous ... objectionable ... disgusting," registers its cleansing effects on him too. He comes upon words that make him feel he is back in his childhood among his family, words he has forgotten "because I never again felt the emotion I needed to express them." Boredom banished, "how avidly I read it!"[47] In the protagonist's transformative experience of reading, Seghers manages to explicitly articulate her pedagogical goals, even directly mentioning the Nazis whose effects she eventually sought to undo.

Whereas Weidel's manuscript transforms the non-Jewish protagonist, *Transit* elides the fact that Ernst Weiss, the model for Weidel, was indeed a Jew. Born in 1882 in Brno, Weiss trained as a doctor and was a good friend of Kafka. He gave up his medical career in 1920, moved to Berlin, and turned to writing. After 1934, he lived in exile in Paris, where he wrote his last novel, *The Eyewitness* (1938), which is about a young German veteran of the First World War, A. H. (clearly intended to be Hitler), who is sent to a military hospital because he is suffering from hysterical blindness. Seghers was acquainted with Weiss in Paris, where he committed suicide in 1940. While there is no definitive evidence that she read *The Eyewitness*, the fact that the protagonist of *Transit* notes that there are other "evil" characters in the story suggests she may have been aware of Weiss's references to Hitler. And the novel's oblique references are indeed typical of the distance with which Seghers often approaches her portrayal of Nazis and their crimes. The German protagonist in *Transit* gains a name only when he takes on the persona of the writer—who can be construed to be Jewish but is not named as such. Jewish difference thus haunts *Transit*, a story about German choices under the Nazis, but its ghost is just strong enough to let Seghers continue to avoid the topic of the Antisemite—and not strong enough to bring actual Jews into her narrative.

These early texts were important precursors for stories she wrote a few years later that explicitly address the transformation of Nazis into East Germans, a topic that necessarily engaged Seghers's own self-identification as a Jewish-born German victim of Nazi persecution whose own mother had been murdered in the Holocaust, even though she does not make her position explicit. She also does not engage explicitly with the Antisemite in these "transformation texts," which may have been a way to avoid digging too deeply into her own pain but certainly contributed significantly to her status with party leaders.[48]

146 THE POSTWAR ANTISEMITE

Writing the Perpetrator

While the Antisemite and the Jew are not entirely absent from the texts Seghers wrote to help transform former Nazis into socialists, they both gradually disappear from her postwar narratives. It was clear that former Nazis in East Germany had to be re-educated, which is to say transformed, before they could be incorporated into the GDR socialist ranks. Less clear, however, was how that was to happen and what role explicit opposition to antisemitism should play in the process. If artists creating culture in the new German state wanted to decry antisemitism, they had to do so extremely carefully, even lightly, particularly if, like Seghers, they had been persecuted as Jews. If they pushed too hard, or in the wrong time and place, they could be criticized for being vengeful. Denouncing a high-ranking Nazi in West Germany could be useful, but accusing a typical East German *Mitläufer* (follower) of antisemitism was trickier, for it could disrupt the smooth transformation of former Nazis into good, socialist citizens and risk privileging Jews over other victims. Seghers represented the Antisemite in these texts as misguided but redeemable, helping us see how antisemitism figured in her vision of postwar East Germans' transformation and what happened when she challenged the boundaries of that vision.

Seghers actually began writing about the foundations of this transformation while she was in exile. Her story "Ein Mensch wird Nazi" (A person becomes a Nazi) appeared in *Freies Deutschland* in 1942. At the beginning of the story, a former SS member named Fritz Müller is about to be brought to justice. The story recounts his childhood and the origins of his antisemitism. At school, a new teacher prefers two boys who are, respectively, the sons of a political "agitator" and a "Schneiderjüdchen" (little Jewish tailor). However, another teacher likes him because he is blond, blue-eyed, a good swimmer, and his father was in the war. Antisemitism begins to imprint upon him: "Because he slept with his brother in one bed, he thought he understood why the German people needed space. Because he disliked the Jewish tailor, he thought he understood why it was the Jews' fault that he was never full."[49] When he attends a Nazi meeting, he learns that Jews and Freemasons are responsible for the misery wrought by the Treaty of Versailles and that Bolshevism is stealing people's souls. There, he is seduced by promises of nice clothes and free parties, and the lessons about hating Jews build on the foundation constructed by his father and school. But even as he learns to hate Jews, he is also taught to hate Russians, which the story recounts in even

ACCUSED AS JEWS   147

more detail, suggesting that his early hatred of Jews is merely a steppingstone to hatred of Russians. As in so many of her stories, Seghers tempers hatred of Jews with equal if not greater hatred of non-Jews, laying groundwork for the postwar redefinition of the Antisemite.

"The End," written between 1944 and 1945, contains a more explicit representation of the Antisemite in the person of Zillich, a former SS concentration camp guard. The narrative begins from the perspective of Volpert, a former concentration camp prisoner who was tortured by Zillich. It recounts Zillich's brutality, in particular toward Jewish prisoners, whom he kicks in the back and forces to lick dirty staircases, though he is brutal to non-Jewish prisoners as well. It is surely no accident that Volpert is never named as Jewish, though he is in the same boat as the Jews, and that Zillich was the name of a well-known, successful, and openly antisemitic author. As the story shifts to Zillich, the reader also learns that he was born a peasant and was bullied as a boy whose ears stick out, a feature that still bothers him as an adult.

After the war, Zillich longs to be back in command but fears that his former prisoners will be out for revenge. He wanders aimlessly from place to place, worried about being caught and held to account, unable to stay at home or find a new home. At one point, he meets a man who wears a yellow aster in his buttonhole and whistles songs, including the antisemitic "Jewish Blood," which appears to be his way of trying to glean Zillich's political leanings: "He's an odd bird, the little man thought. I'll find out soon enough which tune he'll hop to" (343). When Zillich finally makes a derogatory comment about Jews, the little man thinks, "Finally, now I've got you." When Zillich asks the man for his name, he replies: "Me? I'm Peter Nobody"[50] (344). Seghers's pseudonym and the nameless protagonist's adoption of the writer's name in *Transit* suggest that she used names as important markers of Jewishness and non-Jewishness. With the name Nobody, presumably an allusion to *The Odyssey*, Seghers points to the difficulty—and danger—of identifying people as Jews or Nazis in the postwar context.

The character of Zillich also appears in two earlier Seghers novels, *Der Kopflohn* (The bounty, 1932) and *Das siebte Kreuz*, suggesting that Seghers is trying to work out "what kind of person, in flesh and blood, would embody fascism."[51] In *Der Kopflohn*, Zillich is a leader of the local SA (Storm Troopers) and one of several villagers who denounce a young communist worker, Johannes Schulz, after a young Nazi sympathizer betrays him. Zillich seduces villagers living in misery with his demagoguery and willingness to

148 THE POSTWAR ANTISEMITE

use violence to liberate the community.[52] While Seghers hardly idealizes life in the provinces, she clearly aims to elicit sympathy for rural Germans caught up in Nazism. While the novel has a Jewish character, Naphtel, he does not denounce Schulz and has no connection to Zillich. Although the story offers no evidence that Zillich actually is an Antisemite, his brutality and willingness to use violence subtly introduce the notion of the Antisemite into the text. Zillich is one of several Nazis in *Das siebte Kreuz*, where he again does not interact with Jewish characters (though the novel includes a Jewish doctor), and he is not described as an Antisemite. The revelation that, as a rural peasant from Wertheim am Main, "he, too, had got up early in the morning and sweated mightily, though in vain, for he had lost his tiny farm at a forced sale" further tempers his brutality. Seghers uses sympathetic, reasonable excuses such as economic hardship both to show how people like Zillich became Nazis and to suggest that antisemitism is a consequence of difficult life circumstances rather than socially constructed stereotypes.

It is important to understand how Seghers used the Antisemite to shape her portrayals of the fascist and the anti-fascist. For example, Zillich's story indeed signals the terrifying normalcy of powerful fascists, who look like ordinary people.[53] Their unremarkableness is actually germane to the issue of Jews and their assimilation into German society, a topic that Jewish writers had already been addressing for decades. One of main facets of modern antisemitism was the idea that Jews were evil, all-powerful, and all-knowing, yet they blended in and could not be recognized—which made them all the more dangerous. On one hand, Jews were terribly anxious about being able to blend in, and indeed, under the Nazis, to do so was an important survival strategy. On the other hand, the idea that Jews represented a danger because they could not be recognized was a holdover from before the Nazis gained power. Seghers's story suggests that former Nazis join Jews in their similar efforts to survive after the war by blending in. But by depicting the fate of the Nazi in terms that parallel the historical struggle of the Jew, Seghers again reinforces a structure that represses the Jewish experience of suffering. Ultimately in these stories, "lack of humanity" defines the fascist, not antisemitism, which is hardly present at all.[54]

In the story, Zillich does not refer to his victims as Jews, leaving that designation to the readers' imaginations, prompted by the little man Peter Nobody: "Zillich reckoned how many he had strung up, then cut down, then strung up again. He'd gotten a kick out of doing that, especially in the Piaski camp. He said, 'Strange, isn't it, that some are still around.' 'Why?' countered the little man. 'When the ark opened up after the Deluge, it was a Jew who jumped right out."[55] The semi-nameless Peter Nobody—who may or may not be Jewish—is the only one who names those killed at Piaski, the camp where Seghers's mother was murdered, as Jews. This suggests that although Nobody and Zillich share the same postwar dilemma of needing to hide their identities as Jews/Nazis, there is still a distinction between them: it is Nobody alone who recognizes, or cares, that those killed in the camps were Jews

At one point, Zillich equates Jews with communists:

He of all people knew best that no one escapes a manhunt in a big city. They'd always managed to find even the wiliest Jews, the stealthiest Reds. They'd greased the pot with money whenever a denouncer hesitated. And if money didn't work, they used fear, for nobody on this earth wants to die, especially for a total stranger, even for one of his beloved brethren.[56]

With Zillich now on the run, putting Jews in the same category as other targets makes it easier for the reader to imagine him as akin to the Jews he formerly targeted. At one point, Zillich explicitly compares himself to a Jew: "Zillich imagined he could keep tramping around up here forever—restless and hungry, undisturbed and undetected like the Wandering Jew." But within a few lines, he fantasizes about having someone to abuse, as if he needs to refute this comparison by reminding himself—and his reader—of his previous life: "He yearned for a fierce opposition that resisted even when it was kicked, trampled, and stomped on, till it was dripping with blood and writhed, screamed, and whimpered—instead of yielding gently and humbly like grass under a rake."[57] In many ways, this story is about Zillich trying to come to terms with his otherness in the new postwar world. And like so many Jews, including Seghers's friend, author Ernst Weiss, his efforts fail, and he commits suicide at the end of the story. Seghers's refusal to definitively identify Volpert and Peter Nobody as Jews may be a way to subvert inevitable stereotypes, but in contrast to these more ambiguous characterizations of Jews, this story clearly defines the Antisemite as the brutal irredeemable Nazi who, like the Jews, no longer fits in postwar Germany.

Zillich's reflections on vengeance and evil bring up the limits of vengeance and the nature of evil, which were important topics for Seghers and Victor Klemperer: "Yet, even if they were to find him tomorrow, the evil of which Zillich was simply an outgrowth still wouldn't be eliminated, the frost wouldn't disappear. Just as new growth damaged by a freeze won't bloom

150   THE POSTWAR ANTISEMITE

again, the grief in his heart wouldn't be stilled, he wouldn't be any happier."
Volpert knows that his persecution means that he cannot feel joy again, for
"his heart had frosted over" (a phrasing that evokes Zillich's "freeze," once
again aligning the persecuted and the persecutor). Hanisch expresses his
skepticism through sarcasm:

> "Oh sure, much happier," said Hänisch, with whom he now and then spent
> the night in a rail car on the embankment. "Of course, you'll be glad when
> that scoundrel gets hanged, preferably feet first. Who isn't glad to be rid
> of a rat. Evil as such you won't be rid of this way, you can't get rid of Satan
> himself. You'd first have to get rid of this whole ugly world altogether. I'd
> certainly be plenty glad once they had Zillich by the scruff of the neck."[58]

Seghers often uses role reversal to indirectly criticize vengeance and score-
settling without explicitly pointing out the limits of using violence to exact
revenge. In pushing readers to think for themselves about the moral stakes
of revenge, she creates sympathetic portrayals of characters who seek vengeance, as well as their targets. Thoughtful as it may be, this narrative strategy
nevertheless elides the deep-seated antisemitism in German culture that is at
the root of so much of the persecution that generates specific calls for vengeance. If Zillich represents so many Germans, then what form should justice
take? The story ends with his suicide. Perhaps this early story represents
her grappling with the idea that the Nazi cannot be transformed, before
she ultimately engages the East German project of transforming Nazis into
anti-fascists.

The Man and His Name

For Seghers to return to Germany in 1947, she had to repress the
contradictions between the politics of the place where she now lived and her
personal history. As time went on, her persona as a motherly educator of the
German people depended on a "willingness to repress, on her willingness not
to express any anti-German ressentiments, as Christa Wolf so admiringly—
and, one might add, so naïvely—observed."[59] Many have criticized Seghers
for not adequately addressing German complicity in the Nazi regime. Her
contemporary Greta Kuckhoff, who pleaded for a commemoration of

ACCUSED AS JEWS   151

Jewish Holocaust victims in the GDR, felt that *The Seventh Cross* did not go far enough in showing that far too few Germans had taken part in the resistance—and if more Germans had resisted, there would have been fewer victims: "Don't evade the issue! You don't need to feel sorry, sympathy is evasion. It is soothing, it allows one to speak an *ego te absolvo* over the evil deeds one did oneself or at least allowed to happen, an absolution through which nothing is basically changed."[60]

However, constructing an Antisemite in line with the political demands of the East German state allowed Seghers to find a place for herself in her new "old country" according to her own self-understanding. The novella *Der Mann und sein Name* (The man and his name, 1952), set in the East Germany of its time, tells the story of a former SS member named Walter Retzlow who transforms himself into a good socialist German by taking on a dead man's identity.[61] Seghers wrote it and "Die Rückkehr" (The return) after her own postwar return to Germany, when she turned her fictional attention to people who had remained there throughout the war years under the Nazis. Though *Der Mann und sein Name* is the ultimate "fake it 'till you make it" story, a disavowal of antisemitism does not play a role in Retzlow's transformation; indeed, there is only one brief mention of his hatred of Jews as a motivating force for his wartime behavior. In some ways this is not surprising, given the party's desire to downplay antisemitism in East Germany. But the absence of the Antisemite in this transformation is still notable, for it is the primary way that Seghers manages the problem of complicity in postwar East Germany—through disavowing or ignoring antisemitism as an ongoing presence.

The story takes place between 1948 and 1950, during the period in which the Soviet occupied territory became the new state of East Germany. Retzlow, who oppressed anti-Nazi fighters in a Nazi concentration camp, is mistaken for Heinz Brenner, an anti-fascist resistance fighter who has been killed, which Retzlow knows. Seizing the opportunity to shed his burdensome Nazi past, Retzlow takes on the mistaken identity of the anti-fascist as his own. This fortuitous set of circumstances echoes the events of *Transit*, where the anti-fascist takes on the identity of the Jew. Over time, Retzlow as Brenner actually becomes a committed communist. His slowly developing engagement with work and his pride in the recognition he receives as a locksmith lead to real interest and increasing immersion in socialist ideology.[62] But his relationships to his work colleagues and his girlfriend Katharina are

152   THE POSTWAR ANTISEMITE

eventually overshadowed by his *Existenzlüge* (existential lie), which haunts him and continues to bring him into contact with his old life. Only when he thwarts an act of sabotage by a former Nazi colleague does he feel that he has truly become a new person. His friends start to trust him because he is a good worker, not just because they think he is Heinz Brenner. At the end of the story, his deception and true identity are revealed, and he must start anew, stripped of the name under which he hid. And yet all is not lost, for his friends and Katharina begin to trust him again, and the novella ends en route to a possible happy ending, with the caveat that "it won't be easy."

In November 1950, Seghers wrote to Erich Wendt at Aufbau Verlag and told him that she was working on a "big novel or small book" that would probably be called something like "The False Truth."[63] It was then renamed "Man without a Name," though she also referred to it as her "Questionnaire forger-novella" (a reference to the wartime activities questionnaire imposed by the Allied Forces) with a "risquant" theme[64] and "Novella with the Villain."[65] She also noted that "After all, this novella is my 'main social work'" and "a very important novella about Germany (the transformation of a person, etc.)."[66] Still, though she calls her protagonist a villain, the novella provides only a single brief glimpse of Retzlow's lingering antisemitism *after* he has been transformed into a socialist: he denigrates a man who has stolen tires and makes excuses for it, noting, "Such a degenerate steals from his people like a Jew."[67] Even this slight evidence of how antisemitic stereotypes linger seems to undermine the validity of Retzlow's transformation with the taint of the Antisemite.

Though this mention of explicit antisemitism is brief, Seghers received a letter from a Jewish reader in East Germany complaining that it fomented antisemitism. Seghers replied that she was offended by the letter writer's accusation and defensively noted that her own mother had been killed in a camp. However, she did concede that she had written the passage because she did not want to shy away from portraying things as they really were. Seghers clearly intended Retzlow to represent the ordinary Germans who ended up as Nazis, not the fanatics. Unlike her earlier works, "Das Ende," *Ausflug*, and *Die Toten bleiben jung*, which addressed personal guilt and responsibility for Nazi crimes, *Der Mann und seine Name* was not about a protagonist coming to terms with his role in genocide, but rather served as an appeal to readers to transform themselves and become good socialists.[68] The response of one reader decrying the implication of lingering antisemitism in East Germany shows just how precarious it was for her to reveal that.

An early version of *Der Mann und seine Name* appeared in the magazine *Friedenswacht* in February 1952. Seghers finished the book in March and published it in July.[69] However, a number of members of the *Schriftstellerverband* (Writers' Union) complained that the story was not sufficiently positive and did not provide a good example for readers. Seghers replied:

> What does positive mean? Above all, what has a positive effect, so it is justified to describe this person Retzlow in this way. . . . We are a little spoiled at reading. We are usually shown clearly in books what everyone does and must do, and what everyone does after all. From our consciousness and from our experiences, new possibilities arise for our imagination.[70]

While her references to "consciousness" and "imagination" evoke her reflections on her oblique approach to representation in "Das wirkliche Blau," given the goals of East German cultural policy that she now embraced, it should not be surprising that Anna Seghers was committed to pedagogical projects involving the transformation of Germans into good socialists and was willing to exclude the Antisemite from this discussion in order to achieve it. Her own position in East Germany was precarious, and she had to shape her narratives carefully.[71] But reading for the contours of the largely absent Antisemite reveals how it continued to shape her writing.

Victor Klemperer: German-Jewish Patriotism, Zionism, and the Antisemite

Like Anna Seghers, the scholar and diarist Victor Klemperer was horrified to be accused of antisemitism in 1948. "So at the moment I'm an Antisemite and have written an antisemitic book," he complained in a November 1948 letter to SED functionary, writer, and actor Inge von Wangenheim, waxing at once ironic and hyperbolic.[72] A few weeks earlier, he had bitterly remarked in his diary, "The Zion chapter is held to be impossible. . . . I am made out to be an anti-Semite, a pistol is held to my head."[73] Since the war, Klemperer's career had ascended as never before. The first edition of *LTI: Lingua Tertii Imperii*, his study of everyday life under the Nazis—which pointed out how authoritarianism crept into people's lives through language, often without them even realizing it—had been wildly successful. But on the eve of its

154 THE POSTWAR ANTISEMITE

second printing, Klemperer learned that one chapter in the book had been accused of promoting antisemitism. Given his background and experiences, this accusation seemed obscene.

Klemperer was born to a rabbi and his wife in 1881 and converted to Protestantism in 1903. He lost his university position before the war and was temporarily imprisoned by the Nazis, but he survived the war in Germany because he was married to a non-Jewish woman. Though he was on the verge of being deported in February 1945, the bombing of Dresden saved him. Though he no longer self-identified as a Jew, he frequently referenced antisemitism and Jews in his account of Nazi language, and he maintained close relationships with Jews, including his childhood friend, writer Julius Bab.

The first edition of *LTI* sailed smoothly through the editing process with SED party publisher Aufbau Verlag. Klemperer was thus blindsided when editor Erich Wendt and Jewish SED party leader Alexander Abusch informed him that he would have to cut the chapter titled "Zion" for the book's second printing. Party leadership had concerns about the potential antisemitic effects of the chapter, which compared Theodor Herzl to Adolf Hitler, among other things. Neither Wendt nor Abusch explicitly called the book itself antisemitic, however, nor did they accuse Klemperer of being an Antisemite, but they were not acting on their own initiative.

The party leader who was offended by the chapter and insisted it be cut was none other than SED functionary Paul Merker, who had many Jewish colleagues and great respect for the intellectual and political contributions of Jews to an array of issues and causes.[74] In "Hitler's Anti-Semitism and Us," an essay that appeared in *Freies Deutschland* in 1942, Merker decried the unprecedented Nazi crimes against Jews and connected the fight against antisemitism with the class war and the fight against imperialism and capitalism. Where most non-Jewish communists avoided the topic, Merker insisted that antisemitism was a central component of National Socialism and that fighting the persecution of Jews should play a major role in the fight against fascism. Like other communists, he blamed antisemitism on capitalism. However, he realized how easy it was to repeat antisemitic stereotypes when critiquing capitalism and thus stressed the importance of placing the blame on powerful "Aryan" monopolists like Krupp, Thyssen, and others, rather than on Jews. This essay, along with numerous other articles he wrote in exile, revealed his deep engagement with antisemitism and sympathy for Jews.

ACCUSED AS JEWS   155

Merker channeled his engagement into advocacy. He argued, for example, that Jewish property should be restored to its original owners and that antisemitism was widespread in German society and had to be actively opposed. Like some others, he went so far as to suggest that a Jewish homeland in Palestine could be a viable answer. He advocated for making antisemitism and racism state crimes, punishing those who murdered and persecuted Jews and enriched themselves with their property, and making the state pay for exiled Jews to return to Germany or compensating them if they chose not to.[75] Still, Merker never let go of his belief that Germany and Germans were redeemable, even in the face of widespread and persistent German antisemitism. Though he acknowledged that there had not been large-scale resistance against the Nazis, his trust in the "guten Kern unseres Volkes, in der deutschen Arbeiterklasse" (good core of our people, in the German working class) remained unwavering, for he shared the common view that successful communist anti-fascism would eradicate antisemitism.[76] Indeed, he irked the East German authorities precisely because he insisted that his support for Jews was an outgrowth of his communist beliefs, rather than his corruption by American imperialists and Jewish capitalists.[77]

When Merker returned to Germany in 1946, he joined the Party Committee, the Central secretariat, and the Politburo of the SED. In March 1948, he became a member of the provisional Volkskammer (legislature) of what would become the GDR, and he served as secretary of state for agriculture from 1949 to 1950. These positions of power gave him sufficient clout to complain about Klemperer to Wendt and insist that he take action. Wendt wrote to Klemperer to explain the issue on October 13, 1948:

Comrade Merker drew my attention to the Herzl affair. I will consult with some friends here so that we do not encounter unexpected objections later. I have read the whole chapter carefully and would like to say the following: factually everything may be correct, but a comparison of a leader of the nationalist Jewish movement with Hitler after all that Hitler has done to the Jews is, irrespective of the field in which the comparison is made, a very, very bad thing. Six million murdered Jews are an atrocity and a national misfortune beyond compare. Of course, as a Jew, you can feel freer in this regard, but you must not forget that the book is also read by non-Jews and former Nazis, and you must always imagine how it affects such people.[78]

156 THE POSTWAR ANTISEMITE

While Wendt acknowledges the factual accuracy of Klemperer's critique, he also points to the legitimacy of Merker's concerns. However, he had not objected to the chapter the first time around, and now he made it clear that Merker's objections were the impetus for the changes. Indeed, when Klemperer objected, Wendt confirmed that he did not share Merker's feelings and suggested that Klemperer be patient and wait for a change in leadership, after which they would be able to restore the chapter.

The debate about Klemperer's chapter reflects the emerging anti-Zionist position of East Germany and needs to be understood in the context of the long history of German Jews engaging antisemitic stereotypes as a survival strategy. Communist organizations were, for the most part, strongly opposed to all forms of Jewish nationalism—political, cultural, Zionist. But anti-Zionism based on the rejection of Jewish collective self-identification in the name of abstract universalism was not necessarily antisemitic—and in fact only became antisemitic when it allowed national self-determination for everyone but Jews.[79] Long before 1933, the argument that *German* Jews should not be Zionists was an important part of German-Jewish self-identification. The concept of Jewish nationalism was anathema to many German Jews who saw themselves as ardent patriots connected deeply and firmly to German culture (even after the war, some Jews in East and West Germany continued to feel this way). Some even compared Zionists to National Socialists. Julius Bab, another ardent German Jewish patriot and a friend of Klemperer, linked the two in an autobiographical, handwritten essay, dated around 1936: "I cannot understand what (beyond personal inconveniences) a Zionist actually has against a National Socialist in principle? *Basically nothing!*"[80] In a 1933 article, Adolf Bartels had argued that Jewish writers like Bab and Klemperer could not be German writers.[81] Bab believed that Zionist ideology similarly prevented Jews from being German, hence the vehemence of his comparison.

Klemperer's anti-Zionism must be understood in this German-Jewish context. Merker was certainly correct in pointing out the harms caused by comparing Herzl and Hitler after the Holocaust. But in doing so, he subverted Klemperer's use of it to engage his own self-understanding as a Jewish-born German victim of Nazi persecution. In the chapter, Klemperer concedes that Jews *outside* of East and West Germany, including in Austria, had every right to seek national self-determination.[82] In other words, Klemperer did not want to deny Jews the right to a homeland, but rather sought specifically

ACCUSED AS JEWS   157

to preserve an illusory German nationalism for himself and the other Jewish Germans who had been persecuted by the Nazis.

In a foundational article on antisemitism, Shulamit Volkov argues that in the nineteenth century, the abstraction of "Semitism" allowed non-Germans to use antisemitism as a symbolic way to express a range of fears based on modernity and difference. Antisemitism thus became, as she terms it, a "cultural code" that did not necessarily indicate hatred of actual Jews or support for violence against them. While Volkov's notion of antisemitism helps to explain how people could—and can—at once espouse antisemitic beliefs and claim to love Jews, it does not differentiate between the embrace of antisemitic views and the use of those views in a critical, ironic, or even playful way to assert social power. Negative stereotypes about Jews were the purview not only of so-called "Antisemites" but also sometimes of Jews themselves, who could use them to at once subtly capitalize on their disadvantaged situation *and* combat it.[83] Before the Holocaust, this use of antisemitism was an important way for Central European Jews to inscribe the terms of their inclusion in majority non-Jewish populations.[84] Such instances of reclaiming negative stereotypes are important to considering how antisemitism became employed in the construction of the East German state.

We can discern the use of antisemitism as an expression of power in Klemperer's "Zion" chapter, following the lines of claiming the authority to determine the Antisemite, but framed as a way for German Jewish victims of Nazi persecution to express themselves after the Holocaust. Despite the horrors that Central European Jews had experienced between 1933 and 1945, they had to contend with a general population that resented their perceived abandonment of the home front during the war and vengeful attitudes toward non-Jews afterward.

For example, after Klemperer and his wife Eva returned to their home in Dresden in 1945, he seethed with anger when he found that the local grocer who had moved into the house had cheated them, spread false rumors about them, and claimed to have gotten them a mortgage when he in fact did everything he could to get the house into his own hands. Yet Klemperer still felt he needed to restrain his emotions in dealing with the man, identifying the bind for Jews returning to Germany: "I have no reason, moreover hardly any possibility to treat him very considerately. I just don't want to appear the triumphant Jewish spirit of revenge."[85] Klemperer feared that Jews would ultimately be blamed for the circumstances of postwar Germany: "And

158　THE POSTWAR ANTISEMITE

what—this is most on my mind—will be the effect on the future position of the Jews in Germany? Very soon people will be saying: they're jumping the queue, they're taking their revenge, they're the winners: Hitler and Goebbels were right."[86]

Klemperer understood that current expressions of pro-Jewish sentiment did not mean antisemitism had been erased and was no longer a threat. In September 1945, he wrote in his diary about the testimonials made on behalf of people who had been friendly to Jews, linking them to his fears about the perpetuation of antisemitism in Germany: "This whining after testimonials is disgusting. And some time or other the Jews will get the bill for it; I see a new Hitlerism coming, I do not feel at all safe."[87] Here, we see the real irony of Klemperer's position: his concern with the perpetuation of antisemitism was precisely what led to the accusations about antisemitism in his book.

After the war, Klemperer's and Bab's attitudes toward the recovery of German culture diverged. A little over a week before Wendt wrote to him about "Zion," Klemperer wrote to Bab about Bab's unwillingness to live in postwar Germany:

> There is a passage in your letter that I cannot say yes to. They confirm again what touched me so much about their verses, the inescapability of their Germanness. At the same time you write that you will never feel completely at home in your current residence, you indicate a less than favorable situation, mention "good offers" from here and yet you don't want to come for fear of shaking hands with a murderer. I can't agree with that. I also know this fear, I also have a list of the dead, and I have seen with my own eyes and experienced on my own body what one never forgets. But at the time I swore to myself: if I survive, then I want to keep working, so that it will be different. It is impossible for Germany to remain in this horror; it must be able to get up again. . . . Why don't you want to help? I mean, it's like a survivor's duty. Here with us, everyone who is really of good will is so badly needed, there is so much work to be done spiritually. And it has to be done on the spot; over there, everything looks different from a distance. . . . Why don't you want to take part? The murderers will not go away on their own, and if we do not try, they will have offspring.[88]

Though they were both ardent German patriots with few illusions about the widespread antisemitism that remained in Germany, Klemperer was determined to fight from within, while Bab could not bear to return.

ACCUSED AS JEWS   159

Patriotism provides another useful context for considering Klemperer's comparison of Herzl to Hitler, which could also have been a strategy to deflect accusations that Jews were unpatriotic and vengeful. Klemperer considered himself an ardent German patriot and harbored a deep love for the literature of his country of origin. "Zion" quotes Julius Bab's poetry about his love for Germany. Before the Holocaust, Bab was also comfortable with comparisons between Zionists and National Socialists. In this light, Klemperer's critique of Zionism can be seen as the other side of his patriotic embrace of the Germany he and his fellow German Jews so passionately believed in, the one centered on culture and visions of *Heimat* rather than hatred of Jews: "And do you love Germany? A question without meaning! Can I love my hair, my blood, my very being? Is love no longer risk and profit?! Far more blind and profound is my devotion to myself and to this land which is, in fact, myself."[89] In other words, as a German Jew, he saw no need for a Jewish homeland since Germany was his Jewish home. In many ways, this stance is what led Klemperer and other Jews in this book to join the non-Jews who, after the war, sought to fuse antisemitism to Nazism as something wholly different from true German and Austrian culture.

Ironically, there was no better way to prove his patriotism than by deploying antisemitism to support his own argument. Klemperer was not trying to claim that Herzl was like Hitler or that Hitler was not antisemitic. But the comparison allowed him to demonstrate his authority, as a person perceived to be a Jew, to delineate antisemitism (as Wendt suggests, he was "freer in this regard") and, therefore, to dictate the terms of his inclusion as a German (rather than a Zionist) patriot. As a Jew in a position of cultural power in postwar East Germany, he felt he had the authority to declare the state free of antisemitism—but the dictate against his chapter on Herzl undermined his power and, in turn, his authority.

Klemperer's actions in the early years of the Nazi regime provide further context for considering his patriotism in relation to his understanding of antisemitism. In 1933, he actually took the Hitler oath.[90] And Klemperer overtly criticized communism in his diaries. But in 1947, as he prepared to publish *LTI*, he cut all that criticism and focused only on the language of Nazi totalitarianism. The final text of the book hints at continuities between the Nazis and the current government with the phrase "Sprache des vierten Reiches" (language of the Fourth Reich), but the phrase is vague and only appears twice.[91] In his hedging, Klemperer was perhaps not that different from other GDR intellectuals writing in this interstitial

160   THE POSTWAR ANTISEMITE

time: traumatized by Nazism, but not yet aware of the full excesses of Stalinism.

Klemperer's postwar texts reveal his anxious quest for inclusion in an East German *Heimat* based on his nostalgic desire for the prewar ideal of an inclusive German nationalism that didn't hate Jews, which he fantasized might be possible after 1945. At times Klemperer did waver in his view that fascism had been eradicated in East Germany. At one point, he contended that "Germany is a ruined rainworm: both parts twist themselves, both equally infected by fascism, each in its own way."[92] He wavered in particular when confronting the hypocrisy of East Germany's substituting one repressive regime for another. "If I have to join a party, then this one is a lesser evil. For the present at least. It alone is really pressing for radical exclusion of the Nazis. But it replaces the old lack of freedom with a new one! . . . But perhaps I myself am backing the wrong horse?"[93] Given the ambivalence that recurred in his words and actions over the years, it is obvious there was a degree of opportunism in his political positions—as Klemperer himself noted, his commitment to communism was a choice of the lesser evil compared to the West. But there is no doubt that communism also jibed with his real antagonism to Jewish nationalism. Klemperer's stance on Zionism cannot be separated from his complicated relationship to his own Jewish self-identification.[94]

To make his conception of *Deutschtum* (German nationalism) inclusive of Jews like him, Klemperer had to imagine Zionism as on par with Nazi efforts to exclude Jews. In Klemperer's mind, Palestine was a fantasy in which Jews held all the power, socially and structurally, which meant that others were not welcome: "In Zion the Aryan is exactly in the position of the Jew here . . . the Zionists are just as offensive as the Nazis. With their nosing after blood, their ancient 'cultural roots,' their . . . winding back of the world they are altogether a match for the National Socialists.'"[95] And yet, we must keep in mind that Klemperer's deployment of antisemitism, like that of other German Jews, was always qualified by his own anxieties about his position on the margins and limited by the state.[96]

The Irony of Defining the Antisemite

In the intertwined careers of Seghers and Klemperer, we see how a communist government used the Antisemite in the service of fashioning a new East German self-understanding. That Merker could eliminate Klemperer's

ACCUSED AS JEWS   161

"Zion" chapter and that it would be reinstated once Merker was no longer in a position of power crystallizes the influence inherent to such positions in the East German state. Yet, Merker's status was always tenuous. Party leaders were not happy about his stance on Jewish issues, and Walter Ulbricht and others who had spent their exile years in Moscow, as well as Soviet officials, were suspicious of his Western ties. At the beginning of 1947, when the party insisted that Jews should be ranked last in the list of victims of fascism and marked as "Victims of the Nuremberg Racial Laws" and people "forced to wear the yellow star" rather than Jews, Merker worked with Helmut Lehmann, secretary of the Department of Labor and Social Welfare of the Central Secretariat, and Leo Zuckermann, on a counterproposal, as well as on other measures to assist Jewish survivors, including restitution provisions and countering antisemitism. They were not successful.[97]

These actions, as well as the growing instrumentalization of antisemitism in other Eastern European countries, placed Merker under further suspicion. In 1950, he and his Jewish colleagues Leo Bauer, Bruno Goldhammer, Lex Ende, and Willi Kreikemeyer, who had also been in exile in the West, were arrested for espionage, accused of being agents of the West and supporters of Zionism, and expelled from the party. Merker was accused of being an "Enemy of the Nation" for insisting that Germans needed to find a way to assure their Jewish comrades that they would stamp out antisemitism in Germany forever. At a time when Jews in the East German government had become targets of antisemitic purges, Merker in effect actualized the film *Affaire Blum*'s notion that non-Jews could be targets of antisemitism.

In 1952, after Merker's name was brought up in conjunction with the Slánský show trial in Prague, he was arrested and imprisoned. His targeting was based on trumped-up charges of espionage boosted by antisemitic rhetoric.[98] After a trial on March 29–30, 1955, held out of public view, he was deemed to be an informant hostile to the GDR and was sentenced to eight years in prison.[99] However, the charges were dropped and he was released from custody in January 1956.[100] Merker wrote afterward:

> It is completely incomprehensible to them if a gentile, like me, can stand up for the Jews if he is not in their pay or in the pay of Jewish organizations. . . . For them, my standing up for the Jewish people, which was taking place at a time when they were most cruelly persecuted by the Hitler fascists, was sufficient proof that I must be an agent of imperialism and an enemy of the working class.[101]

162   THE POSTWAR ANTISEMITE

The party's use of antisemitic rhetoric in the targeting of Merker—and Merker's own concerns surrounding antisemitism in Klemperer's writing—underscores how the locus of power shifted after the war from determining who was a Jew to determining who was the Antisemite. It also underscored the persistent power of an antisemitic narrative even after the Holocaust, when explicitly denigrating Jews was ostensibly taboo. Government officials had to be able to determine who was an Antisemite because their claim to power rested in part upon not being the Antisemite. They had to make sure nobody could call Klemperer an Antisemite—because if the author of a state-sanctioned book was identified as an Antisemite, the SED would in theory be identified with his antisemitism. The irony is that eliminating the antisemitic chapter of his book served to identify *him*, a Jewish Nazi victim, as an Antisemite.

Prewar antisemitism prevented Klemperer from getting a good academic position, a fact of which he was aware. And yet, in the GDR, he became a celebrated academic, though antisemitism existed there too. Widespread antisemitism before and after the war meant that Klemperer, as a Jewish-born author, always wrote from a position inflected by this socially constructed disadvantage. Klemperer often used Jewish expressions and commented on Jewish mannerisms, and remained wary of Jews' place in positions of power after the war, noting that everything could be taken away at any moment: "Victory—but at what price! Oh Jahwe!"[102] He was pleased when Merker was purged, since "Zion" could return to his book, vindicating his ideas. Distasteful as some of his sentiments may be, the prevalence of systemic antisemitism suggests that they must be considered as part of a Jewish survival strategy.

Regardless of whether and how Klemperer and Seghers wrote about Jews, they were invested in maintaining the idea that East Germany was no home for the Antisemite and in de-emphasizing the persistence of antisemitism. They could not integrate the experiences of Jews in the Holocaust into the socialist vision of the future. But immediately after the war, they did try to do so, in their own limited ways and with varying degrees of success. Ultimately, the only acceptable version of the Antisemite in East Germany was going to be the one portrayed in *Affaire Blum*, who belonged to capitalism and the West and posed its greatest threat to all Germans, not just Jews. Taken together, these texts and films show how determining the postwar Antisemite was a site of contestation and struggle for defining East Germany itself.

As in West Germany, the construction of the Antisemite amid the new postwar taboo on antisemitism reflected the persistence of Jewish difference as a fundamental framework through which people understood themselves and their society. Writers had to balance their own desires to address Nazi crimes with the demands of the Soviet Military authorities and SED functionaries to construct an Antisemite who would complement communist ideology—and how their own use of antisemitic stereotypes played out in the gap between those imperatives. The Antisemite in their texts was inextricably linked to liberal capitalist, bourgeois ideology, but still allowed former Nazis to be reintegrated into society—another thing that continued to link the West and the East, regardless of both Germanys' official disavowals.[103]

PART III
AUSTRIA
The Victim and the Antisemite

5

Hilde Spiel Returns to Vienna

Das andere Leben, The Emperor Waltz, and *The Third Man*

On January 30, 1946, the writer Hilde Spiel (Figure 5.1) made her first trip back to her native Vienna from London, where she had been living in exile for ten years. She had left as an Austrian citizen but returned as a British subject and war correspondent for the *New Statesman*. While she was there, Stefan B., an old friend and fellow journalist, recounted what Spiel called a "blackly farcical" story about a well-known friend and his wife who had hidden an elderly Jewish woman in their home for most of the war. When the woman became gravely ill, a half-Jewish doctor made a risky visit to their home to treat her, but he fled when he determined she had a life-threatening illness that would require an operation. The couple sent their friend to the hospital and got her admitted under the name of the Christian wife. When the woman died after the operation, the husband had no choice but to hold a funeral for his supposed wife, while his actual wife spent the remainder of the war hidden in a locked room in their apartment, essentially a "living corpse" who was "restored to life by the victory of the Allies" three months later.[1] The Jewish woman remained buried in Vienna under the wife's name.

This story about the intertwined fates of Jewish and Christian Austrians epitomizes the complicated web of circumstances Spiel encountered in Vienna a scant five months after the war's end. London had been an alienating city of refuge, and she eventually returned to Austria for good in 1963. By her own account, London never became a place she could truly call home. Like numerous other Austrian émigré writers and intellectuals, she found it challenging to establish herself in a new language and culture. But her return to Austria did not return her to her prewar sense of self-identification. Stefan B.'s story of the women whose identities were transformed by the war evokes the complexity of Spiel's own conflicted emotional relationship to the city she had left behind, which remained buried, as it were, in the past: "Where

---

The Postwar Antisemite. Lisa Silverman, Oxford University Press. © Oxford University Press 2025.
DOI: 10.1093/9780197697757.003.0006

Figure 5.1. Hilde Spiel's early postwar writings reveal the complexity of her emotional relationship to Vienna and her ambivalence about returning to live there after spending years in exile in London. *ÖNB Wien Pf 27.732:C(1)/ Elisabeth Niggemeyer.*

my roots reach deep into the earth as nowhere else, I am a complete stranger, as disconnected in time and space as a ghostly visitor."[2]

Spiel was raised Catholic by parents who converted from Judaism before she was born in 1911. She spent the first two decades of her life in Vienna's vibrant and cosmopolitan cultural milieu, where she had many Jewish friends and acquaintances. She attended the renowned and innovative Schwarzwald School, swam for the successful team Austria, and spent long afternoons among the literati in the Café Herrenhof. In 1933, she published her first novel, *Kati auf der Brücke* (Katie on the bridge), and in 1936, shortly after receiving her doctorate, she left for London, where she married the exiled German writer and journalist Peter de Mendelssohn. Although she left Vienna two years before Germany annexed Austria in 1938, she nevertheless described her departure as a flight from the slow rise of the *Ständestaat* (corporate state) in which she already discerned the kernels of a future Nazi regime.[3]

Spiel never felt comfortable being referred to as a Jewish writer, even after she took up explicitly Jewish topics in her writing. In her memoirs, she describes pleasant childhood memories of Christian festivals, Corpus Christi processions, and her first communion. Though she claims never to have noticed antisemitism in the 1920s, she admits that her father was ashamed of his Jewish origins. She also recalls walking with her paternal grandmother, Laura Birnbaum, who asked her "Ob das sein müsse?" (If that had to be?) when she crossed herself as they passed a church.[4] Her account of this mild rebuke from her Jewish grandmother suggests that Spiel was aware of her difference and the limits of her self-identification as Catholic. She grew up in a milieu where Jewishness mattered at every stage: from the world of her Jewish grandparents, with whom she spent much time as a child, to the Viennese café culture in which she was immersed as a young adult, to an offhand reference to the importance of not seeming "Jewish" at the university.[5]

And yet, Spiel bristled at the thought of others defining her by, as she put it, the Nazis' Nuremberg laws or other racist prejudices; she and de Mendelssohn liked to say that "Hitler hat uns zu Juden gemacht" (Hitler turned us into Jews).[6] Though her maternal grandmother died in Theresienstadt, Spiel felt fortunate that her parents were able to join her in London, even if looking after them became an additional source of stress. At one point her father was interned as an enemy alien; after his release, he was not able to find work. Meanwhile, her mother became deeply lonely and was often emotionally overwrought.

Spiel's postwar writing reveals how conflicted she remained about Austria and Austrians upon her return—she would spend decades unpacking the resulting emotional turmoil, including through essays, fiction, and drama.[7] Like others persecuted as Jews by the Nazis, Spiel had to carefully navigate postwar Austrian attitudes about victimization, war, and continued antisemitism. On the one hand, she describes feeling genuine pleasure revisiting old friends. But the persistence of negative and misguided

170 THE POSTWAR ANTISEMITE

attitudes toward Jews, even amid the general postwar taboo on antisemitism, counterbalances that joy. When the head waiter at the Café Herrenhof, a "master of dignified conduct" back when she was a regular customer, says, "The Frau Doktor was right to leave. The air-raids alone—three times they set the whole city ablaze," he emblematizes the Viennese she criticizes, who remain deeply absorbed in their own wartime suffering and envy what they envisioned as escape, rather than acknowledging her forced exile.[8]

Spiel both sympathizes with Stefan B.'s precarious position as a journalist during the war and bitterly acknowledges that he profited under the Nazi regime while others perished. Likening him to a "small cog in the mechanism which kept the whole appliance working," she reveals the heart of the dilemma that she struggled with throughout her time in Vienna: how to assess her own wartime actions, and the everyday actions of other Austrians, as she observes the changes to a city that nevertheless remains so familiar.[9] This dilemma figures centrally in Austria's postwar narrative about its role in the ascendance of Nazism and the expropriation, exile, and murder of its Jews. As such, it deeply informs the question of complicity in postwar antisemitism, foregrounding the inaccurate and self-serving notion that Austrian Jews faced the same choices as non-Jewish Austrians.

Spiel's *Return to Vienna* is based on the notes she wrote during her trip in 1946, which she drafted and revised several times into a manuscript that was not published until 1968. Unlike the figural Antisemites of some other writers, the Antisemite that Spiel describes is neither a male figure of evil evoked via Jewish-coded qualities, nor a malevolent, murderous Nazi located in the past. Rather, Spiel, like Julius Bab, locates her Antisemite everywhere she turns, in the regular men and women, from waiters in Vienna's cafes to carefree skiers to the woman who won't return her grandmother's silver, whose attitudes toward Jews range from distaste to envy to hatred. These Austrians may not have been committed Nazis and some may have even helped Jews, but in remaining blind to their own roles in upholding the regime, they embed the Antisemite in the everyday life of postwar Austria. Its presence may not be palpable or explicitly articulated, but Spiel has no difficulty finding it in the subtle ways non-Jewish Austrians react to her return.

The earlier drafts of this text, along with Spiel's contemporary letters and newspaper articles, suggest that she later toned down her initial raw and unguarded descriptions of the Antisemite, particularly its female version. In an earlier draft she comments, "There are also new, unpleasant sights. Tyrolean hats worn by all women in this once elegant city. Fur coats in abundance, organized, one supposes, in some Eastern campaign" (i.e., stolen from deported and murdered Jews) and "Jackboots; every female resembling a concentration camp guard." However, in the book she removes the Jewish context by cutting the suggestion that the women's fur coats come from wartime looting, deleting the word "concentration" so the women in boots are just "camp guards," and adding a comparison to prostitutes in 1920s Berlin.[10] Though she still registers her disdain for the Viennese, that disdain is no longer centered on antisemitism.[11]

Spiel's contemporaneous published observations suggest that her criticism varied depending on her audience. In her 1946 article for the Viennese newspaper *Wiener Kurier* titled "Die Wiederkehr" (The return), she is circumspect in describing the postwar impact of the war on the city:

> how the Austrian countryside has swept over Vienna, how the urban has
> , been inundated by the rural, in clothing, language, and way of life. They
> no longer grumble, they scold. They no longer groan, they curse. . . . At
> Demel [a fancy café] the women sit with headscarves, Styrian hats hang in
> the opera cloakroom, men wear Loden coats to the symphony . . . cosmo-
> politanism has given way to the people here.[12]

But in her report for the *New Statesman*, "Vienna," published two months later in English, she sharpens her criticism: "For the Viennese are now as rude to each other and as rancorous to the Russians as they are sugary to the Western occupation troops. Their own language has become coarser, resembling a rural dialect. Their urbane graces have gone."[13] Although she bitterly describes the inadequacies of Austrian denazification procedures leading to the reinstatement of former Nazis in their jobs, she makes no mention of antisemitism. Still, like Hugo Bettauer's satirical description of the provincialization of Vienna after the Jews are expelled in his best-selling 1922 novel *Die Stadt ohne Juden* (The city without Jews), Spiel depicts for both audiences a Vienna changed for the worse without its Jews, without explicitly naming their absence, abruptly changing her tone in the final paragraphs by lauding contemporary Vienna's music, art, and taste.

Though Vienna is Spiel's explicit frame of reference for her own self-identification, her less frequent yet no less evocative descriptions of Austria beyond the city limits frame both the book and the most vivid contours of her Antisemite. She begins and ends the book with memories of leisure activities outside the city and the special role the mountain landscape played in

172 THE POSTWAR ANTISEMITE

counteracting antisemitic stereotypes. As her flight from London descends over the Vienna woods, she remembers her first efforts to ski on their gentle inclines. In the book's final pages, she recalls hiking in the Tyrol with her father, vacationing with her family in Carinthia and the Salzkammergut, and skiing in the Alps, where "[n]othing could match the beauty of these landscapes with their white-encrusted trees, the dust thrown up by the powdery snow and the crackling of the ice, when we flew down the slopes and the cold clean air stung our cheeks."[14]

The countryside, specifically the Alps, was also where deeply rooted antisemitism excluded Jews—and Jews triumphed over the stereotypes that dogged them:

> It was on the Schneeberg and the Rax, too, that the myth of the weakling, cowardly Jewish boy was invalidated.... These young fellows were among the toughest and most daring of the skiers. Some suffered broken limbs not once, but twice in a long winter season, and if they won prizes only in the workers' ski clubs, then it was because since its foundation they were denied membership of the German Alpine Association in Austria. But to all who sat in offices or lecture halls during the week, these Sundays with their tribulations and their splendor represented a continually achieved goal, an eternally renewed reward.

Spiel's trip ends with a day on the ski slopes, where she articulates most clearly how she belongs nowhere, even at home. To belong to the real Austria is to be like the ski instructors she encounters, who possess "the same unselfconscious manner, not feeling subservient or obligated either to one or the other, but just glad to be alive and living off of anyone who comes along." In contrast to the Jewish skiers she has just described, these unfettered Austrians reveal her own continued and inevitable marginalization from Austrianness. They also help her begin to limn the figure responsible for this marginalization, in those who have "the good fortune of having such roots, of depending so little on outward circumstances, of trusting entirely to their own muscles of steel, their confident gaze and total accord with nature."[15]

Spiel shaped her criticism to gently provoke, rather than greatly disturb, Austrians about their recent past. In doing so, she abided by the expectation that Jews who returned should do so as Austrians, not Jews.[16] If the postwar taboo on explicit antisemitism helped enable Austrian Jews to rebuild their lives and participate successfully in the public sphere, the cost was a tacit

HILDE SPIEL RETURNS TO VIENNA   173

agreement to remain silent, or at least not be too loud, about their own suffering, the role of Austrians in the murder and expulsion of the country's Jews, and the persistence of antisemitism. The widely accepted myth of Austria as Hitler's first victim also played a powerful role in delineating the boundaries within which returning exiles could articulate their experiences.[17] The shape of the Antisemite in East and West Germany often depended upon the degree to which Jews could be identified as true German patriots. Austria's similarly self-serving narratives also demanded that Jews pledge allegiance to Austria's postwar sense of itself as the victim, subsuming their victimization under Austria's, which rendered all Austrians victims of the Antisemite and rendered Jews invisible. For Austrians, the Antisemite was the German Nazi who "occupied" Austria since 1938, a figure enhanced in its representation with Jewish-coded traits and conflated with the postwar Allied Forces for an extra boost.

Stefan B.'s story about his friends concisely illuminates how a narrative of easily exchanged victimhood and Jewish absence could provide a soothing entrypoint to uncomfortable issues of Austrian complicity in Nazi crimes. The tale features heroic Austrians who resist the Nazis by risking their lives to shelter a Jewish friend, even (figuratively) dying on her behalf, the reward for which is postwar rebirth. It places the Nazi victimization of Jews and non-Jews on equal footing, which fits right into postwar Austrian political and cultural mythologies: a fantasy of Austrian resistance, martyrdom, and suffering under the Nazis, who thus become fully at fault for the disappearance of Jews from Vienna and their invisibility as victims after the war.

Stefan B.'s story resonated broadly. The Austrian writer Alexander Lernet-Holenia, who was likewise not Jewish, wrote a fictional version, *Der zwanzigste Juli* (The twentieth of July), which appeared in the magazine *Der Turm* in 1946 and was published as a novella in 1947. Alfred Ibach adapted the novella into the screenplay for a film called *Das andere Leben* (The other life), which was directed by Rudolf Steinboeck and released in 1948.[18] The basic plot of the novella and film remains true to the original events: an Austrian Christian woman tries to save her Jewish friend by trading identities so the friend can use her papers for a potentially life-saving, but ultimately futile, hospital visit.[19] But both Lernet-Holenia's story and the film also incorporate postwar issues of complicity and victimization by introducing the figure of a distinct Antisemite who can shoulder the blame for persecuting Jews. In contrast to Spiel's focus on everyday expressions of antisemitism,

174   THE POSTWAR ANTISEMITE

this recourse to the figure of the Antisemite bolsters narratives that retrospectively figure resistance to the Nazis as a moral duty for Austrians.

Der zwanzigste Juli and *Das andere Leben* are typically celebrated as early Austrian attempts to face the complicated nexus of the Second World War, Jews, and antisemitism in Vienna.[20] Their narratives are sympathetic toward Jews and critical of Nazis. But non-Jewish Austrian opposition to antisemitism drives those narratives, which in turn transform decent, moral Austrians into primary targets of the Nazis. As such, both novella and film support the idea that Jewish and non-Jewish Austrian victims of Nazi persecution were indistinguishable, a notion that undergirded Austrians' self-identification as victims of German Nazi aggression. This broad category of victimhood is set in relation to the imagined Antisemite who is subtly coded as Jewish who targets not only Jews but also everyone—and in so doing, diverts attention from everyday Austrian complicity with the Nazis and the postwar persistence of antisemitism.[21]

Three postwar stories created about Austria exemplify the cultural work accomplished by this Antisemite. Significantly, only one of them (*Der zwanzigste Juli/Das andere Leben*) is both by and for Austrians. The other two present images of Austria as envisioned from a distance and aimed at American and British audiences: *The Emperor Waltz*, co-written by non-Jewish American Charles Brackett together with its director Billy Wilder, an Austro-Hungarian-born Jew who had a deep but ambivalent connection to its culture, and *The Third Man*, written and directed by non-Jewish Brits Graham Greene and Carroll Reed, respectively, but commissioned by Alexander Korda, another Austro-Hungarian-born Jew, who asked Greene to write the screenplay for a film set in postwar Vienna. All three are connected by their portrayals of a liminal Antisemite, showing how this figure was useful in addressing the wartime activities of Austrians, even in films originating in the countries of the victorious Allied Forces.

Both Lernet-Holenia's story and the film *Das andere Leben* use Nazi-occupied Vienna as the setting for a tale of Austrian bravery and victimhood. In contrast, Nazis and Jews are fully absent from *The Third Man* (1949), a dark, mysterious tale of murder, the black market, and poisoned children set in post-1945 Vienna. Like *The Third Man*, *The Emperor Waltz* (1948) does not explicitly include Jews or antisemitism, but the cheerful, colorful, operetta-style Hollywood musical set in a Tyrolean village in Austria-Hungary is based upon a reimagined, idealized narrative of Jewish assimilation. In all three films, the Antisemite emerges as a murky non-Jewish bad guy coded as just Jewish enough to signal his position as an outsider who targets everyone, Jews and non-Jews alike. This imagined Antisemite, who is never at home in the Austrias portrayed by these films, nevertheless offers audiences the opportunity to imagine themselves as his targets.

Even as the repression of public antisemitism in the postwar years kept prejudices against Jews below the surface, it enabled the continuation of a hierarchical framework of Jewish difference according to which Austrianness was predicated on the exclusion of Jewishness.[22] The beginning of Austria's postwar era of political consensus demanded that Austrians maintain these taboos, deny their wartime roles, and avoid discussion of political events with painful repercussions.[23] Jewish writers and artists in particular grappled with the terms of their inclusion within this new ethos, even if they no longer lived within its borders. Despite their ambivalences about Austria, both Spiel and Wilder felt the need to address their love for their Austrian *Heimat*—a concept that was fraught for many Jews but remained a longed-for ideal for others.[24] Spiel's critical observations about the Antisemite in Austria complement the unarticulated fantasy of Jewish inclusion presented by Wilder in *The Emperor Waltz*, which reimagines Austria as inhospitable to the Antisemite. Considering these various versions of Austria and Austrians created at the same time but in varying locations underscores how Jews and non-Jews alike had a vested interest in presenting their own definitions of the Antisemite in order to imagine an Austria without one.

Mistaken Identity in *Der zwanzigste Juli* and *Das andere Leben*

Central European literature and film of the twentieth century frequently address issues surrounding Jews and antisemitism through the exchange of identities. Jewish filmmakers in Weimar Germany like Ernst Lubitsch used the motif in comic *Verwechslungkomödien*, comedies of mistaken identity where Jews attempt to appear as non-Jews, as a way to address the difficulties of assimilation. In interwar Vienna, novels like Hugo Bettauer's 1922 *Die Stadt ohne Juden: ein Roman von Übermorgen* and the film on which it based, H. K. Breslauer's *Die Stadt ohne Juden*, used a version of this comic form to satirically address the role of both Jews and non-Jews in perpetuating antisemitic stereotypes.[25] After the war, the genre became much more than a vehicle for humorous tales of Jewish assimilation; it became useful as a

176   THE POSTWAR ANTISEMITE

dramatic tool to buttress support for the idea that the Antisemite's victim encompassed both Jews and non-Jews.[26]

The first major difference between *Der zwanzigste Juli* and Stefan B.'s story of exchanged identities is that Lernet-Holenia turns the anecdote's elderly Jewish woman into Suzette Joël, the *bezaubernde* (enchanting) seventeen-year-old dark-haired daughter of a Jewish doctor (the son of a rabbi), who marries Alberti, a non-Jewish linguist, in 1936. After 1938, Alberti's marriage to a Jew costs him his job, but he is soon back at work, using his linguistic skill on behalf of the new regime's foreign office. Suzette's parents are deported and not heard from again, and Alberti dies in early 1944 of a lung infection, for which he could have gotten treatment abroad were he not married to a Jew. If Alberti is thus a martyr for his Jewish wife, her Jewish parents are simply victims.

Newly vulnerable in the absence of her husband, Suzette seeks shelter from her blonde friend Elisabeth Josselin, who is the daughter of Buschek, an Austrian aristocrat, who disapproved of her marriage to a German Nazi army major of aristocratic French Protestant ancestry—a mixed marriage of sorts—who had, in turn, disapproved of her friendship with the Albertis. Elisabeth risks a great deal to hide Suzette from her husband and the Gestapo agents in Vienna. When that is no longer possible, Elisabeth's father allows Suzette to take shelter in his apartment, arousing the suspicions of his landlady. Various neighbors help Suzette, but eventually she returns to Elisabeth and informs her friend that she is three months pregnant. Elisabeth offers to pawn her jewelry to pay Bukowsky, a smuggler, to get Suzette out of the country, but it isn't worth enough, so instead they use the money for an abortion. When it becomes clear that the abortion has been botched, they call a doctor, who insists that Suzette go to the hospital. As in Stefan B.'s story, Suzette uses Elisabeth's identification to be admitted to the hospital, where she dies.

Here, again, the text diverges from Stefan B.'s story. Rather than spending the rest of the war in hiding, Elisabeth identifies with her friend as she ponders the dissolution of her identity and her marriage, which is close to ruin: "Basically, she was now no longer anyone at all. She was, so to speak, on the death bed in place of Suzette."[27] Elisabeth's identification with her Jewish friend increases as she procures Suzette's forged papers from the smuggler so she can flee in Suzette's place. When her husband learns what has happened, he informs his German army superior of his wife's actions—which he feels bound to do as a German patriot. To his surprise, his boss tells him that his wife has acted admirably and suggests he join their plot to murder Hitler—a reference to the failed assassination attempt of July 20, 1944, which gives the story its name. Josselin's decision to assist with the plot indicates that he has realized he was wrong to believe his commitment to the Nazis was patriotic and now supports Elisabeth's resistance efforts. This is, perhaps, Lernet-Holenia's main intervention in the story: using Josselin to tie together Elisabeth's act of resistance, which symbolizes Austrian resistance, German resistance to Hitler, and patriotism.

The figural Antisemite of this story is the trafficker, Bukowsky. Bukowsky is also an agent of the Nazi *Sicherheitsdienst* (intelligence agency of the SS), albeit for purely opportunistic reasons, and thus further underscores the difference between true patriotism and superficial support for the Nazis. Bukowsky has a mix of Jewish-coded and Antisemitic attributes. In this, he mirrors Elisabeth after Suzette's death, when she is functionally both the Jew and non-Jew, and thus the Antisemite's ideal Austrian target. Although Bukowsky is a Nazi, his dark hair, ambiguous nationality (he is described as a "stranger with unusual connections"), lack of patriotism or principles, sexual perversity (it is implied that he expects Elisabeth to pay for her escape with sex), and residence in the luxurious Grand Hotel code him as a Jew. These codings are reinforced via the actor who plays him, Siegfried Breuer, who played a similarly slimy Jewish character, Kuhn, in the antisemitic Nazi film *Leinen aus Irland* (1939).[28] Reinforcing this identity confusion, Elisabeth's father believes Bukowsky is a Jew because of his Slavic-sounding name. Bukowsky in turn falls in love instantly with Elisabeth/Suzette, dismissing the Nazi law against fraternizing with Jews as a "laughable regulation."[29] This is of a piece with his actual disdain for the Nazi ideology he opportunistically supports (he also claims that the Germans are engaged in a losing, self-destructive operation), which stands in stark contrast to Elisabeth and her husband's moral and patriotic rejection of the Nazis.

When Bukowsky approaches his German Gestapo (Nazi police) colleague, Latheit, with a photograph to obtain a visa for Elisabeth/Suzette so they can flee together, he further reveals himself as the Jewish-coded Antisemite. Initially, Latheit is thrilled to have caught Alberti's Jewish wife, forcing Bukowsky to claim that she is actually not Jewish, in order to get the visa (though he still thinks she is Suzette). Latheit remarks, "Most Germans are anti-Semites without ever having seen a Jew. But it goes too far that you consider a Jewess *not* to be a Jew."[30] In challenging Bukowsky's authority to determine who is a Jew, Latheit asserts his own; in differentiating Bukowsky

178   THE POSTWAR ANTISEMITE

from "most Germans," he subtly suggests that Bukowsky may be a Jew—or at least that he is protecting a Jew.

Bukowsky soon learns (it is unclear how) of Elisabeth's true identity. But he still plans to leave for Switzerland with her the next day, which is also the date of the planned assassination. Before leaving, Bukowsky demands that her husband Josselin be arrested for his role in her deception. His arrest hinders him from participating in the failed assassination plot. Latheit, in the meantime, has also made inquiries and discovered Elisabeth's ruse. When he discovers that Josselin has not participated in it as Latheit would have expected, he misinterprets Bukowsky's order for Josselin's arrest as a sign that Bukowsky had advance knowledge of the plot. Latheit catches Bukowsky at the train station just as he and Elisabeth are about to leave for Switzerland. Bukowsky exits the train, and he and Latheit end up shooting each other dead on the platform, in effect, staging a duel between the Jewish Antisemite and the German Antisemite.[31]

In the story's final passage, Elisabeth begins her journey in a train compartment next to Bukowsky's seat, which is empty until her husband suddenly appears and sits down. Bukowsky's arrest request has indeed saved Josselin from participating in the failed assassination attempt, so he has boarded the train to rescue Elisabeth. This conclusion takes the story's switched identities to their ultimate ideological resolution: Elisabeth and Josselin flee Vienna like Jewish refugees, their "mixed" marriage repaired by their acts of Nazi resistance. Where the dead Suzette and Alberti can be no more than victims, Elisabeth, still masquerading as a Jew, and Josselin, her loving German husband, have transformed their victim narrative into a story of resistance, courage, and patriotism. Leaving the Austria they love is their ultimate act of martyrdom.

Spiel's complicated postwar relationship with Lernet-Holenia, who was not Jewish, sheds some light on the stakes of his engagement with Jewish difference and the Austrian narrative of national martyrdom. Spiel admired Lernet-Holenia as a friend and colleague in PEN Austria, for which he served as president from 1969 to 1972.[32] She praised his novels about switching identities, in particular *Beide Sizilien* (Two Sicilies, 1942), appreciating how he used the motifs of the Doppelgänger and the unknown stranger to address his doubts about his own identity, as well as his father's (as she did).[33] But she also competed with him for status and readership and was aware of his ambivalences toward Jews.[34] She discussed his problematic use of antisemitic language with their friend, writer and doctor Alexander Hartwich, who wrote to her on October 21, 1969, "You will see from the enclosed document that Lernet in no way denies his 'stinking Jews.' He just added 'Saujuden' to them and that version he gave you has already begun. The difference between 'every stinking Jew' and the—individual—'Saujuden' probably needs no interpretation." Three days later, Spiel replied, "You have known Alexander for a long time, much longer than I have. Didn't you already know about his deep-rooted, 'cavalier' antisemitism? Has his nature, his character so far remained hidden to you ... ?"[35]

Lernet-Holenia's adaptation of Stefan B.'s story reflects his ambivalence about his own successes under the Nazis. He never hid his rejection of Nazi ideology, and his name appeared on the first Nazi blacklist of banned books in 1933.[36] In 1941, the Nazi regime prevented the distribution of his novel *Mars im Widder* (Mars in Aries) because they considered it too sympathetic toward Poland.[37] Some Nazis labeled him "unreliable" and suspected he might not be completely Aryan, given his father's unknown origins.[38] A Nazi memo from 1940 complains of his frequent meetings with Jewish women and negative attitude toward the Nazi regime, which did not exhibit the moral character expected of an officer in the German army (into which he had been conscripted in 1939).[39]

However, none of these issues seemed to stand in the way of his career. They certainly did not prevent him from joining the *Reichsschrifttumskammer* (the professional Nazi organization of writers), a requirement for all writers who wished to continue publishing under the Nazis.[40] After he was wounded in the invasion of Poland in 1939, he became the dramaturge for the Berlin military film office at the suggestion of his publisher (it remains unclear why an author with such a negative reputation was able to gain such an important post in the Nazi propaganda office). He was promoted to director of the Entwicklungsstabs der Heeresfilmstelle (Department of Development of Military Films) on September 16, 1941.[41] Although he moved to Bavaria Film the next year, he still wrote the first draft of what would become one of the most commercially successful films of the Third Reich, *Die große Liebe* (1942, The great love).

But in his personal life, Lernet-Holenia had little truck with Nazis. Until 1942, he maintained a close relationship with Maria Charlotte (Lotte) Sweceny, née Stein, who was a half-Jew according to Nazi laws.[42] In the many letters he wrote to Lotte, he expressed critical attitudes toward Hitler, the Nazi regime, and antisemitism, as well as his sympathy for Jews (he called her "Hase" [rabbit], a word he frequently used in place of "Jew" to avoid

180   THE POSTWAR ANTISEMITE

detection by Nazi censors. He offered Jews shelter and tried to help them get emigration papers (prefiguring Elisabeth); but his relationships with Jewish women, whom he often described with the stereotype *schöne Jüdin* (beautiful Jewess), recalling the "enchanting" Suzette, registered a fetishization of the other that is fundamentally, if paradoxically, antisemitic.[43]

Ultimately, Lernet-Holenia's complexity, of which Spiel was so aware, resonates across his life, as well as his novella. Lernet-Holenia served as an officer in the Second World War and styled himself an aristocrat opposed to the Nazis, which renders Buschek, an Austrian who rejects the Nazis, something of an avatar for his creator. But the author also considered himself as much a victim as those who left in 1938, even though, as his friend writer Carl Zuckmayer noted, he was not directly endangered.[44] Though in January 1939, he traveled with Lotte to South America and New York, where they may have contemplated fleeing Germany for good, he returned to Europe and his subsequent experiences in the Army and the Nazi film industry.[45] It is hardly surprising, then, that Lernet-Holenia's engagement with Jewish difference in his postwar works is also indicative of how he aimed to define the Antisemite as a figure removed from himself and Austria. And yet his Antisemite, as embodied in Bukowsky and Latheit, both polices and transgresses the exchange of identities and the confusion around identifying Jews and non-Jews. As a figure who simultaneously evokes and represses ideas about Jews and antisemitism, this Antisemite could, ironically, be said to resemble the author who created him in order to disavow him.[46]

Lernet-Holenia's novella received mixed reviews, but it resonated enough for the newly established Filmstudio of the Theater in der Josefstadt to adapt it for their first film, *Das andere Leben*.[47] Filming began in Vienna in September 1947.[48] Perhaps because the film, like the novel, was by Austrians for Austrians, its story hewed closely to the novella. Its main departure, however, is its increased focus on the relationship between Elisabeth and Suzette, played by Aglaja Schmid and Vilma Degischer.[49] Originally titled *Ich für Dich* (I for you), *Das andere Leben* uses visual cues, including fabric patterns and proximity, to highlight Elisabeth and Suzette's interchangeability. The film's poster (Figure 5.2) advertises its Doppelgänger motif with the women's similar profiles in the foreground and Bukowsky, the dark, Jewish-coded Antisemite who poses a danger to them both, in the background. By bringing Lernet-Holenia's story to the screen, *Das andere Leben* visually highlights its reversal of the terms of the prewar *Verwechslungskomödie*, turning a counterintuitive wartime scenario in which the non-Jew must adopt the identity

Figure 5.2. A poster for director Rudolf Steinboeck's *Das andere Leben* highlights the dark, threatening Antisemite as a danger to both Jewish and non-Jewish women by foregrounding the similarities between the Jewish Suzette Alberti (played by Vilma Degischer, right) and the Christian Elisabeth Josselin (played by Aglaja Schmid, left). *Courtesy of Filmarchiv Austria.*

182 THE POSTWAR ANTISEMITE

of the Jew in order to survive, while the Jew who adopts a non-Jewish identity dies, into a useful postwar narrative that conflates Austrians with the Nazis' Jewish targets.

The film also takes the opportunity to highlight the non-Jewish Elisabeth as the Antisemite's ultimate victim, a status she reaches only after Suzette dies. After Elisabeth adopts Suzette's identity, the film repeats a montage of her on a series of doorsteps receiving food and shelter from Austrians—only this time Elisabeth is the one on the same doorsteps. These scenes highlight how she has taken on the role of victim and provides another opportunity to see how much Austrians helped Jews (or people pretending to be Jews). The antisemitism of regular Austrians toward Jews is not ignored: a man laughs as he knocks off Dr. Joël's hat, a landlord mutters unpleasantries to Suzette as she unlocks the door to her apartment building, and Buschek's landlady implies that she may denounce Suzette for not having a ration card. But in contrast to these examples, the film portrays its ultimate Antisemite as a Jew: a man wearing the white armband of Vienna's *Judenpolizei* (the Nazi-appointed Jewish police who assisted the Gestapo in deporting Jews from their apartments and also hunted fleeing Jews) informs Dr. Joël of his imminent deportation, Joël balks, and the Jewish operative says, in a semi-threatening manner, "You're not going to give me any trouble, are you?"[50] In contrast, one scene at a train station depicts soldiers guarding sleeping, non-Jewish children waiting to be evacuated to the countryside for their protection and expressing tender sympathy for these "poor children."

As in the novella, Bukowsky and Latheit serve as the story's key Antisemites. The film highlights Bukowsky's malevolence via his looks, as well as additional scenes. Evoking Harlan's depiction of Joseph Süss Oppenheimer, Bukowsky is a dark, handsome cosmopolitan who likes expensive jewelry; he is seductive yet sleazy. In the film, he also loves art, in particular, Jewish-coded modern art, like Boris Winkler in *Das dritte Geschlecht* and Jakob Blum in *Affaire Blum*. In fact, his love of art becomes the vehicle that differentiates him as a liminal Antisemite, rather than a straightforward Nazi like Latheit. Shortly after Bukowsky falls in love with the woman he thinks is Suzette, but before he learns that she is actually Elisabeth, he drives her to a monastery outside Vienna that is serving as a storage facility for vast amounts of looted Jewish art. In this scene, the blended qualities of the Antisemite could not be clearer: as a Nazi, he has access to Aryanized property, which he can only appreciate because of his Jewish-coded love of art. Although he hopes to impress Elisabeth with his knowledge, his strategy backfires, for Elisabeth is horrified when she recognizes a Buddha that belonged to the Joëls.[51]

Das andere Leben premiered in Vienna in May 1948 and received positive reviews, which was not surprising, given that it allowed Austrians to identify with its victims and heroes and helped audiences imagine narratives of wartime resistance.[52] The multiple versions of Stefan B.'s anecdote about the Austrian couple who saved a Jewish woman illuminate Austrians' concerns with depicting the best of Austria in their texts and films. In *Der zwanzigste Juli* and *Das andere Leben*, this meant presenting an Austria that was largely inhospitable to the Antisemite. The Austrian Jewish émigré director Billy Wilder was also interested in envisioning an Austria free from the Antisemite, albeit for different reasons and with different implications.

Billy Wilder's *The Emperor Waltz*

Billy Wilder is generally considered alongside German-Jewish émigré directors, like Douglas Sirk and Max Ophüls, but his background and young adult years mark his difference from that group.[53] Wilder was born in the Carpathian mountain town of Sucha, Galicia (today Sucha Beskidzka, Poland), which was part of Austria-Hungary until 1918. He spent his young adult years in Vienna before he moved to Berlin, where he worked as a screenwriter until 1933. Film critic Karena Niehoff picked up on the distinctiveness of Wilder's origins, noting that he "still speaks a flirty, flattering Viennese German" and describing how he differentiated himself from his peers when "he told how the round table of Germans, almost all Berliners, who had come to Hollywood, eagerly and wistfully enumerated the subway stations from Krumme Lanke to Alexanderplatz and intervened furiously if someone neglected to name Klosterstrasse."[54]

We should keep in mind Wilder's gentle ribbing of nostalgia for Berlin as we approach *The Emperor Waltz*: his only film set in Austria, his only musical, his singular foray into nostalgic *Heimat* kitsch, his first color film, and the first film he made after editing the American film about Nazi atrocities *Die Todesmühlen* (*Death Mills*). Wilder claimed to remember nothing about the small town where he was born in 1906, though when the town later named a street after him, he called it "one of the highest points in my life."[55] His father Max managed restaurants along the rail lines around Krakow, which led to the happenstance of his birth in Sucha. During the

184   THE POSTWAR ANTISEMITE

First World War, the Wilders, along with thousands of Jews, relocated to Vienna, where Billy attended high school and began his career as a reporter for *Die Stunde.*

Like many aspiring journalists, he left for better career opportunities in Berlin, which became the setting of his postwar films that deal explicitly with the Nazi past. Vienna, on the other hand, appears only as a subtext in a few of his films.[56] But Wilder's experiences in Europe provide crucial context for his creation of *The Emperor Waltz*, a kitschy Hollywood film that idealizes life in the provincial mountains of Austria-Hungary, on the heels of a trip to Germany where he was immersed in cultural reconstruction after the Nazi genocide of the Jews and searched in vain for information about the fate of his mother, stepfather, and uncle.[57]

Wilder had traveled to Germany as a civilian with the rank of colonel in the Information Control Division (ICD) of the U.S. military. In Bad Homburg, he helped write a 400-page manual for reconstructing the German film industry.[58] He also edited film taken in Dachau and Auschwitz for what would become *Die Todesmühlen (Death Mills)*. These experiences color his well-known film *A Foreign Affair* (1948), in which a U.S. congressional committee travels to occupied Berlin to ensure the morality of U.S. soldiers. In fact, Wilder was still in Germany when he submitted an early proposal for that film to the head of the ICD, General Robert A. McClure, who met with him about it in 1946, shortly before Wilder returned to the United States.[59]

But *A Foreign Affair* was not the first film Wilder made after returning from Germany. In a letter to the U.S. State Department, Wilder claimed that "circumstances beyond my control" had delayed his film on the American occupation of Germany.[60] These circumstances were *The Emperor Waltz*, an operetta-style musical in which an American salesman courts an Austrian aristocrat and saves a batch of mixed-breed puppies from drowning. Most readings of the film focus on its implicit, if obvious, condemnation of Austrian support for Nazi racial policies that are thwarted by an American savior.[61] But this kitschy *Heimat* film also vividly celebrates Austrian culture. Wilder himself undertook great effort and expense to recreate a Tyrolean village in the Canadian Rockies to ground the film's embrace of mountains, music, folk culture, and good-natured, fun-loving, dirndl- and lederhosen-wearing villagers who themselves warmly embrace its American protagonist.[62] *The Emperor Waltz* envisions Austria as a nostalgic fantasyland of pre-1918 clichés—and a country that accepts Jews, at least certain Jews, and rejects Antisemites.[63]

HILDE SPIEL RETURNS TO VIENNA   185

Wilder was not naïve about Austrians' involvement in Nazi crimes, their jubilation about the *Anschluss*, or their unwelcoming attitude toward returning Jewish émigrés. In later years, he explicitly noted his distaste for Austria's claim to victim status:

> The Germans who moved to Austria were absolutely in jubilation. And the Austrians were beating up the Jews, and the German troops, they had to separate the Jews from the Austrians. [Shakes his head.] And now Austria says that they were the first ones who were occupied by Germany! Occupied! Then they were begging to be taken into the great German Reich. . . . And the jubilation in Austria and Vienna when Mr. Hitler came! He is an Austrian, you know. They were very proud of him.[64]

Given this unflinching view of Austria and Austrians, as well as his concerns about the fate of his Jewish family at the time, Wilder's turn to a musical film celebrating Austrian culture seems remarkable. It makes more sense, however, when we understand *The Emperor Waltz*'s nostalgia for a fantasy vision of an earlier era as an effort to separate Nazi Austria from the provincial Austria-Hungary of Wilder's childhood, where Emperor Franz Josef, who appears as a character in the film, enjoyed a widespread reputation among Austrian Jews as their great protector. This idea of the past became particularly important for Jewish émigrés like Wilder, whose opposition to Nazi ideology was visceral and personal, but whose deep attachment to the countries from which they came was difficult to dissolve. Wilder balances politics and nostalgia by envisioning an Austrian past where a Jewish-coded American outsider could be accepted and there was no place for a liminal Antisemite, thus at once rebuking the Nazis while rehabilitating an imagined pre-Nazi Austria.

The screenplay for *The Emperor Waltz*, co-written by Wilder and American writer Charles Brackett, features Bing Crosby as Virgil Smith, an American gramophone salesman who travels with his trusted white terrier Buttons to Emperor Franz Josef's summer palace in the hopes of boosting his Austrian sales with a royal endorsement. Upon arriving at the palace, Smith meets the snooty Countess Johanna Augusta Franziska Stoltzenberg-Stolzenberg (played by Joan Fontaine), who is visiting with her father, Baron Holenia, and is accompanied by her black poodle, Scheherazade, whom she wants to mate with the emperor's black dog.[65] After sumptuous scenes of aristocrats waltzing at the palace and Austrian peasants performing

186   THE POSTWAR ANTISEMITE

charming folk dance and ballet sequences in idyllic settings, as well as a comic interlude that features the anxious poodle under Freudian-style analysis with the Viennese-accented veterinarian Dr. Zwieback, Scheherezade ends up mating with Smith's white terrier instead of the emperor's black dog, just as the initially haughty and dismissive countess falls sway to Smith's lowbrow charms.[66] The birth of spotted puppies reveals the regrettable mating, and Baron Holenia orders Dr. Zwieback to drown them. At the last moment, Smith rescues the pups from Dr. Zwieback, who claims only to have been "following orders." True to his reputation among nostalgic Jews as their tolerant protector, the emperor wants to keep the puppies even though they are mongrels. As further indication of his benevolence, he allows the countess and Smith to marry as the film comes to its generically comic but politically serious end.

To consider how *The Emperor Waltz* engages the categories of Jewish difference, we need to begin with the fact that Wilder's film originated with two other narratives by Jewish writers. The first was *Olympia*, a 1928 play by Budapest-born Jewish playwright Ferenc Molnár, who fled to the United States in 1940. *Olympia* features a countess in love with a Hungarian captain, who as a commoner is unsuitable for marriage. In his diary, Brackett described meeting Molnár in New York in 1943, where he "talked of the great luxury court theaters of Vienna and Budapest." When they discussed how Brackett and Wilder might turn his play into a film, Molnár did not suggest Jewish characters, yet he spoke of his nostalgia for Austria-Hungary, where the emperor was the protector of the Jews: "The Habsburgs were not anti-Semitic. You see, they saw no difference between any people who wore ordinary clothes."[67]

The second was an earlier screenplay Wilder co-wrote with playwright Hyman Solomon Kraft for Paramount in 1936, first titled *Vienna Hall* and then *Moon over Vienna*, in which the American leader of a jazz band travels to Vienna and sets up shop next to a waltz hall. Screenwriters Don Hartman and Frank Butler took over the script and renamed it *Champagne Waltz*. Released in 1937, its American jazzman competes for business with the Waltz Palace, which is run by none other than the king of waltzes himself, Franz Strauss.[68] The blending of these stories in *The Emperor Waltz* (Figure 5.3) incorporates the affinity of many—and Jews in particular—for Vienna as the locus of musical culture, along with Wilder's own longing for the trappings of an earlier Austria that seemed to transcend political, racial, and national differences. To do so, he would need to move the bulk of its setting from Vienna to the Austrian provinces.[69]

Figure 5.3. The caption for this publicity photograph for *The Emperor Waltz*, which incorrectly identifies Billy Wilder's birthplace as Vienna, reads: "For a scene in *The Emperor Waltz*, his next for Paramount, Bing Crosby wears a real silk tie from Austria. Director Billy Wilder, a native of Vienna, is enjoying a nostalgic moment as he examines it." *Photo: Margaret Herrick Library (AMPAS).*

As he prepared to film *The Emperor Waltz*, Wilder spared no expense to recreate a picturesque Austrian landscape in Jasper National Park in Alberta's Rocky Mountains (Figure 5.4). According to Vienna-born Jewish émigré Paul Elbogen, who served as the film's technical advisor, Wilder wanted a

Figure 5.4. At enormous expense, director Billy Wilder arranged for the cast and crew of *The Emperor Waltz* to travel for days by train to the Canadian Rockies, where they constructed a set as a provincial Austrian village according to his exact specifications. *Screen shot from* The Emperor Waltz.

specific, authentic version of one of Austria's most picturesque mountain villages along the lines of Tyrol's Hall, the South Tyrol's Sterzing, or Upper Austria's Hallstatt. The result featured houses whose balconies had real flower boxes, a church, and a village square with a fountain. Other extravagant production elements, as described by Elbogen in a 1948 article in *Neues Österreich*, included an over-the-top Hollywood budget, expensive stars, lavish costumes, 600 extras and dancers, including 460 ball guests (with 120 dancing pairs) and 100 extras cast as Austrian peasants, 30-meter-high wall paintings in the ballroom, 50 real paintings, and a canvas painted to feature the palace of Schönbrunn.[70]

The transportation expense and effort were also over the top: "Three 'Traundln' [Austrian rowboats] made according to my specifications, and several Austrian farm wagons were transported three thousand miles to Jasper; the company followed in a special train. And every morning a train of about thirty cars and trucks—we had to bring our own source of electricity—set off to drive up into the glaciers."[71] Wilder wanted an island constructed in the middle of a lake, a roadway painted just the right shade of ochre, daisies painted a specific shade of blue, extra pine trees hauled in at enormous cost, and a $1,600 recreation of the automobile in which Franz Josef rode in 1905.[72] These extravagances can be understood as expressions of Wilder's desire to recreate the experience, not just the appearance, of the idealized Austria he imagined—and of the ironic impossibility of this return, which was also part of his larger vision.

Wilder's idyllic mountains grew out of a cinematic tradition. Jewish directors such as Ernst Lubitsch, Wilder's mentor, commonly used the trope of the out-of-place Jew in the mountains as a comical way to explore issues related to Jewish assimilation and self-identification.[73] Such codings became particularly important in Austria after 1918, as the political and cultural divide between Vienna and the provinces intensified in the wake of the dissolution of Austria-Hungary. During this time, Austrians often invoked Jewish difference as a way to articulate and reinforce power struggles between city and province.[74]

From the viewpoint of the provinces, interwar Vienna loomed large as a dangerous "Jewish" metropolis—superficial, ugly, crass, corrupt, depraved, socialist, capitalist, materialist, decadent, modern, and immoral, depending on the demands of political or cultural expediency. In turn, the provinces functioned as the site of all that was pure, good, beautiful, respectable, moral, and Christian—values that many sought to include in a new "Austrian" (and thus non-Jewish) sensibility. This coding affected how both Jews and non-Jews engaged these spaces, including narratives in which Jews might fit in if they adapted in the right way, and narratives that Jews themselves created, so long as they rejected urban, Jewish modernity.

Outside the movie theater, the codings of Jewish difference did not mean that Jews were entirely absent from the provinces any more than they implied that Jews were always at home in Jewish-coded Vienna. But they did affect the choices Jews made about living in and traveling to the provinces. Austrian émigré Martin H. Ross explained why his Jewish grandparents chose to continue vacationing in the Tyrol in the 1920s despite their awareness of its antisemitism: "Inasmuch as Tyrol was the gathering place for antisemites, it followed that by going there they felt that they dissociated themselves from the people who were the target of antisemitism."[75] Like the *Sommerfrische* (summer resorts) in the provinces, where antisemitism was also a given, the non-Jewish coded mountains attracted Jews seeking to overcome their own sense of disenfranchisement.

190   THE POSTWAR ANTISEMITE

Nazis seemed to find mountain films aesthetically appropriate for marking heroic occasions.[76] The narratives of mountain films subtly changed under the Nazis. As the language of *Heimat* became increasingly nationalistic, focusing on and defending one's local community became equated with defending the nation.[77] Such elements can be discerned in postwar *Heimat* films that emerged at the end of the 1940s, some of which aimed to present landscapes as spaces of return for *Vertriebene*, ethnic Germans expelled from their homelands in the East.[78] However, rather than turning the mountains into a space of return for native Germans, Wilder's film fantasizes about them as an alternate Austrian space inhospitable to the Antisemite, but which might under certain conditions welcome an outsider.

Wilder and Brackett wrote thirteen films together between 1936 and 1950, including *Ninotchka, The Lost Weekend*, and the Oscar-winning *Sunset Boulevard*.[79] Brackett's diaries provide a rich source of information about their collaboration, as well as how they diverged in their views on Jews and antisemitism. At times, Brackett had difficulty comprehending Wilder's decisions about *The Emperor Waltz*, which he called a "stinker." As Brackett noted, "I don't suppose I ever understood it very well."[80]

Charles Brackett, whose prominent American family had settled in Massachusetts in the seventeenth century, was born in Saratoga Springs in 1892 and was the epitome of American privilege: he attended Williams College and Harvard Law School, and his father, Edgar Truman Brackett, was a New York state senator as well as a prominent lawyer and banker. Brackett genuinely admired Wilder's talent, and his grandson Jim Moore notes that their odd-couple configuration seemed to work well, at least for a time. But Brackett's diary also reveals an abundance of antisemitic attitudes and slurs. He describes a colleague as "a red-faced, pop-eyed Jew who says a play can't be very good because the cinema rights were sold for $11,000."[81] When actor Eleanor Boardman tells him, "I can't bargain. I am not a Jew," in a discussion about rent, he replies, "Nor am I."[82] He notes that film mogul Harry Warner "is certainly the type of ego-ridden Jew that the Jews of the country should most deplore."[83]

Given pervasive antisemitism in American culture, it is no surprise that he made such statements in private conversations and his diary, nor is it surprising that Wilder and Brackett clashed on whether characters should be coded as Jews. For example, in 1949, when working on *Sunset Boulevard* with screenwriter Donald McGill Marshman, Jr., the three disagreed on whether the character played by Jack Webb—Artie Green—should be renamed.

HILDE SPIEL RETURNS TO VIENNA   191

Brackett suggested an Italian name, but Wilder insisted on calling him Artie Hirsch. Brackett notes:

> Suddenly he was accusing us of disapproval of Jewish-Gentile marriages. We informed him that we thought to make the one pleasant and likeable and good person in our current undertaking too obviously Jewish would have the same irritating effect on a public which has been overdosed with *Gentleman's Agreement, Crossfire, Young Lions*, etc. We're all for a touch of Jewish propaganda—that's why I didn't hesitate to take delightful Jack Webb for the role—but don't overdo it by having it bad and irritating propaganda.[84]

Wilder had his own racist and misogynist prejudices. Brackett's diaries illuminate both:

> Billy and I worked all morning but Billy indulged in a digression—his feelings about women: his boredom with them, his scorn for them, his intense dislike. He is a real misogynist (like most intense amorists) and I may say I share his boredom with most of the women he picks out, as dreary and affected a lot of empty-headed females as one could imagine.[85]

During one conversation about their servants, Brackett wrote, Wilder said "he thought all Negroes were lazy. Judith [Wilder's wife] flared up: 'You can't say that any more than you can say all Jews are shysters and cheats!'" After her interjection, Billy backtracked: "'In fact,' Billy replied, 'the only generalization one can make is that all capitalists are sons-of-bitches.'"[86]

Wilder's prejudices did not alter the limitations he faced as a Jew, but Brackett remained indifferent to the painful loss of his family in the Holocaust and unaware of how it might have affected him. The past seemed to weigh heavily on Wilder during the filming of *The Emperor Waltz* in 1946, even though they were making a comedy. Aware of Wilder's dark mood, but unwilling to look beyond his success to acknowledge the Nazi genocide that was certainly fresh in his mind, Brackett wrote:

> A day on the dubbing stage. When I met Billy in the office I knew he was in one of his moods, and his mood proved to be the persecuted one. The Rebel discriminated against. This comes on him now and then—he craves occasional persecution as animals crave salt. With the passing of years, however,

192   THE POSTWAR ANTISEMITE

and his great success, it's getting goddamned hard to find any persecution...
he and I were asked to speak two lines in *Variety Girl* for nothing. At first
he said he would do so for an automobile, then only if $125,000 was given
to the Jewish Blind. I may add that I've never known the Jewish Blind to
haunt his conscience before. Result: *Variety Girl* will have to stagger along
without Brackett and Wilder.[87]

Wilder's emotional struggles may help explain why the original
screenplay's depiction of Austrians—and Virgil's relationships to them—was
not entirely rosy. The film's protagonist, Smith, is carefully depicted as a non-
Jewish character. However, as a clever, cosmopolitan salesman, he is still
coded as a Jew and the opposite of the typical hero of German and Austrian
Heimat films, usually a forester, mountaineer, or hunter, whose natural hab-
itat is the mountains.[88] In a scene whose staging of rural mountain life as a
tourist attraction echoes *Heimat* films, Smith, clad in *Tracht* (Austrian folk
costume), sings a song called "Friendly Mountain." Two Austrians yodel
as he passes and lift their hats to him; he does the same, then realizes he is
wearing his hat the wrong way and turns it around.

An earlier draft of the screenplay, however, casts a shadow over these
pleasant interactions when, driven by a chauffeur, Johanna and her father,
the baron, overtake Virgil and note the phonograph he carries in his back-
pack. Offended by the presence of a "tradesman" who should not "be allowed
to presume on the Emperor of Austria" and his "cur" (a derogatory term for
a mutt), Johanna threatens to have the Austrian police expel him: "You'll
leave by the next train." Virgil scoffs at the notion: "Like fun they will. Listen,
I'm an American citizen and he's an American dog, and I've got a passport
and he's got a license." To which Johanna replies: "If you don't go voluntarily, the gendarmes will take you and your dog by the nape of your necks
and throw you on the train." After sharing a few more barbs, she reinforces
her threat: "The first train out of here. You, your apparatus and your dog.
Especially that dog." Her triple reference to having Virgil deported by train
underscores his vulnerability as a foreigner and associates him with Jews like
Wilder's mother and other relatives murdered by the Nazis. After driving off
and leaving Virgil in a cloud of dust, two more peasants pass by, yodeling.
This time, Virgil tells them, "Shut your stupid Tyrolean traps!" and defiantly
turns his hat around to face the wrong way.[89]

Documents from the studio's censors suggest that the filmmakers
were asked to tone down any scenes that might damage the United States'

relationship with foreign powers, which may account for the elimination of this heated, politically tinged dialogue between Johanna and Virgil from the final film. On the other hand, Brackett notes, after seeing rushes of the scene, the fight between Crosby and Fontaine on the road "bores me more than any in the picture," suggesting that he, too, may have had something to do with eliminating the scene.[90] It might also explain why the revised screenplay inserts an additional scene in which Virgil comes across a group of peasants engaged in folk dancing, whose enthusiasm inspires him to start kicking up his own heels and slapping his knees: "Woodchopper steals girl from man lying by haystack. They start to dance. Virgil, looking down at the scene below, laughs. Man and girl dancing—kick—now Virgil sticks his stick into the ground and does a little imitation of the dancers."[91]

In what is perhaps the film's kitschiest scene, an entire Austrian village emerges with their instruments for a spontaneous performance (Figure 5.5). The screenplay notes that they "have brought out their violins, cellos, and bass viols, and are indulging in a little twilight concert. There is no conductor.

Figure 5.5. Extras in this screenshot from director Billy Wilder's *The Emperor Waltz* are dressed in Austrian provincial costume for an impromptu orchestra concert on the sidewalk of the Canadian set that was designed to look exactly like a village in Tyrol. *Screen Shot from* The Emperor Waltz.

194   THE POSTWAR ANTISEMITE

They are playing from windows, from the doorsteps of their shops, sitting on the fountain in the square."[92] That the villagers appear impossibly culturally sophisticated and welcoming to quick-witted foreigners like Virgil is much more than parody: it is fantasy.[93]

On the other hand, with the Nazi associations of Johanna's character removed, the film's central Antisemite emerges as veterinarian Dr. Zwieback, played by German-Jewish actor Sig Ruman. Through most of the film, Zwieback is comic relief for his attempts to psychoanalyze dogs—an obvious dig at Freud, a motif in several other Wilder films.[94] His Viennese-accented English also signals his attachment to the city and his outsider position in the provinces. His character takes a darker turn when he is about to carry out the baron's directive to kill the puppies. When Smith intervenes in this barely concealed metaphor for killing Jews, Zwieback claims that he is "just following orders." Although the aristocratic Austrian gives the order, Zwieback most evokes the figure of the Antisemite—especially through this common excuse given by Nazi *Mitläufer* (literally, followers) in denazification trials, with which Wilder was familiar. If this association with the Nazis suggests Zwieback is an Antisemite, he is also portrayed via Jewish codes as an out-of-place outsider in a fantasy version of Austria, underscoring the emperor's benevolence. The character of Zwieback, so out of place in the film's Austrian provinces full of friendly villagers, underscores how the prewar role of the Jew as outsider was transformed into its antithesis, the Antisemite/Nazi outsider.[95]

Despite devoting such time and energy to recreating an idyllic Austrian setting and making sure his characters and their costumes appeared as authentically Austrian as possible, Wilder was not pleased with the final result. During the film's first screening in 1947, Brackett noted, "Billy [was] sitting through it very unhappy because he really hates it by now," although Brackett later describes Wilder as excited about the film's successful premiere.[96] But later, Wilder claimed to consider *The Emperor Waltz* an embarrassment: "The less time you consume in analyzing *The Emperor Waltz*, you know, the better. There's nothing to explain, there's nothing to read into *that thing*."[97] Wilder chalked up his dissatisfaction to his inability to produce musicals. The fact that he never explained why he spared no expense in reproducing an entire music-loving Austrian village in Canada directly after learning about the crimes of the Nazis, including those that affected him personally, requires us to take the film more seriously.

HILDE SPIEL RETURNS TO VIENNA   195

Perhaps most telling is an interview where Wilder insists that *The Emperor Waltz* had nothing to do with what had happened in Europe, then immediately contradicts himself by noting that it actually had everything to do with his experience editing *Die Todesmühlen* (*Death Mills*):

> I kind of thought it would be fun to make a musical. I have no talent for a musical . . . I was not up to making a musical. I don't know, I should have gone to a hospital or something, after being in Germany and cutting an hour-and-a-half documentary about the concentration camps in London. . . . There was nothing to direct. It had to be a natural thing that happened that they were just able to photograph. You cannot have corpses built up in a little funeral pyre. No. And there was that one shot that I really loved, a shot that they took in a concentration camp, either Dachau or Auschwitz. There was a field of corpses, a *field*, and one corpse was not quite dead. And he looked and he saw the camera, did not know what it was, and he walked to the corpses, on top of the corpses, and sat down, ultimately, on dead corpses, and stared at us. That was the shot. I was not there when they photographed it. But that was the shot, and I used the whole shot. So I was kind of very eager to do something on the more frivolous side.[98]

In this context, *The Emperor Waltz* was far from frivolous, yet perhaps its frivolity was why he rejected the finished version. The film seems to carry a wish for transformation—to transform that field of corpses back into a prewar image of an ideal Austria. Yet, there is something about this project that fails—perhaps Bing Crosby's Virgil could never pass as the Jewish outsider of Lubitsch's mountain films, while Sig Ruman's Zwieback was too convincing as the figure of the Nazi Antisemite. For Wilder, it may have been the realization of a failed fantasy that made him eager to forget its existence.

Absent Jews, Invisible Antisemitism, and *The Third Man* (1949)

British director Carol Reed's noir murder mystery about a callous man exploiting Vienna's black market to poison children for money makes no explicit mention of Jews or antisemitism. The makers of *The Third Man*, now considered a classic, can be lauded for not playing into stereotypical

196   THE POSTWAR ANTISEMITE

depictions of black marketeers as Jews, but closer examination shows that both the film and the novella upon which it was based deploy codes and tropes that evoke negative Jewish stereotypes even as they foreclose such explicit characterizations. *The Third Man* uses the misery and devastation wrought by the war on a city once known for its sophistication as the backdrop for a suspenseful tale of black market intrigue. Although directed and written by Englishmen, the film featured numerous Austrian actors (including Ernst Deutsch), used Austrian technical workers, and includes a number of untranslated lines spoken by Austrian actors that specifically address Austrian audiences in an unflattering way.[99] Thus grounded in contemporary Austria, it arguably represents Vienna's postwar condition of invisible antisemitism in a land of absent Jews even more deeply than films that aimed to critique antisemitism, such as *Das andere Leben* or *Der Prozeß*. Jews and antisemitism are noticeably absent from both the film *The Third Man* and the Graham Greene novella on which it is based. Both works simultaneously evoke and repress these seemingly absent forces, particularly in their representation of the black market, exemplifying how antisemitism without Jews and Antisemites continued to mark public life in Vienna in the immediate postwar period.[100]

Alexander Korda, the film's Hungarian-born, British Jewish producer, imagined that postwar Vienna, which was not only damaged but divided and controlled by French, British, U.S., and Soviet forces, would serve as the perfect backdrop for a tale of crime and intrigue.[101] He asked Graham Greene, whose screenplays he admired, to work on the film. Greene wrote the story and helped adapt it for the screen, delivering precisely what Korda sought: a gripping tale of death, criminality, and general moral confusion in the early postwar years. The film begins when an American writer of pulp Westerns named Holly Martins (played by Joseph Cotton) travels to Vienna upon the invitation of his friend Harry Lime (Orson Welles). Lime, also an American, officially works for the International Refugee Office but unofficially peddles watered-down, and therefore deadly, penicillin on the black market. After Martins arrives in Vienna, he learns that Lime has been hit by a car, but he later learns that his friend has faked his own death in order to continue his lucrative underground activities, which have resulted in the illness and death of many children. The film culminates in an iconic chase scene through Vienna's vast network of sewers that ends with Martins killing Lime.

The Third Man's masterful and memorable depiction of the city's dark, gritty streets and sewers and its tale of black market racketeering and murder make it as thrilling as any spy film. Countless critics and scholars have written about its merits and themes of morality, guilt, and redemption; many argue that it belongs among the greatest films of all time. However, the realities of postwar Vienna, as well as Greene's earlier publications and proclivities, reveal the film's more ambiguous implications. Austrian and international newspapers of the time were filled with articles highlighting the unpleasant activities of DPs on the black market, often implying that they were Jewish but not identifying them outright as Jews. It was common knowledge that not only DPs, but virtually the entire population of Austria and many foreigners, including members of the Allied Forces, participated actively in the black market. However, despite the widespread nature of this activity and the tiny numbers of Jews in Vienna, newspaper articles and eye-witness reports often foregrounded the role of DPs in the black market and the tensions they caused, both real and imagined.[102]

Although Greene claimed that "real life" was merely a backdrop to a fictional story, he took care to base *The Third Man* on the realities of the postwar situation in Vienna.[103] In an effort to soak up the city's atmosphere, he visited for two weeks in February 1948, staying at the centrally located Hotel Sacher, frequenting seedy nightclubs, and meeting with numerous people savvy to how the city functioned under its bizarre circumstances: jointly controlled by the Allied Forces in the inner district, divided among them beyond its boundaries. According to Elizabeth Montagu, Greene's guide in Vienna, the writer became fascinated with the "run-down, seedy, devastated city of the present," and these meetings greatly influenced the film's story. She recounts that among those he met was Peter Smollett (also known as Hans Peter Smolka, or Harry P. Smolka), a Viennese Jewish correspondent for *The Times* and the *Daily Express*, who had written "highly topical stories concerning the shady aspects of post-war Vienna," including one on a "shadowy man who peddled diluted penicillin" via the city's extensive sewer system, which, to Montagu's consternation, made its way uncredited into both the book and film.[104]

Austria had a long history of associating foreign Jews with underhanded business dealings and the black market, particularly during and after World War I, when thousands of refugees from Galicia and elsewhere arrived in Vienna.[105] Moreover, the idea that Jews adulterated their black market goods to harm children updated centuries-old canards about Jews as well-poisoners and child-killers. The persistence of these rumors can be seen in the June 1946 sentencing of an Austrian woman in Bad Ischl to two months

198 THE POSTWAR ANTISEMITE

in jail for spreading the false rumor that local children had become sick after former concentration camp inmates purposefully gave them marmalade and cake infested with tuberculosis bacteria.[106] The association of Jews harming children with illegally obtained and adulterated substances extended to penicillin, fostered by reports that Jews from the United States sent penicillin in aid packages to Jews in Europe, as well as the fact that the American Jewish Joint Distribution Committee, an international relief organization, sent one million dollars worth of penicillin, then a newly discovered "wonder drug," to Russia for Jewish DPs (as well as 30 million units to Czechoslovakia for the population in general).[107]

In one sense, Greene and the filmmakers can be lauded for not including Jews in their tale of black market intrigue. Indeed, the depiction of a black market without Jews may have more closely reflected the actual situation than did the inflated implications of sensationalist newspaper reports and eyewitness accounts. Nevertheless, both novella and film actually do evoke negative Jewish stereotypes even as they avoid specifically naming characters as Jews. Harry Lime epitomizes the dark, foreign black marketeer, skilled at swindling, who poisons innocent children without compunction and typifies the city's moral decay. Lime opportunistically takes advantage of those in need and ruthlessly uses his cold-blooded business acumen to his own advantage. As such, he perfectly embodies a Jewish character type familiar from pre–World War II English literature, including works by Greene.[108] But portraying this figure as a Jew was now taboo, which meant that Lime necessarily had to be explicitly *not* Jewish, hence his open professions of his Catholicism and continued faith in God, even as he chooses to engage in morally reprehensible behavior.

In one notable scene, Lime peers down from a car of Vienna's famous Ferris wheel and asks Holly Martins whether, if offered money to kill the anonymous "dots" below, he would really turn it down. In short, Lime embodies the characteristics that Max Horkheimer and Theodor Adorno claim the Antisemite ascribes to the Jew: "The fantasies of Jewish crimes, infanticide and sadistic excess, poisoning of the nation, and international conspiracy, accurately define the antisemitic dream, and fall short of its realization."[109] In *The Third Man*, these characteristics operate effectively, if subliminally, to turn a man who is not a Jew into a Jew. In other words, Harry Lime fits the bill as the liminal Antisemite in Vienna's atmosphere of invisible antisemitism.

Greene's explicit references to Nazis in the novella add to its simultaneous evocation and suppression of Jews and antisemitism, though these

HILDE SPIEL RETURNS TO VIENNA   199

mentions did not make their way into the film. For example, in the book, Harry, who works for the International Refugee Office, lives in an apartment requisitioned from an unnamed Nazi in a building whose landlord's wife is named Ilse Koch—the name of the wife of Karl-Otto Koch, the erstwhile commandant of Majdanek and Buchenwald. Infamous for her sadism and for purportedly making lampshades out of tattooed prisoners' skin, the real-life Ilse Koch earned the nickname the "Bitch of Buchenwald" and was sentenced to jail in 1947 for her role in the murder of countless Jews.

But Harry's connection to the Nazi's former apartment is ambiguous: while living there, he is associated not only with the Nazi he displaced but also, implicitly, with the original Jewish owner displaced by the Nazi. According to one source, 80 percent of the 1,200 Jews who returned to Vienna in 1947 found their former apartments undamaged by bombing but occupied by Nazis or Aryanizers who, according to Austrian law, could not be ousted unless they had joined the Nazi party before 1938 or held a key position in the party.[110] Like DPs in the black market, the Jews returning to reclaim their apartments aroused antisemitic sentiment among Austrians dealing with the city's severe housing shortage, even though most of the claims were unsuccessful.[111]

The Third Man's simultaneous evocation and repression of Jews and Antisemites makes sense for a film that depicts contemporary realities. Greene made liberal use of antisemitic stereotypes in his books and his film reviews for *The Spectator* during the 1930s.[112] But in the immediate postwar era, as details about the murder of Europe's Jews came to light, neither Greene nor the filmmakers had any desire to address these topics—just as, in the face of current political tensions, they toned down the novella's negative references to Russians. The postwar taboo against explicit antisemitism was so pervasive that Greene later returned to his earlier novels and cut or toned down such references for later editions, explaining that "[a]fter the holocaust one couldn't use the word Jew in the loose way one used it before the war . . . casual references to Jews . . . a sign of those times when one regarded the word Jew as almost a synonym for capitalist."[113] About *The Third Man*, he remarked, "We had no desire to move people's political emotions; we wanted to entertain them, to frighten them a little, even to make them laugh."[114]

Today, *The Third Man* remains known for its representation of postwar Vienna and its gritty streets filled with black market intrigue as much as, if not more than, pure entertainment. But its postwar context means that this representation attests to the ongoing invisible presence of both antisemitism

200 THE POSTWAR ANTISEMITE

and Jews. While the aesthetics and mood of *The Third Man* are practically antithetical to *The Emperor Waltz*, both films hold up an image of the Austrian *Heimat* "washed clean" of antisemitism. In this regard, the urban environment of *The Third Man* could be exchanged with the provincial environment of *The Emperor Waltz*, for in both, the liminal Antisemite becomes the figure around which the film is ordered. This play on the motif of exchanging roles signals the complexity involved in Jewish self-identification, as Hilde Spiel's experiences illustrate, but it also signals a more insidious effort, as was evident in Lernet-Holenia's *Der zwangzigste Juli*, to diminish the reality of Jewish suffering and dismiss the antisemitism that persisted in everyday Austrian life after the war. While these narratives and films had different intentions and present different stories, they all ultimately uphold the framework of Jewish difference instead of dismantling the hierarchical coding system that still separated Jews from non-Jewish Austrians. Rather than eliminating Jewish difference as a narrative force and reconciling these distinctions, the suppression of antisemitism and the absence of Jews led only to their subtler evocation.

6

False Accusations

Der Prozess and *1. April 2000*

August 1940 must have been a stressful month for the Brunngraber family. The Nuremberg Laws were starting to cause trouble for Louise Brunngraber, her daughter Erika, and her husband Rudolf. Born Aloisia Gettinger in Vienna in April 1901, Louise was the daughter of a Jewish-born mother, Berta Kohn, and a non-Jewish father, Johann Gettinger.[1] Her parents met when Johann was employed as a servant by Berta's parents, Samuel and Regina Kohn. Berta converted to Catholicism in April 1893, and married Johann a month later.[2] Louise and her three siblings were baptized and raised as Catholics.[3] They grew up in the working-class district of Favoriten, where Louise met Rudolf Brunngraber. They moved in together in 1926, Louise left the Catholic church on December 1928, and they married the following month, by which point Rudolf had also left the Catholic church.[4] Their daughter Erika was born in 1930.

To earn money, Louise worked as a secretary in the war office and modeled for art students at Vienna's *Kunstgewerbeschule des Österreichischen Museums für Kunst und Industrie* (Academy of Applied Art of the Austrian Museum for Art and Industry), where Rudolf entered into a course of study for a career as an artist starting in 1926.[5] There, he trained as a commercial artist, mainly by copying the paintings of artist Gustav Klimt.[6] In March 1928, he wrote to Helene Klimt, wife of Gustav's brother Emil, to ask whether he might be able to visit their home to view the artist's paintings, so keen was he to see the original works. She advised him to visit the Klimt exhibit in Vienna's Neue Galerie. She had also suggested that he contact Serena Lederer, whose portrait Klimt had painted, and who, along with her husband, the wealthy industrialist August Lederer, held the largest private collection of the painter's works.[7]

But Rudolf would soon prove better suited for the literary world. The success of his debut novel *Karl und das 20. Jahrhundert* (*Karl and the Twentieth Century*, 1933), which was eventually translated into eighteen languages,

The Postwar Antisemite. Lisa Silverman, Oxford University Press. © Oxford University Press 2025.
DOI: 10.1093/9780197697757.003.0007

202 THE POSTWAR ANTISEMITE

allowed Louise to stop working.[8] By March 1938, Rudolf Brunngraber had left copying paintings behind and become one of Austria's most celebrated authors. Like all other non-Jewish Austrian writers, after the *Anschluss* he was required to join the *Reichsschrifttumskammer* (Reich Chamber of Literature) in order to keep publishing. His application was accepted without incident and he became a member on July 1, 1938.[9] In September 1939, two weeks after the Nazi invasion of Poland, the *Reichs-Rundfunk-Gesellschaft* (Reich Broadcasting Corporation) in Berlin approached him about his novel *Opiumkrieg* (Opium war), which they considered "excellent material for a gripping political radio play, which could be very effective propaganda right now."[10] Rudolf adapted the script, and the play was aired three times.[11]

But in August 1940, to his surprise, Rudolf was suddenly expelled from the *Reichsschrifttumskammer* and forbidden to publish in Austria.[12] Fearing that he would no longer be able to support his family, he hired Berlin lawyer Carl Haensel to file an appeal.[13] Haensel soon learned that the problem was Louise's status as a *Mischling* (Nazi term for progeny of mixed Jewish/non-Jewish ancestry). Although writers classified as *Volljuden* ("full Jews" in Nazi terminology) had long been excluded from *Reichsschrifttumskammer* membership, in 1939 Goebbels tightened the membership requirements to exclude writers with any degree of Jewish classification. The spouses of so-called *Volljuden* and *Halbjuden* ("half-Jews" in Nazi terminology) who had "committed an offense against the state or against National Socialism or otherwise demonstrated that they incline toward Judaism" were also excluded.[14] Rudolf was one of twenty-four authors removed from the *Reichsschrifttumskammer* between August 1940 and April 1941 as a result of these new rules.[15]

Rudolf's expulsion from the *Reichsschrifttumskammer* caused a dilemma for the Brunngrabers. He was keen to maintain his career but aware that he needed to justify Louise's classification. The new guidelines stipulated that authors married to *Halbjuden* might be able to continue as members if they could prove their "disinclination to Judaism," suggesting the reasons for an affidavit Rudolf wrote to accompany his appeal of the decision on September 5, 1940:

> My wife (Aryan on her father's side) is actually Jewish on her mother's
> side, i.e. a Grade I *Mischling*, but my wife's mother was baptized Catholic
> before she gave birth to my wife in conjunction with her marriage many

years beforehand, and this shows that my wife was raised in an entirely un-Jewish house. There was never any mingling with Jewish relatives because they did not exist, and my wife's mother has been dead for years. As for me, I can document that my family tree is documented from the 17th century as from German-Aryan farming stock on both my mother and father's side. My father was also a farmer.[16]

Rudolf carefully crafted his narrative to appeal to its Nazi readers. He did not mention his own political commitment to socialism and strategically included his arrest in 1933 for agitating against the dictatorial Dollfuss regime, which later banned the Nazi party. His claim that he could not join the Nazi party because of his wife's status implies that he otherwise would have done so. After detailing the success of his novels, he concludes by reasserting his Aryan bona fides: "After all this, as well as the fact that my wife, who feels she is an Aryan, has never subjected me to Jewish influence, and after pointing out that we have a nine-year-old daughter to take care of, I believe that my request to revoke the exclusion is reasonable."[17]

When Haensel sent Rudolf's letter of appeal and affidavit to the *Reichsschrifttumskammer*, he included documentation of Berta Gettinger's baptism on April 7, 1893, eight years before Louise's birth, and stressed that all four of her children had been baptized and had married Aryans. Haensel also attempted to distance Louise from her family's Jewishness by emphasizing her pious Christian upbringing under the direction of her Aryan father:

> since she was a woman raised as a Christian who lived completely within these lines of thought and staunchly rejected everything Jewish, Mr. Brunngraber only learned about her status as a *Mischling* much later. It is emphasized that it is specifically the father of Frau Brunngraber— Gettinger—who is Aryan and who determined the family's cultural and ideological outlook.[18]

Throughout that autumn, Rudolf continued to anxiously supply his lawyer with evidence to support his appeal. In September 1940, he wrote to Haensel with additional details about Louise's estrangement from her Jewish family, framing Berta as a victim who had waged (and lost) a legal battle against her Jewish parents after they disinherited her for marrying Johann.[19]

204 THE POSTWAR ANTISEMITE

In May 1941, after the *Reichsschrifttumskammer* rejected Rudolf's appeal, he agreed to take Haensel's advice and file for divorce. But he changed his mind when he realized that divorce would cause significant problems for Louise and Erika and would not guarantee that his membership would be reinstated.[20] Instead, he applied for special permission to work, which was an alternative to membership. In another letter to Haensel, Rudolf stressed his fears for his very existence and begged the lawyer to meet with *Reichsschrifttumskammer* director Hans Hinkel about his case.[21] He also sent Haensel a fresh, detailed account of his past that stressed his disadvantaged, impoverished childhood, casting himself as a victim of his youthful circumstances as well as the Jews. In this account, he shifts from denying the Jewishness of his mother-in-law Berta, whom he had previously portrayed as a victim of her Jewish parents, to playing it up in order to cast himself as *her* victim. He undoubtedly highlighted the indignity of being held back from his writing career by an illiterate Jewish woman only to appeal to Nazi officials and underscore his distance from Judaism. Strategically, the account includes very few details about Louise or other Jews in his life. Instead, he negates the influence of Louise's mother, claiming he "never had *one* coherent conversation" with her, as if attempting to exorcise the family of the last remnants of its Jewishness, and contrasting the strength of his own Aryan background to her feebleness, as he defined himself against the Jewish-tainted family into which he had married:

> After I got married, I was never in close contact with my wife's family. I never addressed her parents with "du," and I never had *one* coherent conversation with her Jewish mother. And this was not due to racism or intellectual/snobbiness, but simply—as strange as it may seem given the origins of my wife's mother—because this mother was downright illiterate (she could not tell time.) *I cite this here not as the argument of a poetically-minded person driven to the point of the grotesque, but rather the expression of despair of a German writer who has been translated into twelve languages, who can prove his Aryan family tree back to the age of the Thirty Years' War, and now, at age forty and having lived a really difficult life, whose intellectual and practical existence is to be taken away on account of a deceased illiterate woman, with whom he never had a personal relationship.* Incidentally, my wife's completely un-Jewish development is also shown by the fact that all her siblings also married Aryans.[22] [Emphasis in original]

FALSE ACCUSATIONS 205

Rudolf's letter abounds with stereotypes about Jews, from the backhandedly positive assumption that all Jews are educated and literate to the insulting implication that they cannot be the equals of Germans like him.[23]

Throughout the 1920s and 1930s, Rudolf maintained close professional and intimate relationships with Jews, and he was well aware of the dangers of Nazi antisemitism.[24] In contrast to the considerable number of non-Jewish Austrians who abandoned their Jewish spouses, Rudolf remained married to Louise.[25] As the wife of an Aryan, Louise was not required to wear a yellow star, and she leveraged this position to help her less advantaged Jewish relatives. At great risk, Louise visited her mother's sister Ernestine in the hospital when she was ill, bringing Erika, who was blond, as cover. She also sent Erika to bring her hot food every day, until Ernestine's deportation and murder in Theresienstadt. Erika and Louise's visits to Ernestine dismayed Rudolf, but he did not forbid them.[26] The contrast between Rudolf's letters to his lawyer and his actions once again show that one did not have to hate Jews in order to construct vivid and effective antisemitic narratives—in this case, to save his family.

To build the case for Rudolf to continue working, Haensel asked him to provide details about other authors in mixed marriages who were permitted to write. Rudolf obliged by describing the circumstances of his friend, poet Wilhelm Szabo, who was married to Valerie Szabo-Lorenz, a *Halbjüdin*, though he said that divulging the information made him feel like a "heel toad" and begged Haensel to keep it confidential. Apparently, Szabo had not been accepted into the *Reichsschrifttumskammer* because of questions about his "unclear parentage" as well as his marriage to a *Mischling*, but he had received permission to write a novel.[27]

Their efforts paid off, and in June 1941 Rudolf was granted preliminary permission to publish his novel *Zucker aus Cuba* (Sugar from Cuba).[28] Then new concerns about his support for the Nazi party arose.[29] Anonymous individuals had denounced him for speaking critically about the state, military operations, and the war, citing, among other comments, a remark about the *Führer* being a man of average intelligence whose success was due to a streak of good luck. He was also accused of spreading rumors about affairs between a Nazi official and several actors. In a haughty letter of defense, Rudolf explained that the inferior intelligence and differences of age, social class, career experience, and spirituality between him and his denouncers had led them to misunderstand him. He noted that he had recently visited and received visits from various Nazi officials.[30] In the end, the denunciations

206 THE POSTWAR ANTISEMITE

were dismissed, and Rudolf was granted final permission to publish his work on November 6, 1941.[31]

At that point, Rudolf became a Nazi favorite, a status that lasted until the end of the war. Some of the benefits accrued to his family: he secured a place for Erika at school until she was sent to the countryside in 1943, as part of the *Kinderlandverschickung,* an evacuation program designed to keep children safe from bombings, while Louise was permitted to accompany her as a group leader.[32] Rudolf stayed behind in Vienna, taking frequent trips to Berlin, though he was able to resist Goebbels's request that he move there. Louise and Erika returned to Vienna in the fall of 1945.[33]

When the war ended, the status of friend of Goebbels shifted rapidly from asset to liability. In response, Rudolf pivoted to representing himself in terms of his conflicts with the Nazis, refusal to join the Nazi party, and prewar socialist affiliations (including his term as chairman of the *Vereinigung sozialistischer Schriftsteller* [Association of Socialist Writers] in the 1930s). Like directors Veit Harlan and Wolfgang Liebeneiner, he scrambled to overcome the challenges his relationship with Goebbels posed to his postwar career. His desire to distance himself from his success under the Nazis, combined with his wartime experiences crafting narratives about Jews in order to ensure that success, provides critical context for his shift to film, particularly screenwriting. During the war, he cast himself and his family as non-Jewish victims of Louise's illiterate, deceased Jewish-born mother in order to satisfy the Nazis who controlled his career. After the war, he portrayed Jews and non-Jews as victims of a liminal Antisemite, which helped distance him—and other Austrians—from those very Nazis. Two films for which he served as screenwriter both rely upon liminal figures of evil in order to frame the innocence of its victims: in one case, Jews are unfairly accused of murder, and in the other, the state of Austria is unfairly accused of disrupting world peace.

Austrian director G. W. Pabst's film *Der Prozess* (The trial, 1948) is a fictionalized account of the false ritual murder accusations Jews faced in Tiszaeszlár, a small town in Austria-Hungary, in 1882–1883. *1. April 2000* (1952), directed by Wolfgang Liebeneiner, was a state-financed comedy that envisioned a still-occupied Austria on trial in the year 2000, unjustly accused of damaging world peace and defending itself from the judgment of an international organization headed by a cold-hearted widow. *1. April 2000* has no Jewish characters and does not mention antisemitism. However, as a courtroom drama it echoes *Der Prozess*'s narrative of unjust accusations, but in this film, the future state of Austria stands in for the wrongly accused Jews of the past, while the delegates of the international organization sitting in judgment, particularly its female leader, parallel their oppressors. By refiguring the courtroom drama of *Der Prozess*'s innocent Jewish victims as one that exonerates the wrongly accused state of Austria, *1. April 2000* references Brunngraber's preceding screenplay, but this time positioning Austrians as the true victims, while at the same time avoiding any explicit references to Jews or Antisemites.

It is no surprise that the plots of both films, one set in the past and the other in the future, would center on trials, given the numerous denazification trials in *Volksgerichte* (local courts in Austria) as well as the high-profile trials of Nazis and collaborators. However, Brunngraber's wartime experience of skillfully framing his relationships with Jews sheds light on how both narratives evoke a constructed Antisemite. This figure is articulated via the codes of Jewish difference in order to underscore the oppression of its victims. In *Der Prozess*, which takes place in the Austro-Hungarian past, Jews and their Christian savior are the focus, and the current state of Austria does not figure at all. In *1. April 2000*, Austria's innocence is foregrounded and both Jews and Antisemites are notably absent, save for its non-Austrian, Jewish-coded outsider. She is a woman of ambiguous origin, known only for her role as the president of the Global Union that puts Austria on trial and her harsh, military-like demeanor, whom the Austrian protagonist softens and charms into marriage. By associating her with the modern art of Gustav Klimt, with which Brunngraber was intimately familiar, she also evokes the artist's Jewish subjects and Aryanized clients. She is the film's liminal Antisemite who evokes both Jews and their antisemitic oppressors.

Both films were written and directed by men who had enjoyed successful careers under the Nazis (Brunngraber, Pabst, and Liebeneiner) but, unlike Veit Harlan, did not make explicitly antisemitic films. Still, both films share another goal: restoring Christianity as the proper moral foundation to postwar Austrian culture. The hero of *Der Prozess* is Károly Eötvös, the defense lawyer for the wrongly accused Jewish victims, who clarifies the nature of his moral rectitude when he asserts that he made his decision to defend Jews "because I am a Christian." *Der Prozess* suggests that opposition to antisemitism is most significant for the opportunity it provides to affirm the superiority of Christianity. *1. April 2000*, on the other hand, uses a courtroom drama set in the future as a vehicle for its characters to present the history of Austria as a defense against accusations of disturbing world peace.

208 THE POSTWAR ANTISEMITE

That defense includes several historical *mises en abyme*: a documentary film presented at the trial featuring the Austrian flag's legendary origins during the Third Crusade (1189–1191); a re-enactment of the celebrated double royal wedding of the grandchildren of Holy Roman Emperor Maximilian I in Vienna's *Stephansdom* (1515); and another documentary that expounds upon the (largely mythical) piety of Holy Roman Emperor Karl V. The film skips over the period after 1918 and omits Jews from Austrian history, yet promotes Christianity as the main evidence of Austria's peaceful origins and intentions.[34]

Der Prozess and *1. April 2000* exemplify how the framework of Jewish difference was kept in place via cultural creations that allowed audiences to deflect confrontation with Austrian complicity in Austrian Jews' absence. Rudolf Brunngraber kept his wife and daughter safe and did not publish overtly antisemitic propaganda for the Nazis. At the same time, however, his career thrived at the time and his wartime letters to Nazi functionaries helped hone his skill in creating narratives in which non-Jewish Austrians appear as victims of Jews in general, or Jewish women in particular, traces of which can be discerned in these films.

In contrast to their German counterparts, whose films directly confronted recent history, postwar Austrian filmmakers tended to look to the more distant imperial past for their film content, at least in part to distinguish themselves from Germany.[35] By focusing on an event that took place in nineteenth-century Austria-Hungary, *Der Prozess* was part of this distancing, while *1. April 2000* sets up a narrative in the future in order to mythologize the past. There is nothing in either film that one could label as promoting antisemitism; indeed, *Der Prozess* is concerned with actively opposing it. However, while both films attempt to present the image of postwar Austria as free of Antisemites, they also ended up reinforcing the absence of its Jews to promote Christian narratives.

A Death in Tiszaeszlár

The late-nineteenth-century blood libel case that inspired the events of *Der Prozess* is key to thinking about how Austrians responded to the issue of their complicity in the Holocaust. While it is evident, as described in the previous chapter, that many cultural creations sought to distance Austria from the genocide of the Jews by omitting representations of antisemitism and Jews,

Der Prozess explicitly takes up the topic of antisemitism. However, by doing so through the motif of the ritual murder, the film places the issue of postwar antisemitism in the context of a mythological past, rather than framing it as an issue of contemporary reckoning. *Der Prozess* remains the best-known dramatization of the Tiszaeszlár blood libel case, but the events also inspired Arnold Zweig's successful 1914 play, "Ritualmord in Ungarn" (Ritual murder in Hungary).[36] Staging Zweig's play in 1920 in Prague reflected Pabst's initial interest in the topic, though he first broached the idea of making a film about it during Hitler's ascent to power and rising political antisemitism in Germany. The original events and Zweig's play lay the groundwork for understanding the historical dynamics of how narratives of Jewish victimhood can be transformed into narratives of Jew as victimizer.

The events in Tiszaeszlár followed a familiar antisemitic script, to which the film hews closely. On April 1, 1882, a fourteen-year-old Christian peasant girl named Eszter Solymosi disappeared on an errand. Before Eszter's body was even found, her mother and other villagers accused thirteen Jewish men of ritually murdering her to use her blood to make matzah for the upcoming Passover holiday. Eszter's body was found on June 18, 1882, with no obvious wounds. The trial began a year and a day later and lasted six weeks. In the end, the accusations were determined to be spurious and the accused Jews were acquitted of all charges. The events typified the blood libel accusations and trials that began in the twelfth century and spiked in Central Europe in the late nineteenth century.[37]

However, Tiszaeszlár stood out from other blood libel cases because of a dramatic conflict between one of the accused, the synagogue sexton József Scharf, and his fourteen-year-old son, Móric. After his father was charged, the young boy was sequestered away from his family for over a year by local functionaries associated with the prosecutor, during which time they turned him against his family and Judaism by offering him a well-paying position and promises of a bright future. At the trial, Móric testified that his father had invited Eszter into their home on the Sabbath to move a candelabra, an act that required a non-Jew (known as a Shabbos goy). He further testified that a beggar then lured her into the nearby synagogue, where, through a keyhole in the synagogue door, Móric claimed to have seen the Jewish butcher slash her throat while his father and other men held her down. The men then dressed her dead body and presumably threw it in the river.[38]

A Hungarian law that allowed defendants to cross-examine witnesses led to a confrontation between Móric and the defendants that included a heart-wrenching plea from his father, József, who denied his son's accusations. According to numerous newspaper accounts at the time, as well as the published memoirs of defense attorney Károly Eötvös, this father-son conflict was the emotional climax of the trial, as Móric exclaimed, "Eh, what do I care about a bunch of ragged Jews!" and renounced Judaism.[39] After a live reconstruction of events proved that Móric could not have seen anything inside the synagogue from the keyhole, the boy recanted. Ten days later, the prosecutor reversed course and asked the judges to exonerate all the defendants. The trial and its aftermath revealed the antisemitism of a number of high-ranking Hungarian government officials, including Jószef Bary, the magistrate assigned to the case, and parliamentarian Géza Ónody, whose antisemitic invectives against the accused inflamed public opinion. Meanwhile, press coverage of Eötvös's eloquent defense captured international attention.

German-Jewish writer Arnold Zweig took advantage of the trial's dramatic possibilities, particularly its intra-Jewish, father-son conflict, to address the topic of Jewish assimilation in his 1914 drama "Ritualmord in Ungarn." Zweig presents Ezster's death, the false accusations against the Jews, and the trial within the framework of a conversation between Satan, who also appears as a character, and the disembodied voice of God, who asserts that the accusation and trial were intended as a test of Jews' loyalty and desire for their Messiah. He also alters historical details to foreground the play's message warning against the dangers of antisemitism and its relationship to Jewish anxieties about the challenges of assimilation. For example, though there was no evidence that Eszter had negative attitudes toward Jews, when the play's Esther first appears, she sticks out her tongue at two Jews and complains that they are extorting everyone in the village, including her mother.[40] Zweig renames Ónody, the antisemitic Hungarian politician, Baron von Onody and makes him responsible for Esther's death: she falls into the river as she tries to escape his unwanted sexual advances. These scenes provide further context for the false accusations against the Jews by pointing to widespread antisemitic stereotypes among different classes.

Zweig also refashions the plight of Móric, now spelled as the German Moritz, as a Jewish tragedy, embellishing the boy's incarceration to include torture so that his character could better represent the suffering of the Jews and their struggles with assimilation.[41] When Moritz is introduced, he is reading the Bible, comparing its pharaoh to the kaiser in Vienna, and dreaming about going to fight as a soldier in a scene that typifies contemporaneous questions raised for Jews about the degree of their loyalty to the state and their anxieties about living as Jews amid ever-present antisemitism.[42] Zweig's play ends when Moritz commits suicide, wrapped in a prayer shawl in the synagogue, wracked with guilt over having implicated his father in a murder he did not commit. In reality, after the trial, Móric renewed his wavering faith in Judaism and moved to Brussels. Zweig's version does not easily resolve the challenges Jews faced at the time regarding assimilation and antisemitism. But it sympathizes with Jews' struggles in a non-Jewish world and offers divine redemption for Moritz via his suicide.[43]

Zweig's artistic adaptation was met with mixed reactions. Although the play won the prestigious Kleist prize for German literature in 1915, it was censored in Germany after the outbreak of World War I, for fear it might offend Hungarians, and was not performed in Vienna until 1918. At that point, it was given a new title to emphasize its Jewish frame and to avoid mentioning Hungary and ritual murder: "Die Sendung Semaels: jüdische Tragödie in fünf Akten" (Satan's message: a Jewish tragedy in five acts). In 1919, one Viennese critic complained that it cast Christians in a negative light.[44] But when Pabst staged Zweig's play at the Neue Deutsche Theater in Prague in 1920, the influential Jewish writer Felix Weltsch confirmed the audience's approval.[45] In its 1948 film version, however, Pabst, Brunngraber, and their colleagues transformed Zweig's Jewish tragedy into a vehicle to serve post-1945 Austrian interests in distancing itself from antisemitism by framing it as a tale of Christian, rather than Jewish, redemption and refashioning Moritz as the narrative's figural, liminal Antisemite.

The Making of *Der Prozess*

G. W. Pabst was born to Austrian parents in 1885, grew up in Vienna, and became a successful film director in Germany. But when Hitler first came to power, he had already left Germany for Paris, where he remained off and on until 1939.[46] When he met up with his colleague Rudolph S. Joseph in France in 1933, he said that the situation in Germany had made him feel closer to the Jews. In response, Joseph reminded him of a line from Zweig's play: "Die Gerechten der Völker sind gleich vor dem Herrn" (The righteous among peoples are equal before the Lord). Pabst, who had directed the play in Prague in 1920, was apparently so taken with the line that he insisted they make their next film about the Tiszaeszlár blood libel accusation.[47]

212 THE POSTWAR ANTISEMITE

This wasn't Pabst's first effort to adapt Jewish material to film. His former assistant Mark Sorkin recalled that in the early 1920s, Pabst's interest in Jewish theater led them to acquire the rights to S. Ansky's classic Yiddish drama *Der Dybuk*. However, the funding for the production fell through because its Jewish backers were concerned that general audiences would not respond well to its themes.[48] The 1933 attempt to make the blood libel film was similarly thwarted. Louis Louis-Dreyfus, the French Jewish businessman who they hoped would be their financial backer, was too anxious about stirring up antisemitism in France to support the film, and Pabst did not want to pursue the project over the objections of his Jewish colleague.[49]

Pabst returned to Austria shortly before the outbreak of World War II, and, to the surprise of many colleagues, continued a successful career making films for the Nazis: *Komödianten* (1941) and *Paracelsus* (1943). Neither is explicitly antisemitic, especially compared to other Nazi films such as Veit Harlan's *Jud Süss*. Still, both fit seamlessly into Goebbels's fascist, antisemitic agenda.[50] Rumors about the reasons for Pabst's decision to remain in Europe and his successes under the Nazis put Pabst's possibilities for a postwar career in jeopardy. In 1946, he wrote to Seymour Nebenzal, a German-born Jewish producer in Hollywood with whom he had worked before the war, attempting to interest him in collaborating on a new project. His letter suggests that Nebenzal brought up the rumors surrounding Pabst's wartime activities, since Pabst describes at length the health issues that suddenly arose in 1939 that precipitated his decision to remain at his family's castle in Styria, Austria, instead of emigrating to the United States as originally planned.[51] By all accounts, Pabst never showed interest in actively supporting Nazi cultural policy.[52] However, one letter Pabst wrote to his wife Trude shortly after the war broke out suggests that a discussion with director Willi Forst may have also helped convince him to stay in Austria. Pabst wrote: "I happened to meet Willi Forst at the barber's. He was visibly interested and kept asking if I wanted to work here in Vienna. I'll tell you more about what he told me when we speak. He was very talkative."[53] After the war, Pabst downplayed his willingness to remain in Austria, but the collaboration with Nebenzal never materialized.

Pabst's work for the Nazis casts a shadow of opportunism over his postwar projects.[54] *Der Prozess* did little to assuage his critics, some of whom had been victims of Nazi persecution. Lotte Eisner, who was imprisoned in Gurs, France, had harsh words for Pabst's choice to make films for the Nazis, as well as for *Der Prozess*. She claimed that during a meeting in Vienna in 1946, Pabst

FALSE ACCUSATIONS 213

bragged that the Allies had wiped away any taint of collaboration. Although he told her, "Bei den Amerikanern und Russen bin ich reingewaschen" (The Americans and Russians cleansed me), Eisner still believed him to be "an opportunist, if not a Nazi."[55] Pabst was one of several Austrians accused of deliberately using Jewish topics to draw attention away from—or attempt to make up for—their antisemitism and/or successes under the Nazis. Lothar Müthel, for example, directed a relatively benign stage version of Lessing's *Nathan der Weise* (Nathan the Wise) in 1945, scarcely two years after producing a "crassly antisemitic" *Merchant of Venice.*[56]

Pabst's postwar texts reflect how little the absence of Jews in Austria mattered to him, even as he made a film about the dangers of antisemitism.[57] In a 1948 article for *Die Zeit* titled "Der österreichische Film," Pabst insisted that the current return to Austria of actors, technicians, authors, and directors from "Americanized" Berlin offered Austria the chance to become a substantial producer of films that reflected the spiritual and cultural depth of the people. Not only did he *not* include a plea for the return of exiled Jews in the film industry from further afield, he seemed to indirectly suggest that Austrians should take advantage of Jews' postwar absence when he proclaimed that films should not rely on profit-seeking, private capital as a source of funding. Notably, Pabst does not mention that, after 1938, almost all of the thirty Austrian film distributors were Jews who were expelled, and half of the 189 Viennese cinema operators were Jews who were stripped of their assets. Their property was not returned after the war, nor were they invited to return.[58] The only way to ensure the artistic merit of Austria's films as a national asset, he claimed, is to gain state support.

Also troubling is Pabst's characterization of the Nazi regime as much more amenable to the film industry than Hollywood: "We should also remember what a powerful instrument the totalitarian states have made domestic film. If their success remained limited, it was only because they propagated negative ideas." On the other hand, Hollywood suffers from an "enormous concentration of power and the monopoly of private capital."[59] In a 1942 speech, Goebbels equated the historical plot of Pabst's 1941 film *Komödianten*, about eighteenth-century actors seeking to purify German theater, with the Nazis' goals of purifying German theater by eliminating Jews, making it difficult to fully unlink Pabst's plea for reshaping postwar Austrian cinema from the Nazis' agenda.[60]

Pabst once again broached the idea for *Der Prozess* in 1947 after a chance meeting in Vienna with Rudolf Brunngraber, who was similarly interested in distancing himself from his professional successes under the Nazis.[61] Brunngraber wrote the screenplay with German author Kurt Heuser (who also wrote the screenplay for Pabst's *Paracelsus*). Hungarian-Jewish writer Emmerich (Imre) Roboz, who had published a two-volume novel based on the Tiszaeszlár blood libel in 1932, was involved at the early stages of the project before bowing out.[62] Brunngraber used the screenplay as the basis for his own novel, *Prozess auf Tod und Leben* (1948), an expanded version of which was serialized in the *Arbeiter-Zeitung* and published as a book under the title *Pogrom* (1953).

Some view Brunngraber's participation in co-writing the screenplay for *Der Prozess* and his subsequent publications based on it as atonement for his success as one of the best-selling, best-earning, and most read authors during the Nazi era (Figure 6.1).[63]

Tensions between Emmerich Roboz and his colleagues became apparent even before the film was released. One cause was the article "Tiszaeszlár és Jud Süss: A magyar népre hárítja a vérvád buñét egy osztrák neo-náci film" (Tiszaeszlár and Jud Süss: An Austrian neo-Nazi film accuses the Hungarian

Figure 6.1. Bestselling author Rudolf Brunngraber signs copies of his book *Überwindung des Nihilismus* (Overcoming nihilism) of 1949. His other books, including his novel *Prozess auf Tod und Leben*, are displayed behind him. ÖNB/ Wien FO400022/02.

FALSE ACCUSATIONS   215

people of blood libel), which appeared in the Hungarian periodical *Képes Figyelö* in January 1948.[64] The article describes the film as an attempt by German and Austrian neo-Nazis to deflect accusations of antisemitism toward Hungary. By comparing the film to *Jud Süss*, the article suggests that its creators intended to rouse antisemitic sentiment for narrative effect. It also notes the career successes of Pabst, Brunngraber, and Heuser under the Nazis, while expressing sympathy for Roboz, claiming his screenplay had been discarded in favor of a version written by "Nazi sympathizers" Brunngraber and Heuser.

In March 1948, Roboz wrote to the Austrian branch of the international writers' club PEN, of which Brunngraber was a member, to request a formal hearing. He alleged that Brunngraber had used their collaborative material for the film to craft a novel on the subject, even though he knew Roboz had already prepared the manuscript for a similar novel.[65] As Klaus Kastberger has pointed out, letters from the publisher Zsolnay suggest that Brunngraber had indeed relied on Roboz's work in order to write his novel, despite Brunngraber's protests to the contrary.[66] To retaliate against Roboz's accusations, Brunngraber published belittling complaints in a Viennese newspaper about his victimization at the hands of an unnamed "foreign colleague," describing him as a "strange man" who "slandered us, who had suffered persecution in the Third Reich, as old Nazis, new fascists, antisemites and profiteers" and the film as an antisemitic hodgepodge.[67] Tensions reached a breaking point in May 1948, when Pabst, Brunngraber, Heuser, and Johann Hübler-Kahla, the film's producer, sued the editor of *Képes Figyelö*, Roboz, and writer Gisi Gruber for defamation. At the trial, they accused Roboz of associating them with Nazis by proclaiming that the film was going to be another version of *Jud Süss*. In the end, Roboz was acquitted.[68]

Roboz was not the only Jew dissatisfied with the film. Even before the film finished shooting, Vienna's diminished Jewish community protested its creation, fearing antisemitic backlash. Jews had good reason to be wary of a film on the topic, given that the Nazis had had the same idea.[69] Journalist Otto Horn claimed, "we just finally want peace for our people" and "all of that is happily over."[70] Brunngraber, however, claimed that the filmmakers had a higher purpose: unlike the Jews, they could not simply "let sleeping dogs lie," since "the dogs had already bitten and worrisome traces of their rabies remained in the blood of those on earth." In an unpublished manuscript regarding public responses to the film, he dismissed what he characterized

216 THE POSTWAR ANTISEMITE

as Jews' "fearful passivity" and "tolerance of antisemitic threats" in favor of the message of "consistent combat" offered by the film. In one especially revealing passage, Brunngraber underscores how he and the other filmmakers continued to think about their mission using the terminology of the Nazis they claimed to oppose: "We saw ourselves above all as Aryan actors within an Aryan realm, contemplating Jewish resistance."[71] Meanwhile, Pabst asserted the film's universal message in a 1948 interview, insisting that the events in Hungary could have happened anywhere: "The Jews are only the object of this film, which is therefore not a film for the Jews, but rather a film against violence."[72]

In the fall of 1947, Hungarian diplomats in Austria also expressed their dismay, warning that a film that portrayed their country in a bad light could damage postwar relations between Hungary and Austria.[73] Wary of the potential backlash, the Austrian government threatened to limit or even suspend screenings.[74] However, neither the government nor anyone else had legal grounds to prohibit the film, and the project went ahead as planned. And despite the Jewish community's protests, the film did receive some Jewish support. Ladislaus Morgenstern, the head cantor in Vienna's main synagogue, played Salomon Schwarz, the *schochet* (butcher), and served as the film's advisor on Jewish rituals. Jewish actor Ernst Deutsch returned to Vienna from exile in Hollywood when Pabst invited him to play the lead role of Josef Scharf.[75] The A-Tempo Verlag in Vienna released a record of Morgenstern singing Jewish songs to coincide with the film's release, proudly proclaiming itself the first label in postwar Europe to produce Jewish synagogue songs for the public.[76] But as this book has made clear, relying upon instances of Jewish support for projects envisioned by people who ultimately aim to uphold the framework of Jewish difference is a strategy that is quite useful for keeping it in place, rather than dismantling it.

A Christian Savior for a Jewish Antisemite

Though it removes Zweig's spiritual frame, *Der Prozess* roughly follows the plot: the film traces the events from Esther's disappearance to the exoneration of Josef Scharf and the other Jews. However, unlike the play, it reveals Esther's disappearance as a suicide, implying that she has killed herself after cruel mistreatment by the mean-spirited woman who employed her. The film was mostly well received by critics, garnering two top prizes at the 1948

Venice Film festival, Best Director for Pabst and Best Actor for Deutsch.[77] Alfred Werner, an Austrian Jewish journalist, acknowledged that the film was a serious attempt to address racial hatred and admitted that it clearly moved the non-Jewish audience at the screening where he saw it in Vienna. He nevertheless objected to the film's depiction of Jews and Jewish rituals, noting that members of the Scharf family had complained about the distorted portrayal of their son's character.[78] Film critic Lotte Eisner similarly complained that Pabst's depictions of Jews were tactless and in poor taste,[79] and a Zurich newspaper critic wrote, "Pabst is a poetic man . . . but he doesn't love Jews. You don't love a person whom you depict that way."[80]

The film's depiction of Jews as the "Other" via stereotypes and the elevation of its Christian hero and heavy use of Christian symbolism remain the film's most contentious aspects, and perhaps best reveal how the film kept the constructed categories of Jewish difference in place even as it purported to oppose antisemitism.[81] As Alfred Werner noted, "The Jews of Tisza Eszlar in 1882 were not strange and fantastical ghetto-dwellers, wearing long beards and caftans, but were what one might call 'assimilated' Jews, looking and behaving more or less like their Christian neighbors."[82] And they are not always portrayed sympathetically: In two scenes, for example, Jews feature as moneylenders, represented as having power over impoverished villagers and a man seeking relief from gambling debts. And long before Hungarian Antisemites ply Moritz with the attractions of secular life, it is a Jew who first supplies Moritz with "braces with silver clasps that only gentlemen in the city wear." Moritz's father Josef, played by Deutsch, is mostly portrayed as calm, pious, and judicious. And yet, in the film, it is Josef who plants the thought in the mind of Esther's mother that Jews may have been responsible for her disappearance when he recalls how, in his youth, Jews were always first to be blamed for murdering missing girls. These scenes subtly implicate Jews in their own persecution.

Moreover, the film's highest narrative tension and harshest instance of verbal antisemitism appear in the courtroom confrontation between the Jewish son and father toward the end of the film, which transforms the Jewish child into a young adult who victimizes the accused Jews, including his own father, who, in turn, curses him, evoking the stereotypical vengeful Jew. Even before the filming was completed, a newspaper article offered a tantalizing morsel of the intergenerational drama with these words: "His own son became his mortal enemy!"[83] Moritz rejects Judaism even before Esther is killed, and is already well on his way to becoming an Antisemite by

218   THE POSTWAR ANTISEMITE

the time the Hungarian prosecutor and others isolate him from his family in order to convince him to give false testimony at the trial. As a key witness, he enters the courtroom dressed and coiffed as a sophisticated young man, in stark contrast to the bearded, caftaned Jewish defendants. Moritz tells the court that he is no longer a Jew and addresses his father with disdain, yelling, "I'll address you how you deserve!" Josef pleads with him not to be inhumane, but finally raises his arms and waves his hands, yelling, "I curse you!" at his son. This exchange between Moritz and Josef tapped into antisemitic tropes about disloyal, protean Jews (Moritz) most recently promulgated via Nazi propaganda, including *Jud Süss*, as well as stereotypes about vengeful Jews (Josef) that played into widespread postwar fears in both Austria and Germany. In this scene, Moritz becomes the film's most effective, liminal Antisemite, and Josef is transformed into the audience's most vengeful Jew.

This scene also provides the opportunity for the Christian Hungarian lawyer, Eötvös, to serve as their savior and to rise to the defense of the Jews "in the name of humanity." Eötvös figures explicitly in the film as a Christian savior; at the halfway point of the film, the film focuses almost exclusively on him and his conflicts with antisemitic Hungarian politicians, effacing its Jewish characters. The final courtroom scene provides visual reinforcement of his superiority: he appears high up in the gallery, above the Jewish defendants, next to the cross formed by the room's window panes, as if he carries the cross on his back.[84] It echoes an earlier scene, when he also appeared on a high balcony, watching Hungarians parading on the street below crying, "Hungary Awake," in a parallel to their German Nazi counterparts; it is at this moment that Eötvös proclaims he defends Jews because he is a Christian, verbally reinforcing his superiority.

There are a few scenes in the film, in addition to this one, that evoke the Nazi persecution of Jews. However, they remain too subtle to actively confront viewers.[85] Instead of candidly addressing the problems of the present, both Pabst and Brunngraber indulged in prewar skills of subtle codings in order to downplay Austrians' treatment of Jews. In this context, the praise the film received raises questions about the function of philosemitism in postwar culture. Antisemitism and philosemitism often exist side by side, utilizing the same stereotypes, albeit for different ends.[86] The intent of the filmmakers was clearly to criticize antisemitism and plead for reason and justice. But their stereotypical representation of Eastern European Jews enabled the persistence of an implicit antisemitic narrative. In a review in *Neues Österreich*, Otto Basil lauds the film's critique of antisemitism and praises its "shockingly real and truthful" portrayal of the "foreign behavior patterns" of Jews. Noting that anyone who complains about this depiction has clearly never visited an Eastern European ghetto or the Jewish quarter in a Central European city like Vienna, Basil holds Jews as the Other, a geographically and culturally bounded group whose difference needs to be described to those who do not understand it.[87] When this fascination is framed positively, it is philosemitism; the negative version is—or can lead to—antisemitism.[88]

In Zweig's play, Moritz is lured by powerful Antisemites into the temptations of assimilation; by denouncing his father, he denounces God. But in the end, he realizes his errors, returns to Judaism, and is redeemed by God through his suicide. In the film, Moritz's transformation begins with the lure of the city and luxury items, both coded as Jewish. At the end of the film, the Hungarians throw Moritz into a jail cell, presumably for having given false testimony. The acquitted Jews come to collect him. No longer dressed in a fine suit, he bows to his knees and throws himself at his father's feet. Josef helps him up, embraces him, and the group walks away together. There is no redemption for Moritz, just forgiveness by the other Jews.

The Jews of *Der Prozess* were—and remain—passive. The powerful Antisemites have been toppled by the Christian who set himself up to be their ultimate enemy. Eötvös replaces the God of Zweig's play, and the Jews remain in their group, powerless to the Antisemites and dependent upon the good Christians who oppose them. As Brunngraber admitted: "We didn't make a film for the Jews, but rather against the antisemites."[89] He explains that the film wasn't intended to advocate against the negative effects of antisemitism; rather, it was to use antisemitism as a vehicle to promote tolerance in general, further underscoring the absence of Jews in Austria after the Holocaust:

> We were striving for an ideological film, and we turned to a story of Jewish fate because, after Auschwitz and Meidanek [*sic*], it was closer to us than was the fate of Blacks, Armenians or Parsi's, because we wanted to make amends for *Jud Süß*, and because, above all, we saw antisemitism ominously simmering. We therefore believed that we could expect that the better part of the public would not under all circumstances welcome the artistic result of our efforts, but would at least welcome them as a matter of principle.[90]

The radical shift in the narrative intent of *Der Prozess* was not lost on Arnold Zweig, who was in exile in Haifa when the film was made. In a letter to author Lion Feuchtwanger, who was in exile in California, Zweig complained

220 THE POSTWAR ANTISEMITE

bitterly that the film distorted his play's Jewish tragedy with a comparison to the master of ironic antisemitism, author Karl Kraus: "Dear Feuchtwanger, you're probably not going to believe this is possible, but the film that Pabst is stealing from me is going to be called 'In the Name of Humanity.' It's not even an invention of K. Kraus—his spirit lives on even without him."[91]

Explicitly castigating antisemitism for humanist ends while implicitly perpetuating Jewish stereotypes and promoting Christian saviors, *Der Prozess* shows how Jewish difference continued to mark culture created in Vienna in the immediate postwar period—and, indeed, held the framework of Jewish difference in place. Ultimately, *Der Prozess* aimed to restore confidence in Austrian and European society. Portraying antisemitism as a historic phenomenon that could be overcome via reason, as well as a hatred that Jews as well as non-Jews could embody, it effectively erased the contemporary Jewish victims of antisemitism as it celebrated tolerance for all.

The Austria Film—*1. April 2000* (1952)

Given Pabst's enthusiasm for state support of film in Austria, it is not surprising that he was involved in planning a state-funded propaganda piece that was at first called the "Austria Film." Along with the "Austria Book," it formed one part of a government initiative aimed at boosting the morale of Austrian citizens and rehabilitating the country's international reputation after the Second World War, as well as proving itself worthy of independence.

In October 1948, the government formed a special committee of functionaries with the idea of creating a film to advertise Austria. One member was Ernst Marboe, the newly appointed head of the cultural section of the Federal Press Service in 1945, a Christian Socialist married to the cousin of Chancellor Leopold Figl. An automobile accident in 1938, shortly after the *Anschluss*, had rendered him unfit for military duty, so he spent the war years working in a gas and coal factory.[92] This government position laid the foundation for Marboe's career: he became leader of the Federal Theater Administration in 1953, and his family remains a force in Austrian culture and media to this day. In one interview, Marboe claimed to have come up with the idea for the "Austria Film" in 1944, as he stood on a balcony looking out over Vienna after a bomb attack. He then turned to director Willi Forst and said, "At one point we should stage the whole of Austria."[93] But it was actually the threat of the film division of the U.S. Information Service, headed

FALSE ACCUSATIONS   221

by Austrian Jewish émigré Ernst Hauesserman, creating a film about Austria that initially drove the committee to decide that an "Austrian Propaganda Film" would be better off if Austrians rather than "foreigners" created it.[94]

By December, the committee had come up with an unusual democratic process to find the perfect screenplay: a contest, in which they invited Austrians to submit ideas for the narrative of an "Austrian Propaganda Film" of "international importance."[95] They received at least 2,200 submissions, which were reviewed by a new committee of filmmakers and film journalists that included directors Pabst, Willy Forst, and Karl Hartl.[96] In the end they awarded four prizes for the best ideas, but the committee decided that none of the submissions were feasible for the project as they had envisioned it. Most of them focused on war, bombs, returnees, prisoners of war, and the general postwar atmosphere, and the committee doubted that a film on such depressing and distressing topics would succeed.[97]

Instead, on October 18, 1949, the film's final editorial committee began working on new ideas. This committee consisted of Marboe, Brunngraber, music critic and musicologist Max Graf, historian Friedrich Heer, and writer Paula von Preradović.[98] However, Marboe and Brunngraber ultimately seized the initiative. They came up with a new concept that wrapped its rendering of Austria as *Heimat* in comedic and satirical layers, including spaceships, and worked out the full screenplay. They presented the first draft to Chancellor Figl and the full committee on May 10, 1950. The committee noted approvingly that they had put together a "large-scale documentary about Austria, which is supposed to express its historical, cultural-political and humanitarian mission in Europe" that went far beyond a mere propaganda film.[99] Though the committee had hoped for international participation in the production, particularly from Americans, filmmakers in Hollywood were wary. Wolfgang Reinhardt, son of Max Reinhardt, explained his concerns in a letter to the Austrian general consul in Los Angeles:

> one has to assume a good, strong action and then, afterwards, try to do as much specifically Austrian—landscape culture art—as possible. The reverse way of first compiling a list of everything that you want to show and then finding an action can never lead to a practically evaluable result.[100]

Brunngraber and Marboe hoped to partner with a private production company in Austria for outside funding, but Austrian studios also found the idea unappealing, so they were forced to rely only on government funds.

222   THE POSTWAR ANTISEMITE

At first glance, the two seem an unlikely pair for this project: Marboe was a Christian-conservative politician with no experience in film, while Brunngraber was a socialist whose cinematic experience was limited to the screenplay for *Der Prozess*. But they were in full agreement that the best way for the film to support Austrian independence was through lighthearted satire. The film begins in the year 2000, when friendly, wholesome Austrians are not bitter, but rather good-naturedly exhausted from fifty-five years of tiresome occupation by the Americans, French, British, and Russians. They just want the rest of the world to recognize that they are a peace-loving nation so they can sing, drink, waltz, and love each other without foreign supervision. But when the Austrian prime minister declares independence, an international Global Union Protection Commission arrives to rectify the situation, flying in on a flying-saucer-like spaceship and guarded by a militia dressed in puffy suits, who resemble nothing so much as cuddly Michelin men with laser guns (Figure 6.2).

In a mockery of forward-thinking feminists, the Global Union is headed by a frosty female Präsidentin (president) played by Hilde Krahl, whose icy stare intimidates anyone who dares to oppose her. The Global Union accuses Austria of disturbing world peace by declaring independence and puts the country on trial. The charming, handsome prime minister, played by Josef Meinrad (who plays the magistrate Bary in *Der Prozess*), offers up a retelling of Austrian history that convinces the tribunal that Austria is indeed a benign nation of wine, women, and song—and convinces the Präsidentin to fall in love with him. Along the way, every possible Austrian actor available performs every Austrian cultural cliché imaginable: a montage of the Lipizzaner horses, the folk hero of the beloved song *Lieber Augustin*, drunken tavern antics, grand waltzes, dirndls, lederhosen, ball gowns, and military uniforms. The film aims to lure tourists by presenting Austria as a harmless, cheerful country, but it does so by using historical documentaries and re-enactments as evidence for its defense in a satirical trial. By the end of the film, the international powers have been charmed enough by Austrian culture to dismiss its political significance, and a delegate unearths a copy of the 1943 Moscow declaration proclaiming the innocence of Austria, convincing all that the Occupation Forces should leave immediately.

Although other actors were considered for the role of Präsidentin, the hardened leader who presides over the trial with the coolness of a dictator, choosing Austrian actor Hilde Krahl helped balance out the fact that the film was directed by her husband, Wolfgang Liebeneiner, a Silesian-born

FALSE ACCUSATIONS 223

Figure 6.2. A silly-looking spaceship descending on Vienna's Schönbrunn Palace, the majestic former summer residence of the Habsburgs, highlights the farcical aim of director Wolfgang Liebeneiner's *1. April 2000*, set fifty years into the future. *Courtesy of Filmarchiv Austria.*

224 THE POSTWAR ANTISEMITE

German.[101] It is unclear whether Pabst and Forst were removed from planning the film or stepped down. However, Pabst's 1948 article bemoaning the promotion of clichés in Austrian film suggests that he decided to leave. In the end, the committee agreed almost unanimously to hire Liebeneiner as director.[102] The fact that he had made major propaganda films for Goebbels—including *Ich klage an* (I accuse, 1941), which promoted euthanasia—did not appear to deter them, for none of the committee's memos mention it. Like Harlan, Liebeneiner never joined the Nazi party, and he would later dubiously claim that *Ich klage an* was not a propaganda film at all, but rather "a document of humanity in an inhuman time" that sought to test whether the public would accept a law permitting euthanasia.[103] Though he was second only to Veit Harlan as an influential, successful director under the Nazis, Liebeneiner kept a much lower profile after the war, which allowed him to escape much of the scrutiny that Harlan has received.[104]

There were lots of reasons for the Austrians to hire Liebeneiner. He was, by that time, an expert in making propaganda films. While he was a German citizen, his birthplace in Lower Silesia meant that he was "not so much a non-Austrian," or so he told the *Wiener Zeitung* when he was trying to play up his Austrian credentials.[105] Liebeneiner had also directed Krahl in the lead role in his 1943 film *Großstadtmelodie* (Melody of a great city) in which she plays a woman who moves to Berlin to pursue a career in photography, encounters many challenges, finds success and falls in love, gives up the man she loves for her work, but finally reconciles with him. As such, the film details the ambivalences of Nazi ideology around womanhood: presenting the reality of women working, tempered by the ideal of femininity as wife and mother.[106] In *1. April 2000*, Liebeneiner again tackles this theme of a strong-willed, capable, career woman softened by love. But in this case, the female protagonist is first vilified as a cold-hearted, unfeeling leader who wants to persecute the man who represents Austria until he teaches her how to properly enjoy life.

But the committee was most concerned about the optics of hiring a German to direct their Austrian propaganda film. To defend their choice, they stressed Liebeneiner's experience with film comedy, although he was not particularly known for this genre.[107] In one memo, they said they needed someone with the skills to direct a "documentary feature comedy" using modern color film—although the film was actually shot in black and white.[108] The committee even managed to get their justification into the newspaper, in a 1951 article that repeats a government memorandum word for word:

FALSE ACCUSATIONS   225

While Austria has a number of successful directors in the field of musical film comedy and film operettas, it lacks a director of film comedy like the late director Lubitsch, as France has several directors (René Clair, Sascha Guitry, Cocteau, Duvivier, etc.) and now Wolfgang Liebeneiner exists in Germany. This finding, regretted by the Austrian authorities, naturally does not in any way mean an evaluation of the qualities of the Austrian directors.[109]

This propaganda for the propaganda film never mentions that the Austria-Germany film nexus lacks talented comedy directors because the Nazis drove out its Jewish directors. Placing Liebeneiner, who made films for the Nazis, on the same plane as Lubitsch, a Jewish film director who emigrated to Hollywood in 1922, elides the events of the recent past and normalizes those who created culture for the Nazis. The article's slide from Lubitsch to French non-Jewish directors to Liebeneiner suggests that this statement has been carefully crafted to link Liebeneiner to a Jewish director and to avoid his activities under the Nazis.[110] When questions did indeed arise about why Liebeneiner had been chosen to direct instead of an Austrian, Marboe was ready with his reply: "The director inevitably comes from the type of material and Liebeneiner is undoubtedly predestined for the comedic style."[111]

The ardent defense of Liebeneiner as the German director of an Austrian propaganda film also indicates the work the film was doing to connect the national myth of *Heimat* Austria to Germany and Western Europe. One last tactic in that defense is the article's claim that:

it has long been clear that narrow national borders are not considered to exist in film at all. As is well known, a number of Austrian directors are continuously producing films in Germany and no one has objected to this from the German side, just as Liebeneiner, on the other hand, has already successfully shot two films in Austria without the slightest objection being raised in the press.[112]

That irony is the only sign of the murder, persecution, and forced exile of Jewish artists during the Holocaust; by hardly mentioning those artists, the article defending Liebeneiner, and the creators of *1. April 2000* who hired him and masterminded his defense, did not have to engage with the issue of complicity in ongoing antisemitism in the postwar period. Instead, they could depict a unity among European nations, with Austria as its cultural

226 THE POSTWAR ANTISEMITE

ideal, that fulfills postwar Western Europe's political objective of getting back to normal as quickly as possible, even if normal now means no Jews.

Austria as Victim . . . Just Kidding!

Both *Der Prozess* and *1. April 2000* tell stories about innocent victims placed on trial for crimes they did not commit. But where *Der Prozess* takes its historical trial seriously and uses it in earnest for political purposes, *1. April 2000* taps into Austrian frustrations with trials by poking fun at them—at least on the surface. Billing the film as a comedy allowed Austrians to indulge their feelings of having been unjustly implicated in Nazi crimes, while avoiding potential opposition from the Allied Occupation Forces to a film critical of their presence by pretending those feelings were not serious.[113]

Brunngraber and Marboe needed only to look to East Germany to find a real-life model for their judgmental Präsidentin, described in the screenplay as a "dreaded dragon," who is charming, attractive, and has "a stern and intelligent expression on her face."[114] In 1948, Hilde Benjamin was a ranking member of the SED, the German Democratic Republic's ruling Socialist party, and a judge on the high court. She was also presiding over a new program in the Eastern zone to train civilians as judges within seven months.[115] She became notorious in the 1950s for presiding over political show trials and issuing harsh sentences, which the Austrian press reported on.[116] As *Time* magazine made clear, "In three months of 1952 alone, she handed down two death sentences, eight terms of life imprisonment, and 109 years at hard labor. In court she shrilly interrupted defense counsel with cries of "go on, go on, we have no time for your silly excuses."[117]

Benjamin was often mistaken for a Jew because she had been married to Georg Benjamin, a Jewish physician killed in Mauthausen in 1942.[118] The Präsidentin thus resembled Benjamin not only as the harsh female judge of a show trial, but also as a vengeful, Jewish-coded widow whose husband had been killed under tragic circumstances. In the film, the Präsidentin's status as a widow balances her severe demeanor, making it more plausible that she could fall in love and have her status as a wife restored by the Austrian prime minister, a redemption that in turn enables her to truly understand—and judge—Austria as a peace-loving country.

Crucially, however, Hilde Krahl as a harsh Präsidentin also evoked the Nazis. Born Hildegard Kolacny in Brod, Austria-Hungary (now Croatia)

FALSE ACCUSATIONS   227

in 1917, she came to Vienna when she was five years old.[119] Krahl joined the Nazi party on January 1, 1936, at a time when it was still outlawed in Austria.[120] In a 1938 interview for *Mein Film*, she praised the *Anschluss*, proclaiming how glad she was that she could no longer be described as a foreigner in this new, great Fatherland, asking rhetorically, "Who wouldn't be happy about that?"[121] Her blacklisting by the British section of the Allied Information Services Branch (ISB) suggests they were aware of her Nazi party membership; however, somehow she was still able to participate in filmmaking beginning in 1949, with a starring role in Liebeneiner's *Liebe '47*.[122]

Krahl's Nazi party membership adds an ominous tone to some of her scenes in *1. April 2000*. For example, soon after the International Committee arrives in Vienna, the Präsidentin demands to be taken to the largest place that a trial can be held in Austria, asking the prime minister: "Where do your murder trials take place?" The lighthearted Austrian prime minister underscores the status of show trial when he suggests that the proceedings take place in the Opera, or even Parliament (a joke about the performative nature of politics that itself connects the show politics of the film's twenty-first-century Austria with postwar political realities). However, the Präsidentin insists that the tribunal should take place "where the murder trials happen," emphasizing how seriously she takes the Austrian declaration of independence as an act of aggression.

The next scene then shows the balcony where Hitler delivered his first speech after the *Anschluss*; immediately following, the setting shifts to Vienna's *Großer Schwurgerichtssaal* (great courtroom) in which we see a large fresco showing a detail from Gustav Klimt's painting *Jurisprudence* (Figure 6.3). In 1894, Klimt had been commissioned to create this and two other works—*Medicine* and *Philosophy*—for the ceremonial hall at the University in Vienna; however, they were never hung there due to controversy surrounding accusations that its naked figures, one of which depicted a pregnant woman, were immoral and pornographic. After a parliamentary committee deemed the works unsuitable for the university, Klimt reacquired the works and later sold them to the Jewish Lederer family. Aryanized by the Nazis after 1938, *Jurisprudence* was destroyed, together with hundreds of other Klimt and Schiele paintings and drawings, in a widely publicized fire at Schloss Immendorf in Lower Austria in 1945.[123]

Portraying the Präsidentin in front of the Klimt painting thus evokes the Jews associated with modern art, as well as the Nazis who typically

228 THE POSTWAR ANTISEMITE

> Einstellung
> Präsidentin: Oper? Ich wünsche den größten Gerichtssaal von Wien. Wo finden Ihre Mordprozesse statt?
> 130 Präsident: In der ehemaligen kaiserlichen Hofburg. Exzellenza.

Figure 6.3. One scene in the film *1. April 2000* features Hilde Krahl prosecuting Austria for the crime of disturbing world peace while positioned directly under the avenging goddess of justice from Gustav Klimt's painting *Jurisprudence* (1901–1907). Its inclusion in *Yes, Oui, OK, Njet*, next to the headline "Gerechtigkeit!" (justice), underscores the book's reinforcement of the bitter sentiment undergirding the satirical film. Ernst Marboe, *Yes, Oui, OK, Njet*, p. 108. © *Verlag Österreich*.

FALSE ACCUSATIONS 229

considered it to be degenerate. Ironically, however, Klimt happened to be one of the most beloved artists of Baldur von Schirach, the highest-ranking Nazi in Vienna. In order to make Klimt's works palatable for Nazi aesthetics, its associations with Austria-Hungary, modernism, and Jewish patronage had to be removed. For example, the famed portrait *Adele Bloch-Bauer I* (1907) was changed to the more anonymous *Damenbildnis mit Goldhinter* (Female portrait with a gold background).[124] And he instigated the largest ever retrospective of Klimt's art in 1943 in Vienna, in which one-third of the works shown had been expropriated from Jewish patrons.[125] It is significant that it serves as the film's only reference to Viennese modernism, the culture created between 1890 and 1910 that is so celebrated today. The state-sponsored culture of the immediate postwar years was decidedly Christian conservative and antimodernist, though not without conflict.[126] Brunngraber may have suspected the potential for Austrians to eventually embrace a new, post-Nazi form of Viennese modernism without Jews. In their absence, it would later be transformed into a symbol of national redemption and a way for Austrians to create distance from their National Socialist past.[127]

Brunngraber's great affinity for Klimt's controversial art, as well as his awareness of Klimt's Jewish clients and portraits of Jewish women, is no doubt reflected in this choice to associate the artist with Krahl's Präsidentin. It also cements her position as stern adjudicator while it mocks her false belief in her ability to adjudicate objective, naked truth. Notably, the screenplay describes the scene as follows:

> On the front wall is a large fresco by Klimt depicting Justitia. In the picture, the head of Justitia underscores the voice of the President: "Justice! Justice is the basis of world peace. Justice without regard to person, country, or power. The basis of justice is truth. But the whole truth. The pure, naked truth." The camera moves back, gradually revealing the naked figure of Lady Justice incarnate in truth, with the President entering the frame below, whom the camera now pans down to be alone in the picture.[128]

In the film, we see the Präsidentin positioned in front of the painting's detail of Veritas, Justitia, and Lex, representing the three pillars of the legal system, with men's heads peeking in between these women who personify them. Her jaw aligns perfectly with that of Justitia, highlighting how the film positioned Austria's postwar self-identification as an innocent victim of harsh international forces—just as Klimt's painting from the turn of the century critiqued

230 THE POSTWAR ANTISEMITE

the state's abuse of the rule of law, so the film associates this tribunal with an unfair system.

Here, the film makes clear its critique that an international commission could ever be a fair arbiter of so-called justice to Austria. Positioning its attractive, yet harsh and masculine-coded leader in front of Klimt's painting allows the film to gently mock her role, setting her up to be softened by the Austrian prime minister's appealing seductiveness and charm. This portion of Klimt's painting plays a central role in the satirical aim, as it portrays not only Justice as a female figure, but also Truth as a naked woman. By having the camera move back to reveal her nakedness, and by putting the Präsidentin alone in the frame with her, the film can underscore its use of gender as a satirical dig at superfluous and dangerous international judgment. Its inclusion in the film hints at the distinctive modern art of Vienna in a mocking way, associated with the false justice personified by the Präsidentin.

Directly after this scene, the Präsidentin accuses neutral Austria of having a secret, hidden stash of offensive weapons, and adds a menacing threat: to have Austria erased from the map: a brilliant transformation of Austria as falsely accused aggressor into targeted victim. As a punishment echoing the genocidal policies of the Nazis, she proclaims: "Its population will be evacuated and the territory will remain uninhabited for the next two centuries." The film plays with the idea that non-Jewish Austrian men can manipulate Jewish women, but its irony does not extend to an awareness of the threats that Jewish women pose to male patriotism. Instead, its idea of national identity circumscribes female power within the gender norms that governed postwar Austrian society.

If we recall Brunngraber's wartime efforts to transform his wife into a non-Jewish Austrian, we can see its echoes in the film's narrative of an Austrian man transforming the Jewish-coded Präsidentin into a warm-hearted lover of Austria. Its inclusion also allows Brunngraber both to lightly mock the Nazis' appropriation of Klimt and to signal his art's symbolic role as a marker of Viennese modernism. A satirical film featuring a show trial resonated with Austrians who were fed up with being unfairly maligned for complicity in Hitler's crimes when they considered themselves his first victim. By associating the trial of Austria with Stalinist show trials in the Soviet Union and the Communist bloc that mostly targeted Jews, the screenwriters further strengthened the connection between Austria and innocent Jewish victim(s) that Brunngraber also made in *Der Prozess*.

FALSE ACCUSATIONS   231

By replacing the innocent Jewish victims of *Der Prozess* with the wrongly accused state of Austria, *1. April 2000* manages to repeat the narrative structure of the earlier film by portraying Austrian non-Jews as the real victims, but it also avoids explicit references to Jews or Antisemites altogether. This very formulation depends upon Nazi tropes, whether intentionally or not. Nazi comedy films used techniques understood to be Jewish, such as irony, wit, and slapstick, and replaced them with more straightforward strategies that they considered morally superior, such as finding comedic moments in mundane situations that appeared more natural or true to life.[129] By returning to "Jewish" comedy modalities of irony, wit, and slapstick in a film with no Jews, *1. April 2000* repudiates Nazi taxonomies at the same time as it perpetuates the foundations of Jewish difference that provide the terms for the continued exclusion of Jews—and now, Antisemites as well—from Austria.

Contemporary critics understood that the film was also hiding a serious point about Austrian independence behind the curtain of satire. A 1952 article in the West German periodical *Der Spiegel* suggested that Marboe was only able to make a film that used comedy to construct a national myth because he was related to Austrian Chancellor Figl and held a high government position. When asked about the film's more serious intent, Marboe revealed the dilemma the committee had faced in selecting a script: "We only had one other option—a film legend. But that would have inevitably led to a Wagner-style production."[130] Instead, they created a film that builds deniability into its very title, April Fools' Day, echoing the negation and denial entailed in Austria's postwar revision of its national self-identification—as well as the ways in which Brunngraber and his peers rewrote their own biographies. Ultimately, *1. April 2000* was a propaganda film with a critical message framed as a comedy, which made it easy to deny serious intent if anyone was offended by its depiction of Austrian history and culture or its mockery of the Allied occupation.

As Brunngraber was writing the screenplay for *1. April 2000*, he was also completing his prose versions of *Der Prozess* and defending himself against Roboz's accusations of antisemitism and Nazism, suggesting that his presentation of Austria's victimhood in *1. April 2000* was intertwined with his own. Despite his ongoing engagement with antisemitism in Hungarian history for his book based on the film, neither antisemitism nor Jews appear in the "Austria Film"; it is as if Jews and Nazis never happened. In an Austrian future without Jews, the state of Austria replaces the Jewish victims, in the

232 THE POSTWAR ANTISEMITE

critical move of the country's postwar identity; *1. April 2000* thus becomes an exemplar of postwar Austrian narratives that simply eliminate material references to the Second World War so that it no longer forms part of Austrian self-identification.[131]

The film's premiere took place on November 19, 1952, with tongue-in-cheek invitations designed to look like Allied-enforced identity cards.[132] It ended up being one of the most expensive films made in Austria, only earning half of its production costs at the box office.[133] The film did worse in other countries; in Holland, for example, where the Nazi occupation had been headed by Arthur Seyss-Inquart, a brutal Austrian, a lighthearted comedy featuring Austria as a victim was especially unwelcome. Ernst Marboe's book, *Yes, Oui, OK, Nyet* (1954), which outlines how the film was made, suggests he was bitter about the film's lackluster reception, as it blamed the high costs of its production on the Allied Forces and made some of the film's complaints about their continued occupation more explicit.[134] One illustration featuring helpless hands drowning under a downpour of question marks accompanies text that equates the required questionnaires of the Nazis with those of the Allied Occupation Forces (Figure 6.4).

The book is also much more direct about the serious intent at the heart of this comic film:

> Austria forces the great men at the table of power to see the foolishness of its fourfold occupation in the pictures of a film comedy. Is there something like a world conscience? What will it say about it? Will it smile, will it be silent, will it just be fun for an hour? As always: icons and film comedy, everything in the name of Austria's freedom![135]

The Book of Austria

It could be said that Austria took on the responsibility of restoring faith in the goodness and morality of European civilization after the Holocaust as part of its quest to cement its status as Hitler's first victim. The Moscow Declaration in effect gave it permission to claim that status, which tempered the question of national complicity in both the events of the war and postwar antisemitism. In comparison to the atrocities perpetrated by Nazi Germany, the everyday antisemitism that Hilde Spiel observed in Vienna could be seen as practically benign. And yet, in reality, postwar antisemitism remained just as damaging and pervasive and became a significant factor in

Figure 6.4. An illustration from *Yes, Oui, OK, Njet*, the book published to complement the film *1. April 2000*, suggests helpless Austrians drowning in a sea of unrelenting questions, equating Nazi questionnaires with the denazification efforts of postwar Allied occupation forces. Ernst Marboe, *Yes, Oui, OK, Njet*, p. 132. © *Verlag Österreich*.

the purported invisibility of antisemitism and the actual erasure of Jewish victims in Austria.

The 544-page *Book of Austria*, which appeared in 1948, the same year as *Der Prozess*, was explicitly designed to construct a vision of Austria as an

234 THE POSTWAR ANTISEMITE

independent state at the center of a humanist, civilized Europe. The book was intended to accompany the "Austria Film," which ultimately became *1. April 2000*. Marboe intended both the book and the film as state-funded projects to redeem Austria to the rest of the world—the result was a massive representation of Austria with hardly any Jews. But before he got to the film, which was envisioned in 1948 as "a particularly effective means of cultural propaganda for Austria, which is extremely suitable for promoting its reputation and popularity all over the world,"[136] he began work on *The Book of Austria*, which had a similar remit.

A 1947 memo for the "Propagandabuch über Österreich" (Propaganda book about Austria) states that its purpose was to correct the impression of Austria that the rest of the world had developed "in the years of Nazi rule" and suggests a 1940 French tourist guide, *Paris, Frankreich, Nord und West*, as a model. But tourism would only be a starting point for the project's real goal: as one memorandum put it, "Tourism propaganda indirectly becomes state propaganda and, moreover, a means of communication between the nations."[137] Indeed, the chancellor's office insisted the book be printed by the state printing office because it is was "state propaganda," not "tourist propaganda."[138] Nevertheless, it functioned similarly to shape Austria's image for the international community,[139] at once promoting the beauty of Austria's physical landscape, expounding on the country's cultural treasures, and actively trying to shift contemporary perceptions of Austrians and their history.

The book's first edition contains traces of culture and history in Austria beginning with the prehistoric figure of the Venus of Willendorf, dating back to 15,000 BCE, and continuing all the way up to 1945. The preface states that its intention is to fill a gap in the world's knowledge of Austria by capturing the (presumably foreign) reader's interest with words and pictures. But it also seems aimed at convincing a specifically Austrian audience that the world outside Austria is actually just like them: "Get to know Austria, for it is a lovely part of the world. Learn to recognise the Austria that is in your very blood, for it is a large part of you."[140]

Marboe's aim was to keep the book's content light and flowing, all "mixed up in an amusing chatter" rather than a structured, pedantic textbook.[141] As with the film, he sought to involve a broad spectrum of Austrians in its production.[142] But the writers from whom he solicited essays were all men who had been members of the *Reichsschrifttumskammer*, Austrian non-Jews who, like Brunngraber, had published under the Nazis. It is perhaps for this reason that the Austrian *Heimat* of *The Book of Austria* has no place

FALSE ACCUSATIONS 235

for Nazis and antisemitism, which means, by extension, it has no place for Jews.[143] In keeping with postwar culture's foregrounding of Christianity, the descriptions in *The Book of Austria* often emphasize churches, cloisters, and monasteries, as well as biblical imagery.[144] Its descriptions feature bucolic provincial landscapes, implying a state of Christian nature, free of civil and political conflict, Nazis, and Jews.

The Book of Austria describes cities, in particular Vienna, similarly. Before the war, "Red" Vienna, the capital city, seat of Social Democracy, and home to the majority of Austria's Jews, was often coded as Jewish. The book acknowledges the city's diversity but ultimately emphasizes its Christianity: "Some choose a life compounded of all those things that the word home stands for: baptism, wedding, the family business: others are lured by the siren call of distant lands of opportunity, the fascination of the unknown, the tearing up of roots, making a fresh home far away." The city is also subsumed by the non-Jewish-coded countryside, which literally embraces and parents it: "the city is a product of the surrounding countryside; in fact, as you will soon see for yourself, it is itself part of the countryside. . . . See how the city is enfolded in the loving arms of bountiful mother nature and the smiling landscape!"[145]

As in *1. April 2000*, its mentions of Viennese modernism are both brief and ambivalent. Although the book contains extensive discussion of baroque art and architecture, as well as a table listing its many paintings and art images and their sources, the art of Vienna 1900 is shown only briefly. Not only is there no text devoted to Klimt, Schiele, or their patrons, but also, unlike all of the other artwork depicted in the book, there is simply no indication given about the source of these images for this book.[146] And yet, the book devotes many pages to praising the notoriously antisemitic Viennese mayor Karl Lueger as the shaper of the city and enabler of social programs, electricity, gas, and other modernizations.[147]

Unlike *1. April 2000*, *The Book of Austria* includes the period after 1918. But it never mentions the specifics of Austria's political situation between 1934 and 1945, including the *Ständestaat* and Austrofascism. Rather, it portrays Austria as a passive victim at the mercy of unemployment and Hitler, a position that ultimately led to a renewed commitment to "understanding and tolerance":

> Austria stood sandwiched between ideological and material forces which soon began to extend their interest across its borders, until finally these

236   THE POSTWAR ANTISEMITE

conflicts destroyed the domestic peace of the small, tormented country. Nor should it be forgotten that the ranks of the various armed organizations such as the Heimwehr, the Schutzbund and the SA were swelled by the unemployed. Yet despite menacing rifts Austria somehow managed to hold off the pressure of the Third Reich until eventually Hitler's troops poured across the frontier and Austria's freedom and independence were extinguished—for the time being. The years 1938–1945 did at least generate one important virtue in the people of Austria—a determination to exercise understanding and tolerance once their freedom was restored.

It illustrates the text mentioning Hitler and the *Anschluss* with photographs of buildings bombed years later in Vienna, including the *Stephanskirche* and Opera house, but omits the crowds that welcomed the annexation and the subsequent expulsion of Austrian Jews.[148]

Although a reader would never know from its descriptions that these years had any impact on Jews, the book does mention a few prominent Austrian Jews. A brief reference implies the post-*Anschluss* emigration of one of the country's most famous (Jewish) directors without actually mentioning it: "Unfortunately, Vienna still lacks a modern Max Reinhardt to transform this wonderful square into a stage set." Freud gets a brief mention that allows Vienna to take the credit for his successes: "It was the Vienna of this period, where the most assorted human types met in frank contact, which gave Sigmund Freud a unique platform for making his penetrating observations into the structure of the human soul and the forces which impelled it." Julius Tandler's achievements in public health are praised for holding up Vienna "as a model to the world." The book does not indicate that they were Jews— or acknowledge the antisemitism they faced in Austria.[149]

The three instances in which *The Book of Austria* explicitly (and briefly) references Jews reveal the implications of their exclusion from its vision of *Heimat*. The book begins with an account of Austria's history, starting with the Venus of Willendorf (ca. 15,000 BCE) and moving on to the Babenbergs and Leopold I (940–994). Jews first appear in relation to usury:

> The concept of money also fell now into bad repute; business and trade were dominated by the granting of credit and the taking of interest. In an attempt to control the abuses of usury, Leopold VI founded a municipal credit bank with a capital of 30,000 silver marks, only to lose his money when the Church sharpened its strictures against the levying of interest, and money

transactions fell more and more into the hands of the Jews. 200% interest on debts were not unknown. The Church's spiritual countermeasures included a ban on any taking of interest, under threat of exclusion from the sacraments and from Christian burial. In a bid to put an effective brake on the impoverishment and proletarianisation of the broad masses of the people, it was declared heretical even to defend money-lending or any financial transaction.

Deploying a widespread and historically inaccurate stereotype, this initial reference figures Jews as threats to the sanctity of the Christian church.[150]

The next mention again subordinates Jews to Christians. It appears in an account of traditional holiday plays, including a popular medieval legend (recalling Josef and Moritz in *Der Prozess*) of a Jewish boy who is miraculously saved by the Virgin Mary after his father throws him into a fire because he has converted to Christianity.[151] The book's account omits both the father and the conversion, focusing on how the Virgin Mary saves the Jewish boy:

The originally simple dialogue pieces soon became regular theatrical performances, their optical effect heightened by minor stage devices. Thus when, for the procession of 1610, the story was performed of the Jewish boy who was cast alive into the fire, it was "pleasing and moving"—this double effect being the primary object—that the Virgin Mary came to the succor of the youth in the flames.[152]

If removing the father cleanses the antisemitic narrative of its most negative elements, the result, which highlights the saving force of Christianity, remains antisemitic.

The book's third and final mention—and erasure—of Jews occurs in the description of Eisenstadt, the capital city of Burgenland:

All these new buildings seem to make the older symbols of the town's historical development stand out even more prominently, the old royal free town, the Esterházy Palace, the Jewish Ghetto in Unterberg, and the more recent settlement of Oberberg. The Wolf Collection in the Provincial Museum has some unique objects of Jewish culture, while a quite different world is represented by the Stations of the Cross in Bergkirche, fascinatingly lifelike painted figures carved in wood, in curious little grottos. Finally a visit to the

238　THE POSTWAR ANTISEMITE

miracle-working picture of the Holy Virgin and to the Haydn mausoleum in the Bergkirche are a good way of rounding off a first visit to Eisenstadt.[153]

Mentioning neither the destruction of the Eisenstadt Jewish community nor its Jews who perished in the Holocaust, the description focuses instead on the remains they left behind. The Jewish wine merchant Sándor Wolf founded the private Wolf Museum, located in his house, in 1926; after he fled to Palestine in 1938, the collection was incorporated into the Burgenland Landesmuseum.[154] An image of a "Synagoge Totenglas" (synagogue funeral glass) with Hebrew letters is presumably one of the collection's "unique objects," contrasting starkly with the "lifelike painted figures" of the Stations of the Cross. Whether the inclusion of the Totenglas is an unconscious or conscious reference to the deaths of Eisenstadt's Jews, focusing on it here at once reduces the presence of those Jews and their history to a religious artifact and establishes that presence firmly in the past, where the *Heimat* once limited it, with no place in the present, except a museum.

Rudolf Brunngraber was one of Austria's most popular authors during and after the Second World War. He was not a member of the Nazi party and refused to abandon his vulnerable wife and daughter. But that did not stop him from reinforcing Jewish difference in postwar narratives that aimed to avoid political responsibility and present Austria and Austrians as outside the bounds of National Socialism. The general unwillingness of Austrian courts to hold its citizens accountable for their crimes under the Nazi regime fits his utilization of trials involving false accusations against innocent victims—both to help rehabilitate his personal image, as well as the image of Austria. But by carrying forth the erasure of Jews and Jewish culture from Austria via its depiction of antisemitism as relegated to a distant time and place in *Der Prozess*, and completely absent from *1. April 2000*, these films and the materials related to them helped perpetuate an antisemitic legacy as it shaped a new form of Austrian self-identification without Antisemites and without Jews.

PART IV
THE UNITED STATES
The Anti-Racist and the Antisemite

7

Laura Z. Hobson Stands Up
for Josephine Baker

Gentleman's Agreement

Judging from the fur wraps and coats, it must have been an chilly evening in New York City on October 22, 1951, when novelist Laura Z. Hobson joined Harlem socialite and civic leader Bessie A. Buchanan and National Association for the Advancement of Colored People (NAACP) executive secretary and noted American civil rights activist Walter Francis White on the picket line to protest racial discrimination at the Stork Club (Figure 7.1).[1] The previous week, the city's toniest night spot had refused to serve popular entertainer Josephine Baker.[2] Buchanan, who had been in Baker's party that night, was three years away from becoming the first Black woman elected to the New York State Assembly. Laura Z. Hobson was neither a civil rights leader nor an activist. But her bestselling 1947 novel, *Gentleman's Agreement*, and the Academy Award–winning film of the same name starring Gregory Peck, had made her famous as an outspoken voice against antisemitism. The participation of a well-known white woman in the protest offered the promise of publicity as well as support. It also provides a salient example of how the constructed Antisemite and the framework of Jewish difference intersected with racism in the United States after the war—an example that remains painfully relevant today.

The plot of *Gentleman's Agreement* was not incidental to this protest. The novel's protagonist, non-Jewish journalist Phil Green, poses as a Jew to research a series of articles on antisemitism. Along the way he faces discriminatory incidents ranging from explicitly hateful insults and acts of prejudice to subtler expressions of discomfort and unease from colleagues and others. Although *Gentleman's Agreement* explicitly focuses on antisemitism, it also contains scenes that condemn racist attitudes.[3] In fact, Hobson said she joined the picket line because protesting discrimination of any kind accorded with the liberal, nonsectarian values that her parents had instilled

The Postwar Antisemite. Lisa Silverman, Oxford University Press. © Oxford University Press 2025.
DOI: 10.1093/9780197697757.003.0008

Figure 7.1. Photographs such as this one, featuring Laura Hobson (second from left) protesting with Bessie A. Buchanan and Walter White on behalf of Josephine Baker outside the Stork Club on October 22, 1951, appeared in newspaper reports throughout the United States. *Courtesy of New York Public Library/Schomburg Collection.*

in her since childhood.[4] "*Gentleman's Agreement* is the reason I'm here," she told reporters. "I've never walked on a picket line in my life before, but there comes a time when sending a protest telegram is not enough. I called and asked Walter White what else I could do, and so I am here doing it."[5] Her presence did indeed make the event newsworthy. Newspapers in New York, Boston, Columbus, Raleigh, and as far away as London featured her photograph on the picket line to illustrate stories about the protest.[6]

The incident that sparked the protest had occurred before midnight on Tuesday, October 16, 1951, when Baker, Buchanan, actor Roger Rico, and Rico's wife, Solange, sat down at a table in the Stork Club's VIP area. Baker had just finished her last performance at the famed Roxy Theater on West 50th Street just off Times Square, part of her triumphal return tour of the United States after decades living in Paris.[7] Born into poverty in St. Louis,

Missouri in 1906, Josephine Freda McDonald started singing and dancing at a young age, joined a traveling theater troupe at age fourteen, and soon began performing on Broadway. She left the United States in 1925 to escape the racism that was holding back her career. By that time she had already been married and divorced twice, the second time to Willie Baker, whose name she kept. In Paris, she became a star at the Folies Bergère and established her own successful nightclub, Chez Josephine. She became a French citizen in 1937 and joined the Resistance during the war, using her celebrity for espionage and to entertain the troops; her efforts earned her numerous accolades, including France's highest order of merit, the Légion d'Honneur.[8] By 1951, Baker was not only one of the most popular and highly paid entertainers in the world, but also had years of activism against fascism, Nazism, racism, and xenophobia in Europe and America under her belt.[9]

What exactly happened at the Stork Club that night depends on who is telling the story. Baker told one newspaper that they ordered crabmeat, steak, and wine but still had not been served after an hour: "One by one they came and said there was no crabmeat, there was no steak, there was no wine. . . . Then the waiters wouldn't come near us. It was just silence."[10] The *New York Times* reported that Baker was informed by the wait staff that the food she had ordered was not available.[11] Solange Rico later confirmed that the other members of their party received their food in a timely fashion, and only Josephine was kept waiting.[12] George Amodio recalled his fellow waiters' decision not to serve Baker as a tacit response to owner Sherman Billingsley's outspoken dismay at her presence in the club that night.[13] The thread through all of these accounts is that Baker was not served, so she left the table to call Walter White and Billy Rowe, a deputy commissioner of the New York City Police Department, to report racial discrimination. Her party left the Stork Club, and Baker and Buchanan went to White's home to discuss their next steps.[14] Racial discrimination was common at New York nightclubs at that time, but the Stork Club and Billingsley had a particular reputation for discriminating against Black people.[15] Still, Baker's complaint caused headlines, for it showed definitively that even the most famous celebrities were not immune to racist treatment.

As Baker planned her next steps, she turned to Walter Winchell, one of the nation's best-known and most influential radio personalities, as well as the inventor of the celebrity gossip column and a Stork Club regular whose livelihood depended upon the access to celebrities it provided him.[16] During the Second World War, Winchell was also one of the only American journalists to

244   THE POSTWAR ANTISEMITE

criticize antisemitism publicly and explicitly. Winchell's grandfather, Chaim Weinschel, was a cantor who had emigrated from Poland in 1881. Winchell was born Walter Winschel in Harlem in 1897; the family eventually changed the name to sound less Jewish. His father, Jacob, worked in the silk business and fashioned himself something of a dandy, wearing spats, carrying a cane, and even calling himself Jack de Winchel in a further effort to distance himself from Jewishness. Walter began his career as a vaudeville performer. Eventually, he became a powerful journalist who made and destroyed reputations.

Winchell first became politically active after the Great Depression, when President Franklin Roosevelt invited him to the White House in the hope that he would promote the New Deal to his vast audience. He maintained a close relationship to J. Edgar Hoover, director of the FBI, who investigated numerous individuals at his behest. Flush with newfound social power, Winchell became a populist champion against racism and antisemitism, which helped keep him in the public eye. In 1939, when many tried to ignore the 20,000 Nazi sympathizers who rallied at Madison Square Garden, Winchell was one of the few willing to publicize the event and speak out as a Jew against Nazism. His support for giving Black soldiers the vote caught the attention of Representative John Rankin, a Mississippi Democrat, who on many separate occasions denounced him as a "kike" on the floor of the House of Representatives. In one particularly vitriolic outburst, he accused Winchell of "doing more to injure President Roosevelt than any other man alive." About Winchell he continued:

> In one of his filthy, indecent insinuations, he stooped to as base a level as that of the loathsome ghoul at night, that invades the sacred precinct of the tomb, goes down into the grave of a buried child, and with his reeking fingers strips from its lifeless form the jewels and mementoes placed there by the trembling hands of a weeping mother.... How much longer will the decent, patriotic Jews of America have to endure the punishment he is to bring upon them? How much longer will patriotic Gentiles have to endure his infamous persecutions?[17]

A *Time* magazine report, noting Rankin's slurs against Winchell, inspired Hobson to write *Gentleman's Agreement* and appears in both the novel and the film.[18]

Winchell's outspokenness over such causes played into his favorite activity, fawning over celebrities like Josephine Baker, whose canny ability to

LAURA Z. HOBSON STANDS UP FOR JOSEPHINE BAKER   245

claim the spotlight fed his own desire to generate colorful narratives about society's outsiders.[19] Baker was likewise delighted by Winchell, whose regular mentions in his columns provided her with helpful public visibility. Several months prior to the Stork Club incident, Winchell attended Baker's performance in Miami—her first after her long hiatus in Europe—at Copa City, a nightclub known for refusing attendance to Blacks. At her insistence, club owner Ned Schuyler allowed Blacks to attend her performance. Winchell sat up front next to former heavyweight champion Joe Louis. That night, Baker told the audience that it was the most important moment of her life: "This is really my first appearance in this, my native land in 26 years. The other times didn't count. Now it is different. I am happy to be here and to be performing in this city under these circumstances when my people can be here to see me."[20] Afterward, Baker was commended by the NAACP for battling racial segregation in Miami. Winchell had nothing but praise for her performance, describing Baker as a "real star."[21]

Their warm relationship was also evident in October at the Stork Club, when Baker and her party stopped to greet Winchell at his regular table on their way to be seated. According to newspaper columnist Jack O'Brien, who was at Winchell's table with his wife that night, Baker stopped to say hello and Winchell replied that "he liked her ponytail." Around an hour later, Winchell and the O'Briens left for a late film screening, unaware of the incident or Baker's discrimination complaint.[22] The next day, to Winchell's surprise, Baker publicly demanded that Winchell confirm her racist treatment and condemn the Stork Club and Billingsley. Given their friendship and his reputation for speaking out against racism, she believed Winchell would be on her side, but she had overestimated him. Despite a flurry of negotiations over the next days, Winchell claimed on his radio broadcast that he had not been at the Stork Club "at the time of the alleged discourtesy" and did not repudiate Billingsley.[23] Instead, he railed against having been branded a racist for not supporting her. He, not Baker, was the true victim.

There is ample evidence that Winchell already knew about Billingsley's racism. Winchell's remarks to Herman Klurfeld, who had long served as his ghostwriter, indicate he was aware of discrimination at the Stork Club—but he saw no problem as long as nobody accused him or Billingsley of racism:

> Look, the Stork discriminates against everybody. White, black, and pink. It's a snob joint. The Stork bars all kinds of people for all kinds of reasons. But if your skin is green and you're rich and famous or you're

246 THE POSTWAR ANTISEMITE

syndicated, you'll be welcomed at the club. Irving Hoffman always brings his Negro friends to the Stork, and it doesn't cause any kind of ruckus. But if I published what I'm telling you, all the damn troublemakers would use it as proof that Sherman and I are bigots or something.[24]

Winchell was not willing to break with Billingsley for Baker and jeopardize his close relationship with the owner of the elite nightclub that provided a crucial source of material for his radio shows and columns.[25] In the weeks that followed, Baker and the NAACP targeted Winchell, Billingsley, and the club in newspapers and on radio talk shows for upholding racism.

But while Billingsley ignored the hubbub, Winchell continued to draw attention to his role in the incident with increasingly unhinged efforts to smear Baker.[26] He bristled at the public pressure and grew increasingly paranoid. He went after her in his columns with every derogatory category he could find: she was pro-Communist, pro-Fascist, antisemitic, anti-Negro, and a political opportunist. He drew attention to her trips to the Soviet Union and numerous interviews in the *Daily Worker*, brought up a brief statement of support for Mussolini she had made before the war, and called upon his friend J. Edgar Hoover to have the FBI investigate her activities. He also excerpted translated passages from *Les Memoires de Josephine Baker*, an updated version of her 1927 autobiography, reissued in 1949, that crassly described American Jews in Harlem as responsible for African American misery.[27]

Baker's autobiography, letters, and conversations indeed indicate she was blind to her own prejudices and at times used antisemitic stereotypes to describe Jews both before and after the war, primarily in the form of complaints about their wealth and control over businesses. But the following month, she appeared as the guest of honor at a meeting of 900 women members of the American Jewish Congress in Chicago, accusing Winchell of distorting her memoirs and insisting that her previous marriage to Jean Lion, a French Jew, meant she could not be anti-Jewish.[28] Similarly, Winchell tried to counteract accusations of supporting racism by rallying Black supporters and friends to highlight his past efforts on behalf of civil rights. Nevertheless, people who have intimate relationships with and personally support individual members of groups that face discrimination can also hold prejudices against them to deploy when it suits their needs. Baker and Winchell's public struggle for the authority to cast each other as Antisemite and Racist—and their blindness to their own prejudices—highlighted how irresistible it was for them to deploy accusations of racism and antisemitism.

In analyzing the harms this caused, we must seriously consider how they were targets of discrimination themselves and how their deployment of accusations engaged this discrimination. Insisting that one of their claims must have more merit than the other forecloses an understanding of the harm that trying to resolve conflicts such as this brings to bear and instead keeps interlocking systems of oppression in place.[29] Nevertheless, although they shared some tactics, it was clear that Winchell had far more power to damage Baker's reputation. The U.S. government already viewed her international efforts to attack racism in the United States as a threat; Winchell's efforts to smear her via his connections at the FBI fueled the fire. During the next years, the State Department undertook substantial efforts to discredit her and make it difficult for her to travel to and from the United States.[30] Winchell's reputation also suffered a hit; the aftermath of the incident was the beginning of his decline, largely because he did himself in.[31]

To be sure, their dispute reflects the long-standing crux of the relationship between racism and antisemitism in America: Jews are perceived as whites who enjoy the privileges of unmarked social power.[32] Overlooked, however, is that this whiteness is conditional.[33] Moreover, equating Jews with non-Jewish whites also masks how white privilege overlaps with antisemitic stereotypes that cast Jews as seekers of control, power, and domination, up to a global scale.[34] One of the consequences of the struggle to define the Antisemite is that it often relies upon perpetuating oppression via other systems of inequality. Intersectionality—which holds that overlapping systems of inequality, such as gender, sexuality, race, class, ethnicity, and other fluid categories, produce compounded effects of discrimination—helps us see how people who are oppressed according to one system may deploy the position of oppressor in another system as a way to engage with their own disadvantaged position.[35] The Baker-Winchell incident illustrates how adaptable the postwar Antisemite could be in the service of reinforcing American racism.

The accusations flung by these formerly cordial colleagues demonstrate how the constructed categories of race, Jewish difference, and gender served as powerful tools in the public sphere. Despite Baker's antisemitic statements, she still faced a humiliating act of racial discrimination at the Stork Club. Winchell's support for Billingsley, refusal to condemn racism at the Stork

248 THE POSTWAR ANTISEMITE

Club, and misogynist efforts to smear Baker did not alter his own vulnerability to antisemitism. However, Baker's and Winchell's prejudices cannot be considered independently of their disadvantages according to these ordering systems. They have to be understood as tools deployed by individuals who would never gain the authority held by an unconditionally white man like Billingsley. Recognizing how much power the ability to define the Antisemite and the Racist conferred in this postwar period helps us understand how it is perpetuated. In the end, both Winchell and Baker's careers suffered in the aftermath of the Stork Club incident, while Billingsley, who had the least to lose, emerged unscathed.

Hobson's Antisemite

Laura Z. Hobson's statements at the Stork Club protests and her book's sympathetic attitude toward Black people make it clear that she supported civil rights. Nevertheless, the critique of antisemitism in *Gentleman's Agreement* actually hinges on keeping racial inequality in place, further revealing how difficult it is to challenge the biases produced by multiple systems of difference. In arguing that Jews deserve to be treated just like other (white) Americans because they can pass for one another, the book reinforces America's white racial frame. In other words, its narrative hinges on the fact that Jews and non-Jews can pass for each other—never mentioning that this happens at the expense of non-white people, many if not most of whom are excluded from the possibility of passing. This reading brings to light how this frame often appears, albeit unarticulated, in other narratives of oppression, keeping the benefits it confers on white people hidden from white people.[36] Like in the European context, the success of a narrative like *Gentleman's Agreement* also suggests that in postwar America, the strength of narratives opposing antisemitism were at least in part attributable to their ability to cast the Antisemite as a figure who denies Jews the benefits of whiteness.[37] It's no coincidence that Hobson's notes and papers demonstrate her emotional investment in showing that Jews did not differ fundamentally from other white Americans.[38]

In *Gentleman's Agreement*, Phil Green's aim is to write from a position of empathy about the people who would "never go to an antisemitic meeting" or "send a dime to Gerald Smith," a reference to the American clergyman and populist political organizer, founder of the Christian Nationalist Crusade

LAURA Z. HOBSON STANDS UP FOR JOSEPHINE BAKER 249

and 1944 presidential candidate.[39] Along the way, his new status exposes him to bigotry of all kinds—from latent to violent—and causes complications in his personal relationships. Although popular, Hobson's book also received criticism. Some felt that it did not adequately foreground Jewish culture and customs. Others considered it less skillful than comparable American novels and films that thematized and critiqued antisemitism in the immediate postwar era.[40] But Hobson's novel was unique for focusing on Americans' complicity in perpetuating everyday instances of antisemitism. She makes it quite clear in her autobiography that she wanted Americans to see how they still discriminated against Jews even when they thought they did not. In fact, Hobson refused to acquiesce to powerful men who tried to soften her arguments about how antisemitism functioned. When Richard L. Simon, her publisher at Simon & Schuster, asked her to change a sentence from "That's how they did it" to "That's how the unconscious antisemites did it," Hobson strongly protested, replying, "Dick, you're asking me to scuttle my whole point, the basic point of the whole book. I'm not going to label them 'unconscious antisemites'—I want to show them in action, let them speak their words, let them behave their behavior. All those nice people who'd tell you they hate prejudice. The book is *about* nice people."[41]

Hobson was not interested in comforting audiences who found the Antisemite distasteful. Rather, she aimed to expose and even trigger discomfort by forcing people to face their own prejudices. But in so doing, she revealed her own comfort with the fact that Jews would benefit from being considered unconditionally white. Born Laura Zametkin in New York City in 1900 to Jewish émigrés from Russia, Hobson grew up aware that her father, a labor organizer and editor of the Yiddish newspaper *Forverts*, had been imprisoned and tortured in Russia. She married non-Jewish publisher Thayer Hobson in 1930, divorced him in 1935, and never married again, although she adopted one child and gave birth to another as a single mother at a time when it was not socially acceptable to do so. She began her career as a reporter and worked for a number of news outlets, including *Time*. As she noted in her autobiography, trying to pass as a non-Jew was part of her experience growing up.

Up until the end of the Second World War, the common view in the United States was that Jews were a race. But the fact that white Jews could often, though not always, pass as Christians meant that they faced subtler obstacles and prejudices than Black people. Mildred Martien Hudgins, a vaudeville performer in the 1920s, identified this hierarchy succinctly when she

250   THE POSTWAR ANTISEMITE

described segregation in Atlantic City, where signs at fancy hotels proclaimed NO DOGS, NO JEWS. But there was no ban on Black people—not because they were welcome, but because it went without saying. As she noted, "They didn't have to put NO N******, because we knew it."[42] This perception of the distinction between, on the one hand, American racism as self-evident, ubiquitous bigotry based on skin color and, on the other, antisemitism as a prejudice that was no less persistent but meaningfully less harmful because Jews could pass as non-Jewish white people is, I argue, what the narrative of *Gentleman's Agreement* unfolds.[43] At the same time, by emphasizing the subtler form of antisemitism found in the United States, as opposed to the murder of millions of Jews in Europe, the novel frames prejudices against Jews in the United States as less harmful and more easily erased than the dangerous real Antisemite in Europe.

The dramatically different experiences of Jewish people and Black people in America, where the color line was the primary determinant of social status, cannot be denied.[44] To be sure, not all Jews are white. However, the majority of Jews in the United States—as well as in the public imagination—were not people of color, so it was, on the whole, much easier for Jews to achieve financial, professional, and social success in white America. A fundamental tension for Jews in America, then, was that many aspired to white, Anglo-Saxon superiority even as they campaigned against bigotry.[45]

Given Hobson's background and the era in which she wrote, it is not surprising that her story reflects not only racism, but also sexist views about differences between women and men. To start, the protagonist of *Gentleman's Agreement* is a non-Jewish male journalist instead of a Jewish woman like herself. As her editor Lee Wright told her, "It [antisemitism] is a great theme, but I think it has to be written by your hero, a liberal Christian man."[46] Wright understood that an article about antisemitism by a Jewish man or woman would be predictable, but an article by a non-Jewish man pretending to be a Jew would fulfill Jewish and non-Jewish fantasies of a Christian savior. In that respect, Hobson cedes her authority to define the Antisemite to her protagonist, affirming that a Jewish woman, like herself, could not be seen to be its ultimate arbiter. Moreover, allowing Phil to pass as a Jew and therefore become the Antisemite's target reinforces the theme of the Antisemite as a primary danger to non-Jews in an American context; the real Antisemite may be murdering Jews in Europe, but in the United States, the Antisemite's real danger is the threat it poses to American democracy. Hobson's Antisemite prefigures what would become a popular and widespread view of American exceptionalism when it comes to antisemitism, which persists to the present day.

But Hobson's postwar Antisemite revealed the fallacy of this notion of exceptionalism by sharing one important trait with its German and Austrian counterparts. Like many of the texts, films, and trials analyzed in this book, *Gentleman's Agreement* also supports the notion that the Antisemite's danger is primarily to a nation's idea of itself (here, to America and Americans) and only secondarily to Jews. At the start of the novel, Phil Green lists the various aspects of antisemitism he intends to explore, including "antisemitism in business," "social antisemitism," and "violence." Finally, he writes, "Link up with growth of anti-alien feeling, anti-Negro, anti-Catholic, all minority. (Threat to US most serious, not to Jew.)"[47] Paralleling antisemitism with other forms of prejudices in the United States deflects victimhood away from the Jews and helps Hobson stay on message and circumvent the "special pleading" that American Jews felt they had to avoid when speaking about antisemitism—just as European Jews tried to avoid sounding vengeful.[48]

Like its European counterparts, Hobson's narrative also includes a liminal Antisemite who, although non-Jewish, mixes Jewish and non-Jewish qualities. In Germany and Austria, the liminal Antisemite is often a non-Jewish outsider whose malevolence emerges via coded references to Jews. In *Gentleman's Agreement*, this figure takes the form of Belle, Phil's sister from Detroit. Belle first appears in the context of a shopping trip while visiting Phil in New York, echoing European stereotypes of Jewish women as consumers. She dismisses Phil's assignment to report on antisemitism by saying it should have been assigned to a Jewish writer and scoffing, "You can't scold people into changing." She and her husband want to sell their house and move into a bigger one, further linking her to superficial consumerism, which morphs into crass antisemitism when she complains that they are having trouble selling the old one because "[t]hat cheap Pat Curran keeps trying to Jew us down." Phil is horrified by how loud, animated, and definitive she is, and he finds her desire for a new house vulgar and ridiculous. Belle is mean-spirited, wasteful, overly consumerist, status-oriented, and nouveau riche: her husband made it big by designing a "new wheel-transmission gadget that did the trick better than the one his company had been using."[49] In other words, Hobson, like her European colleagues, describes the Antisemite in terms typically used to describe—and demean—Jewish women.

Gentleman's Agreement also configures the liminal Antisemite as Jews who aspire to achieve status by denying their Jewishness and criticizing other

252   THE POSTWAR ANTISEMITE

Jews. Phil's first encounter with the Jewish Antisemite occurs when he looks through his bookshelf for books about Jews and finds that not only are the Jews depicted as dishonest, scheming, and repulsive, but the authors of the books are also Jews![50] But the most telling example is Phil's secretary Elaine Wales, a Slavic-looking blonde with a distinctive accent who seems both foreign and interesting. Believing Phil is a Jew, she admits that she is too, but the magazine would not hire her when she applied with her real name, Estelle Walovsky. Elaine scoffs at the irony of this happening at a "liberal magazine" that aims to fight injustice. However, before Phil or the reader can sympathize with the discrimination she faced, she complains that the magazine is now encouraging Jews to apply as secretaries, concluding, "Don't you hate being the fall guy for the kikey ones? ... You know, loud, and too much rouge and all." Indignant at the slur, Phil considers whether she is registering an "unconscious longing, hidden and desperate, to be gentile and have the 'right' to call Jews kikes." But then he realizes what she means: "That was it, then. They were O.K. Jews; they were 'white' Jews; with them about, the issue could lie mousy and quiet."[51] In the book, Phil is careful not to display his irritation as he firmly informs Elaine that she is being antisemitic; she indignantly rejects the label and leaves the room. However, in the film version of the scene, Phil angrily chastises her. While *Gentleman's Agreement* has several virtuous Jewish male characters who decry antisemitism but understand that the correct moral choice is to remain a Jew, the fact that the Jewish woman casts aside her self-identification as a Jew and must be disciplined for propagating antisemitism upholds misogyny.[52]

The point that Jews can also harbor and deploy antisemitic prejudices is important. However, targeting Phil's angriest outburst against antisemitism toward Elaine, a Jewish woman, suggests that those who suffer under antisemitism are expected to be both its moral arbiters and impervious to its power—just as Black people are expected to both rise above racism and be impeccable in their dealings with white people. As with Baker and Winchell hurling insults at each other, this view shows little understanding of these structural disadvantages and their consequences.

If, in the end, the film and book's liminal Antisemites play different roles than they did in Germany and Austria, they serve to buttress an American subtext in which the real, murderous Antisemite remains the Nazi in Europe. As Dave Goldman, Phil Green's Jewish friend and soldier in the U.S. Army, points out, Americans need to oppose antisemitism because antisemitism prevents America from being everything it stands for. "The hell with the

Jews, as Jews. . . . It's the whole thing, not the poor, poor Jews.' He waved toward the windows, as if he were waving to the whole stretch of country beyond."[53] Dave's point underscores the message that being an Antisemite cannot be part of being an American. However, defining the Antisemite as other than what one is—whether nationally or individually—is a powerful way of establishing moral and cultural authority.[54]

The terms of inclusion that Jews fantasized about were, to some extent, more developed in the United States. The New Deal explicitly included Jews and other minorities in its conception of American nationalism, and in the 1930s, Jews began to be visible in positions of leadership in public service. It therefore makes sense that Hobson would confront Americans about their antisemitic prejudices by creating a comfortable space for white people to imagine rejecting prejudices against Jews—that is, by nudging the topic along, rather than destabilizing the coterminous category of race.

In part, the success of *Gentleman's Agreement* reflects the desire of American audiences to buttress their position of moral authority at a time when the government was growing uneasy that postwar criticism of racism in the United States might hinder foreign relations.[55] Asserting U.S. opposition to antisemitism not only helped achieve this goal but perpetuated the portrayal of U.S. soldiers heroically rescuing Europeans from an event that was the antithesis of American values. This construct would become instrumental to American self-identification, the reorganization of Europe in the postwar period, and its cultural counterpart, the development of the Holocaust into the "master moral paradigm," according to which the antisemitic Nazi is the quintessential evildoer.[56] Yet Hobson still had to use her male, non-Jewish savior to make the claim that American identity rested, at least in part, on having the authority to define the Antisemite. *Gentleman's Agreement* does not claim antisemitism is absent in America. Rather, its narrative asks that Jews be viewed as white, which in turn helps delineate American-style antisemitism and detach it from the Nazi Antisemite in Europe, whom U.S. troops had vanquished during the war. The white American, inclusive of Jews, remains the good guy, while the Nazi Antisemite remains confined to Europe.

The reinforcement of white superiority in *Gentleman's Agreement* can help us understand how the framework of Jewish difference and the constructed Antisemite continued to operate in the context of postwar racism, even when Jews and antisemitism were not explicitly referenced. One particularly relevant example is Robert Stemmle's 1952 anti-racist film *Toxi*, about the

254   THE POSTWAR ANTISEMITE

responses of a middle-class, white German family when Toxi, a Black child, is dropped off at their home. The film contains no explicit references to either Jews or antisemitism, but the Nazis' antisemitic agenda is evoked to support the film's anti-racist message via several oblique references. Significantly, the film ends with the performance of a nativity play that offers Toxi the opportunity to appear in whiteface, while the white German child dons blackface. Similar to *Gentleman's Agreement*'s reinforcement of America's white racial frame by suggesting the interchangeability of Jews and Christians as whites, *Toxi* reinforces Jewish difference by highlighting the interchangeability of Blacks and whites as Christians in order to oppose racism. Both films, one American and one German, aim to oppose discrimination. But each film's blind spot is that this opposition is predicated on the support of other discriminatory frameworks.[57]

The liminal Antisemite became a particularly contentious figure following the establishment of the State of Israel in 1948, a development that ultimately resulted in Jews becoming the majority population in their own country. As a figure of oppression, the Jew-as-Nazi proved irresistible—even to some Jews. In 1948, Hannah Arendt, Albert Einstein, and twenty-five other prominent Jews published an open letter to the *New York Times* criticizing Israeli leader Menachem Begin's Freedom Party (Tnuat Haherut) as "closely akin in its organization, methods, political philosophy, and social appeal to the Nazi and Fascist parties," with the goal of achieving a "Leader state," a direct translation of the term *Führerstaat*.[58] As German-Jewish targets of Nazi persecution, Arendt and Einstein understood that everybody was at risk of utilizing fascism and bigotry. Drawing a provocative comparison seemed like an effective way to make their warning more compelling. But employing this comparison as a strategic rhetorical device also entailed significant risk, as the juxtaposition of Israel and Nazi Germany soon became a foundational mechanism for vilifying Jews.

Although all of these represent uses of the figural Antisemite to boost a particular narrative, the necessity of considering who is speaking to whom about what highlights that there is no easy litmus test that abdicates us from carefully considering each and every example in good faith. The struggle for the authority to construct the figural Antisemite—and thus have the power to define antisemitism—continues today.[59] It is worth considering how these arguments often stem from a wide range of people who insist that using this provocative image is their right: not to desire to destabilize the framework of Jewish difference from which antisemitic stereotypes are generated, but rather to use the figural Antisemite as a commanding narrative device, while exempting oneself from its harmful terms. The Antisemite became a placeholder for the enemy, intersecting with other forms of discrimination to give each a powerful postwar boost.

While history is often concerned with the struggle over power and naming, as in the struggle to define the Antisemite discussed here, this book has begun and ended with postwar incidents in which the stories of victims are questioned, avoided, dismissed, or rejected altogether by people trying to avoid their own complicity by insisting that they are its true victims. And insisting on maintaining this status can impede reconciliation. Baker, Hobson, and Winchell actively railed against both antisemitism and racism. But they also erroneously believed that opposing one made them immune from the other.

Jacques Abtey, Baker's colleague in the French Resistance, recounts Winchell's response, in 1963, to the suggestion that he and Baker make amends:

> "She broke me . . . she broke my heart. I, who have done so much for the black cause—" I said, "Listen, since I'm involved in the story, I'm going to see Josephine and arrange a reconciliation." He said "Yes, you could." Then, suddenly, "No, I don't want it. I have the translation of her book, I have the newspaper articles, I was not at the Stork Club when it happened—" It was fantastic, he was like a child, I had to console him. I will always see him in the taxi crying, "She broke my heart, I'm a finished man."[60]

Winchell's account of his victimization by Baker recalls Philipp Jenninger's account of his suffering at the hands of Ida Ehre. Despite his pain and desire, Winchell stops short of pursuing reconciliation with Baker and retreats back to the comforts of imaging himself as her victim. The various political and personal reasons for his refusal evident in this short passage underscore the complexity of Jews'—and others—lived experiences, which are often, and perhaps ironically, absent from stories that aim to define the Antisemite.

Notes

Introduction

1. *Kristallnacht* or *Reichskristallnacht* (night of broken glass) are the terms commonly used to refer to the evening of November 9–10, 1938. "November Pogroms" avoids that term's status as a problematic Nazi euphemism and more accurately reflects the violence of the events, which actually took place during November 7–10, 1938. See Ulrich Baumann and François Guesnet, "Kristallnacht–Pogrom–State Terror: A Terminological Reflection," in *New Perspectives on Kristallnacht: After 80 Years, the Nazi Pogrom in Global Comparison*, ed. Steven J. Ross (Purdue University Press, 2019). On its commemoration as a postwar cultural construction, see Y. Michal Bodemann, *Gedächtnistheater. Die jüdische Gemeinschaft und ihre deutsche Erfindung* (Rotbuch, 1996), 116.
2. Wolfgang Homering, ed., *Ida Ehre. Im Gespräch mit Sepp Schelz* (Ullstein, 1999), 49.
3. In 1943, Ehre was imprisoned in Fuhlsbüttel concentration camp for six weeks. Her husband explained that she was released because he had contacted Nazi leader Heinrich Himmler, whose father had once been assistant principal at the school he and Heinrich attended in Augsburg. Homering, *Ida Ehre*, 66–67. Facing deportation in February 1945, Ehre went into hiding for the final months of the war at the home of actor Marianne Wischmann. Michaela Giesing, "Ida Ehre and Hamburg's Kammerspiele Theater," in *Key Documents of German-Jewish History*, https://keydocuments.net/article/giesing-ida-ehre.
4. I use the terms "Germans" and "Germany" when referring to the period before 1949, and thereafter "East Germans/East Germany/German Democratic Republic (GDR)/Deutsche Demokratische Republik (DDR)" and "West Germans/West Germany/Federal Republic of Germany (FRG)/Bundesrepublik Deutschland (BRD)" where applicable.
5. Ehre also founded the Kammerspiel-Film-Gesellschaft, for which she obtained a license in October 1947. However, its films never proceeded past the planning stages. Peter Pleyer, *Deutscher Nachkriegsfilm 1946–1948* (C. J. Fahle, 1965), 43.
6. After their third visit to her theater, Ehre sent Harlan and Söderbaum a letter requesting that they cease attending. Herlinde Koelbl, *Jüdische Portraits. Photographien und Interviews* (S. Fischer, 1989), 53. However, Harlan's daughter Maria Körber recalls a humiliating incident in which the couple was publicly ejected from Ehre's theater. See Felix Moeller's documentary *Harlan: In the Shadow of Jew Süss* (2008), 58:57.
7. Philipp Jenninger, "Rede am 10. November 1988 im Deutschen Bundestag," https://www.swr.de/swrkultur/wissen/archivradio/philipp-jenningers-rede-am-jahrestag-der-reichspogromnacht-1988-104.html.
8. Oesterle-Schwerin, an Israeli-born daughter of German-Jewish refugees, shouted "Das ist doch alles gelogen!" (That's all a lie!) after Jenninger finished his sentence. She later revealed that the outburst was premeditated—not a reaction to Jenninger's specific words, but to his very presence as a speaker. In the days leading up to the speech, members of the Green Party, Social Democratic Party (SPD), and Free Democratic Party (FDP) had insisted that Heinz Galinski, head of the Zentralrat der Juden in Deutschland (Central Council of Jews in Germany), be the one to speak at the commemorative event. Decades later, Jenninger would blame Galinski for turning politicians against him with his "many tricks." "'Wenn du einmal im Sarg liegst, kommst du nicht mehr raus.' Nach Vorlage genehmigte Niederschrift des Gesprächs mit dem Bundestagspräsidenten a.D., Dr. Philipp Jenninger, am Dienstag, 16. Mai 2006," *Monatshefte* 100, no. 2 (2008): 182. See also *Jenninger. Was eine Rede an den Tag brachte* (NDR, 1989).
9. On the rhetorical weaknesses of the speech, see, "'Irgendwie musste das ja mal endlich gesagt werden.' Die Jenninger-Rede zum 50. Jahrestag der Reichspogromnacht von 1938," in *Die Sprachen der Vergangenheiten. Öffentliches Gedenken in österreichischen und deutschen Medien*, Ruth Wodak, Florian Menz, Richard Mitten and Frank Stern (Suhrkamp, 1994).

258   NOTES TO PAGES 2–5

10. "West German Resigns Post After Kristallnacht Speech," *Washington Post*, November 12, 1988, A17.
11. Ehre was not seated beside Jenninger when he delivered his speech at the podium. Video footage of the event shows that Ehre first bowed her head during the Bonn Bach Society's performance of Mordechai Gebirtig's "s brennt, Brüder, es brennt," then repeated the gesture after reciting Celan's poem while listening to Jenninger's speech. See *Jenninger. Was eine Rede an den Tag brachte* (NDR, 1989).
12. "A 'guilt and shame' speech would have been better than trying to explain why Hitler's dictatorship came about." "'Wenn du einmal im Sarg liegst," 182–83. On the significance of Celan's poem, see Daniel H. Magilow and Lisa Silverman, *Holocaust Representations in History: An Introduction* (Bloomsbury, 2020), 33–41.
13. "'Wenn du einmal im Sarg liegst," 183.
14. For a sample of letters and newspaper reports, see Armin Laschet and Heinz Malangré, eds., *Philipp Jenninger, Rede und Reaktion* (Einhard Rheinischer Merkur, 1989). For an overview of the incident, including its resonances in the GDR, see Constantin Goschler and Anthony Kauders, "Alignments," in *A History of Jews in Germany Since 1945: Politics, Culture, and Society*, ed. Michael Brenner (Indiana University Press, 2018), 356–58.
15. "After reciting my poem, I was so upset that I just cried. I didn't hear Jenninger's speech at all. Some of my friends found it terrible, others didn't understand what the fuss was about. Maybe he just presented it the wrong way." "Das Bild, das um die Welt ging," *Bild*, November 12, 1988, 2; "'Wenn du einmal im Sarg liegst," 186.
16. "'Wir haben sie ungewöhnlich hoch geschätzt!' Helmut Schmidt erinnert sich an Ida Ehre." Ida Ehre Kulturverein, Hamburg. Published on April 5, 2011, 10:42, https://www.youtube.com/watch?v=qrNyB6xaCUE.
17. Dov Waxman, David Schraub, and Adam Hosein, "Arguing About Antisemitism: Why We Disagree About Antisemitism and What We Can Do About It," *Ethnic and Racial Studies* 45, no. 9 (2022).
18. On Jewish difference, see Lisa Silverman, *Becoming Austrians: Jews and Culture between the World Wars* (Oxford University Press, 2012), 7; "Beyond Antisemitism: A Critical Approach to German Jewish Cultural History," *Nexus 1: Essays in German Jewish Studies* (2011); "Reconsidering the Margins: Jewishness as an Analytical Framework," *Journal of Modern Jewish Studies* 8, no. 1 (2009). Zygmunt Bauman proposes the term "allosemitism" (first coined by Artur Sandauer and cited by Baumann in 1998) to refer to the Othering of the Jew in both its positive and negative iterations. See Eliezer Ben-Rafael, *Confronting Allosemitism in Europe: The Case of Belgian Jews* (Brill, 2014), 18–35. However, the inclusion of the term "semitism" undermines its potential to signify a neutral, co-constitutive relationship between the constructed ideals of the Jew and non-Jew.
19. Scholarship on antisemitism is vast. For recent overviews, see Mark Weitzman, Robert J. Williams, and James Wald, eds., *The Routledge History of Antisemitism* (Routledge, 2024) and Jonathan Judaken, *Critical Theories of Anti-Semitism* (Columbia University Press, 2024), 1–20. Judaken proposes using the term "Judeophobia" to allow for more nuanced, intersectional analyses otherwise hampered by the limitations of the term "anti-Semitism." *Critical Theories of Anti-Semitism*, 13. David Nirenberg suggests using the term "anti-Judaism" to refer to a "powerful theoretical framework for making sense of the world." *Anti-Judaism: The Western Tradition* (Norton, 2013), 463–64. However, the terms "Judeophobia" and "Anti-Judaism" continue to conflate the negative iteration of the constructed Jew with the broader theoretical framework from which it emerges. Vivien Laumannn and Judith Coffey distinguish between antisemitism and "goynormativity" (analogous to heteronormativity) to signal the advantage the non-Jew occupies in the dominant, unmarked, and naturalized position. *Gojnormativität. Warum wir anders über Antisemitismus sprechen müssen* (Verbrecher Verlag, 2021). On the unspoken assumption that the constructed Jew is primarily Ashkenazi, white, and male, to the exclusion of Jews of color, Sephardi Jews, Arab Jews, and women, see Jon Stratton, *Coming out Jewish: Constructing Ambivalent Identities* (Routledge, 2000), 3–4. On the persistence and pitfalls of assuming Jews are white, and therefore unmarked, in popular culture, see Jonathan Branfman, *Millennial Jewish Stars: Navigating Racial Antisemitism, Masculinity, and White Supremacy* (New York University Press, 2024). David Schraub explores "conditional whiteness" as it applies to white Jews, emphasizing how their lived experiences diverge from those of white non-Jews in "White Jews: An Intersectional Approach," *AJS Review* 43, no. 2 (2019).

NOTES TO PAGES 5–7   259

20. Evelyn Torton Beck was among the first to promote the analysis of social constructions of the Jew alongside the social constructions of gender, sexuality, and race. See "The Politics of Jewish Invisibility," *NWSA Journal* 1, no. 1 (2022). See also Marla Brettschneider, *Jewish Feminism and Intersectionality* (State University of New York Press, 2016).

21. While the terms "antisemitic" and "anti-Jewish" are often used interchangeably, the term "philosemitic" is most often understood as "pro-Jewish" with the added quality of being superficial or disingenuous. On its relationship to antisemitism and distinction from the term "anti-antisemitism," see Jonathan Judaken, "Between Philosemitism and Antisemitism: The Frankfurt School's Anti-Antisemitism," in *Antisemitism and Philosemitism in the Twentieth and Twenty-First Centuries: Representing Jews, Jewishness, and Modern Culture*, ed. Phyllis Lassner and Lara Trubowitz (University of Delaware Press, 2008), 27–29. On antisemitism and racism in the German context, see Moishe Postone, "Anti-Semitism and National Socialism," in *Germans and Jews Since the Holocaust: The Changing Situation in West Germany*, ed. Anson Rabinbach and Jack Zipes (Holmes & Meier, 1986), 305.

22. See also Cynthia Baker on the symbolic uses of the term "Jew" throughout history in *Jew* (Rutgers University Press, 2017). On postwar constructions of the Jew in France, see Sarah Hammerschlag, *The Figural Jew: Politics and Identity in Postwar French Thought* (University of Chicago Press, 2010). Elad Lapidot and Hannah Tzuberi pinpoint the impossibility of "disfiguring" the Jew without paradoxically erasing it: "The ambivalent thrust of philo-Semitism and any anti-anti-Semitism is that the Jewishness that it befriends, and generates, is a difference that no longer makes any difference." "Jewish Friends: Contemporary Figures of the Jew: Introduction," *Jewish Studies Quarterly* 27, no. 2 (2020): 105.

23. Max Horkheimer characterized the absence of explicit antisemitism during a visit to Frankfurt in 1946 as evidence that anti-Jewish sentiment could be selectively activated—turned on and off as needed. Monika Boll, "Max Horkheimers zweite Karriere," in *"Ich staune, dass Sie in dieser Luft atmen können." Jüdische Intellektuelle in Deutschland nach 1945*, ed. Monika Boll and Raphael Gross (Fischer, 2013), 351.

24. I identify this reductive binary framework not because it accurately represents lived experience, which is clearly more nuanced, but because the lives and works of those discussed here engaged with its oversimplified constructions in order to make meaning. The risk of reifying these constructed binaries, rather than destabilizing them, remains one of the most challenging aspects of interrogating such frameworks. See Silverman, *Becoming Austrians*, 7. On Jewish difference as an aesthetic device that can be used to underscore universal values, see Caroline Kita, "Jewish Difference," in *Migration, Integration, and Assimilation: Reassessing Key Concepts in (Jewish) Austrian History*, ed. Tim Corbett, Klaus Hödl, Caroline A. Kita, Susanne Korbel, and Dirk Rupnow, *Journal of Austrian Studies* 54, no. 1 (2021): 6–10.

25. These categories were not only matters of survival under the Nazis but also played a significant role in the immediate postwar years, influencing the distribution of scarce resources such as jobs, food, housing, and property. Atina Grossmann and Tamar Lewinsky, "Way Station," in Brenner, ed., *A History of Jews in Germany since 1945*, 120.

26. Max Horkheimer and Theodor W. Adorno identified the combined desire for and disavowal of the Jewish as a crucial aspect of antisemitism's logic: both detesting Jews and constantly imitating them. *Dialectic of Enlightenment* (Continuum, 1999), 184. Neil Levi explains that this impulse is best understood not as a desire to be the Jew, but rather as the desire to imitate an externalized image of one's own repressed impulses (mimesis). *Modernist Form and the Myth of Jewification* (Fordham University Press, 2014), 4, 8.

27. Frank Stern, *The Whitewashing of the Yellow Badge: Antisemitism and Philosemitism in Postwar Germany* (Pergamon Press, 1992), xvi.

28. Frank Biess, *Homecomings: Returning POWs and the Legacy of Defeat in Postwar Germany* (Princeton University Press, 2006), 49.

29. See Paul Hanebrink, *A Specter Haunting Europe: The Myth of Judeo-Bolshevism* (Harvard University Press, 2018).

30. On blaming Jews for Germany's misfortunes during the war and erasing the boundaries between Jews and the Allied Forces, see Anna M. Parkinson, *An Emotional State: The Politics of Emotion in Postwar West German Culture* (University of Michigan Press, 2015). On the defensiveness of antisemitic discourse in Austria after 1945, see Ruth Wodak, Peter Nowak, Johanna Pelikan, Helmut Gruber, Rudolf de Cilia, and Richard Mitten, *"Wir sind alle unschuldige Täter!" Diskurshistorische Studien zum Nachkriegsantisemitismus* (Suhrkamp, 1990), 21–22.

260 NOTES TO PAGES 7–8

31. As Hannah Arendt observed, "Allied Policy in Germany is frequently explained as a campaign of successful revenge." According to her, this narrative "serves as a consoling argument, demonstrating the equal sinfulness of all men." "The Aftermath of Nazi Rule: Report from Germany," *Commentary* 10 (1950): 343.

32. Frances Tanzer identifies this phenomenon in postwar Vienna in "Performing the Austrian-Jewish (Negative) Symbiosis: Stella Kadmon's Viennese Stage from Red Vienna to the Second Republic," *Leo Baeck Institute Year Book* 63 (2018):15.

33. See Norbert Frei, "Von deutscher Erfindungskraft. Oder: Die Kollektivschuldthese in der Nachkriegszeit," in *1945 und wir. Das Dritte Reich im Bewusstsein der Deutschen* (Deutscher Taschenbuch Verlag, 2005), 145–55. At a time when few were willing to confront the issue of German guilt for the murder of European Jews, Heidelberg philosopher Karl Jaspers's 1945–1946 lectures to his students stood out as a notable exception. *Die Schuldfrage. Ein Beitrag zur deutschen Frage* (Artemis-Verlag, 1946).

34. For example, an early draft of an Allied Forces directive removed the phrase as a hindrance to fostering democratic values. Parkinson, *An Emotional State*, 27.

35. Moses Moskowitz, "The Germans and the Jews: Postwar Report," *Commentary* 1, no. 2 (1946): 12.

36. Kate Manne suggests that victimhood involves both being morally wronged at the hands of another agent and suffering injury or humiliation because of that transgression. *Down Girl: The Logic of Misogyny* (Oxford University Press, 2018), 223.

37. On each country's development of diverging memories of a shared past, see Katrin Hammerstein, *Gemeinsame Vergangenheit–getrennte Erinnerung? Der Nationalsozialismus in Gedächtnisdiskursen und Identitätskonstruktionen von Bundesrepublik Deutschland, DDR, und Österreich* (Wallstein, 2017). Each national context of course encompassed a range of subcategories of self-identification. For example, Alon Confino points out that national self-understandings could often intensify and transform local self-identifications rather than oppose them. *Germany as a Culture of Remembrance: Promises and Limits of Writing History* (University of North Carolina Press, 2006). Moreover, in order to parse antisemitic discourse, one must also take into consideration varying levels of context, including space, time, speaker, and audience. Wodak et al., "*Wir sind alle unschuldige Täter!*," 337–41. On non-Jewish German self-victimization as part of German memory culture, see Aleida Assmann, *Der lange Schatten der Vergangenheit. Erinnerungskultur und Geschichtspolitik* (Beck, 2006). On non-Jewish German self-identification with Jewish victims as part of that process, see Ulrike Jureit and Christian Schneider, *Gefühlte Opfer. Illusionen der Vergangenheitsbewältigung* (Klett-Cotta, 2010).

38. The five categories of denazification were Hauptschuldige (major offenders), Belastete (offenders), Minderbelastete (lesser offenders), Mitläufer (followers), and Unbelastete (nonoffenders). Jewish community representatives in Germany identified a direct link between denazification and antisemitism: "The more gently it [denazification] is handled, the more firmly rooted the hatred of Jews becomes." "Zuviel ist geschehen," *Der Spiegel* 43, October 24, 1947, 3. On the significance and implications of denazification, see Mikkel Dack, *Everyday Denazification in Postwar Germany: The Fragebogen and Political Screening During the Allied Occupation* (Cambridge University Press, 2023). On denazification and postwar ressentiment as a cultural phenomenon, see Parkinson, *An Emotional State*. On the figure of the Nazi perpetrator and its relationship to the development of postwar German art, architecture, and literature, see Paul B. Jaskot, *The Nazi Perpetrator: Postwar German Art and the Politics of the Right* (University of Minnesota Press, 2012); Erin McGlothlin, *The Mind of the Holocaust Perpetrator in Fiction and Nonfiction* (Wayne State University Press, 2021). On the reintegration and acceptance of former Nazis in West Germany, see Norbert Frei, *Vergangenheitspolitik. Die Anfänge der Bunudesrepublik und die NS-Vergangenheit* (Beck, 2012); in Austria, see Margit Reiter, *Die Ehemaligen. Der Nationalsozialismus und die Anfänge der FPÖ* (Wallstein Verlag, 2019).

39. Stern, *The Whitewashing of the Yellow Badge*, 386–96. Decades ago, Henryk M. Broder identified the West German phenomenon of preferring dead Jews to living ones and its relationship to antisemitism. "Die unheilbare Liebe deutscher Intellektueller zu toten und todkranken Juden," *Eingriffe. Jahrbuch für gesellschaftskritische Umtriebe*, ed. Klaus Bittermann (Tiamat, 1988). On focusing on dead Jews as part of a nationally imposed culture of remembrance in Germany, see Max Czollek, *Desintegriert Euch!* (Hanser, 2018), 81; on the phenomenon in contemporary culture in general, see Dara Horn, *People Love Dead Jews: Reports from a Haunted Present* (Norton, 2021).

40. As the years went on, police and government officials in West Germany downplayed public acts of antisemitism—such as knocking over headstones in Jewish cemeteries or painting swastikas

NOTES TO PAGES 8–9   261

on synagogues—often dismissing them as acts of communists (at worst) or children (at best). Heinz Liepman, *Vom Gestern zum Morgen. Ein deutscher Jude denkt über Deutschland nach* (Ner-Tamid, 1961), 38. On the persistence of acts of antisemitism in East and West Germany, as well as state attempts to minimize them, see Goschler and Kauders, "Alignments," 333–44.

41. Such initiatives were often dismissed in West Germany as communist propaganda. See Ruth Seydewitz and Max Seydewitz, *Anti-Semitism in West Germany* (Committee for German Unity, 1956). For additional publications highlighting antisemitism in West Germany, particularly through the identification of former expressions of antisemitism by people currently in positions of power, see *Antisemitismus in Westdeutschland. Judenfeinde und Judenmörder im Herrschaftsapparat der Bundesrepublik,* published by the Verband der jüdischen Gemeinden in der Deutschen Demokratischen Republik (Berlin, 1967). For example, after Hermann Franz Gerhard Starke became editor in chief of the West German newspaper *Die Welt, Antisemitismus in Westdeutschland* reprinted Starke's glowing review of Veit Harlan's *Jud Süss* from September 26, 1940, in which he praised the film's ability to "capture the essence of world Jewry with all its problems" and show the "incontrovertible nature of their species." Starke's review is published in translation in Anson Rabinbach and Sander L. Gilman, eds., *The Third Reich Sourcebook* (University of California Press, 2013), 597–98. On this topic, see Gavriel D. Rosenfeld, *The Fourth Reich: The Specter of Nazism from World War II to the Present* (Cambridge University Press, 2019), 146; Jeffrey Herf, *Divided Memory: The Nazi Past in the Two Germanys* (Harvard University Press, 1997); Jack Zipes and Anson Rabinbach, eds., *Germans and Jews Since the Holocaust: The Changing Situation in West Germany* (Holmes & Meier, 1989).

42. Early denazification efforts in the Soviet zone, along with initial reporting on localized antisemitic acts and their punishment, eventually shifted focus to West Germany as a central site of antisemitism. Over time, these acts were subsumed under broader categories of racial discrimination. See Angelika Timm, *Hammer, Zirkel, Davidstern. Das gestörte Verhältnis der DDR zu Zionismus und Staat Israel* (Bouvier, 1997), 106–11. On the historical development of legislation outlawing discrimination against Jews in Germany, see Christoph Jahr, *Antisemitismus vor Gericht. Debatten über die juristische Ahndung judenfeindlicher Agitation in Deutschland (1879–1960)* (Campus, 2011). While the GDR included more Jews in active leadership in politics and culture than the FRG, these Jewish leaders were still subject to expulsion depending on the needs of the party. Michael Brenner, "Introduction," in *A History of Jews in Germany Since 1945,* 2; Mary Fulbrook, "East Germans in a Post-Nazi State: Communities of Experience, Connection, and Identification," in *Becoming East German: Socialist Structures and Sensibilities After Hitler,* ed. Mary Fulbrook and Andrew I. Port (Berghahn, 2013), 36.

43. Official policy in the GDR did not always prevent individual Jews from expressing differing views. For example, Helmut Eschwege occasionally subverted the party line, even while maintaining leadership positions. See Alexander Walther, "Helmut Eschwege and Jewish Life in the German Democratic Republic," in *Rebuilding Jewish Life in Germany,* ed. Jay Howard Geller and Michael Meng (Rutgers University Press, 2020).

44. Tara Zahra, "Prisoners of the Postwar: Expellees, Displaced Persons, and Jews in Austria After World War II," *Austrian History Yearbook* 41 (2010): 193. See also Martin Tschiggerl, "Significant Otherness Nation-Building and Identity in Postwar Austria," *Nations and Nationalism* 27, no. 3 (2021).

45. Believing themselves to be the first victims of Nazi aggression allowed Austrians to self-identify as resistors—despite the fact that 700,000 Austrians were members of the Nazi party, many of whom were deeply complicit in its crimes. Heidemarie Uhl, "From Victim Myth to Co-Responsibility Thesis: Nazi Rule, World War II, and the Holocaust in Austrian Memory," in *The Politics of Memory in Postwar Europe,* ed. Richard Ned Lebow, Wulf Kansteiner, and Claudio Fogu (Duke University Press, 2006); "From Discourse to Representation: 'Austrian Memory' in Public Space," in *Narrating the Nation: Representations in History, Media and the Arts,* ed. Stefan Berger, Linas Eriksonas, and Andrew Mycock (Beghahn, 2008); Bertrand Perz, "Österreich," in *Verbrechen erinnern. Die Auseinandersetzung mit Holocaust und Völkermord,* ed. Volkshard Knigge and Norbert Frei (Bundeszentrale für Politische Bildung, 2005). See also Robert Knight, " 'Neutrality' Not Sympathy: Jews in Post-War Austria," in *Austrians and Jews in the Twentieth Century: From Franz Joseph to Waldheim,* ed. Robert S. Wistrich (Palgrave Macmillan, 1992); Brigitte Bailer, " 'They Were All Victims': The Selective Treatment of the Consequences of National Socialism," in *Austrian Historical Memory and National Identity,* ed. Günter Bischof and Anton Pelinka (Transaction, 1997); Oliver Rathkolb, *The Paradoxical Republic: Austria 1945–2020* (Berghahn, 2020); Bruce F. Pauley, *From Prejudice to Persecution: A History of Austrian Anti-Semitism* (University of North Carolina Press, 1992); Ivar Oxaal, Michael Pollak, and Gerhard Botz, *Jews, Antisemitism and Culture in Vienna* (Routledge, 2020). Jews

262 NOTES TO PAGES 9–10

were largely absent from Austria's victim narrative until the 1980s. See Uhl, "From Discourse to Representation," 212. On the diverse meanings of the "victim myth" in Austria, see Meinrad Ziegler and Waltraud Kannonier-Finster, *Österreichische Gedächtnis. Über Erinnern und Vergessen der NS-Vergangenheit* (Böhlau, 1993). On the Austrian victim myth after 1945 and its effects on Jews, see Ruth Beckermann, *Unzugehörig. Österreicher und Juden nach 1945* (Löcker, 1989). Peter Pirker suggests that martyrdom and sacrifice were soon decoupled from Austrian victimhood in order to satisfy various political agendas. "The Victim Myth Revisited: The Politics of History in Austria up until the Waldheim Affair," in *Myths in Austrian History: Construction and Deconstruction*, ed. Günter Bischof and Marc Landry, (University of New Orleans Press, 2020), 151–72.

46. On the importance of gender to antisemitic imagery before 1945, see Stefanie Schüler-Springorum, "Gender and the Politics of Anti-Semitism," *The American Historical Review* 123, no. 4 (2018): 1218.

47. As U.S. high commissioner John J. McCloy noted, "What this community will be, how it forms itself, how it becomes a part of and how it merges with the new Germany will, I believe, be watched very closely and very carefully by the entire world. It will, in my judgement, be one of the real touchstones and the test of Germany's progress towards the light." Conference in Heidelberg held on July 31, 1949, "The Future of the Jews in Germany," minutes by Harry Greenstein, September 1, 1949, Leo Baeck Institute MS 168, cited in Dan Diner, "Banished: Jews in Germany after the Holocaust: An Interpretation," in Brenner, ed., *A History of Jews in Germany Since 1945*, 21.

48. In 1965, the national socialist and antisemitic statements of former Nazi Taras Borodajkewycz, a professor of economic history at the Hochschule für Welthandel in Vienna, sparked student protests and ultimately led to the death of Ernst Kirchweger, who was caught in violent clashes with neo-Nazis. However, it was not until 1986, when Kurt Waldheim was elected president of Austria and refused to take responsibility for his Nazi past, that these issues in Austria gained international recognition. See Rafael Kropiunigg, *Eine österreichische Affäre. Der Fall Borodajkewycz* (Czernin, 2015); Wodak et al., "Die 'Kampagne' und die Kampagne mit der 'Kampagne'—Die 'Waldheim-Affäre'," in *"Wir sind alle unschuldige Täter!,"* 59–120.

49. On this topic, see Jan T. Gross, *Fear: Anti-Semitism in Poland After Auschwitz: An Essay in Historical Interpretation* (Random House, 2006).

50. Andrea Pető, "Conflicting Narratives About a Post-Shoah Blood Libel Case in Budapest in 1946," in *Die "Wahrheit" der Erinnerung. Jüdische Lebensgeschichten*, ed. Eleonore Lappin-Eppel and Albert Lichtblau (Studienverlag, 2008), 24.

51. The charge read: "As far as the plaintiff is aware, there is a custom in the defendant's circles of making Easter biscuits (!) with a drop of Christian blood." See Michael Brenner, *After the Holocaust: Rebuilding Jewish Lives in Postwar Germany* (Princeton University Press, 2021), 54.

52. Susanne Rolinek, *Jüdische Lebenswelten 1945–1955. Flüchtlinge in der amerikanischen Zone Österreichs* (Studienverlag, 2007), 74.

53. Brenner, *After the Holocaust*, 54. In December 1949, in the Bavarian city of Fürth, a person yelled, "They should build gas chambers for you again," at Jewish community leader and town council member Leo Rosenthal; a crowd of 150 people then surrounded him and yelled antisemitic threats. "Fürther Stadtrat wehrt sich gegen Antisemiten," *Allgemeine Wochenzeitung der Juden in Deutschland*, January 13, 1950, 12. Toward the end of 1948, an elderly Jewish Holocaust survivor in Hamburg published a letter in a newspaper requesting assistance from the public. In response, she received dozens of anonymous letters filled with crass insults. Axel Eggebrecht, "Vom Antisemitismus," *Jüdisches Gemeindeblatt. Die Zeitung der Juden in Deutschland*, March 11, 1949, 6. In Vienna, cemeteries that had been Aryanized and desecrated between 1938 and 1945 were neglected by Austrian federal and Viennese city governments alike, and continued to be vandalized after the war. As Tim Corbett points out in his masterful study of Vienna's Jewish cemeteries, unresolved issues surrounding their future and repair signal the persistence of problematic Austrian *Vergangenheitsbewältigung*. *Die Grabstätten meiner Väter: Die jüdischen Friedhöfe in Wien* (Böhlau, 2021), 947. See also "'Like an Overgrown Graden . . . ?': Austrian Historical Memory and the Aftermath of Cultural Genocide at a Jewish Cemetery in Vienna," *Dapim: Studies on the Holocaust* 32, no. 3 (2018).

54. Hal Lehrman, "Austria: Way-Station of Exodus," *Commentary* 2, no. 6 (1946): 565–72; Moskowitz, "The Germans and the Jews: Postwar Report," 12.

55. Ulrike Weckel, *Beschämende Bilder. Deutsche Reaktionen auf alliierte Dokumentarfilme über befreite Konzentrationslager* (Franz Steiner, 2012).

56. Moskowitz, "The Germans and the Jews," 7.

NOTES TO PAGES 10–12   263

57. Heinz Liepman, "The Survivors," *The Menorah Journal* 35 (1947): 310.
58. On West German attitudes toward Jews, see Werner Bergmann and Rainer Erb, *Anti-Semitism in Germany: The Post-Nazi Epoch from 1945 to 1995* (Routledge, 1997), 253.
59. Paul Lendvai, *Anti-Semitism Without Jews: Communist Eastern Europe* (Doubleday, 1971).
60. Artur Rosenberg, "Land ohne Juden?," *Neues Österrich*, March 26, 1946, 1–2.
61. Theodor Körner, "Das Märchen von Antisemitismus in Wien," *Wiener Zeitung*, February 9, 1947, 3–4; Georg Zivier, *Ernst Deutsch und das deutsche Theater. Fünf Jahrzehnte deutscher Theatergeschichte. Der Lebensweg eines großen Schauspielers* (Haude & Spener, 1964), 78. For example, actor Käthe Dorsch insisted that actor Werner Krauss's antisemitic remarks did not prove that Krauss was an Antisemite, since it was the Nazis who had made antisemitism offensive. Käthe Dorsch to the Spruchkammer Stuttgart, March 14, 1947, Archiv der Akademie der Künste, Berlin, Käthe-Dorsch-Archiv-5. Director Wolfgang Liebeneiner similarly dismissed Krauss's antisemitism as a "quirky game," noting "It is clear to me personally that Mr. Werner Krauss's personal antisemitism has absolutely nothing to do with National Socialism." Wolfgang Liebeneiner, statement dated January 10, 1948, Bundesarchiv Berlin-Lichterfelde, R/9361/V 154998.
62. Bernd Marin, "A Post-Holocaust 'Anti-Semitism Without Anti-Semites'? Austria as a Case in Point," *Political Psychology* 2, no. 2 (1980).
63. "The crudest way of coping with the past is to present the Germans as victims, the Jews as victimizers, exploiters, and vampires, motivated by greed and lust, who bring hatred on themselves, with the implication that perhaps their parents who perished in the gas chambers did, too. Contemptuous pity for victims and losers and the weak in general is another. In both cases, anti-Semitism has come full circle via philosemitism, and the Jews are once more the scapegoats, only paradoxically this time for the guilt induced by their own extinction." Ruth K. Angress (Ruth Klüger), "A 'Jewish Problem' in German Postwar Fiction," *Modern Judaism* 5, no. 3 (1985): 232.
64. Examples include the poll "Ist Deutschland antisemitisch? Ein diagnostischer Beitrag zur Innenpolitik" (Institut für Demoskopie, 1949). For other examples of these phenomena, often referred to as "secondary antisemitism," see Werner Bergmann, " 'Störenfriede der Erinnerung.' Zum Schuldabwehr-Antisemitismus in Deutschland," in *Literarischer Antisemitismus nach Auschwitz*, ed. Klaus-Michael Bogdal, Klaus Holz, and Matthias N. Lorenz (J. B. Metzler, 2007), 20.
65. The power of the figural Jew was often based on its ability to blur boundaries. See Bryan Cheyette, *Constructions of 'the Jew' in English Literature and Society: Racial Representations 1875–1945* (Cambridge University Press, 1995), 6. On casting the Jew as the enemy in Nazi propaganda, see Jeffrey Herf, *The Jewish Enemy: Nazi Propaganda During World War II and the Holocaust* (Harvard University Press, 2009). On the Nazi creation of an ideological enemy through art and propaganda, see Jaskot, *The Nazi Perpetrator*, 24–31.
66. On the myth of the "good German" and the development of this figure in both the GDR and FRG, see Mark A. Wolfgram, *Getting History Right: East and West German Collective Memories of the Holocaust and War* (Bucknell University Press, 2010); Pól Ó Dochartaigh and Christiane Schönfeld, eds., *Representing the "Good German" in Literature and Culture After 1945* (Camden House, 2013).
67. Valerie Weinstein, " 'White Jews' and Dark Continents: Capitalist Critique and Its Racial Undercurrents in Detlef Sierck's *April! April!* (1935)," in *Continuity and Crisis in German Cinema, 1928–1936*, ed. Barbara Hales, Mihaela Petrescu, and Valerie Weinstein (Camden House, 2016), 139.
68. Post-1945 narratives also included "surrogate Jews:" non-Jewish characters who took the place of Jews structurally, rather than through Jewish codes or characteristics. Examples include Hermann Broch's *Der Versucher* (1946) and Wolfgang Koeppen's *Tauben im Gras* (1951). Nancy Lauckner, "The Surrogate Jew in the Postwar German Novel," *Monatshefte* 66, no. 2 (1974).
69. The term "secondary antisemitism" is related to postwar phenomena, such as animosity toward Jews stemming from feelings of guilt related to the Holocaust. However, this term does not capture the postwar drive to assert authority over the definition of antisemitism. On secondary antisemitism and the Frankfurt School, see Lars Rensmann, *The Politics of Unreason: The Frankfurt School and the Origins of Modern Antisemitism* (State University of New York Press, 2017), 359–89. On "secondary," "latent," or *"Schuldabwehr"* antisemitism in Germany, see Werner Bergmann, "Störenfriede der Erinnerung," 13–35; Werner Bergmann, "Sekundärer Antisemitismus," in *Handbuch des Antisemitismus. Judenfeindschaft in Geschichte und Gegenwart* 3, ed. Wolfgang Benz (De Gruyter, 2010). For other forms of

264 NOTES TO PAGES 12–14

antisemitism, see Jan Weyand, *Historische Wissensoziologie des modernen Antisemitismus. Genese und Typologie einer Wissensformation am Beispiel des deutschsprachigen Diskurses* (Wallstein, 2016). On postwar antisemitism in Austria, see Oliver Rathkolb, "Zur Kontinuität. Antisemitischer und Rassistischer Vorurteile in Österreich 1945/1950," *Zeitgeschichte* 16, no. 5 (1989).

70. Saul Friedländer describes "redemptive antisemitism" as the Nazis' hatred of Jews above all other "races," linked to the belief that their annihilation would bring redemption. See *Nazi Germany and the Jews*, vol. 1 (Harper Collins, 1997), 87. On selective antisemitism, see Keith Kahn-Harris, *Strange Hate: Antisemitism, Racism, and the Limits of Diversity* (Repeater Books, 2019), 31–35. On the philosophical underpinnings of anti-antisemitism and a critique of the term, see Elad Lapidot, *Jews out of the Question: A Critique of Anti-Anti-Semitism* (State University of New York Press, 2020).

71. Of course, Sartre's analysis of antisemitism encompassed far more than this simple sentence. See Jonathan Judaken, *Jean-Paul Sartre and the Jewish Question: Anti-Antisemitism and the Politics of the French Intellectual* (University of Nebraska Press, 2006); Ingo Elbe, "The Anguish of Freedom: Is Sartre's Existentialism an Appropriate Foundation for a Theory of Antisemitism?," *Antisemitism Studies* 4, no. 1 (2020); Manuela Consonni and Vivian Liska, eds., *Sartre, Jews, and the Other: Rethinking Antisemitism, Race, and Gender* (De Gruyter, 2020).

72. Nathan W. Ackerman and Marie Jahoda, *Anti-Semitism and Emotional Disorder. A Psychoanalytic Interpretation* (Harper & Brothers, 1950), 40 n12.

73. Theodor W. Adorno, et al., *The Authoritarian Personality* (Harper & Row, 1950), 475.

74. Jean-Paul Sartre, *Anti-Semite and Jew* (Schocken, 1965), 54. Pierre Vidal-Naquet suggests that the line is a transposition of Voltaire's noted phrase, "If God didn't exist, we would have to invent Him." See "Remembrances of a 1946 Reader," *October* 87 (1999): 10. One of Sartre's critics on this front, Pierre Birnbaum, notes: "Oddly enough, though historiography frequently contests the portrait of the Jew, it completely accepts the one of the anti-Semite, and even the most critical of writers congratulate Sartre on his analysis of anti-Semitic behavior, even though his analysis . . . is full of stereotypes taken from an obsolete social science." Pierre Birnbaum, "Sorry Afterthoughts on 'Anti-Semite and Jew,'" *October* 87 (1999): 100.

75. Sarte mentions reading *Hitler m'a dit* and repeats several other Hitler quotes he gleans via Rauschning in *The War Diaries of Jean-Paul Sartre, November 1939–March 1940* (Pantheon, 1984), 142, 220, 223. Half a century earlier, Austrian writer Hermann Bahr included this formulation in a compendium of responses to a questionnaire about antisemitism: "If there were no Jews, the antisemite would need to invent another scapegoat or object of hatred." *Der Antisemitismus. Ein internationales Interview* (S. Fischer, 1894), 3. In 1941, Hannah Arendt berated Jewish theoreticians whom she claimed told other Jews they existed only as inventions of antisemites. "Ceterum Censeo," *Aufbau*, December 26, 1941, 2.

76. Rauschning distances himself from his Nazi past by reconstructing and critiquing conversations between high-level functionaries that he claims to have overheard. The book was first published in French as *Hitler m'a dit* in 1939. It appeared shortly thereafter in English as *Hitler Speaks: A Series of Political Conversations with Adolf Hitler on His Real Aims* (1939) and in German as *Gespräche mit Hitler* (1940). Although influential at the time, the book was later found to be fraudulent. On historians' reception of Rauschning's book, see Mikael Nilsson, *Hitler Redux: The Incredible History of Hitler's So-Called Table Talks* (Routledge, 2020), 21–22.

77. "'Non, répondit Hitler, au contraire, si le Juif n'existait pas, il nous faudrait l'inventir.'" Rauschning, *Hitler m'a dit* (Coopération, 1939), 265.

78. Sartre's own expressions of bigotry toward Jews in his relationships and his work compromise his writings opposing antisemitism. See Bianca Lamblin, *A Disgraceful Affair: Simone de Beauvoir, Jean-Paul Sartre, and Bianca Lamblin* (Northeastern University Press, 1996). In later decades, Sartre suggested that he was the target of his own constructed Antisemite: "It is me that I was describing when I thought I was describing the Jew, a type who has nothing, no land, an intellectual"; at one point he also admitted that his Antisemite "was actually his own fantasy projected onto an other." Hammerschlag, *The Figural Jew*, 68–69.

79. On the constructed Jew as the opponent of the constructed non-Jew, rather than its antithesis, see Silverman, "Beyond Antisemitism," 28. On a related point, Elad Lapidot posits that the anti-antisemite rejects both a negative attitude toward Jews and the perception of Jews as constructed entities. *Jews out of the Question*, 8. On the liminality of the figural Jew, see Zygmunt Bauman, "Allosemitism: Premodern, Modern, Postmodern," in *Modernity, Culture and "the Jew,"* ed. Bryan Cheyette and Laura Marcus (Stanford University Press, 1998), 146–47.

NOTES TO PAGES 14–17   265

80. Sander L. Gilman, *Inscribing the Other* (University of Nebraska Press, 1991). Gilman notes that the figural Jew is most often male, which points to the gendered nature of the framework of Jewish difference.

81. David Engel suggests that the drive to define antisemitism impedes thorough investigation of its historical significance. See "Away from a Definition of Antisemitism: An Essay in the Semantics of Historical Description," in *Rethinking European Jewish history*, ed. Jeremy Cohen and Moshe Rosman (Littman Library, 2009).

82. During the war, Lueger's phrase was commonly attributed to Nazi leader Hermann Goering.

83. On this topic, see Peter Melichar, "Who Is a Jew? Antisemitic Defining, Identifying and Counting in Pre-1938 Austria," *Leo Baeck Institute Year Book* 50 (2005); Hammerschlag, *The Figural* Jew, 16–24.

84. For example, director Leni Riefenstahl explicitly denigrated Jews in correspondence with Nazi functionary Julius Streicher, but during the process of denazification, she touted acts of kindness that she showed Jews. See Bill Niven, *Hitler and Film: The Führer's Hidden Passion* (Yale University Press, 2018), 60.

85. Here I use "antisemitized" as distinct from "antisemitic," following Charles W. Mills's use of the term "racialized" as distinct from "racist" to describe the encoded racist tropes in liberalism, which disavows explicitly racist sentiments. *Black Rights/White Wrongs: The Critique of Racial Liberalism* (Oxford University Press, 2017), xv.

86. On the study of well-intentioned people and their unwitting adoption of prejudices and stereotypes, sometimes called "aversive racism," see Eliot R. Smith and Diane M. Mackie, "Aggression, Hatred and Other Emotions," in *On the Nature of Prejudice: Fifty Years After Allport*, ed. John F. Dovidio et al. (Blackwell, 2005), 364. For a recent study of unconscious bias, see Jennifer L. Eberhardt, *Biased: Uncovering the Hidden Prejudice That Shapes What We See, Think, and Do* (Penguin, 2019). On what Yascha Mounk terms "the philo-Semitism of good intentions" toward Jews after 1945, see *Stranger in My Own Country: A Jewish Family in Modern Germany* (Farrar, Straus, and Giroux, 2015), 109.

87. Michael Rothberg suggests the term "implicated subject" to articulate the collective responsibilities borne by those who inherit or benefit from past actions for which they cannot be held directly liable. *The Implicated Subject. Beyond Victims and Perpetrators* (Stanford University Press, 2019), 83.

88. On the problematic exculpation of historical figures from accusations of antisemitism by contextualizing their behavior as mere reflections of widespread bigotry or acts of political opportunism, see Nancy A. Harrowitz, ed., *Tainted Greatness: Antisemitism and Cultural Heroes* (Temple University Press, 1994), 1–14.

89. Diner, "Banished: Jews in Germany after the Holocaust," 10.

90. Brenner, *After the Holocaust*, 45.

91. This number does not include Jews in DP camps. "Jewish Population of Continental Europe, Juy 1948," American Joint Distribution Committee, European Executive Council, Budget and Research Department Report No. 53, September 21, 1948; Eveline Brugger, Martha Keil, Albert Lichtblau, Christoph Lind, and Barbara Staudinger, *Geschichte der Juden in Österreich* (Verlag Carl Ueberreuter, 2013), 538.

92. Brenner, *After the Holocaust*, 45.

93. Lehrman, "Austria: Way-Station of Exodus," 566.

94. Joseph McVeigh, "The Cold War in the Coffeehouse: Hans Weigel and His Circle of Writers in the Café Raimund," *Journal of Austrian Studies* 48, no. 3 (Fall 2015): 66–68.

95. For example, Jewish psychologist Viktor Frankl, whose life, work, and reputation for promoting reconciliation in postwar Austria remain controversial, was a popular lecturer in Vienna after the war. However, his autobiographical accounts of life in the camps did not gain widespread attention until years later. His book *Ärztliche Seelsorge*, first published in 1946, sold out within three days and was reprinted five times by 1948. He published the more autobiographical *Ein Psycholog erlebt das Konzentrationslager* (Verlag Jugend und Volk, 1946) anonymously, hoping its message would be perceived as universal. Friends eventually persuaded him to attach his name to the second edition. However, both editions sold so poorly that the remaining copies had to be pulped. It was only after its translation into English that his autobiographical work became an international bestseller, first as *From Death-Camp to Existentialism* (1959) and then as *Man's Search for Meaning: An Introduction to Logotherapy* (1963). The book was published in German in 1977 as . . . *Trotzdem ja zum leben sagen: Ein Psychologe erlebt das Konzentrationslager* (Kösel, 1977). Frankl had first used the phrase from the refrain of Fritz

266 NOTES TO PAGES 17–18

Löhner-Beda's Buchenwald song in another book he published in 1946, . . . *trotzdem ja zum leben sagen. Drei Vorträge gehalten an der Volkshochschule Wien-Ottakring* (Deuticke, 1946). See *Viktor E. Frankl, Gesammelte Werke*, vol. 1, ed. Alexander Batthyany, Karlheinz Biller, and Eugenio Fizzotti (Böhlau, 2005), 14–16.

96. See Frances Tanzer, *Vanishing Vienna: Modernism, Philosemitism and Jews in a Postwar City* (University of Pennsylvania Press, 2024); Y. Michal Bodemann, "How Can One Stand to Live There as a Jew . . . Paradoxes of Jewish Existence in Germany," in *Jews, Germans, Memory: Reconstructions of Jewish Life in Germany*, ed. Y. Michal Bodemann (University of Michigan Press, 1996); Bodemann, *Gedächtnistheater*.

97. The emotional community that developed around non-Jewish victimhood depended not just on physical location, but also on "fundamental assumptions, values, goals, feeling rules, and accepted modes of expression." Parkinson, *An Emotional State*, 88n9. See also Anna Koch, *Home After Fascism: Italian and German Jews After the Holocaust* (Indiana University Press, 2023), 153–57; Elizabeth Anthony, *The Compromise of Return: Viennese Jews After the Holocaust* (Wayne State University Press, 2021), 125–63.

98. Fritz Kortner, *Aller Tage Abend* (Kindler, 1959), 459.

99. Hilde Spiel, *Return to Vienna: A Journal*, trans. Christine Shuttleworth (Ariadne, 2011), 54.

100. Willi Forst, "Ich Rufe nach Österreich . . . ein offenes Wort an unsere Freunde in der Welt," *Film. Die österrechische illustrierte Zeitschrift* 1 (1946): 5–6.

101. Leiske stated, "You have returned to your fatherland in an exemplary gesture of reconciliation, and have taken up your chair at this university again. Such loyalty demands loyalty in return. We all, therefore, feel that your election to the highest academic office at our Johann Wolfgang Goethe University has been the climax of our own duty to provide restitution and compensation." Cited in Rolf Wiggershaus, *The Frankfurt School: Its History, Theories, and Political Significance* (MIT Press, 1995), 446–47. On compelling Jews to carry out "ideological labor" in postwar Germany, see Y. Michal Bodemann, "The State in the Construction of Ethnicity, and Ideological Labour: The Case of German Jewry," *Critical Sociology* 17, no. 3 (1990). On the other hand, Austrian-Jewish writer and re-émigré Friedrich Torberg coped with antisemitism by embracing his token presence as Austria's "*Jud vom Dienst*" (Jew on Duty). On Torberg's idiosyncratic postwar Jewish self-identification, see Malachi Hacohen, *Jacob & Esau: Jewish European History Between Nation and Empire* (Cambridge University Press, 2019), 542–80.

102. Notably, Horkheimer was called to serve as the only witness for the prosecution in the 1948 denazification trial of former Frankfurt University rector Franz Schmidt. Boll, "Max Horkheimers zweite Karriere," 351–52.

103. Additional German and Austrian films dealing with the Holocaust and/or antisemitism that premiered in the early postwar years include: *Morituri*, dir. Eugen York, 1948; *Ehe im Schatten* (Marriage in the Shadows), dir. Kurt Maetzig, 1948; *Lang ist der Weg* (The Road Is Long), dir. Marek Goldstein, 1948; *Affaire Blum* (The Blum Affair), dir. Erich Engel, 1948. See Robert Shandley, *Rubble Films: German Cinema in the Shadow of the Third Reich* (Temple University Press, 2001), 80. *Roman einer jungen Ehe* (Story of a Young Couple), dir. Kurt Maetzig, 1951, also focuses on the postwar era in Germany and includes scenes depicting the trials of Veit Harlan. In Austria, Karl Hartl directed a film adaptation of émigré Ernst Lothar's 1946 novel *Der Engel mit der Posaune* (The Angel with the Trumpet), recounting the history of a family of Viennese piano-makers, one of whom marries a Jewish woman; a British version of the film, directed by Anthony Bushell, was released as *The Angel with the Trumpet* in 1950. In the United States, *The Search* (1948), directed by Austrian émigré Fred Zinnemann, whose parents were murdered in the Holocaust, centers on a child who survived Auschwitz and embarks on a search for his mother. On the suppression of antisemitism in this film and its evocation in his famous Western *High Noon* (1952), see Darcy Buerkle, "Landscape, Exile, and Fred Zinnemann's *High Noon*," in *Passagen des Exils/Passages of Exile*, ed. Burcu Dogramaci and Elizabeth Otto (De Gruyter, 2017).

104. Kortner's reference to *Der Ruf* as a "jüdischer Kampffilm" (Jewish film highlighting struggle) suggests he was well aware of its potential to provoke German audiences. Alfred Joachim Fischer, "Fritz Kortner dreht einen Kampffilm," *Mein Film*, October 29, 1948, 9–10. Its main Antisemite is a liminal Jew whose identity as the son of a Jewish professor has been concealed from him by his non-Jewish mother. On the differences between Kortner's original treatment and the final film, see Christiane Schönfeld, "Fritz Kortner's Return to Germany and the Figure of the Returning Exile in Kortner's *The Mission* and Josef v. Báky's *Der Ruf*," *Feuchtwanger-Studien* 3 (2013).

NOTES TO PAGES 18–20   267

105. Kortner's Berlin theater production of Schiller's *Don Carlos* in December 1950 generated antisemitic catcalls and hate mail. See Klaus Völker, *Fritz Kortner: Schauspieler und Regisseur* (Edition Hentrich, 1987), 239. Kortner found greater success in West Germany with his drama *Donauwellen*, which premiered in Munich in 1949, perhaps due to its Viennese setting and its critique·of Austrian opportunism through the character of Duffeck, a typical antisemitic *Mitläufer* who owns an Aryanized barber shop and speaks in Viennese dialect. On the other hand, the harsh backlash from the Austrian press suggests that his portrait of the Austrian Antisemite may have hit too close to home to be successful there. Otto Basil, "Das abgebrochene Gastspiel," *Neues Österreich*, December 13, 1950, 1–2. Kortner first published portions of this drama as "Ein Traum—Kein Leben," in the New York newspaper *Austro American Tribune*, no. 11, June 1947, 3–4. The character of the postwar Austrian opportunist is later immortalized by Helmut Qualtinger in the dramatic monologue *Der Herr Karl*, first broadcast on Austrian television in 1961.
106. Ariane Niehoff-Hack, unpublished manuscript. See also Ruth Liepman, *Vielleicht ist Glück nicht nur Zufall. Erzählte Erinnerungen* (Kiepenheuer & Witsch, 1993), 162.
107. Tanzer, "Performing the Austrian-Jewish (Negative) Symbiosis," 15.
108. In 1943, Goebbels appointed Liebeneiner to be head of production at UFA, one of the most important positions in German cinema. His 1941 film *Ich Klage an* (I Accuse) was used as a way for the Nazis to gauge public acceptance of T4, the secret, nonvoluntary Nazi euthanasia program. Felix Moeller, "'Ich bin Künstler und sonst nichts.' Filmstars im Propagandaeinsatz," in *Hitlers Künstler. Die Kultur im Dienst des Nationalsozialismus*, ed. Hans Sarkowicz (Insel, 2004), 162–65. In Feburary 1950, a few months before Veit Harlan's acquittal, prosecutor Gerhard Kramer dismissed a charge filed against Liebeneiner for having committed a crime against humanity by directing *Ich Klage an*. Decades later, Liebeneiner insisted that the film saved lives and led to the termination of the Nazi program, defensively adding that a Czech Jewish playwright, František Langer, had explored the topic of assisted suicide already in 1932 in his drama "Engel unter Uns." See Erwin Leiser, *Deutschland, erwache! Propaganda im Film des Dritten Reiches* (Rowohlt, 1978), 129–31.
109. Homering, *Ida Ehre*, 81–82, and Verena Joos, *"Mutter Courage des Theaters" Ida Ehre* (Munich: Econ, 1999), 146–47. In contrast to the play, the film *Liebe 47* was not successful. See Robert C. Moeller, "When Liebe Was Just a Five-Letter World," in *German Postwar Films: Life and Love in the Ruins*, ed. Wilfried Wilms and William Rasch (Palgrave, 2008), 143.
110. Ida Ehre, *Gott hat einen größeren Kopf, mein Kind* (Rowohlt,1997), 150. German-Jewish writer Curt Riess, whose wife Heidemarie Hatheyer had starred in Liebeneiner's 1941 film *Ich Klage an*, grappled with similar sentiments in his friendship with Liebeneiner: "I find it astonishing that you said you considered *Jud Süss* to be a work of art. To be honest, I can't imagine it, but it was printed in a newspaper." Curt Riess to Wolfgang Liebeneiner, November 18, 1955, Bundesarchiv Koblenz N 1385-51 Riess.
111. Ehre, *Gott hat einen größeren Kopf*, 154.
112. On intermarried families during the Nazi era, see Michaela Raggam-Blesch, "'Privileged' under Nazi-Rule: The Fate of Three Intermarried Families in Vienna," *Journal of Genocide Research* 21, no. 3 (2019).
113. Ralph Giordano, *Die zweite Schuld oder Von der Last Deutscher zu sein* (Rasch und Röhring, 1987), 10.
114. Liepman, "The Survivors," 304.
115. Joachim Prinz, "Memorandum on a Trip to Germany, July 1949," 20. American Jewish Archives, Jacob Rader Marcus Center, Joachim Prinz collection.
116. Intersectionality refers to the ways in which socially constructed systems of oppression function in tandem with one another and thus create particular challenges. Kimberlé Williams Crenshaw, "Demarginalizing the Intersection of Race and Sex: A Black Feminist Critique of Antidiscrimination Doctrine, Feminist Theory, and Antiracist Politics," *University of Chicago Legal Forum* 1 (1989); *On Intersectionality: The Seminal Essays* (New Press, 2012). Because Jewish difference does not neatly overlap and intersect with race, class, and gender, it is often excluded from and can be fueled by discourses on intersectionality. On this problem, see Karin Stögner, "Der Antisemitismus und das Konzept der Intersektionalität," in *Handbuch Intersektio nalitätsforschung*, ed. A. Biele Mefebue et al. (Springer, 2022). On antisemitic stereotypes about Jews as seekers of power, control, and domination, which overlap with the qualities of white privilege, see Schraub, "White Jews," 383–84; Stögner, "Der Antisemitismus," 94–96. On challenges surrounding the relationship between intersectionality and antisemitism, see also Kerry Wallach

268   NOTES TO PAGES 20–25

and Sonia Gollance, "Introduction: When Feminism and Antisemitism Collide," *Feminist German Studies* 39, no. 1 (2023); Karin Stögner, "New Challenges in Feminism: Intersectionality, Critical Theory, and Anti-Zionism," in *Anti-Zionism and Antisemitism: The Dynamics of Deligitimization*, ed. Alvin H. Rosenfeld (Indiana University Press, 2019).

117. For example, in an interview conducted in 1980, Ehre's emotional breakdowns about the fates of Jewish relatives murdered by the Nazis are met with silence. Interview with Ida Ehre, Hamburg, 1980, Harald von Troschke Archiv, 44:50; 49:50, https://troschke-archiv.de/intervi ews/ida-ehre.

118. On the symbolic status of the victim as morally superior, and on the dynamics of competitive victimhood, see Johanna Ray Vollhardt, *The Social Psychology of Collective Victimhood* (Oxford University Press, 2020). Use of the term "agency" is problematic when it invokes competing narratives of so-called true victims, which rely on the false binary between "passive victimhood" versus "active agency." This binary obscures the presence of deeply ingrained racism and misogyny as well as their effects. See Rebecca Stringer, *Knowing Victims: Feminism, Agency and Victim Politics in Neoliberal Times* (Routledge, 2014), and Alyson Cole, *The Cult of True Victimhood: From the War on Welfare to the War on Terror* (Stanford University Press, 2007).

Chapter 1

1. *Niggun* refers to a Hasidic song. The lyrics are identical to those in the song "Der Rebbe hot gehaissen frailech sain" (The rabbi says be merry) recorded by Peter Upcher and reissued on Lukraphon 1135. Gerson was accompanied by the Sid Kays Fellows Orchestra. Horst J. P. Bergmeier et al., *Vorbei—Beyond Recall: A Record of Jewish Musical Life in Nazi Berlin, 1933–1938* (Bear Family Records, 2001), 409.

2. "Voranzeigen: Jüdisches Jugendpflegeamt Norden," *Jüdische Rundschau*, April 2, 1935, 10; "Wann? Wo?," *Jüdische Allgemeine Zeitung*, March 27, 1935, 6.

3. *Het Volk*, May 6, 1933, 13 cited in Katja B. Zaich, *"Ich bitte dringend um ein Happyend." Deutsche Bühnenkünstler im niederländischen Exil 1933–1945* (Peter Lang, 2001), 58. *De Telegraaf*, November 17, 1933, cited in Horst J. P. Bergmeier, *Chronologie der deutschen Kleinkunst in den Niederlanden 1933–1944* (Hamburger Arbeitsstelle für deutsche Exilliteratur, 1998), 411. Another critic lauded her singing and dramatic performances as "grandiose" and indicated she should appear on stage more often. See Friedrich W. Schulz, "Berlin in Ferien," *Moderne Welt* 11, no. 24 (1930): 9.

4. Max Gerson was born in 1866 in Strelno, Pomerania, Prussia. He died on April 15, 1937, in Berlin. Her mother, (Johanna) Hermine Gerson neé Wohl, was born in 1867 in Glatz, Silesia, Prussia. She and Max married in 1895 in Berlin. https://www.geni.com/people/Dorothea-Dora-Gerson.

5. These were *Die Todeskarawane* (The death caravan) and *Auf den Trümmern des Paradieses* (On the ruins of paradise), both directed by Josef Stein.

6. Erwin Leiser, *Leopold Lindtberg: "Du weisst ja nicht wie es in mir schäumt." Schriften-Bilder-Dokumente* (Musik und Theater Verlag, 1985), 210.

7. Jacques Klöters, "'Momente so, Momente so.' Dora Gerson und das erste Emigranten Kabarett 'Ping-Pong'" in *Die Niederlande und das deutsche Exil 1933–1940*, ed. Katinka Dittrich and Hans Würzner (Athenäum, 1982), 177–78.

8. Cited in Bergmeier, *Chronologie*, 34–35.

9. Bergmeier, *Chronologie*, 16.

10. Saul Friedländer, *Nazi Germany and the Jews: The Years of Persecution, 1933–1939*, vol. I (Harper, 1997), 12.

11. Zaich, *"Ich bitte dringend um ein Happyend,"* 57–64. On the fate of the group, see Peter Jelavich, *Berlin Cabaret* (Harvard University Press, 1996), 236–41.

12. Interview with Kurt Egon Wolff, undated. Deutsches Kabarettarchiv, Mainz, Archiv-Sign 2838.

13. Bergmeier, *Chronologie*, 190; Klöters, "'Momente so, Momente so,'" 178–79.

14. Klöters, "'Momente so, Momente so,'" 179–82.

15. Dora Gerson to Kurt Egon Wolff, August 18, 1934, courtesy of Cabaret Ping Pong Archive, administered by Efram Wolff Studios. Cited with permission.

16. Curt Bry mentions composing songs and writing scenes for Nelson's cabaret in Amsterdam when Dora Gerson and Paul Morgan were the stars of the troupe. Curt Bry, unpublished autobiography, 143. Cited with permission.

NOTES TO PAGES 26–27   269

17. An estimated 8,000 Jewish opera and concert singers, actors, musicians, composers, conductors, and employees of theaters were unemployed and lacking income. The group chose Lessing's drama *Nathan the Wise* for its first performance; other works included Stefan Zweig's drama *Jeremias* and Mozart's opera *The Marriage of Figaro*. Bergmeier, *Chronologie*, 53, 81. See also Sylvia Rogge-Gau, *Die doppelte Wurzel des Daseins. Julius Bab und der Jüdische Kulutrbund Berlin* (Metropol, 1999), 64–65; Gabriele Fritsch-Vivié, *Gegen alle Widerstände. Der jüdische Kulturbund 1933–1941* (Hentrich & Hentrich, 2013), 11–12; Rebecca Rovit, *The Jewish Kulturbund Theatre Company in Nazi Berlin* (University of Iowa Press, 2012); Lily E. Hirsch, *A Jewish Orchestra in Nazi Germany: Musical Politics and the Berlin Jewish Culture League* (University of Michigan Press, 2010). Recent studies of Kulturbund branches in other cities also probe how performers challenged the strict division between "German" and "Jewish" music. See Dana Smith, *Jewish Art in Nazi Germany: The Jewish Cultural League in Bavaria* (Routledge, 2022).
18. In a 1948 letter to Harlan that he never sent, Leo Lindtberg reveals his frustration with Harlan's ambivalence toward Jews when he recalls that Harlan had played the role of a Jewish doctor "with charm and human understanding" in 1930, but also remembers "how conversant you were in the not very pleasant Berlin Jewish jargon." Archiv der Akademie der Künste, Berlin, Leopold-Lindtberg-Archiv 1373. Portions of the unsent letter are printed in Leiser, *Leopold Lindtberg*, 209–12. In April 1933, Harlan performed in Nazi dramatist Hanns Johst's *Schlageter*, about a Nazi martyr sentenced to death by the French in the 1920s. Johst dedicated the play's premiere on April 20, 1933 to Hitler "in loving adoration and unwavering loyalty." Joseph Wulf, *Theater und Film im Dritten Reich. Eine Dokumentation* (Rowohlt, 1966), 189. By 1934, Harlan had already received acclaim for Nazi party member Arzén von Cserépy's film *Ein Mädchen mit Prokura* (A girl with the power of authority). For an overview of the positive reviews, see Frank Noack, *Veit Harlan: The Life and Work of a Nazi Filmmaker* (University of Kentucky Press, 2016), 71–72. That same year, Harlan wrote to Reichsfilmintendant Fritz Hippler, who had worked closely with Goebbels, seeking permission to open a Volkstheater. See " 'Sie lachen noch, Herr Harlan . . . ,' " *Jüdisches Gemeindeblatt. Die Zeitung der Juden in Deutschland*, March 11, 1949, 1.
19. Alfred Bauer, *Deutscher Spielfilm Almanach 1929–1950* (Filmblätter Verlag, 1950), 249. Nazi author Friedrich Bubendey adapted the novel into a play in 1934. Hömberg, who later served as film critic for the *Völkischer Beobachter*, also adapted Harlan's film *Jud Süss* for a novel written under a pseudonym. See J. R. George. *Jud Süss* (Ufa-Buchverlag GmbH, 1941). After 1945, Hömberg settled in Austria, where he enjoyed a successful career as a playwright and host of the popular radio program *Hömbergs Kaleidophon*. He considered himself knowledgeable about Jewish humor, and sent Harlan a Jewish joke book for his amusement when he was ill: "Kristina read a lot from your Jewish joke book and made me laugh, even though I didn't really feel like it." Veit Harlan to Hans Hömberg, December 9, 1963. Forschungsintitut Brenner-Archiv (FBA), Innsbruck, Nachlass Hans Hömberg, 133-002-056. See also the transcript to an episode of *Hömbergs Kaleidophon*, "Es Darf gelacht Werden" (undated), in which Hömberg states that he usually "maintains the taboo" on Jewish jokes, although "every now and then you can allow yourself to reminisce." FBA, Innsbruck, Nachlass Hans Hömberg, 133-001-034, 11.
20. Valerie Weinstein, *Antisemitism in Film Comedy in Nazi Germany* (Indiana University Press, 2019), 63–68. On the Nazis' drive to portray Weimar cinema as morally corrupt and Jewish-dominated, see Sabine Hake, *Popular Cinema of the Third Reich* (University of Texas Press, 2001).
21. On Nazi propaganda touting the German cinema as dominated by Jews, see Eric Rentschler, *The Ministry of Illusion: Nazi Cinema and Its Afterlife* (Harvard University Press, 1996), 155–56.
22. In an undated interview before his death in 1982, Hans Hömberg details his career, unsurprisingly omitting any mention of his work on either *Jud Süss* or *Susanne*. However, he does bitterly recall the stinging rejection his earliest foray into screenwriting received from film producers Noë Bloch and Gregor Rabinovitch, both Jews who were later forced to flee Nazi Europe. His anecdote, in which he mimics their use of Yiddish, links the denigration of Jewish film producers in the screenplay for *Susanne* to his personal resentments. Hömberg Interview with Harald von Troschke, undated, Harald von Troschke Archiv, https://troschke-archiv.de/interviews/hans-hoemberg.
23. Weinstein, *Antisemitism in Film Comedy*, 63–68.
24. One reviewer criticized the film for portraying Jews too positively but praised Harlan for his performance. Frank Noack, *Veit Harlan:"des Teufels Regisseur"* (Belleville, 2000), 99. David Stewart

270 NOTES TO PAGES 27–30

Hull claims that the audience booed at the premiere and that Goebbels sent von Cserépy back to Hungary in disgrace. *Film in the Third Reich: Art and Propaganda in Nazi Germany* (Simon and Schuster, 1973), 69.

25. *Völkischer Beobachter* (Vienna edition), September 4, 1938, 9. Another Viennese critic noted that the film provided "a moral image of the disgusting mechanics of filmmaking by former 'filmmakers.' Despite its serious message, it is a cheerful film that effortlessly shows us what we once had to defenselessly withstand." *Mein Film in Wien. Illustrierte Film- und Kinorundschau* 662, September 2, 1938, 20. A portrait of Harlan in his leading role in *Susanne* appears alongside his interview with writer Wilhelm Schnauck, a frequent contributor to the Nazi journal *Nationalsozialistische Monatshefte*. See "Das soziale Problem—filmisch gestaltet. Ein Gespräch mit dem Spielleiter Veit Harlan," *Mein Film in Wien. Illustrierte Film- und Kinorundschau*, August 5, 1938, 2.

26. Veit Harlan, "My Attitude Towards National Socialism," May, 1945, Staatsarchiv Hamburg (SH), Misc 6911, Part I, 4. Harlan included this statement to explain why he did not leave the country when he was first approached to make *Jud Süss* in 1939; he claimed that to do so would have put him at risk of being shot for desertion.

27. The film and trial have received extensive scholarly attention, including: Herbert Pardo and Siegfried Schiffner, *Jud Süss. Historisches und juristisches Material zum Fall Veit Harlan* (Auerdruck, 1949); Siegfried Zielinski, *Veit Harlan. Analysen und Materialien zur Auseinandersetzung mit einem Film-Regisseur des deutschen Faschismus* (R. G. Fischer, 1981); Rentschler, *The Ministry of Illusion*, 149–69; Linda Schulte-Sasse, *Entertaining the Third Reich: The Illusions of Wholeness in Nazi Cinema* (Duke University Press, 47–91.); Susan Tegel, *Jew Süss: Life, Legend, Fiction, Film* (Continuum, 2011); Friedrich Knilli, *Ich war Jud Süss. Die Geschichte des Filmstars Ferdinand Marian* (Henschel, 2010); Ernst Seidl, ed., *"Jud Süss: Propagandafilm im NS-Staat. Katalog zur Ausstellung im Haus der Geschichte Baden-Württemberg* (Haus der Geschichte Baden-Württemberg, 2007); Bill Niven, *Jud Süss. Das lange Leben eines Propagandafilms* (Mitteldeutscher Verlag, 2022). On the cultural significance of Joseph Süss Oppenheimer, see Yair Mintzker, *The Many Deaths of Jew Süss: The Notorious Trial and Execution of an Eighteenth-Century Court Jew* (Princeton University Press, 2019).

28. On the Nazis' continued emphasis on the Jewish domination of German cinema after 1935 and its links to Harlan's portrayal of Süss, see Rentschler, *The Ministry of Illusion*, 155–56.

29. Harlan, "My Attitude," 8.

30. Curt Bry, unpublished autobiography, 122. Cited with permission. By 1938, Gerson's mother was living with them in Amsterdam. Annie Vonk, "Op bezoek bij Dora Gerson," *Het Volk*, October 27, 1938.

31. "I wrote to Veit. Do you think there's any point? When you're in Berlin, will you speak to him to [have him] tell you what I have written? It is very necessary!" Dora Gerson to Friedel (possibly Friedrich Hellmund), August 27, 1942 (emphasis in original). Allard Pierson Museum, University of Amsterdam, Theater Collection. File on Dora Gerson. In court, Harlan testified: "She was sent away. She wrote to me from Amsterdam in 1942/43" but he did not help her because "[i]f Goebbels had noticed anything, she would have been lost." "'Sie lachen noch, Herr Harlan . . . ,'" *Jüdisches Gemeindeblatt. Die Zeitung der Juden in Deutschland*, March 11, 1949, 1. Later, Harlan considered claiming to have made great efforts to help save Gerson. In one draft of a letter he wrote: "I can prove that I went very far in trying to help her" but was unable to get in touch with her, and would not have been able to "move an entire Jewish family with several children from Holland to Berlin, for example, for safety." However, this statement was not included in the final draft of the letter. Veit Harlan to E. A. Lang, June 20, 1962, Filmmuseum Potsdam (FMP), VH DL (N109), Box 18. Over the years, Harlan often insisted that he had never refused any Jews' requests for help. See, for example, Veit Harlan to the Zentralstelle für Berufungsausschüsse, Hamburg, August 17, 1947, SH 6911, 4. In 1956, he told Curt Riess, "There is no Jew or half-Jew, and there is also no communist, who turned to me during the Nazi era without receiving my active help." Veit Harlan to Curt Riess, September 23, 1956, Bundesarchiv Koblenz, 1385-33 Riess.

32. Kurt Egon Wolff, interview, Kabarettarchiv, Mainz.

33. Gabriele Tergit, "Der erste Tag im Veit-Harlan-Prozeß," *Die neue Zeitung*, March 4, 1949. In a February 3, 1948, deposition, Harlan told prosecutor Gerhard Kramer he had heard that his Jewish first wife had died in a concentration camp. SH 213–11 21249–50, Bd. 4, 2.

34. Katja Wyler-Salten, "Veit Harlans Rolle im Dritten Reich," *Neue Zürcher Zeitung*, April 19, 1962, 17. The interview with Harlan aired on April 14, 1962. Anna Katharina Wyler-Salten, daughter

NOTES TO PAGES 30–34   271

of Austrian-Jewish writer Felix Salten, began her career as an actor in Vienna and Berlin in the 1920s; she left for Switzerland in 1935. By 1940 she was a successful writer and translator. Harlan responded to Wyler-Salten's article with an angry six-page letter to the newspaper demanding a retraction, which the newspaper declined. Veit Harlan to Dr. Schlappner, Editor in Chief, *Neue Zürcher Zeitung*, May 5, 1962. FMP VH DL (N109), Box 18.

35. Veit Harlan, "Wie es War ... Erlebnisse eines Filmregisseurs unter seinem allerhöchtsen Chef, dem 'Schirmherrn des deutschen Films,' **Dr. Josef Goebbels.**" (How it was ... A film director's experiences under his very highest boss, the 'guardian of German films,' Dr. Josef Goebbels) (emphasis in original), 57. Unpublished manuscript, ca. 1960. Bayerische Staatsbibliothek, Munich. This manuscript was later published in abbreviated form as Veit Harlan, *Im Schatten meiner Filme. Selbstbiographie*, ed. H. C. Opfermann (Sigbert Mohn, 1966). A subsequent French version includes some of the original manuscript passages that were cut from the German publication. See Veit Harlan, *Souvenirs ou le Cinéma allemande selon Goebbels*, trans. Albert Cologny (Éditions France-Empire, 1974).

36. Harlan, *Im Schatten*, 77.

37. Harlan remained bitter about an alleged affair between Gerson and Jewish actor Ernst Ginsberg. He claimed to have considered announcing it publicly, but decided against it. Veit Harlan, draft of letter to E. A. Lang, June 20, 1962, FMP, VH DL (N109), Box 18.

38. On Harlan's tendency to refer to himself as a victim, see Frank Liebert, "Vom Karrierestreben zum 'Nötigungsnotstand,' *Jud Süß*, Veit Harlan und die westdeutsche Nachkriegsgesellschaft (1945–1950)," in *Das Lüth-Urteil aus (rechts-) historischer Sicht. Die Konflikte um Veit Harlan und die Grundrechtsjudikatur des Bundesverfassungsgerichts*, ed. Thomas Henne and Arne Riedlinger (Berliner Wissenschafts-Verlag, 2005), 115–18.

39. Harlan, "My Attitude," 2.

40. Harlan, "My Attitude," 3.

41. Harlan, "My Attitude," 16–20.

42. Harlan directed twelve films after 1945. Lion Feuchtwanger told his publisher that he was negotiating for a remake of the film: "The plan is to form a committee of leading figures in Germany that will treat the production of the film as a major act of reparation for the injustice committed by Goebbels and Harlan." Letter from Feuchtwanger to Ben Huebsch, December 27, 1952, cited in Jeffrey B. Berlin, "A Relentless Drive for Meaning (Part II): Lion Feuchtwanger's Unpublished Correspondence with His American Publisher Ben Huebsch (1952–1956)," in *Feuchtwanger and Remigration*, ed. Ian Wallace (Peter Lang, 2013), 132. The remake never materialized. For a comprehensive account of the postwar significance of *Jud Süss* and the effects of the boycotts on Harlan's reputation, see Niven, *Jud Süss. Das lange Leben eines Propagandafilms*.

43. Harlan was already acquainted with Prinz before he left Berlin in 1937. Liepman's letter reveals that Harlan and Prinz met during Prinz's visit to Hamburg. Heinz Liepman to Gerhard Kramer, July 27, 1948, SH 213–11 72298. Prinz spoke at Friday evening services in Hamburg on July 23, 1948. "Dr. Joachim Prinz in Deutschland," *Jüdisches Gemeindeblatt für die Britische Zone*, August 11, 1948, 7.

44. Heinz Liepman to Gerhard Kramer, July 27, 1948, SH 213–11 72298. Following their meeting, Prinz published two open letters in various newspapers. The first was a letter from Harlan to Prinz, dated July 24, 1948, asserting that *Jud Süss* was not intended to stir up antisemitism and warning that his trial would have negative consequences for the Jewish community. The second was Prinz's response to Harlan of July 28, 1948 (mistakenly dated July 22), in which he refuted Harlan's claim. However, Liepman's letter to Kramer from July 27, 1948 reveals that Harlan made demands at the meeting with Prinz that were not included in the published letters. During the trial, Harlan brought up the meeting with Prinz and described it as friendly. Filmmuseum Landeshauptstadt Düsseldorf, SLG.VH-116. References to the letters (but not the private meeting) can be found in "Joachim Prinz v. Veit Harlan: A Film on Trial," *AJR Information*, October, 1948, 2; Pardo and Schiffner, *Jud Süss. Historisches und juristisches Material*, 68–70; Erwin Leiser, *Deutschland Erwache! Propaganda im Film des Dritten Reiches* (Rowohlt, 1968), 144–46.

45. Julius Bab, "Der Fall Harlan," *Der Morgen: Monatsschrift der Juden in Deutschland*, no. 3 (August 1931). In his article, Bab admits he had not attended that meeting. Bab mentions this article in a letter to Harlan dated June 28, 1948. Archiv der Akademie der Künste (AdK), Berlin, Julius Bab Archiv, Bab 515. Both Hans Rehfisch, who called for Walter Harlan to step down, and Eduard Künneke, who chaired the meeting, claimed to recall no accusations of antisemitism

272   NOTES TO PAGES 34-38

or financial mismanagement against Walter Harlan. Testimony of Eduard Künneke to Gerhard Kramer, April 24, 1948, SH 213–11 72298.

46. Harlan said he spoke to Bab both before and after the publication of an interview that appeared in the *Völkischer Beobachter* in 1933; Bab does not recall this conversation. Letter from Veit Harlan to Julius Bab, August 23, 1947, AdK Berlin, Julius Bab Archiv, Bab 515. Harlan claims that he was called into the Gestapo office in 1933 "on account of my friendship with Julius Bab." Harlan, "My Attitude," 12.

47. Bab edited the Kulturbund journal *Monatsblätter* and held lectures for its members on German poetry, literature, and other topics. See *Kulturbundbühne* 3, no. 3 (March 1935); *Kulturbundbühne* 3, no. 11 (November 1935): 3–4. On Bab's emigration, see Elisabeth Bab, "Aus zwei Jahrhunderten. Lebenserinnerungen," unpublished manuscript, ca. 1960, Leo Baeck Institute (LBI) Archives, memoir collection, ME 21, 184–85, 191.

48. In the preface to his book *The Wandering Jews* (1937), Joseph Roth openly criticized the group as "an unwarranted concession on the part of the Jews to the barbarous theories of National Socialism. Its basis is not the assumption—accepted by so many Jews today—that they are a separate race, but the implicit admission that they are an inferior one." Cited in Rovit, *Jewish Kulturbund*, 119.

49. Julius Bab to Fritz Wisten, May 19, 1933, and June 9, 1933, AdK Berlin, Fritz Wisten Archiv, Wisten 74/86/994–1030.

50. Julius Bab to Georg Hermann, May 31, 1933, LBI, Georg Hermann collection, AR 7074.

51. Julius Bab to Hans Franck, spring/summer 1933, AdK Berlin, Julius Bab Archiv, Bab 366. After the war, Bab told Franck's son-in-law Heinz Grothe that Franck had worn a swastika in his home in 1933 and had written a drama scapegoating Jews, titled "Erntefestspiel." Julius Bab to Heinz Grothe, October 5, 1950, AdK Berlin, Julius Bab Archiv, Bab 26.

52. Julius Bab, "Kulturbund deutscher Juden," *Der Schild, Zeitschrift des Reichsbundes Jüdischer Frontsoldaten*, September 14, 1933, 148.

53. For a detailed account of their life in the United States, see Elisabeth Bab, "Aus zwei Jahrhunderten." Elisabeth worked in sales, while Julius lectured, wrote for *Aufbau*, and eventually became a regular critic for the *New Yorker Staats-Zeitung und Herold*. On his difficulties with English, see Rogge-Gau, *Die doppelte Wurzel des Daseins*, 192.

54. Julius Bab, "Bildnis einer deutschen Künstlerin im Jahre 1947," *New Yorker Staats-Zeitung und Herold*, XCIX, no. 24, April 15, 1947, 6B: "Then Hitler came. Walter Harlan was dead, and his son, with scruple-free ambition, became involved in staging his plays in ways corrupted with antisemitism to serve as grand Nazi films."

55. Veit Harlan to the Zentralstelle für Berufsausschüsse, Hamburg, August 17, 1947, SH Misc 6911 Part I.

56. Otto Zippel to the Fachausschuss 7, Hamburg, July 26, 1946, SH, Misc 6911 Part I.

57. Veit Harlan to Julius Bab, August 23, 1947, AdK Berlin, Julius Bab Archiv, Bab 515.

58. Veit Harlan to Julius Bab, August 23, 1947, AdK Berlin, Julius Bab Archiv, Bab 515.

59. Veit Harlan to Julius Bab, August 23, 1947, AdK Berlin, Julius Bab Archiv, Bab 515.

60. Veit Harlan to Julius Bab, August 23, 1947, AdK Berlin, Julius Bab Archiv, Bab 515.

61. Veit Harlan to Julius Bab, October 6, 1947, AdK Berlin, Julius Bab Archiv, Bab 515. Here, Harlan is likely responding to Bab's article "Bildnis einer deutschen Künstlerin im Jahre 1947," *New Yorker Staats-Zeitung und Herold*, XCIX, no. 24, April 15, 1947, 6B.

62. Kortner had been a colleague of Harlan's during their early acting careers. In a well-known incident, Harlan punched Kortner, whom he suspected of having an affair with his second wife, actor Hilde Körber. Years later, in 1963, Harlan's illness prompted Kortner to draft a letter expressing disagreement with the way Harlan was being treated—presumably by the press—and suggesting the possibility of a future reconciliation. Fritz Kortner to Veit Harlan, October 7, 1963, AdK Berlin, Fritz Kortner Archiv, Kortner 355. Kortner noted on the draft that he was not sure whether he had ever sent the letter, but writer Hans Gustl Kernmayr later told Harlan that writer and critic Walther Kiaulehn had seen it: "By the way, Kiaulehn himself said that he saw the letter that Kortner wrote to you with his own eyes. But he will speak to Kortner again one of these days." Hans Gustl Kernmayr to Veit Harlan, March 16, 1964, FBA, Innsbruck, Nachlass Hans Hömberg, 133-002-056.

63. Veit Harlan to Julius Bab, October 6, 1947, AdK Berlin, Julius Bab Archiv, Bab 515.

64. Julius Bab to Veit Harlan, November 15, 1947, FMP, VH DL (N109), Box 26.

65. Veit Harlan to Julius Bab, December 6, 1947, AdK Berlin, Julius Bab Archiv, Bab 515.

66. Zentralausschuss für die Ausschaltung von Nationalsozialisten to the Staatskommissar für die Entnazifizierung/Kategorisierung, Hamburg, December 22, 1947, SH Misc 6911 Part II.

NOTES TO PAGES 39–44 273

67. "Veit Harlan entnazifiziert. Empörung über das Fehlurteil des Zentralauschusses," *Telegraf*, December 17, 1947, states that the news of Harlan's exoneration was released that day. See also letters from the Hamburg Jewish community and the Hamburg SPD to the denazification committee, both dated December 18, 1947, SH Misc 6911 Part II.

68. Zielinski, *Veit Harlan*, 43. "Sturm gegen die Entlastung Harlans," *Neues Deutschland*, December 19, 1947, reports that the denazification committee in Hamburg rejected key evidence, which fueled protests. Protests were also reported in the Bremen *Weser Kurier* on December 24, 1947, and *Neues Deutschland* on December 28, 1947. Years later, the denazification committee renewed the exoneration but did not make that decision public because Harlan had already been acquitted in the trials for crimes against humanity. The undated "Vorschlag für die Kategorisierung von Veit Harlan mit dem Entwurf einer Bergründung," indicates the committee took evidence of the Hamburger court's judgment into consideration in March/April 1949. SH Misc 6911 Part I.

69. Fred A. Angermayer's minutes of the meeting from April 14, 1931 indicate that an unspecified individual yelled out "You're an antisemite!," prompting Walter Harlan to protest. Harlan also complained that Fritz Engel—a Jewish writer—had recently refused to shake his hand, and speculated that Rehfisch would likely respond with a cutting remark. FMP, VH DL (N109), Box 29.

70. Hans Rehfisch to Gerhard Kramer, April 12, 1948, SH 213–11 72295.

71. Veit Harlan to Julius Bab, May 29, 1948, AdK Berlin, Julius Bab Archiv, Bab 515. Although the minutes attribute the accusation of antisemitism to an "unspecified individual," Harlan tells Bab that the record shows that Rehfisch called his father an Antisemite.

72. Veit Harlan to Julius Bab, May 29, 1948, AdK Berlin, Julius Bab Archiv, Bab 515.

73. Oberstaatsanwalt Landgericht Hamburg to Julius Bab, May 29, 1948, AdK Berlin, Julius Bab Archiv, Bab 516.

74. Veit Harlan to Julius Bab, June 3, 1948, AdK Berlin, Julius Bab Archiv, Bab 515. In a letter to his brother, Harlan admits Werner Krauss is a lifelong Antisemite and recalls an incident in which Krauss called Max Reinhardt a *Judenlümmel* (Jew lout). Veit Harlan to Peter Harlan, January 4, 1946, FMP, VH DL (N109), Box 2.

75. Julius Bab to Veit Harlan, undated, FMP, VH DL (N109), Box 26.

76. Veit Harlan to Julius Bab, June 3, 1948, AdK Berlin, Julius Bab Archiv, Bab 515.

77. Julius Bab to Oberstaatsanwalt Landgericht Hamburg, June 28, 1948, AdK Berlin, Julius Bab Archiv, Bab 516.

78. Norbert Wollheim to Manfred George, March 10, 1949, AdK Berlin, Julius Bab Archiv, Bab 410.

79. Julius Bab to Manfred George, March 16, 1949, AdK Berlin, Julius Bab Archiv, Bab 410.

80. Julius Bab, "Immer noch Fall 'Veit Harlan'!," *Sonntagsblatt Staats-Zeitung und Herold*, February 4, 1951, 6B.

81. Veit Harlan to Julius Bab, February 21, 1951, AdK Berlin, Julius Bab Archiv, Bab 515.

82. Veit Harlan to Julius Bab, June 18, 1951, AdK Berlin, Julius Bab Archiv, Bab 515.

83. Veit Harlan to Julius Bab, June 18, 1951, AdK Berlin, Julius Bab Archiv, Bab 515.

84. Bab wrote this manuscript in Paris in 1939; in 1957, he referred to it as a eulogy for German Jewry. Julius Bab, "Leben und Tod des Deutschen Judentums," unpublished ms., ca. 1939, LBI, Julius Bab Collection (AR 196/MF 475), Series I.

85. Rogge-Gau, *Die doppelte Wurzel*, 193.

86. Lion Feuchtwanger, "Offener Brief an einige Berliner Schauspieler," originally published in *Aufbau* 7, no. 27, July 4, 1941, 11. The article specifically names Werner Krauss, Eugen Klöpfer, Heinrich George, Albert Florath, and Veit Harlan. Harlan responded to the republication of the letter in the *Weltbühne* in 1947.

87. Veit Harlan to Lion Feuchtwanger, December 12, 1947, SH 6911, Part I, also reprinted in Pardo and Schiffner, *Jud Süss. Historisches und juristisches Material*, 63–66.

88. Harlan's cynical claim that Süss's attractiveness represented a weakening of the film's antisemitic effects ignores the enduring and widespread stereotypes of Jewish men as seductive peddlers of vice. See, for example, Schulte-Sasse, *Entertaining the Third Reich*, 81.

89. Veit Harlan to Lion Feuchtwanger, December 12, 1947, SH 6911, Part I.

90. Veit Harlan to Lion Feuchtwanger, December 12, 1947, SH 6911, Part I. Harlan's reasoning did not sit well with Leopold Lindtberg, who wrote in an (unsent) 1948 letter to Harlan: "But even if you had refused, you wouldn't have been sent to the concentration camp, you wouldn't have been hung by your feet, your teeth wouldn't have been smashed, your skull would not have been trampled on, you wouldn't have been driven naked into the gas chambers to the sound of a waltz and lampshades would not have been made out of your skin." AdK Berlin, Leopold Lindtberg Archiv 1373. The quoted passage is omitted from the unsent letter printed in Leiser, *Leopold Lindtberg*, 209–12.

274 NOTES TO PAGES 44-47

91. Veit Harlan to Lion Feuchtwanger, December 12, 1947, SH 6911, Part I.
92. *Kindertransporte* (children's transports) were a series of efforts undertaken between December 1938 and May 1940 to rescue Jewish minors from Nazi Germany, Austria, and Czechoslovakia by bringing them to Great Britain; the program saved about 10,000 children.
93. After the war, he survived a Nazi death march of prisoners and was eventually liberated by American troops in Schwerin. United States Holocaust Museum Archive, Norbert Wollheim Papers, 1999.A.0031, RG-80.000, biographical note.
94. Wollheim testifed that *Jud Süss* had played a substantial role in sharpening attitudes against Jews among Germans and others. In a letter to Herbert Pardo, he recounted that a functionary of the *Reichsvereinigung der Juden in Deutschland* had told him that Jewish leaders had anticipated that the film would trigger anti-Jewish violence comparable to the pogroms of November 1938. Wollheim also reported that non-Jewish forced laborers told him the film had incited violence when they viewed it. Norbert Wollheim to Herbert Pardo, August 28, 1948, SH 213–11 72296. For Harlan's second trial, Wollheim opted to submit a written statement rather than appear in person to testify—a decision for which he was sharply rebuked by the judge.
95. "Proteste gegen Veit Harlan," *Die Welt*, December 18, 1947, SH 6911, Part II. Some members of the denazification committee were not aware that the meeting would take place, were absent, or had left before it was adjourned. Tegel, *Jew Süss*, 204.
96. Most accounts state that Harlan and Gerson officially separated in 1924.
97. Veit Harlan to Norbert Wollheim, December 18, 1947, reprinted in Pardo and Schiffner, *Jud Süss*, 66–67.
98. See Laura Jockusch and Gabriel N. Finder, eds., *Jewish Honor Courts: Revenge, Retribution, and Reconciliation in Europe and Israel After the Holocaust* (Wayne State University Press, 2015), 5.
99. "Harlan: Jüdisches Ehrengericht," *Die Welt*, December 23, 1947, SH 6911, Part II. See also *Neues Österreich*, December 25, 1947, 5.
100. Norbert Wollheim to Veit Harlan, January 3, 1948, Filmmuseum Landeshauptstadt Düsseldorf, SLG.VH-116. Also reprinted in Pardo and Schiffner, *Jud Süss*, 67–68.
101. For Wollheim, whose day-to-day responsibilities included monitoring the desecration of Jewish cemeteries, the denigration of Jews as black marketeers, the reappointment of former Nazis to positions of power, and addressing the needs of the remnant Jewish communities, Harlan's trial did not rank as an urgent matter. As he reported to the World Jewish Congress, "The trial in Hamburg has resulted in great bitterness in Jewish circles, although the negative outcome was foreseeable. It is not Harlan who is of interest, but rather the broader implications revealed by the court's stance." These concerns included the perception that initiators and perpetrators of antisemitism were not being held accountable for their past crimes, and the fear that anyone could now justify their involvement in Nazi atrocities as acts committed under pressure or in self-defense. Norbert Wollheim to Alex Easterman, April 30, 1950, Central Zionist Archives C21757.
102. During the war he worked in engineering for various companies; by 1944 he led a research laboratory in Berlin for the technical development of radio and sound film. FBA, Innsbruck, Nachlass Hans Hömberg, 133-033-039 Opfermann.
103. Friedrich Knilli, Interview with Hans Carl Opfermann, 1980, Landesarchiv Baden-Württemberg, Staatsarchiv Stuttgart, J 25 Sammlung Knilli, R 20/005 23 A140068/102. Depite the admiration for Harlan that he expressed in this interview, Opfermann distanced himself from his book a year after its publication. "Herr v. Siemens zieht einen Schlussstrich. Ein Nazi für den deutschen Pavillon in Montreal," *Aufbau*, March 17, 1967, 3; "Veit Harlan, Opfermann und der deutsche Pavillon in Montreal," *Aufbau*, May 19, 1967, 7.
104. Friedrich Knilli interview with Hans Carl Opfermann, 1980, Landesarchiv Baden-Württemberg, Stuttgart, J 25 Sammlung Knilli, R 20/005 23 A140068/102.
105. Opfermann later insisted that he had "never identified or agreed with Harlan's political beliefs and actions" and claimed he published Harlan's autobiography as a historical contribution—comparable, he argued, to the publication of Goebbels's diaries and Hitler's conversations. H. C. Opfermann to the Press Office of the Federal Republic of Germany, March 24, 1967, FBA, Innsbruck, Nachlass Hans Hömberg, 133-033-039 Opfermann.
106. Harlan, "Wie es war," 17.
107. Harlan, "Wie es war," 17.
108. Harlan, "Wie es war," 446.
109. Harlan, "Wie es war," 20.

NOTES TO PAGES 47–53   275

110. Harlan, "Wie es war," 43, 115.
111. Harlan, "Wie es war," 26.
112. Harlan, "Wie es war," 437.
113. Harlan, "Wie es war," 437. SS-Lieutenant General Oswald Pohl was head of the SS Economic and Administrative Main Office and chief administrator of the concentration camps.
114. Harlan, "Wie es war," 386–87.
115. Harlan, "Wie es war," 436.
116. Harlan, "Wie es war," 22.
117. Harlan, "Wie es war," 23. Harlan offered even greater praise for Goebbels in private. In a letter to Fritz Hippler (SS officer and former Reichfilmsintendant under Goebbels), Harlan complains that Curt Riess's recently published biography of Goebbels does not do justice to the stature of their former boss. He disparages Riess by comparing him to a dog and describing him as bow-legged (both stereotypical antisemitic slurs) while also appropriating Yiddish expressions. "Whatever Goebbels may have been, what he was, was tremendous. . . . Who is Mr. Goebbels and who is Mr. Riess? What does the moon care if the dog barks at it? . . . There are no stilts high enough for Mr. Riess's crooked legs to reach Goebbels's eyes—so that he could look the devil in the eyes and tell us who the devil is. Mr. Riess is also a devil, but from a joke shop, not from hell. . . . Not everything can be figured out using *chutzpah*." Veit Harlan to Fritz Hippler, December 28, 1949. FMP VH DLN N109 Box 26.
118. Harlan, "Wie es war," 493.
119. Harlan, "Wie es war," 78.
120. Harlan, "Wie es war," 260, 316–19, 328–29, 336, 478.
121. Harlan, "Wie es war," 23, 25; *Im Schatten*, 8.
122. Harlan, "Wie es war," 58–59.
123. Harlan, "Wie es war," 432.
124. Harlan, "Wie es war," 493.
125. Harlan, "Wie es war," 28.
126. Harlan had been even more explicit about his views on Jews and German patriotism in his letter to Fritz Hippler: "Nobody will deny that the Jews were the enemies of Germany in 1939. Whether the National Socialists were to blame or not has no bearing on the war itself. Understandably, they have declared themselves to be Germany's greatest enemies. As repulsive as this hostility is to me personally—and as much as I believe that most of it stems from the National Socialists—every German must still be allowed to hope for and promote victory, just like the soldiers who are prepared to sacrifice their lives for it." Veit Harlan to Fritz Hippler, December 28, 1949. FMP VH DLN N109 Box 26.
127. Alfred Braun testimony, 8, SH 213–11 72297.
128. Harlan, "Wie es war," 82.
129. Harlan, "Wie es war," 83.
130. Harlan, "Wie es war," 139.
131. Veit Harlan to Julius Bab, June 3, 1948, AdK Berlin, Julius Bab Archiv, Bab 515.
132. Harlan, "Wie es war," 312.
133. Harlan, "Wie es war," 209. Harlan's depiction of Jewish rituals seemed intentionally designed to portray Jews as foreign and unfamiliar as possible. See Bill Niven, *Hitler and Film: The Führer's Hidden Passion* (Yale University Press, 2018), 170. On the film's sonic distortions and inconsistencies in the depiction of Jewish rituals, see Ruth HaCohen, *The Music Libel Against the Jews* (Yale University Press, 2013), 343–58.
134. Harlan, "Wie es war," 209.
135. "Harlan ist soeben von einer Reise durch Polen zurückgekehrt," *Der Film*, January 20, 1940.
136. Harlan, *Im Schatten*, 116.
137. Harlan, "Wie es war," 361–62.
138. As he stated defiantly to a reporter in 1963, "About my whole life I have a guilty conscience. About the film *Jud Süss* I have the very best." Hans Friedrich Lehner, "Gastspiel vor dunklem Hintergrund," *Aachener Nachrichten*, October 5, 1963, 18. Harlan sent this article to Hans Hömberg the next day, October 6, 1963. FBA, Innsbruck, Nachlass Hans Hömberg, 133-002-056.
139. Felix Moeller, *Harlan: In the Shadow of Jew Süss* (2008), 1:07:35.
140. Moeller, *Harlan: In the Shadow of Jew Süss*, 27:45. Other family members acknowledge to varying degrees Veit Harlan's personal animosity toward Jews. See David Bathrick, "Felix Moeller's *Harlan: Im Schatten von Jud Süss* as Family Drama," in *Persistent Legacy: The*

276 NOTES TO PAGES 53–63

Holocaust and German Studies, ed. Erin McGlothlin and Jennifer M. Kapczynski (Camden House, 2016), 212–19.

141. In an early draft of his autobiography, Veit Harlan ventured to ascribe the authority to determine the Antisemite to Goebbels, claiming that he had chosen Harlan to direct *Jud Süss* in part because "Goebbels knew: 'Veit Harlan is not an Antisemite.'" This passage is crossed out, however, and does not appear in his final typed autobiography. Filmmuseum Landeshauptstadt Düsseldorf SLG.VH-49 Folder II, 79.

142. Veit Harlan to Julius Bab, August 23, 1947, AdK Berlin, Julius Bab Archiv, Bab 515.

143. Julius Bab to Ludwig Berger, May 5, 1954, AdK Berlin, Julius Bab Archiv, Bab 68.

144. Bergmeier et al., *Vorbei—Beyond Recall*, 409.

Chapter 2

1. "Abschrift," Lebenslauf Karena Niehoff, Deutsche Kinemathek, Museum für Film und Fernsehen, Archiv, Berlin (DKA) 4.3–201305, J. Becker. Harlan's *Jud Süss* was first screened at the Venice Film Festival on September 5, 1940; it premiered in Berlin on September 24, 1940. Susan Tegel, *Jew Süss: Life, Legend, Fiction, Film* (Continuum, 2011), 181.

2. Karena Niehoff, "Zusammenfassung des Komplexes 'Zwischengefälle im Harlanprozess' und deren Folgen," unpublished manuscript, undated, 3, DKA 4.3–201305, J. Becker.

3. Her mother, Jewish actor and singer Rose Niehoff née Brocziner, born October 21, 1887, in Berlin, baptized Karena in 1933, hoping to protect her under the Nazi regime. Karena grew up believing that her mother's husband, geologist and military captain Dr. Kurt Niehoff, was her father. Her biological father was Ernst Erich Kunheim, a married owner of a chemical factory. Jörg Becker, *Karena Niehoff. Feuilletonistin und Kritikerin* (Edition Text & Kritik, 2006), 12, 15.

4. Rose Niehoff, Lebenslauf, unpublished manuscript, undated, 2, DKA 4.3–201305, J. Becker. Since June 1943, she performed forced labor at a cleaning company.

5. After 1945, Niehoff worked as a freelance reporter with *Der Kurier* in Berlin; she later wrote for several other newspapers and the French literary magazine *Das Journal*, with whose editor, Boris von Borresholm, she published a book mocking Goebbels by reimagining his diaries as a mix of fact and fiction. *Dr. Goebbels nach Aufzeichnungen aus seiner Umgebung*, ed. Borris Borresholm with the cooperation of Karena Niehoff (Verlag des *Journal*, 1949).

6. Karena Niehoff, "Und ein Kongreß," *Der Kurier*, October 1, 1946.

7. Karena Niehoff, "Das Welttheater der Verdammten," *Der Kurier*, October 1, 1946.

8. Karena Niehoff, "Das Langsame Leben," *Der Kurier*, March 22, 1947.

9. "Revisionsentscheidung des Obersten Gerichtshofes für die Britische Zone in Strafsachen," in *Entscheidungen des Oberen Gerichtshofes für die Britische Zone in Zivilsachen*, ed. Mitgliedern des Gerichtshofes und der Staatsanwaltschaft beim Obersten Gerichtshof, vol. 2 (De Gruyter, 1950), 291–312.

10. Norbert Muhlen, "The Return of Goebbels' Filmmakers: The Dilemma Posed by Werner Krauss and Veit Harlan," *Commentary* 11, no. 3 (March 1951): 246. As journalist Ralph Giordano later remarked, "The trial was sensational, largely because Harlan was a widely known figure. It stood out for its truly unique character and marked the beginning of a new era in German judicial history." *Jud Süss. Veit Harlans Film und das deutsche Gewissen* (ZDF, 1984).

11. Veit Harlan, "Wie es War . . . Erlebnisse eines Filmregisseurs unter seinem allerhöchsten Chef, dem 'Schirmherrn des deutschen Films,' Dr. Josef Goebbels" (How it was . . . A film director's experiences under his very highest boss, the 'guardian of German films,' Dr. Josef Goebbels) (emphasis in original), 57. Unpublished manuscript, Munich, ca. 1960. Bayerische Staatsbibliothek, Munich. Harlan repeated this complaint in various forms over the years, such as in a letter to his former colleague Fritz Hippler, the Nazi functionary in charge of Goebbels's film department, in which Harlan wrote "I am being hunted as if I had invented antisemitism." Veit Harlan to Fritz Hippler, March 10, 1952. Filmmuseum Potsdam (FMP) VH DLN N109 Box 28.

12. Testimony of Irene Meyer-Hanno, January 3, 1947, Staatsarchiv Hamburg (SH) 6911, Part I; Testimony of Paul Henckels, April 8, 1950, SH 213–1172297.

13. Veit Harlan to Gerhard Kramer, May 8, 1948, 7, SH 213–1121249–50 Bd. 2.

14. Harlan's Süss is effective because the character evokes both repulsion and fascination; he both pursues forbidden desire as well as embodies it. Linda Schulte-Sasse, *Entertaining the Third Reich: Illusions of Wholeness in Nazi Cinema* (Duke University Press, 1996), 82.

15. Verdict, April 29, 1950, 38, SH 213–1172301.

NOTES TO PAGES 63–67 277

16. On the first day of court, one observer reported that Harlan attempted to demonstrate his superior knowledge of Jewish culture by reciting a long prayer in Hebrew. Later, as a testament to the twisted logic of his defense, "Harlan begins to declaim again, this time with solid Jewish curses from the Talmud that were supposed to appear at the end of the film but that Goebbels cut out. Harlan wanted to mark how unforgiving Judaism and vengeful the Jews were. However, [Harlan claimed] Goebbels deleted these scenes to prevent the Jews from appearing heroic." SH 622-1/ 203–317, Heinrich Christian Meier, 3220, March 9, 1949.

17. "It has now been definitively recognized that the film *Jew Suess* was an anti-Semitic film. Yet, despite extensive efforts, nobody could be identified as responsible." Norbert Wollheim to Alex Easterman, World Jewish Congress, London, April 30, 1950, citing Curt Bley, "Harlan: frei–Brundert: 15 Jahre Zuchthaus," *Die Welt*, May 1, 1950, Central Zionist Archives (CZA) C21757. Effects of the decision resonated quickly: Lawyers for SS officer and gas chamber operator Erich Bauer, who was also on trial for crimes against humanity, tried (and failed) to use Harlan's acquittal as a precedent for exonerating their own client. See the judgment of the Landgericht Berlin in the trial of Erich Bauer, May 8, 1950, Pls 3/50, LA Berlin, B Rep. 058, Nr. 1573, 26. Many thanks to Dagi Knellessen for this reference.

18. Karena Niehoff, "Zusammenfassung des Komplexes 'Zwischengefälle im Harlanprozess' und deren Folgen," unpublished manuscript, undated, DKA 4.3–201305, J. Becker.

19. Karena Niehoff, "Zusammenfassung des Komplexes 'Zwischengefälle im Harlanprozess' und deren Folgen," unpublished manuscript, undated, DKA 4.3–201305, J. Becker.

20. Karena Niehoff to Gunhild Schönwiese, November 19, 1963, Landesarchiv Baden-Württemberg (LBW), Staatsarchiv Stuttgart, J 25 Bü 96. Niehoff wrote in reply to a letter from Schönwiese in which she claimed that her parents had named Niehoff as her godmother in 1940, as evidenced by her baptism certificate of September 29, 1940, bearing Niehoff's name. Niehoff did not recall the event.

21. Astrid Metzger described Niehoff as "beautiful, like all Jewish women are when they are young," and alleged that Niehoff and her husband had been romantically involved. Friedrich Knilli interview with Astrid Metzger, May 7, 1979, LBW, Staatsarchiv Stuttgart, J 25 Bü 96.

22. Ludwig Metzger, Eidestattliche Erklärung, August 7, 1946, Bundesarchiv (BArch) Berlin-Lichterfelde, R 9361-V/145998.

23. For example, after he joined the project, Harlan claimed about Ferdinand Marian: "I took him from a "Stürmer"-like script by Wolfgang Eberhard Möller and Dr. Peter Brauer and rewrote it, thereby making a human out of a vicious clown." Veit Harlan to the Zentralstelle für Berufungsausschüsse, Hamburg, August 17, 1947, 2, SH 6911, Part I.

24. Ludwig Metzger, Eidestattliche Erklärung, August 7, 1946, BArch Berlin-Lichterfelde, R 9361-V/145998.

25. Niehoff had already noted that Harlan's additions included Werner Krauss's roles as various Jews and the rape scene. Denazification Commission in Berlin to the Staatsanwaltschaft bei dem Landgericht, March 11, 1949, BA Berlin-Lichterfelde R9361 V, 154966. Niehoff's testimony that day was reported in "Radauszenen um Harlan Prozess," an undated, untitled newspaper clipping available in SH 131–1 II 721.

26. Bill Niven, *Jud Süss. Das Lange Leben eines Propagandafilms* (Mitteldeutscher Verlag, 2022), 31–32. The Metzger-Möller screenplay, as well as a reworked version of Harlan's screenplay, which he likely gave to Goebbels, are both available at the DKA. See Niven, *Jud Süss*, 31.

27. Capt. Sely to Theatre and Music Section, British Information Control Unit (BICU), "Personnel Vetting," July 18, 1946, BArch Berlin, R 9361-V/147849.

28. Ludwig Metzger, Eidestattliche Erklärung, August 7, 1946, BArch Berlin, R 9361-V/145998. To be sure, Metzger likely downplayed his own antisemitsm; a report from the British Information Control Unit (BICU) note claims that he had been heard making antisemitic statements on set. Memo of August 31, 1946, BArch Berlin, R 9361-V/147849.

29. Harlan, "Wie es War," 429.

30. Harlan, "Wie es War," 430.

31. Veit Harlan to Conny Carstensen, March 18, 1949, FMP, VH DL (N109), Box 26.

32. Thomas Harlan, *Veit* (Rowohlt, 2011), 20. Walter Fritz Tyrolf (1901–1971) joined the Nazi party on May 1, 1937, and became a member of several Nazi organizations. He served as judge at the Landgericht Hamburg as of January 1, 1934; on June 5, 1940, he was appointed as a prosecutor for the NS-Sondergericht in Hamburg. Starting in 1943 he handled cases of robbery, for which he frequently argued for the death penalty. He issued 14 death convictions in total, of which 10 were actually carried out. See Carsten Rinio, "Walter Tyrolf, Richter und Staatsanwalt im

278   NOTES TO PAGES 67–75

Dritten Reich (und danach)," *Mitteilungen des Hamburgischen Richtervereins* 1 (2022): 12, 19. Many thanks to Werner Renz for this source.

33. Gerhard Jacoby, a representative from the World Jewish Congress who attended the trial on April 5, 1950, indicated that explicitly antisemitic testimony from witnesses was allowed in the courtroom without objection, in the absence of Kramer. According to him, writer Gerhard Menzel testified: "I want to tell you something on the subject of 'antisemitism.' Antisemitism exists because as long as Jews have existed in the world, they have been the exact representatives of dictatorship, and today again they are influential in dictatorships.... I know the good characteristics of the Jews (of which there are not few), as well as their bad ones. The bad ones originate from their kind of intellect." Gerhard Jacoby to World Jewish Congress, London, April 7, 1950, CZA 21757.

34. The Hamburg police consulted with Harlan's defense team to gather information about Niehoff's testimony. Letter from the Sekretariat der Verteidigung im Verfahren gegen Veit Harlan to the chief press officer of the Hamburg Kriminalamt, May 8, 1950, FMP, VH DL (N109), Box 27.

35. SH 213–11 72297, Protokoll, 16.

36. Kramer, "Report on the Events of the Harlan Trial, Friday, April 14, 1950," SH, 131-II 720.

37. One member of the audience claimed that Niehoff's "arrogant" interruption elicited "good-natured" laughter and insisted that it was in no way indicative of antisemitism or Nazism in the audience; moreover, it was Niehoff who provoked the disturbance with her offensive description of "cursed Nazi gangs." G. J. to Walter Fritz Tyrolf, April 16, 1950, SH 131-II 720.

38. Protokoll, Karena Niehoff, Generalstaatsanwalt bei dem Hanseatischen Oberlandsgericht, Hamburg, April 20, 1950, SH 131–1 II 720.

39. Protokoll, Karena Niehoff, Generalstaatsanwalt bei dem Hanseatischen Oberlandsgericht, Hamburg, April 20, 1950, SH 131–1 II 720.

40. "Du Judensau, du ...,"*Allgemeine Wochenzeitung der Juden in Deutschland*, April 21, 1950.

41. Protokoll, Karena Niehoff, Generalstaatsanwalt bei dem Hanseatischen Oberlandsgericht, Hamburg, April 20, 1950, SH 131–1 II 720.

42. Protokoll, Karena Niehoff, Generalstaatsanwalt bei dem Hanseatischen Oberlandsgericht, Hamburg, April 20, 1950, SH 131–1 II 720.

43. Protokoll, Karena Niehoff, Generalstaatsanwalt bei dem Hanseatischen Oberlandsgericht, Hamburg, April 20, 1950, SH 131–1 II 720.

44. "Du Judensau, du ...,"*Allgemeine Wochenzeitung der Juden in Deutschland*, April 21, 1950.

45. "Kristallnacht-Stimmung in Hamburg. Harlan-Prozess in Adenauers "Freiheitsluft"/ Radaudemokratie für Antisemiten," *Berliner Zeitung*, April 15, 1950, 1.

46. "Das deutsche Volk ist nicht antisemitisch," *Süddeutsche Zeitung*, April 20, 1950, cited in Werner Bergmann, *Antisemitismus in öffentlichen Konflikten. Kollektives Lernen in der politischen Kultur der Bundesrepublik 1949–1989* (Campus, 1997), 100.

47. Dr. Tyrolf, Landgerichtsrat to the Landgerichtspräsident in Hamburg, April 18, 1950, SH 131-II 720.

48. Norbert Wollheim to the Oberstaatsanwalt beim Landgericht Hamburg, March 30, 1950, SH 213–1172297.

49. Tyrolf also compared Wollheim to the notorious Nazi judge Roland Freisler, claiming he and other Nazi victims wanted courts "in the spirit of Freisler, only on an anti-fascist basis. But we must not give in to this, because if we do, we will never be in peace." "Der Harlan-Revisionsprozess: Der Vorsitzende entgleist," *Allgemeine Wochenzeitung der Juden in Deutschland*, April 7, 1950, 6.

50. Dr. Tyrolf to the Landgerichtspräsident in Hamburg, April 18, 1950, SH 131-II 720.

51. "Harlan wurde wieder freigesprochen," *Neue Zeit*, April 30, 1950, 2.

52. Because Metzger's original screenplay was not available, Tyrolf based his evaluation on the testimony of Harlan, other witnesses, and a synopsis from the Terra film company. Urteil, Landgericht Hamburg, Schwurgericht I, April 29, 1950, 32–34, SH 213–1172301.

53. Testimony of Wolfgang Schleif, March 17, 1950, 11, SH 213–1172297.

54. Harlan, "Wie es War," 433.

55. Harlan, "Wie es War," 434. Ralph Giordano observed, "Harlan's exoneration—his release and acquittal—became, in a way, a form of self-exoneration and self-absolution for them. It created a kind of consensus between Harlan and the majority of the public." *Jud Süss. Veit Harlans Film und das deutsche Gewissen* (ZDF, 1984).

56. *Hamburger Freie Presse*, April 19 and April 20, 1950. Excerpts from Max Brauer's speech also appeared in *Die Welt, Berliner Anzeiger*, and *Neue Zeitung*—Munich edition, on April 20, 1950,

NOTES TO PAGES 75–78 279

and in the *Hamburger Abendblatt* and *Hamburger Echo* on April 19, 1950. In addition to casting Niehoff as a communist and blaming the Communist Party, one newspaper report claimed that Brauer described "Judensau" as having been shouted from a crowd of "quite Eastern-looking people." "Brauers Kampf gegen die 'Stosstruppler,' untitled newspaper, April 20, 1950, SH 131–II 721.

57. Niehoff, who had no connection to the Communist Party, was arrested and imprisoned in the Soviet-occupied zone from February 18 to April 1, 1950, while on assignment for *Die Welt*. Karena Niehoff, statement to the Generalstaatsanwalt of the Hanseatischen Oberlandesgericht, April 20, 1950; "Karena Niehoff entlassen," *Tagesspiegel*, April 28, 1950; Kramer, "Report on the Events of the Harlan Trial, April 14, 1950," SH 131-II 720; Report of the Hamburg Police, May 12, 1950, SH 131–II 721.

58. "Ermittlungen In- und Ausländischer Journalisten," DKA 4.3–201305, J. Becker. Brauer had claimed there was no antisemitism in Germany. See also *Stuttgarter Zeitung*, April 21, 1950.

59. D. I. Gabler to Max Brauer, April 22, 1950, SH 131–1 II 721.

60. Dr. Drexelius to D. I. Gabler, April 28, 1950, SH 131–1 II 721.

61. Karena Niehoff, "Zusammenfassung des Komplexes," 9.

62. The fact that Niehoff had just returned from prison in the Soviet-occupied zone and that she had displayed no evidence of communist leanings did not deter Brauer from making this argument.

63. Erik Blumenfeld to Max Brauer, May 19, 1950, SH 131–1 II 721 and Herta Gotthelf to Max Brauer, July 5, 1950, SH 131–1 II 720.

64. Statement of Manfred Jackson, Landgericht Hamburg, December 24, 1951, SH 131–1 II 721. Jackson and other journalists assumed Brauer received information for the press conference from film producer Hans Domnick, an associate of Harlan. See files in SH 131–1 II 720. Enno Eimers, editor of the *Neue Zeitung*, recalled that Brauer claimed Niehoff yelled "Nazischwein" first. Minutes of a public meeting regarding Niehoff v. Hansestadt Hamburg, January 4, 1952, 3, Landgericht Hamburg Zivilkammer, SH 131–1 II 721.

65. See files in SH 131–1 II 721. The first decision in favor of Max Brauer was issued on May 9, 1952, but Niehoff's appeals dragged on for years.

66. Karena Niehoff to Hamburg Senate, July 15, 1957, SH 131–1 II 721.

67. Lüth held this press conference together with Walter Koppel after Harlan and Söderbaum were ejected from the premiere of *Ehe im Schatten*. Erich Lüth, "Veit Harlan provoziert," *Film-Echo* 2, no. 5 (May 1948): 38.

68. Lüth touted himself as a lone voice pushing others to examine their actions in the Third Reich. At the same time, he provided excuses for those "swept away" by Nazi ideology. *Viel Steine lagen am Weg. Ein Querkopf berichtet* (Marion von Schröder, 1966), 191, 261, 264–65.

69. Werner Bergmann and Rainer Erb, *Anti-Semitism in Germany: The Post-Nazi Epoch from 1945 to 1995* (Routledge, 1997), 12.

70. LBW, Staatsarchiv Freiburg, 5–53737, A2, Bad Staatskanzlei 2380, 000142, 000141. Three students were concussed while others suffered injuries from being beaten, kicked, and slapped. The student group that organized the protest received several antisemitic letters. However, journalist Clara Menck interviewed protesters and concluded that most were motivated by a range of political and social resentments, rather than opposition to antisemitism. "Studenten gegen Harlan," *Der Monat* 42, no. 4 (1952): 573, 580.

71. Veit Harlan to *Recht und Freiheit* magazine, March 8, 1952, FMP, VH DL (N109), Box 18.

72. "Fagin in Berlin Provokes a Riot," *Life*, March 7, 1949, 38–39.

73. Niven, *Jud Süss*, 118–22. See also Arne Riedlinger, "Vom Boykottaufruf zur Verfassungsbeschwerde. Erich Lüth und die Kontroverse um Harlans Nachkriegsfilme (1950–58)," in *Das Lüth-Urteil aus (rechts-) historischer Sicht. Die Konflikte um Veit Harlan und die Grundrechtsjudikatur des Bundesverfassungsgerichts*, ed. Thomas Henne and Arne Riedlinger (Wissenschafts-Verlag, 2005). For a helpful overview of the Lüth-Urteil and its implications for Jews in postwar Germany, see Michael Brenner and Norbert Frei, "Consolidation," in *A History of Jews in Germany Since 1945: Politics, Culture, and Society*, ed. Michael Brenner (Indiana University Press, 2018), 245–48.

74. Frank Stern, *The Whitewashing of the Yellow Badge: Antisemitism and Philosemitism in Postwar Germany* (Pergamon, 1992), 284.

75. United States Holocaust Memorial Museum Archive, Wollheim 1999.A.0031–7–4-3, 7–7–157, 7–7–158.

76. Lüth asked Ida Ehre to extend the invitation to Liebeneiner, who responded that he would "of course" be happy to join the group; in the same letter, Liebeneiner pressured Ehre to advise him

280   NOTES TO PAGES 78–83

on whether he should join a campaign protesting the execution of Jewish couple Ethel and Julius Rosenberg: "Did you follow the trial? . . . Please advise me! For what reason did I let you become educated? Now show that you have a sense of interest!" Wolfgang Liebeneiner to Ida Ehre, January 15, 1953, Staats- und Universitätsbibliothek Hamburg, Archiv, Nachlass Ida Ehre, Ba 86 Wolfgang Liebeneiner.

77. Benjamin Sagalowitz to Erich Lüth, January 20, 1954, CZA C3228.
78. For more details, see Niven, *Jud Süss*, 125–28.
79. Although decriminalized in West Germany in 1969, Paragraph 175 was not fully repealed until 1994.
80. Friederike Brühöfener, "Contested Masculinities: Debates about Homosexuality in the West German Bundeswehr in the 1960s and 1970s," in *Gendering Post-1945 German History: Entanglements*, ed. Karen Hagemann, Donna Harsch, and Friderike Brühöfener (Berghahn, 2019), 300.
81. On this film, see Heide Fehrenbach, *Cinema in Democratizing Germany: Reconstructing National Identity After Hitler* (University of North Carolina Press, 1995), 197–202. On the relationship between representations of homosexuality and Jewishness in Weimar cinema, see Valerie Weinstein, "Homosexual Emancipation, Queer Masculinity, and Jewish Difference in *Anders als die Andern* (1919)," in *Rethinking Jewishness in Weimar Cinema*, ed. Barbara Hales and Valerie Weinstein (Berghahn, 2020).
82. Harlan, "Wie es War," 490.
83. Harlan, "Wie es War," 492.
84. *Basler Nationalzeitung*, no. 28, January 18, 1958. Cited in "Mit einem lachenden und einem weinenden Auge," *Der Kreis. Eine Monatsschrift* 26, no. 2 (1958): 2.
85. Niehoff, "Zusammenfassung des Komplexes 'Zwischenfälle im Harlanprozess' und deren Folgen," DKA, J. Becker 4.3-201305.
86. Author interview with Ariane Niehoff-Hack (Niehoff's daughter), February 6, 2020. Costs were finally waived on April 1, 1958. See SH 131–1 II 721.
87. *Hamburger Abendblatt*, January 24, 1951.
88. Harlan informed Carstensen of his plans to publish a complete report only a few weeks after the trial began on March 3, 1949. Veit Harlan to Conny Carstensen, March 18, 1949. FMP, VH DL (N109), Box 26. See also Filmmuseum Landeshauptstadt Düsseldorf (FLD), SLG.VH-75. Harlan first met Lu Schlage in Hamburg, when she worked as secretary to Walter Abraham. Harlan, "Wie es War," 385. Abraham was chief of staff to the command of the Berlin Municipal police, SS-Brigadeführer, general-major of the police and in charge of the police school at Biesenthal, a subcamp of the Sachsenhausen concentration camp. Geoffrey P. Megargee, ed., *United States Holocaust Memorial Museum Encyclopedia of Camps and Ghettos, 1933–1945*, vol. 1 (Indiana University Press, 2009), 1293.
89. Before 1950 the title of the magazine was *Film Revue: ein Querschnitt durch den Internationalen Film*. Gloth first appears as editor in vol. 4, no. 24–25 (1950).
90. BArch Berlin-Lichterfelde R55 23507–51.
91. See also Harald Gloth, "Die Werft im Hinterzimmer," *Jungen, euer Welt. Das Jahrbuch der Hitler-Jugend*, vol. 2 (Zentralverlag der NSDAP, 1939), 101–4.
92. Gerd Treuhaft, "Neues Wasser auf antideutschen Mühlen? Tatsachen werden nicht ungeschehen gemacht, indem man sie verschweigt," *Das Neue Journal* 9 (1960): 34–35.
93. O. Höhl to *Film und Mode Revue (FMR)* 4, no. 15 (1950): 1171.
94. He was also prepared to publish fictitious letters to the editor that buttressed support for Harlan's publicity campaign. In response to a reader who pointed out the article's erroneous attribution of antisemitism to one of Feuchtwanger's characters, Gloth informs Schlage: "If the reader's opinion turns out to be justified, we will probably have to do something quickly with a fictitious letter so that less well-intentioned readers who notice it don't cast doubt on the objectivity of our reporting." Harald Gloth to Lu Schlage, October 20, 1952. FMP, VH DL/N109, Box 18.
95. H. Vetter to *FMR* 4, no. 11 (1950): 1267.
96. K. Reithmeier to the editors of *FMR* 4, no. 16 (1950): 1267.
97. "Justin: Wird Veit Harlan verbrannt" *FMR* 6, no. 4 (1952): 2.
98. Lu Schlage to Harald Gloth, May 8, 1952, FLD SLG.VH-75.
99. Harald Gloth to Lu Schlage, May 16, 1952, FLD SLG.VH-75. In one letter dated July 15, 1952, Gloth asked Schlage, "Will we still get the original letter from the Jewish woman whose husband was gassed in Auschwitz?," FLD SLG.VH-75.

NOTES TO PAGES 83-93 281

100. Lu Schlage to Harald Gloth, May 20, 1952, FLD SLG.VH-75.
101. Lu Schlage to Harald Gloth, April 1, 1952 and April 4, 1952; Veit Harlan to Peter Brauer, May 19, 1952, FLD SLG.VH-75. Brauer had been chief of Terra, the production company for *Jud Süss*, and had originally been slated to direct the film until Goebbels replaced him with Harlan. Brauer wrote to the magazine demanding the author retract false statements about his involvement in the film. Harlan drafted a reply to Brauer in which he insisted he did not know Herr Schmid, the author of the series, but that he told him everything he had written was true. The words "not sent" appear in handwriting on this draft letter.
102. Harald Gloth to Veit Harlan, May 16, 1952, FLD SLG.VH-75.
103. "Der Fall Veit Harlan. Ein Tatsachenbericht," *FMR* 6, no. 6 (1952): 4.
104. *FMR* 6, no. 5 (1952): cover. This film contains some autobiographical elements: Maetzig's father divorced his mother Marie, a Protestant targeted as a Jew according to the Nazis' Nuremberg laws; she escaped deportation by committing suicide in 1944.
105. "Der Fall Veit Harlan. Ein Tatsachenbericht," *FMR* 6, no. 6 (1952): 6.
106. "Der Fall Veit Harlan. Ein Tatsachenbericht," *FMR* 6, no. 22 (1952): 30.
107. "Der Fall Veit Harlan. Ein Tatsachenbericht," *FMR* 6, no. 5 (1952): 4.
108. While he understood that it would not be prudent for the series to feature photographs of Werner Krauss, Gloth was excited about including a photograph of Söderbaum diapering her baby on the set of *Jud Süss*. As he told Schlage, "I am an insightful, good, and amicable person. However, I am determined to publish the photo of Kristina Söderbaum changing her baby during the filming of *Jud Süss*. Who would want to stand up and object?," Harald Gloth to Lu Schlage, May 6, 1952, FLD SLG.VH-75. The photograph appears in *FMR* 6, no. 16 (1952): 17. A portion of the caption reads: "So she had to take Kristian, her three-month-old son, with her to the studio and feed her child during breaks from filming. An outrageous imposition."
109. "Der Fall Veit Harlan. Ein Tatsachenbericht," *FMR* 6, no. 22 (1952): 24.
110. "Der Fall Veit Harlan. Ein Tatsachenbericht," *FMR* 6, no. 7 (1952): 9.
111. "Der Fall Veit Harlan. Ein Tatsachenbericht," *FMR* 6, no. 17 (1952): 29.
112. "Der Fall Veit Harlan. Ein Tatsachenbericht," *FMR* 6, no. 17 (1952): 29.
113. In a letter to Carl Opitz, who had served as press officer for UFA under the Nazis, Harlan insisted that the rape scene did not make Suess unsympathetic, since those who forbid marriages between Jews and Christians were equally to blame. Veit Harlan to Carl Opitz, May 14, 1948, FMP VH DL (N109), Box 26.
114. "Der Fall Veit Harlan. Ein Tatsachenbericht," *FMR* 6, no. 17 (1952): 28.
115. Niven, *Jud Süss*, 32.
116. "Der Fall Veit Harlan. Ein Tatsachenbericht," *FMR* 6, no. 7 (1952): 9.
117. Klaus Völker, "'Wir spielen ...' Helmut Käutners Leben," in *Käutner*, ed. Wolfgang Jacobsen and Hans Helmut Prinzler (Volker Spiess, 1992), 22.
118. Peter Cornelson, *Helmut Käutner. Seine Filme—sein Leben* (Munich: Heyne, 1980), 19. Cited by Roman Brodmann, January 13, 1980, in the TV series *Laterna Teutonica*.
119. Friedrich Luft, *Die Welt*, June 3, 1975. Cited in Cornelson, *Helmut Käutner*, 22.
120. Robert C. Reimer and Carol J. Reimer, "Helmut Käutner (1908–1980)," *Historical Dictionary of German Cinema* (Rowman and Littlefield, 2019), 164.
121. This clip appears in *Aspekte extra. Jud Süss (Jud Süss Oppenheimer) Veit Harlans Film und das deutsche Gewissen*, ZDF, February 13, 1984, 23:30.
122. *Die Gegenwart*, no. 17, March 1948.
123. *In jenen Tagen* premiered to great fanfare at Hamburg's Warterloo cinema in May 1947; the participation of the public was apparently so great that it required a strong police presence to keep order. See "Kunst in Film ist Schmuggelware. Helmut Käutner im Gespräch mit Edmund Luft," in *Käutner*, ed. Wolfgang Jacobsen and Hans Helmut Prinzler (Volker Spiess, 1992), 140.
124. Peter Pleyer, *Deutscher Nachkriegsfilm 1946–1948* (C. J. Fahle, 1965), 56.
125. Daniela Berghahn, *Hollywood Behind the Wall: The Cinema of East Germany* (Manchester University Press, 2005), 71.
126. One review suggests that the antisemitic incident served to rekindle their marriage, leading to their martyrdom. *Mein Film* 39 (September 24, 1948): 9.
127. The program is listed in Pleyer, *Deutscher Nachkriegsfilm*, 390–92.
128. "Kunst in Film ist Schmuggelware," Jacobsen and Prinzler, 131.
129. Veit Harlan, "My Attitude Towards National Socialism," 3, May 1945, SH 6911, Part I.
130. Helmut Käutner to the Zentral-Ausschuss for Entnazifizierung, Hamburg, November 22, 1947, SH 6911, Part I.

282   NOTES TO PAGES 93–105

131. *Kies* means "money" in Yiddish.
132. According to Käutner, Friedmann was not averse to the idea, but turned down the offer "because he feared that his relatives (in Israel, as far as I remember) might not necessarily know what kind of restaurant he had." Helmut Käutner to Dr. Kreifels, May 6, 1961, FLD, Helmut Käutner, K17.
133. "Erschütterte Zeitkritik. Erstaufführung von Helmut Käutners Film *Schwarzer Kies*," *Süddeutsche Zeitung*, April 17, 1961.
134. Helmut Käutner to Ida Ehre, August 28, 1946, FLD, Helmut Käutner, K3.
135. Archiv der Akademie der Künste (AdK), Berlin, Helmut Käutner Archiv, Käutner 2211; "Loeb – polnischer Jude" appears in handwriting, 40. AdK Berlin, Helmut Käutner Archiv, Käutner 2213.
136. Paul Verhoeven to Helmut Käutner, November 1, 1960, AdK Berlin, Helmut-Käutner-Archiv 1808.
137. Karena Niehoff, *Stimmt es—Stimmt es nicht? Porträts, Kritiken, Essais 1946–1962* (Horst Erdmann Verlag, 1962), 194–95.
138. Niehoff continued to receive anonymous hate mail, including letters calling her a *Judensau*, well into the 1960s. Ariane Niehoff-Hack, "Karena," unpublished manuscript.

Chapter 3

1. *Prager Tagblatt*, March 18, 1924, 4. See also Prague city archives,http://katalog.ahmp.cz/praga publica/permalink?xid=60FF8A5F8ADB4828ADA031B8ED6DDD79&scan=39#scan39.
2. Bedrich (Frederic) Kussi joined his father's firm in 1925. Letter from Frederic Kussi to Julius Kussi, December 5, 1938. Courtesy Susan Lowy Lubow Family Archive. Cited with permission.
3. Warren Rosenblum, "Jews, Justice, and the Power of 'Sensation' in the Weimar Republic," *Leo Baeck Institute Year-Book* 58 (2013): 43–44. Hans died around 1931–1932.
4. Josef Bornstein, "Der Mordfall Helling-Haas," *Das Tagebuch* 7 (1926): 1061–71; 1062.
5. Tenholt positioned Schröder on the roof of a building across from Haas's office so that Schröder could later identify Haas and his chauffeur as his kidnappers. Bornstein, "Der Mordfall Helling-Haas," 1064.
6. Ernst Toller to Betty Frankenstein, August 13, 1926, Ernst Toller, *Briefe 1915–1939*, vol. 1 (Wallstein, 2018), 529–30; Carl von Ossietzky, "Nach 12 Jahren," *Die Weltbühne* 22, August 2, 1926, 159–62.
7. Rosenblum, "Jews, Justice," 36.
8. *Israelitisches Familienblatt*, August 5 and 12, 1926.
9. Letter from Alice Kussi to Julius's first cousin Hermann Kussi, USA, December 6, 1938. Susan Lowy Lubow Family Archive. Cited with permission.
10. Archiv der Akademie der Künste (AdK), Berlin, Erich Engel Archiv 202. Stemmle claims he had access to the material of Haas's lawyer Dr. Braun and learned about the views of the right-wing/reactionary side from a prominent justice official. "R. A. Stemmle: Ein Kriminalfall läßt ihn nicht los," *Funk Uhr* 19, May 13–19, 1962, 3.
11. A copy of this radio play is located at the Friedrich-Ebert-Stiftung Library in Bonn.
12. On postwar East German cinema, national identity, memory, and gender, see Anke Pinkert, *Film and Memory in East Germany* (Indiana University Press, 2008).
13. I use "Germans" and "Germany" when referring to the period before 1949, and thereafter "East Germans/East Germany/German Democratic Republic (GDR)/Deutsche Demokratische Republik (DDR)" and "West Germans/West Germany/Federal Republic of Germany (FRG)/ Bundesrepublik Deutschland (BRD)" where applicable.
14. On coded language linking fascism to antisemitism in East Germany, see Jeffrey Herf, *Divided Memory: The Nazi Past in the Two Germanies* (Harvard University Press, 1997).
15. See Ruth Seydewitz and Max Seydewitz, *Anti-Semitism in West Germany* (Committee for German Unity, 1956); *Antisemitismus in Westdeutschland. Judenfeinde und Judenmörder im Herrschaftsapparat der Bundesrepublik* (Verband der jüdischen Gemeinden in der Deutschen Demokratischen Republik, 1967).
16. Michael Brenner, ed., *A History of Jews in Germany Since 1945: Politics, Culture, and Society* (Indiana University Press, 2018), 2; Mary Fulbrook, "East Germans in a Post-Nazi State: Communities of Experience, Connection, and Identification," in *Becoming East German: Socialist Structures and Sensibilities After Hitler*, ed. Mary Fulbrook and Andrew I. Port (Berghahn, 2013), 36. This broader goal did not preclude more localized expressions of sentiment opposing antisemitism.

NOTES TO PAGES 106–107   283

17. Over the next decades, however, this official line on GDR memorializations did not preclude localized events in which Jewish suffering was given more specific consideration. Bill Niven, "Remembering Nazi Anti-Semitism in the GDR," in *Memorialization in Germany Since 1945*, ed. Bill Niven and Chloe Paver (Palgrave Macmillan, 2010); Alexander Walther, "Commemorating the Shoah in the GDR's (Post-)Perpetrator Society," in *The Afterlife of the Shoah in Central and Eastern European Cultures: Concepts, Problems, and the Aesthetics of Postcatastrophic Narration*, ed. Anna Artwinska and Anja Tippner (Routledge, 2022).

18. For an overview, see Harald Schmid, *Antifaschismus und Judenverfolgung. Die "Reichskristallnacht" als politischer Gedenktag in der DDR* (Vandenhoeck and Ruprecht, 2004). Despite their prominence as leaders and members of the Association of Victims of the Nazi regime (Vereinigung der Verfolgten des Naziregimes, VVN), a branch of which was founded in the Soviet zone in 1947, Jews also retained second-class status in favor of communists and other resistors. Jay Howard Geller, *Jews in Post-Holocaust Germany, 1945–1953* (Cambridge University Press, 2005), 101.

19. These were: Stefan Heymann, *Marxismus und Rassenfrage* (Dietz, 1948) and Siegbert Kahn, *Antisemitismus und Rassenhetze. Eine Übersicht über ihre Entwicklung in Deutschland* (Dietz, 1948).

20. They began in 1946 and 1947 in the Soviet-occupied zone of Germany and continued throughout the GDR. Monika Schmidt, *Übergriffe auf verwaiste jüdische Gräber. Friedhofsschändungen in der SBZ und der DDR* (Metropol, 2016), 199.

21. Robin Ostow, "Being Jewish in the Other Germany: An Interview with Thomas Eckert," *New German Critique* 38 (1986): 74. Of course, this reluctance cannot only be ascribed to fear of antisemitism; many reported feeling little connection to Judaism until they became targets of Nazi persecution. See Anna Koch, "'After Auschwitz You Must Take Your Origins Seriously': Perceptions of Jewishness among Communists of Jewish Origin in the Early German Democratic Republic," in *Jewish Lives Under Communism: New Perspectives*, ed. Katerina Capkova and Kamil Kijek (Rutgers University Press, 2022).

22. Since Jews were classified as a religious community, Jewish Communist Party members were expected to be atheists and not part of that community. However, even if they distanced themselves from it, the party continued to target them as Jews. See Koch, "'After Auschwitz," 117; Geller, *Jews in Post-Holocaust Germany,* 293.

23. Many East German writers published on the subject of German civilian suffering. Bill Niven, *Representations of Flight and Expulsion in East German Prose Works* (Camden House, 2014), 36.

24. Dan Diner, "Zwischenzeit 1945 bis 1949. Über jüdische und andere Konstellationen," *Pfad: Aus Politik und Zeitgeschichte* 65 (2015): 16–20.

25. Wolfgang Staudte's much lauded *Die Mörder sind unter uns* (1946) is the first DEFA film and also one of the few to deal with the Holocaust era. However, it remains unclear whether its only "bona fide" victim, the blond, blue-eyed Susanne Wallner (Hildegard Knef), is supposed to be Jewish. David Bathrick, "Holocaust Film Before the Holocaust: DEFA, Antifascism and the Camps," *Cinémas* 18, no. 1 (2007): 115–16. Other films in the early Eastern zone/East Germany dealing with the topic of Jews and the Holocaust include Kurt Maetzig's *Ehe im Schatten* (1947); Helmut Käutner's *In jenen Tagen* (1947); Staudte's *Rotation* (1949); and Friedrich Wolf's *Rat der Götter* (1950). See also Detlef Kannapin, *Antifaschismus im Film der DDR: DEFA Spielfilme 1945–1955/56* (Cologne: PapyRossa, 1997); Elizabeth Ward, *East German Film and the Holocaust* (Berghahn, 2020).

26. As Anne Rothe notes, East German discourse not only adopted the language of victimhood under fascism, but also, to some extent, embraced the Soviet narrative of being victors in an ideological war against the Nazis. "The Third Reich and the Holocaust in East German Memory," in *Comparative Central European Holocaust Studies*, ed. Steven Tötösy de Zepetnik and Louise O. Vasvári (Purdue University Press, 2009), 81.

27. Lisa Silverman, "Der Film ohne Juden: G. W. Pabst's *Die Freudlose Gasse* (1925)," in *Jewishness in Weimar Cinema*, ed. Barbara Hales and Valerie Weinstein (Berghahn, 2020). On the continuation of this trend between 1933–1945, see Sabine Hake, *Popular Cinema of the Third Reich* (University of Texas Press, 2001), 26.

28. Darcy Buerkle, "Gendered Spectatorship, Jewish Women, and Psychological Advertising in Weimar Germany," *Women's History Review* 15, no. 4 (2006): 63.

29. On the development of inequalities between men and women in the GDR, see Lothar Mertens, ed., *Soziale Ungleichheit in der DDR. Zu einem tabuisierten Strukturmerkmal der SED-Diktatur* (Duncker & Humblot, 2002).

284 NOTES TO PAGES 108–116

30. Rosenblum, "Jews, Justice," 48.
31. Arthur D. Brenner, "Feme Murder: Paramilitary 'Self-Justice' in Weimar Germany," in *Death Squads in Global Perspective*, ed. Bruce B. Campbell and Arthur D. Brenner (Palgrave Macmillan, 2000), 58.
32. Bad Tölz was also the site of an SS officer training school.
33. Centralverein Deutscher Staatsbürger Jüdischen Glaubens, *Deutsches Judentum und Rechtskrisis* (Philo-Verlag, 1927), 47.
34. On Jews and popular culture, see Peter Jelavich, "Popular Entertainment and Mass Media: The Central Arenas of German-Jewish Cultural Engagement," in *The German-Jewish Experience Revisited*, ed. Steven E. Aschheim and Vivan Liska (De Gruyter, 2015).
35. His film . . . *nur ein Komödiant* (1935) apparently passed censors because its setting in the eighteenth century veiled contemporary political references.
36. Ellen Blauert, *Vier Filmerzählungen* (Henschel, 1969), 74. Cited in Christiane Mückenberger, "Zeit der Hoffnungen, 1946 bis 1949," in *Das zweite Leben der Filmstadt Babelsberg. DEFA-Spielfilme 1946–1992*, ed. Ralf Schenk (Berlin: Filmmuseum Potsdam, 1994), 16.
37. Statement of R. A. Stemmle in a letter dated June 29, 1961, from lawyer Dr. Fromm (Berlin). Copy sent to Erich Engel. Archiv der Akademie der Künste (AdK), Berlin, Erich Engel Archiv 202.
38. Stemmle later adapted radio plays, theater productions, and several editions of a novel for West German audiences. A radio play was broadcast by the Süddeutsche Rundfunk in 1953; a drama was first performed by the Münchner Kammerspielen in 1961; a television program was aired by Südwestfunk in 1962. Deutsche Kinemathek, Berlin, Papers of R. A. Stemmle, 4-3-83/39-0.
39. Draft screenplays were submitted for approval to the Soviet Military Authority in 1947. One version is dated September 13, 1947; see AdK Berlin, Erich Engel Archiv 90. A second screenplay is dated November 18, 1947. Kannapin, *Antifaschismus im Film der DDR*, 101. The third screenplay, dated December 3, 1947, is stamped "approved, with improvements" by the Russian censor. Bundesarchiv (BArch) DR/117, Nr. 10520, "Affäre Blum" Der Fall Kölling Haas, RA Stemmle.
40. Kannapin, *Antifaschismus im Film der DDR*, 101n3.
41. Rosenblum, "Jews, Justice," 39–40.
42. "Affaire Blum" Screenplay, Deutsche Film-A.G., Deutsche Kinematek, Berlin, SDK 9362, 220.
43. Wolfgang von Gordon was chief dramaturg at Terra-Film from March 1, 1939, to 1945 and helped oversee the rewriting of the script of *Jud Süss*. Wolfgang von Gordon, witness statement from March 17, 1950, Staatsarchiv Hamburg 213-11 72297.
44. Although officially not favoring any one party, the organization was dominated by the Social Democrats.
45. Simowski wanted "to make sure that the fact that Blum is an entrepreneur is not emphasized too much." Bericht über die Besprechung bei Herrn Mj. Simowski, 2. Jan 1948. DEFA-BR DR 117-0003, Bd.3, aaO., cited in Kannapin, *Antifaschismus im Film der DDR*, 102n1.
46. Warren Rosenblum points out that he was registered as both a real estate agent and an arms dealer in Magdeburg. Crohn was also accused of selling weapons to the *Reichsbanner*, which was probably illegal. "Jews, Justice," 45–47.
47. On tropes and themes of the Nazi era in these films, see Detlef Kannapin, *Dialektik der Bilder, Der Nationalsozialismus im deutschen Film. Ein Ost-West-Vergleich* (Karl Dietz, 2005), 61n112.
48. Mückenberger, "Zeit der Hoffnungen," 12.
49. Hajo Funke, "The Unorthodox Approach to Jewish History in the German Democratic Republic: An Interview with Helmut Eschwege," *New German Critique* 38 (1986): 102.
50. On the Jewishness of Soviet cultural authorities in Germany, see Wolfgang Schivelbusch, *In a Cold Crater: Cultural and Intellectual Life in Berlin, 1945–1948* (University of California Press, 1998), 36. Schivelbusch cites the unpublished memoirs of Grigori Weiss (shortened from Weispaper in 1949 due to antisemitism in the USSR) in the Archiv des Instituts für die Geschichte der Arbeiterbewegung, Berlin.
51. Akexander Dymschitz, "Rückblick und Ausblick (Rede auf der Schlußsitzung des 1. Künstlerkongresses am 30. Oktober 1946 in Dresden)," in *Alexander Dymschitz, Wissenschaftler Soldat Internationalist*, ed. Klaus Ziermann (Henschel, 1977), 77.
52. David Schneer, "Singing between two worlds: Lin Jaldati and Yiddish Music in Cold War Europe and Divided Berlin, 1945–1953," *Journal of Modern Jewish Studies* 20, no. 2 (2021): 248–73.
53. See Herf, *Divided Memory*; Mario Kessler, *Die SED und die Juden. Zwischen Repression und Toleranz: politische Entwicklung bis 1967* (Akademie Verlag, 1995); Stefan Meining, *Kommunistische Judenpolitik. Die DDR, die Juden und Israel* (Lit, 2021).

NOTES TO PAGES 116-125   285

54. Kannapin, *Antifaschismus im Film der DDR*, 102n2.
55. Rosenblum notes that the film's character Blum lacks Haas's record of combat in the First World War and does not mention his reputation (good or bad) as an employer and business leader. "He is a pale abstraction and largely passive figure, around whom events swirl." See Rosenblum, forthcoming.
56. Linking luxury, materialism, and fashion to Jewish women was one way in which films of the Weimar era used Jewish difference as a powerful tool to critique oppressive social norms, economic strife, and urban corruption. Silverman, "Der Film ohne Juden."
57. "Aus dem Tagebuch Rudolf Haas,'" *Vossische Zeitung*, August 10, 1926, 1.
58. Rosenblum, forthcoming.
59. By 1923, Richard Schröder, Gabler's real-life counterpart, was already a committed Nazi, and in 1926, *Das Tagebuch* published a postcard featuring a photograph of him in his *Reichswehrsoldat* uniform on one side and, on the other, a handwritten note by Schröder himself, including the title of his fabricated *Burschenschaft* and swastikas. However, the film makes a concerted effort to distance Gabler from explicit representations of antisemitism.
60. One friend of Schröder who was also a member of the "Alania" Burschenschaft told Tenholt that Schröder created the scar on his own face with a razor to boost his reputation. Bornstein, "Der Mordfall Helling-Haas," 1063.
61. Valerie Weinstein, *Antisemitism in Film Comedy in Nazi Germany* (Indiana University Press, 2019), 160-63.
62. After 1933, Busdorf ran into trouble through Richard Hoffmann, one of the judges in the Haas case (though not depicted in the film), who had previously attempted to obstruct Busdorf's investigation into the murder and was subsequently sanctioned by a Berlin court for his interference. Hoffmann's career was later rehabilitated under the Nazis; he was reinstated as a judge and retaliated by accusing Busdorf of disloyalty to Goebbels. As a result, in 1934, Busdorf lost his pension and went on to write a series of indignant letters to Nazi authorities, professing his loyalty to them and minimizing his role in support of Haas, as well as "boasting of his participation in the notorious Koepenick 'blood week' from June 21-26, 1933, when dozens of leftists in a suburb of Berlin were rounded up and brutally mishandled." When he refused to stop sending letters, the Gestapo arrested him in 1937 and sentenced him to four months in the concentration camp Sachsenhausen. After the war, Busdorf managed to rehabilitate his career and was officially recognized as a Nazi victim—until his brutal activities in Koepenick, as well as his SS membership, were exposed. He was arrested again in 1948 and, following a widely-publicized trial alongside dozens of other defendants, was sentenced to 30 years in prison, where he died in 1957. See Rosenblum, forthcoming.
63. After his initial death sentence was commuted to life imprisonment—and following a failed escape attempt—Richard Schröder remained incarcerated until the Russians released prisoners after May 1945. Under the Nazi regime, he repeatedly applied for amnesty, presenting himself as a Hitler enthusiast and as a victim of left-wing Jewish conspiracy, to no avail. After his release, however, he used falsified papers stamped by a U.S. troop commandant identifying him as a former concentration camp prisoner and current agricultural worker. He went on to write a new biography in which he professed a lifelong dedication to communism and claimed to have fought in a community paramilitary formation. His performance was so convincing that he rose to prominence as the leading officer of the local Communist Party in Wanzleben near Magdeburg, became a member of the anti-fascist unification committee, and served as both area leader and propaganda chief for anti-fascist youth organizations. However, in May 1946, only one year after his release from prison, he was denounced by a local official, arrested, retried, and re-convicted. He was sentenced to two more years in prison. See Rosenblum, forthcoming. Before the Haas-Helling affair, Schröder had already killed his own mother. "Dat is'nen Verbrecher," *Der Spiegel* 1 (1949), 7-8.
64. Dorothy Masters, "'Affair Blum' Powerful Film from Germany," *Daily News*, 1949.
65. Bosley Crowther, "The Screen: German Drama at World," *New York Times*, October 18, 1949, 35.
66. The fact that filming began long before the novel was published suggests that the screenplay and novel were written at the same time. R. A. Stemmle, *Affaire Blum* (Deutscher Filmverlag GmbH, 1948); another edition appeared in 1951, titled *Affäre Blum*. In 1956, Hamburg's Verlag der Sternbücher GmbH printed another edition, also titled *Affäre Blum*.
67. It is not clear whether this is because it was not subject to censors at the Deutscher Filmverlag in 1948, or if, as a novel, it was not seen as having the same effect.
68. Stemmle, *Affaire Blum* (1948), 45.

286   NOTES TO PAGES 125–133

69. Stemmle, *Affaire Blum* (1948), 45–46.
70. Stemmle, *Affaire Blum* (1948), 45–46.
71. Stemmle, *Affaire Blum* (1948), 48.
72. Stemmle, *Affaire Blum* (1948), 160.
73. Stemmle, *Affaire Blum* (1948), 187.
74. Stemmle, *Affaire Blum* (1948), 194.
75. Report from Alice Haas, City Hall, January 18, 1934. National Archives of the Czech Republic, Prague—Police Headquarters in Prague—1941–1950-H-Hanselová, Alice sig. H 755/6.
76. Policejni reditelstvi Praha, 1931–1940, H 823/10 Haas Rudolf, Karton 6265, 10–254_Rudolf. National Archives of the Czech Republic, Prague.
77. Letter from Alice Kussi to Herman Kussi (Julius's first cousin), December 6, 1938. Courtesy Susan Lowy Lubow family archive. Cited with permission.
78. Information on the fates of Alice, her mother, her husband Artur, and her son Alfred can be found at Institut Terezinské iniciativy, database of Holocaust victims, www.holocaust.cz.
79. Erich Engel and R. A. Stemmle, "Affäre Blum," Programm, *Volksbühne Berlin* 44 (1960–1961); Heinz Braun, "Am Justizmord vorbei. Der Fall Kölling-Haas," in *Der Neue Pivatal*, ed. Robert A. Stemmle (Kurt Desch, 1965); afterword by Robert A. Stemmle, 137–40.
80. Engel and Stemmle, "Affäre Blum," Programm, 1. Five years later, Alice's brother Bedrich (Friedrich) Kussi, who was familiar with the radio program, the film, and the book, told Stemmle that Alice had been killed in Theresienstadt. Deutsche Kinemathek, Berlin, Stemmle 4-3-83/39-0. See letters dated October 21, 1970, and October 29, 1970.

Chapter 4

1. "*Stürmers* Echo," *sie—die Wochenzeitung für Frauenrecht und Menschenrecht*, no. 40 (October 3, 1948), 10. Reprinted in *Aufbau: Kulturpolitische Monatsschrift* 4, no. 10 (1948), 918. Founded by Ruth Andreas-Friedrich, Helmuth Kindler, and Heinz Ullstein, all dedicated anti-Nazis, *sie—die Wochenzeitung für Frauenrecht und Menschenrecht* was the first women's weekly newspaper to be granted a license by the U.S. military government. The first issue was published in December 1945; the title was changed to *sie—die Berliner Illustrierte Wochenzeitung* in November 1949. The newspaper began publishing articles criticizing cultural politics in Berlin as early as April 1946. Andreas-Friedrich departed in November 1946, partly due to disagreements over Kindler and Ullstein's lack of interest in women's rights. Shortly thereafter, she went on to found *Lilith. Die Zeitschrift für junge Mädchen und Frauen.* Helmut Kindler, *Zum Abschied ein Fest. Die Autobiographie eines deutschen Verlegers* (Kindler, 1992), 346, 348.
2. The Nazis had murdered a number of Seghers's Jewish family members, including her mother, who was deported and murdered in the Piaski Ghetto in 1942. Her father died of a heart attack following the Aryanization of his and his brother's business. Ulrike Schneider, "Verhältnis zum Judentum," in *Anna Seghers-Handbuch. Leben–Werk–Wirkung*, ed. Carola Hilmes and Ilse Nagelschmidt (Metzler, 2020), 324. On the marginalization of Jews in their capacity to know or communicate knowledge about antisemitism, see David Schraub, "The Epistemic Dimension of Antisemitism," *Journal of Jewish Identities* 15, no. 2 (2022).
3. Anna Seghers, "Passagiere der Luftbrücke," *Aufbau* October (1948). Reprinted in *Anna Seghers. Hier im Volk der kalten Herzen. Briefwechsel 1947*, ed. Christel Berger (Aufbau, 2000) and in Klaus Schulte, "'Was ist denn das überhaupt, ein Jude?' Anna Seghers's Einspruch anlässlich der antisemitischen Hetze gegen die Insassen der Berliner Transitlager für 'displaced persons' in der Presse der Vier-Sektoren-Stadt im Jahre 1948. Rekonstruktion, Lektüre, Kommentar," *Jahrbuch für Kommunikationsgeschichte* 4 (2002): 216–19.
4. Seghers, "Passagier der Luftbrücke," cited in Schulte, "'Was ist denn das überhaupt,'" 216.
5. As Schulte notes in his detailed analysis of this text, Seghers's complicated writing repeats stereotypes without adequate rhetorical distancing. Schulte, "'Was ist denn das überhaupt,'" 200–1. For additional details about her use of indirect narrative techniques in this text and the editorial changes that distorted them, see Ute Brandes, "Seghers's Efforts to Write About Postwar Germany," in *Anna Seghers: The Challenge of History*, ed. Helen Fehervary, Christiane Zehl Romero, and Amy Kepple Strawser (Brill, 2020), 187–89.
6. Schulte, "'Was ist denn das überhaupt,'" 204.
7. Seghers, Letter to the Editors of *Aufbau*, cited in Schulte, "'Was ist denn das überhaupt,'" 221.
8. Seghers, Letter to the Editors of *Aufbau*, cited in Schulte, "'Was ist denn das überhaupt,'" 221–22.

NOTES TO PAGES 133–136   287

9. See, for example, an anonymous letter to the Zentralrat der Juden in Deutschland, dated June 11, 1952. United States Holocaust Memorial Museum, Washington, DC, papers of Norbert Wollheim, 1999.A0031-008-001-0046.

10. Atina Grossmann and Tamar Lewinsky, "Part One: 1949-1949. Way Station," in *A History of Jews in Germany Since 1945: Politics, Culture and Society*, ed. Michael Brenner (Indiana University Press, 2018), 100–7.

11. "Ausländische Schleichhändler und inländische Saboteure," *Neues Österreich*, January 30, 1948, 2.

12. Michael Berkowitz and Suzanne Brown-Fleming, "Perceptions of Jewish Displaced Persons as Criminals in Early Postwar Germany: Lingering Stereotypes and Self-Fulfilling Prophecies," in *"We Are Here": New Approaches to Jewish Displaced Persons in Postwar Germany*, ed. Avinoam J. Patt and Michael Berkowitz (Wayne State University Press, 2010), 169.

13. Hal Lehrman, "Austria: Way-Station of Exodus," *Commentary* (1946): 565–72; 569–70. Jewish newspapers in Germany reported on other newspapers' descriptions of Bergen-Belsen as a "Judenlager" that serves as a "black market paradise." "Etwas vom Schwarzhandel . . . ," *Jüdisches Gemeindeblatt für die Britische Zone*, September 13, 1947, 5; "Belsen—das Schwarzhändlerparadies," *Jüdisches Gemeindeblatt für die Britische Zone*, February 19, 1948, 1.

14. This incident marks an early instance of the emerging trend to eliminate explicit associations of Jews with Bolshevism in West German—and other states'—anti-communist politics after 1945. On that phenomenon, see Paul Hanebrink, *A Spector Haunting Europe: The Myth of Judeo-Bolshevism* (Harvard University Press, 2018), 210. The situation in the East was more complicated.

15. Johannes R. Becher, "Bemerkungen zu unseren Kulturaufgaben," in *Gesammelte Werke*, vol. 16, ed. Johannes R. Becher (Aufbau, 1966), 362–66; 751; Stephen Brockmann, *The Writers' State: Constructing East German Literature, 1945–1959* (Camden House, 2015), 30.

16. On the gradual integration of legal and punitive measures against antisemitism into broader frameworks addressing racism in the GDR, see Christoph Jahr, *Antisemitismus vor Gericht. Debatten über die juristische Ahndung judenfeindlicher Agitation in Deutschland (1879–1960)* (Campus, 2011), 326–36.

17. Brockmann, *The Writers' State*, 31.

18. It also reflected the attitudes of many Jews in the GDR, particularly those who believed that identifying as communists and anti-fascists made it unnecessary to articulate distinct self-understandings as Jews. They assumed that antisemitism required no special focus and would naturally fade as part of the broader struggle against capitalism and oppression of the working class. See Anna Koch, "Exile Dreams: Antifascist Jews, Antisemitism, and the 'Other Germany,'" *Fascism: Journal of Comparative Fascist Studies* 9 (2020): 224; and "'After Auschwitz You Must Take Your Origins Seriously': Perceptions of Jewishness among Communists of Jewish Origin in the Early German Democratic Republic," in *Jewish Lives under Communism: New Perspectives*, ed. Katerina Capková and Kamil Kijek (Rutgers University Press, 2022), 117.

19. On the persistence and use of racist stereotypes in East Germany despite socialists' championing of anti-racism, see Quinn Slobodian, "Socialist Chromatism: Race, Racism, and the Racial Rainbow in East Germany," in *Comrades of Color: East Germany in the Cold War World*, ed. Quinn Slobodian (Berghahn, 2015).

20. Brockmann, *The Writers' State*, 15.

21. Jay Howard Geller, *Jews in Post-Holocaust Germany, 1945–1953* (Cambridge University Press, 2005), 91.

22. Christiane Zehl Romero, "Netty Reiling's Student Years at the University of Heidelberg," in *Anna Seghers*, ed. Helen Fehervary et al., 121.

23. Perhaps the most notorious example is the Hungarian Jewish communist leader Mátás Rákosi. In 1949, Rákosi, along with two other Jewish leaders, orchestrated the arrest of eight communists—including three Jews—on fabricated charges such as espionage. Although the primary target of this show trial, László Rajk, was not Jewish, the inclusion of Jews among the accused allowed Rákosi to eliminate a major political rival while simultaneously challenging the perception that Jews were all-powerful, or that Jewish leaders showed favoritism toward their own. Rákosi was also known for making antisemitic remarks. The day after the arrests, an official Communist Party newspaper published an article titled "Imperialist Cosmopolitanism," which employed a range of antisemitic tropes to depict the accused. The article used coded antisemitic descriptors such as "landless," "unpatriotic," and "uncomfortable," and accused them of fantasizing about emigration rather than engaging in honest construction work. Coded

288 NOTES TO PAGES 136–144

words meant the article could even include *both* "Zionism" and "antisemitism" among other labels of contempt for these "rootless cosmpolitans" steeped in "Trotskyism, fascism, Zionism, antisemitism." Rajk and two of the Jewish defendants were sentenced to death and executed. See Róbert G. Szabó, "Anti-Zionism in the Show Trials in Rákosi Era Hungary (1948–1953), *Journal of Modern Jewish Studies*, July (2024): 1–26, https://doi.org/10.1080/14725886.2024.2381637.

24. Achim Roscher, "Wirkung des Geschriebenen: Gespräche mit Anna Seghers," *Neue deutsche Literatur* 10 (1983): 61.

25. Roscher, "Wirkung des Geschriebenen," 67–68.

26. Roscher, "Wirkung des Geschriebenen," 64. Before 1928, she published the story "Grubetsch" (1927) and the novel *Aufstand der Fischer von St. Barbara* (1928) (*The Revolt of the Fishermen*, 1929) under the name "Seghers," without a first name. Hercules Segers (or Seghers) was the name of a Dutch painter, though it remains unclear whether she chose it with him in mind. Romero, "Netty Reiling," 122.

27. Roscher, "Wirkung des Geschriebenen," 69–70.

28. On the range of political views among Jewish and non-Jewish émigrés, see Andrea Acle-Kreysing, "Shattered Dreams of Anti-Fascist Unity: German-Speaking Exiles in Mexico, Argentina and Boliva, 1937–1945," *Contemporary European History* 25, no. 4 (2016).

29. Philipp Graf, "Twice Exiled: Leo Zuckermann (1908–85) and the Limits of the Communist Promise," *Journal of Contemporary History* 56, no. 3 (2020): 772.

30. *The Seventh Cross*, trans. James A. Galston. (Little, Brown, 1942). It was published in German as *Das siebte Kreuz. Roman aus Hitlerdeutschland* in 1943 by El Libro Libre press in Mexico, although the copyright date indicates 1942. See Stephen Brockmann, "Anna Seghers, Walter Janka, Wolfgang Harich, and the Events of 1956," in *Anna Seghers: The Challenge of History*, ed. Helen Fehervary, Christiane Zehl Romero, and Amy Kepple Strawser (Brill, 2020), 198n6.

31. On Zinnemann's complex relationship to the Holocaust in his postwar films, see Darcy Buerkle, "Landscape, Exile and Fred Zinnemann's *High Noon*," in *Passagen des Exils/Passages of Exile*, ed. Burcu Dogramaci and Elisabeth Otto (Edition Text + Kritik, 2017).

32. In a letter to Kurt Kersten dated January 2, 1945, Seghers explains that her mother had been transported to a concentration camp in Poland and that she hasn't heard from her in years. Letter from Anna Seghers to Kurt Kersten, January 2, 1945. Leo Baeck Institute Archive, Kurt Kersten Collection, AR 4061/MF 476, Series II: Correspondences 1939–1961. At that time, Seghers was still in Mexico.

33. Graf, "Twice Exiled," 8. Merker's efforts did not go far enough for some members of the group, such as Bruno Frei and Leo Katz, who departed in the fall of 1943 to deal primarily with Jewish issues and take non-Jewish Germans to task for joining and supporting the Nazis.

34. Also leading in the effort to secure the restitution of Jewish property was Leo Zuckermann, a Jewish Communist, who became active in the party leadership on Merker's recommendation. Graf, "Twice Exiled," 14.

35. Thomas C. Fox, *In the Shadow of the Holocaust: Jewish-Communist Writers in East Germany* (Camden House, 2022), 60.

36. First published in Anna Seghers, *Der Ausflug der toten Mädchen. und andere Erzählungen* (Aurora Verlag, 1946). By that time, Seghers had already engaged Jewish difference in her dissertation, as well as in the short story *Der Skalp*, about a fight between two boys, one Jewish and the other blond, which she published early in exile in 1933 under the name of Anna Brand. Schneider, "Verhältnis zum Judentum," 325.

37. Fox, *In the Shadow*, 35; Julia Hell, *Post-Fascist Fantasies: Psychoanalysis, History, and the Literature of East Germany* (Duke University Press, 1997), 94–95.

38. Anna Seghers, "Excursion of the Dead Girls," trans. Helen Fehervary and Amy Kepple Strawser, *American Imago* 74, no. 3 (2017): 294.

39. Seghers, "Excursion," 300.

40. Seghers, "Excursion," 305.

41. Although the letter is undated, it begins "I arrived back in Berlin exactly three weeks ago." Bergel, *Anna Seghers*, 38–46.

42. Bergel, *Anna Seghers*, 40.

43. Bergel, *Anna Seghers*, 40–41.

44. Roscher, "Wirkung des Geschriebenen," 65–66.

45. Birgit Maier-Katkin suggests that Seghers's texts at this time anticipated the challenges that postwar silence would pose for the reader. See *Silence and Acts of Memory: A Postwar Discourse on Literature, History, Anna Seghers, and Women in the Third Reich* (Bucknell University Press, 2007), 39–43.

NOTES TO PAGES 144–153   289

46. Anna Seghers, *Transit*, trans. Margot Bettauer Dembo (New York Review of Books, 2013), 20.
47. Seghers, *Transit*, 22.
48. On the significance of such absences in her writing, see Jochen Vogt, "What Became of the Girl: A Minor Archaeology of an Occasional Text by Anna Seghers," *New German Critique* 82 (2001): 153–55.
49. Anna Seghers, "Ein Mensch wird Nazi," in *Anna Seghers, Erzählungen 1933–1947*, ed. Silvia Schlenstedt (Aufbau, 2011), 110.
50. Anna Seghers, "The End," trans. Helen Fehervary and Amy Kepple Strawser, *American Imago* 74, no. 3 (2017): 344–45.
51. Vibeke Rützou Petersen, "Zillich's End: The Formation of a Fascist Character in Anna Segher's 'Das Ende,'" *Seminar* 29, no. 4 (1993): 371.
52. Petersen, "Zillich's End," 371.
53. Petersen, "Zillich's End," 378.
54. Petersen, "Zillich's End," 380.
55. Seghers, "The End," 345.
56. Seghers, "The End," 352.
57. Seghers, "The End," 368.
58. Seghers, "The End," 346.
59. Hell, *Post-Fascist Fantasies*, 101.
60. Cited in Dorothy Rosenberg, "Afterword," in Anna Seghers, *The Seventh Cross* (David R. Godein, 2004), 427.
61. Seghers was unique among writers in East Germany thematizing Nazis hiding under other identities. Brockmann, *The Writers' State*, 190.
62. Ute Brandes, ed., *Anna Seghers, Erzählungen 1950–1957* (Aufbau, 2009), 411.
63. November 30, 1950, AS WAV/I, 378, cited in Brandes, *Anna Seghers*, 409.
64. Anna Seghers to Ina Albrecht, end December 1950, AS WAV/1, cited in Brandes, ed., *Anna Seghers*, 381.
65. Anna Seghers to Wladimir Steshenski, 11.7.1952, AS WAV/1, cited in Brandes, *Anna Seghers*, 407.
66. Anna Seghers to Ina Albrecht, end December 1950, AS WAV/1, Brandes, *Anna Seghers*, 380.
67. Anna Seghers, "Der Mann und sein Name," in *Anna Seghers Erzählungen, (II) Auswahl 1947–1967* (Luchterhand, 1977), 136.
68. Stephen Brockmann, "From Nazism to Socialism in Anna Seghers's 'Der Mann und sein Name,'" *German Studies Review* 37, no. 2 (2014): 306. See also Helmut Peitsch, "Antifaschistisches Verständnis der eigenen jüdischen Herkunft in Texten von DDR-Schriftstellerinnen," in *Kulturerbe deutschsprachiger Juden. Eine Spurensuche in den Ursprungs-, Transit- und Emigrationsländern*, ed. Elke-Vera Kotowski (De Gruyter, 2015).
69. Martin Straub discusses the differences in these two versions in "'Sie bauten ihr furchtbar geschlagenes Land auf, selbst furchtbar geschlagen,' Anna Seghers's Erzählung 'Der Mann und sein Name,'" *Argonautenschiff. Jahrbuch der Anna-Seghers-Gesellschaft* 8 (1999).
70. "Der Mann und sein Name. Protokoll einer Diskussion im Schriftstellerverband," in *Der Schriftsteller. Halbmonatsschrift des Deutschen Schriftstellerverbandes* 4 (Verlag Volk und Wissen, 1953), 4–5. Based on her letters, the contents of her library, and some of her fiction, Seghers continued to engage elements of Jewish religion and culture throughout her life. See Caroline Rupprecht, "Melzer and the Dead Sea Scrolls: Anna Seghers's GDR novel *Die Entscheidung* (1959)," *Leo Baeck Institute Year Book* 69 (2024).
71. Seghers faced pressure to portray ordinary Germans as anti-fascist as early as her time in Mexico, when she wrote for *Freies Deutschland*. In a 1950 report to the SED, Alexander Abusch claimed that, as early as 1944, she held a "completely pessimistic attitude" on the subject. When he insisted she avoid condemning all Germans in one of her articles, she responded: "You can't mention the 75 people we still have in Germany in every article." In response, Abusch published a retaliatory piece in *Freies Deutschland* in which he wrote, "Only abstract, unworldly observers could fantasize that there were only a few dozen anti-Nazis left there." Abusch also criticized Seghers's novel *Die Toten Bleiben Jung*, claiming it reflected her pessimism toward Germans. Alexander Abusch, "Skizze der innerparteilichen politischen Diskussionen in Mexiko 1942/45," November 16, 1950, BArch SAPMO DY 30/70987 Noel H. Field Frankreich Mexiko A to N, 49.
72. Victor Klemperer to Inge von Wangenheim, November 28, 1948, in *Warum soll man nicht auf bessere Zeiten hoffen. Ein Leben in Briefen*, ed. Walter Nowojski (Aufbau, 2017), 342–43.
73. Entry dated October 28, 1948, in *The Diaries of Victor Klemperer, 1945–59: The Lesser Evil*, trans. Martin Chalmers (Weidenfeld & Nicolson, 2003), 270.

290   NOTES TO PAGES 154–161

74. Jeffrey Herf, "East German Communists and the Jewish Question: The Case of Paul Merker," German Historical Institute, occasional paper 11 (1994), 12.
75. Herf, "East German Communists," 12.
76. Paul Merker, "An meinen Bruder in London," *Freies Deutschland* 4, no. 6 (1944–1945): 6.
77. Herf, "East German Communists," 24.
78. Erich Wendt to Victor Klemperer, October 13, 1948. *Warum soll man nicht*, 336–37.
79. Interview with Moishe Postone, "Zionism, Anti-Semitism and the Left," February 5, 2010, https://www.workersliberty.org/files/100205postone.pdf.
80. Archiv der Akademie der Künste, Berlin (AdK) Julius Bab Archiv 1559, "Errinern," (1936–1937), 11.
81. Adolf Bartels, "Die deutsche Literaturgeschichte und die Juden. Ein Beitrag zur Verjudung der Geisteswissenschaften in den letzten Jahrzehnten," *Völkischer Beobachter*, May 5, 1933, supplement.
82. In his chapter, Klemperer also pointed out that, given the distinction between Austrian Jewish nationalism and German nationalism, he did not begrudge Jews in Austria-Hungary their Zionism. Julius Bab expressed a similar point of view in a letter to Max Brod dated July 28, 1928: "The core of our difference, of course, comes from the fact that I have a decidedly German sense of the Fatherland, while in your Austro-Bohemian dilemma you do not and perhaps cannot have such a thing." AdK Julius Bab Archiv 180. On the relationships of Jews to the development of ethnonationalisms in Germany and Austria-Hungary, see Malachi Haim Hacohen, *Jacob & Esau: Jewish European History Between Nation and Empire* (Cambridge University Press, 2019).
83. Shulamit Volkov, "Antisemitism as a Cultural Code: Reflections on the History and Historiography of Antisemitism in Imperial Germany," *Leo Baeck Institute Year Book* 23 (1978): 25–46; 39.
84. See Lisa Silverman, "Revealing Jews: Culture and Visibility in Modern Central Europe," *Shofar: An Interdisciplinary Journal of Jewish Studies* 36, no. 1 (2018).
85. Klemperer, entry dated June 20, 1945, in *Diaries*, 5.
86. Klemperer, entry dated June 17, 1945 in *Diaries*, 2.
87. Klemperer, entry dated September 18, 1945, in *Diaries*, 54–55.
88. Victor Klemperer to Julius Bab, October 4, 1948, AdK Julius Bab Archiv 651.
89. Klemperer mentions that Bab began two poems, one written in 1914 and the other in 1919, with these same lines. Victor Klemperer, *LTI* (Bloomsbury, 2013), 208.
90. Steven Aschheim argues that he did so only to further his career. *Scholem, Arendt, Klemperer: Intimate Chronicles in Turbulent Times* (Indiana University Press, 2001), 77.
91. Roderick H. Watt, "Victor Klemperer's 'Sprache des Vierten Reichs': LTI = LQI?," *German Life and Letters* 51, no. 3 (1998): 360–71; 369–70.
92. Klemperer, entry for Silvester 1958, in *So sitze ich*, 733.
93. Klemperer, entry for November 20, 1945, in *Diaries of Victor Klemperer*, 71.
94. Aschheim describes Klemperer's relationship to Zionism as a "negative foil to his equally obsessive insistence upon positively reconstituting *Deutschtum*—as Nazism increasingly became the prevailing reality." Aschheim, *Scholem, Arendt, Klemperer*, 91–92.
95. Klemperer, entry for June 13, 1934, cited in Aschheim, *Scholem, Arendt, Klemperer*, 92.
96. Walter Kaufman claims that the party took twenty years deciding whether to publish his novel *Voices in the Storm*: "During the years 1951–1956, it was reviewed in four publishing houses and was rejected. The criticism was explicit; the publishers took it very seriously. In this book, a German communist helped a Jew by warning him not to return. The detour he took to warn the Jew put the party in danger and resulted in his torture and death. The publishers believed that such action should not be condoned, and that the character should have been more disciplined. I refused to change the text because I feared that if I pulled out that thread, the whole book would come apart." Although he published it first in Japan, England, Poland, Australia, and Holland, he had to wait until there was a less rigid leadership before it was published in the GDR. Marilyn Rueschmeyer, "A Jewish Writer in East Germany," *European Judaism: A Journal for the New Europe* 17, no. 1 (1983): 35–37.
97. Jeffrey Herf, *Divided Memory: The Nazi Past in the Two Germanies* (Harvard University Press, 1997), 86–88.
98. See Abschrift des Vernehmungsprotokolls von Paul Merker, January 16, 1953, Bundesarchiv (BArch), Stasi-Unterlagen Archiv (BStU), MfS, AU, Nr. 192/56, Bd. 4, Bl. 294–295; and the 1955 Urteil gegen Paul Merker, BArch, BStU, MfS, AU, Nr. 192/56, Bd. 6, bl. 73–87, 13, which states, for example: "In order to create support for himself in emigration, he relied not on

NOTES TO PAGES 161–169   291

political but on racial emigration. In doing so, he particularly sought to connect with emigrated capitalist Jewish circles. He demanded that all Jews who emigrated from Germany be compensated without exception." On Merker's relationships with Jews and his support for restitution and Jewish issues, as well as his arrest and imprisonment, see Herf, *Divided Memory*, 106–161; Wolfgang Kiessling, *Partner im "Narrenparadies." Der Freundeskreis um Noel Field und Paul Merker* (Dietz, 1994). One illustrative example highlights the precarious and often perilous position of Jews in the GDR during this period. In a 1952 report on Paul Merker—drafted under pressure from SED functionary Anton Joos—László Radványi, writing under his code name Johann Schmidt, recounts an incident in Mexico when Merker confessed to reprimanding Anna Seghers for visiting party members he had explicitly forbidden her to see. Schmidt further alleges that Seghers personally submitted evidence of Merker's actions to the SED official overseeing his case. Johann Schmidt, "Kurzer Bericht über Paul Merker," August 19, 1952. BArch SAPMO DY-30 70994, 264. Two years later, during an interrogation concerning Merker, Schmidt introduced antisemitic accusations: he claimed Merker maintained especially close ties to "Jewish industrialists and big retailers," whom he allegedly relied on for financial support. "Vernehmungsprotokoll, Schmidt, Johann," (Berlin, May 4, 1954), BstU MfSZ-Archiv, Untersuchungsvorgang no. 294/52, Paul Merker vol. 3, no. 192/56, 57–58. Cited in Herf, *Divided Memory*, 149. For a recent take on Merker and his role in German memory politics, see Alexander D. Brown, *Paul Merker, the GDR, and the Politics of Memory: 'Purging Cosmopolitanism?'* (Palgrave Macmillan, 2024).

99. Not all Jewish émigrés succumbed to the pressure to denounce Merker. In a letter dated September 16, 1950, to the Central Party Control Commission (ZPKK) of the SED, Fanny Rosner, a German-Jewish émigré to Mexico, recounts being denied membership in *Freies Deutschland* in 1942 by Otto Börner and George Stibi, who argued that admitting a Jewish woman recently divorced from her "Aryan" husband would reflect poorly on the movement in the eyes of its antisemitic members. Notably, her ex-husband was granted membership. It was only upon Paul Merker's arrival in Mexico that Rosner was finally permitted to join the group. BArch SAPMO DY 30/70988, 54–57.

100. Jeffrey Herf, "Dokumentation. Antisemitismus in der SED: Geheime Dokumente zum Fall Paul Merker aus SED- und WS-Archivem," *Vierteljahreshefte für Zeitgeschichte* 4 (1994): 635–67.

101. Wolfgang Kiessling, *Paul Merker in den Fangen der Sicherheitsorgane Stalins und Ulbrichts* (Helle Panke, 1995), 25.

102. Aschheim, *Scholem, Arendt, Klemperer*, 93.

103. A Jewish survivor of Auschwitz, Heinz Brandt, who left East Germany in 1956, commented: "A variation of Göring's famous dictum, 'I'll determine who is a Jew,' made the rounds attributed to Ulbricht: 'I'll determine who was a Nazi." *The Search for a Third Way: My Path Between East and West* (Doubleday, 1970), 164.

Chapter 5

1. Hilde Spiel, *Return to Vienna: A Journal*, trans. Christine Shuttleworth (Ariadne, 2011), 58–59. Originally published in German as *Rückkehr nach Wien* (Nymphenburg, 1968) as Spiel's translation of her unpublished English diary titled "The Streets of Vineta." The meeting with Stefan B. occurs in the entry dated February 10, 1946. In the unpublished text, Spiel refers to him—though not by name—as "one of the Herrenhof crowd," in reference to the group of writers who gathered at the Café Herrenhof. Nachlass Hilde Spiel, Österreichische Nationalbibliothek (ÖNB), Literaturarchiv, Vienna. For a comparison of Spiel's texts, see Kerstin Micheler, "Hilde Spiels 'The Streets of Vineta' (1946) und 'Rückkehr nach Wien' (1968). Ein Vergleich" (MA thesis, University of Vienna, 2018).

2. Spiel, *Return to Vienna*, 36.

3. Ingo Hermann, ed., *Hilde Spiel, die Grande Dame. Gespräch mit Anne Linsel* (Lamuv, 1992), 35.

4. Hermann, *Hilde Spiel*, 33; Hilde Spiel, *The Dark and the Bright, Memoirs, 1911–1989* (Ariadne, 2007), 16, 23.

5. Spiel, *Return to Vienna*, 16.

6. Interview with Felix de Mendelssohn, cited in Sandra Wiesinger-Stock, *Hilde Spiel. Ein Leben ohne Heimat?* (Verlag für Gesellschaftskritik, 1996), 52.

7. For a discussion of Spiel's use of fiction to move beyond the boundaries of her autobiography, see Hillary Hope Herzog, *'Vienna Is Different:' Jewish Writers in Austria from the Fin-de-Siècle to the Present* (Berghahn, 2011), 203–13.

292   NOTES TO PAGES 170–177

8. Spiel, *Return to Vienna*, 53–54.
9. Spiel, *Return to Vienna*, 57.
10. Spiel, *Rückkehr*, 37, 48. Micheler, "Hilde Spiels 'The Streets of Vineta,'" 47.
11. The English is from "Streets of Vineta," ÖNB, ÖLA 15/W7, 12.
12. Hilde Spiel, "Die Wiederkehr," *Wiener Kurier*, February 13, 1946, 4.
13. Hilde Spiel, "Vienna," *The New Statesman and Nation*, April 13, 1946, 262; she also published "The Trek to Palestine," *The New Statesman and Nation* 31 (March 23, 1946).
14. Spiel, *Return to Vienna*, 10, 104.
15. Spiel, *Return to Vienna*, 105, 108.
16. Robert Knight, "'Neutrality,' not Sympathy: Jews in Post-War Austria," in *Austrians and Jews in the Twentieth Century: From Franz Joseph to Waldheim*, ed. Robert Wistrich (St. Martin's Press, 1992), 228.
17. Herzog, *Vienna Is Different*, 181–85. Jewish perspectives on Austrian victimhood were also framed as resistance to both the restitution of Aryanized Jewish property as well as compensation for Jewish victims of Nazi persecution. See, for example, "Offener Antisemitismus in Österreich," *Allgemeine Wochenzeitung der Juden in Deutschland*, February 17, 1950, 4.
18. Alexander Lernet-Holenia, *Der 20. Juli. Erzählung* (Vienna: Erasmus, 1947). Originally published as "Der zwanzigste Juli. Erzählung," *Der Turm* 1, no. 12 (July 1946): 378–87 and "Der zwanzigste Juli. Erzählung (Fortsetzung und Schluß)," *Der Turm* 2, no. 1 (August 1946): 23–29. Lernet-Holenia's story in *Der Turm* appeared a few months after Spiel's visit to Vienna in 1946. However, the two did not meet until after October 1947. Spiel, *The Dark and the Bright*, 214.
19. Robert Dassanowsky suggests that Lernet-Holenia criticized his own behavior before and during the war years in *Der Graf von Saint Germain* (1948) and "Der Graf Luna" (1955). *Phantom Empires: The Novels of Alexander Lernet-Holenia and the Question of Postimperial Austrian Identity* (Ariadne, 1996), 140.
20. Frank Stern et al., eds., *Filmische Gedächtnisse. Geschichte—Archiv—Riss* (Mandelbaum, 2007), 113.
21. Elizabeth Anthony, *The Compromise of Return: Viennese Jews After the Holocaust* (Wayne State University Press, 2021).
22. Lisa Silverman, *Becoming Austrians: Jews and Culture Between the World Wars* (Oxford University Press, 2012), 6.
23. Oliver Rathkolb, *The Paradoxical Republic: Austria 1945–2005* (Berghahn, 2010); Heidemarie Uhl, "From Victim Myth to Co-Responsibility Thesis: Nazi Rule, World War II, and the Holocaust in Austrian Memory," in *The Politics of Memory in Postwar Europe*, ed. Richard Ned Lebow, Wulf Kansteiner, and Claudio Fogu (Duke University Press, 2006).
24. Lappin and Tanzer discuss the large number of Austrian Jewish émigrés who remained nostalgic for Vienna. Eleonore Lappin, "Jüdische Lebenserinnerungen. Rekonstruktionen von jüdischer Kindheit und Jugend im Wien der Zwischenkriegzeit," in *Wien und die jüdische Erfahrung 1900–1938*, ed. Frank Stern and Barbara Eichinger (Böhlau, 2009); Frances Tanzer, *Vanishing Vienna: Modernism, Philosemitism, and Jews in a Postwar City* (University of Pennsylvania Press, 2024), 5–7. Tanzer also suggests that in exile, Jews were also able to claim a self-identification as Austrians that had not previously been possible. See Tanzer, *Vanishing Vienna*, 110.
25. On the use of this motif, see Darcy Buerkle, "Caught in the Act: Norbert Elias, Emotion, and *The Ancient Law*," *Journal of Modern Jewish Studies* 8 (2009). On Ernst Lubitsch's use of this motif, see Ofer Ashkenazi, *Weimar Film and Modern Jewish Identity* (Palgrave Macmillan, 2012), 19–22, 149–50.
26. On the Nazi adoption of this motif as an antisemitic trope in film comedy, see Valerie Weinstein, *Antisemitism in Film Comedy in Nazi Germany* (Indiana University Press, 2019), 186–209; Anjeana K. Hans, "'The World Is Funny, Like a Dream': Franziska Gaal's *Verwechslungskomödien* and Exile's Crisis of Identity," in *Rethinking Jewishness in Weimar Cinema*, ed. Barbara Hales and Valerie Weinstein (Berghahn, 2020), 199.
27. Lernet Holenia, "Der zwanzigste Juli," *Der Turm* 1, no. 12, 386.
28. Klaus Dawidowicz, "Antisemitismus und der Nachkriegsfilm in Österreich," in *Antisemitismus in Österreich nach 1945*, ed. Christina Hainzl and Marc Grimm (Hentrich & Hentrich, 2022), 243.
29. Lernet-Holenia, "Der zwanzigste Juli," *Der Turm* 2, no. 1, 24.
30. Lernet-Holenia, "Der zwanzigste Juli," *Der Turm* 2, no. 1, 25. Alexander Hartwich references this line in his letter to Hilde Spiel; the first edition of Lernet-Holenia's book is dedicated to Hartwich.

NOTES TO PAGES 178–183   293

31. The significance of this pair killing each other was not lost on at least one reviewer, who described the "mysterious" Bukowsky pitted against his Gestapo counterpart in the final scene. *Salzburger Volkszeitung*, May 8, 1948, 5.
32. Spiel later addressed her vexed relationships to Lernet-Holenia and renowned Austrian writer Heimito von Doderer in *The Dark and the Bright*, 332–33. Doderer, who joined the Nazi party in 1933 and wrote the antisemitic essay "Rede über die Juden" around 1935–1936, once referred to Spiel as an "Old Testament goddess of revenge." Stefan Winterstein, " 'Und hätte man gleich den letzten Rassejuden aus der Welt geschafft.' Überblick und bisher Verborgenes zu Heimito von Doderers Antisemitismus," *Sprachkunst* 51, no. 2 (2020): 90. On Doderer's antisemitism, see also Alexandra Kleinlercher, *Zwischen Wahrheit und Dichtung. Antisemitismus und Nationalsozialismus bei Heimito von Doderer* (Böhlau, 2011).
33. Hilde Spiel, "Alexander Lernet-Holenia," in *Welt im Widerschein* (Munich: Beck, 1960), 270; "Im Zwischenreich. Zum Tod des österreichischen Schriftstellers Alexander Lernet-Holenia," in *Die Dämonie der Gemütlichkeit*, ed. Hans A. Neunzig (List, 1991), 246.
34. Spiel also had a vexed relationship with Jewish author Friedrich Torberg, who returned to Vienna in 1951 and founded the anti-communist, CIA-funded journal *FORVM* together with Lernet-Holenia and two others in 1954. On Torberg's postwar activities, see Herzog, *Vienna Is Different*, 195–203; Malachi Hacohen, *Jacob & Esau: Jewish European History Between Nation and Empire* (Cambridge University Press, 2019), 557–67.
35. Letter from Alexander Hartwich to Hilde Spiel, October 21, 1969, Nachlass Hilde Spiel, ÖNB, Literaturarchiv, 15/91, folder 2 (1960–1975); Letter from Hilde Spiel to Alexander Hartwich, October 24, 1969, Nachlass Hilde Spiel, ÖNB, ÖLA, 15/91, folder 2 (1960–1975). Both letters are also cited in Christopher Dietz, ed., *Alexander Lernet-Holenia und Maria Charlotte Sweceny. Briefe 1938–1945* (Böhlau, 2013), 75n262 and 75n263.
36. Dietz, *Briefe*, 20.
37. However, it appeared earlier in serialized form as "Die blaue Stunde" in *Die Dame* in 1939–1940. Dassanowsky, *Phantom Empires*, 114.
38. Dietz, *Briefe*, 21.
39. Gauleitung of the NSADP Oberdonau to the Gauleitung of the NSDAP Vienna, October 17, 1940, cited in Dietz, *Briefe*, 24n58.
40. Dietz, *Briefe*, 21.
41. Dietz, *Briefe*, 59; Robert Dassanowsky, " 'Mon Cousin de Liernut': France as a Code for Idealized Personal and Political Identity in the 'Austrian' Novels of Alexander Lernet-Holenia," *Austrian Studies* 13 (2005): 179.
42. Classified by the Nazis as a *Mischling*, she escaped persecution due to her marriage to a non-Jew. Her status may have inspired the characters of Suzette and Elisabeth. Other Jewish women in Lernet-Holenia's life include Olly (Olga) Leitner and Lily Sporer, both of whom fled Austria after 1938. On these relationships, see Dietz, *Briefe*.
43. Dietz, *Briefe*, 2, 17, 72.
44. Carl Zuckmayer, *Als wär's ein Stück von mir* (Fischer, 1986), 62, cited in Dietz, *Briefe*, 23n54.
45. In New York, he met with ex-girlfriend Lily Sporer, who had already fled there. Dietz, *Briefe*, 33. Dietz cites Lernet-Holenia's essay "Ein Ariernachweis" of 1970.
46. Lernet-Holenia's later texts criticize Austrians for their lack of opposition to Germans and often blame Jews in their own downfall. See Bernd Hamacher, "Alexander Lernet-Holenia und das Judentum," *Schuld-Komplexe. Das Werk Alexander Lernet-Holenias im Nachkriegskontext*, ed. Hélène Barrière, Thomas Eicher, and Manfred Müller (Athena, 2004), 54.
47. *Neues Österreich*, September 14, 1947, 2. See also the negative reviews in the *Salzburger Tagblatt*, August 5, 1947, 7, and *Wiener Kurier*, August 30, 1947, 6. More positive reviews of the film can be found in *Linzer Volksblatt*, July 28, 1947, 2, and *Arbeiterwille*, June 17, 1948, 3.
48. *Wiener Kurier*, September 6, 1947, 5.
49. In *Der Prozeß* (1948), Aglaja Schmid plays Esther, a virtuous non-Jewish heroine, whose "moral purity exculpated the Austrian nation," a frequent motif in postwar Austrian film that also appears in the German film *Affaire Blum* (1948). See Maria Fritsche, *Homemade Men in Postwar Austrian Cinema* (Berghahn, 2013).
50. On Vienna's *Judenpolizei*, see Doron Rabinovici, *Eichmann's Jews: The Jewish Administration of Holocaust Vienna, 1938–1945* (Polity, 2011).
51. This scene references the actual storage of Aryanized artworks. On the Aryanization and storage of Jewish-owned art in monasteries and other locations in Austria, the Allied Forces' transfer of such items to the Austrian government after the war, and the decades it took for these works to

294   NOTES TO PAGES 183–188

be returned to their original owners, see Pia Schölnberger and Sabine Loitfellner, eds., *Bergung von Kulturgut im Nationalsozialismus. Mythen-Hintergründe-Auswirkungen* (Böhlau, 2016).

52. One critic praised its "schöner Humaner Haltung," (beautiful, humane attitude): *Die Weltpresse*, May 5, 1948, 6. The *Salzburger Volkszeitung* lauded it as a return to international-level film-making: May 8, 1948, 5; Robert Faber glowingly reviewed plot, actors, and photography in "Der Atem der Wirklichkeit," *Die Welt am Abend*, May 5, 1948, 7. Lernet-Holenia was apparently dis-satisfied with the film even before it was finished, reportedly claiming that the film producers were hard at work turning his novella into "unsuccessful nonsense." "Lernet-Holenia greift Josefstädter Filmstudio an," *Wiener Kurier*, November 7, 1947, 3.

53. After the war, at least one Viennese newspaper erroneously celebrated Wilder's birth in Vienna and assumed it would be the setting for *Emperor Waltz*. *Die Weltpresse*, June 23, 1947, 3.

54. The quote stems from an unnamed text Niehoff published on November 24, 1957, cited in Hans Helmut Prinzler, "Die Feuilletonistin. Eine Verbeugung vor Karena Niehoff," *Süddeutsche Zeitung*, August 24, 1962.

55. "Polish Town Goes Wild over Wilder," *Los Angeles Times*, May 26, 1996.

56. On Wilder's representations of Berlin, see Ashkenazi, *Anti-Heimat Cinema*, 135–60; Gerd Gemünden, *A Foreign Affair: Billy Wilder's American Films* (Berghahn, 2008), 54–75.

57. Biographies of Wilder's life abound. See, for example, Ed Sikov, *On Sunset Boulevard: The Life and Times of Billy Wilder* (Hyperion, 1998); Bernard F. Dick, *Billy Wilder* (DaCapo, 1996).

58. According to Wilder, he received the offer to enlist in the army and help denazify and recon-struct the German film industry shortly before the war ended. Cameron Crowe, *Conversations with Wilder* (Knopf, 2011), 268.

59. "Outline of Discussion Requested by General McClure Concerning Wilder Proposed Film," February 15, 1946, National Archives and Records Administration (NARA), RG 59, Entry P226 Subject Files.

60. "Due to circumstances beyond my control, I have been rushed into another film, but the idea of the German film is still close to my heart and I shall tackle it sometime later this year." Billy Wilder to John Lefebre, January 7, 1946. NARA RG 59, Entry P226 Subject Files.

61. The film is typically read as a castigation of Austria and a glorification of the United States. See Dick, *Billy Wilder*, 125–26; Jacqueline Vansant, *Austria: Made in Hollywood* (Camden House, 2019), 40.

62. Wilder's depictions distinguish him from the more generic versions of *Heimat* generated by German-Jewish directors discussed in Ashkenazi, *Anti-Heimat Cinema*, 8–9.

63. On the film's "surreal-kitsch" quality, see Nancy Steffen-Fluhr, "Palimpsest. The Double Vision of Exile," in *Billy Wilder Movie-Maker: Critical Essays on the Film*, ed. Karen McNally (McFarland, 2011).

64. Crowe, *Conversations with Wilder*, 184.

65. The name of Baron Holenia may be a dig at Alexander Lernet-Holenia's aristocratic aspirations and longing for Austria-Hungary. Dassanowsky, "Home/Sick," 5.

66. Ernst Lubitsch claimed that Wilder stole the idea of a mismatched couple of mating dogs from him. Dassanowsky, "Home/Sick," 3.

67. Anthony Slide, ed., *"It's the Pictures That Got Small": Charles Brackett on Billy Wilder and Hollywood's Golden Age* (Columbia University Press, 2014), 230.

68. Sikov, *On Sunset Boulevard*, 114–15. Wilder and Kraft received writing credits on the film; Kraft claims that the idea was based on an early Lubitsch film. Hyman Solomon Kraft, *On My Way to the Theater* (Macmillan, 1971), 146. See also Dick, *Billy Wilder*, 123–24; Vansant, *Austria: Made in Hollywood*, 47–61.

69. Earlier titles for the film under consideration include *Pomp & Circumstance* and *Viennese Story*.

70. Paul Elbogen, "Hollywood spart," *Neues Österreich*, May 27, 1948, 3. Elbogen, a Jewish writer born in Vienna in 1894, emigrated to the United States in 1941 following imprisonment in two French internment camps. He later praised the Viennese authenticity of another Hollywood production he advised on: Max Ophüls's 1948 film *Letter from an Unknown Woman*, which also starred Joan Fontaine. "Ein Tag in der Blasiusstraße," *Neues Österreich*, December 28, 1947, 3. Elbogen's scathing critique of Wilder's extravagance was likely shaped by their antag-onistic relationship. Brackett recalls that Wilder played several pranks on Elbogen, including instructing a chambermaid to falsely accuse him of making sexual advances and dispatching a fake policeman to demand his immigration papers. Diary of Charles Brackett, entry dated June 7, 1946, Margaret Herrick Library, Academy of Motion Picture Arts and Sciences (MHL), Charles Brackett papers f.1163. Yet, as with Wilder, the Jasper National Park landscape stirred in Elbogen a profound nostalgia for his native Austria. See Paul Elbogen's letters to Rudolf Kalmar, July 1 and July 17, 1947, Literaturhaus Wien, Nachlass Rudolf Kalmar, Box 11.

NOTES TO PAGES 188–197   295

71. Elbogen, "Hollywood spart," 3.
72. The car cost $1,600. Elbogen, "Hollywood spart," 3.
73. Ashkenazi, *Anti-Heimat Cinema*, 5–6.
74. Silverman, *Becoming Austrians*, 78–79.
75. Martin H. Ross, *Marrano* (Branden, 1976).
76. Bill Niven, *Hitler and Film: The Führer's Hidden Passion* (Yale University Press, 2018), 57.
77. Celia Applegate, *A Nation of Provincials: The German Idea of Heimat* (University of California Press, 1990), 54.
78. Johannes von Moltke, *No Place Like Home: Locations of Heimat in German Cinema* (University of California Press, 2005).
79. Brackett served as president of the Writers Guild from 1938 to 1939 and president of the Academy of Motion Picture Arts and Sciences from 1949 to 1955.
80. Sikov, *On Sunset Boulevard*, 269.
81. Slide, *"It's the Pictures,"* May 19, 1934, 59.
82. Slide, *"It's the Pictures,"* March 2, 1942, 176.
83. Slide, *"It's the Pictures,"* April 3, 1944, 241.
84. Slide, *"It's the Pictures,"* March 16, 1949, 366.
85. Slide, *"It's the Pictures,"* May 24, 1947, 312.
86. Slide, *"It's the Pictures,"* September 26, 1946, 294.
87. Slide, *"It's the Pictures,"* October 4, 1946, 294.
88. Gertraud Steiner, "Die Heimat-Macher. Wer bestimmte den österreichischen Heimat-Film nach 1945?," in *Verdrängte Kultur. Österreich 1918–1938, 1968–1988*, ed. Oliver Rathkolb and Freidrich Stadler (Mitteilung des Instituts für Wissenschaft und Kunst, 1990), 36. On *Emperor Waltz's* basis in operettas, see Katherine Arens, "Syncope, Syncopation: Musical Hommages to Europe," in *Billy Wilder Movie-Maker: Critical Essays on the Film*, ed. Karen McNally (McFarland, 2011).
89. "The Emperor Waltz," script, May 31, 1946, MHL, Paramount Pictures scripts, f.E-151, 44–46.
90. Charles Brackett Papers, Diary, August 19, 1946, MHL, f.1163.
91. The Emperor Waltz," script, July 25, 1947, MHL, Paramount Pictures scripts, f.E-152, 9.
92. The Emperor Waltz," script, May 31, 1946, MHL, Paramount Pictures scripts, f.E-151, 85.
93. Dassanowsky sees "embryonic Nazism" in some of the villagers' uniforms. "Home/Sick," 4.
94. Wilder's antagonism toward Freud may have begun when, as a reporter for *Die Stunde* in Vienna, Freud refused him an interview. Wilder mocks Freud via characters in several other films. See Gemünden, *A Foreign Affair*, 122–23n11.
95. Ruman's role represents an early example of casting Jewish actors as Nazi characters. Wilder recreates the Jew-as-Nazi character in *Stalag 17* (1953), in which Otto Preminger is cast as a Nazi. According to Wilder, "He was a big ham and wanted to do the part." Robert Mundy and Mike Wallington, "Billy Wilder: A *Cinema* Interview," *Cinema*, no. 4 (1969): 19–22; 20.
96. Slide, *"It's the Pictures,"* June 16, 1947, 314; Diary of Charles Brackett, entry dated May 28, 1948, MHL, f.1168.
97. Crowe, *Conversations*, 277. Wilder also claimed, "As for *The Emperor Waltz*, I never want to see it again." "Billy Wilder: A *Cinema* Interview," 21. He also rejected the notion that the film was born of homesickness, telling director Volker Schlöndorff in the 2006 documentary *Billy Wilder Speaks*: "Ah, Bullshit! Homesick for the Alps? With the white socks and the Nazis?"
98. Crowe, *Conversations*, 273, 70. It is not clear to which scene Wilder refers here. At 12:02 in the version available at the U.S. Holocaust Memorial Museum, the camera lingers on a man amid a pile of corpses as the voiceover narration declares: "Often prisoners still alive—or rather not quite dead—were thrown among the corpses" https://collections.ushmm.org/search/catalog/irn1000182.
99. Robert Dassanowsky, *Austrian Cinema: A History* (McFarland, 2008), 139.
100. Robert Knight, "National Construction Work and Hierarchies of Empathy in Postwar Austria," *Journal of Contemporary History* 49, no. 3 (2014): 496–97.
101. Graham Greene, *The Third Man, Loser Takes All* (William Heinemann, 1976), 5.
102. Thomas Albrich, *Exodus durch Österreich. Die jüdischen Flüchtlinge, 1945–48* (Haymon, 1989); Susanne Rolinek, *Jüdische Lebenswelten 1945–1955. Flüchtlinge in der amerikanischen Zone Österreichs* (Studienverlag, 2007).
103. Greene, *The Third Man*, 3.
104. Elizabeth Montagu, *Honourable Rebel: The Memoirs of Elizabeth Montagu* (Montagu Ventures, 2003), 399–410. Michael Shelden brought to light Montagu's recollection of Greene's

296   NOTES TO PAGES 197–202

use of Smollett's stories without citation in *Graham Greene: The Enemy Within* (Random House, 1994), 267–77.

105. Leopold Spira, *Feindbild "Jud." 100 Jahre politischer Antisemitismus in Österreich* (Löcker, 1981), 75.

106. "Verbreitung unrichtiger beängstigender Gerüchte," *Salzkammergutzeitung*, June 9, 1946, 6, and "Wegen Verbreitung falscher Gerüchte," *Salzkammergutzeitung*, August 4, 1946, 2.

107. "U.S. Jews Send Gift of Religious Articles to Soviet Jewry; Rabbis Greet Shipment," *Jewish Telegraphic Agency*, October 6, 1947; "Czechislovak Health Minister Thanks JDC for Gift of 30,000,000 Units of Penicillin," *Jewish Telegraphic Agency*, January 28, 1947; Fred Grubel, *Schreib das auf eine Tafel die mit ihnen bleibt. Jüdisches Leben im 20. Jahrhundert* (Böhlau, 1998), 226.

108. Shelden, *Graham Greene*, 122–30; Bryan Cheyette, ed., *Between "Race" and Culture: Representations of "the Jew" in English and American literature* (Stanford University Press, 1996); Andrea Freud Loewenstein, *Loathsome Jews and Engulfing Women: Metaphors of Projection in the Works of Wyndham Lewis, Charles Williams, and Graham Greene* (New York University Press, 1993).

109. Max Horkheimer and Theodor W. Adorno, *Dialectic of Enlightenment: Philosophical Fragments* (Stanford University Press, 2002), 153.

110. "Returning Vienna Jews Unable to Recover Homes from Nazis; Only Two of 1,200 Get Flats," *Jewish Telegraphic Agency*, June 30, 1947.

111. Susanne Kowarc, Georg Graf, Brigitte Bailer-Galanda, and Eva Blimlinger, '*Ariesierung*' *und Rückstellung von Wohnungen in Wien*. Veröffentlichungen der österreichischen Historikerkommission, vol. 14 (Böhlau, 2004).

112. Shelden, *Graham Greene*, 122–30.

113. Graham Greene to Roderick Young, March 28, 1988, in *Graham Greene: A Life in Letters*, ed. Richard Greene (Little Brown, 2007), 398–99.

114. Greene, *The Third Man*, 8.

Chapter 6

1. Both parents are listed in the baptismal register as Catholic, as are her grandparents Ignaz und Karoline Gettinger (neé Ruschitzka) and Samuel und Regina Kohn (neé Schottik). See Ursula Schneider, "Rudolf Brunngraber: eine Monographie" (PhD diss., University of Vienna, 1990), 33.

2. Carl Haensel (CH) (Rudolf Brunngraber's lawyer) to the Reichsschrifttumskammer (RSK), undated, Literaturhaus Wien (LHW), Nachlass N1.7 Rudolf Brunngraber (NRB), Box 5, 2.1.12.

3. CH to the RSK, September 9, 1940. He includes Louise Brunngraber's birth and baptism certificates as well as her parents' marriage certificate and her mother Bertha Kohn's baptism certificate. LHW, NRB, Box 5, 2.2.7.

4. Schneider, "Rudolf Brunngraber," 36n20.

5. E-mail from Erika Brunngraber to author, August 28, 2020.

6. Hella Guth to Dr. G. Koller, July 10, 1988, Kunstsammlung und Archiv, Universität für angewandte Kunst Wien. RB was a student at the Academy between 1926–1930, where he studied with painter Wolfgang Müller-Hofmann (among others). Müller-Hofmann was forced into retirement in 1939 due to his marriage to Hermine Zuckerkandl, daughter of Otto Zuckerkandl and his wife Amalie, both clients of Klimt.

7. In a letter from Helene Klimt to Friedrich Atzelsberger, Sektionsrat, dated February 27, 1928, she suggests that RB contact Serena Lederer, who enjoyed showing Klimt's works to others. In a letter dated April 18, 1928, Helene Klimt advises RB to visit the exhibition of Klimt paintings in the Neue Galerie. LHW, NRB, Box 5, 2.1.5.

8. RB's most popular novel has been characterized as representative of *Neue Sachlichkeit* (new objectivity) for its style featuring innovative references to the statistical methods and socialist-humanist ideals of polymath Otto Neurath, with whom he worked at the Gesellschafts- und Wirtschaftsmuseum (Social and Economic Museum). See Jon Hughes, "Facts and Fiction: Rudolf Brunngraber, Otto Neurath, and Viennese Neue Sachlichkeit," in *Interwar Vienna: Culture between Tradition and Modernity*, ed. Deborah Holmes and Lisa Silverman (Camden House, 2009).

9. President of the RSK to RB, September 18, 1939, LHW, NRB, Box 6, 2.2.1–2.4; and President of the RSK to RB, August 30, 1940, LHW, NRB, Box 5, 1.11–2.1.40.

NOTES TO PAGES 202–205   297

10. Reichsrundfunk Berlin to RB, September 13, 1939, LHW, NRB, Box 5.1.11–2.1.40. *Opiumkrieg*, published by Rowohlt in 1939, was a bestseller and greatly favored by the Ministry of Propaganda.
11. CH to RSK, September 9, 1940, LHW, NRB Box 5, 1.11–2.1.40.
12. President of the RSK to RB, August 30, 1940, LHW, NRB, Box 6, 2.2.1–2.4.
13. Carl Haensel was a successful novelist and as well as a lawyer. After the war, he defended SS operatives at three of the twelve trials of war criminals held before the Nuremberg Military Tribunals from 1947–1948. Wolfgang Liebeneiner was also one of his clients after 1945. See *Das Gericht vertagt sich. Aus dem Tagebuch eines Verteidigers bei den Nürnberger Prozessen* (Claassen, 1950).
14. These rules were amended for all branches. See Jan-Pieter Barbian, *The Politics of Literature in Nazi Germany: Books in the Media Dictatorship* (Bloomsbury, 2013), 155–56.
15. These 24 authors were classified as "three-quarter, half, and quarter Jews" or as married to "full or half Jews." Barbian, *The Politics of Literature*, 155–56.
16. Affidavit, September 5, 1940, LHW, NRB, Box 6, 2.2.1–2.4. A handwritten narrative from 1940 can be found in LHW, NRB, Box 5, 1.11.5.
17. Affidavit, September 5, 1940, LHW, NRB, Box 6, 2.2.1–2.4.
18. CH to RSK, September 9, 1940, LHW, NRB, Box 5, 1.11–2.1.40.
19. RB to CH, September 11, 1940, LHW, NRB, Box 6, 2.2.1–2.4.
20. CH to RB, May 8, 1941, LHW, NRB, Box 5, 1.11–2.1.40. As RB wrote to CH about his conflicted feelings in the spring of 1941: "And you don't easily part with a wife and a ten-year-old child after having lived together for twenty years, especially not when the practical difficulties, such as the fact that wife and child would not be able to get another apartment, may still outweigh the emotional ones." Undated response from RB to CH letter of May 29, 1941, LHW, NRB, Box 6, 2.2.1–2.4.
21. RB to CH, May 16, 1941, LHW, NRB, Box 6, 2.2.1–2.4.
22. Biographical sketch, May, 16, 1941, LHW, NRB, Box 6, 2.2.1–2.4.
23. In truth, Berta had suffered a stroke so severe that it left her unable to speak and confined at home. E-mail from Erika Brunngraber to author, August 28, 2020.
24. RB's novel *Der Weg durch das Labyrinth* (Zsolnay, 1949) also reflects his complicated feelings about Jews, as well as his brief but intense relationship with sociologist Marie Jahoda, with whom he worked at Neurath's Social and Economic Museum in 1932–1933. (They met in October 1932, shortly after she completed her well-known study "Marienthal. The Sociography of an Unemployed Community," though it was not published until June 1933.) Jahoda was 25 years old and separated from husband Paul Lazarsfeld at the time; she had formally renounced Judaism at age 16. The character Lilli Goslar shares many qualities with Jahoda, including a Jewish background, a doctorate in sociology, and deep engagement with Socialist ideology. RB mentions "Dr. Jahoda" by name and details their relationship in several diary entries in 1933. (In the first, he mentions going with her in October 1932 to visit Dr. Schwarzwald [likely Eugenie Schwarzwald, the well-known educator], who offered Jahoda an opportunity to serve as tutor for G.W. Pabst's children on the French Riviera. It is unclear if she accepted.) LHW, NRB, Box 5, entry dated March 21, 1933. Jahoda does not mention RB in her memoirs, writing only: "From the age of 25 to 50, I was a single, self-sufficient woman. I gradually took pride in my independence, although of course I was emotionally dependent on friends—women and men. There were several of both. I owe the most impressive experiences to men, some wonderful, some difficult, some both at the same time and some, foolish as I was, neither nor and best forgotten." *"Ich habe die Welt nicht verändert." Lebenserinnerungen einer Pionieren der Sozialforschung*, ed. Steffani Engler and Brigitte Hasenjürgen (Campus, 1997), 49.
25. For a thorough review of the details and fates of such intermarriages, see Evan Burr Bukey, *Jews and Intermarriage in Nazi Austria* (Cambridge University Press, 2011).
26. Ernestine Kohn was born on August 8, 1861, and married Janosch von Skoda from Pressburg on January 22, 1912. E-mail from Erika Brunngraber to author, August 28, 2020. Soon after the *Anschluss*, the only hospital in Vienna admitting Jewish patients was the *Rothschild-Spital*, frequently raided by the SS, who rounded up Jews and their guests for deportation. See Dieter J. Hecht, Eleonore Lappin-Eppel, and Michaela Raggam-Blesch, *Topographie der Shoah. Gedächtnisorte des zerstörten jüdischen Wiens* (Mandelbaum, 2015), 265–66.
27. RB to CH, May 16, 1941, LHW, NRB, Box 6, 2.2.1–2.4. On RB's stay in Weitra and further details on Szabo, see Christoph Fuchs, "Rudolf Brunngraber (1901–1960)," *Literatur und Kritik* 317–318 (1997): 103–9.

298   NOTES TO PAGES 205-212

28. "Abgeschickt" (sent) appears in RB's handwriting in the margin of this shorter letter. RB to CH, June 20, 1941, LHW, NRB, Box 6, 2.2.1-2.4. On July 31, 1941, CH informed the Reichsminister that RB would have joined the NSDAP if not for his *Versippung* (marriage to a Jew). LHW, NRB, Box 6, 2.1.12.
29. In September 1941, Brunngraber's kinship was apparently no longer a problem, but permission could not be granted for other unnamed reasons. CH to RB, October 21, 1941, LHW, NRB, Box 5, 1.11-2.1.40.
30. RB to CH, "Schilderung der gegen mich gestatteten Anzeige und meine Gegenerklärung," LHW, NRB, Box 6, 2.2.1-2.4.
31. President of the RSK to RB, November 18, 1941, LHW, NRB, Box 6, 2.2.1-2.4.
32. Otherwise, Erika would have been forced to attend the *Volksschule*, given Louise's classification as a *Mischling*. E-mail from Erika Brunngraber to author, August 28, 2020.
33. Louise Brunngraber to RB, October 18, 1945, LHW, NRB, Box 5, 1.11-2.1.40.
34. On the resonance of Christian sites with Austrian audiences in the postwar period, see Oliver Rathkolb, *The Paradoxical Republic: Austria, 1945-2005* (Berghahn, 2010), 201-2. On the relationship between Christianity and antisemitism, see Magda Teter, *Christian Supremacy: Reckoning with the Roots of Antisemitism and Racism* (Princeton University Press, 2023).
35. Maria Fritsche, *Homemade Men in Postwar Austrian Cinema* (Berghahn, 2013), 21.
36. A number of additional works based on this case of blood libel have emerged since then. These include two failed film attempts: one by the Daro-Film company in Vienna in 1936 and one for a Nazi propaganda film in Hungary in 1941. They also include a novel by Hungarian writer Gyula Krúdy published in 1931 that has been adapted into several films and dramas over the years. Heinz Herald and Géza Herczeg, refugees from Germany and Hungary, respectively, wrote the drama *Der Prozess ohne Ende. Der Fall von Tisza Eszlar* in the late 1930s (Herald had staged the premiere of Zweig's play in Berlin in 1920); it was first published in 1947 in English translation by Noel Langley as *The Burning Bush: A Play in Three Acts*. The play premiered in London in 1948 and in New York in 1949, directed by Erwin Piscator. Together with Guy Endore, Herald also adapted the play for the American film *The Vicious Circle* (1948), directed by William Lee Wilder (Billy Wilder's brother) and starring Fritz Kortner; an edited, one-hour television version of this film aired as *The Woman in Brown* in 1950. The film transforms the antisemitic blood libel into a more mundane murder for which Jewish villagers are falsely accused. The television version removes all references to Jews entirely. Helmut G. Asper, "Der Holocaust im fernen Spiegel. Der Prozess von Tisza-Eszlar (1882/1883) in den Filmen *Der Prozess* und *The Vicious Circle* (1947/48)," *Monatshefte* 106, no. 2 (2014): 238-39. On the other hand, the drama "The Burning Bush" played up its anti-antisemitic message when staged in New York in 1949. See Minou Arjomand, *Staged: Show Trials, Political Theater, and the Aesthetics of Judgment* (Columbia University Press, 2018), 15.
37. See Magda Teter, *Blood Libel: On the Trail of an Antisemitic Myth* (Harvard University Press, 2020).
38. Andrew Handler, *Blood Libel at Tiszaeszlar* (East European Monographs, 1980), 124, 130.
39. Peter Hanak, "Acquittal—but No Happy Ending," *New Hungarian Quarterly* 10 (1969): 120.
40. Arnold Zweig, "Die Sendung Semaels" (Kurt Wolff Verlag, 1920), 12.
41. Sebastian Wogenstein, "Jewish Tragedy and Caliban: Arnold Zweig, Zionism, and Antisemitism," *The Germanic Review* 83, no. 4 (2008): 374.
42. Zweig, "Die Sendung Semaels," 15-16.
43. On Moritz as a Jewish tragic figure of redemption, see Wogenstein, "Jewish Tragedy and Caliban," 370-75.
44. "Aus dem Wiener Kunstleben," *Neues Montagblatt*, October 27, 1919, 6.
45. Felix Weltsch, "'Die Sendung Semaels (Ritualmord in Ungarn)' Zur Aufführung im Neuen deutschen Theater," *Selbstwehr* 14, no. 24, June 11, 1920, 2.
46. Pabst's parents lived in Vienna; his mother was visiting Raudnitz, Bohemia, at the time of his birth on August 27, 1885. See Josef Schuchnig, "G.W. Pabst und die Darstellung der neuen Sachlichkeit im Film, aufgezeigt anhand einiger beispielhafter Filme von Pabst" (PhD diss., University of Vienna, 1976), 9.
47. Rudolph S. Joseph, "G.W. Pabst. The Man and the Artist. In Memory of a Great Friend," unpublished manuscript, Deutsche Nationalbibliothek, IVL 92 Rudolph S. Joseph EB 96/111 A.01.0005, 14.
48. "Erinnerungen des Regieassistenten Mark Sorkin," *Die freudlose Gasse*, DVD (Filmmuseum Munich, 2009).

NOTES TO PAGES 212–214   299

49. Joseph, "G.W. Pabst," 16.
50. *Paracelsus* honors a figure the Nazis revered and revels in fantastical portrayals of "mysterious laboratories and frenzied masses." Eric Rentschler, *The Ministry of Illusion: Nazi Cinema and Its Afterlife* (Harvard University Press, 1996), 174; Goebbels had high praise for Pabst's 1941 film *Komödianten*, with its plot about eighteenth-century actors seeking to purify German theater. Pabst's third film under Goebbels, *Der Fall Molander* (The Molander Affair, 1944–45) remained unfinished.
51. Pabst to Seymour Nebenzal, September 23, 1946, Deutsche Kinemathek, Museum für Film und Fernsehen, Archiv (DKA), Nachlass G.W. Pabst Sig. 200517 (NGWP), PA–24967. For Gertrude Pabst's account, see Lee Atwell, *G.W. Pabst* (Twayne, 1977), 122.
52. Nevertheless, in 1942, GWP and Trude Pabst enrolled their son Peter in the prestigious Schule Schloss Salem in Baden-Württemberg, which the Nazis took over after arresting and ousting Jewish founder Kurt Hahn and dismissing other Jewish teachers in 1933. By 1941, the school operated under the supervision of the Inspektion Deutscher Heimschulen (German Home School Inspectorate) and was managed by the SS. See correspondence between Trude Pabst and GWP, March–July 1942, DKA, NGWP, 4.3-05/17-2, Pabst, Gertrude (3/34). On the school's history, see https://www.schule-schloss-salem.de/en/about-us/history/.
53. Letter from GWP to Trude Pabst, September 5, 1939. DKA, NGWP, 4.3-05/17-2, Pabst, Gertrude (10/34). Journalist Pem (pseud. Paul Marcus) recalls that even before Hitler arrived in Vienna, Forst had threatened to have him expelled from Austria because he did not like what Pem had written about him. "Löwen-Mutter Willy Forst," *Jüdisches Gemeindeblatt. Allgemeine Zeitung der Juden in Deutschland*, November 26, 1948, 5.
54. Atwell, *G.W. Pabst*, 123.
55. Lotte H. Eisner, *Ich hatte einst ein schönes Vaterland. Memoiren* (Deutscher Taschenbuch Verlag, 1984), 95.
56. Rathkolb, *Paradoxical Republic*, 192. In the 1950s, Pabst made films critical of Hitler as a way to soften criticism of his successes during the Nazi regime, including *Der letzte Akt* (1955) and *Es geschah am 20. Juli* (1955).
57. After the war, Pabst was determined to direct a film adaptation of *Nathan der Weise* though he feared it was not commercial enough for German distributors. Undeterred, he partnered with a production company in Israel and made plans to shoot the film there, stating that Ernst Deutsch had agreed to the lead role. GWP to producers Ilse Elkins and Siegmund Breslauer, undated. An undated treatment titled "*Nathan der Weise*: Lessings dramatisches Gedicht als G.W. Pabst-Film" is credited to GWP and Rudolph Joseph; on July 31, 1961, Joseph sent GWP an English translation. DKA, NGWP, PA-24703. The appearance of articles in Israeli newspapers accusing GWP of Nazi collaboration, despite his forceful denials, likely hindered the project. GWP to Christian Broda, November 22, 1958. DKA, NGWP, PA-24703.
58. Already in 1936, two years before the *Anschluss*, the Austrian government ceased to employ Jews so that Austrian films could be shown in Germany. Almost all 30 Austrian distributors and half of the 189 Viennese cinema operators were Jews who were stripped of their assets after March 12, 1938. See Fritsche, *Homemade Men*, 33–34.
59. G. W. Pabst, "Der österreichische Film," *Die Zeit*, May 1, 1948, 13–14.
60. See "Rede vor den Filmschaffenden am 28.2.1942 in Berlin," reprinted in Gerd Albrecht, *Nationalsozialistische Filmpolitik. Eine soziologische Untersuchung über die Spielfilme des Dritten Reichs* (F. Enke, 1969), 493. Veit Harlan starred in the leading role in the antisemitic 1935 Nazi propaganda film *Nur nicht weich werden, Susanne!* (Don't lose heart, Susanne!) in which he saves both a naïve young woman and German cinema from private Jewish financiers.
61. Schneider, "Rudolf Brunngraber," 407. Klaus Kastberger, Afterword to *Prozess auf Tod und Leben* by Rudolf Brunngraber (Milena, 2011).
62. Alfred Werner, "On the Horizon: Austria's Anti-Bigotry Film," *Commentary*, December 1, 1948. Werner writes that Roboz agreed to receive payment and a screenwriting credit for his work, but ultimately distanced himself from the final film due to its "misinterpretations of historical facts." See also "Der Prozeß um den 'Prozeß,'" *Arbeiter Zeitung*, September 2, 1948, 4.
63. As Kastberger notes, in RB's novel *Prozess auf Tod und Leben* "the exculpation of Austria is . . . carried out with meticulous care." "Afterword," 198. RB also published the 55-page essay *Wie es kam. Psychologie des Dritten Reichs* (Neues Österreich Zeitungs- und Verlagsgesellschaft, 1946), characterizing Austria as a defenseless country taken over by Germany.

300   NOTES TO PAGES 215–218

64. "Tiszaeszlár és Jud Süss," *Képes Figyelö*, January 4–5, 1948. No author is named.
65. According to the letter, an appointment for the hearing was set for March 30, 1948; it is unclear whether it took place. Alexander Sacher-Masoch to Oskar Fontana, March 3, 1948, Austrian National Library (ÖNB), Handschriftensammlung, H.I.N. 212.177.
66. Kastberger, "Afterword," x. A letter from the Paul Zsolnay Verlag to RB, dated October 15, 1947, suggests that RB visited the publisher on October 9, 1947, and insisted that he had not used Roboz's work for his own novel. ÖNB, Literaturarchiv, Verlagsarchiv Zsolnay, 286/B82. As Kastberger notes, the documents make it clear that the screenplay was not based on RB's novel, as is commonly assumed.
67. "Warum Prozess," *Welt am Montag*, March 15, 1948, 5.
68. "Zivilprozeß um den 'Prozeß'," *Neues Österreich*, September 1, 1948, 3. Hübler-Kahla had been arrested by the Nazis in Berlin in 1937 for carrying forged documents concealing his partial Jewish ancestry. He was sentenced to eight months in prison and prohibited from working in the film industry until the war's conclusion. Fritsche, *Homemade Men*, 66. At the trial, Roboz and writer Gisi Gruber denied authorship of the article, though Roboz suggested it was based on his own comments and illustrated with his photographs. "Prozess um den 'Prozess'," *Neues Österreich*, May 12, 1948, 3.
69. In 1941, UFA obtained consent from the Hungarian government to produce a film about the trial for the purposes of supporting the Nazis' antisemitic campaign against the Jews. "Nazis to Make Blood Libel Film in Hungary," *Jewish Telegraphic Agency*, February 11, 1941. The film was never realized.
70. "Wenn es einer wagt . . . ," *Österreichisches Tagebuch*, July 5, 1947, 9. On Horn, see Burr Bukey, *Jews and Intermarriage in Nazi Austria*, 118–82.
71. RB, "Der Prozess—Film und die Oeffentlichkeit," typescript, LHW, NRB, Box 4, 1.8.2, 8.
72. Rudolf Kalmar, "Tisza-Eszlar im Film," *Aufbau* 14, no. 13, March 26, 1948, 11–12. Kalmar accurately predicted that the film would become an international success. Rudolf Kalmar to Manfred Georg, March 4, 1948, LHW, Nachlass Rudolf Kalmar, Box 21. Nevertheless, enthusiasm for the film's approach to opposing antisemitism abated; in New York, *Aufbau* ran a much more critical review. R. D., "The Trial," *Aufbau* 18, no. 12, March 21, 1952, 20.
73. On the Hungarian response, see Michael L. Miller, "Filming Ritual Murder after the Shoah: Exculpation, Deflection or Contrition?," *East European Jewish Affairs* March (2025): 1–11. https://doi.org/10.1080/13501674.2025.2480732.
74. "Keine Filmzensur," *Wiener Zeitung*, February 27, 1948, 2.
75. Georg Zivier, *Ernst Deutsch und das deutsche Theater. Fünf Jahrzehnte deutscher Theatergeschichte. Der Lebensweg eines großen Schauspielers* (Haude & Spener, 1964), 76. Deutsch had played the role of Moritz Scharf in a production of Zweig's "Die Sendung Semaels" in 1920 in Berlin, directed by Heinz Herald.
76. *Der Neue Weg* 9 (1948), cited in Evelyn Adunka, *Die vierte Gemeinde. Die Geschichte der Wiener Juden von 1945 bis heute* (Philo, 2000), 90.
77. Directly thereafter, Carol Reed sought out Ernst Deutsch for a role in *The Third Man*. Letter from Ernst Deutsche to Ruth Marton (undated), Leo Baeck Institute Archives, New York, Muehsam Family Collection, AR 25021/MF 736.
78. Werner, "On the Horizon." Reviews in Swiss newspapers also complained about the film's representation of Jews as caricatures, spurring a number of subsequent reviews defending both the film and Pabst's reputation. See Otto Basil, "Der Prozeß," *Neues Österreich*, March 21, 1948, 5. Brunngraber continued to express his disappointment with the negative reception of the prize-winning film in a letter to publisher Paul von Zsolnay dated December 28, 1954. ÖNB, Literaturarchiv, Teilnachlass Zsolnay Verlag, 286105, Gruppe 2.1, Signatur 286/B82, Konvolut Rudolf Brunngraber 20.9.1946-31.3.1965.
79. Lotte H. Eisner, *L'Ecran démoniaque: Influence de Max Reinhardt et de l'expressionisme* (Bonno, 1952), 144.
80. "Der Prozess," *Die Weltwoche*, March 12, 1948, 15.
81. Michael Kitzberger, "Das Volk, die Fremden, der Held und die Bilder davon. Zu G.W. Pabsts *Der Prozess*," in *Ohne Untertitel. Fragmente einer Geschichte des österreichischen Kinos*, ed. Ruth Beckermann and Christa Bliminger (Sonderzahl, 1996), 199, 201, 206.
82. Werner, "On the Horizon." Most Jews in Tiszaeszlár were poor peddlers who spoke Magyar and got along well with non-Jewish townspeople. Handler, *Blood Libel at Tiszaeszlar*, 36.
83. "Ein Mädchen verwschindet—ein Weltprozeß entsteht," *Salzburger Tagblatt*, June 30, 1947, 7.
84. Kitzberger, "Das Volk, die Fremden," 207.

NOTES TO PAGES 218–224   301

85. These include the sign "No Dogs and Jews" on the gates to Onody's home. Karl Prümm points out scenes featuring marching Hungarians evoking goose-stepping German Stormtroopers; the destruction of the village synagogue in flames, surrounded by an angry mob; speeches using Hitler-like rhetoric; torture scenes of the Jewish men. "Dark Shadows and a Pale Victory of Reason: The Trial (1948)," in *The Films of G.W. Pabst: An Extraterritorial Cinema*, ed. Eric Rentschler (Rutgers University Press, 1990), 200.

86. Jonathan Judaken, "Between Philosemitism and Antisemitism: The Frankfurt School's Anti-Antisemitism," in *Antisemitism and Philosemitism in the Twentieth and Twenty-First Centuries*, ed. Phyllis Lassner and Lara Trubowitz, 23–46 (University of Delaware Press, 2008), 29.

87. Basil, "Der Prozeß," 5. Austrian critic Otto Basil opposed the Nazis, but his criticism perpetuates negative stereotypes about Jews and shows little understanding for re-émigrés. He accused Fritz Kortner of unfairly attacking Austria in his drama *Donauwellen*, and asserted without proof that Kortner, along with a "small group of like-minded people in Berlin," had instigated a protest campaign against actor Werner Krauss because of his performance in Harlan's *Jud Süss*. Basil asserted he would expect that a person of Kortner's "stature and background" would have shown "more tolerance and understanding for others' mistakes and character weaknesses." "Das abgebrochene Gastspiel," *Neues Österreich*, December 13, 1950, 1–2. In contrast, R. A. Stemmle claimed that the film's lack of realism and crass portrayals were more likely to breed antisemitism than eradicate it. See "Das Problem des Antisemitismus. Gedanken zum Film "Der Prozess." Unpublished manuscript, DKA, Nachlass R.A. Stemmle, 4.3-05/17-0.

88. Judaken, "Between Philosemitism and Antisemitism," 29–30.

89. RB, "Der Prozess—Film und die Oeffentlichkeit." LHW, NRB, Box 4, Mappe 1.8.2—undated essays.

90. RB, "Der Prozess—Film und die Oeffentlichkeit." A shortened, edited version of this essay that does not specifically mention Auschwitz and Maidanek was published as: "Warum Prozess," *Welt am Montag*, March 15, 1948, 5.

91. Arnold Zweig to Lion Feuchtwanger, August 16, 1947, in *Lion Feuchtwanger—Arnold Zweig. Briefwechsel 1933–1958*, ed. Harold von Hofe, vol. I (Aufbau, 1984), 451.

92. See the biography of Ernst Marboe at https://oecv.at/Biolex/Detail/11000648#.

93. "Schön ist's, wunderschön ist's," *Der Spiegel* 40 (1952): 32.

94. Gernot Heiss, "Österreich am 1. April 2000—das Bild von Gegenwart und Vergangenheit im Zukunftstraum von 1952," in *Wiederaufbau in Österreich, 1945–1955. Rekonstruktion oder Neubeginn?*, ed. Ernst Brückmüller (Verlag für Geschichte und Politik, 2006), 103n5.

95. Barbara Fremuth-Kronreif, "Der 'Österreich-Film.' Die Realisierung einer Idee," in *1. April 2000*, ed. Ernst Kieninger, Nikola Langreiter, Armin Loacker, and Klara Löffler (Filmarchiv Austria, 2000), 11–12.

96. *Österreichische Kino-Zeitung*, February 26, 1949, 4. Three prizes of 5,000, 3,000 and 2,000 schillings were offered. Fremuth-Kronreif, "Der 'Österreich-Film,'" 18.

97. Österreichisches Staatsarchiv, Vienna (ÖStA), Archiv der Republik (AdrR), PBMV, Pr. Zl. 11.188/49 in Grz. 10058/49.

98. Marboe was eventually made Produktionsleiter. See Fremuth-Kornreif, "Der 'Österreich-Film,'" 40.

99. ÖStA, AdR, Bundeskanzleramt (BKA), Gz. 10542-Pr.1b/50 in Grz. 7363.

100. Wolfgang Reinhardt/The Selznick Studio to Dr. Friedrich E. Wallner, General Consul in Los Angeles, October 26, 1951, Grz. 20.157-III/51, cited in Armin Loacker, "Das offizielle Österreich dreht einen Film. Ein Resümee zum Staatsfilm *1. April 2000*," in *1. April 2000*, ed. Ernst Kieninger, Nikola Langreiter, Armin Loacker, and Klara Löffler (Filmarchiv, 2000), 345.

101. ÖStA, AdR, PBMV, Pr. Zl. 11105/49 in Grz. 10058/49.

102. Only one person objected to selecting Liebeneiner as director for the film. Loacker, "Das offizielle Österreich," 349.

103. Wolfgang Liebeneiner to Bundesminister, March 16, 1965, reprinted in Erwin Leiser, *"Deutschland Erwache!" Propaganda im Film des Dritten Reiches* (Rowohlt, 1989), 129–31. Notably, *Ich Klage An* also features a trial of a man at the mercy of the justice system. In many ways, *1. April 2000* is also related to Liebeiner's later *Heimat* films and served as a precursor for his two popular German films about the patriotic, anti-Nazi Austrian von Trapp family in Salzburg, *Die Trapp-Familie* (1956) and *Die Trapp-Familie in Amerika* (1958), both based on Maria von Trapp's 1949 memoir, out of which developed the U.S. stage production/film *The Sound of Music*.

302   NOTES TO PAGES 224–232

104. In an exchange with actor Inge Stolten regarding Liebeneiner's career, she asserts: "Maybe it sounds a bit brutal. But I was stunned when you wanted to start working again immediately after the war. For me you were a Nazi." Liebeneiner responds with astonishment: "Who, me? Why?," *Kultur kontrovers. Kunst im III. Reich* (NDR, 1983), 39:41.
105. "Wir blenden auf," *Wiener Zeitung*, June 1, 1952.
106. Irina Scheidgen, "Nachkriegskarrieren II. Der Fall Liebeneiner," *Mendiengeschichte des Films* 6 (2009): 99.
107. ÖStA, AdR, BKA, Pr AZ 9.966–1952 GZ 11213 "Bericht des Bundeskanzlers über den Stand der Arbeiten am Österreich-Film am 22. April 1952," signed by Figl, April 18, 1952.
108. Armin Loacker discusses the weaknesses of the committee's reasoning. "Das offizielle Österreich," 350.
109. "Österreich-Film vor der Verwirklichung. Wolfgang Liebeneiner wird Regie führe," *Wiener Zeitung*, November 9, 1951, 3.
110. On the decision to hire Liebeneiner, see Fremuth-Kornreif, "Der 'Österreich-Film," 41–48.
111. *Österreichische Film- und Kinozeitung*, May 31, 1952, 3.
112. "Österreich-Film vor der Verwirklichung. Wolfgang Liebeneiner wird Regie führe," *Wiener Zeitung*, November 9, 1951, 3.
113. The Allied Forces pressured the Austrian government in dealing with the consequences of the Nazi regime in educational and judiciary measures. Rathkolb, *Paradoxical Republic*, 244.
114. Screenplay, *1. April 2000. Eine Film-Komödie*, 46, Filmarchiv Austria, Vienna, DB 287. There is no evidence that they used Benjamin as a model, but her activities were reported on in the Austrian press.
115. "Volksrichter' in sieben Monaten," *Arbeiterwille*, October 24, 1948, 2.
116. Austrian newspaper reports on Benjamin include "Schauprozeß im Landestheater," *Die Weltpresse*, April 25, 1950, 1, and "Schauprozeß im Landestheater Dessau," *Salzburger Nachrichten*, April 25, 1950.
117. "East Germany: Red Hilde's Law," *Time*, October 18, 1954.
118. His renowned brother Walter Benjamin committed suicide in 1940 in Portbou, on the border between Spain and France, while attempting to escape the Nazis.
119. Hilde Krahl, *Ich bin fast immer angekommen. Erinnerungen* (Munich: Langen Müller, 1998), 11.
120. Bundesarchiv, Berlin-Lichterfelde, AE R 9361-V/110879.
121. *Mein Film*, April 15, 1938, 5.
122. National Archives and Records Administration, 260 E260 282—Wolfgang Liebeneiner.
123. Newspaper reports mentioning the event as late as 1951 include Valentin Gann, "Trümmerfeld des Geistes," *Salzburger Nachrichten*, April 30, 1951, 3.
124. Laura Morowitz, "Reviled, Repressed, Resurrected: Vienna 1900 in the Nazi Imaginary," *Austrian History Yearbook* 53 (2022): 185; and "'Heil the Hero Klimt!': Nazi Aesthetics in Vienna and the 1943 Gustav Klimt Retrospective," *Oxford Art Journal* 39, no. 1 (2006): 109.
125. Morowitz, "Reviled, Repressed, Resurrected," 16.
126. Oliver Rathkolb described the postwar culture that emerged after these struggles as the "traditional fare of 'Great Art from Austria's Monasteries." Rathkolb, *Paradoxical Republic*, 194. On the support of Vienna's City Councilor Viktor Matejka for modernist projects and his efforts to reintegrate Jewish artists into postwar culture, see Tanzer, *Vanishing Vienna*, 87–111.
127. Frances Tanzer outlines this transformation, showing that not all Austrians rejected modernism and the avant-garde in the postwar years, as long as it did not signal the physical return of exiled Austrian Jews. *Vanishing Vienna: Jewish Absence in Post-Nazi Central Europe* (University of Pennsylvania Press, 2024), 112–20.
128. Screenplay, *1. April 2000. Eine Film-Komödie*, 49. Filmarchiv Austria DB 287.
129. Valerie Weinstein, *Antisemitism in Film Comedy in Nazi Germany* (Indiana University Press, 2019), 66–67.
130. "Schön ist's, wunderschön ist's," *Der Spiegel* 40 (1952): 32.
131. Dieter A. Binder, "Kontinuität—Diskoninuität. Notizen zur österreichischen Kultur nach 1945," in *Österreichische Nationalgeschichte nach 1945*, ed. Robert Kreichbaumer (Böhlau, 1998), 737.
132. Original plans justifying the high cost were for two versions of a color film in German and English to market to American and English distributors. As late as the summer of 1950, efforts were made to interest Americans in co-production. ÖStA, AdR, BKA, Pr AZ 7.363–1950 GZ 10560, Memorandum of the administrative Head of the Bundespressedienstes, July 4, 1950. The English version was never made, and the film was not widely shown in the United States.

NOTES TO PAGES 232–241   303

133. Loacker, "Das offizielle Österreich," 351.
134. Archival documents suggest that there had always been plans for a book to accompany the screenplay. ÖStA, AdR, BKA, Pr AZ 7.363–1950, GZ 8470 Bundespressedienst memorandum, March 15, 1950.
135. Ernst Marboe, Yes, Oui, OK, Nyet (Verlag der Österreichische Staatsdruckerei, 1954), 181.
136. "Prüfung und Durchführung eines Propagandafilmes über Österreich," Memorandum of the Head of the Bundespressedienst (BPD) to BKA, March 23, 1950. The memo notes specifically, "A representative Austrian film is a particularly effective means of cultural propaganda for Austria, which is extremely suitable for promoting its reputation and popularity all over the world." ÖStA, Archiv der Republik (AdR), BKA, Pr AZ 7.363–1950 GZ 8470.
137. Memo dated March 14, 1947, ÖStA, AdR, BPD, 16 90.068/1948, Gz. 80.198-III/47.
138. Österreichische Staatsdruckerei to the BKA, BPD, October 10, 1947, ÖStA, AdR, BPD, 16 90.068/1948, Gz. 80.198-III/47.
139. Letters dated March 14 and March 15, 1947, refer to it as a "Propagandabuch über Österreich" that was designed specifically not to compete with official tourist agency publications. ÖStA, AdR, BPD, 16 90.068/1948, Gz. 80.198-III/47.
140. Ernst Marboe, ed., Das Österreichbuch (Österreichische Staatsdruckerei, 1948); The Book of Austria (Österreichische Staatsdruckerei, 1948), x–xi.
141. March 14, 1947, ÖStA, AdR, BPD, 16 90.068/1948, Gz. 80.198-III/47.
142. Report on the status of the Austria Book by Pfaundler, Scheichelbauer, and Marboe, to be signed by Figl, January 9, 1948, ÖStA, AdR, BPD, 16 90.068/1948, Gz. 90.068-III/48.
143. Contributors include Arthur Fischer-Colbrie, a writer who referred to Hitler and the annexation of the border territories of Czechoslovakia warmly in his essay "Ein Tag in Stifters Heimat" in the Nazi propaganda book, Die Landschaft Oberdonau in der Schau zeitgenössischer Dichter, ed. Nationalsozialistische Deutsche Arbeiter-Partei (Leitner, 1944), 81–84.
144. Marboe, The Book of Austria, 286.
145. Marboe, The Book of Austria, 359–60.
146. These include Klimt's Beethovenfries, illustrating a text about Beethoven, and two scenes from Der Tod und Das Leben, illustrating the section on Die Wiener Medizinische Schule. That chapter ends with a brief textual reference to Klimt's Medizin, though it is not shown. A portrait by Egon Schiele completes the book's representation of Viennese modernism, likewise without text and used only to illustrate the brief, four-page chapter on Austria's First Republic.
147. The achievements of Red Vienna do not appear until the edition published in 1967.
148. Marboe, Das Österreichbuch, 414, 535–37.
149. Marboe, The Book of Austria, 373–74, 151–52.
150. Marboe, Das Österreichbuch, 3, 5, 16, 22.
151. Theodor Nissen, "Zu den ältesten Fassungen der Legende vom Judenknaben," Zeitschrift für französische Sprache und Literatur 62, no. 7–8 (1939): 393–403.
152. Marboe, Das Österreichbuch, 342.
153. Marboe, Das Österreichbuch, 22.
154. Wolf died in 1946 in Haifa. On the background of the museum, see https://editionhansposse. gnm.de/wisski/navigate/5888/view.

Chapter 7

1. "Winchell Evaded Jo Baker Issue, Says White. NAACP's Pickets Thrown Around N.Y. Stork Club," Baltimore Afro American, October 23, 1951, 1.
2. AP17—Stork Club, Newswire. Laura Keane Zametkin Hobson papers, Series II, Box 3, University Archives, Rare Book & Manuscript Library, Columbia University Libraries. The protest followed White's telegram to Mayor Vincent Impellitteri alleging the Stork Club's violation of the New York State Civil Rights Act and the New York State Alcoholic Beverage Control Law with an act of discrimination.
3. As Phil notes, "What the hell chance have we of getting decent with thirteen million Negroes if we can't lick the much easier business of antisemitism?" Laura Z. Hobson, Gentleman's Agreement (Simon and Schuster, 1946), 184–85. On Jewish American opposition to racism, see Cheryl Greenberg, "Pluralism and Its Discontents: The Case of Blacks and Jews," in Insider/Outsider: American Jews and Multiculturalism, ed. David Biale, Michael Galchinsky, and Susannah Heschel (University of California Press, 1998), 63–66. For a discussion of Gentleman's Agreement, see Rachel Gordan, "Laura Z. Hobson and the Making of Gentleman's Agreement," Studies in American Jewish Literature 34, no. 2 (2015); on the book and film in

304   NOTES TO PAGES 241–247

the context of postwar American literature and anti-antisemitism more broadly, see *Postwar Stories: How Books Made Judaism American* (Oxford University Press, 2024).

4. She described herself as "liberal, pro-labor, agnostic, internationalist, and non-sectarian." Laura Z. Hobson, biography, May 1, 1953, 3. Laura Keane Zametkin Hobson papers, Series II, Box 2, University Archives, Rare Book & Manuscript Library, Columbia University Libraries.

5. "NAACP Demands Mayor Crack Down on Stork Club," *New York Post*, October 23, 1951. Laura Keane Zametkin Hobson papers, Series II, Box 3, University Archives, Rare Book & Manuscript Library, Columbia University Libraries.

6. Laura Keane Zametkin Hobson papers, Series II, Box 3, University Archives, Rare Book & Manuscript Library, Columbia University Libraries.

7. Jean-Claude Baker and Chris Chase, *Josephine: The Hungry Heart* (Random House, 1993), 306–7.

8. Mary L. Dudziak, "Josephine Baker, Racial Protest, and the Cold War," *Journal of American History* 81, no. 2 (1994): 548.

9. Bennetta Jules-Rosette, *Josephine Baker in Art and Life: The Icon and the Image* (University of Illinois Press, 2007), 218–20.

10. "Josephine Baker Says Stork Club Prejudiced," *The Troy Record*, October 19, 1951.

11. "Stork Club Is Picketed," *New York Times*, October 23, 1951, 35.

12. Lynn Haney, *Naked at the Feast: A Biography of Josephine Baker* (Dodd, Mead, 1981), 256.

13. Ralph Blumenthal, *Stork Club: America's Most Famous Nightspot and the Lost World of Café Society* (Little, Brown, 2000), 164.

14. Some accounts suggest that Bessie Buchanan pushed Baker to make the incident public. Baker and Chase, *Josephine: The Hungry Heart*, 306–9.

15. "Billingsley's Death Recalls Feud with J. Baker," *Jet*, October 20, 1966, 62.

16. "Walter Winchell Is Dead on Coast at 74," *New York Times*, February 21, 1972, 1. Between his syndicated daily column and his weekly radio show, Winchell drew millions of listeners and readers.

17. Representative Rankin, Congressional Record, HR, 78th Cong., 2nd Sess., February 21, 1944, 1925–1926. Rankin was known for his general bigotry and racist statements in Congress.

18. "Will Soldiers Vote?," *Time*, February 14, 1944, 17–18.

19. Charlene Regester, "The Construction of an Image and the Deconstruction of a Star— Josephine Baker Racialized, Sexualized, and Politicized in the African-American Press, the Mainstream Press, and FBI Files," *Popular Music & Society* 24, no. 1 (2000): 36–37.

20. "Miami Success Climaxes Storybook Career," *Ebony*, May 6, 1951, 76.

21. Neal Gabler, *Winchell: Gossip, Power, and the Culture of Celebrity* (Knopf, 1994), 406.

22. Baker and Chase, *Josephine: The Hungry Heart*, 306–7.

23. Accounts about what happened differ. According to Baker and Chase, Josephine Baker eventually admitted that Winchell had not been present when the discrimination occurred; this was verified by Solange Rico, who noted, "He left before we did." Baker and Chase, *Hungry Heart*, 309. Neal Gabler claims Winchell was not aware of the incident of racial discrimination, but was present at the Stork Club when Baker made the phone call to the NAACP and later lied about not being there. *Winchell: Gossip*, 411.

24. Herman Klurfeld, *Winchell: His Life and Times* (Praeger, 1976), 152.

25. Klurfeld notes that Winchell spoke almost daily to Billingsley for over 30 years. *Winchell: His Life*, 157.

26. Baker's son Jean-Claude points out that among Winchell's papers are handwritten memos in which his outrage at her is on full display; on one scrap of paper he wrote: "After all I did for her!" Baker and Chase, *Hungry Heart*, 310.

27. Walter Winchell, ". . . Of New York. Notes of a Newspaperman," *Washington Post*, November 20, 1951.

28. "Josephine Baker Blasts Winchell at Chicago Meeting," *Jet*, December 27, 1951, 8.

29. On the harms of insisting on picking one side in the face of dueling accusations, and how doing so subverts the important step of approaching claims with open receptivity, see David Schraub, "The Epistemic Dimension of Antisemitism," *Journal of Jewish Identities* 15, no. 2 (2022): 162–63.

30. On their partial success in the 1950s, see Dudziak, "Josephine Baker," 565.

31. Gabler, *Winchell: Gossip*, 401, 413, 415.

NOTES TO PAGES 247–250 305

32. The fact that not all Jews are white is also overlooked. On the unspoken assumption that the constructed Jew is primarily an Ashkenazi white male who serves as an Other for the gentile, Western non-Jew, to the exclusion of Jews of color, Sephardi Jews, Arab Jews, and women, see Jon Stratton, *Coming out Jewish: Constructing Ambivalent Identities* (Routledge, 2000), 3–4.

33. Jews' whiteness can be withdrawn at any time in a range of social situations, with outcomes of varying significance. Jews are also targets of white supremacists, who never consider them to be white. See David Schraub, "White Jews: An Intersectional Approach," *AJS Review* 43, no. 2 (2019).

34. Some antisemitic stereotypes targeting powerful Jews overlap with the powers ascribed to white privilege more generally; in this way, characterizing Jews as white can reinforce antisemitism. See Schraub, "White Jews: An Intersectional Approach"; Karin Stögner, "Der Antisemitismus und das Konzept der Intersektionalität," *Handbuch Intersektionalitätsforschung*, ed. A Biele Mefebue et al. (Springer, 2022), 94–96.

35. See also Kimberlé Crenshaw, "Demarginalizing the Intersection of Race and Sex: A Black Feminist Critique of Antidiscrimination Doctrine, Feminist Theory, and Antiracist Politics," *University of Chicago Legal Forum* 1(1989); *On Intersectionality: The Seminal Essays* (New Press, 2012). Because Jewish difference does not neatly overlap and intersect with race, class, and gender, it is often excluded from and can be fueled by discourses on intersectionality. On this problem, see Karin Stögner, "Der Antisemitismus." On challenges surrounding the relationship between intersectionality and antisemitism, see also Kerry Wallach and Sonia Gollance, "Introduction: When Feminism and Antisemitism Collide," *Feminist German Studies* 39, no. 1 (2023); Karin Stögner, "New Challenges in Feminism. Intersectionality, Critical Theory, and Anti-Zionism," in *Anti-Zionism and Antisemitism: The Dynamics of Delegitimization*, ed. Alvin H. Rosenfeld (Indiana University Press, 2019). In the American context, see Carol Siegel, *Jews in Contemporary Visual Entertainment: Raced, Sexed, and Erased* (Indiana University Press, 2022); Jonathan Branfman, *Millennial Jewish Stars: Navigating Racial Antisemitism, Masculinity, and White Supremacy* (New York University Press, 2024).

36. Matthew Frye Jacobson, *Whiteness of a Different Color: European Immigrants and the Alchemy of Race* (Harvard University Press, 1999), 126–27.

37. The term "white racial frame" describes the explicitly and implicitly circulated ideas founded on viewing whites as superior and the white perspective as the norm. Joe R. Feagin, *The White Racial Frame: Centuries of Racial Framing and Counter-Framing* (Routledge, 2013).

38. Gordan, "Laura Z. Hobson," 240.

39. Hobson, *Gentleman's Agreement*, 49.

40. On postwar American literature that discusses antisemitism, see Leah Garrett, *Young Lions: How Jewish Authors Reinvented the American War Novel* (Northwestern University Press, 2015). On the involvement of American Jews in both engaging and opposing racist stereotypes in the culture industry, see Jacobson, *Whiteness of a Different Color*; Eric L. Goldstein, *The Price of Whiteness: Jews, Race, and American Identity* (Princeton University Press, 2006); Branfman, *Millennial Jewish Stars*.

41. Laura Z. Hobson, *Laura Z: A Life* (Arbor House, 1983), 390.

42. Baker and Chase, *Hungry Heart*, 69.

43. On Jewish visibility in twentieth-century Central Europe, see Kerry Wallach, *Passing Illusions: Jewish Visibility in Weimar Germany* (University of Michigan Press, 2017). The narrative of *Gentleman's Agreement* is echoed in subsequent narratives of "cultural blackface." See Laura Browder, *Slippery Characters: Ethnic Impersonators and American Identities* (University of North Carolina Press, 2000), 204–5.

44. Goldstein, *The Price of Whiteness*, 1.

45. Jacobson, *Whiteness of a Different Color*, 126. James Baldwin pinpoints this paradox in an article on persistent prejudices against Jews as exploiters of Blacks in Harlem, in which he comments that few are able to see that "behind the Jewish face stood the American reality." James Baldwin, "From the American Scene: The Harlem Ghetto: Winter 1948," *Commentary* 5, no. 2 (1948). He developed this idea further in "Negroes are anti-Semitic because they're anti-White," in which he writes that the Jew "is singled out by Negroes not because he acts differently from other white men, but because he doesn't." *New York Times Magazine*, April 9, 1967.

46. Hobson, *Laura Z: A Life*, 372. On Hollywood's engagement with antisemitism and its effects on film production in the United States, see Steven Alan Carr, *Hollywood and Anti-Semitism: A Cultural History up to World War II* (Cambridge University Press, 2008); Gregory D. Black, *Hollywood Censored* (Cambridge University Press, 1994).

306 NOTES TO PAGES 251–255

47. Hobson, *Gentleman's Agreement*, 26.
48. Gordan, "Laura Z. Hobson," 236.
49. Hobson, *Gentleman's Agreement*, 8–10.
50. Hobson, *Gentleman's Agreement*, 55.
51. Hobson, *Gentleman's Agreement*, 154–55.
52. Popular Jewish writers in prewar Central Europe criticized Jewish women for luring Jewish men away from their roots via assimilation. See Lisa Silverman, *Becoming Austrians: Jews and Culture Between the World Wars* (Oxford University Press, 2012), 85.
53. Hobson, *Gentleman's Agreement*, 133.
54. As Horkheimer noted in a letter to Isaac Rosengarten, editor of the *Jewish Forum*, on September 12, 1944: "To protect the Jews has come to be a symbol of everything mankind stands for. Anti-Semitic persecution is the stigma of the present world whose injustice enters all its weight upon the Jews. Thus, the Jews have been made what the Nazis always pretended that they were, the focal point of world history. Their survival is inseparable from the survival of culture itself." Cited in Anson Rabinbach, "Why Were the Jews Sacrificed? The Place of Anti-Semitism in *Dialectic of Enlightenment*," *New German Critique* 81 (2000): 53.
55. On the politics of producing *Gentleman's Agreement* and *Crossfire*, another Hollywood film thematizing antisemitism released in 1947, see Eric A. Goldman, *The American Jewish Story Through Cinema* (University of Texas Press, 2013), 50–96.
56. On the Holocaust as the antithesis of American values, see Tim Cole, *Selling the Holocaust: From Auschwitz to Schindler* (Taylor and Francis, 2017). On the Holocaust as "master moral paradigm" in American culture, see Jeffrey Shandler, *While America Watches: Televising the Holocaust* (Oxford University Press, 2000), xviii.
57. See Angelica Fenner, *Race Under Reconstruction in German Cinema: Robert Stemmle's* Toxi (University of Toronto Press, 2011), esp. 102–3 on the symbolic significance of the character of Toxi in postwar German culture. See also Heide Fehrenbach, *Race After Hitler: Black Occupation Children in Postwar Germany and America* (Princeton University Press, 2007) and Priscilla Layne, "'Don't Look Sò Sad Because You're a Little Negro': Marie Nejar, Afro-German Stardom, and Negotiations with Black Subjectivity," *Palimpsest: A Journal on Women, Gender, and the Black International* 4, no. 2 (2015). On early postwar racism in East Germany, see Quinn Slobodian, "Socialist Chromatism: Race, Racism, and the Racial Rainbow in East Germany," in *Comrades of Color: East Germany in the Cold War World*, ed. Quinn Slobodian (Berghahn, 2015); in Austria, see Philipp Rohrbach, "Life Stories of Children of Black US Occupation Soldiers and Austrian Women," *Journal of Austrian Studies* 56, no. 4 (2023). On the origins of white Christian supremacy and its links to the modern marginalization of Jews and Blacks, see Magda Teter, *Christian Supremacy: Reckoning with the Roots of Antisemitism and Racism* (Princeton University Press, 2023).
58. "Among the most disturbing political phenomena of our times is the emergence in the newly created state of Israel of the 'Freedom Party' (Tnuat Haherut), a political party closely akin in its organization, methods, political philosophy and social appeal to the Nazi and Fascist parties. It was formed out of the membership and following of the former Irgun Zvai Leumi, a terrorist, right-wing, chauvinist organization in Palestine. . . . The discrepancies between the bold claims now being made by Begin and his party, and their record of past performance in Palestine bear the imprint of no ordinary political party. This is the unmistakable stamp of a Fascist party for whom terrorism (against Jews, Arabs, and British alike), and misrepresentation are means, and a 'Leader State' is the goal." See "New Palestine Party: Visit of Menachem Begin and Aims of Political Movement Discussed." A Letter to the *New York Times*, December 4, 1948, 12.
59. For example, the controversy over the U.S. adoption of the definition established by the International Holocaust Remembrance Alliance on May 26, 2016, https://www.state.gov/defining-antisemitism/, and the Jerusalem Declaration of Antisemitism that was created in response, https://jerusalemdeclaration.org/, reflects the intensity of the struggle for the authority to define the Antisemite.
60. Baker and Chase, *Hungry Heart*, 312.

Bibliography

Archives

American Jewish Archives, Cinncinnati, OH
Archiv der Akademie der Künste (AdK), Berlin
Archiv der Universität für angewandte Kunst, Vienna
Bayerische Staatsbibliothek, Munich
Bundesarchiv (BArch), Berlin-Lichtenberg, Stasi-Unterlagen-Archiv (BStU)
Bundesarchiv (BArch), Berlin-Lichterfelde
Bundesarchiv (BArch), Koblenz
Cabaret Ping-Pong Archive, Efram Wolff Studios, Seattle, WA
Central Zionist Archives, Jerusalem (CZA)
Columbia University Archives, New York
Deutsche Kinemathek, Museum für Film und Fernsehen, Archiv (DKA), Berlin
Deutsche Nationalbibliothek, Frankfurt am Main
    Exilarchiv
    Textarchiv
Deutsches Filmmuseum, Frankfurt am Main
Deutsches Kabarettarchiv, Mainz
Dokumentationsarchiv des österreichischen Widerstandes, Vienna
FBI Archives, Winchester, VA
Filmarchiv Austria, Vienna
Filmmuseum Landeshauptstadt Düsseldorf (FLD)
Filmmuseum Potsdam (FMP)
Forschungsinstitut Brenner-Archiv, Innsbruck
Friedrich-Ebert-Stiftung Bibliothek, Bonn
Harald von Troschke Archiv, Frankfurt an der Oder
Kabarettarchiv, Mainz
Landesarchiv Baden-Württemberg (LBW)
    Staatsarchiv Freiburg
    Staatsarchiv Stuttgart
Landeasarchiv Berlin
Leo Baeck Institute Archives (LBI), New York
Literaturhaus Wien (LHW)
Margaret Herrick Library, Academy of Motion Picture Arts and Sciences, Los Angeles, CA
National Archives and Records Administration (NARA), College Park, MD
National Archives of the Czech Republic, Prague
Norddeutscher Rundfunk Archiv, Hamburg
Österreichische Nationalbibliothek (ÖNB), Vienna
    Bildarchiv
    Handschriftensammlung
    Literaturarchiv
Österreichisches Staatsarchiv (ÖStA), Vienna
Prague City Archives
Staats- und Universitätsbibliothek Hamburg

308 BIBLIOGRAPHY

Staatsarchiv, Hamburg (SH)
Staatsbibliothek zu Berlin
Südwestrundfunk Archiv, Stuttgart
Susan Lowy Lubow Family Archive, Morristown, NJ
Theater Instituut Nederland, University of Amsterdam Theatercollectie, Amsterdam
United States Holocaust Memorial Museum (USHMM), Washington, DC
Universität für angewandte Kunst, Kunstsammlung und Archiv, Vienna
Wienbibliothek, Vienna
Zentral- und Landesbibliothek Berlin

Selected Periodicals

AJR Information
Allgemeine Wochenzeitung der Juden in Deutschland
Arbeiterwille
Aufbau
Aufbau: Kulturpolitische Monatsschrift
Bild
Commentary
Daily News
Das Tagebuch
Der Film
Der Kurier
Der Monat
Der Morgen: Monatsschrift der Juden in Deutschland
Der Neue Weg
Der Spiegel
Der Turm
Deutsche Allgemeine Zeitung
Die Gegenwart
Die neue Zeitung
Die Welt
Die Welt am Abend
Die Weltbühne
Die Zeit
Ebony
Film und Mode Revue
Film. Die österreichische illustrierte Zeitschrift.
FORVM
Freies Deutschland
Funk Uhr
Hamburger Abendblatt
Het Volk
Israelitisches Familienblatt
Jet
Jewish Forum
Jewish Telegraphic Agency
Jüdische Allgemeine Zeitung
Jüdische Rundschau
Jüdisches Gemeindeblatt. Allgemeine Zeitung der Juden in Deutschland
Jüdisches Gemeindeblatt. Die Zeitung der Juden in Deutschland
Jüdisches Gemeindeblatt für die Britische Zone

Képes Figyelö
Linzer Volksblatt
The Menorah Journal
Mein Film
Neue Zürcher Zeitung
Neues Deutschland
Neues Montagblatt
Neues Österreich
The New Statesman and Nation
New York Post
New York Times
New York Times Magazine
New Yorker Staats-Zeitung und Herold
Österreichische Film- und Kinozeitung
Österreichische Kinozeitung
Österreichisches Tagebuch
Salzburger Nachrichten
Salzburger Tagblatt
Salzburger Volkszeitung
Salzkammergutzeitung
Selbstwehr
sie—die Wochenzeitung für Frauenrecht und Menschenrecht
Süddeutsche Zeitung
Tagesspiegel
Time
The Troy Record
Völkischer Beobachter
Völksbühne Berlin
Vossische Zeitung
Washington Post
Welt am Montag
Weltbühne
Weltpresse
Weser Kurier
Wiener Kurier
Wiener Zeitung

Films

1. April 2000 (1952), dir. Wolfgang Liebeneiner
Affaire Blum (1948), dir. Erich Engel
A Foreign Affair (1948), dir. Billy Wilder
The Angel with the Trumpet (1950), dir. Anthony Bushell
Das andere Leben (1948), dir. Rudolf Steinboeck
Der Engel mit der Posaune (1948), dir. Karl Hartl
Der Fall Molander (1944–45), dir. G.W. Pabst
Der letzte Akt (1955), dir. G.W. Pabst
Der Prozess (1948), dir. G.W. Pabst
Der Ruf (1949), dir. Josef von Báky
Die Mörder sind unter uns (1946), dir. Wolfgang Staudte
Die Todesmühlen (Death Mills) (1945), dir. Billy Wilder and Hanuš Burger
Ehe im Schatten (1948), dir. Kurt Maetzig

310 BIBLIOGRAPHY

The Emperor Waltz (1948), dir. Billy Wilder
Es geschah am 20. Juli (1955), dir. G.W. Pabst
Gentleman's Agreement (1947), dir. Elia Kazan
In jenen Tagen (1947), dir. Helmut Käutner
Jud Süss (1940), dir. Veit Harlan
Lang ist der Weg (1948), dir. Marek Goldstein
Leinen aus Irland (1939), dir. Heinz Helbig
Letter from an Unknown Woman (1948), dir. Max Ophüls
Liebe 47 (1949), dir. Wolfgang Liebeneiner
Morituri (1948), dir. Eugen York
... nur ein Komödiant (1935), dir. Erich Engel
Rat der Götter (1950), dir. Friedrich Wolf
Roman einer jungen Ehe (1951), dir. Kurt Maetzig
Rotation (1949), dir. Wolfgang Staudte
The Search (1948), dir. Fred Zinnemann
Stalag 17 (1953), dir. Billy Wilder
The Third Man (1949), dir. Carol Reed
The Vicious Circle (1947/48), dir. William Lee Wilder

Documentaries and Television Programs

Aspekte extra. Jud Süss (Jud Süss Oppenheimer) Veit Harlans Film und das deutsche Gewissen (ZDF, 1984)
Billy Wilder Speaks (2006), dir. Volker Schlöndorff
Es kann Dir Dein Vater die Welt nicht erklären in einer Stunde. Wolfgang Liebeneiner im Gespräch mit seiner Tochter Johanna (WDR, 1984)
Harlan: In the Shadow of Jew Süss (2008), dir. Felix Moeller
Jenninger. Was eine Rede an den Tag brachte (NDR, 1989), dir. Werner Hill and Horst Königstein
Jud Süss. Veit Harlans Film und das deutsche Gewissen (ZDF, 1984)
Kennwort Kino: Erlebte Filmgeschichte—Helmut Käutner (ZDF, 1988)
Kultur kontrovers. Kunst im III. Reich (NDR, 1983)
Laterna Teutonica (ARD, 1980)
"Wir haben sie ungewöhnlich hoch geschätzt!" Helmut Schmidt erinnert sich an Ida Ehre (2011)
The Woman in Brown (1948), dir. William Lee Wilder

Unpublished Interviews

Niehoff-Hack, Ariane. Interview with author, February 6, 2020
Opfermann, Hans Carl. Interview with Friedrich Knilli, 1980. LBW, Staatsarchiv Stuttgart
Wolff, Kurt Egon. Undated interview. Kabarettarchiv, Mainz

Published Interviews

Crowe, Cameron. *Conversations with Wilder*. Knopf, 2011.
Ehre, Ihre. Interview with Harald von Trotschke, 1980. Harald von Troschke Archiv.
Funke, Hajo. "The Unorthodox Approach to Jewish History in the German Democratic Republic: An Interview with Helmut Eschwege." *New German Critique* 38 (1986): 88–104.
Interview with Moishe Postone. "Zionism, Anti-Semitism and the Left." February 5, 2010. https://www.workersliberty.org/files/100205postone.pdf.

BIBLIOGRAPHY 311

Luft, Edmund. "Kunst in Film ist Schmuggelware: Helmut Käutner im Gespräch mit Edmund Luft." In *Käutner*, edited by Wolfgang Jacobsen and Hans Helmut Prinzler. Volker Spiess, 1992.

Mundy, Robert, and Mike Wallington. "Billy Wilder: A *Cinema* Interview." *Cinema* 4 (1969): 19–22.

Ostow Robin. "Being Jewish in the Other Germany: An Interview with Thomas Eckert." *New German Critique* 38 (1986): 73–87.

"'Wenn du einmal im Sarg liegst, kommst du nicht mehr raus.' Nach Vorlage genehmigte Niederschrift des Gesprächs mit dem Bundestagspräsidenten a.D., Dr. Philipp Jenninger, am Dienstag, 16. Mai 2006." *Monatshefte* 100, no. 2 (2008): 179–90.

Published Memoirs

Brandt, Heinz. *The Search for a Third Way: My Path Between East and West*. Translated by Salvator Attanasio. Doubleday, 1970.

Ehre, Ida. *Gott hat einen größeren Kopf, mein Kind*. Rowohlt, 1997.

Eisner, Lotte H. *Ich hatte einst ein schönes Vaterland. Memoiren*. Deutscher Taschenbuch Verlag, 1984.

"Erinnerungen des Regieassistenten Mark Sorkin." *Die freudlose Gasse*, DVD. Film-museum Munich, 2009.

Frankl, Viktor E. *Ein Psycholog erlebt das Konzentrationslager*. Verlag Jugend und Volk, 1946.

Giordano, Ralph. *Die zweite Schuld oder Von der Last Deutscher zu sein*. Rasch und Röhring, 1987.

Harlan, Thomas. *Veit*. Rowohlt, 2011.

Harlan, Veit. *Im Schatten meiner Filme. Selbstbiographie*. Edited by H. C. Opfermann. Sigbert Mohn, 1966.

Harlan, Veit. *Souvenirs ou le Cinéma allemande selon Goebbels*. Translated by Albert Cologny. Éditions France-Empire, 1974.

Hobson, Laura Z. *Laura Z: A Life*. Arbor House, 1983.

Jahoda, Marie. *"Ich habe die Welt nicht verändert." Lebenserinnerungen einer Pionieren der Sozialforschung*. Edited by Steffani Engler and Brigitte Hasenjürgen. Campus, 1997.

Kindler, Helmut. *Zum Abschied ein Fest. Die Autobiographie eines deutschen Verlegers*. Kindler, 1992.

Kortner, Fritz. *Aller Tage Abend*. Kindler, 1959.

Kraft, Hyman Solomon. *On My Way to the Theater*. Macmillan, 1971.

Krahl, Hilde. *Ich bin fast immer angekommen. Erinnerungen*. Langen Müller, 1998.

Liepman, Heinz. *Vom Gestern zum Morgen. Ein deutscher Jude denkt über Deutschland nach*. Ner-Tamid, 1961.

Liepman, Ruth. *Vielleicht ist Glück nicht nur Zufall. Erzählte Erinnerungen*. Kiepenheuer & Witsch, 1993.

Lüth, Erich. *Viel Steine lagen am Weg. Ein Querkopf berichtet*. Marion von Schröder Verlag, 1966.

Montagu, Elizabeth. *Honourable Rebel: The Memoirs of Elizabeth Montagu*. Montagu Ventures, 2003.

Ross, Martin H. *Marrano*. Branden, 1976.

Seydewitz, Ruth. *Alle Menschen haben Träume. Meine Zeit—mein Leben*. Buchverlag Der Morgen, 1976.

Spiel, Hilde. *The Dark and the Bright, Memoirs, 1911–1989*. Ariadne, 2007.

Spiel, Hilde. *Return to Vienna: A Journal*. Translated by Christine Shuttleworth. Ariadne, 2011.

Spiel, Hilde. *Rückkehr nach Wien*. Nymphenburg, 1968.

Spiel, Hilde. *Welt im Widerschein*. Beck, 1960.

Zuckmayer, Carl. *Als wär's ein Stück von mir*. Fischer, 1986.

312 BIBLIOGRAPHY

Unpublished Memoirs

Bab, Elisabeth. "Aus zwei Jahrhunderten: Lebenserinnerungen." Unpublished manuscript, ca. 1960, Leo Baeck Institute Archives, New York.

Harlan, Veit. "Wie es War ... Erlebnisse eines Filmregisseurs unter seinem allerhöchsten Chef, dem 'Schirmherrn des deutschen Films,' Dr. Josef Goebbels." Unpublished manuscript, ca. 1960. Bayerische Staatsbibliothek, Munich.

Joseph, Rudolph S. "G. W. Pabst: The Man and the Artist. In Memory of a Great Friend." Unpublished manuscript. Deutsche Nationalbibliothek, Exilarchiv, Frankfurt.

Published Diaries

Klemperer, Victor. So sitze ich den zwischen allen Stühlen. Tagebücher 1945–1959. Aufbau, 1999.

Klemperer, Victor. The Diaries of Victor Klemperer, 1945–59: The Lesser Evil. Translated by Martin Chalmers. Weidenfeld & Nicolson, 2003.

Slide, Anthony, ed., "It's the Pictures That Got Small." Charles Brackett on Billy Wilder and Hollywood's Golden Age. Columbia University Press, 2014.

The War Diaries of Jean-Paul Sartre, November 1939–March 1940. Pantheon, 1984.

Published Letters

Berger, Christel. Anna Seghers. Hier im Volk der kalten Herzen. Briefwechsel 1947. Aufbau, 2000.

Berlin, Jeffrey B. "A Relentless Drive for Meaning (Part II): Lion Feuchtwanger's Unpublished Correspondence with His American Publisher Ben Huebsch (1952–1956)." In Feuchtwanger and Remigration, edited by Ian Wallace. Peter Lang, 2013.

Dietz, Christopher, ed. Alexander Lernet-Holenia und Maria Charlotte Sweceny. Briefe 1938–1945. Böhlau, 2013.

Greene, Richard, ed. Graham Greene: A Life in Letters. Little Brown, 2007.

Hofe, Harold von, ed. Feuchtwanger, Lion—Arnold Zweig. Briefwechsel 1933–1958, vol. I. Aufbau, 1984.

Nowojski, Walter, ed. Warum soll man nicht auf bessere Zeiten hoffen. Ein Leben in Briefen. Aufbau, 2017.

Toller, Ernst. Briefe 1915–1939, vol. 1. Wallstein, 2018.

Other Published Primary Sources

Ackerman, Nathan W., and Marie Jahoda. Anti-Semitism and Emotional Disorder: A Psychoanalytic Interpretation. Harper & Brothers, 1950.

Adorno, Theodor W. The Authoritarian Personality. Harper & Row, 1950.

Antisemitismus in Westdeutschland. Judenfeinde und Judenmörder im Herrschaftsapparat der Bundesrepublik. Verband der jüdischen Gemeinden in der Deutschen Demokratischen Republik, 1967.

Bahr, Hermann. Der Antisemitismus. Ein internationales Interview. S. Fischer, 1894.

Bauer, Alfred. Deutscher Spielfilm Almanach 1929–1950. Filmblätter Verlag, 1950.

Becher, Johannes R., ed. Gesammelte Werke, vol. 16. Aufbau, 1966.

Borresholm, Boris von, and Karena Niehoff, eds., Dr. Goebbels nach Aufzeichnungen aus seiner Umgebung. Verlag des Journal, 1949.

Brunngraber, Rudolf. Der Weg durch das Labyrinth. Zsolnay, 1949.

Brunngraber, Rudolf. Karl und das 20. Jahrhundert. Societäts-Verlag, 1933.

BIBLIOGRAPHY 313

Brunngraber, Rudolf. *Opiumkrieg.* Rowohlt, 1939.

Brunngraber, Rudolf. *Prozess auf Tod und Leben.* Zsolnay, 1948.

Brunngraber, Rudolf. *Wie es kam. Psychologie des Dritten Reichs.* Neues Österreich Zeitungs- und Verlagsgesellschaft, 1946.

Centralverein Deutscher Staatsbürger Jüdischen Glaubens. *Deutsches Judentum und Rechtskrisis.* Philo-Verlag, 1927.

Congressional Record, U.S. House of Representatives, February 21, 1944.

"Der Mann und sein Name. Protokoll einer Diskussion im Schriftstellerverband." In *Der Schriftsteller. Halbmonatsschrift des Deutschen Schriftstellerverbandes* 4. Verlag Volk und Wissen, 1953.

Eisner, Lotte H. *L'Ecran démoniaque: Influence de Max Reinhardt et de l'expressionisme.* Bonno, 1952.

Engel, Erich, and R. A. Stemmle. "Affäre Blum." *Volksbühne Berlin* 44 (1960–1961).

Entscheidungen des Oberen Gerichtshofes für die Britische Zone in Zivilsachen. Edited by Mitgliedern des Gerichtshofes und der Staatsanwaltschaft beim Obersten Gerichtshof, vol. 2. De Gruyter, 1950.

Feuchtwanger, Lion. *Jud Suess.* Drei Masken, 1925.

George, J. R. [pseud. Hans Hömberg]. *Jud Süss.* Ufa-Buchverhandlung G.m.b.H., 1941.

Gloth, Harald. "Die Werft im Hinterzimmer." In *Jungen, euer Welt. Das Jahrbuch der Hitler-Jugend,* vol. 2, 101–4. Zentralverlag der NSDAP, 1939.

Gloth, Harald. *Gesicht unterm Helm. Skizzen eines Infanteristen vom Westfeldzug.* Die Heimbücherei, 1940.

Greene, Graham. *The Third Man, Loser Takes All.* William Heinemann, 1976.

Haensel, Carl. *Das Gericht vertagt sich. Aus dem Tagebuch eines Verteidigers bei den Nürnberger Prozessen.* Claassen, 1950.

Herald, Heinz, and Geza Herczeg. "The Burning Bush: A Play in Three Acts." Translated by Noel Langley. Shirley Collier Agency, 1947.

Heymann, Stefan. *Marxismus und Rassenfrage.* Dietz, 1948.

Hobson, Laura Z. *Gentleman's Agreement.* Simon and Schuster, 1946.

Horkheimer, Max, and Theodor W. Adorno. *Dialectic of Enlightenment.* Continuum, 1999.

"Ist Deutschland antisemitisch? Ein diagnostischer Beitrag zur Innenpolitik." Institut für Demoskopie, 1949.

Jaspers, Karl. *Die Schuldfrage. Ein Beitrag zur deutschen Frage.* Artemis-Verlag, 1946.

Jenninger, Philipp. "Rede am 10. November 1988 im Deutschen Bundestag." Landesmedienzentrum Baden-Württemberg.

Kahn, Siegbert. *Antisemitismus und Rassenhetzte. Eine Übersicht über ihre Entwicklung in Deutschland.* Dietz, 1948.

Klemperer, Victor. *LTI.* Bloomsbury, 2013.

Laschet, Armin, and Heinz Malangré. *Philipp Jenninger, Rede und Reaktion.* Einhard Rheinischer Merkur, 1989.

Leiser, Erwin. *Deutschland, erwache! Propaganda im Film des Dritten Reiches.* Rowohlt, 1978.

Leiser, Erwin. *Leopold Lindtberg: "Du weisst ja nicht wie es in mir schäumt." Schriften-Bilder-Dokumente.* Musik und Theater Verlag, 1985.

Lernet-Holenia, Alexander. *Der 20. Juli. Erzählung.* Erasmus, 1947.

Lothar, Ernst. *Der Engel mit der Posaune.* Zsolnay, 1946.

Marboe, Ernst, ed. *Das Österreichbuch.* Österreichische Staatsdruckerei, 1948.

Marboe, Ernst, ed. *The Book of Austria.* Österreichische Staatsdruckerei, 1948.

Marboe, Ernst. *Yes, Oui, OK, Nyet.* Verlag der Österreichische Staatsdruckerei, 1954.

Niehoff, Karena. *Stimmt es—Stimmt es nicht? Porträts, Kritiken, Essais 1946–1962.* Horst Erdmann Verlag, 1962.

Rabinbach, Anson, and Sander L. Gilman, eds., *The Third Reich Sourcebook.* University of California Press, 2013.

Rauschning, Hermann. *Gespräche mit Hitler.* Europaverlag, 1940.

314 BIBLIOGRAPHY

Rauschning, Hermann. *Hitler m'a dit*. Coopération, 1939.

Rauschning, Hermann. *Hitler Speaks: A Series of Political Conversations with Adolf Hitler on His Real Aims*. Butterworth, 1939.

Rudolf, Rainer, Eduard Ulreich, and Fritz Zimmermann. *Hauerland, Bergstädterland. Deutsche Heimat in d. Mittelslowakei*. Verlag der Karpatendeutschen Landsmannschaft in Österreich, 1979.

Salomon, Ernst von. *Der Fragebogen*. Rowohlt, 1951.

Sartre, Jean-Paul. *Anti-Semite and Jew*. Schocken, 1965.

Seghers, Anna. "Der Mann und sein Name." In *Anna Seghers Erzählungen, (II) Auswahl 1947–1967*, 101–66. Luchterhand, 1977.

Seghers, Anna. "Ein Mensch wird Nazi." In *Anna Seghers, Erzählungen 1933–1947*, edited by Silvia Schlenstedt. Aufbau, 2011.

Seghers, Anna. "Excursion of the Dead Girls." Translated by Helen Fehervary and Amy Kepple Strawser. *American Imago* 74, no. 3 (2017): 283–306.

Seghers, Anna. "The End." Translated by Helen Fehervary and Amy Kepple Strawser. *American Imago* 74, no. 3 (2017): 333–82.

Seghers, Anna. *Das siebte Kreuz. Roman aus Hitlerdeutschland*. El Libro Libre, 1942.

Seghers, Anna. *Der Ausflug der toten Mädchen. Und andere Erzählungen*. Aurora Verlag, 1946.

Seghers, Anna. *Erzählungen 1933–1947*. Edited by Silvia Schlenstedt. Aufbau, 2011.

Seghers, Anna. *Erzählungen 1950–1957*. Edited by Ute Brandes. Aufbau, 2009.

Seghers, Anna. *The Seventh Cross*. Translated by James A. Galston. Little, Brown, 1942.

Seghers, Anna. *The Seventh Cross*. Translated by James A. Galston. Afterword by Dorothy Rosenberg. David R. Godein, 2004. Seghers, Anna. *Transit*. Translated by Margot Bettauer Dembo. New York Review of Books, 2013.

Seydewitz, Ruth, and Max Seydewitz. *Anti-Semitism in West Germany*. Committee for German Unity, 1956.

Stemmle, R. A. *Affaire Blum*. Deutscher Filmverlag GmbH, 1948.

Wulf, Joseph. *Theater und Film im Dritten Reich. Eine Dokumentation*. Rowohlt, 1966.

Zweig, Arnold. "Die Sendung Semaels." Kurt Wolff Verlag, 1920.

Selected Secondary Sources

Adunka, Evelyn. *Die vierte Gemeinde. Die Geschichte der Wiener Juden von 1945 bis heute*. Philo, 2000.

Albrecht, Gerd. *Nationalsozialistische Filmpolitik. Eine soziologische Untersuchung über die Spielfilme des Dritten Reichs*. F. Enke, 1969.

Albrich, Thomas. *Exodus durch Österreich. Die jüdischen Flüchtlinge, 1945–48*. Haymon, 1989.

Angress, Ruth K. "A 'Jewish Problem' in German Postwar Fiction." *Modern Judaism* 5, no. 3 (1985): 215–33.

Anthony, Elizabeth. *The Compromise of Return: Viennese Jews After the Holocaust*. Wayne State University Press, 2021.

Applegate, Celia. *A Nation of Provincials: The German Idea of Heimat*. University of California Press, 1990.

Arens, Katherine. "Syncope, Syncopation: Musical Hommages to Europe." In *Billy Wilder Movie-Maker: Critical Essays on the Film*, edited by Karen McNally. McFarland, 2011.

Aschheim, Steven E. *Scholem, Arendt, Klemperer: Intimate Chronicles in Turbulent Times*. Indiana University Press, 2001.

Ashkenazi, Ofer. *Anti-Heimat Cinema: The Jewish Invention of the German Landscape*. University of Michigan Press, 2020.

Ashkenazi, Ofer. *Weimar Film and Modern Jewish Identity*. Palgrave Macmillan, 2012.

BIBLIOGRAPHY 315

Asper, Helmut G. "Der Holocaust im fernen Spiegel. Der Prozess von Tisza-Eszlar (1882/ 1883) in den Filmen *Der Prozess* und *The Vicious Circle* (1947/48)." *Monatshefte* 106, no. 2 (2014): 230–48.

Assmann, Aleida. *Der lange Schatten der Vergangenheit. Erinnerungskultur und Geschichtspolitik.* Beck, 2006.

Atwell, Lee. *G.W. Pabst.* Twayne, 1977.

Bailer, Brigitte. "'They Were All Victims': The Selective Treatment of the Consequences of National Socialism." In *Austrian Historical Memory and National Identity*, edited by Günter Bischof and Anton Pelinka. Transaction, 1997.

Baker, Cynthia. *Jew.* Rutgers University Press, 2017.

Baker, Jean-Claude, and Chris Chase. *Josephine: The Hungry Heart.* Random House, 1993.

Barbian, Jan-Pieter. *The Politics of Literature in Nazi Germany: Books in the Media Dictatorship.* Bloomsbury, 2013.

Bathrick, David. "Felix Moeller's *Harlan: Im Schatten von Jud Süss* as Family Drama." In *Persistent Legacy: The Holocaust and German Studies*, edited by Erin McGlothlin and Jennifer M. Kapczynski. Camden House, 2016.

Bathrick, David. "Holocaust Film Before the Holocaust: DEFA, Antifascism and the Camps." *Cinémas* 18, no. 1 (2007): 109–34.

Bauman, Zygmunt. "Allosemitism: Premodern, Modern, Postmodern." In *Modernity, Culture and "the Jew,"* edited by Bryan Cheyette and Laura Marcus. Stanford University Press, 1998.

Baumann, Ulrich, and Francois Guesnet. "Kristallnacht–Pogrom–State Terror: A Terminological Reflection." In *New Perspectives on Kristallnacht: After 80 Years, the Nazi Pogrom in Global Comparison*, edited by Steven J. Ross. Purdue University Press, 2019.

Beck, Evelyn Torton. "The Politics of Jewish Invisibility." *NWSA Journal* 1, no. 1 (2022): 165–84.

Becker, Jörg. *Karena Niehoff. Feuilletonistin und Kritkerin.* Edition Text & Kritik, 2006.

Ben-Rafael, Eliezer. *Confronting Allosemitism in Europe: The Case of Belgian Jews.* Brill, 2014.

Berg, Nicolas. *The Holocaust and West German Historians.* University of Wisconsin Press, 2015.

Berghahn, Daniela. *Hollywood Behind the Wall: The Cinema of East Germany.* Manchester University Press, 2005.

Bergmann, Werner. *Antisemitismus in öffentlichen Konflikten. Kollektives Lerner in der politischen Kultur der Bundesrepublik 1949–1989.* Campus, 1997.

Bergmann, Werner. "Sekundärer Antisemitismus." In *Handbuch des Antisemitismus. Judenfeindschaft in Geschichte und Gegenwart 3*, edited by Wolfgang Benz. De Gruyter, 2010.

Bergmann, Werner. "'Störenfriede der Erinnerung.' Zum Schuldabwehr—Antisemitismus in Deutschland." In *Literarischer Antisemitismus nach Auschwitz*, edited by Klaus-Michael Bogdal, Klaus Holz, and Matthias N. Lorenz. J. B. Metzler, 2007.

Bergmann, Werner, and Rainer Erb. *Anti-Semitism in Germany: The Post-Nazi Epoch from 1945 to 1995.* Routledge, 1997.

Bergmeier, Horst J. P. *Chronologie der deutschen Kleinkunst in den Niederlanden 1933–1944.* Hambuger Arbeitsstelle für deutsche Exilliteratur, 1998.

Bergmeier, Horst J. P., Jakob Eisler, Rainer E. Lotz, Hirsch Lewin, Moritz Lewin, Beer Maiblatt, Georg Engel, Helmar Lerski, Arno Nadel, Andreas Weissgerber, and Joseph Achron. *Vorbei—Beyond Recall: A Record of Jewish Musical Life in Nazi Berlin, 1933–1938.* Bear Family Records, 2001.

Berkowitz, Michael, and Suzanne Brown-Fleming. "Perceptions of Jewish Displaced Persons as Criminals in Early Postwar Germany: Lingering Stereotypes and Self-Fulfilling Prophecies." In *"We Are Here": New Approaches to Jewish Displaced Persons in Postwar Germany*, edited by Avinoam J. Patt and Michael Berkowitz. Wayne State University Press, 2010.

Biess, Frank. *Homecomings: Returning POWs and the Legacy of Defeat in Postwar Germany.* Princeton University Press, 2006.

Binder, Dieter A. "Kontinuität—Diskoninuität. Notizen zur österreichischen Kultur nach 1945." In *Österreichische Nationalgeschichte nach 1945*, edited by Robert Kreichbaumer. Böhlau, 1998.

316   BIBLIOGRAPHY

Birnbaum, Pierre. "Sorry Afterthoughts on 'Anti-Semite and Jew.'" *October* 87 (1999): 89–106.

Black, Gregory D. *Hollywood Censored*. Cambridge University Press, 1994.

Blauert, Ellen. *Vier Filmerzählungen*. Henschel, 1969.

Blumenthal, Ralph. *Stork Club: America's Most Famous Nightspot and the Lost World of Café Society*. Little, Brown, 2000.

Bodemann, Y. Michal. *Gedächtnistheater. Die jüdische Gemeinschaft und ihre deutsche Erfindung*. Rotbuch, 1996.

Bodemann, Y. Michal. "How Can One Stand to Live There as a Jew . . . Paradoxes of Jewish Existence in Germany." In *Jews, Germans, Memory: Reconstructions of Jewish Life in Germany*, edited by Y. Michal Bodemann. University of Michigan Press, 1996.

Bodemann, Y. Michal. "The State in the Construction of Ethnicity, and Ideological Labour: The Case of German Jewry." *Critical Sociology* 17, no. 3 (1990): 35–46.

Boll, Monika. "Max Horkheimers zweite Karriere." In *"Ich staune, dass Sie in dieser Luft atmen können." Jüdische Intellektuelle in Deutschland nach 1945*, edited by Monika Boll and Raphael Gross. Fischer, 2013.

Brandes, Ute. "Seghers's Efforts to Write About Postwar Germany." In *Anna Seghers: The Challenge of History*, edited by Helen Fehervary, Christiane Zehl Romero, and Amy Kepple Strawser. Brill, 2019.

Branfman, Jonathan. *Millennial Jewish Stars: Navigating Racial Antisemitism, Masculinity, and White Supremacy*. New York University Press, 2024.

Braun, Heinz. "Am Justizmord vorbei. Der Fall Kölling-Haas." In *Der Neue Pivatal*, edited by Robert A. Stemmle. Kurt Desch, 1965.

Brenner, Arthur D. "Feme Murder: Paramilitary 'Self-Justice' in Weimar Germany." In *Death Squads in Global Perspective*, edited by Bruce B. Campbell and Arthur D. Brenner. Palgrave Macmillan, 2000.

Brenner, Michael. *After the Holocaust: Rebuilding Jewish Lives in Postwar Germany*. Princeton University Press, 2021.

Brenner, Michael, ed. *A History of Jews in Germany Since 1945: Politics, Culture, and Society*. Indiana University Press, 2018.

Brettschneider, Marla. *Jewish Feminism and Intersectionality*. State University of New York Press, 2016.

Brockmann, Stephen. "Anna Seghers, Walter Janka, Wolfgang Harich, and the Events of 1956." In *Anna Seghers*, edited by Helen Fehervary, Christiane Zehl Romero, and Amy Kepple Strawser. Brill, 2020.

Brockmann, Stephen. "From Nazism to Socialism in Anna Seghers' 'Der Mann und sein Name.'" *German Studies Review* 37, no. 2 (2014): 297–316.

Brockmann, Stephen. *The Writers' State: Constructing East German Literature, 1945–1959*. Camden House, 2015.

Broder, Henryk M. "Die unheilbare Liebe deutscher Intellektueller zu toten und todkranken Juden." In *Eingriffe: Jahrbuch für gesellschaftskritische Umtriebe*, edited by Klaus Bittermann. Tiamat, 1988.

Brugger, Eveline, Martha Keil, Albert Lichtblau, Christoph Lind, and Barbara Staudinger. *Geschichte der Juden in Österreich*. Verlag Carl Ueberreuter, 2013.

Brühöfener, Friederike. "Contested Masculinities: Debates About Homosexuality in the West German Bundeswehr in the 1960s and 1970s." In *Gendering Post-1945 German History: Entanglements*, edited by Karen Hagemann, Donna Harsch, and Friderike Brühöfener. Berghahn, 2019.

Buchloh, Ingrid. *Veit Harlan. Goebbels' Starregisseur*. Schöningh, 2010.

Buerkle, Darcy. "Caught in the Act: Norbert Elias, Emotion, and *The Ancient Law*." *Journal of Modern Jewish Studies* 8 (2009): 83–102.

Buerkle, Darcy. "Gendered Spectatorship, Jewish Women, and Psychological Advertising in Weimar Germany." *Women's History Review* 15, no. 4 (2006): 625–36.

Buerkle, Darcy. "Landscape, Exile, and Fred Zinnemann's High Noon." In *Passagen des Exils/ Passages of Exile*, edited by Burcu Dogramaci and Elizabeth Otto. De Gruyter, 2017.

BIBLIOGRAPHY 317

Bukey, Evan Burr. *Jews and Intermarriage in Nazi Austria*. Cambridge University Press, 2011.

Carr, Steven Alan. *Hollywood and Anti-Semitism: A Cultural History up to World War II*. Cambridge University Press, 2008.

Cheyette, Bryan, ed. *Between "Race" and Culture: Representations of "the Jew" in English and American Literature*. Stanford University Press, 1996.

Cheyette, Bryan. *Constructions of "the Jew" in English Literature and Society: Racial Representations 1875–1945*. Cambridge University Press, 1995.

Cole, Alyson. *The Cult of True Victimhood: From the War on Welfare to the War on Terror*. Stanford University Press, 2007.

Confino, Alon. *Germany as a Culture of Remembrance: Promises and Limits of Writing History*. University of North Carolina Press, 2006.

Consonni, Manuela, and Vivian Liska, eds. *Sartre, Jews, and the Other: Rethinking Antisemitism, Race, and Gender*. De Gruyter, 2020.

Corbett, Tim. *Die Grabstätten meiner Väter. Die jüdischen Friedhöfe in Wien*. Böhlau, 2021.

Corbett, Tim. "'Like an Overgrown Garden . . . ?': Austrian Historical Memory and the Aftermath of Cultural Genocide at a Jewish Cemetery in Vienna." *Dapim: Studies on the Holocaust* 32, no. 3 (2018): 172–87.

Corbett, Tim, Klaus Hödl, Caroline A. Kita, Susanne Korbel, and Dirk Rupnow, eds. *Migration, Integration, and Assimilation: Reassessing Key Concepts in (Jewish) Austrian History*. Special issue of *Journal of Austrian Studies* 54, no. 1 (2021).

Cornelson, Peter. *Helmut Käunter. Seine Filme—sein Leben*. Heyne, 1980.

Crenshaw, Kimberlé Williams. "Demarginalizing the Intersection of Race and Sex: A Black Feminist Critique of Antidiscrimination Doctrine, Feminist Theory, and Antiracist Politics." *University of Chicago Legal Forum* 1 (1989): 139–67.

Crenshaw, Kimberlé. *On Intersectionality: The Seminal Essays*. New Press, 2012.

Czollek, Max. *Desintegriert Euch!* Hanser, 2018.

Dack, Mikkel. *Everyday Denazification in Postwar Germany: The Fragebogen and Political Screening During the Allied Occupation*. Cambridge University Press, 2023.

Dassanowsky, Robert. *Austrian Cinema: A History*. McFarland, 2008.

Dassanowsky, Robert. "Home/Sick. Locating Billy Wilder's Cinematic Austria in *The Apartment, The Private Life of Sherlock Holmes*, and *Fedora*." *Journal of Austrian Studies* 46, no. 3 (2013): 1–25.

Dassanowsky, Robert. "'Mon Cousin de Liernut': France as a Code for Idealized Personal and Political Identity in the 'Austrian' Novels of Alexander Lernet-Holenia." *Austrian Studies* 13 (2005): 173–90.

Dassanowsky, Robert. *Phantom Empires: The Novels of Alexander Lernet-Holenia and the Question of Postimperial Austrian Identity*. Ariadne, 1996.

Dawidowicz, Klaus. "Antisemitismus und der Nachkriegsfilm in Österreich." In *Antisemitismus in Österreich nach 1945*, edited by Christina Hainzl and Marc Grimm. Hentrich & Hentrich, 2022.

Dick, Bernard F. *Billy Wilder*. DaCapo, 1996.

Diner, Dan. "Zwischenzeit 1945 bis 1949. Über jüdische und andere Konstellationen." *Pfad: Aus Politik und Zeitgeschichte* 65 (2015): 16–20.

Dudziak, Mary L. "Josephine Baker, Racial Protest, and the Cold War." *Journal of American History* 81, no. 2 (1994): 543–70.

Eberhardt, Jennifer L. *Biased: Uncovering the Hidden Prejudice That Shapes What We See, Think, and Do*. Penguin, 2019.

Elbe, Ingo. "The Anguish of Freedom: Is Sartre's Existentialism an Appropriate Foundation for a Theory of Antisemitism?" *Antisemitism Studies* 4, no. 1 (2020): 48–81.

Engel, David. "Away from a Definition of Antiseitism: An Essay in the Semantics of Historical Description." In *Rethinking European Jewish History*, edited by Jeremy Cohen and Moshe Rosman. Littman Library, 2009.

Feagin, Joe R. *The White Racial Frame: Centuries of Racial Framing and Counter-Framing*. Routledge, 2013.

318 BIBLIOGRAPHY

Fehrenbach, Heide. *Race After Hitler: Black Occupation Children in Postwar Germany and America*. Princeton University Press, 2007.

Fenner, Angelica. *Race Under Reconstruction in German Cinema: Robert Stemmle's* Toxi. University of Toronto Press, 2011.

Fox, Thomas C. *In the Shadow of the Holocaust: Jewish-Communist Writers in East Germany*. Camden House, 2022.

Frei, Norbert. *1945 und wir. Das Dritte Reich im Bewusstsein der Deutschen*. Deutscher Taschenbuch Verlag, 2005.

Frei, Norbert. *Vergangenheitspolitik. Die Anfänge der Bunudesrepublik und die NS-Vergangenheit*. Beck, 2012.

Fremuth-Kronreif, Barbara. "Der 'Österreich-Film'. Die Realisierung einer Idee." In *1. April 2000*, edited by Ernst Kieninger, Nikola Langreiter, Armin Loacker, and Klara Löffler. Filmarchiv Austria, 2000.

Friedländer, Saul. *Nazi Germany and the Jews: The Years of Persecution, 1933–1939*, vol. I. Harper, 1997.

Fritsche, Maria. *Homemade Men in Postwar Austrian Cinema*. Berghahn, 2013.

Fritsch-Vivié, Gabriele. *Gegen alle Widerstände. Der jüdische Kulturbund 1933–1941*. Hentrich & Hentrich, 2013.

Fuchs, Christoph. "Rudolf Brunngraber (1901–1960)." *Literatur und Kritik* 317–318 (1997): 103–9.

Fulbrook, Mary. "East Germans in a Post-Nazi State: Communities of Experience, Connection, and Identification." In *Becoming East German: Socialist Structures and Sensibilities After Hitler*, edited by Mary Fulbrook and Andrew I. Port. Berghahn, 2013.

Gabler, Neal. *Winchell: Gossip, Power and the Culture of Celebrity*. Knopf, 1994.

Garrett, Leah. *Young Lions: How Jewish Authors Reinvented the American War Novel*. Northwestern University Press, 2015.

Geller, Jay Howard. *Jews in Post-Holocaust Germany, 1945–1953*. Cambridge University Press, 2005.

Geller, Jay Howard, and Michael Meng, eds. *Rebuilding Jewish Life in Germany*. Rutgers University Press, 2020.

Gemünden, Gerd. *A Foreign Affair: Billy Wilder's American Films*. Berghahn, 2008.

Gilman, Sander L. *Inscribing the Other*. University of Nebraska Press, 1991.

Gilman, Sander L. *Jewish Self-Hatred*. Johns Hopkins University Press, 1985.

Goldman, Eric A. *The American Jewish Story Through Cinema*. University of Texas Press, 2013.

Goldstein, Eric L. *The Price of Whiteness: Jews, Race, and American Identity*. Princeton University Press, 2006.

Gordan, Rachel. "Laura Z. Hobson and the Making of *Gentleman's Agreement*." *Studies in American Jewish Literature* 34, no. 2 (2015): 231–56.

Gordan, Rachel. *Postwar Stories: How Books Made Judaism American*. Oxford University Press, 2024.

Graf, Philipp. "Twice Exiled: Leo Zuckermann (1908–85) and the Limits of the Communist Promise." *Journal of Contemporary History* 56, no. 3 (2020): 766–88.

Greenberg, Cheryl. "Pluralism and Its Discontents: The Case of Blacks and Jews." In *Insider/Outsider: American Jews and Multiculturalism*, edited by David Biale, Michael Galchinsky, and Susannah Heschel. University of California Press, 1998.

Gross, Jan T. *Fear: Anti-Semitism in Poland After Auschwitz: An Essay in Historical Interpretation*. Random House, 2006.

Grubel, Fred. *Schreib das auf eine Tafel die mit ihnen bleibt. Jüdisches Leben im 20. Jahrhundert*. Böhlau, 1998.

Hacohen, Malachi. *Jacob & Esau: Jewish European History Between Nation and Empire*. Cambridge University Press, 2019.

HaCohen, Ruth. *The Music Libel Against the Jews*. Yale University Press, 2013.

Hagemann, Albrecht. *Hermann Rauschning. Ein deutsches Leben zwischen NS-Ruhm und Exil*. Böhlau, 2018.

BIBLIOGRAPHY   319

Hake, Sabine. *Popular Cinema of the Third Reich*. University of Texas Press, 2001.
Hamacher, Bernd. "Alexander Lernet-Holenia und das Judentum." In *Schuld-Komplexe. Das Werk Alexander Lernet-Holenias im Nachkriegskontext*, edited by Hélène Barrière, Thomas Eicher, and Manfred Müller. Athena, 2004.
Hammerschlag, Sarah. *The Figural Jew: Politics and Identity in Postwar French Thought*. University of Chicago Press, 2010.
Hammerstein, Katrin. *Gemeinsame Vergangenheit–getrennte Erinnerung? Der Nationalsozialismus in Gedächtnisdiskursen und Identitätskonstruktionen von Bundesrepublik Deutschland, DDR, und Österreich*. Wallstein, 2017.
Hanak, Peter. "Acquittal—but No Happy Ending." *New Hungarian Quarterly* 10 (1969): 119–25.
Handler, Andrew. *Blood Libel at Tiszaeszlar*. East European Monographs, 1980.
Hanebrink, Paul. *A Specter Haunting Europe: The Myth of Judeo-Bolshevism*. Harvard University Press, 2018.
Haney, Lynn. *Naked at the Feast: A Biography of Josephine Baker*. Dodd, Mead, 1981.
Hans, Anjeana K. " 'The World Is Funny, Like a Dream': Franziska Gaal's *Verwechslungskomödien* and Exile's Crisis of Identity." In *Rethinking Jewishness in Weimar Cinema*, edited by Barbara Hales and Valerie Weinstein. Berghahn, 2020.
Harrowitz, Nancy A., ed. *Tainted Greatness: Antisemitism and Cultural Heroes*. Temple University Press, 1994.
Hecht, Dieter J., Eleonore Lappin-Eppel, and Michaela Raggam-Blesch. *Topographie der Shoah. Gedächtnisorte des zerstörten jüdischen Wiens*. Mandelbaum, 2015.
Heiss, Gernot. "Österreich am 1. April 2000—das Bild von Gegenwart und Vergangenheit im Zukunftstraum von 1952." In *Wiederaufbau in Österreich, 1945–1955. Rekonstruktion oder Neubeginn?*, edited by Ernst Brückmüller. Verlag für Geschichte und Politik, 2006.
Hell, Julia. *Post-Fascist Fantasies: Psychoanalysis, History, and the Literature of East Germany*. Duke University Press, 1997.
Henne, Thomas, and Arne Riedlinger, eds. *Das Lüth-Urteil aus (rechts-) historischer Sicht. Die Konflikte um Veit Harlan und die Grundrechtsjudikatur des Bundesverfassungsgerichts*. Wissenschafts-Verlag, 2005.
Herf, Jeffrey. *Divided Memory: The Nazi Past in the Two Germanies*. Harvard University Press, 1997.
Herf, Jeffrey. "Dokumentation. Antisemitismus in der SED. Geheime Dokumente zum Fall Paul Merker aus SED- und WS-Archivem." *Vierteljahreshefte für Zeitgeschichte* 4 (1994): 635–67.
Herf, Jeffrey. "East German Communists and the Jewish Question: The Case of Paul Merker." German Historical Institute, occasional paper 11. German Historical Institute, 1994.
Herf, Jeffrey. *The Jewish Enemy: Nazi Propaganda During World War II and the Holocaust*. Harvard University Press, 2009.
Hermann, Ingo, ed. *Hilde Spiel, die Grande Dame. Gespräch mit Anne Linsel*. Lamuv, 1992.
Herzog, Hillary Hope. *"Vienna Is Different": Jewish Writers in Austria from the Fin-de-Siècle to the Present*. Berghahn, 2011.
Hirsch, Lily E. *A Jewish Orchestra in Nazi Germany: Musical Politics and the Berlin Jewish Culture League*. University of Michigan Press, 2010.
Homering, Wolfgang, ed. *Ida Ehre. Im Gespräch mit Sepp Schelz*. Ullstein, 1999.
Horn, Dara. *People Love Dead Jews: Reports from a Haunted Present*. Norton, 2021.
Hughes, Jon. "Facts and Fiction: Rudolf Brunngraber, Otto Neurath, and Viennese Neue Sachlichkeit." In *Interwar Vienna: Culture Between Tradition and Modernity*, edited by Deborah Holmes and Lisa Silverman. Camden House, 2009.
Jacobson, Matthew Frye. *Whiteness of a Different Color: European Immigrants and the Alchemy of Race*. Harvard University Press, 1999.
Jahr, Christoph. *Antisemitismus vor Gericht. Debatten über die juristische Ahndung judenfeindlicher Agitation in Deutschland (1879–1960)*. Campus, 2011.
Jaskot, Paul B. *The Nazi Perpetrator: Postwar German Art and the Politics of the Right*. University of Minnesota Press, 2012.

320 BIBLIOGRAPHY

Jay, Martin. "The Jews and the Frankfurt School: Critical Theory's Analysis of Anti-Semitism." *New German Critique* 19 (1980): 137–49.

Jelavich, Peter. *Berlin Cabaret*. Harvard University Press, 1996.

Jelavich, Peter. "Popular Entertainment and Mass Media: The Central Arenas of German-Jewish Cultural Engagement." In *The German-Jewish Experience Revisited*, edited by Steven E. Aschheim and Vivan Liska. De Gruyter, 2015.

Jockusch, Laura, and Gabriel N. Finder, eds. *Jewish Honor Courts: Revenge, Retribution, and Reconciliation in Europe and Israel After the Holocaust*. Wayne State University Press, 2015.

Joos, Verena. *"Mutter Courage des Theaters" Ida Ehre*. Econ, 1999.

Judaken, Jonathan. "Between Philosemitism and Antisemitism: The Frankfurt School's Anti-antisemitism." In *Antisemitism and Philosemitism in the Twentieth and Twenty-First Centuries: Representing Jews, Jewishness, and Modern Culture*, edited by Phyllis Lassner and Lara Trubowitz. University of Delaware Press, 2008.

Judaken, Jonathan. *Critical Theories of Anti-Semitism*. Columbia University Press, 2024.

Judaken, Jonathan. *Jean-Paul Sartre and the Jewish Question: Anti-Antisemitism and the Politics of the French Intellectual*. University of Nebraska Press, 2006.

Jules-Rosette, Bennetta. *Josephine Baker in Art and Life: The Icon and the Image*. University of Illinois Press, 2007.

Jureit, Ulrike, and Christian Schneider. *Gefühlte Opfer. Illusionen der Vergangenheitsbewältigung*. Klett-Cotta, 2010.

Kahn-Harris, Keith. *Strange Hate: Antisemitism, Racism, and the Limits of Diversity*. Repeater Books, 2019.

Kannapin, Detlef. *Antifaschismus im Film der DDR. DEFA Spielfilme 1945–1955/56*. PapyRossa, 1997.

Kannapin, Detlef. *Dialektik der Bilder, Der Nationalsozialismus im deutschen Film. Ein Ost-West-Vergleich*. Karl Dietz, 2005.

Kastberger, Klaus. "Afterword." In *Prozess auf Tod und Leben* by Rudolf Brunngraber. Milena, 2011.

Kessler, Mario. *Die SED und die Juden. Zwischen Repression und Toleranz. Politische Entwicklung bis 1967*. Akademie Verlag, 1995.

Kiessling, Wolfgang. *Partner im "Narrenparadies." Der Freundeskreis um Noel Field und Paul Merker*. Dietz, 1994.

Kiessling, Wolfgang. *Paul Merker in den Fangen der Sicherheitsorgane Stalins und Ulbrichts*. Helle Panke, 1995.

Kitzberger, Michael. "Das Volk, die Fremden, der Held und die Bilder davon. Zu G.W. Pabsts *Der Prozess*." In *Ohne Untertitel. Fragmente einer Geschichte des österreichischen Kinos*, edited by Ruth Beckermann and Christa Bliminger. Sonderzahl, 1996.

Kleinlercher, Alexandra. *Zwischen Wahrheit und Dichtung. Antisemitismus und Nationalsozialismus bei Heimito von Doderer*. Böhlau, 2011.

Klöters, Jacques. "'Momente so, Momente so.' Dora Gerson und das erste Emigranten Kabarett 'Ping-Pong.'" In *Die Niederlande und das deutsche Exil 1933–1940*, edited by Katinka Dittrich and Hans Würzner. Athenäum, 1982.

Klurfeld, Herman. *Winchell: His Life and Times*. Praeger, 1976.

Knight, Robert. "National Construction Work and Hierarchies of Empathy in Postwar Austria." *Journal of Contemporary History* 49, no. 3 (2014): 491–513.

Knight, Robert. "'Neutrality' Not Sympathy: Jews in Post-War Austria." In *Austrians and Jews in the Twentieth Century: From Franz Joseph to Waldheim*, edited by Robert S. Wistrich. Palgrave Macmillan, 1992.

Knilli, Friedrich. *Ich war Jud Süss. Die Geschichte des Filmstars Ferdinand Marian*. Henschel, 2010.

Koch, Anna. "'After Auschwitz You Must Take Your Origins Seriously': Perceptions of Jewishness Among Communists of Jewish Origin in the Early German Democratic Republic." In *Jewish Lives Under Communism: New Perspectives*, edited by Katerina Capková and Kamil Kijek. Rutgers University Press, 2022.

BIBLIOGRAPHY 321

Koch, Anna. "Exile Dreams: Antifascist Jews, Antisemitism and the 'Other Germany.'" *Fascism: Journal of Comparative Fascist Studies* 9 (2020): 221–43.

Koch, Anna. *Home After Fascism: Italian and German Jews After the Holocaust.* Indiana University Press, 2023.

Koelbl, Herlinde. *Jüdische Portraits. Photographien und Interviews.* S. Fischer, 1989.

Kowarc, Susanne, Georg Graf, Brigitte Bailer-Galanda, and Eva Blimlinger. *"Ariesierung" und Rückstellung von Wohnungen in Wien.* Veröffentlichungen der österreichischen Historikerkommission, vol. 14. Böhlau, 2004.

Kropiunigg, Rafael. *Eine österreichische Affäre. Der Fall Borodajkewycz.* Czernin, 2015.

Lamblin, Bianca. *A Disgraceful Affair: Simone de Beauvoir, Jean-Paul Sartre, and Bianca Lamblin.* Northeastern University Press, 1996.

Lapidot, Elad. *Jews out of the Question: A Critique of Anti-Anti-Semitism.* State University of New York Press, 2020.

Lapidot, Elad, and Hannah Tzuberi. "Jewish Friends: Contemporary Figures of the Jew: Introduction." *Jewish Studies Quarterly* 27, no. 2 (2020): 103–75.

Lappin, Eleonore. "Jüdische Lebenserinnerungen. Rekonstruktionen von jüdischer Kindheit und Jugend im Wien der Zwischenkriegzeit." In *Wien und die jüdische Erfahrung 1900–1938*, edited by Frank Stern and Barbara Eichinger. Böhlau, 2009.

Lauckner, Nancy. "The Surrogate Jew in the Postwar German Novel." *Monatshefte* 66, no. 2 (1974): 133–44.

Laumann, Vivien, and Judith Coffey. *Gojnormativität. Warum wir anders über Antisemitismus sprechen müssen.* Verbrecher Verlag, 2021.

Layne, Priscilla. "'Don't Look So Sad Because You're a Little Negro': Marie Nejar, Afro-German Stardom, and Negotiations with Black Subjectivity." *Palimpsest: A Journal on Women, Gender, and the Black International* 4, no. 2 (2015): 171–87.

Leiser, Erwin. *Deutschland Erwache! Propaganda im Film des Dritten Reiches.* Rowohlt, 1968.

Lendvai, Paul. *Anti-Semitism Without Jews: Communist Eastern Europe.* Doubleday, 1971.

Levi, Neil. *Modernist Form and the Myth of Jewification.* Fordham University Press, 2014.

Liebert, Frank. "Vom Karrierestreben zum 'Nötigungsnotstand,' *Jud Süss,* Veit Harlan und die westdeutsche Nachkriegsgesellschaft (1945–1950)." In *Das Lüth-Urteil aus (rechts-) historischer Sicht. Die Konflikte um Veit Harlan und die Grundrechtsjudikatur des Bundesverfassungsgerichts*, edited by Thomas Henne and Arne Riedlinger. Berliner Wissenschafts-Verlag, 2005.

Loacker, Armin. "Das offizielle Österreich dreht einen Film. Ein Resümee zum Staatsfilm *1. April 2000.*" In *1. April 2000*, edited by Ernst Kieninger, Nikola Langreiter, Armin Loacker, and Klara Löffler. Filmarchiv, 2000.

Loewenstein, Andrea Freud. *Loathsome Jews and Engulfing Women: Metaphors of Projection in the Works of Wyndham Lewis, Charles Williams, and Graham Greene.* New York University Press, 1993.

Maier-Katkin, Birgit. *Silence and Acts of Memory: A Postwar Discourse on Literature, History, Anna Seghers, and Women in the Third Reich.* Bucknell University Press, 2007.

Manne, Kate. *Down Girl: The Logic of Misogyny.* Oxford University Press, 2018.

Marin, Bernd. "A Post-Holocaust 'Anti-Semitism Without Anti-Semites'? Austria as a Case in Point." *Political Psychology* 2, no. 2 (1980): 57–74.

McGlothlin, Erin. *The Mind of the Holocaust Perpetrator in Fiction and Nonfiction.* Wayne State University Press, 2021.

McVeigh, Joseph. "The Cold War in the Coffeehouse: Hans Weigel and His Circle of Writers in the Café Raimund." *Journal of Austrian Studies* 48, no. 3 (Fall 2015): 65–87.

Megargee, Geoffrey P., ed. *United States Holocaust Memorial Museum Encyclopedia of Camps and Ghettos, 1933–1945,* vol. 1. Indiana University Press, 2009.

Meining, Stefan. *Kommunistische Judenpolitik. Die DDR, die Juden und Israel.* Lit, 2021.

Melichar, Peter. "Who Is a Jew? Antisemitic Defining, Identifying and Counting in pre-1938 Austria." *Leo Baeck Institute Year Book* 50 (2005): 149–74.

322 BIBLIOGRAPHY

Mertens, Lothar. *Soziale Ungleichheit in der DDR. Zu einem tabuisierten Strukturmerkmal der SED-Diktatur.* Duncker & Humblot, 2002.

Micheler, Kerstin. "Hilde Spiels 'The Streets of Vineta' (1946) und 'Rückkehr nach Wien' (1968): Ein Vergleich." MA thesis, University of Vienna, 2018.

Miller, Michael L. "Filming Ritual Murder after the Shoah: Exculpation, Deflection or Contrition?" *East European Jewish Affairs* March (2025): 1–11. https://doi.org/10.1080/13501674.2025.2480732.

Mills, Charles W. *Black Rights/White Wrongs: The Critique of Racial Liberalism.* Oxford University Press, 2017.

Mintzker, Yair. *The Many Deaths of Jew Süss: The Notorious Trial and Execution of an Eighteenth-Century Court Jew.* Princeton University Press, 2019.

Mitten, Richard. "Jews and Other Victims: The 'Jewish Question' and Discourses of Victimhood in Postwar Austria." In *Austria in the European Union,* edited by Günter Bischof, Anton Pelinka, and Michael Gehler. Transaction, 2002.

Moeller, Felix. "'Ich bin Künstler und sonst nichts.' Filmstars im Propagandaeinsatz." In *Hitlers Künstler. Die Kultur im Dienst des Nationalsozialismus,* edited by Hans Sarkowicz. Insel, 2004.

Moeller, Robert C. "When Liebe Was Just a Five-Letter Word." In *German Postwar Films: Life and Love in the Ruins,* edited by Wilfried Wilms and William Rasch. Palgrave, 2008.

Moltke, Johannes von. *No Place Like Home: Locations of Heimat in German Cinema.* University Of California Press, 2005.

Morowitz, Laura. *Art, Exhibition and Erasure in Nazi Vienna.* Routledge, 2024.

Morowitz, Laura. "'Heil the Hero Klimt!': Nazi Aesthetics in Vienna and the 1943 Gustav Klimt Retrospective." *Oxford Art Journal* 39, no. 1 (2006): 107–29.

Morowitz, Laura. "Reviled, Repressed, Resurrected: Vienna 1900 in the Nazi Imaginary." *Austrian History Yearbook* 53 (2022): 169–89.

Mounk, Yascha. *Stranger in My Own Country: A Jewish Family in Modern Germany.* Farrar, Straus, and Giroux, 2015.

Mückenberger, Christiane. "Zeit der Hoffnungen, 1946 bis 1949." In *Das zweite Leben der Filmstadt Babelsberg. DEFA-Spielfilme 1946–1992,* edited by Ralf Schenk. Filmmuseum Potsdam, 1994.

Neunzig, Hans A., ed. *Die Dämonie der Gemütlichkeit.* List, 1991.

Niether, Hendrik. *Leipziger Juden und die DDR. Eine Existenzerfahrung im Kalten Krieg.* Vandenhoeck & Ruprecht, 2015.

Nilsson, Mikael. *Hitler Redux: The Incredible History of Hitler's So-Called Table Talks.* Routledge, 2020.

Nirenberg, David. *Anti-Judaism: The Western Tradition.* Norton, 2013.

Nissen, Theodor. "Zu den ältesten Fassungen der Legende vom Judenknaben." *Zeitschrift für französische Sprache und Literatur* 62, no. 7/8 (1939): 393–403.

Niven, Bill, ed. *Germans as Victims: Remembering the Past in Contemporary Germany.* Palgrave, 2006.

Niven, Bill. *Hitler and Film: The Führer's Hidden Passion.* Yale University Press, 2018.

Niven, Bill. *Jud Süss. Das lange Leben eines Propagandafilms.* Mitteldeutscher Verlag, 2022.

Niven, Bill. "Remembering Nazi Anti-Semitism in the GDR." In *Memorialization in Germany Since 1945,* edited by Bill Niven and Chloe Paver. Palgrave Macmillan, 2010.

Niven, Bill. *Representations of Flight and Expulsion in East German Prose Works.* Camden House, 2014.

Noack, Frank. *Veit Harlan:"des Teufels Regisseur."* Belleville, 2000.

Noack, Frank. *Veit Harlan: The Life and Work of a Nazi Filmmaker.* University of Kentucky Press, 2016.

Ó Dochartaigh, Pól, and Christiane Schönfeld, eds. *Representing the "Good German" in Literature and Culture After 1945.* Camden House, 2013.

BIBLIOGRAPHY 323

Oertel, Christine. *Juden auf der Flucht durch Austria. Jüdische Displaced Persons in der US-Besatzungszone Österreichs.* W. Eichbauer, 1999.

Oxaal, Ivar, Michael Pollak, and Gerhard Botz. *Jews, Antisemitism and Culture in Vienna.* Routledge, 2020.

Pardo, Herbert, and Siegfried Schiffner. *Jud Süss. Historisches und juristisches Material zum Fall Veit Harlan.* Auerdruck, 1949.

Parkinson, Anna M. *An Emotional State: The Politics of Emotion in Postwar West German Culture.* University of Michigan Press, 2015.

Pauley, Bruce F. *From Prejudice to Persecution: A History of Austrian Anti-Semitism.* University of North Carolina Press, 1992.

Peitsch, Helmut. "Antifaschistisches Verständnis der eigenen jüdischen Herkunft in Texten von DDR-Schriftstellerinnen." In *Kulturerbe deutschsprachiger Juden. Eine Spurensuche in den Ursprungs-, Transit- und Emigrationsländern,* edited by Elke-Vera Kotowski. De Gruyter, 2015.

Pelinka, Anton. "Taboos and Self-Deception: The Second Republic's Reconstruction of History." In *Austrian Historical Memory and National Identity,* edited by Günter Bischof and Anton Pelinka. Transaction, 1997.

Perz, Bertrand. "Österreich." In *Verbrechen erinnern. Die Auseinandersetzung mit Holocaust und Völkermord,* edited by Volkshard Knigge and Norbert Frei, 170–82. Bundeszentrale für Politische Bildung, 2005.

Petersen, Vibeke Rützou. "Zillich's End: The Formation of a Fascist Character in Anna Segher's 'Das Ende.'" *Seminar* 29, no. 4 (1993): 370–78.

Pinkert, Anke. *Film and Memory in East Germany.* Indiana University Press, 2008.

Pleyer, Peter. *Deutscher Nachkriegsfilm 1946–1948.* C. J. Fahle, 1965.

Postone, Moishe. "Anti-Semitism and National Socialism." In *Germans and Jews Since the Holocaust: The Changing Situation in West Germany,* edited by Anson Rabinbach and Jack Zipes. Holmes & Meier, 1986.

Postone, Moishe. "Zionism, Anti-Semitism and the Left." February 5, 2010. https://www.workersliberty.org/files/100205postone.pdf. Accessed March 16, 2023.

Prümm, Karl. "Dark Shadows and a Pale Victory of Reason: The Trial (1948)." In *The Films of G.W. Pabst: An Extraterritorial Cinema,* edited by Eric Rentschler. Rutgers University Press, 1990.

Rabinbach, Anson. "Why Were the Jews Sacrificed? The Place of Anti-Semitism in *Dialectic of Enlightenment.*" *New German Critique* 81 (2000): 49–64.

Rabinovici, Doron. *Eichmann's Jews: The Jewish Administration of Holocaust Vienna, 1938–1945.* Polity, 2011.

Raggam-Blesch, Michaela. "'Privileged' Under Nazi-Rule: The Fate of Three Intermarried Families in Vienna." *Journal of Genocide Research* 21, no. 3 (2019): 378–97.

Rahden, Till van. "Clumsy Democrats: Moral Passions in the Federal Republic." *German History* 29, no. 3 (2011): 485–504.

Rathkolb, Oliver. *The Paradoxical Republic: Austria 1945–2005.* Berghahn, 2010.

Rathkolb, Oliver. "Zur Kontinuität. Antisemitischer und Rassistischer Vorurteile in Österreich 1945/1950." *Zeitgeschichte* 16, no. 5 (1989): 167–79.

Regester, Charlene. "The Construction of an Image and the Deconstruction of a Star: Josephine Baker Racialized, Sexualized, and Politicized in the African-American Press, the Mainstream Press, and FBI Files." *Popular Music & Society* 24, no. 1 (2000): 31–84.

Reimer, Robert C., and Carol J. Reimer. *Historical Dictionary of German Cinema.* Rowman and Littlefield, 2019.

Reiter, Margit. *Die Ehemaligen. Der Nationalsozialismus und die Anfänge der FPÖ.* Wallstein Verlag, 2019.

Rensmann, Lars. *The Politics of Unreason: The Frankfurt School and the Origins of Modern Antisemitism.* State University of New York Press, 2017.

324   BIBLIOGRAPHY

Rentschler, Eric. *The Ministry of Illusion: Nazi Cinema and Its Afterlife.* Harvard University Press, 1996.

Riedlinger, Arne. "Vom Boykottaufruf zur Verfassungsbeschwerde. Erich Lüth und die Kontroverse um Harlans Nachkriegsfilme (1950–58)." In *Das Lüth-Urteil aus (rechts-) historischer Sicht. Die Konflikte um Veit Harlan und die Grundrechtsjudikatur des Bundesverfassungsgerichts,* edited by Thomas Henne and Arne Riedlinger. Wissenschafts-Verlag, 2005.

Rinio, Carsten. "Walter Tyrolf, Richter und Staatsanwalt im Dritten Reich (und danach)." *Mitteilungen des Hamburgischen Richtervereins* 1 (2022): 11–20.

Rogge-Gau, Sylvia. *Die doppelte Wurzel des Daseins. Julius Bab und der Jüdische Kulutrbund Berlin.* Metropol, 1999.

Rohrbach, Philipp. "Life Stories of Children of Black US Occupation Soldiers and Austrian Women." *Journal of Austrian Studies* 56, no. 4 (2023): 77–88.

Rolinek, Susanne. *Jüdische Lebenswelten 1945–1955. Flüchtlinge in der amerikanischen Zone Österreichs.* Studienverlag, 2007.

Romero, Christiane Zehl. "Netty Reiling's Student Years at the University of Heidelberg." In *Anna Seghers: The Challenge of History,* edited by Helen Fehervary, Christiane Zehl Romero, and Amy Kepple Strawser. Brill, 2019.

Roscher, Achim. "Wirkung des Geschriebenen. Gespräche mit Anna Seghers." *Neue deutsche Literatur* 10 (1983): 61–75.

Rosenblum, Warren. "Jews, Justice, and the Power of 'Sensation' in the Weimar Republic." *Leo Baeck Institute Year-Book* 58 (2013): 35–52.

Rosenfeld, Gavriel D. *The Fourth Reich: The Specter of Nazism from World War II to the Present.* Cambridge University Press, 2019.

Rothberg, Michael. *The Implicated Subject: Beyond Victims and Perpetrators.* Stanford University Press, 2019.

Rothe, Anne. "The Third Reich and the Holocaust in East German Memory." In *Comparative Central European Holocaust Studies,* edited by Steven Tötösy de Zepetnik and Louise O. Vasvári. Purdue University Press, 2009.

Rovit, Rebecca. *The Jewish Kulturbund Theatre Company in Nazi Berlin.* University of Iowa Press, 2012.

Rueschmeyer, Marilyn. "A Jewish Writer in East Germany." *European Judaism: A Journal for the New Europe* 17, no. 1 (1983): 35–37.

Rupprecht, Caroline. "Melzer and the Dead Sea Scrolls: Anna Seghers's GDR Novel *Die Entscheidung* (1959)." *Leo Baeck Institute Year Book* 69 (2024): 163–81.

Schivelbusch, Wolfgang. *In a Cold Crater: Cultural and Intellectual Life in Berlin, 1945–1948.* University of California Press, 1998.

Schmid, Harald. *Antifaschismus und Judenverfolgung. Die "Reichskristallnacht" als politischer Gedenktag in der DDR.* Vandenhoeck and Ruprecht, 2004.

Schmidt, Monika. *Übergriffe auf verwaiste jüdische Gräber. Friedhofsschändungen in der SBZ und der DDR.* Metropol, 2016.

Schneer, David. "Singing Between Two Worlds: Lin Jaldati and Yiddish Music in Cold War Europe and Divided Berlin, 1945–1953." *Journal of Modern Jewish Studies* 20, no. 2 (2021): 248–73.

Schneider, Ulrike. "Verhältnis zum Judentum." In *Anna Seghers-Handbuch. Leben–Werk–Wirkung,* edited by Carola Hilmes and Ilse Nagelschmidt. Metzler, 2020.

Schneider, Ursula. "Rudolf Brunngraber. Eine Monographie." PhD dissertation, University of Vienna, 1990.

Schölnberger, Pia, and Sabine Loitfellner, eds. *Bergung von Kulturgut im Nationalsozialismus. Mythen-Hintergründe-Auswirkungen.* Böhlau, 2016.

Schönfeld, Christiane. "Fritz Kortner's Return to Germany and the Figure of the Returning Exile in Kortner's *The Mission* and Josef v. Báky's *Der Ruf.*" *Feuchtwanger-Studien* 3 (2013): 475–94.

BIBLIOGRAPHY 325

Schraub, David. "The Epistemic Dimension of Antisemitism." *Journal of Jewish Identities* 15, no. 2 (2022): 153–79.

Schraub, David, "White Jews: An Intersectional Approach." *AJS Review* 43, no. 2 (2019): 379–407.

Schuchnig, Josef. "G.W. Pabst und die Darstellung der neuen Sachlichkeit im Film, aufgezeigt anhand einiger beispielhafter Filme von Pabst." PhD dissertation, University of Vienna, 1976.

Schüler-Springorum, Stefanie. "Gender and the Politics of Anti-Semitism." *The American Historical Review* 123, no. 4 (2018): 1210–22.

Schulte, Klaus. " 'Was ist denn das überhaupt, ein Jude?' Anna Seghers' Einspruch anlässlich der antisemitischen Hetze gegen die Insassen der Berliner Transitlager für 'displaced persons' in der Presse der Vier-Sektoren-Stadt im Jahre 1948. Rekonstruktion, Lektüre, Kommentar." *Jahrbuch für Kommunikationsgeschichte* 4 (2002): 196–231.

Schulte-Sasse, Linda. *Entertaining the Third Reich: The Illusions of Wholeness in Nazi Cinema.* Duke University Press, 1996.

Seidl, Ernst, ed. *'Jud Süss. Propagandafilm im NS-Staat. Katalog zur Ausstellung im Haus der Geschichte Baden-Württemberg.* Haus der Geschichte Baden-Württemberg, 2007.

Shandler, Jeffrey. *While America Watches: Televising the Holocaust.* Oxford University Press, 2000.

Shandley, Robert. *Rubble Films: German Cinema in the Shadow of the Third Reich.* Temple University Press, 2001.

Shelden, Michael. *Graham Greene: The Enemy Within.* Random House, 1994.

Siegel, Carol. *Jews in Contemporary Visual Entertainment: Raced, Sexed, and Erased.* Indiana University Press, 2022.

Sikov, Ed. *On Sunset Boulevard: The Life and Times of Billy Wilder.* Hyperion, 1998.

Silverman, Lisa. "Absent Jews and Invisible Antisemitism in Postwar Vienna: *Der Prozess* (1948) and *The Third Man* (1949)." *Journal of Contemporary History* 52, no. 2 (2017): 211–28.

Silverman, Lisa. "Beyond Antisemitism: A Critical Approach to German Jewish Cultural History." *Nexus 1: Essays in German Jewish Studies* (2011): 27–45.

Silverman, Lisa. *Becoming Austrians: Jews and Culture between the World Wars.* Oxford University Press, 2012.

Silverman, Lisa. "Der Film ohne Juden: G.W. Pabst's *Die Freudlose Gasse* (1925)." In *Jewishness in Weimar Cinema*, edited by Barbara Hales and Valerie Weinstein. Berghahn, 2020.

Silverman, Lisa. "Reconsidering the Margins: Jewishness as an Analytical Framework." *Journal of Modern Jewish Studies* 8, no. 1 (2009): 103–20.

Silverman, Lisa. "Revealing Jews: Culture and Visibility in Modern Central Europe." *Shofar: An Interdisciplinary Journal of Jewish Studies* 36, no. 1 (2018): 134–60.

Slobodian, Quinn. "Socialist Chromatism: Race, Racism, and the Racial Rainbow in East Germany." In *Comrades of Color: East Germany in the Cold War World*, edited by Quinn Slobodian. Berghahn, 2015.

Smith, Dana. *Jewish Art in Nazi Germany: The Jewish Cultural League in Bavaria.* Routledge, 2022.

Smith, Eliot R., and Diane M. Mackie. "Agression, Hatred and Other Emotions." In *On the Nature of Prejudice: Fifty Years After Allport*, edited by John F. Dovidio, Peter Glick, and Laurie A. Rudman. Blackwell, 2005.

Spira, Leopold. *Feindbild "Jud." 100 Jahre politischer Antisemitismus in Österreich.* Löcker, 1981.

Steffen-Fluhr, Nancy. "Palimpsest: The Double Vision of Exile." In *Billy Wilder Movie-Maker: Critical Essays on the Film*, edited by Karen McNally. McFarland, 2011.

Steiner, Gertraud. "Die Heimat-Macher. Wer bestimmte den österreichischen Heimat-Film nach 1945?" In *Verdrängte Kultur. Österreich 1918–1938, 1968–1988*, edited by Oliver Rathkolb and Freidrich Stadler. Mitteilung des Instituts für Wissenschaft und Kunst, 1990.

Stern, Frank. *The Whitewashing of the Yellow Badge: Antisemitism and Philosemitism in Postwar Germany.* Pergamon, 1992.

326 BIBLIOGRAPHY

Stern, Frank, Julia B. Köhne, Karin Moser, Thomas Ballhausen, and Barbara Eichinge, eds. *Filmische Gedächtnisse. Geschichte—Archiv—Riss.* Mandelbaum, 2007.

Stögner, Karin. "Der Antisemitismus und das Konzept der Intersektionalität." In *Handbuch Int ersektionalitätsforschung,* edited by Astrid Biele Mefebue, Andrea D. Bührmann, and Sabine Grenz. Springer, 2022.

Stögner, Karin. "New Challenges in Feminism. Intersectionality, Critical Theory, and Anti-Zionism." In *Anti-Zionism and Antisemitism: The Dynamics of Deligitimization,* edited by Alvin H. Rosenfeld. Indiana University Press, 2019.

Stratton, Jon. *Coming out Jewish: Constructing Ambivalent Identities.* Routledge, 2000.

Straub, Martin. " 'Sie bauten ihr furchtbar geschlagenes Land auf, selbst furchtbar geschlagen.' Anna Seghers' Erzählung 'Der Mann und sein Name.' "*Argonautenschiff: Jahrbuch der Anna-Seghers-Gesellschaft* 8 (1999): 103–16.

Stringer, Rebecca. *Knowing Victims: Feminism, Agency and Victim Politics in Neoliberal Times.* Routledge, 2014.

Szabó, Róbert G. "Anti-Zionism in the Show Trials in Rákosi Era Hungary (1948–1953)." *Journal of Modern Jewish Studies* (2024): 1–26. https://doi.org/10.1080/14725 886.2024.2381637.

Tanzer, Frances. "Performing the Austrian-Jewish (Negative) Symbiosis: Stella Kadmon's Viennese Stage from Red Vienna to the Second Republic." *Leo Baeck Institute Year Book* 63 (2018): 1–19.

Tanzer, Frances. *Vanishing Vienna: Jewish Absence in Post-Nazi Central Europe.* University of Pennsylvania Press, 2024.

Tegel, Susan. *Jew Süss: Life, Legend, Fiction, Film.* Continuum, 2011.

Teter, Magda. *Blood Libel: On the Trail of an Antisemitic Myth.* Harvard University Press, 2020.

Teter, Magda. *Christian Supremacy: Reckoning with the Roots of Antisemitism and Racism.* Princeton University Press, 2023.

Timm, Angelika. *Hammer, Zirkel, Davidstern. Das gestörte Verhältnis der DDR zu Zionismus und Staat Israel.* Bouvier, 1997.

Tschiggerl, Martin. "Significant Otherness: Nation-Building and Identity in Postwar Austria." *Nations and Nationalism* 27, no. 3 (2021): 782–96.

Uhl, Heidemarie. "From Discourse to Representation: 'Austrian Memory' in Public Space." In *Narrating the Nation: Representations in History, Media and the Arts,* edited by Stefan Berger, Linas Eriksonas, and Andrew Mycock. Berghahn, 2008.

Uhl, Heidemarie. "From Victim Myth to Co-Responsibility Thesis: Nazi Rule, World War II, and the Holocaust in Austrian Memory." In *The Politics of Memory in Postwar Europe,* edited by Richard Ned Lebow, Wulf Kansteiner, and Claudio Fogu. Duke University Press, 2006.

Vansant, Jacqueline. *Austria: Made in Hollywood.* Camden House, 2019.

Vogt, Jochen. "What Became of the Girl: A Minor Archaeology of an Occasional Text by Anna Seghers." *New German Critique* 82 (2001): 145–65.

Völker, Klaus. " 'Wir spielen . . .' Helmut Käutners Leben." In *Käutner,* edited by Wolfgang Jacobsen and Hans Helmut Prinzler. Volker Spiess, 1992.

Völker, Klaus. *Fritz Kortner. Schauspieler und Regisseur.* Edition Hentrich, 1987.

Volkov, Shulamit. "Antisemitism as a Cultural Code: Reflections on the History and Historiography of Antisemitism in Imperial Germany." *Leo Baeck Institute Year Book* 23 (1978): 25–46.

Vollhardt, Johanna Ray. *The Social Psychology of Collective Victimhood.* Oxford University Press, 2020.

Wallach, Kerry, and Sonia Gollance. "Introduction: When Feminism and Antisemitism Collide." *Feminist German Studies* 39, no. 1 (2023): 1–23.

Wallach, Kerry. *Passing Illusions: Jewish Visibility in Weimar Germany.* University of Michigan Press, 2017.

Walther, Alexander. "Commemorating the Shoah in the GDR's (Post-)Perpetrator Society." In *The Afterlife of the Shoah in Central and Eastern European Cultures: Concepts, Problems, and the Aesthetics of Postcatastrophic Narration*, edited by Anna Artwinska and Anja Tippner. Routledge, 2022.

Walther, Alexander. "Helmut Eschwege and Jewish Life in the German Democratic Republic." In *Rebuilding Jewish Life in Germany*, edited by Jay Howard Geller and Michael Meng. Rutgers University Press, 2020.

Ward, Elizabeth. *East German Film and the Holocaust*. Berghahn, 2020.

Watt, Roderick H. "Victor Klemperer's 'Sprache des Vierten Reichrs': LTI = LQI?." *German Life and Letters* 51, no. 3 (1998): 360–71.

Waxman, Dov, David Schraub, and Adam Hosein. "Arguing About Antisemitism: Why We Disagree About Antisemitism and What We Can Do About It." *Ethnic and Racial Studies* 45, no. 9 (2022): 1803–24.

Weckel, Ulrike. *Beschämende Bilder. Deutsche Reaktionen auf alliierte Dokumentarfilme über befreite Konzentrationslager*. Franz Steiner, 2012.

Weinstein, Valerie. *Antisemitism in Film Comedy in Nazi Germany*. Indiana University Press, 2019.

Weinstein, Valerie. "Homosexual Emancipation, Queer Masculinity, and Jewish Difference in *Anders als die Andern* (1919)." In *Rethinking Jewishness in Weimar Cinema*, edited by Barbara Hales and Valerie Weinstein. Berghahn, 2020.

Weinstein, Valerie. "'White Jews' and Dark Continents: Capitalist Critique and Its Racial Undercurrents in Detlef Sierck's *April! April!* (1935)." In *Continuity and Crisis in German Cinema, 1928–1936*, edited by Barbara Hales, Mihaela Petrescu, and Valerie Weinstein. Camden House, 2016.

Weitzman, Mark, Robert J. Williams, and James Wald, eds. *The Routledge History of Antisemitism*. Routledge, 2024.

Welzer, Harald, Sabine Moller, and Karoline Tschuggnall. *"Opa war kein Nazi." Nationalsozialismus und Holocaust im Familiengedächtnis*. Fischer, 2002.

Weyand, Jan. *Historische Wissensoziologie des modernen Antisemitismus. Genese und Typologie einer Wissensformation am Beispiel des deutschsprachigen Diskurses*. Wallstein, 2016.

Wiesinger-Stock, Sandra. *Hilde Spiel. Ein Leben ohne Heimat?* Verlag für Gesellschaftskritik, 1996.

Wiggershaus, Rolf. *The Frankfurt School: Its History, Theories, and Political Significance*. MIT Press, 1995.

Winterstein, Stefan. "'Und hätte man gleich den letzten Rassejuden aus der Welt geschafft.' Überblick und bisher Verborgenes zu Heimito von Doderers Antisemitismus." *Sprachkunst* 51, no. 2 (2020): 69–100.

Wodak, Ruth, Florian Menz, and Richard Mitten. "'Irgendwie musste das ja mal endlich gesagt werden.' Die Jenninger-Rede zum 50. Jahrestag der Reichspogromnacht von 1938." In *Die Sprachen der Vergangenheiten. Öffentliches Gedenken in österreichischen und deutschen Medien*, edited by Ruth Wodak. Suhrkamp, 1994.

Wodak, Ruth, Peter Nowak, Johanna Pelikan, Helmut Gruber, Rudolf de Cilia, and Richard Mitten. *"Wir sind alle unschuldige Täter!" Diskurshistorische Studien zum Nachkriegsantisemitismus*. Suhrkamp, 1990.

Wogenstein, Sebastian. "Jewish Tragedy and Caliban: Arnold Zweig, Zionism and Antisemitism." *The Germanic Review* 83, no. 4 (2008): 365–89.

Wolfgram, Mark A. *Getting History Right: East and West German Collective Memories of the Holocaust and War*. Bucknell University Press, 2010.

Zaich, Katja B. *"Ich bitte dringend um ein Happyend." Deutsche Bühnenkünstler im niederländischen Exil 1933–1945*. Peter Lang, 2001.

Ziegler, Meinrad, and Waltraud Kannonier-Finster. *Österreichische Gedächtnis. Über Erinnern und Vergessen der NS-Vergangenheit*. Böhlau, 1993.

Zielinski, Siegfried. *Veit Harlan. Analysen und Materialien zur Auseinandersetzung mit einem Film-Regisseur des deutschen Faschismus*. R. G. Fischer, 1981.

328 BIBLIOGRAPHY

Ziermann, Klaus, ed. *Alexander Dymschitz, Wissenschaftler Soldat Internationalist.* Henschel, 1977.

Zimányi, Vera. "Comments on Fritz Zimmermann's 'The Role of the Burgenland in the History of the Habsburg Monarchy.'" *Austrian History Yearbook* 8 (1972): 80–83.

Zipes, Jack, and Anson Rabinbach, eds. *Germans and Jews Since the Holocaust: The Changing Situation in West Germany.* Holmes & Meier, 1989.

Zivier, Georg. *Ernst Deutsch und das deutsche Theater. Fünf Jahrzehnte deutscher Theatergeschichte. Der Lebensweg eines großen Schauspielers.* Haude & Spener, 1964.

Index

For the benefit of digital users, indexed terms that span two pages (e.g., 52–53) may, on occasion, appear on only one of those pages.

Figures are indicated by an italic *f* following the page numbers.

1.April 2000, 206–8, 220–26, 233*f*, 233–34, 235, 238, 301n.94, 301n.95, 301n.100, 301n.103, 302n.114, 302n.128

Abraham, Walter, 81, 280n.88
Abtey, Jacques, 255
Abusch, Alexander 138–39, 140, 154, 289n.71
Ackerman, Nathan, 13
Adenauer, Konrad, 10, 71–72
Adorno, Theodor W., 13, 198, 259n.26
Affaire Blum, 104–5, 106–24, 108*f*, 128, 134–35, 161, 162, 182–83, 293n.49
Allgemeine Wochenzeitung der Juden in Deutschland, 57*f*, 70, 71–72
Allied Forces, 6–7, 8, 9, 10, 65, 71–72, 152, 173, 174, 196–97, 232
Allied Information Services Branch (ISB), 226–27
allosemitism, 258n.18. *See also* antisemitism
Alps, 171–72, 295n.97
American Jewish Joint Distribution Committee, 197–98
Amsterdam, 25, 29*f*, 125–26, 142–43, 268n.16, 270nn.30–31
Anderson, Lale, 23–25
Andreas-Friedrich, Ruth, 286n.1
Angermayer, Fred. A., 273n.69
Anschluss, 9, 27, 168–69, 185, 201–2, 220–21, 227, 236
Ansky, S., works by: *Der Dybuk*, 212
anti-antisemitism, 12, 259n.21, 264n.70, 303–4n.3. *See also* antisemitism
anti-fascism, 8–9, 18, 105–7, 112, 115, 121–22, 129, 134, 138, 139, 148, 150, 151–52, 155, 278n.49, 285n.63, 287n.18, 289n.71
anti-Jewish policies, 1. *See also* antisemitism
anti-Judaism. 258n.19. *See also* antisemitism
anti-Zionism. 156–57. *See also* Zionism
antisemitism
antisemitization, 15–16, 265n.85

assocations of infanticide with, 174–75, 195–96, 197–98
associations of well-poisoning with, 132, 197–98
blood libel, 208–9, 211–12, 213–15, 298n.36
defining, 12–15, 32, 33, 36, 37, 38, 39–40, 43, 46–47, 53–55, 59–63, 69, 73, 77–78, 80–81, 86, 87–90, 94, 95, 96–97, 115–16, 129, 134, 136, 146–47, 149, 162, 175, 180, 198, 204, 247–48, 250–51, 252, 253, 254–55, 263–64n.69, 265n.81, 306n.59
International Holocaust Remembrance Alliance definition, 306n.59
Jerusalem declaration on Antisemitism, 306n.59
latent, 12, 248–49, 263–64n.69
Radauantisemitismus, 12
redemptive, 12, 264n.70
Schuldabwehrantisemitismus, 263n.64, 263–64n.69
secondary, 12, 263n.64, 263–64n.69, 264n.70
selective, 12, 264n.70
See also Jews, characteristics of; stereotypes of
Arendt, Hannah, 254, 260n.31, 264n.75, 306n.58
Aryanization. 182–83, 199, 207, 227, 262n.53, 267n.105, 286n.2, 292n.17, 293–94n.51. *See also* restitution of Jewish property
Aryans, 12, 26, 35–36, 49–50, 85, 107, 117, 122–23, 154, 160, 179, 202–3, 204, 205, 215–16, 291n.99
Ashkenazim, 258n.19, 305n.32
Association of Film Producers in the British Zone, 38–39
Association of Nazi Persecutees, 80–81
Association of Persecutees of the Nazi Regime – Federation of Antifascists. *See* Vereinigung der Verfolgten des Naziregimes – Bund der Antifaschisten

330 INDEX

Association of Socialist Writers. *See* Vereinigung
  sozialistischer Schriftsteller
Aufbau, 40, 272n.53, 300n.72
Aufbau-Verlag, 152, 154
Aufbau: Kulturpolitische Monatsschrift, 130–34
Auf Wiedersehen, Franziska, 90
Auschwitz, 11, 29, 29*f,* 33, 39, 44–45, 72, 84,
  106, 127–28, 184, 195, 219, 266n.103,
  280n.99, 291n.103, 301n.90
Australia, 126–27, 129
Austria, 4, 7–8, 9–11, 16–18, 23–25, 27–28,
  47, 51, 54–55, 60, 77, 119, 133–35,
  156–57, 159, 167–200, 201–38, 251, 252,
  259n.30, 261–62n.45, 262n.48, 262n.53,
  263–64n.69, 265–66n.95, 266n.101,
  267n.105, 269n.19, 274n.92, 290n.82,
  292n.17, 292n.24, 293n.42, 293n.46,
  293n.49, 293–94n.51, 294n.61, 294n.70,
  299n.58, 299n.63, 301n.87, 301n.103,
  302n.113, 302nn.126–127, 303n.136,
  303n.146, 306n.57
Austria (sports club), 168–69
Austria-Hungary, 174–75, 183, 184, 185, 186,
  189, 206–7, 208, 226–29, 290n.82,
  294n.65
Austrian Federal Press Service, 220–21
Austrian Federal Theater Administration,
  220–21
Austrian Patriotism, 230, 301n.103
Austrofascism, 235

Bab, Elisabeth, 34, 42, 54, 272n.53
Bab, Julius, 25–26, 33, 34–42, 43, 45, 50–52,
  53–55, 86, 154, 156, 158–59, 170, 271–
  72nn.45–47, 272n.53, 273n.84, 290n.82,
  290n.89
Babenberg, House of, 236
Babi Yar, 138–39
Babylon Theater, 108, 108*f*
Bad Homburg, 184
Bad Ischl, 10, 197–98
Bahr, Hermann, works by, *Der Antisemitismus.*
  Ein internationales Interview, 264n.75
Baker, Josephine, 241–48, 252, 255
Baldwin, James, 305n.45
Bartels, Adolf, 156
Bary, Jószef, 209–10, 222
Basil, Otto, 218–19, 301n.87
Bauer, Erich, 277n.17
Bauer, Leo, 161
Bavaria, 101, 125, 262n.53
Bavaria Film, 179
Bayreuth, 9–10

Becher, Johannes, 134, 135–36
Begin, Menachem, 254
Benjamin, Georg, 226
Benjamin, Hilde, 226
Benjamin, Walter, 302n.118
Bergen-Belsen 287n.13
Berger, Ludwig, 54
Bergner, Elisabeth, 39–40
Berlin, 16, 19–20, 23–26, 33, 34, 37, 43, 44–45,
  47, 51, 54, 56–57, 63–64, 67, 75, 76,
  77, 80, 90, 106, 108*f,* 109–10, 118, 119,
  122–23, 124, 128, 130, 131*f,* 132–33,
  138–39, 140, 142–43, 145, 170–71, 179,
  183–84, 201–2, 206, 213, 224, 267n.105,
  268n.4, 269n.18, 270n.31, 270–71n.34,
  274n.102, 276n.1, 276n.3, 276n.5,
  277n.17, 280n.88, 285n.62, 286n.1,
  288n.41, 294n.56, 298n.36, 300n.75,
  301n.87
Bettauer, Hugo, works by, *Die Stadt ohne Juden:*
  ein Roman von Übermorgen (The City
  without Jews), 171, 175–76
Biesenthal, 280n.88
Billingsley, Sherman, 243, 245–46, 247–48
black market, 93, 130–34, 174–75, 195–98, 199–
  200, 274n.101
Bloch, Noë, 269n.22
blood libel. *See* antisemitism
Blum, Léon, works by, *Souvenirs sur l'Affaire,*
  113
Bolsheviks, 6–7
Bonn, 1
Bonn Bach Society, 258n.11
Börner, Otto, 291n.99
Borodajkewycz, Taras, 262n.48
Borresholm, Boris von, works by, *Dr.*
  Goebbels nach Aufzeichnungen aus
  seiner Umgebung. 276n.5. *See also*
  Niehoff, Karena
Brackett, Charles, 174, 185–86, 190–93, 194,
  294n.70, 295n.79
Brandt, Heinz, 291n.103
Brauer, Max, 75–77, 80, 278–79n.56, 279n.65
Brauer, Peter, 281n.101
Braun, Alfred, 51
Breslauer, H.K., works by, *Die Stadt ohne Juden*
  (film), 175–76
Breuer, Siegfried, 177
British Military Zone (Germany) 33, 38–39, 40,
  44–45, 58–59, 72
Broch, Hermann, works by, *Der Versucher,*
  263n.68
Broder, Henryk M., 260n.39

INDEX   331

Brunngraber, Erika, 201, 204, 205, 206
Brunngraber, Louise, 201–2, 203–5, 206,
    296n.3, 298n.32
Brunngraber, Rudolf, 201–8, 211, 213–16,
    218–19, 221–22, 226, 227–29, 230–32,
    234–35, 238, 298n.29
Brunngraber, Rudolf, works by:
    1.April 2000, 206–8, 220–26, 233*f*, 233–34,
        235, 238, 301n.94, 301n.95, 301n.100,
        301n.103, 302n.114, 302n.128
    Der Weg durch das Labyrinth, 297n.24
    Karl und das 20. Jahrhundert, 201–2
    Opiumkrieg, 201–2, 297n.10
    Pogrom, 213–14
    Prozess auf Tod und Leben, 213–14, 214*f*
    Überwindung des Nihilismus, 214*f*
    Zucker aus Cuba, 205–6
Bry, Curt, 23–25, 268n.16
Buchanan, Bessie A., 241, 242*f*, 242–43
Bundestag, 1, 2, 3*f*, 4, 20
Burgenland, 237, 238
Busdorf, Otto, 112–13, 117, 128, 129, 285n.62
Byk, Maria, 86

cabaret, 18, 23, 25, 51, 90, 268n.16
Café Herrenhof, 168–70, 291n.1
Canada, 193*f*, 194
Canadian Rockies, 184, 188*f*
capitalism, 8–9, 11–12, 104–5, 106–7, 110, 111,
    115–17, 118, 120–23, 128, 129, 132–33,
    134–35, 154–55, 162–63, 189, 191, 199,
    287n.18, 290–91n.98
Carinthia, 171–72
Carpathia, 183
Carstensen, Conny 280n.88
Catholicism, 137, 168–69, 198, 201, 202–
    3, 296n.1
    anti-Catholicism, 251. *See also* Christianity
CDU, *See* Christian Democratic Union
Celan, Paul, works by, "Todesfuge" (Death
    fugue), 1, 2–4, 20, 258n.11, 258n.12
Central Committee of Liberated Jews in the
    British Zone, 33, 40, 44–45, 72
Central Council of Jews in Germany. *See*
    Zentralrat der Juden in Deutschland
Chile, 1
Christian Democratic Union (Christlich
    Demokratische Union, CDU), 2
Christian Social Party (Christlichsoziale
    Partei), 220–21
Christianity, 28, 43–44, 52–53, 82, 86, 126, 137,
    167–68, 169, 173–74, 181*f*, 189, 203,
    207–8, 209, 211, 217, 218, 219, 220,

222, 227–29, 234–35, 236–37, 247–51,
    253–54, 262n.51, 281n.113, 298n.34,
    306n.57. *See also* Catholicism
Christlich Demokratische Union. *See* Christian
    Democratic Union
Christlichsoziale Partei. *See* Christian Social Party
Cold War, 76, 93, 106
comedy, 26, 45, 94, 191, 206–7, 224–25, 226,
    231, 232, 292n.26
Commentary, 10, 16–17
communism, 8–9, 61–62, 75–76, 105, 106–7,
    110, 112, 113–14, 115–17, 120, 121–22,
    129, 134, 136–37, 138–39, 140–41,
    147–48, 149, 151–52, 154–55, 156,
    159–60, 163, 230, 246, 261n.40, 261n.41,
    270n.31, 278–79n.56, 279n.62, 283n.18,
    285n.63, 287n.18, 287–88n.23, 288n.34,
    290n.96
    anti-communism, 114, 287n.14, 293n.34
Communist Party, 278–79nn.56–57, 283n.22,
    285n.63, 287–88n.23
    Central Committee, 138–39
Copa City, 244–45
Cotton, Joseph, 196
Crohn, Paul, 103–4, 114, 284n.46
Crosby, Bing, 185–86, 187*f*, 190, 192–93
Crossfire, 191, 306n.55
Cserépy, Arzén von, works by
    Ein Mädchen mit Prokura, 269n.18
    Nur nicht weich werden, Susanne!, 26,
        269–70n.24
Cultural Association of German Jews. *See*
    Kulturbund deutscher Juden
Czechoslovakia, 101–3, 102*f*, 117, 127–28, 140,
    197–98, 267n.108, 274n.92

Dachau, 184, 195
Daro-Film 298n.36
Das andere Leben (film), 173–75, 180–83,
    181*f*, 195–96
DDR. *See* German Democratic Republic
DEFA (Deutsche Film-Aktiengesellschaft), 91,
    92–93, 104–5, 113, 114–15, 283n.25
Degischer, Vilma, 180–82, 181*f*
Demokratische Post, 138–39
denazification, 8, 106–7, 112, 171, 194, 207,
    233*f*, 260n.38, 261n.42, 265n.84,
    266n.102, 294n.58
Der Engel mit der Posaune, 266n.103
Der Herr Karl, 267n.105
Der Stürmer, 26, 28, 63, 71–72, 73, 130,
    277n.23
Deutsch, Ernst, 195–96, 216, 299n.57, 300n.77

332 INDEX

Deutsche Demokratische Republik (DDR). *See* German Democratic Republic

Die Mörder sind unter uns, 92–93, 112, 114–15, 283n.25

Displaced Persons (DPs), 58, 130 *See also* black market

Doderer, Heimito von, works by: "Rede über die Juden" 293n.32

Dollfuss, Engelbert, 203

Domnick, Hans 279n.64

Dorsch, Käthe, 263n.61

Dresden, 115, 154, 157–58

Dreyfus Affair, 113

Duke of Württemberg (Karl Alexander), 27–28

Dymschitz, Aleksandr, 114–15

East Germany. *See* German Democratic Republic

Eckert, Thomas, 106

Ehre, Ida, 1–4, 3*f*, 18–19, 20, 91–92, 94, 255, 257n.3, 257n.5, 257n.7, 258n.11, 268n.117, 279–80n.76

Ehrhardt, Kurt, 117

Eimers, Enno, 279n.64

Einstein, Albert, 254

Eisenstadt, 237–38

Eisner, Lotte, 212–13, 216–17

Elbogen, Paul, 187–88, 294n.70

Ende, Lex, 161

Endore, Guy, 298n.36

Engel, Erich, works by

Affaire Blum (film), 104–5, 106–24, 108*f*, 128, 134–35, 161, 162, 182–83, 293n.49

Affäre Blum (drama), 128

Engel, Fritz, 273n.69

Eötvös, Károly, 207–8, 209–10, 218, 219

Eschen, Fritz, 131*f*

Eschwege, Helmut 115, 261n.43

euthanasia, 222–24, 267n.108

Evans, Karin, 108*f*, 117

Farkas, Karl, 18

fascism, 8–9, 91, 105–6, 107, 108–9, 110, 115, 134–35, 141, 147–48, 154, 160–61, 212, 215, 242–43, 246, 254, 282n.14, 283n.26, 306n.58

FBI (Federal Bureau of Investigations), 244, 246, 247

FDP. *See* Free Democratic Party

Fechenbach, Felix, 113

Federal Republic of Germany (Bundesrepublik Deutschland, BRD), 1–4, 7–10, 17–18, 19, 20, 56, 59–61, 71–72, 75, 77–78, 79, 80, 90, 91, 105–7, 115–16, 118–19,

128, 134–35, 146, 156–57, 163, 172–73, 231, 257n.4, 260nn.38–39, 261n.40, 261nn.41–42, 263n.58, 263n.66, 267n.105, 271n.42, 279n.73, 299n.57

Fehrbellin (labor camp), 56–57

Feme-Committee, 108–9

Feuchtwanger, Lion, 43, 45, 219–20, 271n.42, 280n.94

Feuchtwanger, Lion, works by: *Jud Süss* (novel), 27–28, 33, 43

Figl, Leopold, 220–21

Film und Mode Revue, 81, 82–90, 88*f*

Fischer-Colbrie, Arthur, 303n.143

Florath, Albert, 273n.86

Folies Bergère, 242–43

Fontaine, Joan, 185–86, 192–93, 294n.70

Forst, Willi, 212, 220–21, 222–24, 299n.53

Forverts, 249

FORVM (journal), 293n.34

France, 29, 29*f*, 34, 35–36, 103–4, 113, 138, 139–40, 176, 196, 211–13, 222, 225, 234, 242–43, 246–47, 255, 259n.22, 294n.70, 297n.24, 302n.118

Franck, Hans, 35, 272n.51

Frankfurt am Main, 2, 17–18, 259n.23, 266n.102

Frankfurt School, 263–64n.69

Frankfurt University, 266nn.101–102

Frankl, Viktor, works by: *Ärztliche Seelsorge; From Death-Camp to Existentialism; Man's Search for Meaning: an Introduction to Logotherapy; . . . Trotzdem ja zum leben sagen: Ein Psychologe erlebt das Konzentrationslager*, 265–66n.95

Franz Josef, Emperor, 185–86, 188–89

Free Democratic Party (Freie Demokratische Partei, FDP), 257n.8

Freedom Party (Tnaut Haherut, Israel), 254, 306n.58

Frei, Bruno, 138–39, 288n.33

Freie Demokratische Partei. *See* Free Democratic Party

Freies Deutschland, 138–39, 146–47, 154, 289n.71, 291n.99

Freisler, Roland, 278n.49

French Resistance, 242–43, 255

Freud, Sigmund, 185–86, 194, 236, 295n.94

Fürth, 262n.53

Furtwängler, Wilhelm, 47

Galicia, 183, 197–98

Galinski, Heinz, 257n.8

gas chambers, 54, 143, 263n.63, 273n.90, 277n.17
GDR. *See* German Democratic Republic
Gebirtig, Mordechai, works by: "'s brennt,
Brüder, es brennt," 258n.11
Gentleman's Agreement (film), 191, 241–42,
248–52, 253–54, 303–4n.3, 305n.43,
306n.55
George, Heinrich, 273n.86
George, Manfred, 40
German Alpine Association, 172
German Democratic Republic (GDR)
(Deutsche Demokratische Republik,
DDR), 7–9, 11–12, 16, 71–72, 75, 104–7,
110, 112–13, 115–17, 118–19, 121–22,
123–24, 126–27, 128, 129, 130–36,
139–41, 145–46, 150–52, 153, 155,
156–57, 159–61, 162–63, 172–73, 226,
257n.4, 258n.14, 261nn.42–43, 263n.66,
282n.12, 282n.14, 283n.17, 283n.20,
283n.23, 283nn.25–26, 283n.29,
287n.16, 287nn.18–19, 289n.61,
290n.96, 290–91n.98, 291n.103,
301n.103, 306n.57
German Federal Constitutional Court, 80
Germany, 1–12, 16–20, 23, 25–29, 32–37,
39–46, 47–51, 53–55, 58–61, 62–63,
65, 68–72, 75–77, 81–83, 85–91, 92–94,
95–97, 101–5, 106–29, 130–63, 168–69,
172–73, 174, 175–78, 179, 180, 183–85,
190, 192, 194, 195, 202–3, 204–5, 208–9,
210–12, 213–15, 217–18, 222–26, 232–
33, 251, 252, 253–54, 257n.4, 257n.8,
259n.21, 259n.30, 260n.37, 260nn.38–
39, 261n.40, 261n.42, 262n.47, 263n.63,
266n.101, 266nn.103–104, 267n.108,
269n.17, 269n.21, 273n.84, 274nn.92–
94, 275n.126, 279n.58, 289n.71,
290n.82, 290–91n.98, 293n.46, 298n.36,
299n.58, 299n.63
cinema, 26, 78, 267n.108, 269n.21, 270n.28,
299n.60
collective guilt, 260n.33
"Good German," 60–61, 85–86, 97, 141, 263n.66
nationalism, 50–51, 69, 97, 110, 119, 120–21,
127, 156–57, 160, 290n.82
patriotism, 8, 35–36, 44, 45–46, 50–51, 53–
55, 60–61, 65, 69, 70, 81, 85–86, 111–12,
156, 158–60, 172–73, 176–78, 275n.126
theater, 299n.50
Gerson, Dora, 23, 24*f*, 29*f*, 30, 33, 37–38, 43–44,
49–50, 54, 61–62, 84, 88–89, 268n.16,
270n.31
Gerson, Hermine, 268n.4

Gerson, Max, 268n.4
Gesellschafts- und Wirtschaftsmuseum
(Vienna), 296n.8
Gestapo, 56–57, 117, 128, 141, 176, 177–78,
182, 272n.46, 285n.62, 293n.31
Gettinger, Berta (née Kohn), 21–97, 201–38,
297n.23
Giese, Dr. Hans, 78
Ginsberg, Ernst, 271n.37
Giordano, Egon, 70
Giordano, Ralph, 19–20, 276n.10, 278n.55
Gloth, Harald, 81–83, 280n.89, 281n.108
Goebbels, Joseph, 26, 27, 28, 30, 31, 32*f*, 33,
36–38, 39–40, 41–42, 43, 46–49,
51–53, 61–62, 63, 79, 81, 83, 84, 85,
87, 88–89, 157–58, 202, 206, 212, 213,
222–24, 267n.108, 269n.18, 269–70n.24,
270n.31, 271n.35, 271n.42, 275n.117,
276n.141, 276n.5, 276n.11, 277n.16,
277n.26, 281n.101, 285n.62, 299n.50
Goering, Hermann, 265n.82
Goldhammer, Bruno, 161
Gordon, Wolfgang von, 114, 284n.43
Gottschalk, Joachim, 84–85
goynormativity, 258n.19
Graf, Max, 221
Great Britain, 27–28, 37, 83, 106, 167, 174, 196,
266n.103, 274n.92
Great Depression, 244
Green Party (Grüne), 2, 257n.8
Greene, Graham, works by: *The Third Man*,
174, 195–97, 198–200, 295–96n.104
Grodzinsky, Thea, 38
Grothe, Hans, 272n.51
Gruber, Gisi, 215, 300n.64
Grüne. *See* Green Party
Gurs, 212–13

Haas, Alfred, 286n.78
Haas, Alice (Kussi), 101–3, 102*f*, 104, 107, 117,
127–29, 286n.78, 286n.80
Haas, Hans, 127
Haas, Louis, 101
Haas, Ottilie, 101
Haas, Rudolf, 101, 102*f*, 104, 107, 113, 126–29
Haensel, Carl, 202, 203–4, 205, 297n.13
Hahn, Kurt, 299n.52
Hamburg, 1–2, 18, 19–20, 30–31, 34, 36,
38–39, 46, 56, 57*f*, 63–64, 65–66, 67,
71–72, 74*f*, 75–77, 80, 84, 85–86, 90,
93, 104, 262n.53, 271n.43, 273nn.67–
68, 274n.101, 277–78n.32, 278n.34,
280n.88, 281n.123, 285n.66

334 INDEX

Hamburg Kammerspiele, 1–2
Hamsun, Knut, 47
Hamsun, Knut, works by: *Segen der Erde*, 52
Hansel, Artur, 127–28, 286n.78
Hanselová, Alice. *See* Haas, Alice
Harlan, Kristian, 281n.108
Harlan, Thomas, 53–54
Harlan, Veit, 1–2, 8, 18, 19–20, 23–55, 56–97,
　　116, 206, 207–8, 222–24, 257n.6,
　　269nn.18–19, 269–70nn.24–25,
　　270n.26, 270–71n.34, 271n.38, 271n.42,
　　273n.74, 275–76n.140, 276n.11,
　　280n.94, 281n.101
　ability to manipulate Goebbels, 48
　acquittals for crimes against humanity, 33,
　　73–74, 74*f*, 80, 267n.108, 273n.68,
　　277n.17
　admiration for Goebbels, 48–49, 275n.117,
　　276n.141
　antisemitic denigration of Curt Riess,
　　275n.117
　autobiography of, 30, 33, 46–53, 271n.35,
　　276n.141
　boycotts of films of, 76–80
　charges of crimes against humanity, 18, 34,
　　39, 40, 58–59, 89
　claims of victimization by Goebbels, 48
　claims of victimization by Jews, 45–46, 49–50
　claims of victimization by Antisemites, 33,
　　42, 44, 49–50, 86
　claims of victimization by the Nazis, 30, 37–
　　38, 44, 49–50
　conflict with Erich Lüth, 77–78, 80–81, 82,
　　279nn.67–68, 279–80n.76
　criticism of Goebbels, 49, 51–52
　denazification of, 27, 28, 30–31, 34, 36, 37,
　　38–39, 43, 44, 45–46, 64, 67, 82, 93,
　　273nn.67–68
　disavowals of antisemitism by, 30–32, 34
　　to Curt Riess, 270n.31
　German patriotism of, 50–51, 53–54, 61, 85,
　　275n.126
　leading role in *Nur Nicht weich werden,
　　Susanne!*, 26–28, 269n.22, 299n.60
　meeting with Joachim Prinz, 271nn.43–44
　relationship with Dora Gerson, 23, 24*f*,
　　25–26, 29–30, 38, 44, 45, 49–50, 88–89,
　　270n.31, 270n.33, 271n.37, 274n.96
　relationship with Fritz Kortner, 272n.62
　relationship with Goebbels, 27, 48–49, 51–
　　52, 63
　relationship with Julius Bab, 33, 34, 36–42,
　　272n.46, 272n.61, 273n.71

　relationship with Lion Feuchtwanger, 33, 43
　relationship with Norbert Wollheim, 33,
　　40, 44–46
　relationships with Jews, 33, 37, 45, 52–
　　53, 84–85
　request to appear before a Jewish honor
　　court, 45–46
　trials for crimes against humanity, 8, 28, 30,
　　33, 56, 58–97, 116, 266n.103, 277n.16,
　　280n.88
Harlan, Veit, works directed by:
　*Das dritte Geschlecht (Anders als du und ich
　　[§175])*, 78–80
　Das unsterbliche Herz, 37–38, 40
　Der grosse König, 32*f*
　Die goldene Stadt, 68, 74
　Hanna Amon, 77
　Immensee, 74
　Jud Süss, 1–2, 27, 28–33, 36, 39–41, 43–47, 51,
　　52–53, 56, 58–59, 61–66, 68–69, 72, 73,
　　74–75, 76–77, 78, 79, 80–83, 84–85, 86–
　　89, 88*f*, 90, 112–13, 122, 212, 214–15,
　　261n.41, 267n.110, 269n.19, 269n.22,
　　270n.28, 270n.26, 271n.42, 271n.44,
　　273n.88, 274n.94, 275n.133, 275n.138,
　　276n.141, 276n.1, 276n.14, 277n.23,
　　277n.25, 281n.101, 281n.108, 281n.113,
　　301n.87
　Jugend, 68
　Kolberg, 84–85
　Krach im Hinterhaus 27
　Kreutzersonata, 46
　Opfergang, 74
Harlan, Walter, 34, 37–38, 39, 40–41, 271–
　　72n.45, 272n.54, 273n.69
Harlan, Walter, works by: *Das Nürnbergische
　　Ei*, 37–38
Harlem, 241, 243–44, 246, 305n.45
Hartl, Karl, 221, 266n.103
Hartwich, Alexander, 178–79, 292n.30
Hasidism, 52–53, 268n.1
Hatheyer, Heidemarie, 267n.110
Hauesserman, Ernst, 220–21
Hauff, Wilhelm, works by: *Jud Süss* (novella),
　　27–28
Heer, Friedrich, 221
Heidelberg University, 137
Heimat, 159, 160, 175, 183–84, 190, 199–200,
　　221, 225, 234–35, 236, 238
Heimat films, 184, 190, 192, 301n.103
Heine, Heinrich, 43
Heinemann, Gustav, 71–72
Helling, Hellmuth, 101–3, 108, 111

Hellmund, Friedrich, 270n.31
Henckels, Paul, 38, 61–62
Herald, Heinz, works by, *Der Prozess ohne Ende. Der Fall von Tisza Eszlar/ The Burning Bush: a Play in Three Acts*, 298n.36, 300n.75
Herczeg, Géza, works by, *Der Prozess ohne Ende. Der Fall von Tisza Eszlar/ The Burning Bush: a Play in Three Acts*, 298n.36
Hermann, Georg, 35
Herzl, Theodor, 154, 155–57, 159
Heuser, Kurt, 213–15
Heyde, Bernhard, 1, 19
Heyde, Ruth, 1
Heymann, Stefan, 106
High Noon, 266n.103
Hindenburg, Paul von, 108–9, 110, 117
Hinkel, Hans, 41–42, 204
Hippler, Fritz, 32*f*, 269n.18, 275n.117, 275n.126, 276n.11
Hitler, Adolf, 1, 2, 3–4, 8, 9, 13–14, 23, 31, 39–40, 45, 46–47, 48, 49–51, 53, 65, 67, 81, 85, 89–90, 93, 105, 108–9, 110–11, 115, 141–42, 145, 154, 155, 156–58, 159–60, 161, 169, 172–73, 176–77, 179–80, 185, 208–9, 211, 227, 230, 232–33, 235–36, 258n.12, 264n.75, 264n.77, 272n.54, 274n.105, 285n.63, 299n.53, 301n.85, 303n.143
Hitler, Adolf, works by, *Mein Kampf*, 48, 108–9
Hitler Youth, 140–41
Hobson, Laura Z., 241–42, 244, 248–51, 253, 255
Hobson, Laura, Z., works by, *Gentleman's Agreement* (novel), 241, 242*f*, 244, 248–54, 303–4n.3
Hobson, Thayer, 249
Hochschule für Welthandel (Vienna), 262n.48
Holland. *See* Netherlands
Hollywood, 17, 18, 51, 174–75, 183, 184, 187–88, 212, 213, 216, 221, 225, 294n.70, 305n.46, 306n.55
Holtorf Troupe, 23
Hömberg, Hans (pseud. J. R. George), 269n.19, 269n.22, 275n.138
Hömberg, Hans, works by, *Jud Süss* (novel, pseud. J.R. George) 269n.19, 269n.22
Hömbergs Kaleidophon, 269n.19
homophobia, 79–80
homosexuality, 78–80, 280n.81
Hoover, J. Edgar, 244, 246
Horkheimer, Max, 13, 17–18, 198, 259n.23, 259n.26, 266n.102, 306n.54

Horn, Otto, 215–16
Hörsing, Otto, 103
Horthy, Miklós, 138
Hotel Sacher, 197
Hübler-Kahla, Johann, 215, 300n.68
Hudgins, Mildred Martien, 249–50
Hungary, 9–10, 12, 214–16, 218, 269–70n.24, 298n.36

I. G. Farben, 44–45
Ibach, Alfred, 173–74
Impellitteri, Vincent, 303n.2
imperialism, 154, 161
intermarriage, 107, 267n.112, 297n.25
International Holocaust Remembrance Alliance, 306n.59. *See also* antisemitism
intersectionality, 247, 258n.19, 267–68n.116, 305n.35
Irgun Zvai Leumi (Palestine), 306n.58
Israel, 254–55, 257n.8, 282n.132, 299n.57, 306n.58

Jackson, Manfred, 70, 279n.64
Jacoby, Gerhard, 278n.33. *See also* World Jewish Congress
Jahoda, Marie, 13, 297n.24
Jasper National Park, 187–89, 294n.70
Jaspers, Karl, 260n.33
Jenninger, Philipp, 2–4, 3*f*, 9, 20, 255, 257n.8, 258n.11, 258n.15
Jerusalem declaration, 306n.59. *See also* antisemitism
Jewish Cultural Association. *See* Jüdischer Kulturbund
Jewish difference, 5–6, 9, 12, 14, 15–16, 18, 27–28, 52, 54, 60, 61–62, 87, 96–97, 106, 110, 113, 115–16, 119, 120–21, 123–24, 129, 135–36, 139, 141–42, 145, 163, 175, 178–79, 180, 186, 189, 199–200, 207, 208, 216, 217, 220, 231, 238, 241, 247–48, 253–55, 258n.18, 259n.24, 265n.80, 267–68n.116, 285n.56, 288n.36, 305n.35
Jewishness, 11–12, 104–5, 106, 107, 110, 113, 118, 122–23, 124, 126, 128, 137–38, 147, 169, 175, 203, 204, 243–44, 251–52, 259n.22, 280n.81, 284n.50
Jews
    art, 182–83
    artists, 225–26, 302n.126
    Austrian Jews, 16, 23–25, 54–55, 170, 172–73, 183, 185, 208, 216–17, 220–21, 236, 266n.101, 270–71n.34, 290n.82, 292n.24, 302n.127

336 INDEX

Jews (cont.)
   cemeteries, 9–10, 106, 261n.40, 262n.53,
      274n.101
   characteristics of, 12, 32, 116–17
   as characters, 1–2, 12, 26, 52, 77, 91, 114,
      117–18, 122–23, 147–48, 177, 186, 192,
      198, 206–7, 218, 252
   conditional empowerment of, 136
   conditional whiteness of, 247, 249, 258n.19
   Court Jews, 27–28
   Eastern European, 218–19
   émigrés, 13, 25, 33, 34, 51, 114–15, 167–68,
      183, 185, 187–88, 189, 220–21, 249,
      266n.103, 288n.28, 291n.99, 292n.24
   German Jews, 1–2, 10, 25–26, 27–28, 32, 33,
      34, 42, 50–51, 54–55, 75–76, 77–78,
      96, 97, 114, 115, 118–19, 124, 156–57,
      159, 160, 183, 194, 210, 254, 257n.8,
      267n.110, 273n.84, 291n.99, 299n.62,
      306n.50
   Gesinnungsjuden, 122–23
   Halbjuden, 56–57, 67, 69, 70, 86, 112, 202, 205
   Holocaust victims, 150–51, 286n.78
   humor, 269n.19
   ideological labor of, 266n.101
   Jewish nationalism, 156, 290n.82
   Judaism, 5–6, 36, 137, 168–69, 202, 204,
      209–11, 217–18, 219, 277n.16, 283n.18,
      297n.24
   Judenpolizei, 182, 293n.50
   Orthodoxy, 30, 137
   Rassejuden, 122–23
   re-émigrés, 8, 16–18, 105, 106, 266n.101,
      301n.87
   self-identification of, 5–6, 17, 137–38, 145,
      154, 156, 160, 189, 199–200, 251–52,
      253, 266n.101, 287n.18
   stereotypes of, 5–7, 11, 12, 14, 15–16, 18, 26,
      32, 45, 60, 87, 91–92, 94, 117, 122–23,
      124, 130, 132, 133–34, 135–36, 137–38,
      140, 147–48, 149, 152, 154, 156, 157,
      163, 171–72, 175–76, 179–80, 195–96,
      198, 199, 205, 210, 217–19, 220, 237,
      246–47, 251, 254–55, 264n.74, 265n.86,
      267–68n.116, 273n.88, 277n.21,
      285n.56, 286n.5, 287n.19, 301n.87,
      305n.34, 306n.52
   as surrogates, 263n.68
   victims of Nazi persecution, 16, 105–6, 139,
      157, 232–33, 260n.37, 292n.17
   Volljuden, 70, 202
   "white Jews," 12

women, 7–8, 20, 30, 44, 65, 84, 88–89, 91–92,
   107, 132, 140, 167–68, 176, 179–82,
   181*f*, 183, 204, 208, 229–30, 246–47,
   250–52, 258n.19, 266n.103, 277n.21,
   285n.56, 291n.99, 293n.42, 305n.32,
   306n.52
Johst, Hanns, works by, *Schlageter*, 269n.18
Joloff, Friedrich, 79
Joos, Anton, 290–91n.98
Joseph, Rudolph S., 211
Jud Süss (1940 film, Harlan), 1–2, 27–33, 36–41,
   43–47, 51–53, 56, 58–59, 61–66, 68–69,
   72, 73, 74–75, 76–77, 78, 79, 80–82, 83,
   84–85, 86–87, 88*f*, 90, 112–13, 116, 214–
   15, 217–18, 261n.41, 267n.110, 269n.19,
   269n.22, 270nn.26–27, 271n.42,
   271n.44, 274n.94, 275n.138, 276n.141,
   278n.40, 281n.101, 281n.108, 301n.87
Jud Süss (1934 film, Mendes), 27–28
Jud Süss (1916-1917 drama, Feuchtwanger),
   27–28
Jud Süss (1925 novel, Feuchtwanger), 27–28
Jud Süss (1827 novella, Hauff), 27–28
Jud Süss (1941 novel, Hömberg (pseud. J.R.
   George)), 259n.22, 269n.19
Judaism. *See* Jews
Judeophobia. 258n.19. *See also* antisemitism
Jüdischer Kulturbund/Kulturbund deutscher
   Juden (Jewish Cultural Association/
   Cultural Association of German
   Jews). 25–26, 34–36, 41–42, 269n.17,
   272nn.47–48

Kadmon, Stella, 18
Kahn, Siegbert, 106, 283n.19
Kalmar, Rudolf, 294n.70, 300n.72
Kammerspiel-Film-Gesellschaft, 257n.5
Kandinsky, Wassily, 124–25
Karl Alexander, Duke of Württemberg, 27–
   28, 73
Karl V, Holy Roman Emperor, 207–8
Karwinski, Baron Karl, 133–34
Katz, Leo, 138–39, 288n.33
Katz, Otto, 138–39
Kaufman, Walter, 290n.96
Käutner, Helmut, 1–2, 90–96, 282n.132,
   283n.25
Käutner, Helmut, works directed by:
   In jenen Tagen, 1–2, 91–93, 281n.123,
      283n.25
   Schwarzer Kies, 90, 93–97
Képes Figyelö, 214–15

INDEX 337

Kernmayr, Hans Gustl, 272n.62
Kiaulehn, Walther, 272n.62
Kielce Pogrom, 9–10
Kinderlandverschickung, 206
Kindertransporte, 44–45, 274n.92
Kindler, Helmuth, 286n.1
Kisch, Egon Erwin, 139
Klee, Paul, 124–25
Kleist Literature Prize, 138, 211
Klemperer, Eva, 157–58
Klemperer, Victor, 135–36, 149–50, 153–61,
  162, 290n.82, 290n.89
Klemperer, Victor, works by, *LTI: Lingua Tertii
  Imperii*, 153–54, 159–60
Klering, Hans, 114
Klimt, Emil, 201
Klimt, Gustav, 201, 207, 227–30, 228*f*, 235,
  296nn.6–7, 303n.146
Klimt, Helene, 201, 296n.7
Klöpfer, Eugen, 273n.86
Klüger, Ruth, 11
Klurfeld, Herman, 245, 304n.25
Koch, Ilse, 198–99
Koch, Karl-Otto, 198–99
Koeppen, Wolfgang, works by, *Tauben im Gras*,
  263n.68
Kölling, Johannes, 101–4, 110, 123–24
Kölling-Haas Affair, 129
Königskinder (film), 94
Körber, Hilde, 36, 38, 78–79
Körber, Maria, 257n.6
Korda, Alexander, 174, 196
Kortner, Fritz, 17, 18, 38, 266nn.104–105,
  272n.62, 293n.37, 301n.87
Kortner, Fritz, works by
  Der Ruf (film), 18, 266n.104
  Donauwellen (drama), 267n.105, 301n.87
Kraft, Hyman Solomon, works by, *Moon Over
  Vienna (Champagne Waltz)* (film), 186,
  294n.68
Krahl, Hilde, 18–19, 222–24, 226–27,
  228*f*, 229–30
Kramer, Gerhard, 34, 39–40, 66, 68, 71,
  267n.108, 270n.33
Krause, Willi (pseud. Peter Hagen), works by,
  Nur nicht weich werden, Susanne!, 26
Krauss, Werner, 39–40, 47, 51–52, 64–65, 73,
  263n.61, 273n.74, 273n.86, 277n.25,
  281n.108, 301n.87
Kreikemeyer, Willi, 161
Kristallnacht. See November Pogroms
Krúdy, Gyula, 298n.36

Krupp, Gustav, 154
Kruyt, Herman, 23–25
Kuckhoff, Greta, 150–51
Kühne, Fritz, 84–85
Kulturbund (East German), 140
Kunheim, Ernst Erich, 276n.3
Künneke, Eduard, 271–72n.45
Künsterkolonie Schmargendorf (Berlin), 25–26
Kunstgewerbeschule des Österreichischen
  Museums für Kunst und Industrie
  (Vienna), 201
Kussi, Alice. *See* Haas, Alice
Kussi, Bedrich (Friedrich), 282n.2, 286n.80
Kussi, Julius, 101, 104

La Habanera, 87, 88*f*
Lang ist der Weg, 266n.103
Langer, František, works by, *Engel unter Uns*,
  267n.108
Langley, Noel, 298n.36
latent antisemitism. *See* antisemitism
Lazarsfeld, Paul, 297n.24
Leander, Zarah, 87
Lederer, August, 201, 227
Lederer, Serena, 201, 227, 296n.7
Lehmann, Helmut, 160–61
Lehrman, Hal, 10
Leiferde assassin, 109–10
Leinen aus Irland, 177
Leiske, Walter, 17–18, 266n.101
Leitner, Olly (Olga), 293n.42
Lendvai, Paul, 10–11
Leningrad, 138–39
Leopold I (Margrave), 236
Leopold VI (Duke), 236–37
Lernet-Holenia, Alexander, 173–75, 176–77,
  178–82, 199–200, 292n.19, 293n.32,
  293n.34, 293n.42, 293nn.45–46,
  294n.52, 294n.65
Lernet-Holenia, Alexander, works by
  Beide Sizilien, 178–79
  Der zwanzigste Juli, 173–75, 176–79, 180–82,
    199–200, 292n.18
  Die große Liebe, 179
  Mars im Widder, 179
Lessing, Gotthold Ephraim, works by, *Nathan
  der Weise*, 212–13, 269n.17, 299n.57
Lessing, Theodor, 306n.50
Liebeneiner, Wolfgang, 18–19, 77–78, 93,
  206–8, 222–27, 223*f*, 263n.61, 267n.108,
  267n.110, 279–80n.76, 297n.13,
  301nn.102–104, 302n.110

338   INDEX

Liebeneiner, Wolfgang, works directed by:
  1.April 2000, 206–8, 223*f*, 224–32, 233*f*, 233–
    34, 235, 238, 301n.103
  Großstadtmelodie, 224
  Die Trapp-Familie, 301n.103
  Die Trapp-Familie in Amerika, 301n.103
  Ich Klage an, 222–24, 267n.108, 267n.110
  Liebe 47, 18, 267n.109
Lieber Augustin (song), 222
Liepman, Heinz, 10, 18, 19–20, 34, 271n.43,
  271n.44
Lindemann, Alfred, 113
Lindtberg, Leopold, 23–25, 269n.18, 273n.90
Lion, Jean, 246–47
Lipizzaner horses, 222
Löhner, Fritz (Beda), works by, . . . *trotzdem ja*
  zum leben sagen (song), 265–66n.95
London, 167–69, 168*f*, 171–72, 195, 241–42,
  298n.36
Lothar, Ernst, works by, *Der Engel mit der*
  Posaune (novel), 266n.103
Louis Haas AG, 101–3, 127
Louis-Dreyfus, Louis, 212
Louis, Joe, 244–45
Lubitsch, Ernst, 90, 175–76, 189, 195, 225,
  292n.25, 300n.66, 300n.68
Lueger, Karl, 14, 50, 235, 265n.82
Luft, Friedrich, 90
Lügenpresse, 110–11
Lukraphon, 25–26, 268n.1
Lüth, Erich, 77–78, 80–81, 82, 279nn.67–68,
  279–80n.76
Lüth-Urteil (Lüth verdict), 80, 279n.73

Maetzig, Kurt, 84, 114–15, 266n.103, 281n.104,
  283n.25
Maetzig, Kurt, works directed by,
  Ehe im Schatten, 84, 92, 114–15, 266n.103,
    279n.67, 283n.25
  Roman einer jungen Ehe, 266n.103
Magdeburg, 101, 103–4, 108–9, 110, 111–12,
  123, 284n.46, 285n.63
Magdeburger Justizskandal (Magdeburg
  Dreyfus Affair), 103–4, 107
Mainz, 137
Majdanek, 198–99
Mannheim, Lucie, 37
Marboe Ernst, 220–22, 225, 226, 231, 232, 233*f*,
  233–35, 301n.92, 301n.98
Marboe, Ernst, works by
  1.April 2000, 206–8, 220–26, 233*f*, 233–34,
    235, 238, 301n.94, 301n.95, 301n.100,
    301n.103, 302n.114, 302n.128

The Book of Austria, 232–38
  Yes, Oui, OK, Njet, 228*f*, 232
Marcus, Paul (pseud. Pem), 299n.53
Marian, Ferdinand, 43, 73, 86–87, 88*f*,
  277n.23
Marin, Bernd, 10–11
Marseilles, 138–39, 144
Marshman, Donald McGill Jr., 190–91
Matejka, Viktor, 302n.126
Maximilian I, Holy Roman Emperor, 207–8
May, Karl, 23
McCloy, John J., 71–72, 262n.47
McClure, Robert A., 184
Meinrad, Josef, 222
Memmingen, 9–10
Menck, Clara, 279n.70
Mendelssohn, Francesco von, 38
Mendelssohn, Peter de, 168–69
Menzel, Gerhard, 278n.33
Merker, Paul, 138–40, 154–57, 160–61, 288n.34,
  290–91nn.98–99
Metzger, Astrid, 63–64, 277n.21
Metzger, Ludwig, 56, 62–66, 68–69, 72, 73,
  278n.52
Mexico, 138–39, 140, 143, 288n.30, 288n.32,
  289n.71, 290–91nn.98–99
Meyer-Hanno, Hans, 61–62
Meyer-Hanno, Irene, 61–62
Miami, 244–45
Minsk, 138–39
misogyny, 5, 37, 69, 191, 247–48, 251–52,
  268n.118
mixed marriages. *See* intermarriage
Mogilewer, Mark, 115
Mohn, Sigbert, 46–47
Möller, Eberhard Wolfgang, 64–65, 81, 277n.23,
  277n.26
Montagu, Elizabeth, 295–96n.104
Morgan, Paul. 268n.16
Morgenstern, Ladislaus, 216
Morituri, 266n.103
Moscow, 160–61
Moscow Declaration, 9, 222, 232–33
Moskowitz, Moses, 7, 10
mountain films, 190, 195
Muhlen, Norbert, 59–60
Müller-Hofmann, Wolfgang, 296n.6
Munich, 16, 47, 267n.105
Müthel, Lothar, works directed by, *Merchant of*
  Venice, Nathan der Weise, 212–13

National Association for the Advancement of
  Colored People (NAACP), 241

INDEX 339

National Socialism (Nationalsozialistische
Deutsche Arbeiterpartei (NSDAP)),
1–3, 4, 6–9, 10–12, 14–15, 18–20, 25–26,
27, 29–32, 34–36, 37, 38, 39–42, 43, 44,
45, 46–52, 53–55, 56–60, 61–62, 65, 66–
69, 70, 71–72, 73, 74, 75, 77, 78–82, 84–
87, 89, 90, 91–94, 95, 97, 104–7, 109–11,
112, 114, 115, 116–17, 119, 121–24,
126–29, 130, 131f, 132, 134–35, 137,
138–39, 141–42, 143–49, 150–52, 153–
55, 156–57, 159–61, 162, 163, 168–70,
171, 172–75, 176–78, 179–85, 190, 191,
192, 194, 195, 198–99, 201–2, 203, 204,
205–6, 207–8, 212–16, 217–19, 222–24,
225, 226–29, 230–32, 233f, 234–35,
238, 242–43, 244, 252, 253–54, 259n.25,
261–62n.45, 262n.48, 263n.61, 263n.65,
265n.84, 267n.108, 267n.112, 269n.20,
269n.22, 270n.25, 270n.31, 274n.92,
274n.101, 276n.3, 278n.37, 279n.68,
284n.47, 285nn.62–63, 288n.33,
289n.61, 290n.94, 291n.103, 295n.93,
295n.95, 295n.77, 298n.28, 299n.50,
299n.52, 299n.57, 302n.104, 302n.113,
302n.118, 306n.54, 306n.58
anti-Nazis, 51–52, 59, 85, 104–5, 114, 139,
151–52, 286n.1, 289n.71, 301n.103
antisemitism of, 43, 61–62, 110–11, 159, 205,
264n.70, 300n.69
atrocities and crimes, 4, 8, 9, 12, 15, 30, 58–
61, 106–7, 112, 116, 135, 143, 154, 163,
173, 183–84, 185, 191, 194, 226, 238,
258n.10, 274n.101, 286n.2
characters, 11–12, 92–93, 94, 145–50, 151–
52, 174–75, 177–78, 182–83, 194, 198–
99, 226–27, 260n.38, 295n.95
laws and terminology, 44, 70, 86, 154, 169,
179–80, 184, 202, 215–16, 230, 257n.1,
281n.104, 293n.42
leaders and officials, 8–9, 18, 46–49, 51–52,
57–58, 59, 61–62, 81, 106, 109–10, 141,
146, 204, 205–6, 208, 227–29, 257n.3,
265n.82, 276n.11, 278n.49, 281n.113,
285n.62
membership in, 13–14, 18, 19–20, 26, 35,
49–50, 64, 65, 67, 78, 101–3, 123–24,
129, 203, 226–27, 264n.76, 269nn.18–
19, 277–78n.32, 285n.59, 288n.33,
293n.32
Ministry of Propaganda, 32f, 48, 49, 64,
297n.10
Nazi Germany, 9, 27, 69
neo-Nazis, 74, 214–15, 262n.48

persecution, targeting, and victimization by,
1–2, 6, 7–8, 9, 16, 19–20, 30, 31, 37–38,
41, 42, 81, 85, 91, 105–6, 122–23, 126–
27, 128, 130, 134–35, 139, 141–42, 145,
156–57, 162, 169–70, 173, 174, 180–82,
192, 212–13, 218–19, 254, 261–62n.45,
268n.117, 278n.49, 283n.21, 285n.62,
292n.17
propaganda, 1–2, 6–7, 8, 18, 27, 31, 41, 47–
48, 49, 56, 58–59, 61–62, 81, 87, 95, 130,
190, 208, 212, 217–18, 269n.22, 270n.28,
292n.26, 298n.36, 299n.60, 303n.143
refusal to join, 206, 222–24, 238
resistance to, 31, 44, 61, 112, 139, 144–45,
150–52, 155, 173–74, 176–77, 178,
179, 180, 183, 215–16, 242–43, 244,
261–62n.45, 283n.18, 283n.26, 292n.17,
301n.87
Sicherheitsdienst des Reichsführers-SS (SD),
41
SS (Schutzstaffel), 81, 123–24, 146–47, 151,
177, 275n.113, 275n.117, 277n.17,
280n.88, 284n.32, 285n.62, 297n.13,
297n.26, 299n.52
Sturmabteilung (SA), 67, 81, 147–48, 235–36
Nazism. See National Socialism
Nebenzal, Seymour, 212
Nelson, Rudolf, 25
neo-Nazis. See National Socialism
Netherlands, 25, 29, 143, 232, 270n.31, 290n.96
Neue Sachlichkeit, 296n.8
Neurath, Otto, 296n.8, 297n.24
New Deal, 244, 253
New York, 34, 36, 37–38, 39, 40–41, 54, 84, 138,
180, 186, 190, 241–42, 243, 249, 251,
293n.45, 298n.36, 303n.2
Niehoff, Karena, 18, 56–59, 57f, 60–61, 62–72,
75–77, 79–80, 86–87, 90, 95–97, 183,
276n.5, 277nn.20–21, 277n.25, 278n.34,
278n.37, 278–79nn.56–57, 279n.62,
279n.64, 279n.65, 282n.138, 294n.54
Niehoff, Kurt, 276n.3
Niehoff, Rose, 56–58, 276n.3, 276n.4
Nordische Rundfunk, 104
November Pogroms, 1, 2, 91, 105–6, 257n.1
NSDAP. See National Socialism
Nur nicht weich werden, Susanne!, 26–28,
299n.60
Nuremberg laws, 160–61, 169, 201, 281n.104
Nuremberg trials, 8, 19–20, 57–58, 60–62,
297n.13

O'Brien, Jack, 245

340 INDEX

Odessa, 138–39
Oesterle-Schwerin, Jutta, 2, 257n.8
Oliver Twist, 77
Olympia, 186
Ónody, Géza, 209–10, 301n.85
Opfermann, H.C., 46–53, 274n.103, 274n.105
Ophüls, Max, works by, Letter from an Unknown Woman, 183, 294n.70
Opitz, Carl, 281n.113
Oppenheimer, Joseph Süss, 27–28, 86, 88–89, 182–83, 270n.27. See also *Jud Süss*
Organization Consul (OC), 108–9
Ossietzky, Carl von, 103–4

Pabst, Georg Wilhelm (G.W.), 112–13, 206–9, 211–17, 218–20, 221, 222–24
Pabst, Georg Wilhelm (G.W.), works directed by,
  Der Fall Molander, 299n.50
  Der letzte Akt, 299n.56
  Der Prozess, 112–13, 206–20
  Es geschah am 20. Juli, 299n.56
  Komödianten, 212, 213, 299n.50
  Nathan der Weise, 299n.57
  Paracelsus, 212, 213–14, 299n.50
Pabst, Trude, 212, 299nn.52–53
Palestine, 115, 155, 160, 238, 306n.58
Paramount Pictures, 186, 187f
Paris, 138–39, 140, 145, 149, 211, 242–43, 273n.84
Peck, Gregory, 241
PEN (writers' club), 178–79, 215
Penicillin, 58, 196, 197–98. See also black market
philosemitism, 8, 12, 77–78, 80–81, 96, 218–19, 259n.21, 263n.63. See also antisemitism
Piaski Ghetto, 148–49, 286n.2
Picasso, Pablo, 124–25
Ping-Pong (cabaret), 25. See also cabaret
Piscator, Erwin, 23, 298n.36
Pohl, Oswald, 48, 275n.113
Poland, 9–10, 52–53, 94, 179, 183, 201–2, 243–44, 288n.32, 290n.96
Prague, 31–32, 44, 52–53, 101, 127–28, 161, 208–9, 211
Preminger, Otto, 295n.95
Preradović, Paula von, 221
Prinz, Joachim, 20, 34, 78, 271nn.43–44
Protestantism. 71–72, 137, 154, 176, 281n.104. See also Christianity

Qualtinger, Helmut, 267n.105

Rabinovitch, Gregor, 269n.22
race, 5, 9, 25, 122–23, 247–48, 249–50, 253, 259n.20, 264n.70, 267–68n.116, 272n.48, 305n.35, 306n.57
racism, 155, 204, 241, 242–43, 244, 245–48, 249–51, 252–54, 255, 259n.21, 261n.42, 265n.85, 268n.118, 287n.16, 306n.57
  anti-racism, 287n.19
  aversive racism, 265n.86
  blackface, 253–54
  cultural blackface, 305n.43
  opposition to racism, 303–4n.3
  racialization, 265n.85
  unconscious bias, 265n.86
Radauantisemitismus. See antisemitism
Radványi, László (pseud. Johannes Schmidt), 137, 138, 290–91n.98
Rajk, László, 287–88n.23
Rákosi, Mátás, 287–88n.23
Rankin, John, 244, 304n.17
Rauschning, Hermann, works by, *Hitler m'a dit* (*Hitler Speaks: A Series of Political Conversations with Adolf Hitler on his Real Aims*), 13–14, 264nn.75–77
Rehfisch, Hans, 39, 271–72n.45, 273nn.69–70, 273n.71
Reichs-Rundfunk-Gesellschaft, 201–2
Reichsbanner Schwarz-Rot-Gold, 114, 284n.46
Reichskristallnacht. See November Pogroms
Reichsschrifttumskammer, 179, 201–4, 205, 234–35
Reichstag burning, 138
Reinhardt, Max, 23, 221, 236, 273n.74
Reinhardt, Wolfgang, 221
Reitling, Netty. See Seghers, Anna
Rembrandt, 137
restitution of Jewish property, 106, 115–16, 139–40, 160–61, 266n.101, 288n.34, 290–91n.98, 292n.17. See also Aryanization
Rico, Roger, 242–43
Rico, Solange, 242–43, 304n.23
Riefenstahl, Leni, 265n.84
Riess, Curt, 267n.110, 270n.31, 275n.117
Roboz, Emmerich (Imre), 213–16, 299n.62, 300n.64, 300n.66
Roosevelt, Franklin D., 244
Rosenberg, Artur, 10–11
Rosenberg, Ethel and Julius, execution of, 279–80n.76
Rosenthal, Leo, 262n.53
Rosner, Fanny, 291n.99
Ross, Martin H., 189

Roth, Joseph, works by, *The Wandering Jews*, 272n.48
Rothschild-Spital, 297n.26
Rowe, Billy, 243
Roxy Theater, 242–43
Ruman, Sig, 194, 295n.95

Sachsenhausen, 280n.88, 285n.62
Sagalowitz, Benjamin, 78
Sakimura, Shigeki, 56–57
Salten, Felix, 270–71n.34
Salzburg, 301n.103
Salzkammergut, 171–72
Sartre, Jean-Paul, 13–14, 264n.71, 264n.74, 264n.75, 264n.78
Scharf, József, 209–10
Scharf, Móric, 209–11
Scharf family, 216–17
Schiele, Egon, 227, 235, 303n.146
Schiller, Friedrich, works by, "Don Carlos," 267n.105
Schlage, Lu, 81, 82–83, 280n.88, 280n.94, 281n.108
Schleif, Wolfgang, 73
Schlesinger, Otto, 109–10
Schloss Salem school, 299n.52
Schmid, Aglaja, 180–82, 181f, 293n.49
Schmidt, Franz, 266n.101
Schmidt, Helmut, 4
Schmidt, Johannes. *See* Radványi, László
Schmidt, Leonard F. *See* Schlage, Lu
Schnauck, Wilhelm, 270n.25
Schönbrunn, 187–88, 223f
Schönwiese, Gunhild (Metzger), 63–64, 277n.20
Schriftstellerverband, 153
Schröder, Richard, 101–4, 110, 282n.5, 285n.59, 285n.60, 285n.63
Schuldabwehrantisemitismus. See antisemitism
Schuyler, Ned, 244–45
Schwarzwald, Eugenie, 297n.24
Schwarzwald school, 168–69
Seghers, Anna, 130–54, 131f, 160–61, 162, 286n.2, 288n.32, 288n.36, 288n.45, 289n.61, 289n.70, 289n.71, 290–91n.98
Seghers, Anna, works by,
    Aufstand der Fischer von St. Barbara, 288n.26
    "Das Ende," 147–50
    Das siebte Kreuz, 147–48, 288n.30
    "Das wirkliche Blau," 143–44, 153
    "Der Ausflug der toten Mädchen," 141–42
    Der Kopflohn, 147–48
    Der Mann und sein Name, 151–53

"Der Skalp" (pseud. Anna Brand), 288n.36
Die Toten Bleiben Jung, 152, 289n.71
"Ein Mensch wird Nazi," 146–47
"Grubetsch," 288n.26
"Passagiere der Luftbrücke," 130–33, 286n.5
Transit, 144–45, 147, 151–52
Sephardim, 258n.19, 305n.32
sexism, 5
sexuality, 5, 12, 20, 89, 247, 259n.20
Seyss-Inquart, Arthur, 232
Sid Kays Fellows Orchestra, 268n.1
sie – die Wochenzeitung für Frauenrecht und Menschenrecht, 130, 286n.1
Silesia, 222–24
Simon & Schuster, 248–49
Simon, Richard L., 248–49
Simowski, Samuil, 114, 284n.45
Slánsky trial, 140, 161
Sluizer, Abel Juda, 29, 29f
Sluizer, Max, 29, 29f
Sluizer, Miriam, 29, 29f
Smollett, Peter (pseud. Hans Peter Smolka, Harry P. Smolka), 197, 295–96n.104
Social Democratic Party of Germany (Sozialdemokratische Partei Deutschlands, SPD), 38–39, 41, 257n.8, 273n.67
socialism, 11–12, 76, 113, 139–40, 146, 151–53, 162, 189, 203, 206, 222, 249, 287n.19, 296n.8, 297n.24
Socialist Unity Party (Sozialistische Einheitspartei Deutschlands, SED), 106–7, 115–16, 130, 135, 139–40, 153–54, 155, 162, 163, 226, 289n.71, 290–91nn.98–99
Society for Christian-Jewish Cooperation, 76
Söderbaum, Kristina, 1–2, 28, 31–32, 44, 46–47, 53, 68, 81, 84–85, 87, 279n.67, 281n.108
Söhnker, Hans, 90
Solymosi, Eszter, 209
Sommerfrische, 189
Sorkin, Mark, 212
Soviet Union, 115–16, 119, 132, 134, 140–41, 160–61, 230, 246, 283n.26
Soviet Military Authority, 113–14, 115, 124, 130, 134, 163, 196, 284n.39, 284n.50
Soviet occupation zone, 8–9, 57–58, 91, 104–5, 112, 113, 114–15, 139–40, 151–52, 261n.42, 279n.57, 279n.62, 283n.18, 283n.20
Sozialdemokratische Partei Deutschlands (SPD). *See* Social Democratic Party of Germany

342 INDEX

Sozialistische Einheitspartei Deutschlands
(SED). *See* Socialist Unity Party
Spiel, Hilde, 17, 167–74, 175, 178–79, 180, 232–
33, 291n.7, 292n.18, 293n.32, 293n.34
Sporer, Lily, 293n.42, 293n.44
Stahlhelm, 108–9, 110
Stalinism, 106, 159–60, 230
Ständestaat, 168–69, 235
Starke, Hermann Franz Gerhard, 261n.41
Staudte, Wofgang, works by, *Die Mörder sind
unter uns*, 92–93, 112, 114–15, 283n.25
Stein, Josef, works by, *Die Todeskarawane; Auf
den Trümmern des Paradieses*, 268n.5
Steinboeck, Rudolf, 173–74, 181*f*
Stemmle, Robert A., 104–5, 108*f*, 112–13, 115,
117–18, 119, 122, 123–24, 128–29, 253–
54, 282n.10, 284n.38, 286n.80, 301n.87
Stemmle, Robert A., works by
Affaire Blum (film), 104–5, 106–24, 108*f*, 128,
134–35, 161, 162, 182–83, 293n.49
Affaire Blum (novel), 124–27, 128–29
Affäre Blum (drama), 128
Justizwillkür ges.gesch. Ein Hörspiel, 104
Toxi, 253–54, 306n.57
Stibi, George, 291n.99
Stolten, Inge, 302n.104
Stork Club, 241, 242*f*, 242–45, 247–48, 255,
303n.2, 304n.23
Strauss, Franz, 186
Streicher, Julius, 26, 51–52, 63, 130, 265n.84
Sweceny, Maria Charlotte (Stein), 179–80
Switzerland, 25, 29, 34, 77, 78, 138, 178,
270–71n.34
Szabo-Lorenz, Valerie, 205
Szabo, Wilhelm, 205, 297n.27

Tandler, Julius, 236
Tenholt, William, 101–4, 110, 123–24, 128,
282n.5, 285n.60
Terra (production company), 73, 278n.52,
281n.101, 284n.43
The Angel with the Trumpet, 266n.103
The New Statesman, 167, 171
The Search, 266n.103
The Sound of Music, 301n.103
The Third Man, 174–75, 195–200
The Vicious Circle, 298n.36
The Woman in Brown, 298n.36
Theresienstadt, 57–58, 127–28, 169, 205,
286n.80
Thyssen, Fritz, 154
Time, 226, 244
Tiszaeszlár, 206–7, 208–9, 211, 213–15, 300n.82

Toller, Ernst, 103–4
Torberg, Friedrich, 266n.101, 293n.34
tourism, 234
Trapp, Maria von, 301n.103
Treblinka, 127–28
Trier, Walter, 124–25
Trümmerfilme, 91
Tulpanow, Sergei, 114–15
Tyrol, 170–72, 174–75, 184, 187–88, 189,
192, 193*f*
Tyrolf, Walter Fritz, 67, 70, 71–73, 75, 274n.94,
277–78n.32, 278n.49, 278n.52

UFA (Universum-Film Aktiengesellschaft), 93–
94, 95, 267n.108, 281n.113, 300n.69
Ulbricht, Walter, 160–61, 291n.103
Ullstein, Heinz, 286n.1
Union of Jewish Communities in
Switzerland, 78
United States of America, 9, 17–18, 19–20,
35–36, 42, 76, 106, 124, 127–28, 138–39,
184, 186, 192–93, 197–98, 212, 241–55,
266n.103, 272n.53, 294n.61, 294n.70,
302n.132, 305n.46
American nationalism, 253
American patriotism, 244
House of Representatives, 244
Information Service, film division, 220–21
Military, Information Control Division
(ICD), 184
State Department, 184, 247
UNRRA (United Nations Relief and
Rehabilitation Administration),
130, 131–33
Upcher, Peter, works by, "Der Rebbe hot
gehaissen frailech sain," 268n.1
Upper Austria, 187–88

Veit, Conrad, 83
Venice Film Festival, 216–17, 276n.1
Venus of Willendorf, 234, 236
Verband Deutscher Bühnenschriftsteller
(Association of German Dramatists), 34
Vereinigung der Verfolgten des Naziregimes
– Bund der Antifaschisten (Association
of Persecutees of the Nazi Regime
– Federation of Antifascists, VVN), 41,
283n.18
Vereinigung sozialistischer Schriftsteller
(Association of Socialist Writers), 206
Vergangenheitsbewältigung, 7, 260n.37, 262n.53
Verhoeven, Paul, 95
Verwechslungskomödie, 180–82

INDEX 343

Vienna, 2–3, 10–11, 16–17, 18, 138–39, 167–69, 170–72, 173–76, 178, 180–84, 185, 186–88, 187*f*, 189, 195–98, 199–200, 201, 206, 207–8, 210–11, 212–14, 215–17, 218–19, 220–21, 223*f*, 226–29, 230, 232–33, 235, 236, 260n.32, 262n.48, 262n.53, 265–66n.95, 267n.105, 270–71n.34, 292n.18, 292n.24, 293n.34, 293n.39, 293n.50, 294n.53, 294n.70, 295n.94, 297n.26, 298n.36, 298n.46, 299n.53, 302n.126, 303n.147

Vihrog, Jessica, 26

Völkischer Beobachter, 27, 37, 38, 39, 40, 269n.19, 272n.46

Volksbühne (Berlin), 23, 34, 128

von Báky, Josef, works by, *Der Ruf*, 18, 266n.104

VVN. *See* Vereinigung der Verfolgten des Naziregimes – Bund der Antifaschisten

Wagner, Richard, 231

Waldheim, Kurt, 262n.48

waltz, 185–86

Waterloo Cinema (Hamburg), 84

Webb, Jack, 190–91

Weber, Willi, 109–10

Weinschel, Chaim, 243–44

Weiss, Ernst, works by, *The Eyewitness*, 145, 149

Welles, Orson, 196

Wendt, Erich, 152, 154, 155–56, 158, 159

Werner, Alfred, 216–17

Wessely, Paula, 78–79

West Germany. *See* Federal Republic of Germany

White, Walter Francis, 241–42, 242*f*, 243

whiteness, 247, 248. *See also* Jews, conditional whiteness of

Wilder, Billy, 174, 175, 183–95, 187*f*, 188*f*, 193*f*, 294n.53, 294nn.56–57, 294n.58, 294n.62, 294n.66, 294n.68, 294n.70, 295nn.94–95, 295n.97, 295n.98, 298n.36

Wilder, Billy, works by,
A Foreign Affair, 184
Die Todesmühlen (Death Mills), 183–84, 195
The Emperor Waltz, 174–75, 183–95, 199–200, 294n.53, 295n.88, 295n.97
The Lost Weekend, 190
Ninotchka, 190
Stalag 17, 295n.95
Sunset Boulevard, 190–91

Wilder, Judith Frances, 191

Wilder, William Lee, 298n.36

Winchell, Walter, 243–48, 252, 255, 304n.16, 304n.23, 304n.25, 304n.26

Wolf, Christa, 150–51

Wolf, Sándor, 238

Wolff, Meta, 84

Wolfgang Borchert, works by, *Draußen vor der Tür*, 1–2, 18

Wollheim, Norbert, 33, 40, 43, 44–46, 72, 77–78, 274n.94, 274n.101, 278n.49

World Jewish Congress, 34, 274n.101, 278n.33

World War I, 138–39, 145, 183–84, 197–98, 211, 285n.55

World War II, 1, 6–7, 14–15, 19–20, 46–47, 106, 174, 180, 198, 212, 220, 231–32, 238, 243–44, 249–50

Wright, Lee, 250–51

Württemberg, Duke of. *See* Karl Alexander

Wyler-Salten, Anna Katharina (Katja), 30, 270–71n.34

xenophobia, 242–43

Yiddish, 23, 26, 212, 249, 269n.22, 275n.117, 282n.131

Young Lions, 191

Zentralrat der Juden in Deutschland (Central Council of Jews in Germany), 2, 93–94, 257n.8, 287n.9

Zinnemann, Fred, 139, 266n.103, 288n.31

Zionism, 114, 156, 159–61, 287–88n.23, 290n.82, 290n.94. *See also* anti-Zionism

Zivier, Georg, 76

Zsolnay Verlag, 215, 300n.66, 300n.78

Zuckerkandl, Amalie, 296n.6

Zuckerkandl, Hermine, 296n.6

Zuckerkandl, Otto, 296n.6

Zuckermann, Leo, 138–39, 160–61, 288n.34

Zuckmayer, Carl, 180

Zurich, 25, 30, 78, 216–17

Zweig, Arnold, works by, *Ritualmord in Ungarn/Die Sendung Semaels: jüdische Tragödie in fünf Akten*, 128, 208–9, 210–11, 216–17, 219–20, 298n.36, 300n.75